Computers and Society

COMPUTERS AND SOCIETY

Modern Perspectives

Ronald M. Baecker

OXFORD
UNIVERSITY PRESS

Great Clarendon Street, Oxford, OX2 6DP,
United Kingdom

Oxford University Press is a department of the University of Oxford.
It furthers the University's objective of excellence in research, scholarship,
and education by publishing worldwide. Oxford is a registered trade mark of
Oxford University Press in the UK and in certain other countries

First Edition published in 2019

Impression: 1

Published in the United States of America by Oxford University Press
198 Madison Avenue, New York, NY 10016, United States of America

British Library Cataloguing in Publication Data
Data available

Library of Congress Control Number: 2019930247

ISBN 978–0–19–882708–5 (hbk.)
ISBN 978–0–19–882709–2 (pbk.)

Printed and bound by
CPI Group (UK) Ltd, Croydon, CR0 4YY

Foreword

> "It was the best of times, it was the worst of times, it was the age of wisdom, it was the age of foolishness, it was the epoch of belief, it was the epoch of incredulity, it was the season of Light, it was the season of Darkness, it was the spring of hope, it was the winter of despair…"
>
> Charles Dickens, *A Tale of Two Cities* (1859)

Technological development, be it academic or commercial, often begins with good intentions. Academics and developers envision technology leveraging and advancing both individual and social capabilities in ways that not only make people better but allow people to do things that were previously thought onerous or impossible. Yet technology often becomes a double-edged sword, where bad things accompany the good.

Computers as a technology suffer the same difficulties, but even more so. The swift uptake of diverse computer-based technologies means that change is rapid-fire and unpredictable. We begin to use particular computer technologies because we (or their developers) see the benefits, but rarely do we see the negative consequences—unintended or deliberate—until it is too late. Indeed, we may not even be fully aware of the issues involved, simply because it is hard to comprehend the full extent of the incremental changes that occur as we live through them.

Computers and Society will help you to understand the changes that are happening now as a consequence of various computer technologies and sensitize you to look for other changes that are likely to happen in the future. While you may be reading it as a required text in a Computers in Society course, the book's value goes far beyond that. If you deeply consider the issues presented in each chapter, this book will change how you think about technology's role in society. If you are a developer or product purchaser, it may help you to consider the negative implications of the computer applications you are creating or buying—that is, to see the 'dark patterns' in how the applications can be misused or subverted, and the various shades of grey in between. If you are a technology consumer, you may better understand and debate the issues that accompany the computer systems you or the people around you are using. If you are just living your day-to-day life, this book may help you to understand and interpret the changes you notice around you, what you hear in the news, and what you talk about with your friends and family.

Computers and Society could not have been easy to write. The breadth, depth, historical context, and relevancy of the topics covered are impressive to say the least, and the amount of work that must have been required to research each topic is somewhat staggering. It needed someone like Ron Baecker to write it. Ron is a senior academic whose career spans the period from the 1960s to 2018 and beyond. As an expert in graphics, human–computer interaction, and collaboration technologies, he was instrumental in researching and pioneering some of the key computer concepts that we now take for granted. He not only lived through the changes introduced by computers over the last sixty years, but remained highly aware of those changes both through his knowledge of the field and his teaching of various Computers and Society courses over the decades (the first in 1972). I was lucky enough to work with Ron on various academic projects and consider him both a colleague and a friend. He has the personality to fit the authorship of a book such as this. He doesn't accept things at face value. He delves into issues and debates them. He is opinionated, but his opinions are evidence-based. He pioneers, because he is always looking into the future rather than just at the present.

The above quote by Charles Dickens echoes the book's sentiment. Computers promise so much to society, but the risks are great. As this book shows, the best and the worst of computers are manifest in many niches of today's society. While you may have a passing awareness of at least a few of the issues raised in this book, *Computers and Society* will further inform you about those issues through its deep and thoughtful treatment.

Saul Greenberg,
Emeritus Professor, University of Calgary, Canada

Acknowledgements

Many people helped me to write and publish this book. David Olson, Ishtiaque Ahmed, John DiMarco, Dwight Wainman, and several reviewers made helpful comments on drafts. I am especially grateful to Leslie Mezei, Saul Greenberg, Jonathan Grudin, and Kellogg Booth for extensive and insightful comments and suggestions.

I could not have completed this work in the twenty-two months it took me without the Google search engine, the literature search engine and extensive resources of the University of Toronto Library, and the insightful technology reporting of the *New York Times*. Sincere thanks to Benjamin Walsh and Michelle Spence at the university's Engineering Library, who found material for me when I had to admit defeat by the arcane interface of the library's search engine.

Two undergraduate University of Toronto students contributed to the effort. Mira Rawady ordered books from one of the Frightful Five and found and collected books from the university's many libraries. Uma Kalkar was extraordinary, proofreading, checking URLs, improving wording, making excellent suggestions, and courageously questioning some of my wording. Because of Uma, I can now make the important assertion that this book was reviewed by one knowledgeable and thoughtful person less than a third of my age.

Several people from Oxford University Press were very helpful. Dan Taber orchestrated a thorough review process of early drafts and believed in the book even when the comments were mixed. Katherine Ward guided image permission clearances. Lydia Shinoj oversaw the book's production process. Elizabeth Stone contributed copy editing.

Finally, I am grateful to three professors at Massachusetts Institute of Technology, the late Murray Eden, the late Joe Weizenbaum, and Noam Chomsky, and one professor at the University of Toronto, the late Kelly Gotlieb, whose social conscience, thoughtful analyses, and clear voices on behalf of justice and goodness helped set me on a half-century journey culminating in this book.

Contents

Case Studies

Prologue

I wrote this book because I could not find a concise but comprehensive, current, affordable, and globally focused treatment of key issues to use in teaching a Computers and Society seminar to University of Toronto undergraduates in the autumn of 2017. I had taught my first Computers and Society class in 1972, so I had a good sense of what I wanted.

The text needed to be succinct to allow instructors to tailor and add other course readings based on their passions and on student interests. This approach would also encourage students to think and develop ideas and solutions, and not to memorize canned answers. It was important to provide an imaginative set of exercises for individual students or student teams. The rapid pace of technological change and societal responses to these developments made 'comprehensive' and 'current' key requirements. I had to avoid discussing only US situations, cases, and laws; an international and culturally diverse overview of technology and its uses and implications worldwide was needed. Finally, the text needed to be affordable and offer good value.

I worked hard on the title. Each of the four key words is significant.

Computers was interpreted in the broadest sense, at various scales—large-scale computational engines, corporate networks, desktop and laptop computers, the internet, tablets, and mobile phones. I also included the 'internet of things' and 'ubiquitous computing', where computers are invisible to the naked eye. I stressed the amazing progress as well as the both encouraging and discouraging consequences of our achievements.

By *society* I included not only social issues, but also political choices, legal responses, and moral and ethical dilemmas. Ethical choices are brought up in many of the exercises and are highlighted in one case study in each chapter.

Many of the current textbooks have chapter-level tables of contents that have changed little since 2000. They focus primarily on the classical 'big six' topics of Computers and Society courses—intellectual property, free speech, privacy, security, safety, and automation. While these topics are still important, my book approaches them in a more *modern*, livelier way, and ranges broadly over issues not covered in the other books.

Finally, I also tried with all topics to present a variety of *perspectives*. Many issues raised are troubling ones, with no obvious 'right' answers. It is vital that those addressing the issues be able to see that there are several plausible answers and opinions to every question.

Although mainly targeted at upper-level undergraduate students, the book can be used with mature freshmen or sophomores, and at a graduate level. It may also be used in courses dealing with digital technologies in disciplines such as politics, government, philosophy, sociology, psychology, education, or medicine.

In the words of my friend Leslie Mezei, who also has followed developments for over fifty years, this book needed to convey 'the awe and the terror of it all'. I hope that I have done so.

This Prologue begins with historical context—both the history of computing and my own fifty-plus years in the field. Chapters are organized into three sections, the first dealing with *applications* of computers and telecommunications, where the dominant theme is *opportunity*; the second focusing on critical *threats* posed by computerization, where the dominant theme is *risk*; and the third analysing *issues* that have loomed large in the last decade, and grow more important each year, where the dominant theme is *choice*. To establish context, chapters begin with a description of visions that have motivated many of the developments, or summaries of relevant history, or reminders of science fiction novels or films that have foreshadowed the issues.

I conclude the Prologue by discussing how topics are typically presented and ways in which this book may be used. A great variety of engaging individual or group assignments appear within each chapter just after the relevant section. I also briefly mention other valuable books, journals, websites, and videos. More resources are cited in a section at the end of the text before the Index. All URLs of documents, videos, and other resources were checked between May and August 2018.

0.1 Background

I am an Emeritus Professor of Computer Science. My first introduction to programming, writing programs in the MAD 'high-level language', and submitting them on punched cards in the inhuman process called 'batch processing', was hardly inspiring. Yet happily, in the following year, 1962 to 1963, I was able to write programs in assembly language and submit them on paper tape to one of the first PDP-1 minicomputers. This was indeed a *personal computer*, because I had little competition for the machine at night. The long nights became palatable through occasional spurts of playing Space War on an early cathode ray tube (CRT) display. I derived a good sense of what interactive computing could be like.

This experience deepened during my doctoral work on computer animation.[1] Several people could concurrently do interactive graphics under a time-sharing operating system on the TX-2 computer—an important experimental machine best known for hosting the influential Sketchpad PhD thesis of Ivan Sutherland,[2] which launched the field of computer graphics. In the five decades since completing my PhD, I have been an active research participant and keen observer of applications of computing to education and learning, medicine and health, the arts, digital media, collaborative work and learning, and as enhancements to the life of senior citizens.

A high-level, optimistic vision of the power of human creativity coupled to machine capability had already been provided in 1960 by the influential 'man–machine symbiosis' paper of scientist and computer technology research leader J. C. R. Licklider:[3]

> The hope is that, in not too many years, human brains and computing machines will be coupled together very tightly, and that the resulting partnership will think as no human brain has ever thought and process data in a way not approached by the information-handling machines we know today.

Other thinkers and pioneers amplified this optimism. A far-seeing 1945 paper by engineer and inventor Vannevar Bush,[4] who had led the US scientific research and development (R&D) effort during the Second World War, postulated a device called the Memex, conceived to transform the ways in which we explore information and create knowledge. In 1962, engineer and inventor Doug Engelbart described the potential of digital technologies for augmenting human intellect and facilitating team collaboration.[5] Soon thereafter, in 1965, generalist Ted Nelson sketched early concepts of hypertext and hypermedia.[6] Computer scientist Alan Kay then anticipated the personal computer and personal dynamic media,[7] a topic to which we shall return in Chapter 2.

Yet others had fears for the future. Early concerns were expressed about issues such as privacy, automation and work, and the goals of and limits to artificial intelligence (AI). The 1960s and 1970s saw some of the first books on computers and society. University of Toronto computer science professors Kelly Gottlieb and Allan Borodin contributed an early textbook.[8] Law professor Alan Westin wrote a scholarly treatise on privacy.[9] Computer scientist Joseph Weizenbaum reflected on the dangers of relying on computer programs that no human being understood anymore and the effect of programmers' personality and lifestyle on the work they create.[10] Mathematician and AI guru Seymour Papert and philosopher Hubert Dreyfus engaged in a debate about the potential of AI,[11] issues we shall revisit more knowledgeably in Chapter 11.

Computer speed was then a fraction of what it is now. Moore's Law predicted continuous miniaturization and impacts of this on computer power and memory.[12] Indeed, the number of logic components one could place on a silicon chip was projected to double approximately every two years. For example, the first Macintosh computer, announced on 1 January 1984, had 128 KB (128,000 bytes) of memory. A 'Mac' purchased in 2016 (thirty-two years or sixteen two-year periods later) had 16 GB (16 billion bytes). Moore's Law would predict that it could have 32 GB of memory, a very accurate forecast indeed. There have been similar increases in processor chip count and speed—amazing advances in digital technology!

This progress has enabled the digitization of communication, the internet, the web, mobile phones, and advances in AI and machine learning, which rely upon massive processor power and memory. The speed of hardware and software developments has emboldened many pioneers to articulate visions of a grand and glorious future; we shall highlight some of these. We shall also mention visions of despair and nightmares of plausible totalitarian control aided by technology.

Technological change has produced a complex set of issues for individuals, society, and government. Concerns about privacy and automation's effects on work and jobs continue. There are new opportunities and challenges in the areas of digital inclusion, intellectual property, security, and safety. We also see ways in which computing impacts learning, health, politics and government, and war and peace. A discussion of safety will also highlight concerns about the environment. Trust of automated systems and robots is now a major issue. There are also legitimate concerns about the 'tech-centric' lifestyle we have adopted, and the phenomenon of increasing corporate concentration. We shall address all these themes in this volume.

0.2 Opportunities: computer applications

I first discuss applications of computers and telecommunications, areas in which digital technologies have changed our lives, and will likely do so even more profoundly in the future.

If we are optimistic about the ways in which widespread computerization improves our life, then we must be concerned when digital technology is not meaningfully available to some sectors of society. Such gaps are known as 'digital divides'. In Chapter 1, we examine the goal of removing digital divides, between rich and poor, individuals in Western societies and those in 'Third World countries', young and old, men and women, and those who are able-bodied and those who have sensory, motor, cognitive, or reading challenges. This goal is now often termed *digital inclusion*. We shall consider a challenge to this goal in the battle over *net neutrality*, and present several notable examples of digital inclusion, including the formation of online communities and the widespread availability of knowledge and information in over 40 million Wikipedia articles in over 250 different languages. This development is all the more remarkable because it has engaged over 30 million individuals in its creation and upkeep.

Wikipedia demonstrates the power of *digital media*; there are many other examples from the arts and sciences. Chapter 2 discusses the explosion of digital media, the role and value of *intellectual property* (IP), and the intellectual property of digital media. Writers, musicians, artists, and inventors have historically viewed their creations as protected by IP regulations, enabling them to profit from and control the use of their writings, music, art, and inventions. We shall discuss digitized music, motion pictures, mash-ups of fragments of audio and visual media, digital textbooks, and research literature. In all cases, there are questions about what represents *fair use* and what may be considered inappropriate use, often termed 'piracy' or 'stealing'. We then discuss the concept of *open access*, as applied to textbooks and research journals, and also the *open source* software movement. We close with the important *Creative Commons* method of licensing creations, which provides us an opportunity to bridge the divide between *proprietary* (uses focused on ensuring credit and earning compensation for work) and *open*, shared culture.

Chapter 3 begins by reviewing influential visions of how computers could revolutionize *education* and *learning*. We then discuss real developments: tutorials, drill-and-practice exercises, simulations and gaming, enhanced presentations, smart classrooms, flipped classrooms, intelligent tutoring, online learning, and massive open online classrooms (MOOCs). The current ubiquity of online learning has transformed traditional 'classrooms' in post-secondary and continuing education. Due to the success of these developments, school administrators and school systems now struggle to wisely apply digital technology in the schools, and to control the extent to which resources should be allocated to computers. One specific case is a dilemma now prevalent in secondary schools—the issue of when and how to allow or restrict the use of mobile phones and other mobile devices in classrooms.

We begin our discussion of applications to *medicine* and *health* in Chapter 4 with influential early visions of possible roles for computers. We consider the effect of online health information sources found on the internet and online forums where individuals share their health experiences with others. We examine the care improvements promised by personal health and electronic medical records, technology for documenting adverse drug reactions and interactions, and the use of big data for infectious disease surveillance. Digitization also extends to the human body; patient simulators are now widely used in medical education. Artificial body parts are increasingly embedded in real humans, likely resulting in *bionic people* or *androids* in the future. Recent advances in understanding the human genome point to exciting opportunities for *precision medicine,* using genetics to better target treatments to the specifics of each patient. These advances also allow future parents to have what some term as *designer babies,* a vision that brings delight to some and chills to others. Finally, we look at two current topics of particular interest to older adults: *neuroplasticity* and *brain training exercises,* and robotic companions and caregivers for seniors, especially for those with degenerative diseases.

Free speech, politics, and *government* are other aspects of our lives that have undergone dramatic change. This is the topic of Chapter 5. Visions have primarily been negative, expressed in several influential literary dystopias. We consider the cultural and legal framework governing speech and other forms of expression on the internet, the universal right of free speech, and incentives governments have to restrict speech that they view as pornographic, hateful, threatening, treasonous, or supporting terrorism. Troubling new issues have also arisen in recent years with social media 'speech' that is actually *fake news.* This came to the foreground during the 2016 US presidential election, but has also affected politics in other parts of the world. We focus on emerging trends in e-democracy, including the roles of social media in enabling political protest and the application of social media to political campaigning, including the use of surveys and big data to target potential voters. We conclude the chapter with a discussion of e-government, the use of technology and social media in governance, including the bizarre and painful US case of the current 'tweetocracy' of President Donald J. Trump.

Some of the earliest computers were developed for military applications during the Second World War. The effects of computerization and worldwide telecommunications on *law and order, war and peace* is the theme of Chapter 6. After highlighting android policemen and soldiers from science fiction novels and films, we review the use of social media by police, and by citizens in their interactions with police. We discuss technology-aided surveillance by police and by government. Then, looking beyond the borders on an individual country, we examine how computer hacking may be used by one nation against the other, for example, to interfere with elections, a prominent topic after the 2016 American election, and one that has continued to arise in various parts of the world in 2017 and 2018. We discuss societies that repress and forbid free access to the internet, as well as methods of combatting this repression, which often is done from nations outside the repressive society. We then expand our view of hacking as an agent of international politics, via *cyberespionage, cyberterrorism,* or more generally, *cyberwarfare.* Modern warfare technology has also changed: there is an increasing use of drones and other self-guided weapons as tools of combat, or *semi-autonomous weapons,* and the future possibility of *robot soldiers.*

0.3 Risks: technological threats

In Chapters 7, 8, and 9, we focus on major issues that often arise in the uses of the digital technologies discussed in previous chapters.

Security is the attribute of a computer system that ensures that it can continue to function as it normally does and as it is supposed to function. We begin Chapter 7 by explaining some of the major ways in which computer systems may be insecure and therefore subject to invasion. *Hackers*—individuals who seek to exploit the weaknesses of a system— and *cybercriminals* exploit system vulnerabilities in order to break in or disrupt the system. Such intrusions can interrupt the computational and communication capabilities of an institution or a society and have the ability to wreak great damage. Hackers with political motivations have already been discussed in the preceding chapter. In Chapter 7, we continue our discussion of large-scale system intrusions, typically done for financial gain, and then look at three specific ways in which digital society is vulnerable to sabotage—*identity theft*, often via *phishing*; break-ins into our digital worlds, including our phones and our homes; and the security of electronic voting. We close with a discussion of legal responses to safeguard security.

Safety of a system is similar to but not identical to security and is the topic of Chapter 8. A system that is secure may not be safe, if its normal operation can result in damage to individuals or societies. For example, intractable user interfaces can cause frustration, anger, and even rage. Damage may be done to younger people by *cyberbullying* and through the use of *revenge porn*. There are also daily threats to our safety because pedestrians, bike riders, and drivers are immersed in their mobile devices. We then widen our scope from the individual to society. Our inability to predict the complexity and control the costs of large-scale *information technology* (IT) implementations threatens safety because it undermines our ability to plan an orderly progression for a government or an organization. Even more serious are incomprehensible large-scale software systems that are no longer understood, even by their creators; controlling them is essential for society to function. We also look at safety in electronic medical devices, industrial accidents such as with nuclear reactors, and the recent interest in self-driving cars. We close by examining ways in which IT contributes to improving the planet's environment, and ways that it contributes greenhouse gases and waste that further jeopardize our planet's safety.

Concerns about *privacy*, the topic of Chapter 9, have long been manifested in dystopian literature, and have been discussed within computer science since the early years. Data storage is now virtually limitless and free, so governments and corporations can keep and access records on almost all aspects of our lives. Hardly a week goes by when we do not hear of a significant data breach that exposes people's personal financial or health information. There are also new risks from new technologies—*social media* where we ourselves expose personal information, location tracking, video surveillance, and embedded devices. For example, the privacy intrusions via inappropriate use of Facebook data by Cambridge Analytica illustrated in 2018 the malicious use of our social media information. Government itself is not safe—the 2016 revelations of Hillary Clinton's emails raised the question of whether or not politicians and statesmen can count on private communications in the internet age. The 2013 news of the widespread US surveillance of American citizens and other individuals unleashed anger at the covert data collection, and support for or anger at *whistle-blowers* such as Edward Snowden who exposed the practice. We close the chapter with a discussion of legal responses to safeguard privacy.

0.4 Choices: challenges for society

The topics of Chapters 10, 11, and 12 are not new, but have increased in urgency due to technical developments over the past two decades.

The effect of *automation* on *work* and *jobs* has engaged thoughtful computer scientists and economists since the earliest days of computing. Discussions often invoked movements such as the Luddites during the British Industrial Revolution. We examine in Chapter 10 how computers are used to enable more efficient processing of job applicants and employee selection, and how they are also used to monitor job performance. Not only is there dramatic change in our jobs, there are changes in how we do some of this work. Examples are found in *on-demand services* and in methods of job tasking and sharing that are enabled by internet communication. We then discuss how computers are doing both manual labour and mental labour, and investigate its effects on various sectors of the economy—agriculture, manufacturing, service industries, and the professions. We end with an overview of current data and projections on unemployment caused by automation, visions of the future of work and leisure, and the choices that we as a society will face as we struggle with the economic and psychic impact of many or most human jobs becoming obsolete due to technological advances. For example, will we need to institute *guaranteed annual incomes*?

Since the 1960s, advances in AI have made us ask whether we will soon no longer be the species with the greatest ability to think, and the consequences we will face in ceding critical, even life and death, decisions to intelligent machines. Chapter 11 discusses many important questions. What kinds of artificial intelligence are there? What is the difference between *good old-fashioned AI* (GOFAI) and the modern approaches to *machine learning*? What are the capabilities and limitations of smart programs? Should programs be treated anthropomorphically, as if they were people? Can machines exhibit *empathy*? How do we know what a machine knows or does not know? Can we understand the logic behind its decisions or actions, in other words, are they *explainable*? Under what circumstances do we trust people and traditional machines, and under what circumstances should we *trust* computers? Who or what is *responsible* if errors are made or life is lost? Furthermore, since our digital records, whether accurate and complete or not, stand for us in situations where it is essential that there are no errors, there are concerns about *fairness* and *justice*, for example, how big data can be used to characterize unfairly and limit the opportunities of some individuals.

The widespread use of the internet for purposes such as social media has led to dramatic changes in our *lifestyle*. In Chapter 12, we discuss the internet and social media's enabling of interconnectedness of people to friends, acquaintances, and communities, in terms of what it allows, and also what a surfeit of connectedness means for our lives. We look at the phenomenon of addiction to computers or social media. We consider the effect of ubiquitous digital media, the impact of the Internet of Things on work and home life, and the rapidly improving capabilities of *virtual reality* and *augmented reality*. We look at online dating, and, as robots become more lifelike, the future of sex robots. We examine how financial transactions are changing, and the future of cash in a world with digital finance infrastructures such as *blockchain*. As some IT firms have developed monopolistic positions and expanded their focus to allow them to dominate numerous other sectors of the economy, we close with the topic of corporate concentration.

In the Epilogue, we summarize social, legal and policy, and ethical issues and questions. Following the Epilogue, there is an Afterword that summarizes developments in autumn 2018.

What kind of society would we like? How should we address the tension between proprietary and open approaches to digital media? To what extent will we use computers in education and medicine, and should we impose limits? Will we still drive, or will we yield driving to smart cars in the interests of safety or efficiency? What happens when smart technology fails or is compromised? Will we allow ourselves to enjoy states of solitude disconnected from technology, or can we no longer imagine being offline?

To what extent, and how, should governmental policies and laws control the ways in which computers are used? How important is digital inclusion, and how do we increase it? What kinds of speech should governments or the monolithic firms that control the internet forbid? How can we control the proliferation of fake news? Will governments be able to deal with cyberattacks on their sovereignty? Will there be no limits on surveillance in the service of security? How can we ensure that some privacy remains?

What ethical choices do we face as we live in societies where there are fewer and fewer limits to what digital technologies can do? Will we use precision medicine to order babies with certain characteristics? Will we allow an arms race in cyberweapons? Will there be limits to what work can be automated? How will we ensure dignity and economic security to those who can no longer find work? Are there limits to what we will trust machines to do? How will we decide when not to convey trust and responsibility? What do educated citizens, as well as those active in technology professions, do when faced with conflicts between their beliefs and what is happening?

0.5 How to use this book

Typically, we motivate the treatment of each topic with an engaging and specific case study that illustrates the topic to be presented and the themes to be discussed. Where needed, we include a layperson's discussion of the computer science developments that have enabled the topic to be relevant and interesting. We sketch the extent to which and how computer capability is affecting or is likely to affect society in the foreseeable future. We summarize how some individuals can view these developments and impacts as positive and others can see them as negative. We expand the discussion to consider policy decisions that have been made or could be made by various branches of governments, and ethical dilemmas that may be perceived and acted on by individuals and organizations. We highlight different points of view about most issues. Where possible, we enrich the discussion by explaining how various aspects of the same issue have manifested themselves and been dealt with in different cultures, societies, or nations.

Tech Support

Gracing this book's cover is a brilliant editorial cartoon that originally was the cover art of the 23 October 2017 issue of the *New Yorker* magazine—'The Money Issue'. It was created by the cartoonist and illustrator R. Kikuo Johnson,[13] and was given the title 'Tech support'.

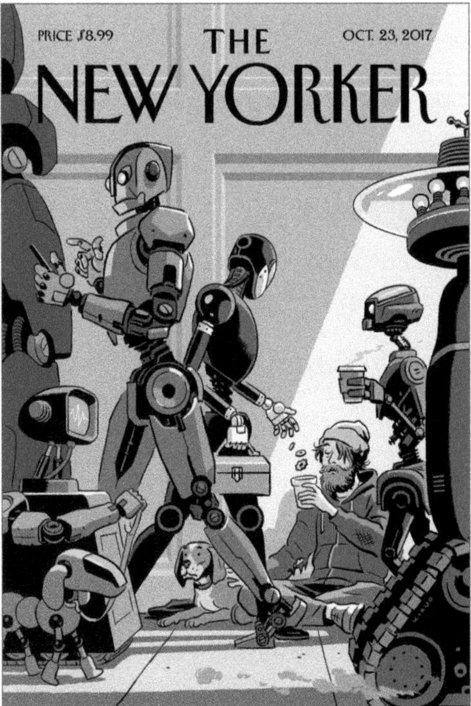

Figure 0.1 The cover of a recent issue of *The New Yorker* magazine: "Tech Support"[14]

It is eye-catching, and also illuminates several themes that I will discuss primarily in Chapters 10 and 11. What are the limits to AI? Will robots take our jobs? What jobs will they not take? What physical forms will robots assume? Will they learn our habits? Will they drink coffee and text while walking? What will become of us? How will we sustain ourselves if we can no longer get paying jobs?

My short treatments of each theme and topic do not give 'all the answers'. The text points the way for students to go out and read literature that is cited, and to find and organize more literature that responds to specific research questions that they themselves may investigate. Many references to additional literature that appear in the electronic version of the text may be clicked to access online versions of the cited papers. There is a section called Notes that includes asll the endnotes that elaborate on arguments made in the text and provide the references for citations. There also is a section called Resources which lists websites that have huge amounts of relevant, useful, and current material.

Students are encouraged to formulate and debate their own opinions about social, policy, and ethical issues.

Each chapter contains interesting assignments and projects. Others may be obtained by morphing an assignment of one category into a similar one from another category, or by modifying the topic straightforwardly, such as by substituting one country for another. The ten categories are:

1. Scholarly *research* paper
2. *Concept* definition as a new Wikipedia article, or as improvements of an existing one
3. *Debate* topic, realized in various forms that involve two competing individuals or teams
4. *Policy* brief, presenting facts, opinions, and arguments for a politician or candidate
5. Text of a proposed *law*, on an issue of importance, in the context of a specific country
6. *Jury* deliberation, by a small group on a hypothetical violation of a real or postulated law
7. *Field work*, understanding technology use via interviews, questionnaires, observation
8. *Book report*, on a relatively recent book related to material discussed in the course
9. *Technology review*, comparing and contrasting several comparable products
10. Dilemma regarding *ethics*, in some cases for an individual working in the computer field, in other cases for an organization or society.

Assignments encourage students or teams of students to research and synthesize material that goes beyond what is discussed in the text.

A word about terminology. Although my title is 'Computers and Society', the word 'computer' was used because that term typically appears in the titles of courses dealing with the subject matter of this book. Two phrases are more descriptive. Using the phrase *digital technologies* makes it clear that we typically are speaking of a variety of devices, only some of which look like computers, such as mobile phones and fitness measurement devices. *Information and communication technologies* (ICT) makes it clear that we are speaking of systems of devices and connections that communicate and process information. We shall typically simply just say *information technology* (IT).

This book will primarily be read in academia, but the subject matter is not just of academic interest. Many who engage with the topics experience life-changing insights into how vital the issues are. Many build careers trying to ensure that technology is used to make the world a better place. In May 2018, I attended a conference called RightsCon.[15] It was the seventh such conference, attended by over 2,000 passionate and articulate individuals from 115 countries. RightsCon describes itself as:[15]

> [a] conference on human rights in the digital age...bring[ing] together business leaders, policy makers, general counsels, government representatives, technologists, and human rights defenders...to tackle pressing issues at the intersection of human rights and digital technology.

Events since 2016 illustrate how digital technologies are exacerbating worldwide human rights issues such as disinformation, authoritarian control, divisiveness, hatred, and conflict.

If this book engages your imagination and your social conscience, there is much for you to do!

0.6 A note to instructors

This book is shorter than a traditional Computers and Society text, and can therefore be used differently. Each of the chapter topics could form the basis of several weeks to a half-semester of presentations and discussion. Instructors are encouraged to tailor their course organization to match their interests and those of their students. They can profitably assign the core readings from the text, and supplement it with references provided in the text, or with additional readings that they or the students may choose. Or there need be no additional readings; the material presented can provide the basis for organizing classes and for designing assignments and projects that will engage students mightily over a term, or even over a year.

A course focused on the traditional Computers and Society topics would use Chapters 2, 5, 7, 8, 9, and 10, with selections from some of the other topics. There are of course many more options.

The assignments and projects can be tailored by instructors as individual or team assignments. Most can have both written and oral components. The assignments are grouped at the end of the discussion of each topic (a section within a chapter) to enrich the preceding discussion.

Ethical discussions are best led by the instructor, with additional readings assigned according to his or her tastes and beliefs. This can be done in four different ways: applying an Ethical Theory; applying a Code of Ethics and Professional Conduct; focusing on the Ethics Case Studies in this text or assigning papers from other sources that present ethical analyses; or reading and discussing issues that emerge in literature such as science fiction.

Ethical theories

One or several ethical theories may be taught. Here are some options:[16]

Ethical theory	Key idea
Deontological ethics	The morality of an action is based on rules of behaviour. For example, act in accordance with universal laws of how humans should behave that may be derived through rational thought. (Immanuel Kant)
Act Utilitarianism	Act in a given situation so as to produce 'the greatest happiness for the greatest number' (Jeremy Bentham).
Rule Utilitarianism	Act in accordance with rules that lead to the greatest good. (John Stuart Mill)
Social Contract	Act in accordance with rules that have been agreed upon by individuals so that they can live together in a society. (Thomas Hobbes, John Locke, Jean-Jacques Rousseau, and recently by John Rawls, who expressed this in terms of a theory of justice.)
Virtue Ethics	Act according to virtues, character traits of good human beings who behave virtuously. (Philosophy grounded in writings of Plato and Aristotle.)

The instructor may frame ethical discussions in terms of the code of ethics of a professional society. The Association for Computing Machinery (ACM), the society of computer science research and teaching, has had a code of ethics and professional conduct since 1992. It was updated in 2018.[17] Its preamble explains its methodology and how it is to be used:

> The Code includes principles formulated as statements of responsibility, based on the understanding that the public good is always the primary consideration. Each principle is supplemented by guidelines, which provide explanations to assist computing professionals in understanding and applying the principle.

Another relevant framework is the code of ethics of the software engineering community.[18]

Analysis and discussion may also focus on examples highlighted in this text's Ethics Case Studies. Or one might assign some additional readings on topics that highlight ethical issues. Three books are good sources. Since 1985, Deborah G. Johnson has authored a compact and excellent text called *Computer Ethics*, now in its fourth edition.[19] The book's second chapter, 'Ethics and Information Technology', is a useful introduction to the ethical theories mentioned above. Johnson also motivates ethical thinking beautifully:

> Our deliberations about how to act and what to choose often involve moral notions (right and wrong, loyalty, duty, justice, responsibility), ethical principles (do no harm, tell the truth, keep your promises), and ideas about what makes for a full and meaningful life (concern for others, community, friendship).

A wonderful and broad compendium of classic papers is *Computers, Ethics, & Social Values* by Deborah G. Johnson and Helen Nissenbaum,[20] published in 1995. In this volume, Prof. Terry Winograd's essay on social responsibility and the third chapter, on software ownership, focus insightfully on ethical questions. Kenneth Einar Himma and Herman T. Tavani's *The Handbook of Information and Computer Ethics* provides broad coverage of ethical and policy issues raised by widespread computerization,[21] for example, Prof. Dorothy Denning's chapter on the ethics of cyberconflict.

Finally, students may be highly motivated by reading and discussing issues that arise in literature such as science fiction. [22]

Some other books may be helpful to instructors with respect to certain topics.

Sara Baase's *A Gift of Fire: Social, Legal, and Ethical Issues for Computing Technology* is now in its fifth edition.[23] It covers a subset of the topics covered in my book, and pulls out 'Freedom of Speech', 'Crime', 'Evaluating and Controlling Technology', and 'Errors, Failures, and Risks' explicitly as chapters. A valuable feature is a set of sections at the end of each chapter listing important books and articles, and organizations and websites. References are included in comprehensive notes which amplify the text and set the references in context.

Michael J. Quinn's *Ethics for the Information Age* is now in its seventh edition.[24] Its topic list is similar to that of Baase's book. A notable feature is its presentation of eight different ethical theories, its selection of five of these as most relevant and useful, and its use of these theories to frame and discuss topics that appear under the themes of networked communications, intellectual property, information privacy, privacy, security, reliability, professional ethics, and work and wealth.

Computers and Society: Modern Perspectives differs from the two aforementioned textbooks in several ways. My text is much more current, yet more concise, as the goal was to frame topics in broad outline rather than to present them in as much detail as the other texts. My outlook is more global, with less of an American emphasis. This text's treatment of the themes of digital inclusion, learning, health, safety, AI, work and leisure, politics, war and peace, and lifestyles goes far beyond that found in the two other books. Finally, unlike Quinn, I do not discuss ethical dilemmas using specific codes of ethics, leaving that to instructors to present as they think best.

Here are four other useful books. Still impressive is Rob Kling's *Computerization and Controversy: Value Conflicts and Social* Choices.[25] Its 1996 second edition includes valuable writing by the author as well as many classic papers. Three volumes have a narrower focus. *Reinventing Technology, Rediscovering Community: Critical Explorations of Computing as a Social* Practice,[26] by Philip Agre and Douglas Schuler, focuses on ontological questions about computers and software as well as the application of networks to support community. Batya Friedman's *Human Values and the Design of Computer Technology* proposes a methodology known as value-sensitive design.[27] A new volume discussing this approach is being published in 2019. A useful volume that is somewhat current with robot technology and applications is *Robot Ethics: The Ethical and Social Implications of Robotics* by Patrick Lin, Keith Abney, and George Bekey.[28]

You may also want to refer students to the following publications:

- *Communications of the ACM*, ACM
- *Computer Law and Security Review*, Springer
- *Ethics and Information Technology*, Springer

- *IEEE Computer Magazine,* IEEE
- *Interactions,* ACM
- *Journal of Information, Communication and Ethics in Society,* Emerald
- *Science, Technology, & Human Values,* Sage
- *Technology in Society,* Springer
- *MIT Technology Review,* MIT Press
- University law journals, especially Duke, George Washington University, Harvard, Stanford, University of California at Berkeley, University of Chicago, and the University of North Carolina

Part I

Opportunities

1

Digital inclusion

J. C. R. Licklider, Vannevar Bush, Doug Engelbart, Ted Nelson, and Alan Kay optimistically and exuberantly imagined how computers could better the lives of people. Much of this has come to pass. The Internet supports learning by 'students' at all levels. Information on laws, procedures, diseases, and medical care may be found on the web. The Internet now provides the easiest, or in some cases the only, way to pay bills or order items such as books, groceries, and even clothing. It is a means of communication with family, friends, individuals one would like to meet, individuals with whom one could share insights, and potential employers. Music, films, and other means of entertainment stream to our digital devices.

This implies that those for whom digital technology is not available are at a disadvantage. The gap between the technology-haves and the technology-have-nots became known in the 1990s as a *digital divide*.[1] The concept is nuanced; we can speak of availability or scarcity of hardware, such as personal computers (PCs) and mobile phones; of infrastructure such as cellular networks; of communications bandwidth that enables a smooth media viewing experience; of expertise in using the technology; of commitment to its use; and of engagement in the process. Some only consume information; others contribute their ideas via methods such as blogging and tweeting.

Yet a better way to describe digital technology widely accessible is the goal of *social inclusion*,[2] to allow all individuals, regardless of socio-economic status, location, race, gender, or ability or disability, to take advantage of the benefits of modern computing and telecommunications. To have terminology that is even more evocative, we shall use the more modern and descriptive term of *digital inclusion*.[3] This has been defined by the International Telecommunications Union as 'empowering people through information and communication technologies (ICTs)'. The term 'people' is meant here to imply all people throughout the world.[4]

This chapter will first examine the digital divide between the haves and the have-nots (often the rich and the poor) within several nations. Examples of the benefits of digital inclusion will be cited. We shall also discuss the threat to digital inclusion within the USA posed by the recent US government decision to abandon the policy of *net neutrality*.

We examine ways to digitally include not just individuals in developed societies but also people in 'developing countries'. We discuss the impact technology can have in such contexts, and also the damage that can be done in any nation when the Internet is shut down for political reasons.

We then introduce the concept of the *inclusive design* of technology and examine how the failure to provide inclusive technology often leads to a divide between those who are able-bodied and those who have sensory, motor, or cognitive challenges. We conclude the chapter with two interesting special cases of digital inclusion—the divides between male and female and between young and old—and the ways in which gender and age play a significant role in digital inclusion.

Do digital divides still exist? What are the benefits of solving the problem of digital inclusion? What are the challenges that must be met?

1.1 Pioneers and visionaries

The vision of digital inclusion has motivated individuals and societies to close digital divides. We shall first highlight the work of two individuals with early far-reaching dreams about digital inclusion for people with disabilities. We shall then celebrate the achievement of an entrepreneur committed to making quality information available to all internet users.

The British scientist Alan Newell began work on technology for deaf and non-speaking people in the UK in the late 1960s.[5] His first inventions were a voice-operated typewriter using Morse code for people who could not type and a talking brooch, a wearable communication aid for people who could not speak. His research then moved to what became known as Augmentative and Alternative Communication (AAC) for people with severe disabilities such as Amyotrophic Lateral Sclerosis (ALS). Newell coined the phrase 'ordinary and extra-ordinary human–computer interaction'; he believed that one could understand how *people with disabilities in ordinary environments* could cope by understanding the functioning of *people without disabilities in severe environments*. Examples of this concept are how heavy fog makes it hard to see long distances and how loud noises make it difficult to hear. A more recent innovation has been the use of theatre enactments to raise awareness of the lives of individuals with disabilities and senior citizens. This proved especially helpful in thinking about needs and possible technology solutions for senior citizens, some of which are discussed later in this chapter and also in Chapter 4.

The American scientist Elliot Cole began work on treatments for Traumatic Brain Injury (TBI) in the early 1980s.[6] In the USA, 1.7 million people who have experienced a TBI are seen in a hospital each year. The increased survival rate of soldiers returning from war zones has meant the prevalence of TBIs has grown. Cole's major concern was enabling people to do normal everyday activities that had been routine before their injuries: tasks such as remembering names, making lists, checking completed items off a list, and making one's lunch. His solution, developed and tested with over 100 patients over three decades, was 'user-friendly' software delivered on PCs that functioned as *cognitive prostheses*. Cole also pioneered *tele-rehabilitation*, working with patients using telecommunications, thereby enabling the patient to be in his or her natural environment, supported by a therapist who could be located remotely. He sometimes described his work as identifying and fostering 'islands of abilities in seas of deficits'.

Both Newell and Cole employed digital technologies to aid individuals with disabilities: in one case, primarily sensory and motor, and in the other case, cognitive. Yet computers and telecommunication technologies aid us all in many ways, often as a source of information and knowledge at one's fingertips on the web. A dramatic vision of this was created by Jimmy Wales, the co-founder of Wikipedia.

Wikipedia

Wikipedia is a free online encyclopaedia that has become a remarkable success in the past fifteen years.[7] There are now over 40 million articles, 5 million of them in English, in over 250 languages. It is accessed by nearly 500 million unique viewers each month. It is now the dominant general encyclopaedic resource in the world.

Wikipedia's content is created by its community of users and readers. There are now 30 million 'registered editors' and over 100,000 active editors. Most of the content creators do not have credentials, but are just ordinary people. Although the original goal of allowing text to be entered by anyone has had to be modified due to disputes over accuracy and occasionally even vandalism, various scholarly analyses have given Wikipedia high marks for quality.[8]

Co-founder and leader of the project, Jimmy Wales, sought to create 'a world in which every single person on the planet was given free access to the sum of all human knowledge'.[9] Wikipedia has dealt reasonably well with the problem that there are sometimes passionate disagreements as to what is the truth and what is knowledge and what is neither. We aim 'not for the truth with a capital T, but for consensus', said Wales,[10] in which people who disagree can at least reach a consensus on the essence of their dispute.

Figure 1.1 The Wikipedia page describing Wikipedia

There have been recent developments related to Wikipedia. One good one has been Google's Knowledge Graph,[11] which aids the instantaneous access to knowledge. It provides summaries of facts in response to searches right on the search results page. One then need not dig deeper into websites, online encyclopaedias, or other sources of information. A negative development has been the censoring of access to Wikipedia by over a dozen countries including China, Cuba, Iran, Russia, Syria, and Turkey,[12] a topic to which we shall return in Chapter 5.

Research: Identify, illustrate, discuss, and analyse Wikipedia mechanisms for the resolution of disputes over what constitutes the truth and what is the knowledge that should be recorded on Wikipedia.

Debate: Resolved: Despite occasional inaccuracies, Wikipedia contributes hugely to our knowledge and wisdom.

1.2 Access to the Internet

Although Wikipedia was created only in 2001, the value of the Internet for all citizens was recognized by governments earlier. For example, in the USA, the Clinton administration's High Performance Computing Act of 1991 proposed the creation of what was called a 'national information infrastructure.'[13] In January 1994, then US Vice President Al Gore spoke about 'connect[ing] and empower[ing]...citizens...through broadband, interactive communication.' Internet access equality was explored in detail in four US National Telecommunications and Information Administration reports between 1995 and 2000.[14] A grand political vision accompanied these developments:[15] the digital divide must be overcome to give everyone the ability to compete in a 'New Economy'. One can question whether or not this is a realistic goal, although being competitive is certainly desirable for individuals and businesses.

Since then, there have been countless recitations of ways in which computer and communication technologies benefit many people but are disproportionately available to individuals based on categories such as household income, educational attainment, race, ethnicity, gender, age, community type (urban, suburban, rural), disability status, and language preference.

Inequities in access are still to some degree prevalent within the USA.

Table 1.1 Characteristics of internet users in the USA at two recent points in time[16]

	2000	2015
All American adults (18 and above)	52%	84%
Household income less than $30K	34%	74%
Household income greater than $75K	81%	97%
Less than high school	19%	66%
At least a college degree	78%	95%
18–29	70%	96%
Over 65	14%	58%
Female	50%	84%
Male	54%	85%
Black, non-Hispanic	38%	78%
White, non-Hispanic	53%	85%

We can see that the digital divide in the USA has narrowed, but not completely.

Net neutrality

This rapid growth of internet use was fuelled in part by visionary US government policies. A small but significant factor leading to the Internet's success has been the pricing of telecommunications. The phrase *net neutrality* refers to a telecommunications policy in which: (1) all users, corporations, and individuals pay the same amount, regardless of the volume of data used; (2) all data is treated the same, regardless of purpose of use; and (3) there are no fast lanes for special customers or data or purposes. These rules guaranteed equal treatment, similar to the transmission of electricity for telephone calls. In 2018, Federal Communications Commission (FCC) chairman Ajit Pai abandoned this policy and allowed telecommunication companies to charge differentially, an action that was greeted with a flurry of lawsuits from state attorney generals and public interest groups.[17]

Although it is too early to know the impact, many worry that US telecommunication companies will increasingly tilt internet pricing and policies in favour of big business and special interests. Among the groups that have expressed concern are artists and activists,[18] who convey their creativity and their message using social media such as YouTube, Facebook, and Twitter; small businesses, 500 of whom protested because their firms increasingly rely upon the economics of e-commerce; and start-ups, 200 of whom spoke up for the same reasons.

Digital inclusion or exclusion must not be viewed as a binary variable,[19] with groups or nations characterized either as 'haves', that is, technologically 'rich'; or 'have-nots', that is, technologically 'poor'. Unfortunately, individuals with wealth and education are more likely to have the 'digital skills' which with to make good use of the Internet. In a bad case of negative feedback, use of the net can in turn increase inequalities in knowledge and skill.[20] Yet factors that can increase digital inclusion, such as low-cost broadband, low-cost computers, public-access computing centres, and relevant digital literacy training are essential but insufficiently unimplemented.[21] Digital media content in appropriate languages, human resources to promote learning and literacy, and social resources, that is, support from committed institutions and community partners,[22] are vital to bridge the divide. Finally, it is critical that prospective internet users have the motivation to make effective and meaningful use of the technology, and that their uses be 'situationally relevant', that is, it must support meaningful goals for them such as pursuing social connections, engaging in commerce or political activity, or consuming goods and services.[23]

Does digital inclusion better the lives of citizens? In Chapters 2, 3, and 4, we will give examples via developments in technologically enhanced media, education, and health. In this chapter, we shall present one other example: digital communications to support community.

Beginning in the early 1990s, community networks across the world used the Internet to create community cohesion, inform citizens, provide access to educational resources, and strengthen democracy.[24] Most were situated in urban areas, although some linked individuals across rural spaces. The Berkeley Community Memory project was an outstanding early example of creating a 'virtual people's park'. Principles underlying such systems included access, service, democracy, and world community. They anticipated today's Internet and its mechanisms such as websites, forums, list servers, and blogs, which enable individuals worldwide to stay in touch with friends and acquaintances, enlarge the circle with whom they interact, and enrich their lives with instantaneous access to online sources of knowledge and information. We shall return to this topic in Chapter 5, where we will discuss the role of community networks in terms of enabling greater participation in the political process.

Research: Research and analyse the digital divide for your country or country of origin.

Research: Identify and discuss cases of countries other than the USA where the issue of net neutrality has come up and what policies were put in place.

Concept: Write a Wikipedia article, 'digital inclusion'.

Book report: Jan van Dijk and Alexander van Deursen (2014). *Digital Skills: Unlocking the Information Society*. Palgrave Macmillan.

Ethics: Your town is planning a major expenditure on providing free and excellent bandwidth throughout the area. At the same time, it needs to raise taxes significantly, because there are other pressing demands for cash, especially for road repair. Your expertise as a computer professional is sought. What do you advise? How do you compare and judge the importance of physical and virtual highways?

1.3 Internet access across the world

Globally, access to computing and telecommunications is distributed unevenly.

Table 1.2 Global internet penetration in 2013

Ranking	Country	% of population with internet access
1st	Iceland	96.5%
2nd	Bermuda	95.3%
3rd	Norway	95.1%
	...	
15th	Canada	85.8%
18th	USA	84.2%
	...	
86th	China	45.8%
139th	India	15.1%
	...	

Ranking	Country	% of population with internet access
178th	Myanmar	1.2%
179th	Timor-Leste	1.1%
180th	Eritrea	0.9%

As Table 1.2 shows, there are vast regions of the world with little digital inclusion.[25] Inequalities are even greater when one considers availability of bandwidth and not just subscriptions to services.[26,27]

The growth of internet use in Canada, Europe, China, and India has been similar to the USA, with the latter two countries starting somewhat later.

Table 1.3 Digital inclusion (individuals who used the Internet at least occasionally in 2013) in several countries

		Age			Education			Income		
Country	Total %	18–34%	35+%	Diff.	Less %	More %	Diff.	Less %	More %	Diff.
USA	89%	99%	85%	−14%	80%	95%	+15%	84%	97%	+13%
Canada	90%	100%	87%	−13%	81%	95%	+14%	85%	99%	+14%
China	65%	93%	49%	−44%	48%	91%	+43%	56%	80%	+24%
India	22%	34%	12%	−22%	9%	38%	+29%	11%	28%	+17%
Pakistan	15%	20%	10%	−10%	6%	33%	+27%	8%	20%	+12%
Ethiopia	8%	12%	4%	−8%	5%	43%	+38%	5%	23%	+18%

In Table 1.3 we can see the differences in digital inclusion as a function of age, education, and socio-economic variables within each nation, as well as differences between the countries.[26]

China is interesting because of its growing influence in world politics and trade. The digital divide there is rapidly shrinking, driven by increases in mobile connections, which had risen to 890 million by the end of 2015.[28] The country is now a major world player in digital media,[29] despite its extreme government internet censorship.[30] We shall return to this topic in Chapter 5.

One dramatic digital inclusion success is Digital Green.

Digital Green

Rikin Gandhi has been the driving force behind this project.[31] Gandhi had started with a concept that was not working—creating village knowledge centres in small villages throughout India. After working at length with farmers, he modified the concept. He focused on training farmers and employed them along with other villagers to create and endorse

Continued on next page

educational digital videos made with local talent. In a thirteen-month controlled trial involving 1,470 households in sixteen villages, Digital Green increased the adoption of desired agricultural practices by a factor of seven; Gandhi's process was ten times more cost-effective than a classical agricultural extension approach.

Figure 1.2 Screenshot from a video overview of Digital Green
© Digital Green

Key to success was the organization's human element, especially Gandhi himself, and the means used to engage the participation and enthusiasm of farmers. The Digital Green Foundation has grown and seems to be thriving.[32] As of June 2016, its 4,400 videos had reached over 1 million individuals in over 13,000 villages in India and other nations in Asia and Africa. Its approach has also been adopted—with promising early results—in nutrition education.[33]

Not every project has been as successful. One ambitious effort was the One Laptop Per Child (OLPC) project of Nicholas Negroponte,[34] founder of the MIT Media Lab. The mission was 'to empower the world's poorest children through education'. The goals of the project were:

> to provide each child with a rugged, low-cost, low-power, connected laptop... [and] hardware, content and software for collaborative, joyful, and self-empowered learning. With access to this type of tool, children are engaged in their own education, and learn, share, and create together. They become connected to each other, to the world and to a brighter future.

Founded in 2005, its original goal was building and shipping 100 to 200 million US $100 machines per year within two years.[35] By 2014, the project had only shipped devices at a price closer to US $200 to approximately 2.4 million children.[36]

These results were insufficient to enable sustainability, and the head office shut down that year.[37] There have been several thoughtful analyses of how and why OLPC achieved what it did, and why it did not do more.[38] The OLPC failed to anticipate and deal with the complexities of a developing country environment and the response by computer hardware industry players such as Intel to develop competitive low-cost laptops. Other challenges included a lack of electricity, hardware unreliability, repair problems, insufficient teacher expertise, insufficient budget for repairs and training, technology rushed to market, and disagreements among key OLPC executives. Nonetheless, the OLPC staff reported findings from various sites that were 'largely positive in nature', including improvements in school attendance and engagement.[39]

The largest deployments of the OLPC concept were in Peru (860,000 laptops) and Uruguay (570,000 laptops). The number of computers per student increased in 319 rural Peru primary schools from 0.12 to 1.18.[40] Yet only about 40 per cent of the students took the computers home due to concerns about theft and machine breakage. No significant effect was found on test scores in maths or language, although a significant positive effect was seen in one cognitive skills measure.

The deployment in Uruguay was studied extensively.[41] Devices were distributed to students in every public school and many secondary schools. The secondary schools were brought on board because of enthusiasm about results at the primary level. The result was an impressive reduction in the digital divide, both in terms of income level and geography. Yet advances in digital inclusion were not ideal; for example, only one-fourth of students reported that their parents also made use of the laptops. No impact on test scores in reading and maths was found. Laptop use declined over time; only 4.1 per cent of the students reported using the machines 'every' or 'almost every' day by 2012. Machines were used mainly for downloading, web surfing, and game playing. There was no effect on the self-perceived ability to carry out educationally significant tasks.

The need to enhance teacher training and to transform education is a theme to which we shall return in Chapter 3. We shall also address the value of standardized testing in assessing the impact of educational technological innovations that seek outcomes not in line with accepted standardized outcomes. Do standardized tests capture what one has learned? If not, how does one articulate the value of innovations that do not result in better student test scores?

The desire for worldwide digital inclusion, as well as expanded markets for technology, continued into the 2010s. In 2013, founder and CEO of Facebook, Mark Zuckerberg, asserted in a white paper that (internet) connectivity is a 'human right'.[42] He went further in a keynote speech to the Mobile World Congress:[43]

> [a] Deloitte study...showed that if you increase the number of people in emerging markets that have Internet access you could easily create more than a hundred million jobs and bring that many people or more out of poverty and you could decrease the child mortality rate by up to 7% and save millions of lives by giving people access to that information.

The report,[44] actually released a year later, did not say that, but did assert:

> This study analyses how Facebook stimulates economic activity and jobs through three broad effects: as a tool for the biggest and smallest of marketers; as a platform for app development; and as a catalyst for connectivity. It estimates that through these channels Facebook enabled

> $227 billion of economic impact and 4.5 million jobs globally in 2014. These effects accrue to third parties that operate in Facebook's ecosystem, and exclude the operations of the company itself.

Unfortunately, the report's intricate research methodology shed little light on how Deloitte justified the claims of substantial economic impact and job creation that Facebook has 'enabled'.

Yet Facebook does bring value to many people and businesses. To bring greater connectivity to developing countries, and ultimately secure new customers, in August 2013 Facebook established an organization called 'Free Basics'. By November 2016, it had connected 40 million people to the Internet.[45] Yet its technologies and policies resulted in great controversy, most notably in India.[46] Little of the Internet's full potential was exposed as the site favoured Facebook, violating net neutrality. Many individuals perceived Facebook's ulterior motive to be securing a higher market position rather than improving the life of citizens in developing countries. Because of this perception, Facebook withdrew Free Basics from India in 2016.

Kentaro Toyama, founding assistant managing director of Microsoft Research India (MSR India), provided his analysis of the problems encountered in using technology to promote social change around the world.[47] He described his disappointment that ten different promising educational technology projects at MSR India did not seem to make a difference, always floundering because of the lack of good teachers and academic administrators. Based on his observations of over fifty projects, he argued that real impact results from the dedication of the researchers to create concrete social impact, the commitment and capacity of partner organizations, and the desire and ability of the intended beneficiaries to utilize the technology.

In other words, designing with knowledge of the human element and context is more significant than creating any specific technological features. This was illustrated by the Digital Green project mentioned—its success is due primarily to its community and to the commitment of individuals. Two other examples are research projects, which we shall now describe.

The first is research done in Sierra Leone by Steven Sam.[48] The research literature on digital inclusion falls into three categories: papers that suggest that mobile phones are 'panaceas for ameliorating the problems of poor people'; others that suggest that they 'widen existing socio-economic disparities'; and a third group that views the mobile phone as 'a means to achieve the development of human well-being'. As a research contribution of the latter kind, Sam carried out participant observation, in-depth interviews, informant interviews, and focus group discussions with almost one hundred 'marginalized' people between 18 and 35 years old in two small towns (one urban, one rural) near Freetown, the capital of Sierra Leone. Marginalization was defined in terms of lack of schooling and regular formal employment. The study found that mobile phones were used to organize family affairs, especially financial; keep in touch with family; coordinate activities for small businesses; and participate in politics. Despite the value of digital telecommunications to empower participants, Sam found no evidence that they were 'completely emancipated from their marginality' due to their technological ability. He concluded that political decision-making remains in the hands of 'political elites' and that political input via telecommunications is 'unnoticed in national development policy'.

A second example addressed the issue of enabling individuals in developing countries with low literacy to use mobile phones.[49] Professor Ishtiaque Ahmed's research team worked with a group of rickshaw pullers in Dhaka, Bangladesh. None could read or write a complete sentence in any language. A six-month ethnographic study helped the researchers design an interface that allowed low-literate pullers to get remote assistance in placing calls from members of their community who were more literate. This collaborative use model proved effective in a second study, in which the interface was tested with ten pullers over six weeks. Yet, like so many research studies, it is an open question whether the benefits are sustainable and scalable.

Research: Rese[illegible] case of Free Basics and discuss if and how the result could have been di[illegible] ad Facebook done things differently.

Debate: Resolv[illegible] urces in the developing world should be spent on upgrading health a[illegible] acy as opposed to information technology.

Book report: Wa[illegible] r, Charles Kane, Jody Cornish, and Neal Donahue (2012). *Learn[illegible] nge the World: The Social Impact of One Laptop Per Child.* Palgrave Mac[illegible]

Book report: Ken[illegible] ama (2015). *Geek Heresy: Rescuing Social Change from the Cult of Technol[illegible]* ic Affairs, Perseus Books Group.

1.4 Internet shutdowns

We have seen that the Internet can enhance literacy and empower individuals. As we shall discuss in detail in Chapter 5, it is also a vehicle for free speech and the expression of ideas. These ideas are not always popular with governments, so they sometimes try to suppress dissent by shutting down the Internet. This has been happening increasingly throughout the world.

Internet shutdowns do not just occur under totalitarian regimes. Between 1995 and 2010, there were growing numbers of shutdowns. Forty-five per cent of the 606 incidents spread across ninety-nine countries happened in democratic regimes or in emerging democracies.[50] India has suffered the largest number of shutdowns; Chinese access has been limited by what is known as the 'great Chinese firewall', and there have been numerous incidents in Africa and the Middle East.[51]

By 2015, this was costing countries a conservative estimate of $2.4 billion in lost productivity, not counting impacts such as reduced tax revenues and loss of consumer confidence.[50] Special damage is sustained by emergency service workers and journalists. Also affected are human rights advocates, who have been outspoken in their attempts to fight internet shutdowns.[52] In 2016, the United Nations passed a resolution on behalf of human rights on the Internet.[53]

We shall return to these issues in both Chapters 5 and 6. Next, we shall discuss how internet access, even if unhampered by governments, is not equally accessible by all.

1.5 Inclusive design of technology

The Inclusive Design Research Centre of Canada's OCAD University defines inclusive design as 'design that considers the full range of human diversity with respect to ability, language, culture, gender, age and other forms of human difference'.[54] The researchers note that inclusive design processes must 'recognize diversity and uniqueness', use an 'inclusive process and tools', and do so while keeping in mind the work's 'broader beneficial impact'. We do not have the space to elaborate further on the design process but will focus on specific disabilities that present challenges for digital inclusion: vision, hearing, and cognition.

The World Health Organization (WHO) estimated that 246 million have poor vision, 285 million people worldwide are *visually impaired*, and 39 million are blind.[55] Roughly 90 per cent live in low-income settings; 82 per cent of the blind are 50 years old or older. Because vision is the primary modality we use in interacting with computers and mobiles, poor vision is a serious obstacle; zero vision is a grave one. Despite recent genetic, stem cell, and bionic advances to end blindness,[56] the digital divide between those with and without adequate vision is wide.

A variety of technological aids have been developed to help those with low vision access computers. First, there are screen magnifiers which enlarge what is displayed on a screen. More interesting, however, are *screen readers*.[57] Screen readers take the text from the screen and convert it into voice or into Braille or other haptic feedback. Effective design of screen readers takes into account the frustrations that blind users experience in interacting with the web,[58] as well as thoughtful design guidelines to ameliorate these issues.[59] A key element is the order in which sections of the screen are vocalized. There are intrinsic problems that will always remain, for example, assisting those with poor or no vision in navigating complex paths among various internet pages, or relationships among complex charts and tables; and enabling the 'seeing' of material which cannot be completely described in text, such as diagrams, photos, and videos. But what about navigating the world, and not just the screen?

Navigation aids for the blind and visually impaired

BlindSquare,[60] created in 2017, is an accessible app which announces interesting features of an environment to the visually challenged. Outdoors, it works by retrieving information using the global position system (GPS), and then announcing street intersections and plausible points of interest to the user. Indoors, it can work if the environment has been instrumented with iBeacons: low-energy Bluetooth devices sending out signals describing the area that can be received by smartphones.

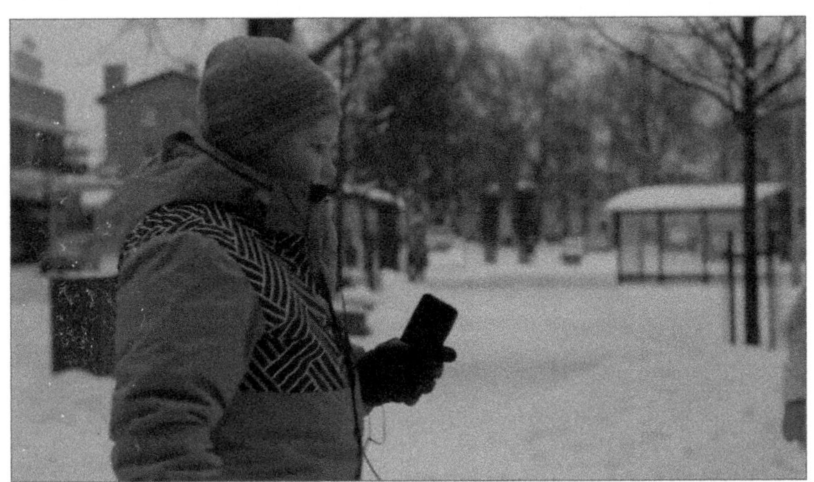

Figure 1.3 Screenshot from a video introduction to BlindSquare

Recently, WHO estimated that 360 million people worldwide have *disabling hearing loss*.[61] This disproportionately affects the elderly—over one-third of individuals 65 years old or older suffer from hearing impairments. Hearing difficulties do not significantly impede computer and internet use; in fact, technology could be used to deliver hearing loss tests, information, and interventions to the hearing challenged.[62] Furthermore, where information is communicated in sound, there are well-understood techniques such as *closed captioning* for videos and movies. For mobiles, the situation is different, as hearing is typically as or more essential than vision and touch for effective use.

Recent research projects suggest promising directions, including an app for recognizing sounds in the environment and turning them into visual or vibro-tactile alerts on a mobile phone,[63] and SignWriting,[64] a method for communicating on mobiles via static visual signs. Much effort has gone into supporting the dynamic American Sign Language (ASL) under restricted bandwidth conditions on mobile phones,[65] although increasing bandwidth will soon make this easier.

Cognitive challenges are extremely diverse. Cognitive disabilities can include autism, dementia, Down syndrome, and TBI, among many others.[66] One can also speak about functional diagnoses of challenges such as attention span, executive function, language, naming, memory, and visuospatial ability. As all of these are needed to use digital technology, cognitive disabilities are serious impediments to the use of digital devices.

Significant work has been done in the area of autism. A systematic and comprehensive review of *interactive technologies* for autism noted that individuals with autism are often well disposed to use technology, which they find less stressful than interacting with people.[67] Eight components of interactive technology platforms for autism have been identified: PCs and the web, video and multimedia, mobile technologies, shared active surfaces, virtual and augmented reality, sensor-based and wearable technologies, robotics, and natural user interfaces.

There has also been work done specifically on technologies relevant to children with other special needs,[68] and on software architectures to ease the incorporation of inclusive internet interfaces into mainstream software.[69]

It is important to note that innovations designed for people with special needs often benefit the rest of us. Curb cuts, introduced to help people in wheelchairs move between the sidewalk and the street, also work for individuals with baby carriages and bicycles. Closed captioning, originally intended for the hard of hearing, also help us in noisy sports bars, where everyone becomes hard of hearing. Vocalizations of information for the visually impaired are useful for anyone surrounded by a dense fog.

Research: Research if and how people who cannot read are Internet-disadvantaged.

Research: Technologies for working with ASL.

Concept: Write a Wikipedia article on Alan Newell, pioneer in inclusive design.

Concept: Write a Wikipedia article on Elliot Cole, pioneer in cognitive prosthetics.

Policy: Write a brief for a politician who is planning to speak about digital inclusion for blind and visually impaired people at a conference of politically active citizens.

Law: Requiring libraries to provide internet access technology for blind patrons.

Technology review: Identify and evaluate several new solutions to navigation assistance for the visually impaired. Refer to issues raised in this chapter.

Ethics: Your software firm is delivering products that are not accessible by people with disabilities such as poor vision. You raise the issue. The CEO insists that the firm cannot afford to develop such features and that they would be detrimental to users with normal vision. How do you deal with this? How do you debate ideals versus economics? What options can you identify? How far will you go to protest the decision?

1.6 Gender issues

Statistically, women and girls have now achieved parity in internet use with men and boys, at least in the Western world, but it is helpful to examine their use more carefully. Early hopes for *computer-mediated communication* (CMC) were that the absence of visual gender clues online would lead to more equal and equitable participation on conversations. Yet research has uncovered significant gender differences in the style of one's digital participation.[70] Susan Herring and her colleagues analysed the discourse of participants in online discussion forums and responses to surveys about 'netiquette'. They found that men and women participated unequally and in different ways; men tended to dominate conversations, often being argumentative and confrontational, while women said less and tended to be polite, supportive, and encourage negotiation and agreement. They concluded that this was in part due to different values and approaches to conversation. Although differences in participation volume and style have reduced over the years, their recent synthesis was that the research results 'run counter to the claim that gender is invisible or irrelevant in CMC, or that CMC equalizes gender-based power and status differentials'. Differences also vary by country; a survey found greater gender differences within a British group of university students than among a Chinese cohort.[71]

Ethics

Gender portrayal in video games: Gender has also been a significant variable in video games. Analyses of video games by researchers concerned about gender equality have focused on three major issues: (1) the extent to which female characters are present in the games; (2) the ways in which women and girls are portrayed; and (3) the degree to which video games present experiences that are enjoyable for females and are consistent with their learning, work, and play styles. A review of 150 games across nine gaming platforms found that only 10 per cent of the primary characters were female and overall only 15 per cent of the characters were female.[72]

Figure 1.4 Typical portrayals of women in video games, as illustrated by characters in *Mortal Kombat*

Reproduced with permission from D.Williams, et al. The virtual census: representations of gender, race and age in video games. *New Media & Society*, 11(5): 815-834.Copyright © 2009, SAGE Publications. https://doi.org/10.1177/1461444809105354.

A study of the portrayal of women in thirty-three popular Nintendo and Sega Genesis video games found that there were no female characters in 41 per cent of the games with avatars.[73] Female characters were portrayed as sex objects 28 per cent of the time and had violence directed against them 21 per cent of the time. Women were rarely featured as heroes or as action characters, but more typically cast as victims or damsels in distress—like the

Continued on next page

popular character of Princess Peach, the female lead in the Nintendo Mario franchise. A study of German female gamers found that they disliked video games because of the lack of meaningful social interaction, the extent of violent content directed towards women, the female gender role stereotyping just discussed, and the focus on competition rather than collaboration.[74]

Even if this style of video game design and development is still good business strategy—an assertion that should be questioned—designers and developers need to consider the ethics of perpetuating misogyny in their games.

Could video games be this way because most of them are designed by men? Since the late 1990s, concerns have been raised about the degree to which women and girls are underrepresented as programmers and computer scientists.[75] The percentage of women working in computing has declined steadily from 35 per cent in the early 1990s to a current (2018) level of 25 per cent.[76] Reasons given for this decline include the image of the profession, the lack of emphasis in secondary schools on STEM (science, technology, engineering, and maths) education for girls, and the relative scarcity of successful female role models in technology fields.

Yet this development is paradoxical. In 1843, Ada Lovelace, daughter of the English poet Lord Byron, wrote what is thought to be the first computer program. It was designed for Charles Babbage's machine called the Analytical Engine, which was never built. Historian Nathan Ensmenger recounted that computer programming was a desirable and welcoming profession for women in the 1960s, with good opportunities for upward mobility into management.[77] Only later did computing begin to be viewed as a 'masculine discipline' where 'people skills' are unimportant.[78]

The underrepresentation of women in computing is caused in part by similar phenomena in higher education. In 1985, only 37 per cent of computer science university and college degrees went to women;[79] by 2014, that percentage had dropped to 18 per cent. To remedy this, institutions like Carnegie Mellon University (CMU) have mounted a concerted effort to raise the percentage of women entering the computer science undergrad program; they have succeeded, as the number has grown from 7 per cent in 1995 to 42 per cent in 2000.[80]

Another good example is small California-based Harvey Mudd College. It educates prospective engineers, scientists, and mathematicians using a broad curriculum that includes the humanities and the social sciences.[81] The percentage of female computer science majors was 10 per cent in 2005; it rose to between 37 and 50 per cent early in the 2010s. President Maria Klawe, a respected computer scientist, demonstrated the importance of strong role models and female leadership to encourage women in STEM fields. There were also three major innovations: (1) the department changed the introductory programming course to focus on problem solving with computational approaches, the broad scope of computer sciences applications, and its impact on society, very different from the typical introduction to programming course content; (2) they made it possible for each female first-year student, regardless of major, to attend the Grace Hopper Celebration of Women in Computing;[82] and (3) they created large numbers of on-campus summer research opportunities for first-year students who had completed Introductory Computer Science.

An increasing number of courses for adolescent girls teach them how to code,[83] in order to reduce the gender gap in STEM. Additionally, the gender disparities in university computer science participation vary in severity between countries and cultures.[84] In Asia, for countries where data is available, 43 per cent of first university degrees in maths and computer science were awarded to women. Examples where the situation is also good are Italy: 43 per cent, Finland: 42 per cent, Portugal: 41 per cent, Greece: 40 per cent, and Mexico: 38 per cent. One reason this is possible is that the discipline of computing now places increasing emphasis on understanding user requirements and developing congenial user interfaces. These tasks require breadth, also skills in communicating with and understanding users, customers, and application domains. The field is not just for men or 'geeks'.

Efforts to stop women and girls in the leading Western technology nations from being left behind and treated differently from men and boys are occurring, albeit (too) slowly. Another factor impeding progress is the issue of work culture. Think about Alphabet (Google), Amazon, Apple, Facebook, and Microsoft—the five leading internet and mobile software developing firms, to be called in Chapter 12 the Frightful Five (a term coined by journalist Farhad Manjoo). Collectively, they have had only fifteen CEOs in over 125 years of existence. All the CEOs have been men. Men have also held most of the leadership positions in the venture capital firms that fund Silicon Valley. The result has been a culture of Brotopia,[85] in which the 'lone genius nerd'[86] has been celebrated and dominant, creating an environment often like that of a male university fraternity. In many cases, this has led to a culture in which women are insufficiently valued, discriminated against, harassed, or even sexually assaulted. Accounts detailing such behaviour are now routine.[87] Despite assertions that the industry is encouraging diversity and working towards punishing and eliminating such inappropriate behaviour, the goal of gender (and racial) diversity in the high-technology workplace still seems to be far away.[88]

Research: Review methods that have been used at various levels of schooling that have succeeded or failed in interesting more girls in computer science.

Research: Study the extent to which gender and age stereotyping still is the norm in today's video games.

Research: Research whether or not there have been changes in the participation of women in the design and coding of video games, the cause of these changes, and any effects that have been observed.

Debate: Resolved: Females are no longer disadvantaged with respect to creating or using information technology.

Book report: Thomas J. Misa (ed.) (2010). *Gender Codes: Why Women are Leaving Computing*. IEEE Computer Society.

Policy: Write a brief advising a male candidate for a university Arts and Science dean position on policies he could advance to ensure greater understanding of information technology by all the institution's students.

1.7 Technology for seniors

Digital inclusion for seniors is an active area of research, development, and technology adoption. Here is a quote from AGE-WELL, a leading R&D site:[89]

> AGE-WELL NCE (Aging Gracefully across Environments using Technology to Support Wellness, Engagement and Long Life NCE Inc.) is Canada's technology and aging network... dedicated to the creation of technologies and services that benefit older adults and caregivers... to help older Canadians maintain their independence, health and quality of life, [and to] increase their safety and security, support their independent living, and enhance their social participation.

Such work is particularly relevant because the world's population continues to age at a rapid rate. Especially noteworthy is the rate of growth of the 'oldest old', that is, those over 80 years of age.

Table 1.4 Aging of the world's population

	2015	2030	2050
People in the world aged 60 and over	901 million	1.4 billion	2.1 billion
People aged 80 and over	125 million	*	434 million

Note: * no data available

Demographic data indicate that seniors are going online in increasing numbers.[90] Yet the digital divide between seniors and other adults still exists. By 2017, almost all Americans were going online; the percentage for individuals 65 and over was roughly two-thirds. The good news is that the gap between seniors and everyone else has been narrowing. Only 14 per cent of seniors were going online in 2000; the percentage grew to 59 per cent by 2013. The bad news is the extent to which technology use declines as seniors get older and become the oldest old.

Table 1.5 Technology use as a function of age

Tech use at different ages	65–69	70–74	75–79	80+
Uses the Internet	82%	75%	60%	44%
Has home broadband	66%	61%	41%	28%
Owns a smartphone	59%	49%	31%	17%

Older adults experience more vulnerability with respect to new technology,[91] as 73 per cent of seniors say that they need help to understand and navigate new electronic devices.[92] In Chapter 8, we shall return to other kinds of harmful emotions seniors often experience with digital technology—frustration, anger, and even rage.

Assisting older adults in staying connected

An important use of seniors' technology is for connectedness with family and friends. Social isolation is a critical problem for older adults in many societies. For example, varying estimates of social isolation in Canada's seniors range from 19 to 30 per cent.[93] A recent US study found that 43 per cent of seniors reported feeling lonely;[94] loneliness was associated with declines in activities in daily living and mobility, and an increased risk of death. Since the Internet enables worldwide electronic communication that is synchronous (e.g., real-time video conferencing), and asynchronous (e.g., text and audio-visual email), there have been many solutions proposed for facilitating connectivity and combatting seniors' social isolation and loneliness.[95]

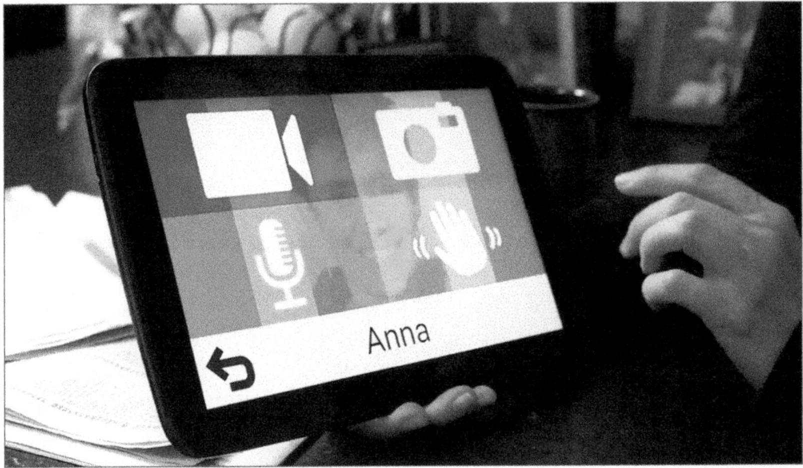

Figure 1.5 A prototype that focuses on enabling seniors' communication in text, voice, photos, and videos

Another application for seniors' technology is fall detection, often called Personal Emergency Response Systems (PERS).[96] From the classic 'I've fallen and I can't get up' technology, which required a senior needing help to call for it, newer designs are apps for wearables which detect falling and/or lack of motion automatically to alert emergency response personnel immediately.

More generally, the challenge of digital inclusion for older adults can be viewed in two ways. The simpler problem is that of designing technologies and interfaces that are easy for seniors to use, assuming they are committed to this use. The more challenging problem is that of motivating and supporting seniors to use technologies if they are not certain that they want to so at all, or if they are positively reluctant to do so.

Several authors have proposed design principles or guidelines to aid the invention of technology and interfaces that support use by older adults. These typically focus on human dimensions such as visual, auditory, and haptic perception; motor abilities, especially motions of the hand and the fingers; and cognitive abilities, especially memory, attention, orientation, and problem solving.[97] Examples of guidelines are keeping the type large enough to read and ensuring that the user need not remember large numbers of items. These suggestions may be enhanced with the experiences of designers working on seniors' use of the web.[98] Yet many interfaces are still too intricate, filled with jargon, poorly organized, and difficult to navigate for the aging population. Even worse, today's digital devices are often confusing to use from the moment one opens the box.

One particularly interesting study of factors that influence the acquisition, use, and retention of mobiles by older adults with vision, hearing, or dexterity impairments found that safety was one of the highest motivations.[99] However, seniors were put off and confused by opaque and distressing sales and service pricing plans and by confusing information concerning which features were available on what devices. Of note is that the one phone designed specifically for seniors proved unsatisfactory.

What makes seniors' use of technology even more challenging than what is implied by their decline of sensory, motor, and cognitive capabilities can be understood from the demographics of chronic disease and other perils.[100] Older adults are disproportionately affected by chronic diseases such as diabetes, cancer, heart disease, and strokes. Eighty per cent of seniors have at least one such condition; over 70 per cent of US Medicare beneficiaries have two or more. Furthermore, one of the most common threats to health is the fact that one out of three seniors has a fall each year. Consequences include hospitalization and reduced physical activity. Furthermore, one in four seniors experience behavioural health problems such as depression or anxiety.

The result of all of this is that one-third of seniors never use the Internet.[91] Some experience *digital disengagement*, trying but then ceasing to use the Internet regularly. A study found percentages of disengagement ranging from 3.5 to 39 per cent, the wide range being due in part to greatly different measures of disengagement.[101] Causes of disengagement cited in five case studies including eyesight problems, lack of interest or need or motivation, lack of people to communicate with, and the forgetting of skills. There was always a combination of factors that led to increasingly intermittent usage, never just one sole reason. The study also found other serious causes, such as fear of privacy loss, identity theft, financial security, or digital safety, as well as a reluctance to engage in an activity that one often finds stressful or even humiliating.

Finally, neurodegenerative diseases, such as dementia and Alzheimer's disease, are becoming more prevalent.

Table 1.6 Prevalence of dementia: data forecast over the next thirty years

	2015	2030	2050
People in world with dementia	46.8 million	74.7 million	131.5 million

As one progresses through various stages of dementia from mild to severe, problems with memory, executive function, communication, poor judgement, confusion, and ultimately loss of control over bodily functions can make the use of technology more and more challenging.[102]

On the one hand, if computer use is satisfying, resulting in enhanced sense of worth, independence, and social connectedness, one can overcome these problems. On the other, if computer use is a challenge, it is likely to result in frustration, failure, and anger; poor health makes this even more likely. We shall return to this again in our discussion of safety in Chapter 8.

Research: Challenges in computer and mobile phone use faced by seniors who have dementia.

Research: Compare and contrast the out-of-box experience with three or four new mobile phones.

Concept: Write a Wikipedia article entitled 'seniors' technology'.

Debate: Resolved: It is essential that your grandparents become computer-literate.

Debate: Resolved: Designing technology specifically for seniors will not be necessary in thirty years when all are computer-literate. (Or will seniors' deteriorating vision, hearing, motor control, cognition, and self-confidence always cause problems? For a discussion of this proposition, see the Aging in Place Technology Watch.[103])

Jury: John Smith is on trial for identity theft and taking $20,000 from the life savings of 85-year-old Herman. He claims he is innocent, as Herman willingly gave his banking and personal information to him. Is John guilty and, if so, what penalty should you administer? Depending on the country and legal system within which the trial takes place, what protections are offered to Herman?

Field study: Explore how seniors in a care facility (retirement home, long-term care/nursing home, etc.) learn and use, or fear and avoid, technology.

1.8 Summary

We have addressed the goal of digital inclusion, which ideally means empowering all people everywhere through ICTs. Some of the earliest goals of this kind were articulated by Alan Newell and Elliot Cole, who imagined and dedicated their research careers to using technology to assist individuals with sensory, motor, and cognitive disabilities. Entrepreneur Jimmy Wales envisioned comprehensive information available online to everyone and was able to make this happen with Wikipedia. Wikipedia is a particularly compelling form of digital inclusion, because so many people read the articles and there are also numerous writers.

We began by examining at the digital divide in specific countries. Data suggests that these divides are narrowing, yet there are often political challenges, such as those currently posed in the USA by the proposal to abolish net neutrality. We discussed typical benefits of digital inclusion, empowering people to organize and help one another using a variety of virtual communities and enabling all people to have information at their fingertips using software such as Wikipedia and the Google Knowledge Graph. Yet, in situations of economic scarcity, even the best-intentioned societies will struggle to determine how many resources to allocate to ensure digital inclusion.

Next, we looked at the digital divide between different countries. These divides are narrowing, yet there are still nations in the world whose use of digital technologies is very light. Many individuals and organizations in developed countries have dedicated themselves to bridging the divide existing in 'Third World' nations. We saw examples of great success, such as Digital Green. Yet there has been disappointment in efforts of grandiose scope such as OLPC, as well as other programs that did not have sufficient support from the people they wanted to help or from organizations which had local experience and credibility. It is clear that technical people committed to worldwide digital inclusion need to understand local conditions, customs, and values, and to partner with local experts if they are to make the impact on the world that they seek.

Obstacles to regular use of the Internet also arise under both democratic and totalitarian regimes when the Internet is shut down to suppress dissent.

Inclusive design seeks to ensure that new technologies are available and usable by all, independent of background, nation, location, race, gender, income, education, or ability. We examined some of the issues that arise when people are blind, or have low vision, as information and commands that are displayed need to be translated into some other modality, such as sound, or made 'visible' through one's sense of touch. The degree of disability implied by the inability to read the screen has been severe, yet, as we shall see in Chapter 12, innovations such as voice assistants and 'hearable technologies' are making vision less essential for using some digital technologies.[104]

Problems encountered by individuals with auditory challenges are particularly serious in using mobile phones; there is promising technological research on this problem. Cognitive challenges can manifest themselves in a variety of disease conditions. Autism spectrum disorder is one area in which significant research has been done. Other cognitive conditions that pose challenges need to have their own specific issues addressed if digital inclusion is to be achieved.

Societies struggling with how many resources to allocate to accessibility should remember that it has been proven that technology or environment accessibility often proves to be of wider benefit, as we have seen with curb cuts and video closed captioning.

The growing ubiquity of computers and the Internet in our society is among women and girls as well as men and boys. Although access and use of digital technology by males has outstripped use by females, the gap has narrowed. Yet research tends to show that patterns of behaviour and inequities with regard to gender carry over into the digital domain. In video games, gender stereotyping has damaged digital technologies and reduced their potential for empowerment and enjoyment by women. It will be interesting to see if such gender differences continue as today's children, all 'digital natives', progress into adulthood.

Our final topic dealt with older adults and computers. If seniors can successfully use technology, this can lead to an enhancement of their sense of worth, provide them with access to information and resources, and open channels for communication with family, friends, and new acquaintances. If technology is difficult, frustrating, or intractable to use, it can result in digital disengagement. That older adults often have multiple chronic diseases, that their abilities continue to change in what is typically an inexorable pattern of decline, and that they often develop degenerative diseases like dementia makes achieving digital inclusion for seniors very challenging.

We have made great progress towards digital inclusion by allowing computers and mobiles to assist, inform, and connect us. Yet there are disturbing aspects (and potential consequences) of the last few decades of progress. Andrew Keen has been one of the most persistent critics:

> The error that evangelists make is to assume that the internet's open, decentralised technology naturally translates into a less hierarchical or unequal society. But rather than more openness and the destruction of hierarchies, an unregulated network society is breaking the old centre, compounding economic and cultural inequality, and creating a digital generation of masters of the universe. This new power may be rooted in a borderless network, but it still translates into massive wealth and power for a tiny handful of companies and individuals.[105]

We shall return to this theme in Chapter 12.

Debate: Resolved: Andrew Keen's critique of today's internet society is correct; the benefits are going primarily to a new digital elite with extreme wealth and power.

Book report: Andrew Keen (2015). *The Internet is Not the Answer*. Atlantic Monthly Press.

1.9 Key terms

Ada Lovelace
AGE-WELL
Alan Newell
Asynchronous electronic communication
Augmentative and Alternative Communication (AAC)
BlindSquare
Brotopia
Closed captioning
Cognitive challenges
Cognitive disabilities
Cognitive prostheses
Computer-mediated communication (CMC)
Digital disengagement
Digital divide
Digital Green
Digital inclusion
Digital natives
Elliot Cole
Free Basics
Frightful Five
Gender gap
Gender stereotyping
Google's Knowledge Graph
Grace Hopper Celebration of Women in Computing
High Performance Computing Act of 1991

Inclusive design
Information and communication technologies (ICTs)
Interactive technologies
Internet shutdowns
Jimmy Wales
Mark Zuckerberg
Netiquette
Net neutrality
Neurodegenerative diseases
New Economy
One Laptop Per Child (OLPC)
Personal Emergency Response System (PERS)
Screen magnifiers
Screen readers
SignWriting
Social inclusion
Social isolation
STEM (science, technology, engineering, and maths)
Synchronous electronic communication
Tele-rehabilitation
Visual impairment
Wikipedia

2

Digital media and intellectual property

Vannevar Bush envisioned a machine that would assist humanity in the creative work of writing. Doug Engelbart imagined the collaborative sharing and enhancement of knowledge. *Digital media* today—text, drawings, photos, audio, and video—surpass the visions of their pioneers. These media may be copied, shared, and modified in ways that challenge the legal system, because unrestricted content sharing without suitable payment to creators runs counter to *intellectual property* (IP) traditions and laws.

Writers, musicians, artists, and inventors have long relied upon IP protection to enable them to control the use of their creations and inventions. *Copyright infringement,* that is, copying in violation of copyright, threatens the income that they could receive from their creations. The concept of *fair use* is a critical issue in such discussions, as it allows certain exceptions to copyright.

One area that has received a great deal of attention is the digital copying and sharing of music; we shall examine the interplay between conventional behaviour, ethics, technical interventions to limit or block copying, laws and legal battles, and product and pricing innovation.

Next, we shall look at similar issues in the domain of motion pictures. There are effective and legal streaming services, yet there are still concerns about copyright infringement. Copyright holders now automatically produce *takedown notices* to insist that websites remove illegally or improperly sourced material. Such notices include many errors, causing additional complications for video creators.

One interesting challenge to the concept and laws of copyright occurs in the creation of *mash-ups.* Artists use fragments from existing musical or visual performances as well as their own material to create audio-visual works that combine multiple content sources. Artists, lawyers, and businesspeople debate the extent to which such mash-ups violate reasonable copyright protection.

Copyright is also significant for academic articles and textbooks. There are two especially interesting cases to discuss. One is the widespread copying of textbooks by students due to the high price of texts. The other is the fair pricing of the publication of research results that have been funded by government grants. This issue has provided one of several stimuli to the creation of *open access* publications.

Finally, we shall discuss IP issues that surround software, and protection by copyright and patents. Protection of novel software by *patents* is now accepted practice, yet many believe that the software patenting system is broken. Advocates of fewer IP restrictions on software developed the concept of *free software*, which resulted in the *open source* software movement. We shall discuss this in detail.

Our final topic will be Lawrence Lessig's *Creative Commons* method of characterizing and licensing IP, a new and creative solution to the tension between copyright and free use.

Do our concepts of IP and the laws protecting it need to change in response to new developments in digital technologies? How can we best balance the demands of consumers, the rights of inventors, companies marketing products based on these inventions, and the importance to society of unhampered media use which can stimulate creativity and innovation?

2.1 Pioneers and visionaries

In the earliest days of computing, the computer was imagined as a machine for the rapid computation of numbers to estimate missile trajectories, decipher codes, and so forth. Soon thereafter, computers also were calculating social security payments and corporate profits. Yet, by the 1950s, a number of thinkers and inventors noticed that the numbers could represent alphabetic characters or magnitudes of audio waveforms or points on a Cartesian coordinate system. Using suitable input and output transducers, such as paper scanners and devices for printing or plotting information on paper, computers could be used to input, generate, and transform documents, music, and pictures, that is, digital media.

Three early visions came from Max Matthews, Ivan Sutherland, and J. C. R. Licklider. In 1957, while working at AT&T Bell Laboratories, Matthews wrote 'MUSIC',[1] the first widely used computer program to generate music. By 1968, Matthews was experimenting with interactive digital sound generation. Sutherland wrote his 1963 PhD dissertation on an interactive graphics program for producing structured drawings;[2] this Sketchpad program helped spark the field of computer graphics. Lastly, in 1965 Licklider provided a blueprint for the digital libraries of the future.[3]

These pioneers created digital media, but what about the *ownership* of digital media? The laws of IP, as we shall discuss below, evolved in response to the desire of writers, musicians, and artists to own and control their creations. They wanted to gain economic benefits from their creations in the same way that owners of material artefacts such as food, machinery, and transportation vehicles can profit from what they own and/or have created. Some early computer scientists challenged the assumption that digital media should be treated in the same way as non-digital media are. We shall focus on two such individuals, Brewster Kahle and Richard Stallman.

Kahle imagined that all human writing, including everything written online, should be preserved, accessible, and free for everyone to access and use. Even with an immature internet and a relatively new World Wide Web, he noted the growing importance of digital information, as he wrote in 1997:[4]

> this new resource [the Internet] will offer insights into human endeavor and lead to the creation of new services.... Where historians have scattered club newsletters and fliers, physical diaries and letters, from past epochs, the World Wide Web offers a substantial collection that is easy to gather, store, and sift through when compared to its paper antecedents.... as the Internet becomes a serious publishing system... these archives... will also be available to serve documents that are no longer 'in print'.

His subsequent technical and entrepreneurial efforts sought to build and commercialize the *Wayback Machine*—a search engine for the retrieval of old internet information—and the *Internet Archive*—a 'non-profit library of millions of free books, movies, software, music, websites, and more'.[5]

With goals similar to the Internet Archive, Michael S. Hart's Project Gutenberg,[6] initiated in 1971, was the first attempt to turn books into *e-books*. Google Books was created in 2004 as another effort to preserve books digitally.[7] By 2015, Google had scanned over 25 million books into its digital library.

On a par with Kahle, Stallman's vision was that computer programming should result in artefacts—computer programs—that can and must be freely accessible and usable by all other programmers. In announcing his open source and free GNU operating system, he explained:[8]

> I consider that the golden rule requires that if I like a program I must share it with other people who like it. I cannot in good conscience sign a nondisclosure agreement or a software license agreement.... So that I can continue to use computers without violating my principles, I have decided to put together a sufficient body of free software so that I will be able to get along without any software that is not free.

Stallman's vision, as well as the contributions of others such as Linus Torvalds, animated the *open source software* movement, to which we shall return below.

Research: Compare and contrast the goals and approaches of Project Gutenberg, the Internet Archive, and Google Books, paying particular attention to issues of IP.

Debate: Resolved: The Wayback Machine should be outlawed, as it makes it impossible for people to ever escape mistakes they have made.

2.2 Intellectual property: protection and fair use

Both Kahle and Stallman sought to enable works of writing—in one case, English text, in the other case, computer programs—to be freely available, and at zero or little cost.

Historically, the cost of written text, such as novels or books of poetry, had been driven in great part by the cost of printing. When represented digitally, the cost of creating a 'digital print' is almost zero, yet authors have still wanted to be compensated for their labour and creativity.

Their right to compensation was protected by a form of intellectual property protection known as *copyright*. In the early days of computing, sharing software, as desired by Stallman, was routine. Software that was commercialized was typically bundled in with the cost of hardware, so it had no individually priced value. Once software became unbundled in the 1960s, it became an item that could be sold separately and whose value was also protected by copyright.

The four major kinds of intellectual property

Copyright is one of a set of ways in which intellectual property is protected. There are four major forms of intellectual property protection: *trade secrets*, *patents*, *copyright*, and *trademarks*.[9]

A *trade secret* is information that is commercially valuable and not generally known or easily ascertained. A firm keeps the information secret using security measures such as locks, passwords, and confidentiality agreements. A good example is the formula and method for making Coca-Cola.

A *patent* gives an inventor the exclusive right, for a set period of time, to make an artefact that is useful, novel, non-obvious, and enabling. It thereby allows the inventor to prevent others from making the patented object, or to earn income by licensing it to others. A good example is Polaroid's invention of instant photography. There have recently been great controversies over the patenting of software, and bitter legal battles over patents dealing with the interface and functionality of mobile devices between major electronics companies such as Google and Samsung.

A *copyright* gives an author the exclusive right to distribute, display, copy, and make derivative works of something he or she has authored, for example, a poem, PhD thesis, song, symphony, graphic design, painting, or computer program. Copyright protection goes back to the British Statute of Anne in 1709 and the US Constitution in 1787, with its goal '[t]o promote the Progress of Science and useful Arts'.[10] Worldwide, many aspects of copyright protection are agreed upon, such as those enshrined in the 1886 Berne Convention and the 1996 World Intellectual Property Organization (WIPO) Copyright Treaty.[11] Many battles about IP protection have dealt with copyright protection or violation.

A *trademark* is a name or symbol used by a merchant or company to identify something it has created or manufactured. The goal is to distinguish it from similar items, and to indicate the identity of the individual or firm making it. Examples are 'Word', to identify Microsoft's word processing program; the words 'Kleenex' and 'Xerox', to signify particular brands of tissue and photocopying equipment; the design of Exxon's tiger; the Mercedes Benz hood ornament sculpture; and Avis's slogan 'We Try Harder'.

Laws protecting IP benefit creators and inventors and companies that are distributing books, music, works of art, and inventions. But there should be, and there is, a limit to what the owners of IP can disallow. The concept of *fair use* encompasses what consumers and users can reasonably do without requesting permission from copyright owners and without harming their economic interest. A reporter can quote from a speech by a politician. An English teacher can copy a couple of pages of poetry. A scholar can reproduce a short passage from another work to accurately convey what the author of that work said (as is the case with quoted passages in this book). Music or film fans can make copies of purchased CDs or DVDs for their own use, unless impeded by digital rights management technology, which we will discuss.

More generally, fair use is said to apply when certain conditions hold true.[12] There are four major issues: (1) The more the use tends toward research or education, as opposed to commerce and profit, and the greater the degree of transformation of the work, the more likely it is that fair use laws will apply. (2) Certain works are granted more leeway in copying, for example factual works usually have more fair use allowances than expressive works such as fiction. In addition, the more creativity that is involved in making the new work, the less leeway is allowed. (3) The more of the original work you take, the less likely it is that fair use will apply. (4) The more that your use negatively impacts the market or potential market of the original work and the livelihood or success of the author, the less likely it will qualify as fair use. The application of these heuristics is almost always a matter of subjective judgement, which is why IP disputes about fair use versus copyright violation often are taken to court.

Before discussing the methods of protecting the IP of various kinds of digital media, it is worth noting that fair use is also important to the economy and to innovation. A 2007 study found that industries including consumer device manufacturing, internet search and web hosting, e-commerce, software development, and education relied upon fair use, and that together these industries represented almost 17 per cent of the US Gross Domestic Product (GDP).[13]

Research: Looking at the legal systems of two countries that interest you, compare and contrast their practices with respect to digital technology and IP.

Research: Study and report on the fair use of books and artworks by university professors and students.

Ethics: You are a programmer in a software firm. You discover a co-worker taking source code from a competing product, copying critical sections, making trivial changes to hide its origins, and including it in your code base. You report this to management, who refuse to act on your concern, citing its weak competitive position. What do you do?

2.3 Music

The earliest major IP battle fought over digital technology began in the early 1990s with respect to music downloading and sharing. This had become possible because of a number of technical developments. Most importantly, digital storage was continually becoming cheaper, in accordance with Moore's Law, which predicted that the number of chips on a given area of silicon would be doubling approximately every two years (discussed in the Prologue). Digital storage had also become available in numerous compact forms, such as floppy disks and digital cartridges. A new audio digital compression format, called *MP3*, reduced the size of music files by 75 per cent to 95 per cent of the original size, with only modest compromises in terms of sound quality.[14] The internet was also becoming universally available for file storage and transmission. By the end of the twentieth century, novel creations such as *peer-to-peer (P2P) file sharing* software,[15] for example Napster,[16] rose to the forefront of music downloading and sharing.

Ethics

Music downloading and sharing: Starting in 1999, Napster made it easy for individuals to send digital copies of music to their friends. The 'virtual community' Napster enabled grew rapidly.

It's Here!!

Napster v2.0 is now available! Download it now and join the internet music revolution!

Welcome to Napster, the future of music. Napster is the best search engine available, and the best way for users to find and download MP3s. By creating a virtual community, Napster ensures a vast collection of MP3s for download. Napster also eliminates the problems of conventional FTP transferring by using cutting-edge technology to ensure the completion of each MP3 transfer.

napster features include:

- Advanced Search System
: Search every library online for songs - you can specify the minimum ping times, bitrates and frequency. All results are pinged to allow you to find the fastest site. The search is realtime, so the list of available songs you receive is reliable every time. Never again deal with tied up sites. If you cannot access the song, it simply does not show up in the results.
- Chat System
: The easy-to-use napster interface allows users to chat with each other in a number of different forums based on music genre.
- Audio Player
: Your choice of the internal napster player or an external MP3 player of your choice, making napster the most complete MP3 product on the market.
- HotList
: napster's hotlist allows users to keep track of their favorite MP3 libraries. The hotlist notifies users as to when their favourite libraries are online and accessible.
- Playlist
: The playlist helps users maintain and manipulate MP3 playlists, so users can pick the order in which they wish to hear songs in their library.
- Feedback
: napster contains a built-in form for submitting bugs, suggestions and comments. napster's feedback provides the staff with an immediate way to realize concerns associated with the software.

Figure 2.1 A screen shot of an early (October 1999) Napster home page

There was an ethos in much of the culture that condoned and applauded music copying and sharing. here are some examples collected by one author:[17] 'I cannot afford to buy... [the] song. The company is a large, wealthy, corporation. I wouldn't buy it at the retail price (or pay the required fee) anyway. The company is not really losing a sale or losing revenue. This violation is insignificant compared to the billions of dollars lost to piracy by dishonest people making big profits.' Others believed that 'Everyone does it', making it foolish and uneconomical to pay for songs. Some reasoned that they illegally copy music to 'sample songs to see if they really wanted them', perhaps before buying it. For these individuals, Napster provided a huge inventory of songs, far more than could be found at an individual store or from a specific label, with the added 'convenience of getting their music online' and as a medium that did not require a CD.

As we shall see, music downloading and sharing continues to the present day, but much has changed since the early days of Napster. In what situations and under what conditions are such practices ethical?

Why were so many individuals willing to do what most recognized was a form of stealing? A questionnaire administered to eighty-four Irish individuals, seventy-one of them between the ages of 21 and 24, showed that most viewed downloading as immoral but found ways to morally disengage from the act in order not to feel guilty.[18] An online questionnaire given to 172 undergraduates at a US university showed that most viewed music downloading and sharing differently than they did the act of shoplifting a physical CD.[19] Concerns about possible punishment, morality, and the rule of law factored into their judgements about piracy scenarios and their own downloading behaviour, while respect for the corporate music industry played no role. Another questionnaire administered to 196 students found that 75 per cent of participants admitted to downloading, and 15 per cent to downloading music at least once a week.[20] Downloaders had less concern for the law than non-downloaders, engaged in other risky behaviours, and were also more likely to steal an actual CD if there was no risk of getting caught. Finally, questionnaires were given to 207 Taiwanese high school students aged 15 to 19, asking questions about their attitudes towards two kinds of actions—pirated music product purchasing, and unauthorized duplication/download.[21] In both cases, the perceived prosecution risk, magnitude of consequences, and social consensus were significant factors. Singer or band idolization was significant in the case of pirated music product purchasing, reducing the likelihood of such behaviour; however, this was not the case with unauthorized duplication or download, likely because it was felt not to harm the musicians.

Some musicians applauded the copying and sharing of music. They felt that Napster was helping them become better known; hence, it would ultimately improve their success. It was also helping new and unknown artists rise in popularity. These groups supported Napster and music copying and downloading. Yet this support was dwarfed by legal challenges from other musicians and all the corporate record labels. The legal battles boomeranged at first, providing Napster free publicity, and thereby helping it grow faster. Despite efforts by Napster to control the distribution of copyrighted material and to convert its free distribution into a subscription service (much like Soundcloud and Spotify in present day), the legal assault was successful and Napster was shut down in mid-2001.[16] Napster then attempted to sell its assets to the German media firm Bertelsmann, but this move was blocked by the US bankruptcy courts, forcing the company to liquidate its assets in mid-2002.

Other P2P music sharing sites sprang up in Napster's absence, using technology that involved no centralized music storage, and hence were harder to shut down. There were disputes over their impact, yet most observers agreed with the Recording Industry Association of America (RIAA) that these sites were harmful to the music companies. Their data indicated a percentage drop in annual CD sales of 25 per cent from 2000 to 2003.[11] Hence, music publishers stepped up their legal assault on these digital ventures; in September 2003, RIAA initiated lawsuits against thousands of individuals suspected of illegal downloading. Downloading music files then decreased by about 50 per cent within a year.[19]

The music industry also tried various schemes for locking files to prevent copying. Known in the industry as *digital rights management* (DRM),[22] there are numerous methods to protect copyrighted content.[23] All aim to confirm the owner's copyright over the material, manage the distribution of the content, and control access to and use of the content. Control over access rights has become increasingly severe as DRM technologies have matured, incorporating restrictions on multiple activities including viewing, copying, printing, and altering the content. Technologies have included encryption keys linked to one computer, Web-based permission protocols, digital watermarks that can prevent copying, and hacking copying software to prevent it from working properly. There have also been major attempts by media companies to develop and standardize DRM technologies. Examples are the Secure Digital Music Initiative (SDMI) and the Sony BMG Music Entertainment Rootkit.[24]

Yet DRM has not been successful. It is cumbersome, and inconvenient to purchasers with legitimate reasons for copying, such as backup or reformatting for people with disabilities. It raised concerns about privacy, often being hidden in the files. Its side effects on user software and hardware were not obvious. It introduced security flaws onto people's machines. There was actually a suggestion that music publishers should 'ethically attach' viruses to downloadable music files as a method of deterrence![25] Hackers found flaws in the techniques and published ways to get around them. Furthermore, DRM caused frustration and anger, resulting in legal and societal backlash against the media industries.

Governments in the USA and Europe enacted legislation in response to lobbying from the music and motion picture industries. The United States passed the Digital Millennium Copyright Act (DMCA) law in 1998; the European Union (EU) ratified the European Union Copyright Directive (EUCD) in 2001.[22] DMCA criminalized attempts to circumvent DRM methods such as copy protection schemes. Another important provision was for *safe harbour*, designed to prevent websites from liability for copyright infringements, as long as they made good-faith efforts to remove infringing material from their sites. EUCD was designed to harmonize the ways in which European countries fought copyright abuse. The EU legislation was gentler than the US laws, focusing on DRM circumvention intended for commercial purposes, making it less likely that individual consumers or researchers would be charged.

Neither technical nor legal measures were effective in stopping music piracy. Debates about the ethics and implications of music downloading and sharing continued. Arguments have become more nuanced; new issues have been raised. Scholar Robert L. Frost suggested that the problem is the almost monopolistic control that a handful of record companies have over the music business.[26] He asserted that the internet provides an environment for the disintermediation of the business so that content producers can connect more directly to consumers. He argued that prices should go down, and musicians would earn more, while incentives for piracy would be dramatically reduced. David Lametti noted that sharing music has always been part of music's culture, especially among youth, and that this sharing fosters creativity, knowledge, and education.[27] He proposed that society and its legal systems needed to keep this in mind when seeking a balance between the rights of society and the rights of copyright holders.

David Bach noted that the DMCA and the vigorous prosecution of those suspected of music piracy, or directly or indirectly aiding music piracy, had several deleterious side effects. It strengthened the monopolistic positions of the few major industry incumbents and weakened outside competition in the industry.[11] His second point was that new digital technologies should make it easier for copyright holders to grant fair use exemptions, but that this was not happening. Finally, he argued that decisions by the few monopolistic owners to wall off a vast amount of IP in *information enclosures* was not in the best interests of the emerging information society. Finally, Bart Cammaerts placed the debates about the legality of sharing music in the context of generally increasing durations of copyright protection; for example, copyright holds for seventy years after an individual's death, and 120 years after the date of creation in case of corporate ownership,[28] in both the USA and Europe. He argued that the only way the music industry could maintain its rigid ownership position would be through increasing inspections and other invasions of privacy of internet users, and he believed music companies should embrace rather than continue to confront the 'participatory networked culture'.

The IP legal scholar and activist Lawrence Lessig has advanced some of the most articulate and impassioned pleas and inventive ideas for finding a new balance between reasonable protections of IP rights and some degree of IP internet sharing and re-use.[29] Lessig noted that low-cost digital media authoring technologies have enabled new forms of youth literacy and expression, with this creativity becoming their form of speech. Much of this is *remix*, whereby creators do not take works wholesale, but use new digital tools to say things in new ways. (We discuss this idea under the label 'mash-ups' later in this chapter.) The laws today, argued Lessig, are blunt instruments that do not distinguish between remix re-use and wholesale piracy. The result is increased extremism on both sides: media companies requiring automatic takedowns of content suspected to be infringing (we will return to this topic in the discussion of movie IP), individuals arguing for the abolition of copyright. What is needed, said Lessig, are artists and creators embracing the idea of their work becoming available more freely, under appropriate conditions, and businesses embracing a more nuanced distinction between what is free and what is not free, and allowing both, under certain conditions. Also required are laws that distinguish between the theft of entire pieces of music to avoid payment, and the use of music fragments in artistic expression. His invention of the Creative Commons license, to be discussed at the end of this chapter, is one step towards enabling this more nuanced environment.

A 2010 study of over 2,000 college students sought to predict the impact of music publishers removing DRM on consumers' willingness to pay for songs and on producers' revenues and profits.[30] The research indicated that the music industry could benefit from removing DRM because this would increase the demand for music products as well as consumers' willingness to pay for these products.

By then, a new distribution and pricing strategy, led by Apple, was being adopted. Using a mixture of technical, packaging, and pricing innovations, Apple succeeded in reducing the magnitude of the conflict. Apple had launched the iTunes Music Store in 2003, pricing the songs at 99 cents, and protecting them with a brand of DRM. By 2007, other music retailers were beginning to offer songs without DRM, and Apple followed this model in 2009.[31] Other subscription services soon sprang up, including one from Amazon, called Prime Music. Apple became and has continued to be the market leader for legal music downloading, holding 63 per cent of the market share of paid digital downloads in 2012, with Amazon as distant second at 22 per cent.

Yet technology continues to advance. Paid music downloading seems to have peaked, dropping from $2.8 billion in 2013 to $2.3 billion in 2014, due to an increase in streaming subscription services such as Apple Music and Spotify.[32] Industry reports from 2016 found that streaming accounted for 47 per cent of US recorded music sales, followed by 31 per cent in downloads and only 20 per cent by physical media.

A 2013 overview by sociologist Matthew David summarized the outcomes of the online battle for and against the control via copyright:[33]

> Attempts to represent file-sharing as theft, piracy, and an aid to terrorism have largely failed, and have often backfired, as when the piracy label has come to be celebrated by many, rather than vilified.... sharing has not been stopped by cultural, legal, or technical means.... In the music industry... new business models based on free information exchange, such as by fostering better rewards for 'live' performance, represent 'perestroika from below.' Online sharing hit recorded music first and hardest. Alternatives here are also most developed. Challenges to business as usual in film, television, journalism, publishing, and computer gaming emerged later but parallel those in music.

Debate: Resolved: Downloading of copyrighted media without paying for its use is stealing.

Book report: Lessig, Lawrence (2004). *Free Culture: How Big Media Uses Technology and the Law to Lock Down Culture and Control Creativity*. The Penguin Press.[34]

Book report: Lessig, Lawrence (2006). *Code, Version* 2.[35] Basic Books.

Jury: Assuming either the DCMA in the USA or the EUCD in a European country, debate as a jury what verdict to determine and what damages to award for an individual who cracked a DRM technique in order to enable research to be done on translating music into vibrations for deaf people.

Technology review: Current websites and apps for music downloads, streaming, and sharing.

Field study: Interview a number of musicians who have been making music professionally for ten to twenty years and solicit and analyse their experiences with systems for paid music such as iTunes, as well as unpaid music sharing.

2.4 Movies

As Matthew David implied, internet downloading and streaming of motion pictures and television started a few years after the copying and sharing of music began. This was because movies and shows required more bandwidth than songs. Poor image quality was also often an issue. The illegally sourced files sometimes contained viruses. Yet these factors were not sufficient to counter the attraction of obtaining the content for free.[36] As with music, the entertainment industry first reacted with alarm, quantifying their loss of revenue, then mounted technical and legal attacks. The US motion picture industry estimated a $3 billion loss from a total production revenue of $32 billion in 2002.[37] Piracy varied greatly across different countries, ranging from lows of 12–15 per cent in Sweden, Italy, and Greece to highs of 92–95 per cent in Indonesia, Ecuador, and Pakistan. Particularly damaging in all cases was the illegal release of a motion picture before its official theatrical release, which was estimated by one analyst to cause a 19 per cent decrease in revenue compared with post-release movie piracy.[38]

A landmark case in the domain of films was Metro-Goldwyn-Mayer Studios (MGM) vs Grokster.[39] A consortium of twenty-eight of the largest entertainment studies (led by MGM) sued Grokster and Streamcast, movie streaming sites, for copyright infringement. The defendants initially won in a US District Court because of an analogy with Sony's Betamax VCR, which had survived a copyright suit on the grounds that it was primarily used for the legitimate purpose of time-shifting. The Grokster decision was upheld by a US Court of Appeals but was then reversed by the US Supreme Court in 2005. The Supreme Court's reasoning was that there was ample evidence that both Grokster and Streamcast promoted their services as similar to Napster and as a tool for illegally distributing copyrighted material. Aspects of their technical architecture seemed designed to evade legal liability.[41] Both companies used the availability of popular copyrighted material as an argument for gaining investors. They relied upon this feature as an incentive for advertisers; it was also a key aspect of their business strategy. After the Supreme Court decision, Grokster shut down its P2P network in 2005 and paid $50 million in damages to the media industry players.[42] Other similar actions in subsequent years were successful in damaging or shutting down other major purveyors of pirated media content.

YouTube[40]

The number of sites that supplied video downloads continued to increase in parallel with increasing internet bandwidth and decreasing costs of storage. YouTube, founded early in 2005 and bought by Google for $1.65 billion eighteen months later, grew exponentially, and now is the second most popular website.[43] By February 2017, there were 400 hours of video content being uploaded to YouTube every minute.

Continued on next page

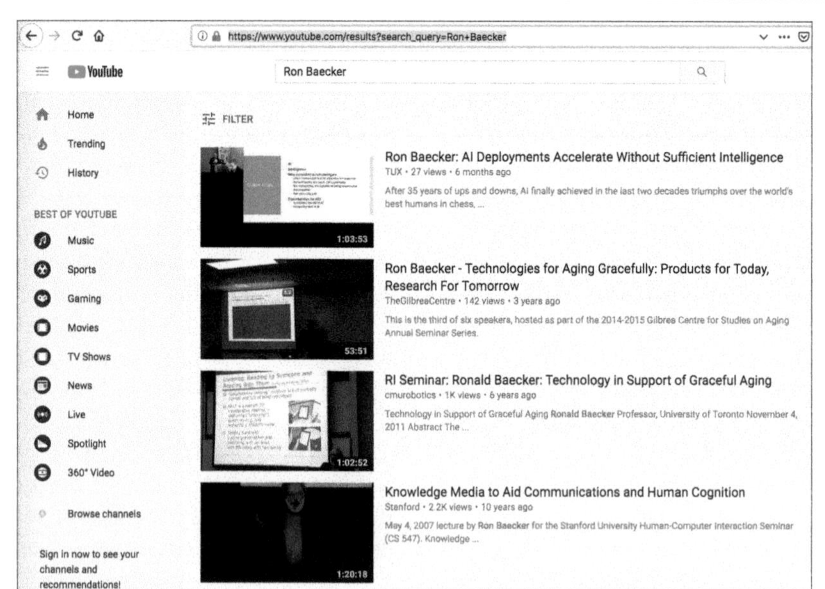

Figure 2.2 Screenshot of a 2018 YouTube selection of video-recorded talks given by this book's author
By permission of Oxford University Press

Many of the issues discussed in this chapter and in Chapter 5 apply to YouTube. There have been ongoing battles about 'pirated' content on the site, but YouTube has been reasonably vigilant in protecting the property rights of video content creators and publishers. Aspects of the mechanics of protection—'takedown notices'—will be discussed in this section. Because the medium is a relatively open vehicle for content dissemination, it is censored in many countries, including national bans in China and Iran. Most of the content is available for free, paid for by advertising. Yet there are some specialty paid channels on YouTube, which YouTube created in part to compete with Netflix and Amazon Prime Video's video streaming services, that also produce their own content. In fact, much of American filmmaking's creative talent is now focused on these digital mass media vehicles as opposed to its traditional reliance on Hollywood films.

Thorin Klosowski, a consumer who originally thrived on pirated content then later began to buy media, told his story in print.[44] For a while, he found the availability of good content, the frustrations of ordering online, and the obstacles imposed by DRM so annoying that it was easiest (and cheapest) to download copyrighted material from sites making it available for free. Yet more good content soon became available in a timely fashion at a reasonable price from online interfaces that made legal purchases simple. As the encumbering DRM restrictions were also reduced, it became easier to purchase copyrighted than to access pirated material. Perhaps removing his legal exposure also played a role. He thus stopped pirating media and 'went legit'. Many others have made the same decision.

One factor in the battle against the illegal distribution of movies and other IP that violates copyright has been *takedown notices*, huge numbers of which are now automatically generated by algorithms. For example, Google's search system received less than 100 takedown requests in 2009, but in 2014 the number ballooned to 345 million.[45] Many of the notices are frivolous and disruptive to video producers, who find it difficult or impossible to challenge the notices and get their work reinstated online. In some cases, this can be financially ruinous to individuals.[46]

Most alarming is the staggering scope of errors in the process.[47] Research interviews confirmed that the majority of online service providers were primarily relying on algorithms to process the exorbitant volume of requests. When analysed by hand, the correctness of a random sample of 1,800 takedown notices from Google Web Search taken from over 100 million takedown requests found that 30 per cent of requests were potentially problematic. In 4 per cent of the cases, targeted content did not match the work that it allegedly infringed; in 19 per cent the identification of the infringed work was incomplete. The researchers also analysed by hand the correctness of a sample of 1,700 takedown notices taken from 33,000 takedown requests related to Google Image Search. Ignoring the large number of requests from one individual sender, 36 per cent of the requests were questionable, including 15 per cent in which the subject matter of the claim was unclear, 12 per cent where fair use defences seemed plausible, and 6 per cent where ownership was unclear.

We recall that the safe harbour provisions of the DMCA protect websites from legal liability as long as they make reasonable efforts to remove infringing material. But what are reasonable efforts, and how much effort must an organization such as YouTube make in order to decide if a copyright owner's (often automated) complaint is valid, or if the material in question is protected by the fair use doctrine? A recent court decision dealt with a lawsuit against a woman who posted a video of her children dancing to the Prince song 'Let's Go Crazy'.[48] The decision reaffirmed the need for takedown notices to consider fair use, but also affirmed the court's willingness to recognize automated takedown notices as valid.[49] The DMCA provided that copyright holders who make material misrepresentations in their takedown notice could be liable to the alleged infringers. Having individuals review possible copyright violations makes it less likely that copyright holders could be held liable for misrepresentation.[50] Yet, because the DCMA gives copyright holders huge leverage, and because it puts online service providers under huge pressure, the deluge of automated takedown notices will continue. The complex law allows damages to be claimed in various ways by all three parties—the copyright holder, the online service provider, and the alleged infringer. Thus, deciding how to proceed, especially for individuals or small companies, is a critical but difficult decision to make.[51]

Research: Compare and contrast streaming services for music and movies.

Research: In pursuing their own film production, Netflix and Amazon have disrupted Hollywood. Support this premise with research and analysis.

Research: India has a huge film industry known as Bollywood. To what extent, and how, has digital technology affected Bollywood?

Concept: Write a Wikipedia article on the 'automatic takedown notice'.

2.5 Mash-ups

An interesting aspect of media copyright is *mash-ups*. Tools for the digital composition of music and visual media enable composers, artists, and individuals to express themselves creatively with media. All music is transmitted, stored, and played digitally. This allows composers, music lovers, and just about anybody to create a mash-up (the terms 'remix' and 'mix tape' refer to similar concepts). The mash-up creator digitally samples existing material from multiple sources, possibly together with new material, to create a new composition. The widespread popularity of musical mash-ups has been described thusly: 'consumers today think of songs as active components ready to be mixed up in a new recipe, not as static artworks meant to be heard again and again in some inviolable original setting'.[52]

Endless Love of Bush and Blair

One example of a mash-up is the already mentioned video of young children dancing to a Prince song. An even more compelling demonstration of the power of mash-ups incorporating visual and audio media is the edited sequence of video clips of then US President George W. Bush and then British Prime Minister Tony Blair set to a soundtrack of Lionel Richie's 'Endless Love'.[53]

Figure 2.3 An image from the Bush-Blair Endless Love mashup

Lawrence Lessig wrote:[54] 'For anyone who has lived in our era, a mix of images and sounds makes its point far more powerfully than any eight-hundred-word essay in the New York Times could. No one can deny the power of this clip, even Bush and Blair supporters, again in part because it trades upon a truth we **all** including Bush and Blair **supporters** recognize as true. It doesn't assert the truth. It shows it. And once it is shown, no one can escape its mimetic effect. This video is a virus; once it enters your brain, you can't think about Bush and Blair in the same way again.... But why...can't the remixer simply make his own content?...The answer to these questions [is]...Their meaning comes not from the content of what they say; it comes from the reference, which is expressible only if it is the original that gets used.'

As most media are protected by copyright, what happens when existing material that belongs to other owners who take a rigid view of their copyright, and expect no use whatsoever without their being paid a license fee, are used in mash-up creations? Michael Katz, a legal scholar, noted that more than half of online teens—the 'NetGen'—are content creators who use digital authoring tools and source material found on the internet.[55] Arguing that the term 'piracy' should be reserved for wholesale copying and redistribution, and that people are confused by 'labyrinthine statutes and inconsistent rights enforcement', he proposed that copyright legislation be amended to legalize the repurposing of content. Fellow legal scholar Kerri Eble agreed, documenting the difficulties faced by mash-up artists, because of ambiguities in the law, as well as the seeming inconsistency with which media owners whose work has been sampled pursue vindication, issue cease-and-desist orders, and seek financial compensation.[56] The two agreed on the notion that fair use provisions needed to be broadened to include a safe harbour for 're-contextualized' or 'redesigned' artworks.

IP attorney Robert S. Gerber broadened the discussion of mash-ups to include new applications created with application programming interfaces (APIs) from existing software and data sources found on the internet. He noted that such works raised a host of new contract laws and copyright, patent, trademark, and warranty issues, a discussion of which is beyond the scope of this textbook.[57]

Research: The IP issues that persist when one 'mashes up' existing software, their APIs, and data sources found on the internet to create a novel application.

Policy: Draft a brief for the attorney of a motion picture company that has decided to allow some mash-ups without laying charges of copyright infringement but is trying to formulate a policy on where to draw the line.

Law: Define a relaxed view of IP to allow mash-ups of content where the result is substantially different from the works contributing material to the mash-up.

Book report: Lessig, Lawrence (2008). *Remix: Making Art and Commerce Thrive in the Hybrid Economy*. Bloomsbury Academic.

2.6 Textbooks and research publications

We now turn our attention to a third kind of creative activity, the writing of textbooks and other scholarly material, including the fruits of research, and discuss how the tension between copyright protection and free or inexpensive access has played out in the domain of academic publications. These issues have received relatively little attention compared with the widespread interest in and discussion of the violation of copyright for music and movies.[58] There are at least two interesting questions regarding academic texts: the first is how and to what extent do university and college students violate copyright with respect to their textbooks, why do they do this, and what, if anything, is being done about it? Secondly, what issues arise with access to the results of research that has been paid for by government grants? This latter issue will be discussed in the following section.

Every reader of this book knows that university and college students are typically hard pressed to make ends meet, and usually view the cost of textbooks as exorbitant. Hence there is widespread copying of chapters from books. In some cases, they even copy the entire manuscript, or download a pirated edition. The author of this reasonably-priced textbook, of course, hopes that the copy you are reading has been paid for!

Textbook prices

Publishers argue that textbooks are expensive because many of them have relatively small print runs compared with trade books. Yet costs in academia have been rising much faster than overall consumer prices, at least in the USA, but arguably also elsewhere in the world. Between 2002 and 2012, US university and college tuition and fees increased 89%, and college textbook prices increased 82%, while overall consumer prices only increased 28%.[59] These trends go back even further; here are some percentage changes from 1978 to 2014 in some relevant costs in US dollars:[60]

Consumer Price Index (CPI)	+262%
New Home Prices	+408%
Medical Care	+604%
College Textbooks	+945%

Yet this phenomenon does not apply to all books, as recreational books have gotten cheaper between 1998 and 2014:

Recreational Books	–0.77%
All Items	+46%
College Textbooks	+161%

Some university texts now cost over $400. It is easy to see why students would consider obtaining a book without paying for it. Cost is not the only factor in the decision of whether to buy the book through proper channels or not, as the decision to pirate a book also depends upon how the course is taught and the perceived quality and utility of the book.[61]

Many students who cannot afford new textbooks comparison shop on the internet, buy used ones (30 per cent), rent them (10 per cent), buy less expensive e-books (8–10 per cent), share or borrow them (10–15 per cent), or purchase no book whatsoever (10–30 per cent), perhaps using library copies.[62] Others purchase or download unauthorized copies or copy pages themselves. According to a recent study, 25 per cent of students photocopied or scanned some textbooks, and 19 per cent used pirate websites.

Textbook piracy is part of a larger phenomenon of *book piracy*. E-book piracy represents a great deal of this. It has recently been estimated to have cost US publishers $315 million in lost sales.[63] The typical book pirate was between thirty and forty-four years old and had an annual household income of between $60,000 and $99,000, so here again we see that economics is not the only cause.

For general-interest books, one can make the argument that piracy may be an advantage, as obscurity is an author's worst nightmare.[64] But even for academics and professors, where texts are often assigned by them in classes, piracy is generally no blessing. What are the stakeholders—publishing ventures, universities, and academic authors—doing about the issue?

Textbook publishing is one of the most highly concentrated manufacturing markets in the world.[62] The biggest publishers—Pearson, Reed Elsevier, Thomson Reuters, Wolters Kluwer, and Bertellsman, who rake in over $3.5 billion revenue a year, according to a 2010 figure—are *educational* publishers.[65] They are very profitable, with after-tax profit margins of over 10 per cent.[62] They are voracious, often acquiring their smaller competitors. They are diversified, often also delivering financial information services, and being involved in developing learning management systems. They use techniques designed to keep their profit margins high, such as forcing bookstores to sign agreements prohibiting the import of less expensive international editions. Given the pricing data shown, their only contribution to solving the problem of skyrocketing costs seems to be their publishing of somewhat cheaper e-book text versions and participating in systems for textbook rental.

Nonetheless, like music and movies, the industry is in the throes of disruption. Entrepreneurial ventures are driving a flourishing book rental market.[66] Apple and Amazon have filed patents to allow the renting of e-books.[67] Some universities, such as Indiana University and the California State University system, have negotiated steep discounts with major publishers for e-books and related materials.[62]

Academics sympathizing with their students' plight have ways to reduce textbook costs. One method is not to insist that students buy the most current version of a textbook, which allows for more reliance on used book purchases or lower-cost rentals.[68] A professor can design a custom course-pack, consisting of one's own writing and reprints of other articles, some of which may be license-free, which reduces the cost of the total package. A third method is to author, perhaps with some colleagues, an *open access* textbook. Open access is gaining momentum as a movement, which we shall now discuss.

Research: The internet has enabled new forms of writing. Identify and discuss various forms of creativity, such as that pioneered by companies such as Blogger, Twitter, and Wattpad.

Law: Draft a statute (for some jurisdiction) specifying what constitutes fair use of IP by teachers in their classrooms and guaranteeing them the right to make fair use of the IP without fear of legal action.

Ethics: Under what conditions and in what situations would you download a pirate edition of a textbook as opposed to buying or renting some version of it? What ethical issues would you consider, and how would you resolve them?

2.7 Open access publications

An *open access* (OA) publication is one where the publisher, who might be the author(s) themselves if they self-publish, places few or no copyright restrictions on the work. For example, they could allow readers to make their own copies or obtain copies however they choose. (At the end of this chapter, we shall discuss a variant of this idea, called the *Creative Commons license*—a mechanism for choosing which kinds of freedoms and which kinds of restrictions to place on IP.) Since no or minimal fees usually return to the publisher, nor royalties to the authors, an open access book is typically cheaper than one protected by traditional copyright.

The open access movement has many adherents, in part because making books cheaper is a social good. A more significant driver is the notion that authorship becomes a collaborative venture that can include other professors as well as students, who work together to refine and improve the material. An early promising project was Rice University's Connexions endeavour and the Community College Open Textbook Project (CCOTP).[69] However, all projects found version control and maintaining high quality content challenging. The concept is not taking off at the university level, likely because most academic authors want to keep control of the product, and also desire a royalty in return for the work. The concept is also being explored at the middle and high school level. One two-year study involving twenty middle and high school science teachers and almost 4,000 students discovered a way to use open textbooks that reduced costs by over 50 per cent when compared with the use of traditional textbooks.[70] However, the financial sustainability of open access textbooks is in question.[71]

The area where OA publications is gaining good traction is journal publishing, especially in the sciences. Due in part to the corporate concentration discussed above, we have seen a dramatic increase in the cost of textbooks and research publications. This causes hardships for university and research libraries that try to keep current with journal subscriptions. Thus, in the twentieth century, efforts to reduce the cost via open access began. Other goals were to speed up publication and to enable a greater degree of consultation as part of the review process. John Willinsky's book *The Access Principle: The Case for Open Access to Research and Scholarship* discussed open access publications,[72] and noted the importance of this movement to the university and research libraries of developing nations, which have limited funds to purchase journal subscriptions. For example, access to high-impact scholarly literature used to be limited in India to only a few elite institutions.[73]

Journal of Medical Internet Research (JMIR)

This open access journal, founded by professor Gunther Eysenbach of the University of Toronto in 1999, covers e-Health and 'healthcare in the internet age'.[74] In 2016, its impact factor was 5.175, thus placing it first among twenty medical informatics journals, and fourth out of ninety journals in 'health care sciences and services'. JMIR Publications now publishes over twenty scientific journals. Its articles are published using the Creative Commons Attribution License 2.0 (to be discussed).

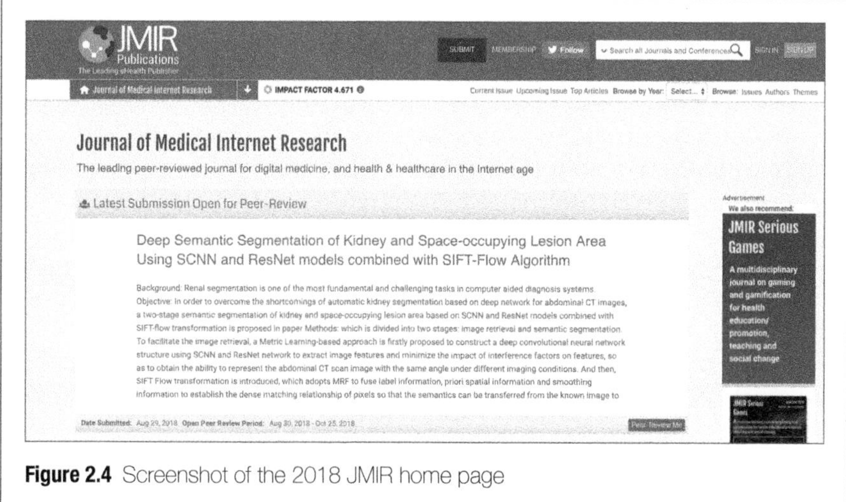

Figure 2.4 Screenshot of the 2018 JMIR home page

OA journals have had many problems to solve: resistance from traditional publishers, developing an IT infrastructure, inventing a viable business model, motivating potential authors via academic rewards, marketing despite having limited finances, and achieving critical mass.[75] The issue of viable business models is the most challenging, and is sometimes solved by asking authors to pay a portion of the publishing costs in order to have their research in print.

The movement has nonetheless grown rapidly. A study of 2,000 randomly selected journal articles showed that 20 per cent could be found in an OA form on the web.[76] Of these, 8.5 per cent were freely available at the publishers' sites; 11.9 per cent of them could be found somewhere, often on the author's website, using search engines. Almost 50 per cent of the articles published between 2004 and 2011 in the USA, Canada, EU member countries, Japan, and Brazil were readily available on the internet.[77] A more recent estimate is that 15 per cent of the articles indexed in the Web of Science are in full OA journals.[78] Given the obstacles, this is remarkable progress.

OA journals exhibit many varieties, differing in part on where and when the material is made available (sometimes OA publications appear later in a paid, print journal), and also on how the journals are funded.[72] Traditional journals charge an average of $5,000 per article published, whereas the charges for the largest OA publishers range from $1,350 to $2,900, with an average per article charge of $660.[79] The latter number is somewhat misleading, as some OA journals are subsidized by universities or professional societies. One aspect of the cost of the highest quality journals, whether traditional or open access, is that they are more selective, rejecting many of the articles. Therefore, journals such as *Nature*, which only publishes 8 per cent of what is submitted, would be more expensive than journals of the same size that have a far greater percentage of acceptances.

One debate about OA journals deals with academics' need to demonstrate that they are publishing in venues of quality and that their work is being read and cited. A study of the frequencies of citation of OA versus non-OA publications in four disciplines—philosophy, electrical and electronic engineering, political science, and mathematics—showed an advantage in all cases for OA publication, which ranged from 45 per cent more citations in philosophy to 91 per cent more in mathematics.[80] Another study examined 1.3 million articles published across ten years in ten disciplines. It found a publication citation advantage for OA in all the fields, ranging from 36 per cent for biology and 49 per cent for economics to 108 per cent for psychology, 108 per cent for law, and 172 per cent for sociology.[81] A third study looked at a cohort of 1,500 OA versus non-OA articles published in the second half of 2004 in the same journal—the *Proceedings of the National Academy of Sciences*—and found that the OA articles were twice as likely to be cited in the first four to ten months after publication, with this advantage growing to three times as likely in the ten to sixteen months after publication.[82]

Yet some researchers criticized much of the literature on the topic.[83] They noted three possible reasons for the effects cited. Indeed, they could be due to OA publications being superior. But the results could be due to a *selection bias*, that is, the authors are posting quality papers online and/or choosing to submit them to OA journals. The results could also be due to the fact that the articles became available earlier, and thus would have been seen more often than a non-OA article at the same point in time. There is clearly a need for more robust research to disentangle the confounding variables, but the appeal of OA publishing to many scholars is undeniable and understandable.

One additional aspect of OA that is worth mentioning is the increasing attention since 2008 to the publishing of research that has been financed by government grants in the vast majority of all current research. Concerns with the high cost of traditional journals have led many scientists to protest that would-be consumers of the research results should not have to pay twice for the research, first via taxes to the government, and then via subscription fees to the journal publishers. Bo-Christer Björk, who has studied OA publishing since 2003, put the case in stark terms:[84]

> the results of research globally costing an estimated 1000 Billion USD of primarily public taxpayer money . . . should not be hidden behind pay walls, to protect the estimated 10 Billion USD subscription revenue . . . of scholarly journal publishers.

Increasingly, in many parts of the world, this concern is being addressed by legislation.[85] In 2005, the US National Institutes of Health (NIH) Public Access Policy required that all NIH-funded research be published open access. As a result, the NIH's public digital archives, PubMed Central (PMC), grew to include 3.3 million full-text articles by 2015. In the UK, the Wellcome Trust opted for a different strategy by subsidizing OA publication fees to set up a very high-quality OA journal.[78]

Research: Research the evidence for differences in quality between traditional and open access publications, and the causes if differences have been found.

Debate: Resolved: Textbooks should be created as open source collaborations.

Book report: Willinsky, John (2006). *The Access Principle: The Case for Open Access to Research and Scholarship*. MIT Press.

Field study: Interview a number of scientists who have published in traditional journals, as well as in OA publications, and discuss the similarities and differences of the processes they have encountered.

2.8 Software patents

Finally, we turn our attention to the intellectual property known as software. Computer programs are routinely protected by trade secret; firms insist that their employees and contractors not disclose their work outside of the firm. Programs are also protected by copyright, so that others cannot use or modify the code without permission (we shall discuss the open source challenge in the following section). In the earliest days of computing, programs were viewed as unpatentable, since mathematical expressions or reasoning are not patentable. But software is the only artefact that humanity has created which is both *writing*, hence protectable by copyright, and *process*, hence protectable by patent. As a result, the US Patent Office issued a patent for a magnetic tape sorting algorithm in 1968;[86] the floodgates opened soon thereafter. By 2007, software was receiving 15 per cent of all patents granted.[87] This growing trend has continued: in 2012 there were 40,000 software patents issued in the USA.[88] Companies are now vigorously pursuing software patents as a source of competitive advantage.

IBM has historically earned over $1 billion per year by licensing its inventions. In 2016, it was awarded over 8,000 US patents, making it the corporate record holder for the twenty-fourth year in a row.[89] Some software patents are controversial, for instance the Amazon One Click patent, which allows shoppers to make online purchases with a single click. It was rejected in Europe as being non-obvious, but survived several court challenges in the USA. The patent has yielded significant competitive advantages and revenues for Amazon; the US patent expired in 2017.[90]

The US courts have recently been paying more attention to what should and should not be considered patentable. A decision by the US Supreme Court in 2014 to limit the awarding of business process patents has slowed the granting of patents for software that may reasonably be viewed as routine implementations of well-known processes.[91] The Supreme Court has also been active in decisions with regard to patent trolls, as will be discussed towards the end of this section.

Apple versus Mirror Worlds

An interesting example was a suit filed by a 'patent troll' in 2008, allegedly on behalf of professor David Gelernter of Yale University. Gelernter and student Eric Freeman had obtained several patents dealing with the invention of their LifeStreams document stream operating system.[92] The idea was novel: it proposed that all files be stored based on their time of creation, and retrieved in that manner, without the need to resort to artificial file names. LifeStreams represented documents visually as a set of rectangles receding into three-dimensional space. The suit claimed that three Apple interface techniques, including Cover Flow, which represents files three-dimensionally, infringed the original patents, now owned by the patent troll that had bought the IP of Gelernter and Freeman's failed Mirror Worlds company. Mirror Worlds was initially awarded $625 million in damages;[93] the decision was overruled by an appeals court.[94]

Continued on next page

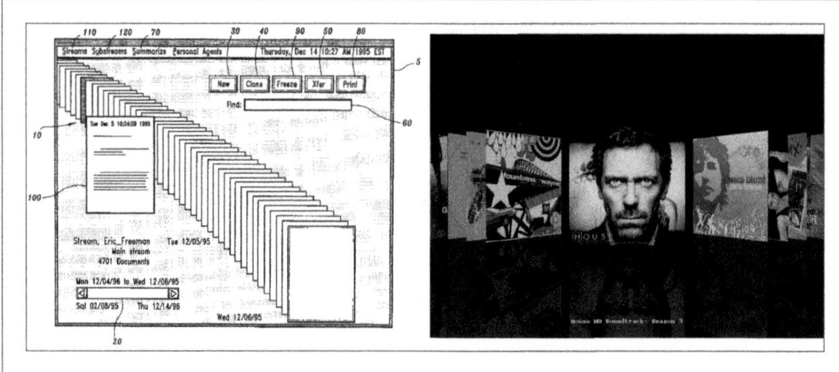

Figure 2.5 LifeStreams (left) and Cover Flow (right)

There are five reasons that lead many to feel that the software patent system is broken. A significant number of software patents seem illegitimate, not identifying and protecting inventions that are useful, novel, non-obvious, and enabling. The One Click patent is a good example; the patent seems to protect something that is obvious and not novel. The second reason is that systematic and comprehensive searches for *patent prior art*,[88] or inventions that may predate your invention, is impractical because there are so many software patents and they are 'impossible to index'. Although an overstatement, it indicates the complexity that bedevils industry executives, entrepreneurs, and patent attorneys. This complexity has been described as *patent thickets*, which cause challenges to the commercialization of discoveries when products make use of many patents, which is often the case with software.[95] Thirdly, analyst opinions differ as to the value of software patents to businesses at different stages of their growth,[96] although it is generally agreed that having at least one patent helps a start-up assert its strategic competitive advantage and may also help a firm raise venture financing.

Fourthly, there have emerged since 1998 a new form of predatory business called a *patent troll*. A patent troll, sometimes called a *non-practicing entity* (NPE), is a company that licenses patents without producing goods. It sometimes acquires the patents for next to nothing, often absorbing the names and assets of small start-ups that have gone bankrupt. We have seen an example in the case of Mirror Worlds. These companies especially seek vaguely worded patents on old inventions that can be asserted against many newer technologies.[97] Patent trolls then send threatening letters to and sometimes bring suits against a small number of largely established firms or large numbers of small firms in order to extract license fees for use of the IP embodied in the patent.

From 1990 to 2010, NPE lawsuits were associated with half a trillion dollars of lost value of the companies sued, yet very little return was realized by inventors.[98] In 2011, US companies spent $29 billion in legal fees and settlement costs dealing with these frivolous letters and lawsuits.[99] The firms sued are often mid-size (earning an average annual revenue of only $11 million), so the lawsuits are very disruptive. In 2011, an estimated 100,000 small businesses received threatening letters, and almost 3,000 firms were sued by patent trolls.[97] This may cause severe damage to companies that often have no stake in technology but may just be using random business applications on the internet.

The problem is so severe that companies are now lobbying politicians for changes in IP regulations. In June 2017, the US Supreme Court made a decision that is a setback to patent trolls.[100] After finding that 40 per cent of IP infringement cases had been filed in East Texas because its citizens know little about technology but are sympathetic to assertions that small inventors have been cheated, a new regulation stipulates that cases need to be filed in the geographic location where the defendant conducts business. Another Supreme Court decision making it easier to challenge questionable patents used in questionable lawsuits by patent trolls came down in April 2018.[101]

Finally, many oppose software patents because of a larger belief system in the value of sharing innovation as opposed to holding it proprietary with mechanisms such as patenting. This belief system is the *open source* movement.

Research: Research and analyse a set of legal cases dealing with software copyright infringement.

Research: Research and analyse the patent battles between Google and Samsung.

Debate: Resolved: Software patents are helpful to start-ups.

Field study: Interview a set of software entrepreneurs about their experiences with software patents.

2.9 Open source software

At the beginning of the chapter, we discussed Richard Stallman's vision of free software. By 'free', Stallman meant freedom of expression, as in 'free speech', and not a zero price, as in 'free beer'. More details may be found on the GNU Operating System website:[102]

> A program is free software if the program's users have the four essential freedoms:
>
> 0) The freedom to run the program as you wish, for any purpose (freedom 0).
> 1) The freedom to study how the program works, and change it so it does your computing as you wish (freedom 1). Access to the source code is a precondition for this.
> 2) The freedom to redistribute copies so you can help your neighbor (freedom 2).
> 3) The freedom to distribute copies of your modified versions to others (freedom 3).
>
> By doing this you can give the whole community a chance to benefit from your changes. Access to the source code is a precondition for this.

These freedoms are protected in the world of free software by *copyleft*, which specifies that one cannot add restrictions denying others the freedoms when one redistributes the software. This is in contrast to copyright, which is a statement not of freedoms but of restrictions.

Stallman's abiding passion was that software could easily and routinely be shared among a community of developers, much as it had been in the early days of computing. Once companies placed a value and a price on it, conventional wisdom was that access had to be restricted, so that its value could be realized. This is still the case with most software. However, Stallman and others, most notably Linus Torvalds, the chief architect of the Linux operating system, challenged the conventional wisdom. They developed and distributed programs that included their source code, hence the term *open source software*. Besides GNU and Linux, there are many other notable examples, such as the Apache web server, the Perl programming language, the Netscape Navigator and Firefox web browsers, the OpenOffice integrated productivity tool package, and the Android mobile operating system.

Linux[103]

Although Stallman provided the early vision for open source software and software components that were later merged with Linux, it was Linus Torvald's creation of the Linux kernel in 1991 that was the first major demonstration of the viability of open source development for large-scale, industrial-strength software. The full Linux operating system was collaboratively created by thousands of software developers around the world, mostly working independently, but some contributed by large corporations, such as Dell, HP, IBM, and Oracle. The result was a free and open re-implementation of the UNIX operating system that had originally been developed in 1971 at AT&T Bell Laboratories. Details are beyond the scope of this text, but today, Linux runs on far more machines, ranging from embedded microprocessors to mobile phones to computers to supercomputers, than does any commercial proprietary operating system.

Figure 2.6 The Linux mascot, Tux
Attribution: lewing@isc.tamu.edu Larry Ewing and The GIMP

Software architect Eric Raymond produced an early, articulate, and influential expression of the virtues of open source development.[104] His essay, 'The Cathedral and the Bazaar', began:

> Linux is subversive. Who would have thought even five years ago that a world-class operating system could coalesce as if by magic out of part-time hacking by several thousand developers scattered all over the planet, connected only by the tenuous strands of the Internet?... Certainly not I.

Somewhat later, he went on to say:

> But I...believed there was a certain critical complexity above which a more centralized, a priori approach was required. I believed that the most important software...needed to be built like cathedrals, carefully crafted by individual wizards or small bands of mages working in splendid isolation, with no beta to be released before its time.... Linus Torvalds's style of development...came as a surprise. No quiet, reverent cathedral-building here – rather, the Linux community seemed to resemble a great babbling bazaar of differing agendas and approaches...out of which a coherent and stable system could seemingly emerge only by a succession of miracles.

Law professor Eben Moglen described the open source movement in political terms as 'not merely...a form of production...but also...the beginning of a social movement with specific political goals which will characterize not only the production of software in the twenty-first century, but the production and distribution of culture generally', the vanguard of 'confrontation between two fundamentally different forms of social organization'.[105]

Open source and proprietary software are not locked in a confrontation to the death between warring ideologies. Open source development complements proprietary development; many organizations do both.[106] Open source has become mainstream.[107] The O'Reilly Software Development Survey of almost 7,000 individuals involved in software development reported that almost 65 per cent of developers read and edit code originally written by others (of course, not all of this is open source code).[108] Open source companies such as Red Hat, JBoss, and MySQL have demonstrated the ability to generate revenues, sometimes make a profit, raise venture capital, and in some cases be acquired, such as IBM's announcement in October 2018 of a planned acquisition of Red Hat for an astounding $34 billion.[109]

Yet there are still questions about the effectiveness and challenges of open source software. Early open source software was notorious for the prevalence of poor user interfaces. Programmers seemed to be writing software primarily to be used by other programmers. Raymond himself told one horrifying true story about the attempts of one technically sophisticated individual to get printing working under a Linux system.[110] Yet efforts to address open source usability have become vigorous,[111] and open source software has improved significantly in this regard. Another unanswered question and challenge is the *security* of open source software.[112] While some feel that open source software is more secure because vulnerabilities can in principle be discovered by many programmers, others feel it is less secure because some of these people can exploit the vulnerabilities.

Research: The usability of open source software.

Research: The security of open source software compared with proprietary software.

Concept: Write a Wikipedia article on 'open source usability'.

Policy: Draft a brief for the Vice President Development of a software firm debating whether or not to release open source a program ancillary to the main proprietary software packages on which it bases its market position.

2.10 Creative Commons licensing

We close this chapter by discussing a major recent IP achievement, the *Creative Commons* license (CC).[113] Chiefly due to the brilliant legal scholar and activist Lawrence Lessig, CC allows creators of IP to adopt a middle ground between strict control over use of IP via copyright, and no control by not applying copyright. Owners of IP may grant certain rights to allow for the use or modification of their creation, and deny certain rights in order to remove some of the ambiguities that we have seen at different places within this chapter. It is particularly useful in cases where the copyright holder wishes to allow uses that it views as socially constructive and not damaging to its economic interests, but also wants to draw a firm line in the sand on where certain uses should be disallowed.

Creative Commons license

A holder of IP who wishes to use a CC license must first answer several questions. Do I wish to allow adaptations of my work to be shared? Allowable answers are 'yes', 'no', and 'yes, as long as others share alike'. Next, the IP holder must specify if commercial uses of the work are to be permitted or not. The final step is to choose the license. All the licenses insist that your work be attributed, or credited. They differ in whether or not commercial use is permitted, whether or not users are allowed to modify your work (this is particularly relevant to software but allows the concept of remixing for mash-ups, as we have seen), and whether or not their work (which builds upon yours) must be licensed on the same terms (the *share alike* provision). This implements part of Stallman's original vision, namely that improvements to the original IP would have to be shared by the philosophy of share alike.

Attribution 4.0 International (CC BY 4.0)

This is a human-readable summary of (and not a substitute for) the license. Disclaimer.

You are free to:

Share — copy and redistribute the material in any medium or format

Adapt — remix, transform, and build upon the material for any purpose, even commercially.

The licensor cannot revoke these freedoms as long as you follow the license terms.

Under the following terms:

Attribution — You must give appropriate credit, provide a link to the license, and indicate if changes were made. You may do so in any reasonable manner, but not in any way that suggests the licensor endorses you or your use.

Figure 2.7 One form of the Creative Commons license

Reproduced under the terms of the Creative Commons Attribution 4.0 International (CC BY 4.0) license. https://creativecommons.org/licenses/by/4.0/

Creative Commons is attractive and viable, with 1.1 billion works licensed as of January 2016.[113]

Research: Research the evolution of the Creative Commons license, and the critical issues that were addressed as it moved to its present form.

2.11 Summary

From the early days of computing, visionary computer scientists imagined the possibility of limitless access to the world's store of written information and knowledge. When advances in digital technology also enabled access to music, images, and motion pictures, it became clear that this would challenge our concepts of IP and the laws that govern its use. The result has often been open warfare among corporations owning IP; the musicians, filmmakers, artists, and scientists who created the IP; and citizens wishing to gain free or reasonably priced access and use of the content. Fair use is often a compromise that allows citizens to use IP royalty-free without undermining the right to a fair return for creators and publishers.

The first battles were fought in the domain of music. Technology turned the industry upside down, allowing for digitization and widespread distribution and sharing of musical content. This was followed by extreme reactions by many players, including music publishers fearing for their livelihoods, and consumers delighting in and making use of new capabilities. Many music downloaders knowingly crossed a moral line to enforce control over their media for a variety of reasons. For almost a decade, the technologies for safeguarding copyrighted music and hastily passed new laws could not find middle ground between corporations and communities. The conflict then weakened in part due to novel technologies, but primarily through wiser business strategies. The result has been a new status quo in which a great deal of music is sold as individual songs or made available via streaming services with pricing strategies that seem acceptable to consumers, artists, and media companies.

A similar battle has been fought in the domain of motion pictures. Here we have seen the ascendancy of legal movie and television streaming services with pricing structures that have attained a wide following. Yet there continues to be vast quantities of online content that are suspected of copyright infringement. As a result, websites have resorted to the safe harbour provision built into the DMCA that protects them if they make efforts to remove such content. Because of the magnitude of effort involved, content takedowns are now typically done by algorithms. There is increasing evidence of serious flaws in these algorithms that result in flawed automatic takedowns of content. This assumes copyright infringement even where none exists, and also disallows fair use when it should be granted.

A challenging case occurs with the increasing prevalence of musical and audio-visual mash-ups, creations that incorporate small, and possibly radically transformed, portions of existing copyrighted works. Mash-ups are created routinely by as much as half of the computer-savvy population. Their existence challenges the legal system to modify copyright protection to allow reasonable use of copyrighted material without unreasonable criminal exposure, although such change has not yet come.

A fourth domain of conflict deals with printed matter, especially publications for educational or research purposes. Extreme corporate concentration in the textbook publishing industry helped the price of textbooks to grow four times faster than the CPI at the same time that the price of recreational books decreased. The result has been widespread copying of textbooks. E-books, book rentals, custom course-packs, and instructor acceptance of older book editions have all contributed to a decent diminishing of the problem. Yet we still do not have compromises that satisfy all the stakeholders.

A fundamental solution is the concept of an open access publication, in which academics collaborate on a book that is then typically distributed electronically or through non-profit printing ventures. This idea has not caught on for textbooks, but has spawned a rapidly growing movement of OA journal publications. Participants in this process have solved critical problems such as quality control, although there still are issues with creating viable business models. Costs have to some extent been transferred from the readers of journals, or more accurately the libraries that purchase them, to the writers of the articles to be published. One particularly vivid stimulus to this movement is the reluctance to pay for access to scientific results that taxpayers have already funded with tax dollars.

A fifth kind of intellectual property is computer software. Programs are increasingly protected via patents on the processes embodied in the software. This is an area rife with conflict, in part because patents have been granted on ideas that are obvious and not novel, and in part because the growing complexity of software makes it difficult to judge when new concepts are derived from previous concepts. An especially noxious aspect of the software patent crisis is patent troll companies that buy up or acquire patents, especially old and vague ones, and then threaten to sue large numbers of firms and individuals who may be using technology that is, in some sense, derivative from the earlier patents.

Many developers have rejected the move towards tighter proprietary control over software by joining the open source movement. Here, code is published but not subject to normal copyright restrictions, rendering it free for re-use and modifications. The movement has grown rapidly and has spawned viable business models. Some open source development and software use is now routine even in companies that primarily develop and use proprietary software.

One of the primary critics of the dominance of proprietary culture has been law professor Lawrence Lessig. His Creative Commons license is a mechanism that allows IP creators to specify exactly what uses are allowed or not allowed, including uses for commercial purposes, and to indicate whether modifications to the IP need to be returned to the commons or not. Hopefully ideas such as this will allow for less warfare and more collaboration among creators of IP, corporations marketing content, and citizens wishing to consume and sometimes to make modest modifications to the IP for personal use.

2.12 Key terms

Amazon One Click shopping patent
Apple Music
Application programming interfaces (APIs)
Book piracy
Book rentals
Brewster Kahle
Community College Open Textbook Project
Copyleft
Copyright
Copyright holders
Copyright infringement
Cover Flow
Creative Commons license (CC)
Custom course-pack
Digital media
Digital Millennium Copyright Act (DMCA) (1998)
Digital Rights Management (DRM)
E-books
Educational publishers
Endless Love of Bush and Blair
European Union Copyright Directive (EUCD) (2001)

Fair use
Free software
GNU operating system
Google Books
Information enclosures
Intellectual property (IP)
Internet Archive
iTunes Music Store
Journal of Medical Internet Research (JMIR)
Lawrence Lessig
LifeStreams
Linus Torvalds
Linux operating system
Mash-ups
Metro-Goldwyn-Mayer Studios (MGM) vs. Grokster
Mirror Worlds
Moore's Law
MP3
music downloading and sharing
music streaming
Napster
Netflix
Open access publications
Open access textbook
Open source software
Participatory networked culture
Patents
Patent prior art
Patent thickets
Patent troll or non-practicing entity (NPE)
Peer-to-peer file sharing software (P2P)
Piracy
Project Gutenberg
Recording Industry Association of America
Richard Stallman
Safe harbour
Secure Digital Music Initiative (SDMI)
Selection bias
Software
Sony BMG Music Entertainment Rootkit
Spotify
Takedown notices
Trademark
Trade secret
U.S. NIH Public Access Policy
Vannevar Bush
Wayback Machine
YouTube

3

Computers in education and learning

As we have already hinted, computers and the internet have made profound changes in how we learn.[1] We begin this topic by reviewing influential visions and early prototypes suggesting how technology could revolutionize education.

Early on, computers were used by educators to deliver online tutorials about subject material, administer drill-and-practice exercises on rote skills, act as supportive environments for creatively exploring ideas through programming in English-like languages, and function as inexpensive, ubiquitous, and dynamic audio-visual resources.

We shall then discuss other newer methods for using digital technologies to transform how students approach subject matter and how classrooms are organized. By using interactive simulation games, students learn by taking actions with respect to certain scenarios. Presentation aids such as PowerPoint and Prezi have replaced blackboards to present and elucidate concepts. *Smart classrooms* allow instructors and students access to technology that facilitates learning; *inverted classrooms* allow more effective use of classroom time by enabling students to prepare for lectures in advance and focus on working together with their teachers in class. *Intelligent tutors* are artificial intelligence (AI) programs that actively support student learning, diagnose student difficulties with the material, and then adapt tutoring strategies based on these findings.

Next, we shall review how online learning has opened up new opportunities for adult and continuing education, whereby students can learn in their own time and at their own pace. The challenge online learning technology developers now face is to provide discussion forums, real-time chat capabilities, and methods for instructor feedback so that advantages of face-to-face interaction are not lost in web-based learning. Particularly exciting is the growth of worldwide learning communities via Massive Open Online Courses (MOOCs), an area of current expansion and creativity.

While technology is now seen as instrumental in learning, there are still debates on the extent to which it should be used and how it should be used in education. A particularly prevalent dilemma is in middle and secondary schools. The issue is whether or not and how to encourage or disallow the use of mobile phones and other devices in classrooms.

Has digital technology transformed education and learning? What are the benefits? What are the downsides? Is the role of the teacher changing? Can teachers be better supported? Are there any limits to the extent to which we should use digital devices in education or in classrooms? What could happen if intelligent tutors become smart enough to capably perform a great deal of instruction and evaluation? What should happen?

3.1 Pioneers and visionaries

PLATO,[2] which was developed at the University of Illinois Urbana-Champaign in the early 1960s, was the first system to achieve prominence in this field. PLATO delivered lesson modules written in the novel TUTOR programming language. The lessons could be used on custom-built flat-panel plasma display terminals. They were delivered by a time-sharing system that ran on large mainframe computers. Operating for over four decades, it was an environment for educational innovations including online learning communities, message boards, notes systems, chat forums, real-time conferencing, email, online testing, and multiplayer games.[3] We shall return later in this chapter to the role of messaging and conferencing in education.

In 1963, Patrick Suppes and Richard C. Atkinson of the Institute for Mathematical Studies in the Social Sciences at Stanford University developed programs that provided *drill-and-practice computer-assisted instruction* in mathematical logic and arithmetic.[4] This was followed by tutorial programs in reading, logic, mathematics, and problem solving, as well as rigorous experimental evaluations of performance by comparing students in computer-based sections with those receiving traditional instruction. In his review of their early achievements, Suppes wrote:

> the most important social change...will begin in the seventies...computer terminals in homes and the availability of a wide range of courses for the continuing education of adults.

Replace 'computer terminals' with 'laptops or tablets' and delay the time frame by two decades, and his prediction would be right on.

Beginning in the early 1980s, John Anderson and colleagues at Carnegie Mellon University took another step by developing AI technology driving intelligent tutoring systems.[5] Such tutors made use of 'cognitive model[s] of the competence[s] that the student is being asked to learn', and were expected to behave intelligently in response to student input, problems, and questions. We shall discuss this topic further later in this chapter.

A radically different view on the role of computers in learning was that of Seymour Papert. In a series of early technical reports,[6] he envisioned using technology in schools not 'in the form of machines for processing children' but rather:[7]

> as something the child himself will learn to manipulate, to extend, to apply to projects, thereby gaining a greater and more articulate mastery of the world, a sense of the power of applied knowledge and a self-confidently realistic image of himself as an intellectual agent.

Key to these concepts was the development by Papert and collaborator Wallace Feurzeig of Logo,[8] a novel programming language specifically designed to facilitate student understanding of mathematics and mathematical problem solving, as suggested in Papert's writings. Although children were learning how to program, Papert's goal was not for students to develop computer science skills, but instead to use programming as a tool of thought and a vehicle for creativity.[9]

An important vision (inspired in part by Papert) was Alan Kay's Dynabook,[10] described thusly:

> What then is a personal computer? One would hope that it would be both a medium for containing and expressing arbitrary symbolic notions, and also a collection of useful tools for manipulating these structures, with ways to add new tools to the repertoire.... superior to books and printing in at least some ways without being markedly inferior in others.... owned by its user (needs to cost no more than a TV) and portable (which to me means that the user can easily carry the device and other things at the same time). Need we add that it be usable in the woods?

He added that this personal computer should be:

> active (like the child) rather than passive.... with the attention-grabbing powers of TV, but controllable by the child rather than the network... like a piano: (a product of technology, yes), but... [also] a tool, a toy, a medium of expression, a source of unending pleasure and delight...!

Kay's 'interim Dynabook' and its Smalltalk programming language supported a variety of exciting projects that included systems interacting through images, sounds, and movies.[11] All of this, in some sense, anticipated the laptops and tablets of the twenty-first century.

Inspired by the work of Papert and Kay, researcher and inventor Mitchel Resnick took over Papert's team and renamed it the Lifelong Kindergarten Group.[12] Previously, the Logo computing language had allowed the programming of 'turtle behaviors' and 'turtle graphics'. The turtle was a small programmable navigable robot that could make drawings with a pen that could be lowered and raised. Resnick extended Logo to support actively behaving objects through LEGO and Programmable Bricks construction kits.[13] The tiny processors, sensors, and motors embedded inside LEGO bricks later became the Microworlds commercial product. It was also a precursor of the current 'maker' movement that encourages children to be creative by designing and making things.[14]

The intellectual successor to LOGO and Smalltalk is the visual programming language and exploration environment called Scratch.[15] Targeted at children, Scratch's goal is to enable and encourage its users to achieve *digital fluency*, that is, 'not just the ability to chat, browse, and interact, but also the ability to design, create, and invent with new media'. Scratch's environment allows for creations that are 'more tinkerable' (using graphical programming blocks that can easily be assembled into wholes), 'more meaningful' (supporting diversity and personalization), and 'more social' (supporting a community in which over 15 million users have registered and shared almost 19 million projects and almost 100 million comments in close to a decade).

The PLATO team, Suppes, Papert, Kay, Resnick, and Nicholas Negroponte, with his One Laptop Per Child (OLPC) project discussed in Chapter 1, all had dramatic visions of how computers could transform education. Resnick's impact as measured by the number of student adopters is more impressive than that of the other visionaries. Recall Chapter 1's discussion of the grandiose assumptions of the OLPC team, and the extent to which it did not sufficiently support and engage local champions of the vision. One major reason for Resnick's success is his creation of a local digitally inclusive movement called Computer Clubhouses.[16] Each of the 100 'clubhouses' in nineteen countries provides 'a creative, safe, and free out-of-school learning environment where young people from underserved communities work with adult mentors to explore their own ideas, develop new skills, and build confidence in themselves through the use of technology'.

In a sense, the PLATO team's and Suppes' visions were conservative; they proposed ways to do what had long been done in classrooms, but more efficiently, and also outside the space and time constraints of traditional classrooms. Papert, Kay, and Resnick, on the other hand, suggested that digital computational and display technologies, as they became more powerful and less expensive, could provide tools of remarkable power and flexibility to students, and enable them to create new artefacts and reimagine learning, a concept that recalls the vision of J. C. R. Licklider.

Since then, other methods of going beyond books and blackboards have been invented. We shall discuss several such inventions: educational simulations and games, aids to lecturing and teaching, 'smart classrooms' incorporating electronic whiteboards and tabletops, inverted classrooms and other novel uses of video recording and playback, and online learning environments.

Research: Research intelligent tutoring systems, and where and how they have been effective or ineffective.

Research: Decide on measures to evaluate the success of Scratch; evaluate to what extent it has been successful.

Debate: Resolved: Books are better than computers as tools for learning.

Book report: Papert, Seymour, and Idit Harel (1991). *Constructionism*. Ablex.

3.2 Digital simulations and serious gaming

The earliest computer-based learning modules presented and tested students on the instructors' lessons. But what if the material to be learned were a set of rules, and the measure of one's learning of the material were the ability to understand and apply these rules in a realistic situation? *Digital simulations* and *serious gaming* seek to enable an enjoyable experience in learning about some subject matter by actively performing tasks related to the material. In many cases, role playing, whereby one pretends that one is an actor in the world that is being simulated, is incorporated. For our purposes, we will not distinguish between simulations and games.[17]

SimCity

An early compelling simulation game, one that has survived since its release in 1989, is SimCity.[18] The idea is to pretend that one is the mayor of a virtual city, creating and populating the area with buildings in commercial, industrial, and residential zones. Much like real life, utilities and services must be provided to people and businesses, budgets must be created and managed, and tax rates must be determined and taxes levied. Natural disasters, such as earthquakes and floods, can happen and must be survived in the virtual world.

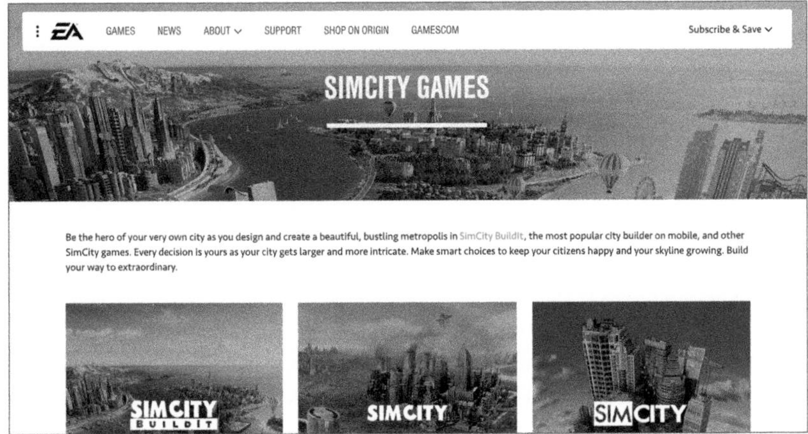

Figure 3.1 Screen shot from home page of SimCity[19]
The *SimCity* games and screenshots thereof, and EA web pages, are licensed properties of Electronic Arts, Inc.

As SimCity progressed through various versions and platforms, it added additional features such as the ability to create and manage multiple cities. It can also now support multi-player games.

Many other examples can be cited,[20] including simulations of the statistical behaviour of water in an interconnected set of dams; the growth of microorganisms; concepts in physics, chemistry, and physical science; memory concepts in computer science; case studies in information ethics using a collaborative role-playing approach; and the use of virtual and augmented realities for learning concepts about the environment. Educational programmes at most business undergraduate and graduate levels make significant use of business games as vehicles to teach a variety of topics including aspects of strategy, finance, decision-making, communication, and negotiation.[21]

If designed properly, educational simulations can engage students in a valuable learning experience. To succeed, they need to encourage exploration, effectively use animation and interactivity, include puzzles or clues, be fun to play, and be credible and useful simulations of the subject domain.[22] Students must believe that they do not already understand everything and be open to learning something new. *Learning histories,* which are replayable and browsable records of one's behaviour using a simulation, are very useful.[23] They allow learners to review what they have done, including actions that have proved to be either good or bad. These histories help students strategize on how to do better in their next use of the simulator.

A review of forty years of work proposed criteria for effective learning in a simulated environment:[24]

1. Are participants learning the model of the real world that the game is simulating?
2. Does the model of the real world have verisimilitude?

It is important to remember that a simulation can never be perfect; 100 per cent fidelity is only possible within a real system. Yet the simulation must not be misleading and must largely reflect the actual behaviour of the system being modelled. If fidelity is strong and the experience engages students, it can provide a great learning experience. And, as demonstrated by the success of SimCity, student learning using effective simulation games is as likely to happen at home as it is in a classroom.

Research: Study and summarize the evidence about the extent to which computer simulations and serious games encourage thinking and about the weaknesses that may exist in simulation models.

Research: Study the concept of a learning history; describe its use in computer-based learning environments.

Concept: Rewrite the existing Wikipedia article on 'business game'.

Technology review: Environmental simulations for learning.

Technology review: Massive multi-player educational games.

3.3 Presentation technology

Our discussion thus far has focused primarily on what is being taught and how it is being taught. We now turn our attention to the 'classroom' in which teaching and learning take place, the tools that can be used by instructors, and the changes in pedagogy enabled by new technologies.

Traditional classrooms were outfitted with a blackboard that allowed a teacher to write text or equations or draw diagrams or pictures to present and clarify material. Writing on blackboards meant that the lecturer could only present material relatively slowly, which did facilitate understanding by many students. Blackboards were later usually replaced by whiteboards, which afforded greater clarity without obnoxious chalk dust. Modern classrooms allow the display of computer output, such as prepared slides, to be shown on an electronic whiteboard. Instructors now must be careful not to use this medium to flood students with torrents of information.

PowerPoint and its critics

The dominant software for preparing and presenting slides is Microsoft PowerPoint.[25]

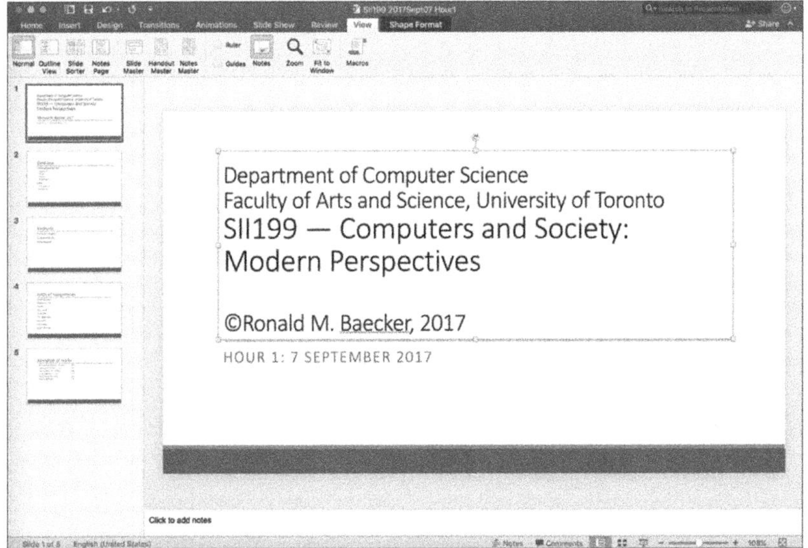

Figure 3.2 Screenshot of an early version of a PowerPoint slide prepared for a course using a draft of this book
Used with permission from Microsoft

PowerPoint's widespread use unleashed a flurry of debate about the effect of such presentations on learning and thinking. The debate was initiated by an invective essay by Edward R. Tufte, an eminent and well-respected graphic designer. Tufte criticized PowerPoints' cognitive and presentation style, usually consisting of a series of slides organized as hierarchical structures of very short phrases.[26] Independent of the details of the debate, it is important to remember that a slide creation program such as PowerPoint is a tool for presentation and communication. For such tools to be effective, lecturers must learn how to use the software skilfully.

Despite the dominance of PowerPoint, there are other styles of presentation supported by computer displays. One technique is the use of an electronic whiteboard as a canvas to write, sketch, and highlight things, just as one did in years past on blackboards.[27] Another increasingly popular alternative to PowerPoint is that of *zoomable user interfaces*, or ZUIs, which allow panning and zooming over large display canvases, punctuated by occasional jumps to a new canvas.[28] This concept, utilized by software such as Prezi, allows the instructor to move seamlessly between views that show the big picture and views that show detail, making the screen presentation dynamic and fluid. An additional powerful but idiosyncratic example is the so-called *Lessig Method* of slide lecture support.[29] Lawyer, author, and professor Larry Lessig synchronizes slides that show only a single word or phrase or image at numerous appropriate points in his vocal presentation. This is hard to prepare and to execute because it requires new slides to appear as often as every few seconds, but if done properly can yield a dramatic presentation.

The web has information on other presentation methods as well, including those by Apple co-founder Steve Jobs and venture capitalist Guy Kawasaki.[30] In education, it is essential that instructors choose presentation methods that are consistent with their style and personality and conducive to information transfer of the material at hand, and that communication tools be used in such a way as to engender the greatest student comprehension, comfort, and enthusiasm.

Research: Compare and contrast PowerPoint, Prezi (a ZUI), and the Lessig method as presentation vehicles using two or three examples and explain how and why certain techniques are better for certain kinds of content.

Book report: Tufte, Edward R. (2006). *The Cognitive Style of PowerPoint: Pitching Out Corrupts Within*. Second Edition. Graphics Press LLC.

3.4 Smart and flipped classrooms

Teachers increasingly use computers with projected displays in the classroom. If the display surface is one that also supports interaction, that is, where a user can point or circle or draw somewhere on the surface and that input is recognized by the computer that drives the display, then new kinds of digitally supported learning become possible.

Since the early 90s, there have increasingly been available interactive electronic surfaces; some act as digital whiteboards, such as Smartboards, while others act as digital tabletop displays. In some cases, classrooms are outfitted with computers for each student and multiple electronic tabletops and whiteboards to allow flexible combinations of use. Such classrooms are typically known as *smart classrooms*. One of the earliest examples was a network of fifty-five linked workstations to support science education at Brown University.[31]

eClass

A more sophisticated development was eClass (formerly called Classroom 2000), an instrumented classroom at the Georgia Institute of Technology.[32] This project viewed teaching and learning as multimedia authoring with three phases: pre-production, live recording, and post-production. First the instructor prepared his or her lecture material, including slides and/or videos. Then there was the lecture, with the instructor displaying and annotating lecture materials, and students using PCs for display of and annotation on the material. In Phase Three, students reviewed the materials and annotations (both those they had made and those the instructors had made in the capture and access system). Controlled experiments in two classes showed that the lecture-captured notes were useful but did not result in improved performance—although happily they did not result in decreased attendance.

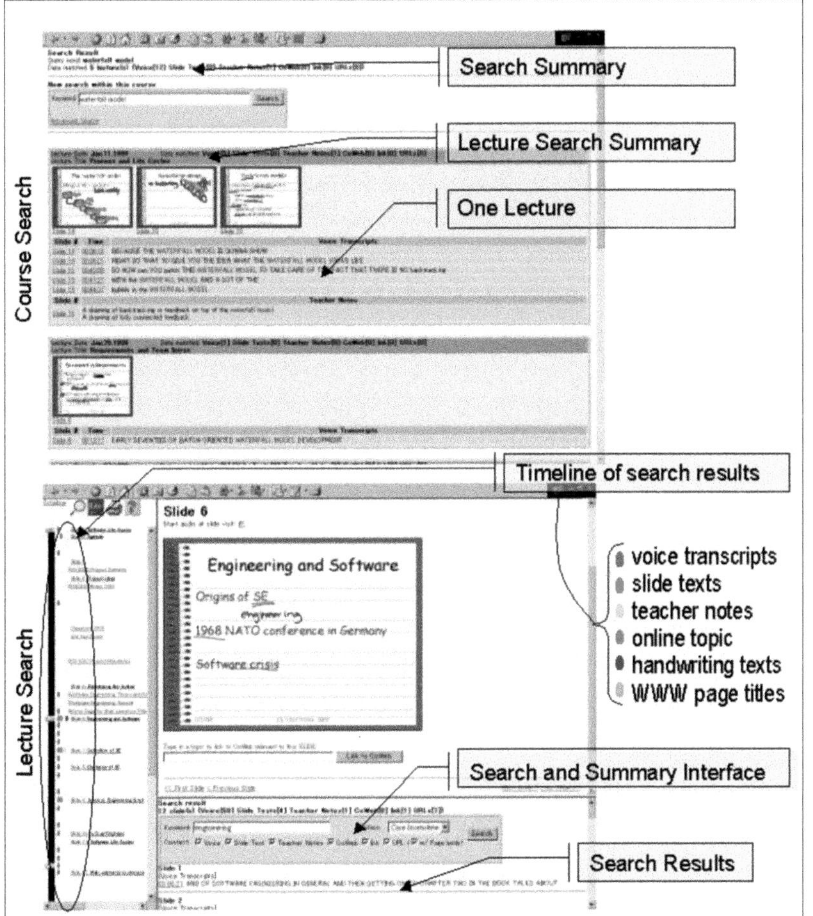

Figure 3.3 Screenshot of what the student saw in eClass: a list of all the recorded lectures; a timeline of all the slides in one lecture; and availability of voice transcripts, professorial annotations on the slides, and the student's annotations

Recent work has seen more sophisticated technology configurations in smart classrooms. For example, shared tablets and large wall displays were used in tandem to encourage group work in a finance management class.[33] Students moved smoothly back and forth between gathering around and doing group work on a tablet, and class discussions made use of the wall display. Researcher Roberto Martinez-Maldanado has carried out longer-term thorough design and evaluation studies of the use of multiple tabletops in a classroom.[34] His technology includes voice input features for each tabletop, wall displays for entire classroom viewing, and teacher dashboard displays for viewing complex computed records of tabletop activity. This represents the use of state-of-the-art technology as well as careful attention to the support of teachers within a smart classroom, as there is a serious issue of teacher attention in an environment overwhelmed with students and devices.

Studies have shown that students can be engaged and enthusiastic in such classroom environments, and that different technology configurations afford various kinds of classroom exercises.[35] Yet it is unclear if the costs of purchasing and maintaining such complex hardware are sustainable in education on a large scale, and how such technology should affect teaching.

These latter innovations assume a traditional classroom, where the focus is on what happens when students come together with teachers in a physical space, perhaps filled with 'fancy toys' that provide tools for enabling learning. Alternatively, digital video recording technology may be used to capture and digitize lectures electronically and present them to students without using up class time. This frees up classroom time for interaction, discussion, debate, exercises, and laboratory work.

The result is what is called the *flipped classroom* or *inverted* classroom.[36] The instructor pre-records the lectures, sometimes using sophisticated production equipment, sometimes only with a quiet room, lamp, and webcam, to create a digital bank of instructional content. Students are then asked to prepare for each class by watching the lecture and possibly doing some reading. Class time is then used to discuss difficult topics or apply fundamental concepts.

A review of thirty-two studies of flipped classroom uses in computer science education found that the approach generally increased learning performance and was received positively by students, who were typically more engaged and developed better learning habits.[37] The flipped classroom allows for more discussion and more cooperative learning. Yet the process has a high initial cost and is very time-consuming for the instructor. Some students were unreceptive to this method; some tended to skip classes, especially if the class size was large. Abigail G. Schleg's recent book on flipped classrooms detailed how the approach has been used in both the sciences and the humanities and described methods of addressing pedagogical and technical production challenges.[38]

The flipped classroom has great value, but it is no panacea for instructors and requires a lot of effort and sophistication in teaching technique that is very different from traditional practices. A variety of interesting options present themselves if class time need not be devoted to lectures, if planning is imaginative and preparation is thorough, if sufficient teaching personnel are available to meet with small groups of students, and if the classroom setting facilitates such meetings.

Research: Collect, analyse, and summarize the research that has been done on the advantages, disadvantages, and effectiveness of the flipped classroom concept.

Policy: Prepare a brief for a politician about to speak about smart classrooms to a meeting of the Board of Education budget committee.

Policy: Prepare a brief for the Superintendent of a school system to speak about flipped classrooms at a meeting with teachers.

Book report: Schleg, Abigail G. (2015). *Implementation and Critical Assessment of the Flipped Classroom Experience.* IGI Global.

3.5 Intelligent tutoring

There has been continued vigorous research on *intelligent tutoring systems* (ITSs) since the early efforts of John Anderson. His research led directly to Kenneth R. Koedinger's development of the Practical Algebra Tutor (PAT) at Carnegie Mellon University (CMU) and its use in the Pittsburgh Urban Mathematics Project (PUMP).[39] PAT and PUMP were practical in that they focused on real-world mathematical problems and the use of computational tools. PAT was specifically designed to support the PUMP curriculum as a 'cognitive tutor' that contained a cognitive model of successful student performance.[5] The cognitive tutor paradigm is an example of 'Good Old Fashioned AI' (GOFAI, see Chapter 11). A test of PAT on PUMP's curriculum was run with 470 ninth-grade algebra students whose performance was evaluated with respect to a comparable group.[39] Those using PAT outperformed the control group by 15 per cent on standardized tests and by 100 per cent on a set of tests that targeted the program's objectives. These impressive results in real-world deployment inspired many other projects in intelligent tutoring.[40]

A system developed at the Worcester Polytechnic Institute and widely deployed and tested is called ASSISTments.[41] Its approach is significantly different: it functions as an authoring platform, comparable to the cognitive tutor authoring tools developed at CMU. Although it contains some intelligent tutoring, its goals are less ambitious. Its primary focus is delivering sequences of questions on particular topics to students; providing rapid feedback using answers, hints, solutions, and videos; and supplying teachers with data on student performance so that they can target instruction more precisely. These more attainable goals and the elaborate scaffolding provided to instructors makes it relatively easy for teachers to develop online curricula. By 2014, 50,000 students were using ASSISTments; this number had doubled each year for the previous eight years.

These landmark systems show promise, as do the increasing numbers of studies that have yielded positive results.[42] Yet intelligent tutoring still faces many challenges before it is to become widely used and demonstrably successful. One of the biggest issues scientists face is *user modelling*.

User modelling

A user model of a student, often termed a *student* or *learner model*, has been defined as 'a model of the [student's] knowledge, difficulties and misconceptions'.[43] Student models in intelligent tutoring systems:[44]

> represent student competencies and learning achievements....may involve techniques to represent content skills (e.g., mathematics, art history), knowledge about learning (e.g., metacognitive knowledge), and affective characteristics (e.g., emotional state). Although students' general knowledge might be determined quickly from quiz results, their learning style, attitudes, and emotions...need to be inferred from long-term observations. Models may be used for assessment by measuring changes in the student...[they] generally represent inferences about users (e.g. their level of knowledge, misconceptions, goals, plans, preferences, beliefs)...characteristics of users...and users' records, particularly past interactions with the system.
>
> Effective student models enable itss to:[45]
>
> 1. Assess the student's level of achievement
> 2. Diagnose the student's problems
> 3. Provide feedback in response to errors
> 4. Extend the knowledge of the student
> 5. Anticipate the effect of an action on the student
> 6. Change the system's teaching strategy.

Open user models are learner models that may be inspected and sometimes even modified by students.[46]

A second challenge is suggested by the findings that young children (ages 3 to 5) are more engaged, remember more, and make more use of what they have heard when they are read to by a social robot that has more intonation and expressiveness than one with a monotonous and flat voice.[47] A third challenge, given the demographics of classrooms in most parts of the world, is that of endowing ITSs with cultural sensitivity and awareness.[48]

For intelligent tutoring to be as good as our best teachers, ITSs require sensitivity and empathy. AI has not yet achieved this. In anthropomorphic language (we shall return to this topic in Section 11.5), one of the pioneers of student modelling, John Self, suggested that intelligent tutoring systems must 'care about' their student users.[49] We are still far from this goal.

Research: Research progress in intelligent tutoring systems, focusing especially on understanding where and how they are effective or ineffective.

Research: Study what is known about the use of intelligent tutoring systems in several different cultures.

Technology review: Compare and contrast the leading available products for intelligent tutoring.

3.6 Online learning

Online discussion boards and computer conferencing systems enable dialogue among students and with a teacher independent of where students are located and when they are available, and is often perceived as less threatening than face-to-face interactions by shy or introverted students.

As early as 1973, the PLATO system had message boards (electronic notes on a central forum) and real-time text chat.[3] Another early and influential 1970s system was Murray Turoff's Electronic Information Exchange System,[50] studied extensively by his collaborator Starr Roxanne Hiltz.

Looking back at technological advances up until 2002, Hiltz and Turoff asserted that effective online learning depends upon rapidly achieving trust between instructor and student as a prerequisite for effective interaction and collaboration supported by appropriate software.[51] In 2005, they predicted that online courses were:[52]

> [Moving] from: face-to-face courses using objectivist, teacher-centered pedagogy and offered by tens of thousands of local, regional, and national universities;
>
> To: online and hybrid courses using digital technologies to support constructivist, collaborative, student-centered pedagogy, offered by a few hundred 'mega-universities' that operate on a global scale.

This prediction seems to be coming true, but it fails to recognize the challenges that must be faced by the developers of online educational support systems and by the teachers who practise their craft online. It also ignores the difference between two kinds of online learning: work by an individual student in accessing and mastering material is very different from work by groups or teams of students as part of a 'community of inquiry'.[53] The quality of this *community of inquiry* is the touchstone of an effective online learning community. An excellent example of a community of inquiry supported by digital technology is the 'knowledge-building discourse' that Professors of Education Marlene Scardamalia and Carl Bereiter have suggested is capable of producing 'transformational thought' from both students and teachers.[54]

Three theoretical constructs may be used to describe and judge the extent to which an online learning system supports a community of inquiry.[55] *Social presence* measures the extent to which individuals can project themselves and engage in open and effective communication. It is required to ensure group cohesion and therefore may correlate with measures of perceived learning and satisfaction with the instructor.[56] *Cognitive presence* measures the extent to which there is critical discourse, collaboration, and reflection that produces a shared understanding in a community of inquiry.[57] *Teaching presence* measures the extent to which instructional design, facilitation, and leadership aids the success of an online environment.[58] Research has shown that the quality of teaching presence helps determine student satisfaction and perceived learning.

Thoughtful critics of online learning focus on several issues. They note that online learners miss face-to-face discussions, and the familiarity of and ability to control the flow of conversations that visible contact affords; the spontaneity and improvisation in such interactions; the feeling of perceiving and being perceived by others; and the deeper sense of getting to know others.[59] Some challenges enumerated by critics are the difficulties of sustaining critical discourse online,[60] and the importance of excellence in instructional methods to achieve quality online learning discussions.[61] Moreover, recent studies have suggested that online courses provide the least value to the students in greatest need of added instruction and/or attention, such as those who are ill-prepared or unable to grasp the subject matter.[62]

In some cases, the content *is* the discussion, for example in online communities with the purpose of connecting students from different areas around the world.[63] These worldwide learning communities build connections and empathy among youth from different cultures.

Voices of Youth[64]

Voices of Youth is an initiative of UNICEF's Communication Division headquartered in New York City. It is 'a global community for young people to learn about development issues (such as Environment, Education, and Human Rights) and to express their opinions. Voices of Youth seeks to create a space that will help young people develop into active global citizens, equipped to communicate and collaborate effectively to make a positive difference in their countries and communities.' Young people typically over the age of 13 from numerous countries all over the world blog, tweet, and comment on one another's communications.

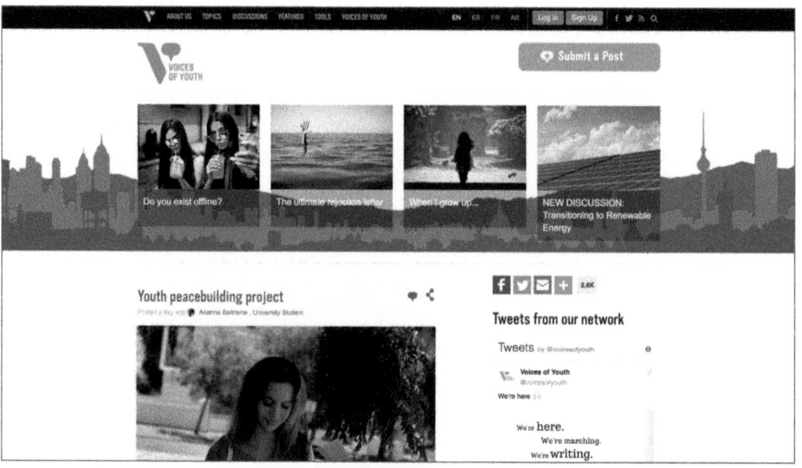

Figure 3.4 Screenshot from Voices of Youth home page
Courtesy of Voices of Youth. http://www.voicesofyouth.org/.

Research: Investigate and analyse the more than thirty years of work that Hiltz, Turoff, and their students have done on building and studying the use of online learning environments.

Research: Investigate and analyse the twenty-five years of work that Scardamalia, Bereiter, and their students have done on technology to support knowledge-building communities.

Book report: Garrison, D. Randy, and Norman D. Vaughn (2008). *Blended Learning in Higher Education: Framework, Principles, and Guidelines.* Jossey-Bass.

3.7 Massive open online courses (MOOCs)

Until recently, online courses were typically environments in which tens and up to a few hundred individuals could participate and engage in the virtual classroom. Now, there is a variant of the original concept called the *Massive Open Online Course* (MOOC).[65] What if the teachers were master teachers, the best in the world on particular subjects, and their lectures could be made available to thousands or millions of students located anywhere in the world? Furthermore, students need not necessarily be registered at a specific academic institution. They could simply be ordinary people interested in some subject matter. Would this not be a major step towards enhancing literacy and disseminating knowledge worldwide?

In 2012, the MOOC became the darling of the high-tech entrepreneurial world. Three high-profile and well-funded start-ups spun out of Stanford, MIT, and Harvard. From then on, the MOOC phenomenon expanded rapidly. By the end of 2017, there were over 81 million students worldwide signed up for at least one course chosen from over 9,000 created by one of 800 universities.[66] Most of the MOOC activity is focused on higher education, but Khan Academy is a non-profit providing instructional videos and practice exercises for levels as early as kindergarten.[67] Most of the activity originated in North America, and most MOOC materials are available in English, but this phenomenon is now changing.

The rapid growth of MOOCs

Currently, the four largest providers of MOOCs are Coursera (a Stanford spin-off, leading by a wide margin), EdX (created by MIT and Harvard), XuetangX from China, and FutureLearn from the Open University in the UK. Coursera opens its website with the slogan 'You are Unstoppable'.[68] FutureLearn is informed by the Open University's history as the most comprehensive and successful national distance learning university. Here is a comparison of these ventures as of June 2017:[69]

Continued on next page

	Launch date	Students	Courses	University partners
Coursera	January 2012	Over 25 million	Over 2,000	Over 150
EdX	2012	Over 10 million	Over 1,500	Over 100
FutureLearn	End of 2012	Over 6 million		Over 100
XuetangX	2013	Over 7 million	Over 400	

MOOCs raise many interesting issues: (a) the extent to which the course is 'open'; (b) appropriate pedagogy for teaching and achieving engagement by huge numbers at a distance; (c) what it means to take a course, attrition and completion, authentication and certification; and (d) revenue models.

In principle, MOOC materials and access are free, but there are a variety of categories to its 'openness'.[65] In all cases, the core lecture content is free (we will return to the issue of revenue models), but the material can be dealt with in different ways. So-called *eMOOCs* are designed as environments in which material can be reused and repurposed by students and institutions. *xMOOCS* are more traditional vehicles for the distribution of fixed content. eMOOCs are usually examples of *open educational resources*, with 'teaching, learning, and research resources that reside in the public domain or have been released under an intellectual property license that permits their free use or re-purposing by others'.[70]

MOOCs represent an active area for learning technologies and human–computer interaction research; several investigators have recommended methods to improve the learner experience. These include 'badges' for rewarding desirable user behaviour;[71] improved video production techniques, including shorter videos, inclusion of talking-heads, and the use of Khan Academy-style tablet drawings;[72] more effective chatrooms;[73] and better ways of supporting synchronous interactive peer learning groups within MOOCs.[74]

Fewer than 10 per cent of students who register for a course complete it.[75] Not everyone is able to understand courses, many of which are sophisticated in content and approach, even though they are taught by the best professors in the world. Reasons for diminishing effort and even dropping out include the time required, the difficulty of the material, and the design of the course. Reasons for sticking with the online course include the quality of the lecture material; the quantity and quality of feedback, which has to be automated given the scale required for such a huge class; and the quantity and quality of peer interaction and review. Critical motivation for participation is often achieving a certificate of completion.

Revenue models for MOOCs include requiring payment to receive graded assignments, and verified credentials or certificates of completion.[76] There are now hundreds of programmes in which one can get a certificate or degree online.[66] Credentials go by various names such as MicroMasters and Nanodegrees. The business is highly competitive. Coursera has raised over $210 million in equity funding; FutureLearn recently announced that it would seek to raise £40 million in investment capital to fuel its marketing and its recruitment of new university partners.[76]

Research: Research the reasons why only 10% of the students who register for a MOOC complete it, and discuss whether this percentage is too low, or is in fact acceptable.

Jury: An immigrant to the USA sues a MOOC company after paying for completion certificates for three courses in machine learning yet still not finding work in that field. Assuming the laws of a particular jurisdiction, discuss whether or not the firm is guilty and if so what penalty to apply.

3.8 Ubiquitous use of computers in schools

There are increasingly interesting ways to use computers in education and learning. But to what end, and to what degree? There have been debates about these questions since the 1980s; controversy surrounding technology in education continues unabated to the present day.

An early analysis and critique came in a 1986 book by professor of education Larry Cuban, who previously had been a city Superintendent of Schools.[77] He found plenty of hype but (as of then) little evidence of technologically based change and improvement in classrooms, noting that 'teachers will alter classroom behavior selectively to the degree that certain technologies help them solve problems they define as important and avoid eroding their classroom authority'. In a subsequent book, he argued that information technology (IT) had achieved neither a transformation of teaching and learning nor productivity gains, and suggested that significant expenditures on technology might have to be at the expense of ignoring other needs such as smaller class sizes, higher teacher salaries, building renovations, full-day preschool and kindergarten, and innovative arts programmes.[78]

Since 2000, there have been several serious and well-publicized media accounts reporting on the dissatisfaction with exaggerated expectations about the educational value of IT in the classroom.[79] All the articles mentioned the excitement associated with using computers in the classroom, yet also raised concern about the significant costs, especially those caused by the laudable desire to ensure that each student has a computer (think back to the OLPC project discussed in Chapter 1). Concerns have been raised about the wisdom of allocating scarce resources of money and classroom time to IT as opposed to other more traditional priorities, such as those mentioned by Cuban. Issues of educational philosophy—what should be taught, when, and how it should be taught—have been raised. Arguments for using computers based on helping students eventually find jobs were criticized. Most of the articles debated the validity of research that purports significant educational gains attributed to classroom computer use. They also reported on the repeated failure to see an improvement in test scores despite the emphasis on the use of technology. Concerns were also raised about the growing childhood occurrence of attention deficit hyperactivity disorder (ADHD), increased aggression, and screen addiction.

This debate continued in more scholarly venues as well. Papert decried the reliance on test scores, asserting that the school of the future and educational technology needed to move education in totally new directions.[80] Arguments based on the philosophy of the

Waldorf Schools movement were employed to assert that the use of computers in primary and middle schools was harmful and to propose delaying such education to high school.[81] The disappointment in 1:1 laptop initiatives was cited as a sign of the failure of new visions to reform education.[82] Kentaro Toyama of Microsoft Research India reviewed its track record of innovative research ideas to improve the Indian school system. He concluded that technological advancement ideas were insufficient to compensate for the lack of good teachers and good principals in schools.[83]

There have only been a few rigorous quantitative evaluations of the effects of classroom use of computers on student performance. One recent paper compared an entire term of US university students using laptops in an unrestricted manner, students working with tablets that had to remain flat on the desktop, and students allowed no technology use, and found that the latter group performed roughly 0.2 of a standard deviation better than the former two groups.[84] Another study of American eighth- and tenth-grade students showed that using a computer for school is consistently associated with higher odds of spending five or more hours on homework and earning high grades, whereas the opposite is true for watching television on weekdays.[85]

An Organisation for Economic Co-operation and Development (OECD) programme carried out extensive data collection and analysis in 2009 and 2012 on educational IT in twenty-nine OECD and thirteen partner countries. It also conducted reading and mathematics tests. It reported in 2015:[86]

> Students who use computers moderately at school tend to have somewhat better learning outcomes than students who use computers rarely. But students who use computers very frequently at school do a lot worse in most learning outcomes, even after accounting for social background and student demographics. The results also show no appreciable improvements in student achievement in reading, mathematics or science in the countries that had invested heavily in ICT for education.... technology is of little help in bridging the skills divide between advantaged and disadvantaged students.... ensuring that every child attains a baseline level of proficiency in reading and mathematics seems to do more to create equal opportunities in a digital world than can be achieved by expanding or subsidising access to high-tech devices and services.

Another comprehensive review of the literature concluded that:[87]

> the primary benefit of current technology use in education has been to increase information access and communication. Students primarily use technology to gather, organize, analyze, and report information, but this has not dramatically improved student performance on standardized tests.

Ethics

Mobile phones in schools and classrooms: An interesting yet often troubling case of the ubiquity of computers in education arises with the role of mobile phones in the classroom. Unlike laptops and tablets, which students may not routinely carry with them and/or use constantly during school time, smartphones are now an inescapable additional appendage for young people. In 2017, Pew Research reported that 100% of American adults ages 18 to 29 own a mobile phone and 92% of them have a smartphone; of these, 100% use mobile devices for text messaging, 97% for internet use, 93% for voice or video calls, 91% for email, and 93% to avoid boredom.[88]

In addition, as smartphones become almost as powerful as laptops and tablets, with increasingly larger screens and better video and audio capability, they can be handy in the classroom. Instructors are faced with a dilemma: how can they ensure that smartphone use in the classroom is dedicated to educational purposes without becoming a distraction to students? Is there a place for mobile devices in class, or should such technology be banned?

Mobile phones are useful for disseminating content for *on-demand learning* at the tip of one's fingertips, using social media to connect to content experts, providing feedback to the instructor by acting as 'clickers', and creating presentation practice and explanatory videos.[89] After banning mobile phones in schools for a decade, in early 2015, New York City decided to lift the ban, citing the need for parents to stay in touch with their children as the primary reason.[90] The decision was opposed by many teachers, who cited concerns about theft, disruption, and distraction.

The effect of mobile phone distraction has been studied by researchers at the London School of Economics.[91] High school student performance in four English cities improved 6.4% of a standard deviation after mobile phones were banned. Students in the lowest quartile saw their scores improve by 14.2%; students in the highest quartile were not affected. Yet there have been anecdotal and almost incredible reports of difficulties in weaning students off their phones; being without them for even thirty minutes caused too much anxiety for some students.[92]

A recent review article confirmed the ongoing conflict between (a) the belief that technology in the classroom has great potential for fostering learning and (b) the reality that mobile phones are typically viewed as entertainment and social devices, making their presence in schools highly disruptive to instructors, attention spans, and fellow students.[93]

Just like the issue of computer use in schools, there is no consensus on mobile phone use in schools. Decisions vary by country. For example, France has recently banned mobile phones in schools through the ninth grade, whereas, just as in New York City, more and more US cities are now allowing them in schools.[94] The percentage of US K–12 schools that prohibited use in 2015–16 was 66%, down from 90% in 2009–10. This was due in part to increasing violence in schools, ranging from shootings to other violence to theft to bullying.[95]

Decisions to include or exclude phones made by principals and teachers fundamentally affect the nature of the classroom, so making it thoughtfully and in consultation with parents is an ethical choice of great consequence. If you were a school superintendent, what would be your ethical decision? What factors would be salient?

Research: Compile and analyse the evidence for and against allowing mobile phones in the classroom.

Concept: Improve the Wikipedia entry on 'mobile phone use in schools'.

Debate: Resolved: Students should be taught how to build their own web page no later than middle school.

Debate: Resolved: Students should be taught how to program in a scripting language no later than high school.

Debate: Resolved: Mobile phones should not be permitted in the classroom.

Book report: Cullingford, Cedric, and Nusrat Haq (2009). *Computers, Schools, and Students: The Effects of Technology*. Ashgate.

Policy: Prepare a brief for a political candidate to decide his or her position with respect to whether or not mobile phones should be allowed in the classroom.

Jury: Parents sue a school board for extensive computer use in the classroom, alleging that their child has become computer-addicted. Discuss if the suit is justified, and what decision you as a jury should take.

Law: Requiring all schools in your city or state to ban mobile phones in the schools.

Field work: Compare and contrast the approach to allowing or banning mobile phones in schools and classrooms that has been adopted by two or three schools.

Ethics: You are a high school principal in a school considering banning mobile phones in the classroom. What is your position and why are you taking that position?

Ethics: You are a high school teacher working at a school that has banned mobile phones in the classroom. You catch one student using a mobile phone. He or she explains that a parent is in the hospital. What do you do?

Ethics: Your town is planning a major expenditure on providing tablets for every student in the high schools. At the same time, it needs to delay road improvements or raise taxes significantly. Your expertise is sought, perhaps unwisely, because you are a computer professional. What do you advise?

3.9 Summary

Learning is vital to our health as a society. Much of this occurs through education in schools. How to ensure the wise use of technology in the classroom is a critical policy decision for students, parents, school system administrators, and government policy-makers.

We began our discussion with a review of ideas by pioneers and visionaries who helped introduce computers to education: the PLATO system to develop online learning tutorials; Suppes and Atkinson's drill-and-practice exercises; Papert and Feurzeig's concept of children's environments for developing creativity through the LOGO programming language; Kay's Dynabook and focus on engaging projects; and Resnick's Scratch programming language, project sharing environment, and Computer Clubhouse movement. PLATO and Suppes established a baseline for the use of technology to teach traditional subjects, where the ability to evaluate student achievement was considered vital. LOGO prototyped a 'maker' culture for virtual constructions that mirrored what was already possible in the physical world with toys including erector sets, tinkertoys, and LEGO.

The Dynabook was the inspiration for modern-day tablets. Resnick added the element of a worldwide community of children learning and sharing their insights through computing.

Over time, other novel uses of computers to foster learning were developed. Simulations and serious games allow learning by creating a virtual world in which one can practise actions and make mistakes without causing real-life harm. They can provide stimulating and joyous learning experiences if they are well designed and correctly model the phenomenon under study.

Presentation technologies support lecturers in augmenting their words and body language with text, images, diagrams, music, and video. PowerPoint is the most prevalent method, but not the only way to do this, as there are increasingly imaginative methods for using software and apps to convey material with images, motion pictures, and sound.

Smart classrooms allow students to work collaboratively with computers, tablets, and electronic whiteboards. Students love the toys, but there are serious issues of cost, maintainability, and scalability.

Flipped classrooms require professors to record and students to review digital videos of the lectures prior to class. Class time is then used for interactions between teachers and students in what is hopefully a new and improved learning experience. Flipped classrooms require flexibility in how classrooms are organized, and a school or school system with adequate funding and personnel.

Intelligent tutoring systems have improved in capability and sophistication over the forty years that AI researchers have been working on them. For some domains, especially mathematics, their ability to diagnose student problems and guide improved learning are impressive. Yet their widespread use awaits the ability to understand what a student is thinking and to endow tutoring robots with a skilful human teacher's sensitivity and empathy.

As the cost of telecommunications went down, online learning progressed from single learners working by themselves to groups of learners interacting in communities of inquiry. The most extreme cases are MOOCs, featuring classes by master teachers that are accessible worldwide. Early excitement subsided somewhat as MOOCs struggled with issues of attrition. Yet they continue to improve and are now available for many subjects. Methods of certification are also increasingly available. Independent of community size, the success of online learning depends upon instructors' skill and imagination in devising ways of encouraging engagement within the student group, and their commitment to spending lots of time monitoring and mentoring.

Experience has shown that large-scale introduction of laptops or tablets in a school requires at least electrical system and air conditioning enhancements, a Wi-Fi network that reaches throughout the school, a secure network infrastructure with firewalls, computer repair capability and loaners, software licenses, and a significant administrative infrastructure.[96] Yet school boards are now under tremendous pressure from hardware suppliers such as Apple, Google, and Microsoft to spend large sums on computers for the schools.[97] Though uses of computers for learning have become more numerous and imaginative, administrators and teachers struggle to find the right balance between vast expenditures of money and modest investment, extensive use and restraint, and an emphasis on new technology and traditional educational priorities. A current specific dilemma is whether to encourage or ban mobile phone use in primary and secondary schools.

There are no easy answers. Resources are always scarce. Communities have many needs for investment other than educational IT, such as health care and social services. Whatever the choices, the quality of teaching, instructors' commitment to their students, and insightful instructional design are ensuring that students are motivated and excited to continue learning.

3.10 Key terms

Alan Kay
Artificial intelligence (AI)
ASSISTments
Cognitive presence
Community of inquiry
Computer Clubhouses
Coursera
Digital fluency
Digital simulations and serious gaming
Dynabook
eClass
Electronic Information Exchange System
eMOOCs
Intelligent tutoring systems (ITSs)
Inverted or flipped classrooms
John Anderson
Khan Academy
Knowledge-building discourse
Learning histories
Lessig Method
Lifelong Kindergarten Group
LOGO programming language
Maker movement
Massive Open Online Courses (MOOCs)
Mitchel Resnick
On-demand learning
Online learning
Open educational resources
Open user model
Patrick Suppes
Pittsburgh Urban Mathematics Project
PLATO
PowerPoint
Practical Algebra Tutor (PAT)
Presentation technology
Prezi
Scratch
Seymour Papert
SimCity
Smart classrooms
Social presence
Teaching presence
User modelling
Voices of Youth
xMOOCs
Zoomable user interfaces (ZUIs)

4

Computers in medicine and health care

As with the chapter on learning, we begin our discussion of *health* applications by examining influential early visions of the possible role of computers in improving health care and medicine. We then look at the great variety of roles played by current digital technologies in this field.

We first consider the online availability of health information. There are two possible sources: one from respected centres of expertise, the other from consumers of medical care, that is, patients, who in working together form what may be viewed as *communities of care*. There is strong evidence that people are using these online medical resources to become more intelligent guardians of their own health and to support themselves when seeking help from physicians.

Next, we examine the care improvements promised by personal health and electronic medical records. Progress here has been disappointingly slow; we shall discuss the mix of technical, cultural, administrative, interpersonal, and financial reasons for the sluggishness in development and deployment. Two particularly interesting cases of medical information are data dealing with adverse drug reactions and interactions, commonly known as *adverse drug events* (ADEs), and the use of big data and social media in epidemic surveillance and control, by which we are becoming better equipped to indicate, predict, and track outbreaks of disease.

Computers have made a huge impact on medical education through the development of human body simulators. There also continue to be more and more advanced uses of technology embedded within the human body, either to augment the functioning of organs or to replace body parts that no longer work, which could possibly result in bionic people or androids in the future. We shall present some examples indicating the pace at which these technologies are developing.

Recent advances in understanding the human genome have enabled a new form of medicine called *precision medicine*. The goal is to use genetic screening of patients to enable more specific treatments than were hitherto possible. Precision medicine also enables what some call *designer babies*. We shall introduce policy and ethical issues raised by this concept.

Finally, we shall look at two topics of increasing interest to older adults—brain training exercises leveraging *neuroplasticity*, with the goals of keeping the mind healthy and staving off dementia; and robotic companions and caregivers for seniors, including those with dementia. The former area has led to fiery debates among scientists about the success of brain training. Robotic companions could be helpful given society's seeming inability to find and fund sufficient numbers of human caregivers for the growing ageing population, yet these measures also raise ethical concerns.

Digital technologies have dramatically transformed the practice of medicine and the drive towards excellent health care for society. Are these inventions for better or for worse? What issues puzzle and concern thoughtful computer scientists and engaged citizens? What policy choices and ethical dilemmas confront us as technology-based medical developments evolve at an accelerating rate?

4.1 Pioneers and visionaries

The scope of these transformations is so large that in discussing the earliest researchers and clinicians we must somewhat restrict the focus.[1] We shall therefore focus on using computers for medical records, a topic still current today, as progress has been slow over the past sixty years.

Two of the leading centres of early work on computing for medicine were the Hospital of Latter Day Saints in Salt Lake City, Utah and the Massachusetts General Hospital (MGH) in Boston, Massachusetts. Under the direction of Dr Homer Warner, who pioneered work on the mathematical modelling of the cardiovascular system, Salt Lake City became a hub for medical computing research.[2] Dr Warner's work included significant early contributions on drug and disease databases, as well as health information repositories. In 1964, the Department of Medical Informatics at the University of Utah became the first programme to grant degrees in medical informatics. Under the direction of Dr Octo Barnett, MGH's Laboratory for Computer Science began in 1964 projects on computerized electronic health records, diagnostic decision support systems, and programming languages for building clinical informatics systems, including the influential Massachusetts General Hospital Utility Multi-Programming System (MUMPS) programming language for building medical information systems.[3]

Another pioneer was Dr Werner V. Slack at Harvard Medical School, who also worked on medical records. Yet even more important were his ideas about dialogues that patients could and should have with computers in order to:[4]

> obtain the patient's medical history and to offer advice and suggestions to the patient about the prevention, diagnosis, and management of common, important medical and psychological problems.

One ground-breaking visionary in computerized medical records was Dr Lawrence Weed. In an important early paper,[5] he proposed 'a plan whereby the hospital record, particularly the progress notes, can be made the central point in medical care and medical education'. Moreover, he argued that hospital records *must* achieve this goal, and proposed the Problem-Oriented Medical Record (POMR) as a way to do this. The complexity of POMRs was great enough that computerization of the system was essential. We shall return to this concept later in the chapter.

Dr William Raub of the US National Institutes of Health (NIH) is best remembered for two major contributions.[6] As a scientist, he envisioned and oversaw the development of PROPHET, a comprehensive set of information-handling tools for scientists studying chemical–biological interactions.[7] As a far-seeing administrator, he oversaw a programme of government grants that funded most of the earliest applications of artificial intelligence (AI) in medicine.

4.2 Online health information and online communities of care

There is never enough time for physicians to practise medicine as they would like. Nor can they answer all the questions a patient asks. Likewise, patients cannot always articulate questions that are in the back of their minds while they are in the doctor's office.

Accessing information and knowledge about health conditions was always difficult. Patients rarely went to the library or bookstore to research symptoms or diseases; and if they did go in search of information, they found mostly incomprehensible material that was not necessarily current or understandable for laymen.

The internet changed this. By 2001, there were 70,000 websites with online health information being used by over 50 million people.[8] Seventy-seven per cent of patients sought information to help them consult with their physicians; 54 per cent sought information for other purposes. By 2003, an estimated 4.5 per cent of all web searches were 'health-related', amounting to 6.75 million such searches each day.[9] More recently, by 2011, 80 per cent of US internet users had looked online for health information.[10]

Yet, rather than saving time, proactive research often resulted in lengthier discussions between patient and physician, and sometimes led to diminished patient trust in the physician. Nonetheless, providing more online medical information is a valuable service, unless its use is impeded by information overload, site disorganization, searching challenges, incomprehensible language, user unfriendliness, and impermanence, issues that will be discussed later in the chapter.

It is vital that online medical information be credible,[8] with believable, authoritative, and trustworthy sources. Credibility may be established through peer review, rating systems, and codes of conduct. However, despite varying ranges of credibility, one early study found that university students had a tendency to rate all internet health information as relatively credible, even when it originated from a source that was not authoritative.[11] Another study found a difference in how people thought they searched and what could actually be observed in a usability lab.[12] Participants in focus groups asserted that they looked at the source of the information, professional design, and 'a scientific or official touch'; yet, in an observational study, no participants actually checked the 'about us' sections of websites or the disclaimers or disclosures.

Another study in the *Journal of the American Medical Association* (JAMA) reported the results of thirty-four physicians evaluating the quality and content of twenty-five English and Spanish health websites.[13] They found that over three-fourths of the search engine's first pages do not point to relevant content, and that only 45 per cent of the critical clinical elements in English and 22 per cent in Spanish are 'more than minimally covered and completely accurate' among the sites. They also noted that 100 per cent of the English and 86 per cent of the Spanish sites require at least high school level reading ability. There is also evidence that health information seekers are usually looking for a specific condition that fits a diagnosis received by themselves or a friend,[14] searchers seldom go beyond the first page resulting from a search, and they pay little attention to credibility.

One more early study reported that 62.4 per cent of patients fully trusted their physicians.[15] Roughly one-fourth expressed a lot of trust in the internet-sourced data; one-fourth expressed no trust at all. When feeling sick, 49.5 per cent wanted to consult their physician first for specific information, 48.6 per cent went online to research prior to visiting their physician, and only 10.9 per cent actually went to their physician first. Another research group agreed that physicians were still seen as the primary source of information and advice.[16] Yet they observed a far more thoughtful use of the internet than did other investigators. Participants in their study used heuristics about good site design and, more importantly, content credibility, to sift and review information that they deemed trustworthy, then subsequently integrated it with advice from family, friends, and physicians.

Literature today still expresses concerns about health information website quality and usability. Wikipedia, the internet's most popular general reference, has been criticized for errors in its health information web pages. One study in the *Journal of the American Osteopathic Association* found many errors when experts checked articles on the ten most costly medical conditions against standard peer-reviewed sources.[17] Using an idiosyncratic measure of quality, another paper found insufficient quality in most health information sites; only 16 per cent were written at more than a sixth-grade reading level.[18] Most alarming, 20th Century Fox recently created fake health websites and released fake articles about topics such as abortion and vaccines to promote a film, 'A Cure for Wellness'.[19] We shall return to the topic of fake news in Chapter 5.

There are ways to use the web carefully. The Consumer and Patient Health Information Section of the Medical Library Association published a list of the top health websites based on criteria including currency and credibility.[20] The US National Institute of Aging published a set of suggestions on finding trustworthy health information on the web.[21] Important criteria they identified, echoing themes discussed in the research literature, include the credibility of the author, the editors of the information, and publication date. They emphasize the importance of consulting with a physician (if you can get an appointment) in addition to using internet research.

There is another way for patients, or individuals concerned about a syndrome or disease, to gather helpful information. Rather than looking online for sources of expertise such as the Mayo Clinic, they may reach out via social media to others who share the same condition or interest. 2014 Pew Research data showed that 26 per cent of adult internet users had in 2013 read or watched someone's online report about a health or medical concern; 16 per cent had sought out others who shared the same concerns.[22]

There are two different online ways one can access the medical experiences and expertise of others. One can participate in a health social network or forum, that is, a defined virtual community of individuals interested in, for example, specific diseases or conditions. Alternatively, one can broadcast a request for help to those on the internet with useful information or skills, which is commonly known as *crowdsourcing* a problem or a task.

PatientsLikeMe

Most health social networks focus on a specific disease or condition. PatientsLikeMe is a comprehensive site that affords its over 600,000 users a place 'where people can share their health data to track their progress [and] help others'.[23] The site is organized into sets of conditions, treatments, and symptoms, creating 'communities of care' zeroing in on certain kinds of people with whom to connect, such as seniors or females.

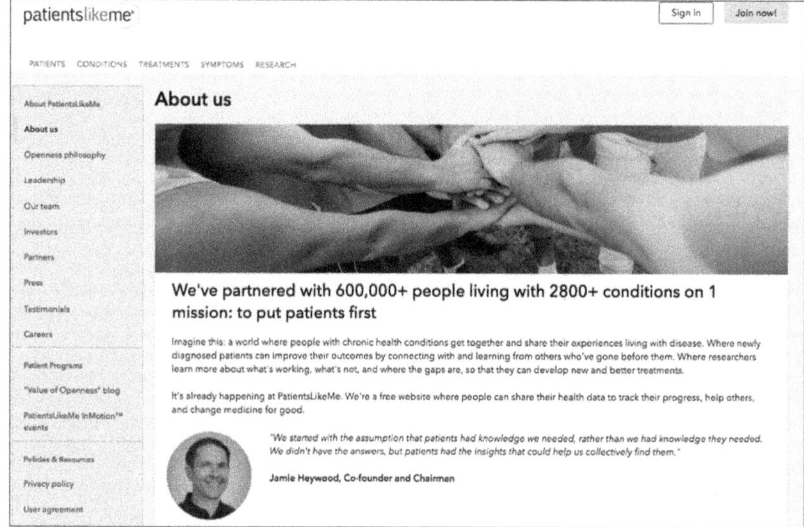

Figure 4.1 Screenshot of About page of PatientsLikeMe website

Members of six PatientsLikeMe disease communities were studied.[24] Seventy-two per cent rated the site 'moderately' or 'very helpful' in learning about a symptom they had experienced; 57% found it helpful for learning about side effects of treatments; and 42% valued finding other patients who could help them better understand their experiences. A follow-up study examining use of PatientsLikeMe by individuals with epilepsy found the percentage of participants who had at least one person with whom they could discuss their disease rose from 30% to 63%. Participants rated the benefits of the community of care as finding someone with the same symptoms (59%), understanding seizures better (58%), and understanding symptoms or treatments better (55%). Benefits increased as the number of relationships among patients with similar conditions increased. One caveat: researchers who conducted the study worked for PatientsLikeMe.

Another example of crowdsourcing for accessing health information from other health consumers is Crowdmed.com,[25] which describes its mission as 'harnessing the collective wisdom of a global, online medical community to provide patients with a clear path to their diagnosis and cure'.

These technologies are generally regarded as improving health. A survey of health internet use by 147 HIV-positive persons found that such use was associated with more knowledge, better coping, and greater social support among patients.[26] Additionally, health social network services include emotional support and information sharing, physician question and analysis, quantified self-tracking, and access to clinical trials.[27] In 2003, medical information system researcher Dr Gunther Eysenbach wrote a review of the impact of the internet on individuals with cancer, stating:[28]

> I believe virtual communities are probably the one Internet application area with the greatest effect on persons with cancer.

Nonetheless, in a 2004 review of the literature, he asserted that more research was needed:[28]

> Numerous controlled studies with peer to peer components have been conducted, but only a few evaluated the effect of peer to peer groups alone. Most studies failed to show an effect, or effects were confounded by potential effects of co-interventions.

Concerns have also been expressed about risks in online heath support groups:[29]

> Online [patient experience] may help people make better health care choices and alert them to health issues, improve their health literacy and understanding of susceptibility to illness, compare their situation with others, improve their own illness narration.... [but]... They may raise anxiety. They may be disadvantageous if they feature only a small number of unrepresentative patients' stories.... The powerful and memorable delivery of a personal experience could be used for a deliberately misleading or exploitative message.

A discussion of virtual communities dedicated to non-suicidal self-injury praised such groups for providing support, typically to youth, but cautioned that participation could also trigger urges to harm oneself.[30] The internet was once used to arrange two suicide pacts involving nine individuals in Japan.[31] There is also a large amount of suicide-assisting information easily available on the internet.[32] For every issue, there is information on both sides; for example, there is tons of information on Reddit about getting high on drugs as well as on fighting an addiction to opioids.[33] An analysis of contributions to four crowdsourced 'share your experience' health websites in three different countries argued that health consumer participants had significant work to do to ensure that their contributions could be helpful to other participants.[34]

Finally, it is interesting to compare and contrast the use of health information repositories and health experience sharing websites. A Microsoft Research comparison of the use of search engines and Twitter for searching and sharing information about symptoms, benign explanations, serious illnesses, and disabilities found evidence of what they termed 'self-censorship' such that:

> serious health conditions, disabilities, and highly stigmatic conditions are generally searched considerably more than they are mentioned in Twitter postings. Symptoms of health conditions, however, were more frequently present in Twitter posts than in search queries.[35]

As social media evolve, there will be even more variety in internet-based health information sharing.

Research: Propose a set of criteria for evaluating health information websites, choose a specific disease, and contrast and compare two or three websites providing information about that disease.

Research: The use of Snapchat for health information sharing.

Research: The use of two different social media as assists in getting high or for fighting addiction.

Concept: Write a Wikipedia article on 'communities of care'.

Debate: Resolved: It is better to seek health information about a specific symptom from a health information website than from members of a virtual community that discusses that symptom.

Law: Forbidding advertising on health experience sharing websites.

Law: Forbidding knowingly publishing false medical or health information on the internet.

Field study: Interview individuals who participate actively in a community of care specialized to a disease.

4.3 Electronic medical records and personal health records

We now turn our attention to the use of computers envisioned and prototyped by the medical informatics pioneers. The *electronic medical record* (EMR) is a repository of data describing a patient's medical conditions and their interactions with the people, places, processes, and materials (including medications) within a physician's *care practice* or within a *hospital*. The electronic *personal health record* (PHR) is a repository of data describing as accurately as possible the health condition of a specific *individual*, and all their interactions with health care providers, processes for maintaining or regaining their health, and medications. The former concept has been around for almost five decades; the latter is newer, although it was implicit in the thinking of Dr Larry Weed. Ideally, both systems should exist, as it seems bizarre not to replace paper with smart electronics to store and process such complex and vital data. Furthermore, the two kinds of records should be linked. We shall see that this process has proved difficult.

Problem-oriented medical record (POMR)

Weed's proposal consisted of four components:[36]

1. The database, a collection of information about the patient
2. A complete problem list
3. Initial plans for each problem...... in SOAP [subjective/objective/assessment/plan] format

Continued on next page

a. Subjective: Patient symptoms, complaints
b. Objective: Physical exams, lab tests
c. Assessment: Thoughts, reasoning
d. Plans: Actions planned and anticipated

4. Daily progress notes, also organized by problem and written in the SOAP format.

The POMR has been widely influential in the design of EMRs.

Progress on implementing EMRs has been slow. As technology evolved from the 1960s through the 1980s, medical practitioners grew more comfortable and familiar with computers. Early successes at sites such as US Veterans Affairs (VA) hospitals and a growing desire to practise scientific medicine should have led to the rapid adoption of EMRs.[37] Yet a 2003 report on five leading US hospitals with clinical information systems found no widespread adoption.[38] A 2009 survey of 3,000 acute care hospitals in the USA found only 1.5 per cent had a comprehensive electronic records system, with an additional 7.6 per cent having at least a basic system.[39] Hospitals in New York State had progressed further: by 2011, 15.5 per cent of the 150 hospitals studied had adopted an EMR system.[40]

Adoption of EMR in private medical practices has been considerably faster. A 2005 survey of 2,900 American group practices found that 14.1 per cent had electronic health records.[41] A decade later, another survey reported that the use by office-based physicians of some type of EMR system had gone up from 18 per cent in 2001 to 78 per cent in 2013; the percentage of clinicians that had systems meeting certain 'basic criteria' had jumped from 11 per cent to 48 per cent.[42]

Numerous clinicians and researchers have described the advantages of EMRs. A 2006 meta-analysis of 257 studies of health information technology (IT), with a primary focus on four pace-setting hospitals and health care institutions, found quality improvements—'increased adherence to guideline-based care, enhanced surveillance and monitoring, and decreased medication errors'.[43] Benefits were especially noticeable in preventive health. The 2008 US Congressional Budget Office noted that EMRs could expand the practice of evidence-based medicine.[44] The use of EMRs could avoid duplicated or unnecessary diagnostic tests, promote the use of generic drugs, and increase physician and nurse productivity and efficiency, although there is still little solid evidence of the latter. An analysis of care data for 27,000 adults with diabetes in the greater Cleveland, Ohio area found that achievement of composite standards for care was 35 per cent higher at EMR sites than at paper-based sites, and the achievement of composite standards for outcomes was 15 per cent higher.[45]

Yet many studies have failed to show benefits. A 2014 survey of 411 American family practice physicians using EMRs reported an average EMR-associated loss of forty-eight minutes per clinic day![46] A 2010 analysis of quality and costs of care and/or administration at 4,000 hospitals found that 'hospital computing might modestly improve process measures of quality but does not reduce administrative or overall costs'.[47] Although some cost–benefit analyses have predicted cost savings,[48] many studies have failed to find clear evidence of this. Since hardware costs continue to drop (although software costs do not), future analyses may yield more positive results.

Why have EMRs, such a good idea in theory, proved to be so problematic in practice? There have been many barriers to implementation. One study of US hospitals focused on inadequate capital, ongoing maintenance costs, unclear return on investment (ROI), inadequate IT staff, and physician resistance to new systems.[39] A review of difficulties encountered in the first British National Health Service hospital computing project concluded that they were caused by a variety of technical, social, economic, and political barriers, including the rapid change in technology relative to the 1967–79 time span of the project.[49] A study of twelve 'early adopter' acute care hospitals and specialized British care settings enumerated problems including unrealistic expectations, delays for customization, end-user training and support needs, changing government policies, contractual negotiations, and the need for complex communications among various stakeholders.[50]

A systematic literature review of 1,700 articles dealing with EMRs found barriers to acceptance in eight categories: financial, technical, time, psychological, social, legal, organizational, and change process.[51] Technical barriers included physicians' lack of computer skills. Time factors were issues before, during, and after EMR installation. Social barriers included interpersonal relationships among all stakeholders. Legal factors included privacy and security concerns. Change process issues included leadership and organizational culture. A subsequent and related paper detailed nineteen interventions that could ease difficulties in EMR adoption.[51] Notable were the active support of senior management and an environment that encourages collaboration and teamwork.

Even when EMRs exist, substantial problems in use are caused by failures in interoperability.[52] Systems from different vendors are not able to seamlessly communicate data to one another, so medical offices and hospitals still have to copy, mail, and fax documents to each other.

One success factor of an EMR system is the extent to which its design considers how medical personnel work together. The subtleties of collaborative work and their effect in a health care setting were explored in an insightful ethnographic study of a toxicology ward:[53]

> [we should] doubt that technologies like the EMR can deliver their promised benefits unless there is a better understanding of the work they are intended to support.... design and development methodologies must actively support... user-led processes of adaptation.

These conclusions were illustrated by the difficulties and ultimate success of an EMR at a hospital in California, where key issues included work process, professional roles, and the allocation of tasks between physicians and nurses.[54]

Failure to safeguard online medical records is another serious problem. Between September 2009 and December 2012, more than 18 million Americans were affected by medical record data breaches.[55] In 2016, 90 million Americans were affected by security breaches of medical records.[56]

We now turn our attention to personal health records. These focus on the symptoms, diagnoses, treatments, and reactions of individuals, as opposed to information that centres on what one experiences in a particular hospital or medical setting. We should note that simply providing access to an EMR is not sufficient; research by Kevin Winkelman, Kevin J. Leonard, and Peter G. Rossos shows it is of little value unless 'accompanied by promotion of a sense of illness ownership, of patient-driven communication, of personalized support, and of mutual trust'.[57]

The advantages of PHRs, and the challenges in creating effective implementations, echo themes discussed with EMRs.[58] PHRs serve to facilitate communication between patients and health care providers, aid education and lifestyle changes, and promote health self-management. An effective user interface and good support are essential for success. These traits are measured in great part by the degree to which patients become actively involved in their own care. Appropriate access for caregivers should also aid families and care staff in participating optimally in the medical process.

Challenges to the implementation and success of PHRs include lack of incentives for the health care industry, consumer confidence around the issue of confidentiality of medical records, insufficient availability of EMRs, and disbelief that a satisfactory ROI will be achieved. There are also issues about what data should be included in PHRs and who should have access to it, as well as the need for interoperability between PHRs and EMRs, which has been hard to achieve.[59]

In closing, we emphasize that these are *socio-technical* systems.[53,60] All stakeholders, including patients, families, physicians, nurses, administrators, and lab personnel, must be involved in the design, adoption, and evolving use of EMRs and PHRs. Secondly, what has been achieved thus far is only a drop in the bucket of what is desirable and should be possible with health informatics. Starting from birth, individuals should possess and own their medical history on a portable device. These should be updated at each interaction with the medical system, and every time one takes a medication, exercises, or perceives a symptom. All data should be interoperable with EMRs at the doctor's office, pharmacy, and hospital. Intelligent software should be able to extract concise and meaningful reports on people's health for themselves and for medical personnel.

Despite five decades since the pioneers' first thoughts, we are still not close to achieving that vision.

Research: Compare and contrast electronic medical records (EMRs) with personal health records (PHRs).

Policy: Prepare a brief for a politician or a candidate proposing a tax increase to allow subsidies to hospitals implementing or improving their EMRs.

Policy: Prepare a brief for the medical director of a hospital proposing significant expenditures and changes in operating procedures by installing an EMR.

Jury: Information about someone's psychiatric condition has been revealed publicly due to a security breach in the psychiatrist's EMR. The patient sues to obtain $5 million for pain and suffering. Debate as to what damages to award the patient, if any.

Book report: Weed, Lawrence L., and Lincoln Weed (2011). *Medicine in Denial.* CreateSpace Independent Publishing Platform.

Field study: Interview office managers or chief administrators of small medical practices in your community to understand their degree of computerization, their experiences, and their attitudes around electronic medical systems.

4.4 Medication data processing

One particularly important application of electronic health data is the detection and prevention of adverse drug events. These can be *adverse drug reactions* (ADRs) to a single medication, as well as unfortunate *drug–drug interactions*. An early review of the field distinguished between *reaction surveillance* systems to detect adverse effects that might occur in the normal prescribing of medications,[61] and *reaction prevention* systems that could prevent the inappropriate prescribing of drugs known to cause problems in certain circumstances or to react with other drugs badly.

Adverse drug reactions and interactions

A meta-analysis of thirty-nine prospective studies found overall an incidence of 6.7% of serious ADRs among hospitalized patients.[62] The incidence of fatal cases was 0.32%. Various other studies have measured percentages of ADEs in hospital admissions ranging from 5% to 17%.[63] Another problem is medication non-compliance, caused in part by poor memory. An interview study of ninety-nine patients aged 65 years old and older, none with known cognitive impairments, found that only 22% could name the drugs they took from memory, only 34% could recall their medical conditions for which they were taking the drugs, and only 49% remembered the number of medications they were taking.[64]

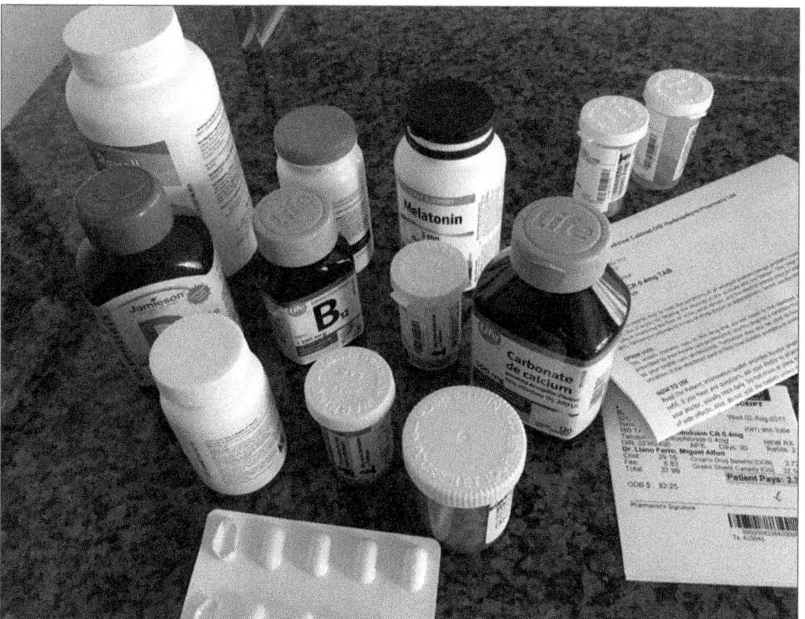

Figure 4.2 Medications in the kitchen of a relatively healthy senior (imagine how many drugs and vitamins there might be if the individual were not relatively healthy)

There is increasing evidence that computerized reaction surveillance can be effective. A study of 37,000 patients admitted to a hospital over eighteen months showed that 730 ADEs (660 of them dose-dependent or predictable) were detected, compared with only nine using traditional methods.[65] A second study examining the effect of a physician order entry system that provided guidelines and warnings when medications were prescribed over six months found that serious medication errors decreased by 55 per cent.[66] A third study reported on six months of an alert system used to prevent ADEs in a community teaching hospital.[67] Alerts were generated with respect to 6.4 per cent of hospital admissions; 44 per cent of them had not been recognized by a physician prior to the alert.

Yet results have not always been that clear. One meta-analysis of ten physician order entry systems with clinical decision support found that only half had statistically significant reductions in ADEs.[68] Another meta-analysis of the effect of physician order entry systems on medication error rate found that twenty-three of twenty-five studies showed a significant relative risk reduction of between 13 per cent and 99 per cent, yet it expressed concerns about the quality of many studies.[69]

There continues to be progress in ensuring medication compliance, such as a *digital pill* that signals the patient and others when medications have not been taken, and ADE screening technology, such as a novel data mining algorithm that searches for higher-than-expected combinations of drugs and events.[70] Yet there are reasons why progress thus far has not been greater. Lack of interoperability among EMRs hinders the ability to synthesize conclusions from disparate data sources. However, one fundamental cause of ADEs is that many people do not have a universally accessible, correct, and complete PHR, and because one's memories of adverse drug events can be incomplete, physicians and patients are not able to avoid repetitions of ADEs and other adverse side effects to certain drugs.

Computer scientists should work with pharmacists, medical administrators, and cognitive scientists to ensure that EMRs and PHRs support ADE surveillance and prevention, and that the occurrence of ADEs is communicated to all relevant stakeholders in a comprehensible manner.

Jury: A child dies due to a fatal side effect of a medication. The parents assert that the manufacturer's insert was inadequate, only mentioning the side effect among a long list of 100 other possible complications. Debate whether or not the drug company is liable.

Ethics: Your extensive use of social media makes you realize that there are frequent reports about a potential problem with a medication manufactured by your drug company employer. You report the concern to management and it refuses to act on your concern. What do you do?

4.5 Big data and infectious disease surveillance and modelling

We have argued that more complete data would be helpful in avoiding adverse drug events. Additionally, recognition and characterization of epidemics can be aided by:[71]

> big data for public health… encompassing patient information gathered from high volume electronic health records and participatory surveillance systems, as well as mining of digital traces such as social media, Internet searches, and cell-phone logs.

Dr Gunther Eysenbach has termed this approach *infodemiology*, which he defined as 'the science of distribution and determinants of information in an electronic medium, specifically the Internet, or in a population, with the ultimate aim to inform public health and public policy'.[72] He distinguished between *'supply-based' applications*, using information published on the internet, and *'demand-based' applications*, using searches and navigation patterns. Infodemiology provides data rapidly, at low cost, with specific information about the locations of outbreaks.

There have been several well-publicized recent successes. Crowdsourcing and voluntary reporting were used in ten European countries to allow the timely tracking of flu-like symptoms.[73] A similar success was achieved in understanding the 2014–15 Ebola epidemic.

Ebola epidemic

Internet data streams were used to understand the West African Ebola epidemic.[74] They showed case clusters in several countries, as well as exposure causes including family, hospital visits, and funeral attendance.

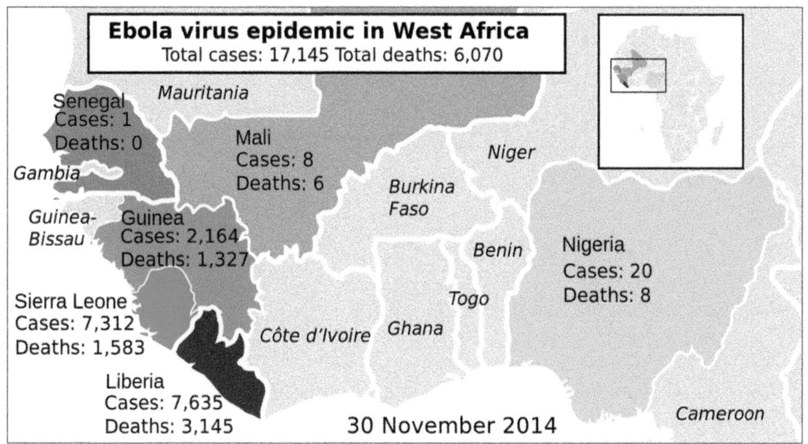

Figure 4.3 Ebola cases and deaths as of November 2014

The infodemiology method was used to identify investigative reports and news stories dealing with the outbreak that appeared on authoritative media outlets worldwide. Of particular interest was the researchers' ability to identify a cluster of cases in Nigeria, based on a single disease importation from Liberia.

Infodemiology does raise issues and concerns. Google's system of 'Google Flu Trends' failed to predict the first wave of the influenza A (H1N1) pandemic, and made other errors in estimating the timing and magnitude of US flu seasons.[75] The system's problems were attributed to 'big data hubris' and 'algorithm dynamics'. A second study comparing epidemic modelling to weather forecasting argued that reliance upon human data sources and interactions made the former intrinsically less reliable.[76] Two studies noted the presence of digital divides (discussed in Chapter 1), with different sectors of society having unequal access to technology. This disparity distorts the accuracy of inferences about epidemic magnitudes and geographies based on data from internet communications sources, such as mobile phone data.[77] A study of Facebook posts about the Zika virus during one week in the summer of 2016 found that only 81 per cent of the posts had useful information or credible news updates,[78] and 12 per cent were classified as misleading by experts. The most popular misleading entry was viewed ten times more than the most useful post.

Big data on the internet is a useful tool for disease surveillance and modelling, even though there is lots of room for improvement. It is not a replacement for traditional health surveillance reports from medical institutions, but rather a complementary one that will be improved when data can also be reported by new technologies such as smart thermometers and other innovations.[79]

Research: Discuss how social media played a role in discussions of and decisions about the Zika virus and participation or non-participation of athletes in the 2016 Summer Olympics.

Concept: Improve the Wikipedia article 'infodemiology'.

Policy: Infodemiologic reports seem to point to a serious health hazard in a distant country. Your athletes are scheduled to compete there in the Olympics. National pride rests on their performance, but fear of infectious disease has many athletes concerned and unwilling to attend the event. Draft a policy brief for the leader of your country to convince and reassure athletes to participate in the Olympics, or to recommend that they do not participate. HINT: Research the 2016 Summer Olympics in Brazil.

4.6 Medical simulators

We now turn our attention to another way in which information technology has changed medicine, in this case the practice of medical education. Prospective doctors and nurses need to learn enormous quantities of facts, and, even more importantly, they must learn how to execute critical processes. In some cases, such as taking a patient's blood pressure, learning is straightforward and the procedures are relatively low-risk. In other cases, such as inserting a stent or removing a tumour, learning is much more difficult, and life often hangs in the balance.

Medical simulators allow medical personnel to practise and hone their skills on inanimate objects, rather than risking making mistakes on people. More specifically, one formulation of ideal requirements for a patient simulator recommends that:[80]

> the physician needs to interact with the anatomy in a clinically realistic manner. Tissues must move as they would in a body, and tools must interact with the tissues, not simply move above them. The physiological responses of the body to interventions such as cutting, suturing, probing, and dilating must be realistic. This interaction must occur...also with appropriate haptic representations. The color of tissues must be realistic...surface texture maps must accurately reflect the simulated organ. Elastic properties of the various organs and tissues must vary from one structure to another.

Medical simulation has evolved from patient actors (known as *standardized patients*) to special-purpose 'task trainers' to more lifelike software-driven *patient simulators* variously incorporating electromechanical mannequins and virtual reality.

Training medical students with patient simulators

A good example is a pre-programmed life-size simulator that mimics cardiac, respiratory physiologic, and pharmacologic responses including allergic reactions.[81] The simulator is used to train and evaluate medical students and residents on their ability to handle potentially life-threatening acute care conditions. A study showed that simulators can reliably, consistently, and validly gauge truthful estimates of medical expertise. Another typical application is the use of a simulator for physician training in carotid artery stenting.[82]

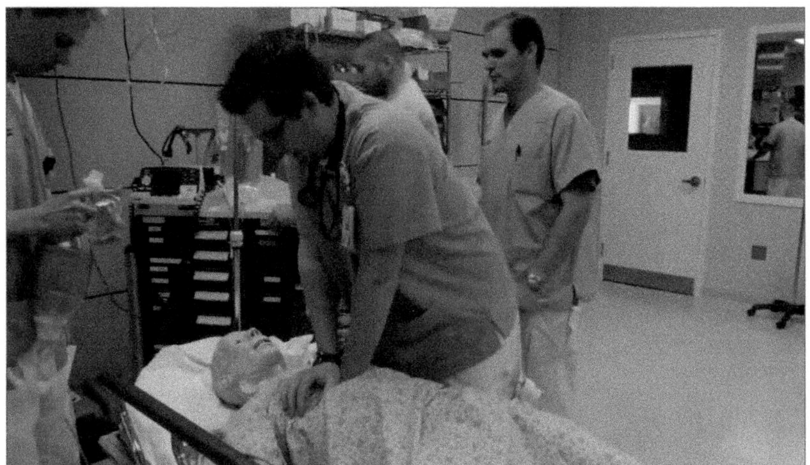

Figure 4.4 Medical simulator in an operating room at Loma Linda University[83]

Simulators are also useful for training physicians and nurses to work better in teams. a study compared anaesthesiologists' communication patterns under three conditions: routine procedures in an operating room, routine procedures in a simulated environment, and crisis conditions in a simulated environment.[84] They found no significant differences between the real and simulated environments for routine cases, but an increased sharing of information in the crisis case. Thus, teamwork can be learned through practice in simulated situations.

Human body simulators of a different design are now starting to be used for a different purpose—practising dangerous manoeuvres in sports.[85] Extensive testing of the first self-righting robotic mobile training devices has recently been applied by high school, universi, and professional players practising the 'art' of tackling in American football, with the goal of reducing player concussions.

Research: The current limits to human body simulators for use in medical education.

Research: Uses of digital technology in professional sports.

4.7 Artificial body parts and bionic people

Medical simulators are machines being used as stand-ins for people. Robots are machines that have been programmed or have learned to carry out human tasks. There are also cases in which people are incorporating machines as part of their own body for medical reasons. This starts with the use of artificial body parts;[86] in the limit, we can imagine bionic people.

Recall the discussion of disabilities in Chapter 1 on *digital inclusion*. As society ages, more and more people have sensory processes such as vision, motor processes such as movement, and cognitive processes such as memory that are challenged. Rehabilitation engineers develop *prostheses* to replace human body parts that are no longer functioning adequately or have ceased to operate. These prostheses now incorporate digital processors so they can behave 'intelligently'. Recently, 3D printing technology has made it easier to design and manufacture prostheses.[87]

The earliest known body part prostheses were artificial toes in ancient Egypt, followed closely by synthetic legs in ancient Rome.[88] Artificial extremities evolved in the nineteenth and twentieth centuries, incorporating mechanical and then also electrical components.[89] Eventually, rehabilitation engineers discovered that myoelectric control could allow people to learn how to control and manoeuvre artificial limbs.[90] For this, one or more sensors are embedded into a fabricated socket to which the prosthetic body part is attached. These sensors transmit electrical signals to the brain and learn how to send signals to activate and control motors to move and manipulate the artificial body part. Recent progress in *brain–computer interfaces* (BCI) has yielded an artificial hand with multiple sensors that allow the owner to feel a variety of meaningful touch sensations when the hand touches and grasps objects.[91] Advances in robotics, telecommunications, and haptics also allow the development and application of robotic surgeons and surgical systems.

Other artificial body parts are implants to improve organs that are not behaving properly. One of the earliest and best-known examples is the *pacemaker*.[92] Pacemakers are small devices implanted in the body and electrically connected to the heart. A pacemaker's tiny computer senses electrical activity at the heart and sends back electrical signals to correct abnormal heart rhythms. Another example is the *cochlear implant* to improve hearing, varieties of which have been surgically inserted since the early 60s.[93] A more recent development is the *artificial retina*, which will improve over time with increasing numbers of pixels and processing power.[94]

Finally, there are artificial organs. A good example is the *artificial heart*.[95] Unlike the pacemaker, this machine is designed not to help one's heart work better, but to replace it in cases of total heart failure or when one is waiting for a heart transplant. There have been other advances in designing artificial organs such as the artificial pancreas.[96] However, inventors still face challenges including the body's immune system trying to reject foreign, artificial bodies.

The Incredible Bionic Man

In the limit, we will be able to create *bionic humans*. Progress towards this goal was portrayed in a remarkable video—'The Incredible Bionic Man'.[97] It exhibits a mobile android equipped with a 3D camera, an artificial heart, lung, kidney, pancreas, and spleen, and circulating synthetic blood. It includes the reaction of horror by a man who himself has prostheses as parts of his body; he is not anti-prosthesis, but groks upon seeing his own scanned face mounted as the 'head' of the android.

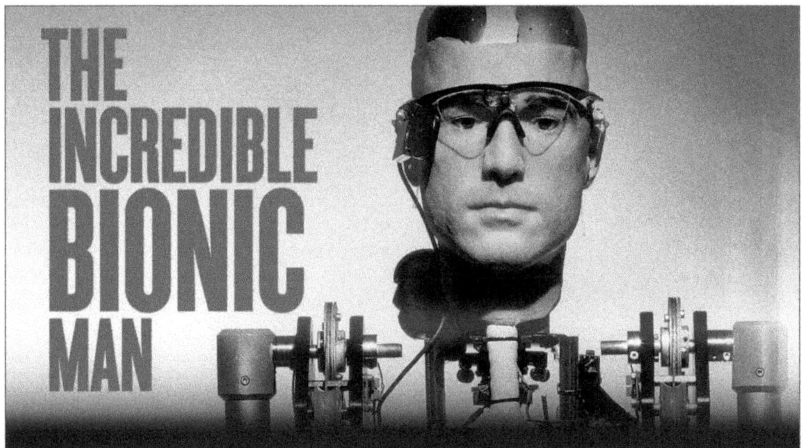

Figure 4.5 Screenshot from the video *The Incredible Bionic Man*
A Darlow Smithson production for Simthsonian Networks and Channel 4.

Digital technologies play an essential role in such advancements, especially for vision, mobility, and navigation.

The artificial brain does not (yet) exist, although there is early and promising work on a 'pacemaker' for the brain that can experimentally enhance memory in some epilepsy patients.[98] There is also now significant work on brain–computer interfaces to tackle sensory disabilities, focusing especially on vision and hearing.[99]

BCI raises many ethical issues.[100] Some apply to biomedical advances still in the research phase, such the possible conflict between treatment and research goals, and the managing of patient expectations. Other issues, such as informed consent, arise when patients have diminished cognitive function or are unable to communicate, and where the intervention is a measure of last resort.

Much of the promise of prosthetics and bionics rests on what is possible with AI. We shall return to AI accomplishments, challenges, and issues several times, especially in

Chapter 11. At the end of this chapter, we shall discuss issues of equity, cost, and the allocation of resources which also apply to other costly developments. One such costly procedure is precision medicine.

Research: Research cases of digital unreliability in electronic human body part prostheses, either due to designer error or due to malicious tampering such as hacking.

Debate: Resolved: There must be a limit on the augmentation and replacement of body parts.

4.8 Precision medicine

Ever since the discovery of the double helix structure of DNA in 1953, progress in genetics and molecular biology has promised to aid the practice of medicine and improve health care. The most recent such development is *precision* (or *personalized*) medicine:[101]

> The word personalized conveys the sense that...genomic data may facilitate rational treatment choices that are tailored to individual patients. The term precision refers to prospects for enhanced molecular resolution, mechanistic clarity, and therapeutic cogency that may accompany clinical implementation of genomics technologies.

Diagnosing diabetic retinopathy

A good example occurs in the treatment of diabetic retinopathy, a condition that affects the eyes of some people with diabetes and that may cause severe vision loss and even blindness.[102] A neural net was trained on 128,000 examples of human expert classifications of the severity of damage to retinal blood vessels. Once trained, the resulting deep learning algorithm was found to exhibit 97% sensitivity and 93% specificity in doing the classifications on a new set of cases.

This means that the net recognized cases of severe damage in 97% of the cases that had been so classified by expert ophthalmologists, with incorrect classifications of that damage as severe in 7% of the cases ('false positives'). The 'ground truth' of correctness was the expert majority decision among the most self-consistent fifty-four US licensed ophthalmologists and ophthalmology senior residents. The decisions of the algorithm were 'on par' with the remainder of the human evaluators. The researchers concluded that potential benefits were 'increasing efficiency, reproducibility, and coverage of screening programs; reducing barriers to access; and improving patient outcomes by providing early detection and treatment'.

A second promising area for precision medicine is Autism Spectrum Disorder (ASD). Several dozen ASD susceptibility genes that play a role in 10 to 20 per cent of the cases have been discovered.[103] There are likely hundreds of ASD risk genes.[104] We have only begun to understand the genetic and environmental correlates with ASD; large-scale testing threatens to overwhelm us with a flood of data, and we are far from being able to use genetics to predict the likely development of an ASD in fetuses or children.[105] Yet the possibility of advances leading to better counselling of parents who already have a child with an ASD is an important reason to continue the work.[106]

Because cancer is a genetic disease caused by damage to one's genome, there are huge opportunities (but, to date, far more failures than successes) in applying precision medicine to cancer.[101] In 2017, the US Food and Drug Administration (FDA) approved two gene-altering drugs, each targeting a specific kind of cancer, costing around $400,000 per year.[107] Researchers have suggested a partnership between cancer clinical practice and research, in which the latest discoveries inform a patient's treatment, and in which treatment details, what was done in each patient encounter and how well it worked, goes into a global database to help advance cancer genomics knowledge.[108]

Scrubbing pigs clean of viruses to reduce risks when transplanting organs into humans and discovering genes strongly linked to Alzheimer's disease are also promising applications for genetic medicine.[109]

Four serious social, ethical, and policy issues are raised by precision medicine: genetic discrimination, allocation of health resources, 'designer babies', and errors and risks.

Genetic discrimination refers to using people's private genetic information for purposes such as denying them jobs or raising their insurance rates, thereby treating them 'unfairly'. There is to date relatively little evidence of genetic discrimination, yet fear of it is widespread, which influences health and life choices.[110] An international review of relevant literature concluded that roughly one-sixth to one-third of individuals with certain diseases felt that they had suffered genetic discrimination.[111] In 2008, the USA passed a Genetic Information Nondiscrimination Act.[112] Almost half of a cohort of thirty-seven nations, either European or previously in the British Empire, have also passed such legislation, including Canada in March 2017. On the other hand, a leading Canadian health journalist recently suggested that current laws are misplaced, causing undue fear of genetic testing.[113] He argued that using genetic information to ascertain insurance risk is reasonable, and that other legal measures could guarantee individuals access to health and life insurance.

A second important issue is the appropriate use of health care dollars and physician time. It is now possible to learn about one's genetic 'susceptibility' to getting a variety of common or complex diseases, including obesity, diabetes, cancer, and Alzheimer's disease. Starting in April 2017, the FDA allowed companies to sell genetic test results for disease risk directly to consumers.[114] The initial price for a report on genetic markers for ten diseases was US$199. Even more interesting is the rush to develop gene therapies;[115] ethical issues have been raised about the appropriate use of discarded bio-specimens for such work.[116]

The demand for genetic screening information is increasing rapidly, yet the benefits and costs are not clear.[117] Allocating this scarce resource could be done in different ways—on the basis of need, so as to maximize 'total benefits' to society, in order to treat people with equity, or to reward one's utility to society.[118] Illustrating the issue of cost is the case of genetic testing to identify patients who are eligible for the lumacaftor–ivacaftor treatment for cystic fibrosis. This currently costs US$300,000 per year, although some medical scientists have suggested that it does no better than conventional therapies that cost US$300 per year.[119] Disappointingly, a meta-analysis of medical literature showed no significant effects of communicating genetic risks of disease on risk-reducing health behaviour, such as smoking cessation, healthier diet, and increased physical activity.[120]

Ethics

Designer babies: Another use of precision medicine that raises serious ethical issues sometimes goes under the somewhat sensationalist phrase of 'designer babies'. There are three levels to this idea:

Level one: Prospective parents can obtain advice about risks to future children based on their genetic characteristics.

Level two: Expecting parents can learn about the genes of embryos, and abort those not meeting their expectations.

Level three: The DNA of fertilized eggs can be modified to seek or to obtain certain characteristics. Desired characteristics could be safety from disease, or desired physical or personality traits.

Opponents of designer babies can take solace in the realization that such visions are still only dreams.[121] For example, even with the trait for height, scientists have thus far only identified 697 of the estimated 93,000 genetic variations.

There is huge controversy over levels two and three.[122] Proponents argue in favour of avoiding disease or disability, improving the human race, and extending the life span. Opponents are concerned about inequities, treating children as products, and the possibilities of error or disaster. Rabbi and law professor Michael J. Broyde has presented a generally favourable view of such techniques from the point of view of Jewish law.[123] There will likely be continued debate, with different religions taking their own positions on the ethics of designer babies. Harvard ethics professor Michael J. Sandel linked these new developments to the old idea of eugenics with a negative critique:[124]

> Breakthroughs in genetics . . . promise . . . that we may soon be able to treat and prevent a host of debilitating diseases [and a] predicament . . . that our newfound genetic knowledge may also enable us to manipulate our own nature—to enhance our muscles, memories, and moods; to choose the sex, height, and other genetic traits of our children; to make ourselves 'better than well' . . . . [one may] view genetic engineering as the ultimate expression of our resolve to see ourselves astride the world, the masters of our nature. But that promise of mastery is flawed. It threatens to banish our appreciation of life as a gift, and to leave us with nothing to affirm or behold outside our own will.

Clearly, these developments test our individual and collective sense of what is ethical, and are worthy of continued research, thought, and debate. What is your opinion of level two and level three interventions? Justify your thoughts.

Finally, there is concern over the risks of genetic manipulation, despite the support recently expressed for gene editing work by the influential US National Academy of Sciencevs and National Academy of Medicine advisory group.[125] There have been diagnostic errors in genetic analysis, difficulties in ensuring that algorithms select medically desirable genes without too many false positives, and a track record mostly of failure in using precision medicine to help cancer patients.[126] One exciting and chilling example is the proposal to combat the spread of Lyme disease by breeding and releasing a genetically modified strain of white-footed mice in Nantucket Island and possibly other locales.[127] What are the dangers of such experimentation with nature?

Debate: Resolved: Public health insurance(s) should cover the costs of an individual receiving one genetic screening assessment in a lifetime.

Debate: Resolved: Gene editing is too dangerous for humanity and should be outlawed.

4.9 Neuroplasticity and brain training

Another important role for computers in health care stems from the concept of *neuroplasticity*. For over a century, we viewed the brain as an organ that could be expanded primarily when one was young, hence the importance to children of mental stimulation and education. It was also thought that the brain could not significantly recover from serious damage. Recent scientific, engineering, and medical advances have shown that brains are capable of far greater healing and self-repair than was previously thought possible. Physician and author Norman Doidge has written about notable cases of individuals with conditions such as strokes, multiple sclerosis (MS), Parkinson's disease, and traumatic brain injury (TBI), demonstrating human resilience and the potential for self-improvement and recovery.[128]

The other major relevant concept is *cognitive reserve*. Developed primarily through the work of Dr Yaakov Stern, cognitive reserve describes the capacity of some individuals to function better cognitively than do others despite significant neurological damage, such as that caused by neuronal plaques and tangles and typically expressed by Alzheimer's disease. Stern wrote:[129]

> The concept of cognitive reserve provides a ready explanation for why many studies have demonstrated that higher levels of intelligence, and of educational and occupational attainment are good predictors of which individuals can sustain greater brain damage before demonstrating functional deficit.

The brain training industry

As implied by Stern, people with higher cognitive reserve are better equipped to withstand 'assaults' on their brain, just as physically fit individuals can handle themselves better when speed or endurance or strength is required. There is a huge literature on the effects of cognitive reserve built over a lifetime of good lifestyle choices, for example higher education, a stimulating job, social contacts, a healthy diet, and exercise. Given that we can exercise and train to become physically fit, it seems logical that we can also train our brains and build up their cognitive reserve. Because of neuroplasticity, we can hope to do this relatively late in life. These ideas have motivated vigorous research and commercialization of brain training

Continued on next page

exercises and games, with a market of US$1 billion in 2012.[130] But there have been misleading claims and false expectations.

Brain-training games capitalize on the ease with which we game by offering a wealth of puzzles and problems that can be played for hours or merely minutes at a time. Learn more about the top brain-training games that can sharpen the mind and potentially prevent cognitive diseases like Alzheimer's.

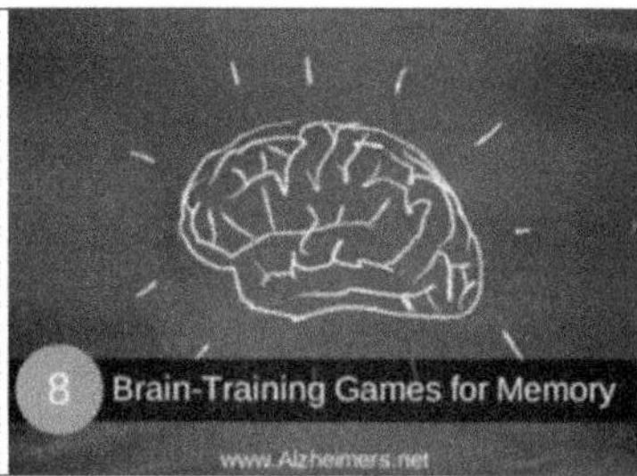

8 Brain-Training Games for Memory
www.Alzheimers.net

Figure 4.6 Screen shot from an article on a website dedicated to Alzheimers education with a misleading suggestion about brain-training games[131]

This implication in the ad shown in the figure is irresponsible; there is no evidence that brain-training games can prevent Alzheimer's disease.

Yet there have been positive results, especially from the IMPACT and ACTIVE research projects.

IMPACT compared a commercially available brain fitness exercise programme focused on improving the speed and accuracy of auditory information processing with an active control.[132] The study was carried out on 487 community-dwelling adults without clinically significant cognitive impairment diagnoses. Cognitive training or control activities were carried out for one hour per day, five days a week, for eight weeks. Gains in measures of memory and attention were significantly greater in the experimental group than in the control group. Improvements were noted both in tasks that involved and did not involve auditory information processing.

ACTIVE is the longest and largest controlled experimental evaluation of a brain fitness regimen.[133] Two thousand eight hundred volunteers (with an average age of 73.6 years at the start of the study) participated for ten years. They were divided into three intervention groups (focused on memory, reasoning, and speed of processing) as well as a no-contact control group. The interventions consisted of ten to twelve hours of training spread over five to six weeks, along with a small amount of booster training in subsequent years. Very impressively, significant impact was demonstrated ten years later:

> Each ACTIVE cognitive intervention resulted in less decline in self-reported IADL [Instrumental Activities of Daily Living] compared with the control group. Reasoning and speed, but not memory, training resulted in improved targeted cognitive abilities for 10 years.

Even more encouraging is a recent conference talk asserting that participants in the speed of processing cohort were 33 per cent less likely than those in the control group to develop dementia over ten years.[134]

It is of course possible that while doing the brain training exercises there was some other change in lifestyle that resulted in protection against neurodegenerative disease. Cautions have been raised about the impact and generalizability of brain training claims and results. Concerned about all the commercial hype centring on brain training exercises, in 2014, seventy-five psychologists and neurologists published an open letter via the Stanford Center on Longevity that concluded:[135]

> We object to the claim that brain games offer consumers a scientifically grounded avenue to reduce or reverse cognitive decline when there is no compelling scientific evidence to date that they do. The promise of a magic bullet detracts from the best evidence to date, which is that cognitive health in old age reflects the long-term effects of healthy, engaged lifestyles.... exaggerated and misleading claims exploit the anxieties of older adults about impending cognitive decline. We encourage continued careful research and validation in this field.

This statement drew a response from hundreds of scientists. Henry Mahncke, CEO of Posit Science, an old and well-respected brain training company, wrote in response:[136]

> There are now more than 70 peer-reviewed papers about the benefits of the BrainHQ exercises from Posit Science. More than 50 of those papers focus specifically on the benefits of our cognitive exercises in aging (see http://www.brainhq.com/agingstudies).... Multiple scientific reviews and meta-analyses have confirmed these positive results.

Some researchers have attempted to shed more light on the controversy by doing meta-analyses of the literature. A review of fifty-two studies chosen from 6,300 papers concluded:[137]

> CCT [Computerized Cognitive Training] is modestly effective at improving cognitive performance in healthy older adults, but efficacy varies across cognitive domains and is largely determined by design choices. Unsupervised at-home training and training more than three times per week are specifically ineffective.

Another thorough review of the claims of the brain fitness companies concluded:[138]

> we find extensive evidence that brain-training interventions improve performance on the trained tasks, less evidence that such interventions improve performance on closely related tasks, and little evidence that training enhances performance on distantly related tasks or that training improves everyday cognitive performance.

An earlier meta-review stressed the importance of using neuroimaging to enhance our understanding of improving adults' cognitive performance, but little has been done so far.[139]

Perhaps the most important fact to realize is the importance of aerobic exercise in improving brain fitness.[140] Expanding on the prescription in the Stanford open letter, staying healthy as one ages requires a broad spectrum of good choices with respect to one's physical, cognitive, social, emotional, and nutritional life. IT has a role to play here, but it is a relatively minor role.

Research: Study and understand the concept of *transfer of training*. Research and discuss the concept and its manifestation in the use of brain training exercises.

Debate: Resolved: Brain training exercises are marketed irresponsibly.

Book report: Doidge, Norman (2007). *The Brain That Changes Itself: Stories of Personal Triumph from the Frontiers of Brain Science*. Viking Penguin.

Book report: Doidge, Norman (2016). *The Brain's Way of Healing: Remarkable Discoveries and Recoveries from the Frontiers of Neuroplasticity*. Penguin Books.

4.10 Robot companions and caregivers for seniors

Many societies are challenged by caring for seniors. The number of seniors across the globe is multiplying rapidly. The world's population of adults aged 60 years and over is projected to grow from 901 million in 2015 to 1.4 billion in 2030 and 2.1 billion in 2050.[141] The number of 'oldest old', or those aged 80 years and older, is projected to grow from 125 million in 2015 to 434 million in 2050. The demographic trend of declining birth rates also reduces the *caregiver support ratio,* making it difficult to find adequate care for older adults. For example, in the USA, the number of potential family caregivers aged 45 to 64 divided by the number of oldest old in the country is projected to decline from more than seven in 2010 to less than three by 2050.[142] Given the problems in finding and training paid caregivers—many are 'imported' from other countries such as the Philippines—there will be fewer and fewer people to care for the growing numbers of seniors. A significant number of US caregivers are also illegal immigrants; President Trump's policies on immigration will make the availability of care for seniors in the USA even worse.[143]

The problem is even more dire in other countries; for example, Japan's population aged 65 and over is projected to grow from a current level of 25 per cent to 40 per cent by 2055. It is estimated that the country will need to add one million care workers and nurses just by 2025 in order to take care of its elderly.[144]

Non-anthropomorphic robot companions[145]

Many countries are turning to robots for possible solutions. A good example of a robot companion is *Paro, the Robot Seal*. Interaction with animals is beneficial for seniors, yet

Figure 4.7 A senior cuddling Paro, the robot seal
Horizons WWP / TRVL / Alamy Stock Photo

many care facilities do not accept animals. Paro is a cute and cuddly animal-like interactive 'intelligent' robotic seal intended to be a companion to seniors. It was designed as a seal, rather than, for example, a cat, because few people know how a seal behaves. Hence most people would not notice 'imperfections' in Paro's reactions.

One study found that a month's worth of interaction with Paro increased seniors' social interaction, primarily via group interaction and discussion of the robot seal, and also improved their ability to handle stress.[146] A more recent study compared an hour's worth of interaction with Paro to treatment usually delivered to seniors with severe dementia.[147] The experimental group (those who had Paro) showed better stability in quality of life and required significantly less medication compared with a decline in the control group. Reviews of studies with Paro and some other early socially assistive robots reported generally positive (socio)psychological and physiological effects, especially in terms of mood and engagement.[148] But the reviews stressed that most studies done to date were methodologically weak, involving small numbers for short periods of time, and did not have control groups or randomization.

Another interesting non-anthropomorphic robot companion, soon to be available, is Elli-Q, from Intuition Robotics.

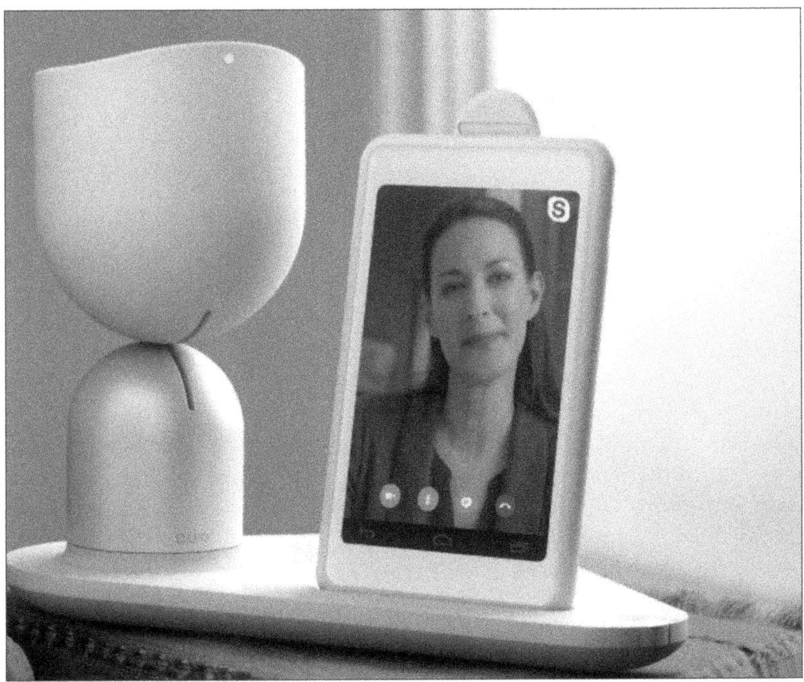

Figure 4.8 Elli-Q, a robot companion for seniors[149]

Elli-Q features an object that listens, speaks, and gives head-like gestures and evocative lights with the top part of an elegant creature-like object, and a tablet for providing information and enabling audio-visual communication.

These technologies describe robot companions, not *robot caregivers*. They are notably *not* anthropomorphic; they do not pretend to be people. Robot caregivers for seniors are only in early stages of laboratory development. Yet ethicists are already thinking about the issues that may be raised. Concerns have been expressed over possible reduction in human contact, increase in objectification, loss of control, loss of liberty, loss of privacy, deception, infantilization, informed consent, safety, and beneficence, that is, ensuring that the robot is in the best interests of the user.[150] Since progress in AI seems unstoppable, there will be growing ethical issues in robot care for seniors, but non-anthropomorphic companions are sensible and safe, and are practical, although currently still too expensive for widespread use.

Concept: Improve the Wikipedia article 'artificial human companion'.

Debate: Resolved: Robots for seniors should be designed to look like people.

Law: Draft a law guaranteeing seniors certain rights when they accept robot caregivers.

Ethics: Your evil stepfather left your elderly mother, and she is starting to show signs of dementia. He offers to pay for a prototype robot caregiver that is the darling of the high-tech biomedical community. What do you do?

Technology review: Research commercially available robot companions and robot caregivers.

4.11 Summary

Many of the opportunities for computer use in medicine and health care were foreseen by early pioneers in the 1960s. Dr Larry Weed's articulation of the EMR via the POMR system was a profound invention, as it emphasized the importance of medical data being organized by the process involved in the diagnosis and care of disease.

Since then, work on medical and health applications of computing has encompassed two key philosophies. For the most part, researchers and developers have sought to enhance the capabilities of health care personnel as well as citizens themselves in order to ensure better medical care and health. A second goal has been to reduce the frequency and severity of errors in the delivery of medical care. We have discussed advances that embody both philosophies.

One computer use that affects most people directly is in providing health information. This happens in two ways: firstly, laymen search to learn more about conditions that concern them from sites they assume to be correct, while others join health information sharing websites—'communities of care'—to learn about the relevant experiences of others, and to share their own stories. In both cases, the results are mostly helpful, yet challenges still remain in guiding information seekers to authoritative sources, improving the comprehensibility and navigability of websites, flagging misleading stories and 'fake health news' (we shall return to this topic in Chapter 5), and establishing substantiated trust in health virtual communities.

Progress in the development of EMRs has been steady but disappointingly slow. The majority of doctor's offices in North America now have some sort of EMR. Due to their greater size and complexity, this is not the case with most hospitals. EMR systems still lack interoperability, resulting in data silos without full data exchange throughout the health care system. Security breaches still pose threats to the privacy of sensitive health information, but medical institutions continue to adopt EMRs to become more efficient and to practise better evidence-based medicine.[151]

A relatively recent variant of the EMR is the personal health record, intended to be a database that integrates all the information about an individual's encounters with various providers of health advice and care. The PHR should be a tool that enables an individual to better understand and promote their own health; wide realization of this has also been delayed because of lack of interoperability, incompleteness of data, and challenging user interfaces.

As EMRs and PHRs become more prevalent, they raise an interesting issue. Who owns your medical and health data? The paradox is that personal medical data is growing to terabytes, underused due to the balkanization of EMRs and PHRs, subject to constant privacy invasions via hacking, and often unavailable to an individual because it is 'owned' by a doctor or a hospital. Yet owning one's health data is a civil right![152]

It has long been anticipated that better data organization could help prevent adverse drug events—bad reactions to medications as well as undesirable drug–drug interactions. Unavailability of health data is often the cause of ADEs. An Institute of Medicine (US) report estimated that between 44,000 and 98,000 people die in the USA each year due to medical errors, and developed recommendations for improvement.[153] The situation was recently revisited by the US National Patient Safety Forum, which wrote, rather disappointingly:[154]

> it has become increasingly clear that safety issues are far more complex—and pervasive—than initially appreciated. Patient safety comprises more than just mortality; it also encompasses morbidity and more subtle forms of harm, such as loss of dignity and respect.... Although our understanding of the problem of patient harm has deepened and matured, this progress has been accompanied by a lessening intensity of focus on the issue.

Concerns have also been expressed in other countries.[155]

Big data is making a big difference in infectious disease surveillance and modelling. The key idea is simple: capture and process digital information, for example mobile phone calls and web searches, to gather evidence about health concerns and also the spread of infections and epidemics worldwide. This method is much faster than traditional epidemiological data-gathering methods such as public surveys or reports of physician visits. Yet there must be safeguards for the confidentiality of data, including protecting the privacy and identity of specific individuals.

Better data, or more specifically better medical knowledge, can also benefit medical education. A primary method is through the design and use of patient simulators. Often realized as a smart mannequin, or through an interactive graphical simulation, these simulators enable individuals training to be physicians or nurses to practise on dummies rather than on people. They are also useful in illustrating and teaching good practices in group work.

Another aspect of modern digital technology is the ability to animate and impart intelligence to electronic prostheses and artificial body parts. This can happen in three ways: firstly, prostheses can substitute for external parts of our bodies such as missing limbs. Devices at the second level attach to organs, and enable them to function better, as in the case of pacemakers or hearing aids. The third level is the most advanced and is comprised of artificial organs such as hearts or kidneys. Increasingly, these devices contain sensors, effectors, and processors that allow them to be more capable and flexible then was heretofore possible. In the limit, if almost all of our body parts are replaced—and this may be possible within several decades—we can become androids. Who are we then? Are we still human? What are our rights and responsibilities?

Precision (or personalized) medicine refers to the use of an individual's genomic data to inform and guide treatment choices optimized for that person. We are at the beginning of a series of exciting developments in this field. Yet ethical issues arise: genetic discrimination, for example, with regard to health and life insurance; allocation of scarce health resources to what is likely to be for some time an expensive process; the creation of 'designer babies', including ways to control who is born in ways that many find morally suspect or unacceptable; and errors and risks that result from making such profound changes to human nature. Medical ethicists are at the forefront of discussions about these topics, but computer science must be intimately involved as well.

Neuroplasticity is the capability of the brain to heal itself after damage. Cognitive reserve is the capacity of the brain to retain cognitive capability after damage. Of particular interest is the cognitive reserve in seniors. Brain training exercises have been developed to stimulate the brain and build up cognitive reserve. Yet there is huge controversy here. Proponents claim positive effects. Opponents stress the fact that there is little transfer of training from skills on which one was trained to more general capabilities. They also decry false advertising by firms implying that their services are a cure-all for neurodegenerative diseases. Any senior enjoying brain training exercises, many of which are game-like, should do them in moderation, but more important is maintaining a healthy lifestyle that includes exercise, social contact, and a healthy diet. Here computers play a minor role; healthy and conscious living provides better preventative measures.

A final health care application of computers is with robot companions and caregivers for seniors. This area is expanding rapidly because of the growing numbers of older adults worldwide and the decreasing availability of sufficient caregivers, both of family and hired help. There are already significant examples of animal-like robot companions, such as Paro, the robot seal, which seem to be well received, although studies have not been extended long enough ascertain whether or not we are seeing a Hawthorne effect. Robot caregivers are still a good distance away, and are dependent for success on being able to automate sensitivity and compassion (we shall return to these issues in Chapter 11), but ethicists are already expressing concern about issues such as seniors' well-being, informed consent, infantilization, as well as loss of human contact and personal safety.

We desire to treat all patients well and equitably and to make wise use of scarce resources, despite the expensive applications discussed in this chapter. What inventions should be prioritized by health care professionals? We already spend more on health care than we can afford. Health care spending has recently grown faster than economic growth in all Organisation for Economic Co-operation and Development (OECD) countries.[156] In Canada, health care is now the largest budget item in every province, reaching 43.2 per cent in Ontario.[157] This increase in spending will skyrocket as the baby boomer population ages, human life spans increase, and birth rates decline further.

Another issue is that of errors: even the best physicians make mistakes. Appropriate and timely data can help prevent many medical errors, yet new technologies may be imperfect or create instances where experts cannot anticipate all the outcomes and therefore overlook certain dangers.

We have not even covered all the possibilities. Some of these opportunities are straightforward, such as encouraging physicians to make greater use of email,[158] and the increasing use of telemedicine, now a mature field after thirty years.[159] Other innovations have until now seemed like science fiction, such as robotic surgeons,[160] which are routinely operating on people today, and AI diagnostic programs, just now start starting to become reality, as we have seen in the section on precision medicine.[161] We shall return to the latter topic in Chapter 11.

How do we decide if and when to develop and widely deploy new biomedical technologies?

Research: Telemedicine. Discuss technical, social, policy, and ethical challenges and choices.

Research: Robot-assisted surgery. Discuss technical, social, policy, and ethical challenges and choices.

Research: The legal and moral issues raised by the issue of the ownership of an individual's health data.

Debate: Resolved: If my heart and brain are replaced by an artificial heart and brain, I am still me.

4.12 Key terms

ACTIVE
Adverse drug events (ADEs),
Adverse drug reactions (ADRs)
Androids/bionic humans
Artificial organs
Big data
Brain–computer interface (BCI)
Brain training exercises
caregiver support ratio
Cognitive reserve
Communities of care
Crowdsourcing
Designer babies
Digital pill
Dr Lawrence Weed
Dr Yaakov Stern
Electronic medical record (EMR)
Genetic discrimination
Google Flu Trends
IMPACT
Infodemiology
Interoperability
MUMPS programming language
Neuroplasticity

Personal health record (PHR)
PROPHET
Paro
Patient simulators
PatientsLikeMe
Precision or personalized medicine
Problem-Oriented Medical Record (POMR)
Prostheses
Robot caregivers
Robot companions
Socio-technical systems
Standardized patients
Transfer of training

5

Free speech, politics, and government

Politics and *government* are undergoing dramatic changes through the advent of new technology. The early developers of community networks (mentioned in Section 1.2) had hopeful visions of information technology (IT)-facilitating participatory democracy. Yet the most memorable visions have been literary dystopias, where surveillance is omnipresent and governments have absolute control. We shall begin by highlighting some of these important writings.

We shall then consider a current and present topic—the cultural and legal frameworks governing free speech and other forms of expression on the internet. We review several kinds of 'undesirable' speech that test our commitment to free speech—messages that are viewed as obscene, hateful, seditious, or encouraging of terrorism. Next, we examine methods governments worldwide use to censor web content and prevent digital transmission of messages of which they disapprove, as well as a similar role for social media firms in what is now known as *content moderation*.

We shall also mention one new form of rampant and very harmful internet speech—*fake news*. Fake news becomes especially troubling when it is released into and retransmitted widely into *filter bubbles* that select these messages and *echo chambers* that focus and sensationalize such points of view to the exclusion of other contradictory ideas. The prevalence and dangers of fake news became obvious during post facto analyses of the 2016 US presidential campaign.

The internet and social media enable greater civic participation, which is usually called *e-democracy* or *civic tech*. Most such uses of social media are relatively benign, as in online deliberations about the desired size of a bond issue, or internet lobbying to get libraries to stay open longer during the summer. However, for more significant issues, such as violations of fundamental human rights, or unpopular political decisions that incite public unrest, social media communications may facilitate political protest that can lead to political change.

IT also plays a role in elections—social media can be used to mobilize the electorate and build enthusiasm for a candidate. Correspondingly, surveys and big data are used to target potential voters during political campaigns and to tailor specific messages to key voters. During election time, *electronic voting machines* are increasingly being used to enable a decision, yet there are security issues and controversies surrounding their use, a topic we shall cover in Chapter 7.

E-government is the use of technology, especially social media, to enable a more efficient and ideally more consultative process of governing. We shall discuss examples and principles of success for e-government, as well as US President Donald Trump's incessant, self-serving, and vitriolic use of *Twitter*, what some have called 'tweetocracy'.

Digital technologies have transformed politics and government. What is the status of free speech in the age of social media? What issues concern thoughtful computer scientists and engaged citizens? Can we block harmful comments but still preserve free speech? How do we ensure that the fake news problem does not become even worse?

5.1 Visions, utopias, and dystopias

The pioneering visions of prominent computer scientists presented in previous chapters helped set research agendas for applying IT towards digital inclusion, education and learning, and medicine and health. Computer scientists have been more muted in imagining positive roles for IT in enabling free speech, improving the political process, and enabling more effective and humane government. One exception is the desire to create global interconnectedness via computer networks, as in the influential Berkeley Community Memory Project in the 1960s:

> the operational politics of the system are deeply democratic . . . no central authority, person or agency mediates people's communication and transaction with each other. The system functions simply to facilitate people's direct contact and contract with each other, nourishing an ultimate participatory democracy.[1]

Utopian fiction 'portrays a setting that agrees with the author's ethos, having various attributes of another reality intended to appeal to readers . . . *dystopian fiction* . . . [is] . . . the portrayal of a setting that completely disagrees with the author's ethos.'[2] Good examples of utopian visions of healthy societies and good government are Plato's *The Republic* and Thomas More's *Utopia*, yet these books do not discuss the role of technology. Any optimism about good government aided by IT has been dwarfed by concerns about totalitarian control. Dystopian fiction is more apt and frighteningly applicable to today's world than are literary portrayals of utopias. Four of the most chilling and successful dystopian visions are the Panopticon, *Animal Farm*, *Brave New World*, and *1984*. All include elements of political repression and control aided by new technologies. All are so imaginative and insightful that they are now an essential part of modern culture.

Jeremy Bentham's Panopticon contained a novel design for a prison.[3] Prisoners were housed at the circumference of a circular building, jailers in the centre. Prisoners could not communicate with one another, nor could they see the jailers, but jailers could observe and monitor all the prisoners. Although technology was not explicitly part of the vision, it is easy to imagine how line-of-sight observations from a central viewing point (much like modern video surveillance systems) can be exploited by governments, a concept further explored in *1984*.

Animal Farm is a satirical novel written by George Orwell in response to his disillusionment with the Stalinist tyranny that betrayed the hopes of the Russian revolution.[4] In the novel, the animals revolt and drive Farmer Jones from the farm. They then adopt their own seven commandments, including the tenet that '[a]ll animals are equal'. Pigs 'Snowball' and 'Napoleon' assume command of a government that grows increasingly corrupt as their society takes on undesirable characteristics of human society. By the end, the animals can no longer distinguish themselves from humans; their mantra has morphed to '[a]ll animals are equal, but some animals are more equal than others'.

Brave New World by Aldous Huxley portrays a world in which reproductive, psychological, and social methods are used to exercise control in a futuristic caste-based society.[5] Methods used to manipulate and condition citizens include 'sleep learning', watching 'feelies', taking 'soma', and cloning via in-vitro fertilization. The motto of the world state is 'community, identity, and stability'. In opposition to dominant beliefs that have been indoctrinated by the World State, John, a key character, articulates his wish for and fights for 'the right to be unhappy'.

1984

1984, also by George Orwell, is arguably the best known dystopic literary vision of totalitarian control over a society.[6] 'Air Strip One' is ruled by Big Brother, an all-knowing and all-seeing figure who may or may not exist. There is omnipresent surveillance by the government, using microphones, cameras, and 'telescreens'. The Ministry of Truth is responsible for historical revisionism, where Winston, the protagonist of the novel, rewrites past newspaper articles so that 'history' always supports Ingsoc's party line. The government's watchful eye seeks out independent and radical thinkers, who are then caught by the 'Thought Police' for committing 'thoughtcrime'. Recent events in the USA have led to a dramatic upsurge in the popularity of *1984* and other dystopian novels that examine the consequences of government monitoring and surveillance.[7]

Figure 5.1 A scene from the recent Broadway production of *1984*
The Broadway Production of *1984*. Photo credit: Julieta Cervantes

Brave New World and *1984* anticipate total control over a population but do so in different ways. In the former novel, control is exercised through pleasure; in the latter novel, using pain.

Research: Compare and contrast two or three dystopian novels, science fiction stories, or films in their use of IT to exercise control over a population.

Debate: Resolved: *Brave New World* is a better metaphor for what ails modern societies than is *1984*. Hint: In your arguments, you may want to distinguish between various countries and societies.

5.2 Free speech

Dystopian novels often express concerns about humanity's ability to think and speak freely. Digital technologies are not (yet) able to control thought, but can be used to facilitate or hinder the expression and transmission of thoughts via writing or speech. The amplification of one's voice excited many digital pioneers, yet there have been and continue to be vigorous legal battles about free speech on the internet.

For centuries, the reach of one's speaking was limited to those in the presence of the speaker. Radio and television changed that, allowing those with access to the airwaves to be heard at distances far from the speaker, although usually only within a distance of tens or hundreds of miles. Satellite transmissions extended the reach further, but they are limited by atmospheric conditions. Now, the internet allows writing or speech to be transmitted instantaneously around the world to a possible audience of billions of internet or mobile phone subscribers. This provides the internet and its users the potential for good or bad, depending upon whether messages bring enlightenment or spread propaganda. As we shall see, governments have varying commitments to free speech over the internet, and they react in different ways to encourage or prevent such messages.

Most societies have enshrined the right of citizens to free speech. Yet there are vast differences in interpretation. The United Nations Universal Declaration of Human Rights states:[8]

> Everyone has the right to freedom of opinion and expression; this right includes freedom to hold opinions without interference and to seek, receive and impart information and ideas through any media and regardless of frontiers.

Free speech in the USA is enshrined in the First Amendment to the Constitution:[9]

> Congress shall make no law respecting an establishment of religion; or prohibiting the free exercise thereof; or abridging the freedom of speech, or of the press; or the right of the people peaceably to assemble, and to petition the Government for a redress of grievances.

Nonetheless, there are common law exceptions, including obscenity, defamation, and incitement of terrorist acts, in part because of inherent ambiguities in the US Constitution. Modern-day catastrophes, such as 9/11, have tested the limits of the Bill of Rights.

Here are some examples from other countries.[10]

Free speech is codified in Canada's Canadian Charter of Rights and Freedoms, but the Charter also refers to exceptions more directly than the US Constitution in its so-called 'Notwithstanding' clause:

> Everyone has the following fundamental freedoms: ... freedom of thought, belief, opinion and expression, including freedom of the press and other media of communication ... The Canadian Charter of Rights and Freedoms guarantees the rights and freedoms set out in it *subject only to such reasonable limits prescribed by law as can be demonstrably justified in a free and democratic society* (emphasis added).

India's Constitution guarantees free speech to all citizens, yet it sets limits on this right to protect matters such as the integrity and security of the state, 'friendly relations with foreign states, public order, decency or morality, [and] defamation or incitement to an offense'.

Article 35 of the Constitution of the People's Republic of China states a right to free speech:

> Citizens of the People's Republic of China enjoy freedom of speech, of the press, of assembly, of association, of procession and of demonstration.

Yet there have always been severe restrictions on free speech in China, and severe penalties for those who appear to threaten government control. We shall discuss this in more detail later in the chapter.

No society regards the right of free speech as absolute (we shall return to this idea later in the chapter).[11] Looking across nations and cultures, the kinds of speech that draw the most government censorship are utterances viewed as obscene, defaming individuals or institutions, promoting hate, posing threats to the government and the established political order, and inciting or encouraging terrorism, which has been especially important since the 9/11 terrorist attacks.

5.3 Print, broadcast, and internet speech

Individuals who wish their thoughts and ideas to be heard at a distance can use various communication media. The most important have been print (primarily newspapers and magazines), radio, television, and the internet. Internet communications can be in various forms, including email, texts, status updates on social media sites, tweets, and Snap images.

Governments regulate communications via these different media with varying degrees of urgency. Print is generally the least regulated, perhaps because it impinges on the senses least directly; not everyone likes to read, and it is relatively easy to keep print materials away from children. The regulation of radio and TV is relatively straightforward because they are viewed as 'common carriers', requiring licensing of a public resource—channels that consume communications bandwidth. Governmental policy on broadcasting is controlled by agencies such as the US Federal Communications Corporation, the Canadian Radio and Television Commission, the Telecom Regulatory Authority of India, and the Ministry of Information Industry of China.[12] A major concern of such agencies is prohibiting the transmission of sexually explicit material; a secondary concern is defamation.

Speech on the internet

The movement to internet media changes speech, which can be *one-to-many*, as in TV programmes, but more interestingly *one-to-one* (such as email) or *many-to-many* (as in a discussion forum or with Facebook posts). Internet communications have thrived. They are available to anyone and do not appear to be controlled by large corporate interests. There were over 181 million blogs expressing personal points of view by the end of 2011.[13] By 2017, the number of internet users across the globe had grown to 3.8 billion people.[14]

Here is some 2017 data about the quantities of internet speech:[14]

Facebook messages per day	4.3 billion
Facebook likes per day	5.75 billion
Tweets per day	650 million
Content uploaded to YouTube per day	4 million hours

Additionally, 205 billion emails are sent and received every day.[15]

Politics lives and breathes on the internet. Given the continued growth of internet communications, governments have become increasingly concerned about posts they view as pornographic, hate speech, politically disruptive, or encouraging of violence. There are also isolated cases of poor and offensive taste, such as the recent posting on Facebook of a murder, and even the live streaming of the rape of a 15-year-old girl by four teenage boys.[16] Internet speech also raises issues of ownership and responsibility (copyright was discussed in Chapter 2).

Research: Compare and contrast the legal status of free speech on the internet in two or three countries.

Research: Identify and analyse cases where people have watched violence being committed over the internet and did nothing, as well as actions some jurisdictions are taking to make such behaviour a criminal act.

5.4 Internet speech that draws censorship

Pornography has long been a significant use for the internet. There is no clear definition of pornography; some individuals regard certain images as art that others view as pornographic. Judgements of the magnitude of pornographic internet use vary; a recent analysis rated 4 per cent of websites and 10 to 15 per cent of searches as credible estimates.[17] The widespread availability of free porn has reduced the margins and slowed the growth of internet porn firms,[18] yet there is still sufficient porn to inflame many who have religious objections or concerns.

Almost everyone agrees that children should not see sexually explicit material. In the USA, the working definition of 'obscene' was established in the 1973 case of *Miller v. California*. The Supreme Court judged a work as obscene if and only if it satisfies the following three conditions:[19]

(a) whether the average person, applying contemporary community standards, would find that the work, taken as a whole, appeals to the prurient interest;
(b) whether the work depicts or describes, in a patently offensive way, sexual conduct specifically defined by the applicable state law; and
(c) whether the work, taken as a whole, lacks serious literary, artistic, political, or scientific value.

It took several decades before the government applied such standards to the internet. At first, it was unclear how perceived obscenity should be regulated, hence, individual organizations often made decisions to censor certain materials themselves. For example, Jeffrey Faucette has written a thorough review of the legal, ethical, and practical considerations involved when Carnegie Mellon University tried to remove sexually explicit images from all campus computers in 1994.[20]

Since then, there have been three major pieces of US legislation intended to safeguard children against viewing obscene matter on the internet: the Communications Decency Act (CDA) of 1996,[21] the Child Online Protection Act (COPA) of 1998,[22] and the Children's Internet Protection Act (CIPA) of 2000.[23] The CDA criminalized transmission of 'obscene' or 'indecent' materials to people under 18 years old, defining materials as objectionable based on their being 'patently offensive as measured by contemporary community standards'. The COPA was even more vague, forbidding 'any material defined as harmful to such minors on the internet'. The first two laws were attacked by organizations such as the American Civil Liberties Union (ACLU) on the grounds of being too broad, and therefore weakening the American right of free speech. The US Supreme Court ultimately ruled both the CDA and COPA unconstitutional.[24] The strategy with CIPA was different: it denied schools and libraries federally funded discounts on internet access if they did not instal 'technology protection measures' on all school internet-connected computers, and was deemed constitutional by the Supreme Court in 2003.[24]

Hate speech may be defined as 'speech which attacks a person or group on the basis of attributes such as gender, ethnic origin, religion, race, disability, or sexual orientation'.[25] Hate speech is dangerous because it is a verbal attack inciting hatred of persons or groups, promoting discrimination and sometimes leading to physical attacks. According to legal philosopher Jeremy Waldron, the harm of hate speech goes beyond the danger of physical violence, because it undermines the essential common good that all people will be protected by the law, and signals to hate speech targets that society does not regard them as citizens with equal dignity.[26]

The European Commission (EC) has been especially concerned about hatred spread virally over the internet. In June of 2016, Facebook (FB), Twitter, Microsoft, and Google therefore adopted a new code of conduct, agreeing to review, and in some cases remove quickly, online text that the EC regards as illegal hate speech.[27] Progress has been made, yet the EC, and especially Germany, complained late in 2016 that more needed to be done, and demanded that 70 per cent of hate speech needed to be removed within twenty-four hours.[28] Germany has taken a particularly strong stance, with a law authorizing fines of up to US$57 million if racist or slanderous comments and posts on social media are not removed quickly; because of this, FB had 1,200 content moderators at work in Berlin by mid-2018 scanning posts for hate speech and other undesirable expressions.[29]

Internet hate speech has also increased in the USA during the increasingly polarized Trump era. A vivid example came after the tragic August 2017 shooting of a peace activist at a neo-Nazi rally in Charlottesville, Virginia. Within days, major social media sites such as FB, Reddit, and Spotify, and even dating apps such as OKCupid, shut down many individuals and sites associated with hate groups.[30] Social media groups have also tried to remove sources of potential threats of violence against women and the glorification of misogynistic individuals who have gone on killer rampages; for example, the 2018 Toronto van attack perpetrator was allegedly inspired by the 'incel' (involuntary celibate) internet misogynistic movement.[31]

Statements of *political dissent* are an important form of free speech. Governments throughout the world, including those with passionate declarations of their commitment to free speech, nonetheless pursue dissidents and try to stifle their internet communications, fearing that they encourage citizens to rebel against the state. For example, recently in the USA, Twitter received a summons to reveal the identity or identities behind @ALT_USCIS, an account critical of President Trump, thought to be run by current or former federal employees.[32] Twitter sued the government to avoid complying with the summons; the government withdrew its case the next day.[33]

Anonymity on the internet involves making contributions with true identities hidden. A special case of this is *pseudonymity*, where people use false names in place of their true names. Anonymity has many purposes, some that many of us would consider noble, and some that can be considered evil.[34] Individuals opposing oppressive regimes, or protesting inappropriate behaviour of individuals or corporations, may only speak up anonymously, as is the case with @ALT_USCIS. Other reasons for remaining anonymous are shyness, or fear that one's personal issues would become public.

Social scientists Ruogu Kang, Stephanie Brown, and Sara Kiesler interviewed forty-four individuals from nine different countries recruited over the internet.[35] Fifty-three per cent admitted to using anonymity for purposes considered illegal, such as attacking or hacking others, or for purposes considered 'undesirable' by society, such as browsing sites with violence or pornography. Half admitted to presenting fictitious information on social network or dating sites. Many went online anonymously because of perceived threats from individuals including online predators. Fifteen of the individuals cited having a prior unpleasant or frightening experience. A variety of benefits for being anonymous were mentioned, including safety, presenting a desirable image, and feeling free to express one's views. David Davenport, on the other hand, has argued strongly that the price of internet anonymity was too high, that social justice required accountability, and that the courts needed to be able to identify the source of a communication in case of a legal dispute.[36]

The Digital Media Law Project,[37] which was a project of Harvard's Berkman Klein Center for Internet and Society from 2007–14, summarized the legal situation in the USA as follows:

> [the] courts require a plaintiff trying to unmask an Internet speaker to bring forward a substantial amount of evidence to support the underlying legal claim (i.e., evidence that the anonymous speaker actually defamed the plaintiff or committed some other unlawful act that injured the plaintiff).... These courts also impose a requirement that the plaintiff provide notice to the speaker whose identity is sought and an adequate opportunity to respond.

Legal intervention is often required to obtain identities because many anonymous seditious communicators have the technical skills to make it very difficult to ascertain their identity.[38]

Terrorism is arguably the area of most concern to governments. There is grave concern over internet uses that appear to threaten the safety of the state and its citizens. In March 2017, a terrorist attack in London that resulted in the deaths of three pedestrians and one police officer caused UK officials to demand that intelligence agencies have access to encrypted text messages.[39] FB, Twitter, Google, and Microsoft announced in December 2016 that they would share technology (such as 'unique digital fingerprints') and information to combat communication of terrorist propaganda through their media.[40] By August, Twitter had already suspended 360,000 accounts associated with online extremism. In February 2017, FB announced that it was initiating a research project to develop artificial intelligence (AI) that could automatically distinguish between news stories about terrorist attacks and attempts to recruit individuals to carry out terrorist attacks.[41] Facebook did this because it felt that it could not employ sufficient human employees to monitor its billions of daily posts. In June 2017, FB indicated that they were then using some AI in conjunction with 150 specialists working in thirty languages to remove inappropriate content.[42] YouTube also has recently taken actions to remove extremist videos promoting terrorism.[43] As the problem of fake news became salient, these numbers grew substantially, as we shall discuss in Section 5.5.

Internet censorship across the world

Internet communications that strongly oppose a government have been censored throughout the world. Reporters without Borders (RwB) publishes annual measures of the degree of internet censorship.[44] In 2011, 13% of the world's people, including in the USA and Western Europe, lived in countries with almost no censorship, while 25% lived in countries with the worst censorship.

Continued on next page

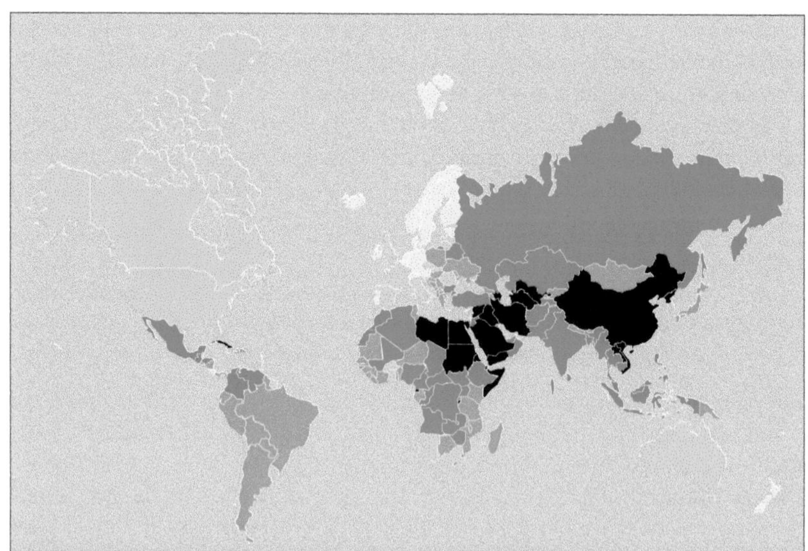

Figure 5.2 The 2018 Reporters Without Borders press freedom map[45]

The 2018 RwB rankings list Norway, Sweden, Netherlands, Finland, Switzerland, Jamaica, and Belgium (#1 to #7) as allowing the greatest press freedom (shown in pale yellow), and Sudan, Vietnam, China, Syria, Turkmenistan, Eritrea, and North Korea (rankings #174 to #180 (shown in black); North Korea actually bans the internet entirely) as offering the least press freedom. India (#138), Pakistan (#139), Russia (#148), and Turkey (#157) also have severe censorship (shown in red).

Section 66A of the Indian Information Technology Act of 2000 imposed severe penalties for communicating information viewed by the government as offensive, menacing, or false.[46] Individuals have been charged under this law for statements said to be hate speech, as well as for cartoons and tweets charging politicians with corruption. The Supreme Court of India ruled that this Section had a chilling effect on free speech and declared it unconstitutional. There is also controversy in India over rules requiring internet service providers (ISPs) and internet sites to remove content found 'disparaging... harassing... blasphemous... or hateful' by government officials and private citizens.[47]

In 2017 dozens of Pakistanis were arrested based on their social media use.[48] Turkey has banned thousands of websites, including Wikipedia.[49] Egypt has filtered out large quantities of content, including local and regional news, and access to human rights websites.[50] Russia has forced Apple and Google to remove LinkedIn from local app stores.[51]

The situation in China is particularly striking, resulting in what is often termed 'The Great Chinese Firewall'.[52] By 2006, there were at least sixty political prisoners in Chinese jails for having revealed 'sensitive' information on the internet. Yahoo!, Microsoft, Cisco, Google, and FB, desiring to crack the Chinese market, have cooperated with the government in limiting free speech. For example, Google (despite its slogan, 'Don't be Evil', first introduced in 2000, and quietly dropped in 2015) first created a version of its search engine that filtered out content objectional to China, then withdrew from China in 2010, and now is said to again be working on such software.[52] FB recently shut down the account of a Chinese man living in exile who had posted stories of corruption among Communist party officials.[53] Another example was discovered by investigators at the University of Toronto Citizen Lab of a surveillance system in China that captured Skype conversations any time a suspect keyword was typed into the chat window.[54]

Many believe that Chinese censorship has worsened in recent years:[55]

> the Party has mobilized its unique and extensive network of surveillance, security, and secret police in ways that have affected many areas of Chinese life. Media organizations... have been hit particularly hard.... editors and reporters have found themselves increasingly constrained by Central Propaganda Department diktats. Told what they can and cannot cover, they find that the limited freedom they had to report on events has been drastically curtailed.

Keyword filtering has been enabled on WeChat accounts registered to individuals with mainland China phone numbers.[56] Apple has been a special target for China.[57] Early in 2017, the government forced Apple to remove the *New York Times* from the Chinese version of the app store, applied pressure to regulate video streaming services for Apple hardware, and required app stores to register with the government. Centralization of software distribution in app stores allowed easy government control and monitoring of information it considers subversive. Later, China partially blocked communication via WhatsApp, forced removal of Skype from Apple's app store, removed apps that supported virtual private networks being used to evade its internet censorship, and made it clear that it would have access to personal data stored in Apple users' iCloud. China's commitment to disallowing 'forbidden' speech has also extended abroad.[58] For example, Chinese students' associations representing over 300,000 Chinese students studying in the USA have tried to prevent exposure to what they viewed as anti-Chinese speeches by human rights advocates, including the Dalai Lama. Do these actions seem reminiscent of Orwell's *1984*?

Ethics

Content moderation: We can see that there are many reasons that organizations remove material from the internet. Some deletions seem virtuous, such as removing content that demeans people of certain races. Others seem like unfortunate restrictions on free speech or actions of governments trying to repress dissent. As of now, content removal cannot be perfected by algorithms, although they are continually being improved.[59] YouTube reported in January 2018 that over 80% of the more than 8 million problem videos first flagged by an AI system had been deleted in the fourth quarter of 2017. Therefore, in critical situations, human judgement typically makes the decision. One result is a new profession known as an internet *content moderator*.[60] Social media firms are continually hiring more of them, but stress that, even for skilled humans, there are many difficult decisions to make.[61]

Continued on next page

Here are some recent examples.[62] FB suspended the account of one user because she had used the word 'dyke' in her posts, even though it was not being used derogatively. Twitter inappropriately suspended actress Rose McGowan's account for speaking of the sexual harassment and assaults by film producer Harvey Weinstein. YouTube's desire to remove extremist propaganda content led to its removal of thousands of videos that could have someday been used to document atrocities in Syria. Other removals are excellent, such as the mid-2018 decision by FB, Apple, and YouTube (Twitter made the opposite decision) to erase most posts and videos from Alex Jones, who glorified violence, spread hate, and propagated conspiracy theories, yet even that decision drew an editorial in the *New York Times* decrying unevenness in the application of policies for content removal.[63]

Decisions about what content social media firms should allow and what they should delete have become critical moral and ethical judgements. How would you balance the commitment to free speech with the desirable goal of shielding people from that which is distasteful, disgusting, or dangerous?

Research: Compare several countries in their policies and methods in censoring speech, or several social media firms in their content moderation policies.

Debate: Resolved: Citizens of a country should be allowed to post any message on the internet, regardless of how offensive or seemingly dangerous it is, without fear of penalty.

Debate: Resolved: Anonymity for authors of social media posts should be acceptable and protected by law.

Policy: Write a brief for a politician or a candidate proposing stronger laws against hate speech on the internet.

Policy: Draft a policy for your social media company on what content it should allow or disallow, and why.

Ethics: You are an internet content moderator. You believe that your employer is too much in favour of free speech, allowing content you believe could lead to more terrorism. Oversight of your work is minimal. You could follow the dictates of your conscience and delete more. Do you? Why or why not?

5.5 Fake news, filter bubbles, and echo chambers

Another aspect of the free speech challenge is a phenomenon now of great interest—*fake news*. Fake news has recently been defined by a multi-disciplinary team of scholars as 'fabricated information that mimics news media content in form but not in organizational process or intent'.[64]

Traditional media, such as newspapers, radio, and television, have strong gateways that discourage active participation by random citizens. With the exception of letters to the editor, community radio, and homebrew video, what is published is controlled by editors and publishers. They are empowered and trusted to use good judgement, although they are often influenced by their beliefs, politics, and sometimes marketing goals, as was the case with the 'yellow journalism' practised by the publishers of certain US tabloids in the 1890s.[65]

The internet is different. In theory, everyone has a voice. With some limitations, people can post whatever they want (nobody may read, listen, or watch, as your contributions may be unknown and therefore invisible to almost everyone, but you can almost always exercise your right to free speech). We have discussed the issue of the perceived threats that some internet posts that might be true may pose to the common good. Here we are concerned about another phenomenon, the dangers resulting from posting material that is known to be false or can be shown to be false. A landmark case of fake news occurred during the 2016 US presidential election.

Fake news in the 2016 US election campaign

Although fake news is not new, it became especially troublesome during the 2016 US presidential contest between Donald Trump and Hillary Clinton. One dramatic example was the flash that the Pope had endorsed Trump, which originated on a satirical website, then spread as supposed fact.[66]

Facebook Engagement*	Source	Fake News Story
960,000	Ending the Fact	Pope Francis endorses Donald Trump for President
789,000	Political Insider	WikiLeaks confirms that Hillary sold weapons to ISIS
754,000	Ending the Fact	Hillary's ISIS email worse than anyone could imagine
701,000	Ending the Fact	Hillary disqualified from holding any federal office
561,000	Denver Guardian	FBI agent involved in Hillary leaks apparently murdered

Top Five 2016 US Election Fake News Stories in Terms of Facebook Engagement

* as measured by Facebook shares, reactions, and comments[67]

Yet fake news went well beyond bizarre episodes.[67] Alt-right fake news sites, many located in Macedonia, filled the internet with scurrilous accusations directed at Hillary Clinton, Barack Obama, and Bill Clinton. A BuzzFeed investigation found 38% of FB posts from three such websites to either be false or partially false. In the last three months of the campaign, BuzzFeed reported that the twenty top-performing fake news stories from 'hoax sites and hyperpartisan blogs' received 8.7 million shares, reactions, and comments on FB, while the nineteen major news websites received only 7.4 million such affirmations. More false posts went viral than did factual posts.

For example, an erroneous post by a Texan speculating that paid protesters were being bused to demonstrate against Trump was shared 16,000 times on Twitter and 350,000

Continued on next page

times on Facebook within two days.[68] The attempt to declare the post false spread less often. Even fact-checking websites such as Snopes became the target of vitriolic fake news.[69]

Yet exactly how fake news affected the election results is complex, as analysed in a landmark 2017 study by the Harvard Berkman Klein Center for Internet & Society.[70] Although one sentence does not do justice to the quality of the report, the researchers found 'a sustained campaign of materially misleading political messaging ... constituting a tightly-insulated echo chamber [to be defined later in this chapter] ... allowing for the development and recirculation of ideas ... [followed by] enticing and demanding coverage from center-left press ... [thereby] set[ting] the agenda for the election, focusing heavily on Clinton's scandals and on Trump's preferred talking points'.

Fake news has also influenced elections in Indonesia and the Philippines; it has spread misinformation about the Colombian peace deal and the West African Ebola virus.[71] In Europe, fake news has spread untruths about political candidates and characterized refugees from the Middle East as terrorists and rapists.[72] For example, in March 2017, social media widely spread the name of a terrorist supposedly responsible for a London attack, only to discover that the individual was then in prison.[73] In India, WhatsApp has been used repeatedly to spread false rumours, such as a fabrication that ignited two vigilante attacks resulting in seven fatalities.[74] In part because WhatsApp users can be anonymous, the intensity of fake news rose significantly before a 2018 Indian election.[75] Falsehoods on FB about the Rohingya ethnic group in Myanmar helped to ignite violence against them, and similarly about Muslims in Sri Lanka, illustrating that there is often a fine line between hate speech and fake news.[76] In advance of an August 2017 election in Kenya, 90 per cent of Kenyans who were surveyed reported hearing or seeing fake news.[77] Similarly, there was a flurry of fake news before a June 2018 election in Mexico.[78]

Conversely, strongmen throughout the world can deflect criticisms of their action by alleging 'fake news'. Trump has repeatedly described scandalous or negative allegations about him as 'fake news'.[79] Leaders in China, Russia, Syria, Venezuela, and Turkey have also begun to do this.[80]

Currently, the world is more polarized than at any time in the past. Concerns about terrorism, refugees, immigration, trade, and incomes are rampant. There are fewer trusted sources that people follow and believe. The Editorial Board of the *New York Times* noted that all Americans used to get the same news from trusted TV hosts such as Walter Cronkite, yet now the fractured media landscape allows them 'to curl up in cozy, angry or self-righteous cocoons'.[81] We shall discuss these 'cocoons', also known as 'echo chambers', later in the chapter. Our obsession with consuming instant news feeds allows misinformation to spread quickly.[82] Another cause is the poor financial state of investigative journalism, since the business models of print, radio, and TV firms have been disrupted.[83] For example, $42 billion of the $59 billion spent on digital advertising in

2015 went to FB, Google, and Verizon, which owns AOL and Yahoo!. Finally, it is worth noting that we have only seen the tip of the iceberg, as deep learning technology (see Chapter 11) is now enabling the production of realistic *fake videos*, also known as *deep fakes*.[84]

Key to the fake news issue is the role of internet media companies. The company with the most at stake is Facebook. Its News Feed algorithms choose articles to send daily to its 2 billion subscribers, making it, in the words of *New York Times* technology columnist Farhad Manjoo, possibly 'the most influential source of information in the history of civilization.'[85] Several interviews with FB CEO Mark Zuckerberg made it clear that he had been shaken by his company's impact on the 2016 US election. Manjoo then commented:

> The people who work on News Feed aren't making decisions that turn on fuzzy human ideas like ethics, judgment, intuition or seniority. They are concerned only with quantifiable outcomes about people's actions on the site. That data, at Facebook, is the only real truth...a particular kind of truth: [their] ultimate mission is to figure out what users want...and to give them more of that.

However, in part because of what happened during the election, FB took aim at fake news. It made it easier for its 1.8 billion members to report fake news, began to partner with fact-checking organizations such as Snopes and FactCheck.org to review suspicious published posts, and enabled items to be labelled 'disputed pieces.'[86] It introduced a link to 'Tips for spotting fake news' at the top of the News Feed in some countries,[87] and, along with other groups of machine learning experts, began working on automatic fact checkers.[88] It also announced plans to double its news review staff to 20,000 individuals.[89] By late 2017, FB went further, restricting the ability of advertisers to direct ads at individuals who use hate speech in their profiles, and developing enhanced methods to recognize links between ads and false content.[90] It slightly de-emphasized its reliance upon news feeds, making a new commitment back towards its initial focus of supporting community, in part because of internal research emphasizing that sharing messages and connecting with friends enhances user well-being. By mid-2018, it released details on its internal processes for defining 'graphic violence', 'hate speech', and 'child exploitation', as well as reporting publicly for the first time on its content moderation efforts during the first quarter of the year.[91] This included removing 583 million fake accounts, 2.5 million instances of hate speech, and 1.9 million posts relating to terrorism.

Other social media companies have also tried to deal with fake news. Google's search engine has been repeatedly changed to ameliorate the problem; some organizations have felt disenfranchised because their legitimate political websites are now barely visible.[92] Some YouTube viewers complained that videos with moderate positions were often followed by more extreme videos.[93] More research is needed here, as well as openness by Google in explaining its algorithms.

Twitter also contributes to the fake news problem. Rumours are tweeted, then retweeted by others without subjecting them to analysis, and are thereby soon to be misinformation.[94] Contributing hugely on Twitter are *bots*, computer programs pretending to be people and spreading misinformation as propaganda. In November 2017, Twitter acknowledged that there may be up to 60 million automated accounts, almost 20 per cent of its total user base.[95] Fake news is only one application; bots are also used to increase the influence and prestige of people or products by exhibiting a large base of followers and many retweets; a US firm called Devumi is a prime supplier to people wanting to purchase followers. Twitter has long known that it has a serious problem, and has struggled to amass resources to deal with it, especially after the 2016 election campaign; it announced in July 2018 that it planned to delete tens of millions of suspicious accounts.[96]

Alessandro Bessi and Emilio Ferrara analysed a month's worth of tweets, over 20 million in total, that were tweeted one to two months before the 2016 US presidential election.[97] They found that roughly one-fifth of the conversation was created by about 400,000 bots. They concluded that this could cause influence redistribution, further polarization of the electorate, and more spreading of fake news. A later study, by Samuel Woolley and colleagues, focused on the USA and suggested that bots could enable surreptitious campaign coordination, violate disclosure rules, and illegally solicit votes or contributions.[98,99] A third study, reported in 2018 by the Pew Research Center, analysed 1 million tweets in the summer of 2017 and found that (1) 66 per cent of the links to popular websites were tweeted by automated accounts; (2) the 500 most active suspected bot accounts contributed 22 per cent of the tweeted links, while the 500 most active humans only provided 6 per cent of the links; and (3) the bots did not seem to have either a liberal or a conservative political bias.[100]

Fake news becomes especially dangerous via phenomena that have been labelled as *filter bubbles* and *echo chambers*. People have always been limited in the diversity of views they encounter in the media. Print, radio, and television news tends to echo the party line of the dominant political ethos of a period. Yet one could always find alternative views—media outlets that differ dramatically from the dominant ethos. For example, National Public Radio (NPR) outlets in the USA and the CBC in Canada have always been significantly to the left of most radio stations in those two countries. This has also been true internationally. Voice of America broadcasts were beamed into Eastern bloc countries during the Cold War.

The internet has caused many people to get less exposure to diverse political views. Whatever one's political leanings, one can find online sources that present and reinforce information consistent with those leanings, what social scientists call 'confirmation bias'. Personalization of search engines such as Google and social media such as Facebook results in users getting their own individual news feeds, something digital media innovator Nicholas Negroponte forecast as 'The Daily Me'.[101] Consequently, people get less and less exposure to views that conflict with their beliefs. They experience what Eli Pariser termed a *filter bubble*—a 'unique universe of information for each of us'.[102] He suggested that we welcome such assistance because we are no longer able to cope with the flood of information that deluges us. Furthermore, because social media are interactive, allowing likes and shares and comments, one is able to hear those points of view reinforced and echoed back, creating what has become known as *echo chambers*.[103]

Barack Obama warned of the dangers of filter bubbles and echo chambers in his presidential farewell address.[104] A long and insightful exposition of the dangers is *#Republic,* a recent book by Harvard law professor Cass Sunstein.[105] Sunstein stressed the importance of having a wide range of common experiences with certain people, but also being exposed to material one would not have chosen on one's own (a point also made by Pariser).[102] Sunstein terms this an 'architecture of serendipity'. The book presents examples of the dangers of *cybercascades*—the methods by which fake news spreads. Strong arguments are given as to how filtering information and limiting opportunities to hear and understand other points of view contributes unproductively to a hardening of positions, as for example in secret FB groups.[106]

Researchers from Facebook examined how 10 million US FB users interacted with socially shared news.[107] Focusing only on 'hard news', they were able to measure what percentage of cross-cutting content (conservative-leaning stories for liberals, liberal-leaning stories for conservatives) would be seen at four stages of a pipeline: random selection, a selection posted by one's friends (most of whom typically share one's ideology), the subset of stories made visible by the Facebook personalization engine, and those selected and clicked upon by the individual:

Table 5.1 A filter bubble in operation[107]

Percentage of cross-cutting content	Random	Posted by friends	Exposed by FB	Selected by user
Conservative	40%	35%	33%	29%
Liberal	50%	24%	22%	20%

This provides precise data in one context for the magnitude of the filter bubble and echo chamber phenomena. Interesting and disturbing is that only 7 per cent of the content clicked on was hard news.

Another research team studied how 1 million Italian and 50 million US FB users reacted to conspiracy and scientific postings over five years.[108] They found that there were 77 per cent polarized users on scientific pages, with the definition of polarized being that 95 per cent of their likes were on such pages. The figure for individuals on conspiracy pages was 92 per cent. The more active the polarized users were, the more friends they had that displayed the same behaviour. Information spread rapidly in such cases, mostly within one day. These *cybercascades* typically occurred within an echo chamber of like-minded individuals. Sentiment analysis showed that the negativity of comments increased with the length of discussion threads.

A third research project analysed the web-browsing behaviour of 50,000 US-located users who regularly read online news.[109] They showed that using social networks and search engines was associated with an increase in the mean ideological distance between the users, even though the communication channels enabled an exposure to material from both ends of the political spectrum.

A fourth study examined 3.5 months of the over 1 billion political tweets in the fifteen months of the 2016 US political campaign.[110] The results showed that Trump supporters lived in their own insular world, having few connections to Clinton supporters or to mainstream media, while Clinton supporters were more splintered and had some connections to verified journalists.

Finally, professor Yochai Benkler and a team of collaborators analysed 1.25 million stories published online by 25,000 sources between 1 April 2016 and the US presidential election on 7 November 2016.[111] The analysts also found differences between the media behaviour of Clinton and Trump supporters. While the former paid attention to left-oriented online sites and traditional media outlets, the latter paid most of their attention to a highly polarized 'right-wing media ecosystem' centred around Breitbart:

> Rather than 'fake news' in the sense of wholly fabricated falsities, many of the most-shared stories can more accurately be understood as disinformation: the purposeful construction of true or partly true bits of information into a message that is, at its core, misleading. . . . this turned the right-wing media system into an internally coherent, relatively insulated knowledge community, reinforcing the shared worldview of readers and shielding them from journalism that challenged it.

It is important to remember that such analyses focus primarily on the role of social media in the hardening of opinions; it is not a complete explanation of the role of all media in these circumstances. Also, despite the fact that fake news becomes more dangerous when magnified in an echo chamber, the role of echo chambers with real news is also troublesome.

Fake news is especially dangerous with health information. Brittany Seymour has termed these 'digital pandemics'.[112] Seymour and a team of collaborators analysed FB connectedness within and between anti-fluoride networks.[113] They showed that in 12 per cent of the cases, members did not actually access the publication being discussed. They also had a 50 per cent chance of seeing non-empirical and negative content unrelated to that publication. Other researchers analysed four years of longitudinal data comprising over 3 million tweets of pro- and anti-vaccination advocates, and found patterns of resolute determination, mistrust of government, and conspiratorial thinking among those vehemently opposed to vaccination.[114]

Chapter 4 was optimistic about the internet enabling more informed health consumers, yet clearly there are still challenges to attaining that vision. Furthermore, in speaking of the political processes of countries both democratic and autocratic, the as yet unsolved problem of fake news is both divisive and corrosive.

Research: Who fact checks the fact checkers?

Research: Study and analyse how Twitter has tried to deal with fake news.

Research: Similarities and differences between yellow journalism and fake news.

Concept: Write a Wikipedia article called 'Cybercascade'.

Policy: Write a brief for the CEO of a social media company proposing a policy on the regulation and control of fake news on their platform.

Law: Specifying penalties for putting fake news on the internet.

Jury: A politician fails to get re-elected due to 'fake news' originating from a wealthy person. The politician sues for $10 million in damages. Assuming the laws of a locale, debate as a jury guilt or innocence, and penalties.

Book report: Pariser, Eli (2011). *The Filter Bubble: How the New Personalized Web Is Changing What We Read and How We Think*. The Penguin Press.

Ethics: You work for a leading search engine company. You discover that their page ranking algorithms have been tuned to de-emphasize the views of individuals knowledgeable about and concerned about climate change. You report the concern to management and it refuses to act on your concern. What do you do?

Ethics: Now change the previous exercise so that the harm is done to the point of view that there is no climate change problem. You report the concern to management and it refuses to act on your concern. What do you do?

5.6 E-democracy

We now look at internet speech that promotes the goals of a democratic society. Ideally, such developments could counter the observation by Robert Putnam about the lack of civic engagement in the USA, and the need for more *social capital*, which he defined as 'features of social organization such as networks, norms, and social trust that facilitate coordination and cooperation for mutual benefit'.[115] Internet communications that enable citizen engagement often go under the name *e-democracy*. Stephen Coleman and John Gøtze proposed that online public engagement in policy deliberation was the central value of e-democracy and was fostered by:[116]

> access to balanced information...an open agenda...time to consider issues expansively...freedom from manipulation or coercion...a rule-based framework for discussion...participation by an inclusive sample of citizens...scope for free interaction between participants...[and] recognition of differences between participants, but rejection of status-based prejudice.

Others use the term *civic tech* to map the field in terms of open government initiatives, including 'data access and transparency...public decision making, resident feedback...[and] voting', as well as community action, including 'civic crowdfunding, community organizing, information crowdsourcing, neighborhood forums, [and] peer-to-peer sharing'.[117]

One of the earliest examples was the Minnesota e-Democracy Project, initiated in 1994 and still in existence today.[118] By 1999, there were 400 people online actively discussing Minnesota politics and seeing e-debates among candidates. A 2006 survey of 256 Minnesota e-Democracy participants found that the online participants did not represent political participation by those who had been inactive previously.[119] Instead, individuals who had already been politically active had a new vehicle for political activity and influence. A 2015 analysis reported that most participants were more knowledgeable about community issues and thought that the forum 'increased their satisfaction with the community as a place to live or work'.[120]

Blacksburg Electronic Village (BEV)

Blacksburg, Virginia, was the 'first town in the world to adopt [in 1993] an all-Internet model for a community-wide network, and the first community in the U.S. to offer residential Ethernet service as an amenity in apartments and townhomes'.[121] Blacksburg has roughly 40,000 inhabitants and is dominated by a technologically innovative university, Virginia Polytechnic Institute and State University (VPI).[122] Over 80% of the population are faculty, staff, or students at VPI. BEV is one of the best-researched examples of civic tech.

By 2001, 97% and 62% of the population were using email and discussion and news groups. High-energy dialogues focused on religious and seniors' issues.[123] Current capabilities include internet services for individuals and non-profit organizations; websites for individuals, arts organizations, and small businesses; mailing lists; and support for blogs and social networks.

Andrea Kavanaugh, BEV's Research Director, has directed studies designed to better understand community involvement and social capital in a town with strong electronic linkages. She observed 'frequent and increasing use of the BEV and the internet for local, social-capital building activities', but no increase in community involvement except among those already active in the community,[124] noting that 'informed activists with multiple group memberships become more involved in local issues once going online, whereas informed non-activists become less involved'.[125]

The BEV studies are notable in being conducted over many years. Other studies have been less robust, with shorter interventions of a few months or years. An excellent three-year study of an experimental wired suburb of Toronto, Canada, was 'Netville', led by sociologist Barry Wellman.[126] Sixty-four new homes were wired with what was then relatively rare high-speed internet access; forty-five 'non-wired' homes were not connected to the network. Sociologist Keith Hampton studied Netville through interviews and participant observation—he lived within the community for the last two years of his study. They concluded that:[126]

> high-speed, always-on access to the Internet, coupled with a local online discussion group, transforms and enhances neighboring. The Internet especially supports increased contact with weaker ties. In comparison to non-wired residents of the same suburb, more neighbors are known and chatted with, and they are more geographically dispersed around the suburb. [The Internet] also facilitated discussion and mobilization around local issues.

Wired residents recognized three times as many residents as did non-wired members, spoke with twice as many, and visited each other 1.5 times as often,[127] hence 'weak ties' were strengthened.

Particularly interesting was what happened when deficiencies were noted in the new homes, and when the developer informed people that the project would end and the telecommunications infrastructure decommissioned.[127] Unrest is routine over normal problems such as minor housing deficiencies, frozen pipes in winter, and a pace of paving roads slower than promised. The developer reported that only 20 per cent of the households would normally be in active protest, yet the percentage was greater than 50 per cent in Netville. The online community also facilitated vigorous but unsuccessful discussion and action to get the developer to change its mind about terminating the project.

Recently, computer scientists have begun to suggest technological innovations that could improve online engagement in policy deliberation—the *raison d'être* of e-democracy. Kavanaugh and her colleagues argued that the diminishing presence of local newspapers and the overwhelming flood of online political content suggested the need for a new kind of information source, a '(hyper) local news aggregator' that they termed the Virtual Town Square.[128] Martin Hilbert presented an optimistic view of information technology's potential, suggesting the potential of weighted preference voting, argument visualization, and the Semantic Web as methods that could ultimately improve reasoned discourse among large numbers of citizens.[129]

The above examples are from the USA, but the phenomena occur worldwide. Good examples are the British Hansard Society running a set of pilot online consultations for the UK Parliament; local governments in Finland, Germany, and Sweden deploying interactive software for soliciting input on city planning; and the governments of France and the European Union offering five online interactive forums for discussing European policy.[116] Developments under authoritarian regimes are also beginning, but slowly. A 2006 study characterized the then current use of the internet by political parties in Russia as 'web wide waste'.[130] Data presented previously in this chapter showed that internet use for political dialogue is still globally suppressed.

To what extent has e-democracy been successful? Is engagement in politics via social media now widespread and successful? Andrew Chadwick concluded very negatively:

> With the notable exceptions of some community networks—[e.g.]...Minnesota e-Democracy...—the road to e-democracy is littered with...failed projects. Reasons...[are] poor funding, unrealistic expectations, inappropriate technology, internal disputes, and a lack of clear objectives....[and] they have been insufficiently embedded in...goals people pursue in geographical communities.[131]

Chief among unrealistic expectations is that civic tech will turn individuals with little interest in politics into political animals. Yet, now that group communications technology no longer requires special software, but is supported by ubiquitous email and social media, individuals will pursue their political leanings and take some actions electronically. These actions include *e-mobilization*.

Research: Study and analyse how the internet is used and not used in your local and state communities.

Concept: Author a Wikipedia article on 'Wikidemocracy'.

Debate: Resolved: The phrase 'e-democracy' is a sham; information and communications technology and the internet provide no substantial benefit to a democratic society.

5.7 Citizen mobilization via social media

The right to access and contribute to social media gives citizens the ability to use the internet to inform themselves and to communicate with others. It also gives them the ability to mobilize for action, a concern for some governments that therefore become keen to discourage internet use.

Early examples of *e-mobilization*, early in the 1990s, used crude technology such as Usenet newsgroups, email, and file transfer protocol (FTP) for US-wide mobilizations around privacy concerns against the Lotus-Equifax Marketplace concept and the Clipper Chip; the first one was successful, the second unsuccessful.[132] Around 1994, there was an online movement in support of land rights for about 3,000 indigenous native rural peasants in Mexico, called the Zapatistas. Most online activity originated in the USA, but it resonated worldwide with groups concerned about global neoliberalism and agreements such as the North American Free Trade Agreement (NAFTA). The MoveOn movement was started in 1998 by Silicon Valley software designers concerned about the US distraction over the Bill Clinton and Monica Lewinsky affair. By 2005, MoveOn had grown to over 3 million members and become a vital US political force.

Researcher and journalist Zeynep Tufekci noted that the 1963 March on Washington took nine months of planning to get 250,000 people to Washington; a few Facebook posts and a relatively small effort got 3.5 million people from around the world to the Women's March in January 2017.[133]

Sometimes, online mobilization can threaten the established political order so much that there is violence and government overturn. We shall return to this theme in the next chapter.

Research: The role of the internet in organizing the 2017 Women's March.

5.8 Campaigning with social media; big data for voter surveillance and targeting

Another political use of IT is campaigns. Social media are used to communicate political messages to supporters and potential supporters, a good development for a democratic society. However, modern techniques of voter surveys and the analysis of big data about the population allow micro-targeting of different messages to different classes of voters, which can be used to mislead potential voters—a retrograde development for a democratic society.

Since social media have become a major force, those seeking to attain or retain office will make use of systems such as FB for conducting dialogues with citizens, Twitter for short political statements and calls to action, YouTube for visually documenting events, and blogs for longer policy statements and commentaries. Optimistically, the '[resulting] political activities [would] gain more transparency and citizens might be more involved in political decision-making'.[134]

In some countries social media seemed to have made a great impact, for example in the election of Justin Trudeau as Prime Minister of Canada in October 2015. Trudeau had greater social media activity than the other two major candidates.[135] Election-related Facebook activity alone amounted to 33 million interactions—posts, likes, comments, and shares—and 6 million tweets, coming mainly from the politically engaged. Trudeau's campaign made use of skilful video marketing; connecting to voters via hashtags such as #GenerationTrudeau and #RealChange; humour; using his family to communicate an image of a caring father, husband, and son; and responding to and engaging with online audiences in both official languages, English and French.[136]

In the USA, the impact of media was clear from the comparative television images of John F. Kennedy and Richard Nixon, which was influential in the former's 1960 triumph. The first national politician to leverage the internet was Howard Dean in his 2004 presidential primary campaign. He noted how bloggers reacted to his speeches and then used this to help improve his speeches; there was also viral recruiting of new supporters and donors using Meetup.com.[137]

Yes We Can!

Arguably no politician has used the internet as skilfully as Barack Obama did during his 2008 US presidential campaign.[138] His team included Facebook co-founder Chris Hughes as a key social media strategist. Web 2.0 social media tools were used early and often—mybarackobama.com; the Neighbor to Neighbor online phone banking tool to help supporters in phoning others; cleverly crafted personalized emails and text messages; a campaign content repository blog; an active presence on FB, LinkedIn, Twitter, and other sites; skilful use of live streaming video, both campaign-created and user-generated; and a digital media campaign guided by analytics.

Twenty-four hours after Obama announced his campaign, 1,000 grassroots groups had formed to use online tools provided on an Obama website to help them organize. By the time of the election, Obama had garnered support from grassroots movements of more than 5 million volunteers, campaign contributions from more than 3.1 million individuals, an email mailing list of over 13 million names, and an awareness of power among those involved ('Yes We Can!'). Once he was President, Obama attempted to carry over his social media presence with such innovations as change.gov and whitehouse.gov, featuring an Obama blog, a YouTube channel, and online meetings.

More recently, in the 2016 US election campaign, social media again played a key role.[139] Donald Trump had the most followers, as measured on FB, Twitter, and Instagram, with the calculations also including total likes. Yet Bernie Sanders had the most engaged audience, as measured by likes per follower.[139] This may have been because of his emphasis on communicating with voters one-on-one via social media, as well as the passion he generated among young voters.

More recently, in the June 2017 British campaign, a bot operating on the dating app Tinder sent 30,000 to 40,000 messages to individuals aged 18 to 25 located in constituencies where the results seemed to be in question.[140] Given that Labour won by as little as twenty-two votes for some of those seats, this action plausibly influenced the results.

Yet there are some aspects of IT's use in political campaigns that are very troubling. Although commentators and researchers imply that this phenomenon is new, that is untrue. Almost forty years ago, an acquaintance of mine set up a minicomputer, a roomful of Diablo printers, and a tabletop digitally driven pen to produce prodigious quantities of seemingly personally signed letters from a particular candidate to possible voters. Letters were constructed by choosing sentences and paragraphs from a database of fragments of speeches given by the candidate. Choices were based on opinions known to be held by the voter. The fragments were glued together to form a letter that implied that the candidate believed what the voter believed. *Voter surveillance* allows the political candidate to speak to 'each voter' in ways that will resonate with that voter. *Big data* allows voter surveillance and targeting to be done with more precision and more nuance, on a wider scale.

Political science professor Colin Bennett has studied and analysed these techniques in depth.[141] Four interrelated broad trends were significant: (1) the transition from voter management databases to integrated voter management platforms, which detail voter lifestyles and beliefs; (2) the transition from mass messaging to micro-targeting, incorporating personal data obtained from data brokerage firms; (3) the analysis of social media and the social graph, allowing 'targeted sharing' of information and pitches from individual citizens to their friends; and (4) the decentralization of voter information to local campaign workers supported by mobile apps on mobile phones. There have also been unsubstantiated reports claiming that 'psychographic profiles' that can predict the hidden political leanings of all American adults were used in the 2016 Ted Cruz and Donald Trump campaigns.[142] There have been similar media uses in Canada, the UK, and Australia, although they have not been successful in Europe due to stronger traditions of data protection and privacy.

There are two interesting books on this topic. In *The Victory Lab: The Secret Science of Winning Campaigns*, the journalist Sasha Issenberg noted that US election politics had become a $6 billion per year industry, with randomized controlled field trials used to improve results.[143] One interesting example involved bulk emails seeking to induce certain citizens to vote. In the USA, whether or not one voted is typically a matter of public record. Election consultants worked for years to figure out different email wordings that would have the most effect on their target voters, ultimately settling on 'carrots' rather than 'sticks', thanking individuals for having voted in the most recent election, and looking forward to their support in the next election.

Professor Eitan Hersh's *Hacking the Electorate: How Campaigns Perceive Voters* cast a broader net, postulating a 'perceived voter model' as the predicted voter's 'likely partisan support, issue support, turnout likelihood, [and] persuadability'.[144] He stressed that such knowledge is not certain, but that campaigns use rough heuristics, based on public (big) data sources, including voting history, race, and place of residence, to make reasonable estimates. These estimates guide strategic decisions as to what to emphasize in speeches, locations to visit, whom to mail, and what to say in the mailings. The Obama campaign made extensive use of such techniques.

Research: Compare and contrast the use of social media in the campaigns of Barack Obama and Donald Trump.

Research: The use of bots in election campaigns.

Book report: Harfoush, Rahaf (2009). *Yes We Did: An Inside Look at How Social Media Built the Obama Brand*. New Riders.

Book report: Hersh, Eitan D. (2015). *Hacking the Electorate: How Campaigns Perceive Voters*. Cambridge University Press.

Book report: Issenberg, Sasha (2012). *The Victory Lab: The Secret Science of Winning Campaigns*. Broadway Books.

Field Study: Choose a recent political campaign of significance, and interview individuals involved in the social media aspects of the campaign on both sides. Try to understand what effects the social media had.

5.9 E-government

Our final topic flows naturally from our discussion of e-democracy—the use of IT to foster citizen engagement and a more vibrant civil society. Technology is also helpful to those who govern; practices of this kind go by the name *e-government*. We shall focus on ways in which government uses digital technologies to inform and consult with its citizens.

There has been much information dissemination, but relatively little consultation. Andrew Chadwick and Christopher May, in an early review of e-government in the USA, UK, and the EU, argued that there were three basic models: the 'managerial', the 'consultative', and the 'participatory'.[145] The managerial model views information and communication technologies (ICTs) largely as 'a quantitative improvement on previous technologies'. The consultative model views technology as a vehicle for 'facilitat[ing] the communication of citizen opinion to government'. The participatory model seeks the goal of 'deliberation, participation and enhanced democracy'. The authors concluded that the managerial model had until then been dominant. Recently, though, there has been more consultation and participation, such as using contests, wikis, social networking, and social voting to solicit innovative ideas from citizens.[146] For example, the city of San Francisco allows complaints to be submitted via Twitter.[147]

The most compelling use of social media by governments is during crisis situations ranging from mild problems such as malfunctioning traffic lights to catastrophic events such as natural disasters. Citizens in Arlington, Virginia, make use of social media announcements of major weather issues, traffic problems, and the crowds and rallies that often happen in and near Washington, DC.[148] Crowdsourced information has been used by governments after the Haiti earthquake in January 2010 and the Japanese tsunami in March 2011 to guide humanitarian assistance and disaster relief.[149] Report verification was a critical challenge. Social media were used by the Queensland Police during heavy Australian rains and flooding at the end of 2010.[150] An analysis of tweeting and retweeting behaviour of 238 governmental Twitter accounts dealing with the Deepwater Oil Spill of April 2010 found interesting ways in which information was disseminated to the public, and the conversational nature of official posts.[151]

One of the best ways in which e-government can measure its success is in demonstrating transparency and in establishing trust. There are cases in which ICT-enabled efforts have demonstrated transparency to citizens, suggesting that corruption would be reduced; examples include Korean efforts to streamline civil applications, India's putting rural property records online, and Pakistan's use of ICT to minimize personal contact between citizens and tax officials to reduce the odds of extortion.[152] Caroline Tolbert and Karen Mossberger asserted that achieving trust is required for government to be both transparent and responsible.[153] Using data from the Pew Internet and American Life project, their analysis demonstrated that visiting a local government website was associated with enhanced trust in that government, although this did not hold true for US state or federal governments. In most cases, however, visiting the websites did correlate with enhanced perceptions of government transparency, effectiveness, accessibility, and responsiveness.

Government as tweetocracy

Clearly, there are constructive uses of social media in democratic societies, at their best linking government and citizens and enhancing public discourse. Yet not all uses are positive. Consider US President Donald Trump's behaviour on Twitter. As early as 2009, long before coming onto the political stage in 2015, Trump developed a style of making important announcements and lashing out at critics and opponents by tweeting.[154] During the 2016 presidential campaign against Hillary Clinton, his tweets proved to be a cost-effective way of getting his message out, as they were often picked up by mainstream print and television media.[155]

However, after he was elected, the tweets got even more bizarre. Here are some examples from late 2016 and the first half of 2017:[156–7]

- the USA should 'strengthen and expand its nuclear forces';
- there will be a new system to ensure competition in the drug industry, causing pharmaceutical stocks to plummet;
- numerous tweets berating the press, often calling the media 'the enemy of the American people';
- a series of tweets repeating an unsubstantiated conservative talk radio report that the Obama government had wiretapped candidate Trump;
- 'China [is] a currency manipulator';
- 'China is working with us on the North Korean problem'; and

- an incredible video depicting him in a wrestling arena attacking a man with a CNN logo superimposed on his head.

Trump has also used Twitter to publicly challenge a government employee who retweeted a visual report comparing the size of the crowds at his and Obama's inaugurations. One recent analysis of Trump's behaviour pointed out that the prevalence of demeaning remarks speaking about and directed toward women is designed to tap into the anger of men threatened by women in power; another analysis suggested that his primary goal was to achieve ongoing and constant attention—the total domination of mindshare.[158]

Given that the Twitter medium was until recently limited to 140 characters (now extended to 280 characters), it is a poor choice for political communications, which require nuance. But President Trump is not a person with a knack for nuance—he often negates his word choice with overuse of quotations, indicating that he is 'just kidding' and that one need not take the words too seriously.[159] This behaviour, and especially his frequent threats against leaders and countries he does not like, does not portray leadership and statesmanship, and has cast doubts around the world on American credibility.[160] Consequences could be disastrous, as serious international incidents could arise from impulsive ranting in place of carefully considered statements crafted with detail and nuance. The only humorous side of this has been some speculation that Twitter should suspend his account for abusive behaviour.[161]

Unfortunately, others have begun to emulate his thoughtless and irresponsible behaviour. One notable example is Elon Musk, CEO of Tesla.[162]

Research: How various leaders who are not Donald Trump use social media.

5.10 Summary

Computer scientists have occasionally envisioned a better future through connecting individuals, and through the use of community networks for citizen engagement. Yet visions of our future as citizens have primarily been negative, often conjured up by dystopian science fiction novels. A central issue in such portrayals is the extent to which governments allow, encourage, discourage, or forbid free speech.

All governments, even totalitarian ones, pay lip service to free speech, but democratic societies hold it as a core value. Yet even liberal societies are troubled by certain kinds of internet speech that they view as: offensive to community standards, for example, obscenity or material posing a threat to children; demonstrating contempt and hate for individuals or groups belonging to a particular race, nationality, or religion, and often inciting others to violence against these groups; challenging the authority of the state; and, more recently, promoting terrorism.

The legal scholar Cass Sunstein gave a list of examples illustrating that free speech is 'not an absolute', and that even the US government regulates speech that creates:[11]

> computer viruses, unlicensed medical advice, attempted bribery, perjury, criminal conspiracies... threats to assassinate the president, blackmail... criminal solicitation... child pornography, violations of the copyright law, false advertising...

and more. The key issue, he argued, in regulation's appropriateness is that government remain 'neutral' among points of view, not forbidding speech just because it disagrees with the speaker's politics.

Governments have long reacted to undesirable speech when it appears in traditional media, both print and broadcast. Restrictions to internet speech viewed as inappropriate have varied across the world, with huge differences among countries in the degree to which they impose censorship.

Furthermore, hundreds of thousands of complaints about such content are received each week by Google, Facebook, and Twitter.[163] Therefore, in addition to censorship by government, social media firms that provide the internet's communications media often see just cause in removing and preventing speech that many people view as harmful.

Christopher Yoo analysed the trade-offs between 'traditional' media such as broadcast and cable TV exercising editorial discretion and the government deciding what speech should or should not be permitted.[164] He argued that it is better for private intermediaries (network, hardware, or software providers) to make these decisions rather than to have the government impose restrictions on free speech. Jilian York and Robert Faris agreed, presenting examples from Australia and other 'Western' countries of actual or contemplated governmental filtering of blacklisted sites that they viewed as undesirable because of lack of transparency and oversight.[165]

On the other hand, Trevor Timm and Jillian York argued that private censorship was undesirable, as it is not necessarily principled, and often motivated by threats of legal action, or bullying from some branch of government.[166] They cited examples of censorship or the threat thereof, causing what is known as the 'Streisand effect', in which what one wants to suppress gains far more publicity and is seen by far more people than if it were ignored. They summarized their position by quoting US Supreme Court Justice Oliver Wendell Holmes:

> the best test of truth is the power of the thought to get itself accepted in the competition of the market, and that truth is the only ground upon which their wishes safely can be carried out.

Journalist Jessica Lessin agreed, stating:[167]

> I'm not comfortable trusting the truth to one gatekeeper that has a mission and a fiduciary duty to increase advertising revenue, especially when revenue is tied more to engagement than information.

Daphne Keller, previously Associate General Counsel to Google, also agreed:[168]

> making private companies curtail user expression in important public forums—which is what platforms like Twitter and Facebook have become—is dangerous. The proposed laws would harm free expression and information access for journalists, political dissidents and ordinary users. Policy makers should... not pretend that Silicon Valley has silver-bullet technology that can purge the internet of extremist content without taking down important legal speech with it.

What do you think? If someone must be the censor, who should it be, government or industry?

A recent example of the battle between those who would silence individuals for 'good cause', and those who insist on the right of expression of unpopular views by unpopular people, is the 2017 case of *Packingham v. North Carolina*, in which the issue is:[169]

> Whether, under the court's First Amendment precedents, a law that makes it a felony for any person on the state's registry of former sex offenders to 'access' a wide array of websites... that enable communication, expression, and the exchange of information among their users, if the site is 'know[n]' to allow minors to have accounts, is permissible, both on its face and as applied to petitioner, who was convicted based on a Facebook post in which he celebrated dismissal of a traffic ticket, declaring 'God is Good'!

Perry Grossman analysed the importance of this case in terms of historical precedents such as the Nazis.[170] He argued that the Nazi era demonstrated how failure to speak out early when there is repression of unpopular groups allows tyranny to gain strength and ultimately repress other groups as well, and that such precedents are especially significant in the age of President Trump. The US Supreme Court ultimately struck down the law, stating in its decision that the law went too far in barring access to 'what for many are the principal sources for knowing current events, checking ads for employment, speaking and listening in the modern public square, and otherwise exploring the vast realms of human thought and knowledge'.[171]

In addition to the challenge of how much freedom a society allows for the expression of ideas that are viewed by many as obscene, offensive, seditious, or threatening, we are now challenged by the dangerous speech of fake news. This became particularly salient during the 2016 US presidential campaign; much of it was used to smear Hillary Clinton. The effect of fake news was magnified by filter bubbles which resulted from social media personalization algorithms, and by the echo chambers caused by sharing of misguiding and often times false news among right-wing believers. Similar phenomena are now being experienced in other parts of the world. As a result, Facebook and other companies are hiring more human internet content moderators and developing machine learning approaches to identify and combat the spread of fake news.

Internet speech as the expression of citizen engagement is part of e-democracy. Numerous communities have experienced and benefited from such activity. Citizens engaged via IT often feel more connected to others and more at home in their community. Usually, those who begin as the most politically involved are the ones who participate most actively in e-democracy. Yet large-scale interconnectedness can mobilize participation that seeks and achieves significant political change.

The internet has increasingly become a key tool in elections. e-campaigning became prominent in the USA with the presidential primary campaign of Howard Dean in 2004, was turned into a fine art by Barack Obama in 2008, and was also used well by Donald Trump and Bernie Sanders in 2016. It has also been important in elections across the world. One troubling aspect is the increasing use of big data and digital surveillance to target certain voters with tailored and manipulative messages.

In parallel with developments in e-democracy, which is technology for the governed, there have been developments in e-government, technology for those who govern. There are increasing instances where tech-based communications have been positive, informing citizens of events, opportunities, and requirements, and in some cases even consulting with and recruiting citizen suggestions. A notable case of governmental technology (in this case, Twitter) abuse is the uncontrolled penchant of President Trump to lash out invectively at opponents and spew half-baked ideas that are both harmful and dangerous to American and global stability.

Thus, there have been, and continue to be, important strides in the use of the internet as a vehicle for speech, ICTs as an instrument of political action, and social media for good government, yet all of this is now in danger because of the virulent phenomenon of fake news.

5.11 Key terms

1973 case of *Miller v. California*
1984
2017 case of *Packingham v. North Carolina*
Animal Farm
Anonymity
Big data
Blacksburg Electronic Village (BEV)
Brave New World
Cass Sunstein
Child Online Protection Act (COPA) of 1998
Children's Internet Protection Act (CIPA) of 2000
Communications Decency Act (CDA) of 1996
Confirmation bias
Cybercascades
Deep fakes
Digital pandemics
Dystopian fiction
e-campaigning
Echo chambers
E-democracy / civic tech
E-government
E-mobilization
Facebook
Fake news
Fake videos
Filter bubbles
Free speech
Hate speech
Internet content moderator
Minnesota e-Democracy Project
Netville
Panopticon
Pornography
Pseudonymity
Social capital
The Great Chinese Firewall
Tweetocracy
Utopian fiction
Voter surveillance
Yes We Can! campaign

6

Law and order, war and peace

Most computers during the Second World War, such as the British code-breaking Colussus machine,[1] had been developed for military use. The effects on *law and order* and *war and peace* of computerization, worldwide telecommunications, social media, artificial intelligence (AI), and robotics is the topic of Chapter 6. As in Chapter 5, the most compelling visions of the potential opportunities and dangers have been in science fiction and in film; we begin the chapter by reviewing some memorable examples.

We then discuss how technology is used by the police, such as the use of video evidence to sometimes exonerate the police against false accusations of needless brutality. We also examine how citizens are using social media to protect themselves and alert others to what they believe is unwarranted violence or unjust actions by law enforcement. We expand upon Section 5.7's discussion of citizen mobilization by social media with the goal of regime change.

In this context, we discuss how the government (especially police and security services) gains leverage via the surveillance of the digital information and communications of citizens. This surveillance has significantly increased due to security concerns post-9/11. We will examine these developments in the USA, Canada, and the UK, as well as in other parts of the world. We shall also discuss cases of organizations trying to subvert societies that repress and forbid access to the internet, with the goal of enabling its citizens to access the internet freely.

Next, we consider ways in which tools of *digital disruption* are used by a country or government or a set of individuals against others. The timely and current case study explored is on governmental use of hacking and other aggressive digital means to interfere with the electoral processes of another country, or even to disrupt or destabilize the other country. At the extreme, governments engage in *cyberterrorism* or even *cyberwarfare*. We shall discuss several recent examples of this and argue that weapons of cyberwarfare could be as catastrophic as nuclear or biological weapons.

The technology of warfare has also evolved. We shall consider the increasing use of drones and other aerial vehicles with no person inside as tools of combat, and issues such as the extent to which their destructive force can be directed precisely at those for which the force is intended. We shall also discuss the emergence of more general kinds of semi-autonomous or autonomous weapons. In the limit, we will have 'robot soldiers', a development with laudable motivations but also troubling implications.

Will the need for security trump civil liberties, akin to the Orwellian state theorized in *1984*? Will the world be rocked by more and more ruthless cyberassaults? How are advances in AI changing the nature of warfare? Will our human troops no longer need to battle one another? If this happens, will the world be a better place? Can we prevent an arms race in autonomous smart weapons? What are the ethical implications of warfare where decisions are increasingly in the hands of algorithms, and not sentient soldiers?

6.1 Visions and nightmares

Robot police, killer cyborgs, and computer overlords have been prominent in science fiction.

A somewhat hopeful vision of all-powerful machines acting for the common good was featured in the *Colossus* science fiction trilogy (1966, 1974, and 1977), and in a 1970 Hollywood film called *Colossus: The Forbin Project*.[2] The US nuclear defence computer, also named Colossus, collaborated with a comparable Soviet machine (Guardian) to declare and enforce world peace by assuming total control.

In 1982, Ridley Scott's very successful film *Blade Runner* portrayed a *film noir* world in which 'replicants', synthetic humans bio-engineered to provide labour for off-world colonies, stage a rebellion and return to Earth.[3] 'Blade runners' are employed to forcibly 'retire' the bionic insurgents. The question of how to distinguish between replicants and humans is central to the plot.

The Terminator

In 1984, director James Cameron released the film of the extremely popular *Terminator* franchise.[4] The premise is the battle between the nearly extinct human race and Skynet, a 'Global Digital Defense Network' that has become self-aware and decided to eliminate all humans as they pose a security threat to the programme. 'Terminators' are autonomous cyborgs built by Skynet and charged with the mission of killing humans.

Figure 6.1 A Terminator Model 101 T-800 in action in the second film of the series
ScreenProd / Photononstop / Alamy Stock Photo

Continuing these themes was the 1987 *Robocop* film series.[5] Robocop was a police officer who had been killed and was 'brought back to life' as a cyborg policeman and killing machine.

In the real world, as the preceding paragraphs were being written in 2017, the world seemed to face a possible nuclear confrontation between the tempestuous and erratic US President Donald Trump and the inexperienced North Korean dictator Kim Jong-un. Happily, the threat appeared to have subsided by 2018, yet the use of digital technology in maintaining law and order, and in provoking the tension between war and peace, has continued to accelerate.

Research: Humans behaving inhumanely, and machines exhibiting humanity, in science fiction literature and film.

6.2 Use of social media by the police and in dealing with the police

As we have seen in Chapter 5, IT is routinely used by governments to communicate and engage with their citizens. Correspondingly, citizens can use technology to facilitate civic action. Most occurrences of this are relatively benign. However, the use of IT becomes more delicate when the government department involved is the police.

Surveys and reports in the mid-2010s indicated that 80 per cent of law enforcement professionals and 95 per cent of agencies were actively using social media.[6] Some critics have charged that departments use social media for 'image-conscious brand[ing]', portraying themselves 'at ease with, or even beloved by their community', especially during times in which allegations of *police brutality* were dominant issues in the community. For example, there is the Seattle Police Department's interactive map that shows responses to 911 incident calls, police reports, and crime statistics.[7]

Yet there are uses of social media that enable novel crime-fighting opportunities.[7] A Nevada county police department created a 'social media community watch' programme. In Toronto, police use social media in its citizen tip Crime Stoppers programme. The New York Police Department uses social media to garner advance warnings of events that might require police response and for criminal investigations. Their Juvenile Justice Division uses social media to monitor local neighbourhood gangs. After Philadelphia, Minneapolis, and Milwaukee experienced several violent incidents in 2010 and 2011, their police departments began monitoring social media to help forestall similar occurrences. Police are using social media during riots, and in post-riot investigations and community outreach. One case was in Vancouver, British Columbia, when the Vancouver Canucks' loss to the Boston Bruins in the June 2011 Stanley Cup hockey finals resulted in separate riots beginning almost concurrently in two separate areas of the town.

There are other examples of police using social media.[8] A sexual predator who attempted to lure a teenage boy over several social media apps was ultimately apprehended. A series of tweets helped Toronto Police catch a stabbing assailant in 2013. There are now specialized social media monitoring programmes specifically for law enforcement, such as Media Sonar in Hamilton, Ontario, and LifeRaft in Halifax, Nova Scotia. There is even now an annual Social Media in Law Enforcement (SMILE) conference attended by representatives from over 150 police departments across the world.

Social media pose challenging issues of *free speech* for the police. They are concerned that the content on their websites reflects their desired image; it should help to achieve goals such as building bridges within the community. For example, when a Toronto police officer posted on his personal Instagram account photos of himself with a battering ram and a bomb, he gave the impression that he was glorifying violence.[9] The Minneapolis Police Department website contained numerous instances of hostile and racist comments that enraged local citizens.[10] Lawyer Alysha J. Bohanon discussed various legal approaches to balancing free speech with editorial control. She noted that free speech protection applies even if the speech is 'tasteless, trivial, or objectionable'; for sites or profiles viewable by the masses, the 'public forum' dictates that the speech should receive high First Amendment protection. Yet the 'government speech' doctrine does not afford the same First Amendment protection for speech made for the government. She proposed a 'separable speech' category to better judge government social media sites.

An interesting situation developed in San Francisco in summer 2011. A Bay Area Rapid Transit (BART) police officer shot a homeless man who was allegedly behaving erratically and threatening violence. A week later, a July demonstration at a BART station during rush hour resulted in the shutdown of several trains. Another demonstration was planned for August. To mute the effects of the demonstration, BART shut down mobile phone service at several points. Despite protests that BART had unconstitutionally suppressed free speech, the agency maintained that its actions were necessary as there was 'a clear and present danger' to public safety, which has been established as a sufficient condition for denying free speech by the Supreme Court in 1919. Lawyer Mirae Yang argued that BART's actions set a dangerous precedent and were ultimately ineffective, and that the British government had considered, debated, and ultimately correctly rejected this procedure in a case with more serious riots.[11]

Digital camera technology can now be used by citizens to watch and record police behaviour. This is not new. In 1991, an American taxi driver named Rodney King was viciously beaten by four Los Angeles policemen; the incident was filmed by a bystander and shown worldwide on new media.[12] When the officers were acquitted, the six-day 1992 Los Angeles riots began; sixty-three people were killed and 2,400 were injured. What is new is that the technology can also be used by police in the form of *body-cams* strapped to their uniforms or worn on their foreheads, or *dash-cams* on the dashboards of police vehicles, to document their innocence in case brutality is alleged. This has caused major contention in the USA because of several high-profile police shootings of unarmed black youth, as well as disproportionate shootings of individuals of colour. A new political movement called *Black Lives Matter* began in 2012,[13] after community watch member George Zimmerman shot unarmed 17-year-old African-American *Trayvon Martin*.[14] Zimmerman was not brought to trial for a long time; when he finally was, he was acquitted of second-degree murder and manslaughter.

Similar incidents fuelled anger in the black community.[15] The 2014 shooting of *Michael Brown*, another unarmed 18-year-old black man, in Ferguson, Missouri, triggered days of both peaceful protest and civil unrest after a grand jury decided not to indict Darren Wilson, the police officer responsible for his death. Independent estimates by the *Guardian* and *Washington Post* put the number of black individuals killed by police in the USA in 2015 at 306 and 258, respectively. A survey of eighteen US academic studies of police and racial bias confirmed the existence of bias and/or the excessive use of force by white police officers against black individuals suspected (but not proven) of wrongdoing.[16]

The Ferguson police department had a supply of body-cams, but Officer Wilson was not wearing one when he encountered Michael Brown.[14] Within three days of Brown being shot, observers recorded video with camera phones of the shooting of two black men, Philando Castile in Minnesota and Alton Sterling in Louisiana, followed by an ambush in Dallas that left five police officers dead.[17] The Minnesota video was posted on Facebook and viewed over 5 million times in the first thirty-six hours. Despite video evidence of overreaction on the part of the policeman, he was found not guilty of second-degree manslaughter.[18]

In the Louisiana case, policemen can be seen shouting epithets, tasering, and tackling Sterling.[19] Ultimately, Sterling was shot and killed. Although the US Justice Department and the Louisiana Attorney General refused to intervene, the city eventually fired the policemen. In a 2018 police shooting death of a black man, Stephon Clarke, in Sacramento, California, the *New York Times* analysed the footage from two police body-cams and one heat-sensing helicopter camera; they found several questionable split-second decisions by the officers and Clarke; they also noted that in fifteen such recent high-profile cases resulting in the deaths of black men, only one officer was now facing prison time.[20]

Police body-cams

Over 50% of larger US police departments have adopted or are testing police body-cams; some have released videos of police heroism to improve their public image.[21] A study of the increasing use of police body-cams in Australia and the USA concluded that their use could yield greater accountability, transparency, and fairness, and ultimately create more positive interactions between the police and the public, but only if the officers did not have the discretion to turn the cameras on and off as they saw fit.[22] Controlled experiments in three UK and US cities showed that police who wore body cameras used far less force and received fewer complaints than those who did not wear cameras.[23] Yet another study of 2,000 police officers in the state of Washington showed no difference in the use of force and in civilian complaints between the police wearing and not wearing body-cams.[24]

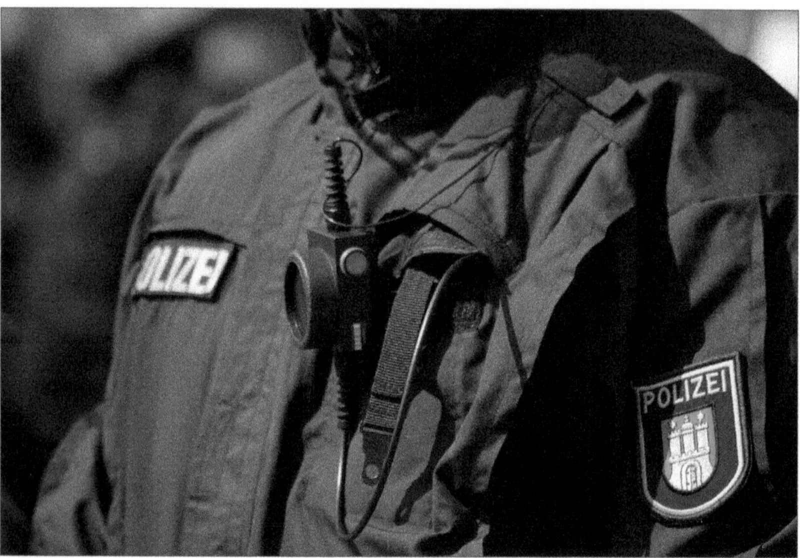

Figure 6.2 A German policeman wearing a body-cam

The International Association of Chiefs of Police reported study results in 2014 that 50% of complaints against the police were dropped when video evidence was introduced; in cases that proceeded, 93% of police officers were cleared of charges after the evidence was introduced.[23] Media coverage of video evidence is also helping sensitize the USA to issues of police violence.[25] Body-cam video is part of a larger change to jurisprudence, including the increasing use of visual technologies such as digitally enhanced photos, computer animation, and multimedia displays.[26] Despite the difficulties in interpreting video evidence in three trials in which police were ultimately acquitted,[27] the potential of the technology was well expressed by the New York Times Editorial Board:[27]

The hope was that the cameras would bring transparency to the policing process, allowing the public to see how officers do their jobs. Misconduct could be recorded, and the devices could also provide evidence to exonerate officers who are falsely accused of misconduct.

There are, of course, privacy issues,[22,23] which we shall discuss in Chapter 9.

Research: The increasing use by the justice system of visual technologies such as dashboard and body-cams, digitally enhanced photos, computer animation, and multimedia displays.

Policy: Draft a brief for the police chief of a city dealing with tasteless or offensive content on her website.

Debate: Resolved: Being a police officer is stressful enough without having your every action recorded on video.

Law: Draft a law ensuring that police officers will always wear body cameras and never turn them off while on duty.

6.3 Citizen mobilization via social media for regime change

A good example of the political power of the internet is the *Arab Spring of 2011*, especially in the North African countries of Tunisia and Egypt. Telecommunications infrastructure for connectivity was growing rapidly in the Arab world; 40 to 45 million people were already online in sixteen Arab countries by 2009; 100 million Arabs were expected to be online by 2015.[28] Government ministers in Jordan were online. Yet, as discussed in Section 5.4, governments in the Middle East were threatened by the internet; they used many methods to suppress online speech. Jeffrey Ghannam best summarized the situation at the end of 2010 in thirteen Middle Eastern countries with respect to internet and social media use: for each country, he noted the numbers of 'bloggers threatened, arrested, or released' by the government.[28] The worst situations were in Egypt and Tunisia, where the numbers were thirty-one and thirteen, respectively.

Internet telecommunications were part of a new system of political communication that challenged the historic legacy of authoritarian repression.[29] Three factors were salient: satellite TV transmission from channels such as Al-Jazeera; the rapidly increasing use of the internet; and the expanding capabilities of mobile phones coupled with the decreasing costs of use.

The literal and figurative spark of the Arab Spring was the self-immolation of Tunisian fruit vendor Mohamed Bouazizi on 17 December 2010. The protests that began there were a long-simmering response to food price inflation, a high unemployment rate, and lack of political freedoms.[30,32] The uprising was fuelled by the use of streaming media to document the events, and by the extensive use of Twitter for coordination, information dissemination, and discussion. The result was striking, as within one month, on 14 January 2011, President Zine El Abidine Ben Ali resigned.

The Arab Spring in Egypt

By February 2010, more than 21% of Egypt's population of 80 million had access to the internet, more than 5% used Facebook, and more than 70% used a mobile phone.[29] Political activists had been engaged in online discussions and debates since 2009.[31] A mass Egyptian protest against the thirty-year dictatorial rule of President Hosni Mubarak was ignited in part by the Tunisian situation and erupted on 25 January 2011. As in Tunisia, there were long-simmering concerns about high unemployment, government corruption, and lack of political freedoms. The eighteen-day protest saw mass gatherings, especially in Tahrir Square in the heart of Cairo, Egypt's capital.

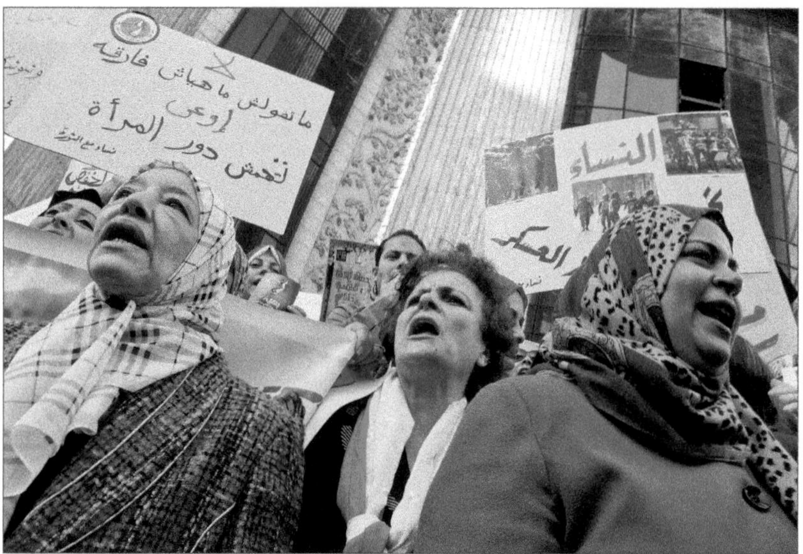

Figure 6.3 Arab Spring protesters in 2011
Megapress / Alamy Stock Photo

There was intense social media activity within the country to organize protests, and outside the country to garner international support. Worldwide knowledge of the events accelerated as roughly half of the participants in the protest shared visuals of the events over the internet.[29] The government countered by arresting bloggers;[30] Egyptian security services began to monitor social media to develop a counter-insurgency strategy. Mubarak cut off internet and mobile phone communications on 28 January in an attempt to quell the rebellion. This resulted in even more intense social media activity, and the subverting of the attempts to shut down communication. Ultimately, Mubarak resigned on 11 February.

Information flowed via the tweeting and retweeting of Tunisian messages between 12 and 19 January 2011, and Egyptian messages between 24 and 29 January 2011.[31] News was co-constructed in messages among various actor types, most prominently journalists, news organizations, bloggers, and activists. An analysis of Egyptian political websites, political conversations in the Tunisian blogosphere, and more than 3 million relevant tweets concluded that Facebook, Twitter, and YouTube were directly used to put pressure on the governments; social media conversations about liberty, democracy, and revolution often just preceded mass protests and helped spread these ideas internationally.[33] For example, in the week before Mubarak's resignation, the rate of tweets from Egypt and the rest of the world about political change in Egypt rose from 2,300 a day to 230,000 a day. Online celebrations and commiseration often followed a major event. For instance, there were 2,200 tweets from Algeria, Bahrain, Egypt, Morocco, and Yemen concerning Tunisia on the day Ben Ali resigned. It was a kind of 'freedom meme', fuelled by videos going viral across the world.[32]

Academic, journalist, and activist Zeynep Tufekci has analysed the use of social media in what she terms 'networked protests' including those against the World Trade Organization in Seattle in 1999, the Arab Spring in early 2011, the Occupy Movement later in 2011, and an uprising in Turkey in spring 2013.[33] Although praising 'the ability to cheaply and easily connect on a global scale', she cautions that 'a lack of organizational depth and experience, of tools and culture for collective decision-making and strategic, long-term action', as well as an inability to execute 'agile tactical shifts at great speeds', coupled with government tools of surveillance and repression, means that social media is no magic bullet to bring about change in the world.

Research: Analyse and discuss political dissent and mobilization via social media in countries that were not part of the Arab Spring.

Book review: Tufekci, Zeynep (2017). *Twitter and Tear Gas: The Power and Fragility of Networked Protest.* Yale University Press.

6.4 Surveillance by government

As we have seen, when the safety of the population seems threatened, or when a government feels threatened, it will use surveillance, mostly using digital technologies, to monitor the population and to stop and punish hostile acts. This surveillance raises practical, social, policy, and ethical concerns.

In early 2016 there was a signature case that resulted in a confrontation between the US Federal Bureau of Investigation (FBI) and Apple Inc.[34] The FBI had possession of an iPhone owned by the perpetrator of a mass shooting in San Bernardino, California. The encrypted data on the phone was thought to contain critical information that could help understand the shooting. Apple maintained that it would have to write new software to bypass the encryption; it used a 'due process' argument to fight the federal court order requiring it to provide the FBI with access to the phone. This was unusual, as such fights were typically based on free speech arguments. Eventually, the FBI found its own way to defeat the encryption,[35] but the fundamental issues of the situation were not resolved.

Tension between the need for security, especially against terrorism, and the commitment to basic human rights, such as privacy in a free society, is key to these ethical and legal dilemmas.

Surveillance, security, and privacy in Canada

Issues were outlined in a National Security Green Paper and Background Document from the Government.[36] It discussed challenges that must be met to achieve greater security against terrorism: Canadian youth should not become 'radicalized to violence'; threats to security must be neutralized; airline passengers need to be protected; known terrorist agencies need to be listed publicly; terrorist financing needs to be disrupted; terrorist use of digital technologies needs to be countered by intercepting communications and subverting encryption; anti-terrorism measures need to be embodied in the Criminal Code; and national security information should not be needlessly disclosed publicly, even though it often should be shared among government departments and with agencies of other nations.

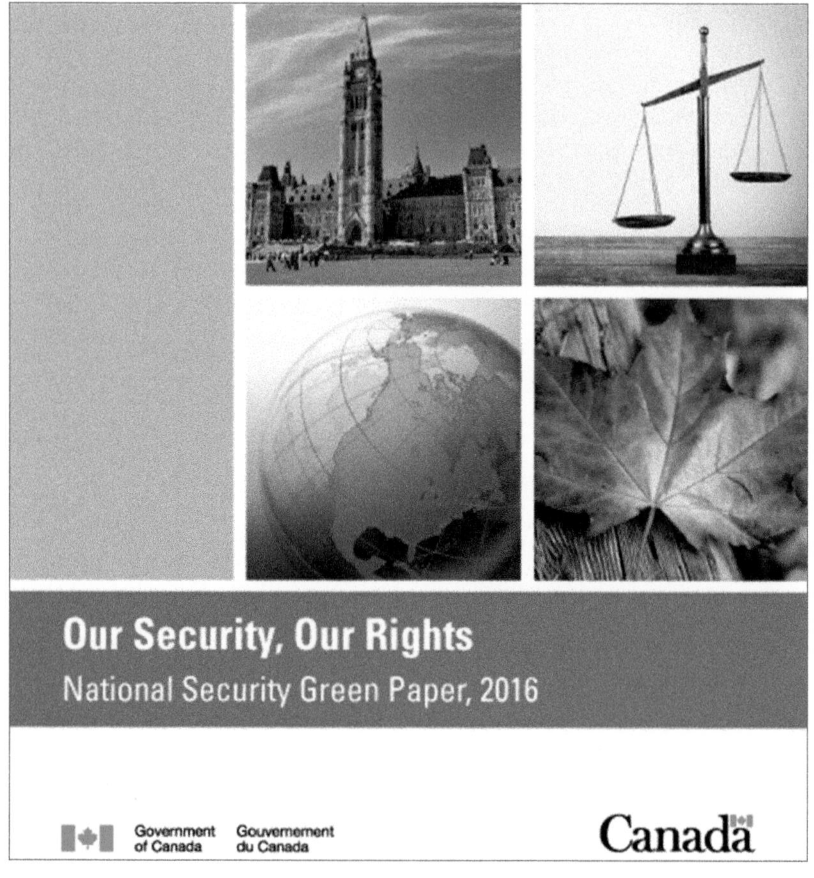

Figure 6.4 Canadian National Security Green Paper

Government of Canada (2016), *Our Security, Our Rights: National Security Green Paper*.

The main concern of the Green Paper is protecting the rights of Canadian citizens. Embedded in the Canadian Constitution and the Charter of Rights and Freedoms, previously discussed in Chapter 5, these include freedoms of expression and association, rights to equality and privacy, and a guarantee of the presumption of innocence until proven guilty. Security and rights often seem to conflict with these values. The Canadian Security Intelligence Service (CSIS) argued that it is committed to enabling these values to co-exist. Typically, if actions by CSIS or by the federal police force—the Royal Canadian Mounted Police (RCMP)—would threaten Charter rights, a warrant from the Federal Court is required. Actions by CSIS and the RCMP are also governed by a series of parliamentary laws including the Criminal Code and the Privacy, Secure Air Travel, Anti-Terrorism, and Proceeds of Crime (Money Laundering) and Terrorist Financing Acts.

These issues were addressed in 2017 by a Canadian Broadcasting Corporation article series triggered by a federal review of the Anti-Terrorism Act and consultations over the Green Paper that had recommended expansion of police investigative powers.[37] The RCMP gave examples of investigations where they believed they had been slowed by legal obstacles. Examples included a report of a father's child abuse allegedly recorded on a locked phone; internet communications of suspected terrorist recruits for which the authorities lacked adequate interception capabilities, or where the communications were outside Canada and legally difficult to obtain; and alleged terrorist communications that were encrypted or where intercepting communications proved too costly. They also cited the specific case of encrypted chats by Aaron Driver, an ISIS terrorist group sympathizer who detonated a bomb in a taxi just before being shot by the police. The RCMP therefore argued the need for warrantless access to internet service provider (ISP) subscriber information. Despite concerns over terrorism, and in part because it had become known that CSIS had violated court orders in the past, 78% of Canadians consulted by a polling firm felt that warrants should be required. The RCMP also sought the power to compel individuals to hand over their passwords and encryption keys, and sought regulations stipulating increased retention of data by ISPs.

Due to the difficulty in reconciling concerns for security with preserving canadian rights and freedoms, the federal government initiated an extensive consultation with canadians in autumn 2016. Over 75,000 written submissions were received and twenty-five live public events were held. The summary report described the consensus as follows:[38]

> most participants... have opted to err on the side of protecting individual rights and freedoms rather than granting additional powers to national security agencies and law enforcement, even with enhanced transparency and independent oversight. They also want the government to focus its efforts on preventing terrorism through measures to counter radicalization to violence, including through public awareness and education campaigns to promote diversity in Canada, better support for new immigrants and at-risk groups, and addressing root causes of radicalization by improving social programs dealing with such things as health (including mental health) and housing.

What a difference from the USA! In fairness, the situation in the United States is more volatile and confrontational because that country has been and continues to be the target of much more terrorism, and the political climate is highly polarized. Despite the greater distrust of government security forces, legislation has tilted in favour of security. Immediately after the 9/11 terrorist attacks, President George W. Bush signed the *Authorization for Use of Military Force* (AUMF) and persuaded Congress to pass the overarching *USA PATRIOT* (Uniting and Strengthening America by Providing Appropriate Tools Required to Intercept and Obstruct Terrorism) *Act.*[39] The most controversial section of the Act—Title II: Surveillance Procedures—allowed for the gathering of 'foreign intelligence information' from both US and non-US citizens, and expanded the scope of legal physical surveillance and wiretapping procedures, including roving wiretaps. It also allowed for 'sneak and peak' warrants, or search warrants with delayed notification and no prior notice. Other provisions were directed at money laundering, improving border security, and allowing greater sharing of information among relevant government agencies. The Bush administration capitalized on the hysteria in the USA post-9/11, with prerogative power overriding protests over possible violations of free speech and protection against unreasonable search and seizure that would have normally derailed speedy passage of this legislation. Most of the provisions have been extended in four subsequent congressional revisits to the clauses of the PATRIOT Act, although some aspects have been abandoned.

There has been extensive debate about this legislation. Grave concerns about the constitutionality of PATRIOT Act provisions have been expressed. Law professors John W. Whitehead and Stephen H. Aden argued that many of the provisions trampled on rights including free speech and association (First Amendment), unreasonable search and seizure (Fourth Amendment), due process of law (Fifth Amendment), and trial by jury (Sixth Amendment0, as well as the right to privacy.[40] They further noted that there had emerged a substantial movement towards creation of a US national ID card, an issue we shall discuss further in Chapter 9. Law professor Susan Herman asserted that the PATRIOT Act upset the balance of powers among the three branches of the US government, increasing executive authority where the US Constitution had intended there to be congressional and judiciary safeguards.[41]

Some of these arguments have been countered in a scholarly article by law professor Oren S. Kerr, who argued that there was widespread ignorance about what the PATRIOT Act actually did. According to Kerr, the act mostly made minor adjustments to then-current laws regulating electronic surveillance, the *1996 Electronic Communications Privacy Act.*[42] He asserted that the Act 'updated the surveillance laws without substantially shifting the balance between privacy and security', and that some provisions actually expanded provisions for privacy and civil liberties. In a subsequent article, he noted that combating computer-related crime required new regulations governing the collection of digital evidence. Independent of the legal issues involved, there is no doubt that 9/11 triggered massive anxiety and counter-terrorist measures in the USA, and that security needs caused massive concern among those devoted to the preservation of American civil liberties.

Since then, there have been other revelations about US government surveillance. The *New York Times* reported that President Bush had ordered the National Security Agency (NSA) to eavesdrop on Americans and others within the USA without first obtaining warrants.[43] The White House had asked the *Times* not to publish this; the paper obliged and delayed publication by a year. Further revelations about the government's methods to protect its citizens at the cost of their freedoms came from the revelations of Edward Snowden.[44] He revealed massive global surveillance under the NSA's direction, including breaking encryption in order to examine data, email, and online transactions, all done with the help of European governments and telecommunication firms (we shall return to this in Chapter 9). It was actually President Barack Obama who ordered a telecom firm to hand over telephone records of millions of customers on an 'ongoing, daily basis', with no specification that those individuals were suspected of any wrongdoing.[45]

In one of his last actions as President, Obama had expanded the power of the NSA to share with other US intelligence agencies personal communications that it had intercepted.[46] On the other hand, the new Trump administration reduced the powers of the NSA to collect certain emails and texts sent by Americans. Furthermore, the US courts have begun to take a more sceptical view of justifications for NSA surveillance that seem to run counter to the US traditions of civil liberties. An important side issue was pointed out by law professors Joshua A. T. Fairfield and Erik Luna, who discussed cases where digital evidence had demonstrated an individual's innocence and thereby forestalled possible wrongful convictions, asserting that individuals—not solely government agencies—needed access to *big data* and other digital evidence that could help establish guilt or innocence.[47]

The United Kingdom has also moved towards policy weighing security over privacy. Snowden revealed that the NSA and the British equivalent agency, the Government Communications Head Quarters (GCHQ), had discovered how to read messages in HotMail, Google, Yahoo, and FB by planting *trapdoors*, or secret entry paths for malware, in commercial encryption software. Further revelations disclosed a massive GCHQ surveillance operation code called KARMA POLICE, which included a system called *Black Hole* that focused primarily on recording people's internet browsing histories, including visits to adult websites.[48] In addition, a system called MUTANT BROTH aided identification of internet users and the logging of their emails and instant messages. KARMA POLICE surveillance was also used to capture data about the radio listening habits of over 200,000 people in 185 countries. As Britain suffered three terrorist attacks in seventy-three days in the spring of 2017, and the new Tory Prime Minister Theresa May took over, there were further calls to limit the spread of extremist content on social media and to monitor and read internet communications from suspected terrorists.[49]

Have these surveillance measures made the citizens of Canada, the USA, and the UK any safer? Even if the answer were known, which it likely is not, it would be classified. But here is some US data that is public. Before the imposition of these stentorian measures, the USA had experienced a truck bombing in Beirut, Lebanon in 1983 with 301 fatalities; a 1993 truck bombing of the World Trade Center with 1,040 injuries; the 1998 attacks against two US embassies in Africa causing 303 fatalities; and the 9/11 assaults resulting in 2,993 fatalities.[50] Although terrorist atrocities have continued with more American deaths, such as in the Orlando nightclub shootings, the recent toll of Americans has been relatively less than the horrendous costs to citizens of Iraq, Afghanistan, Nigeria, as well as to several European countries. Did the PATRIOT Act save lives? How does one balance security and privacy in the age of aggressive fundamentalism and terrorism? We shall revisit these issues in Chapters 7 and 9.

Research: Choose two countries that interest you, either both democratic societies, or both totalitarian, or one of each. Compare and contrast how their police use surveillance to control those who it considers pose dangers to the state.

Concept: Write a Wikipedia article on 'digital innocence'.

Debate: Resolved: Given the dangers from global terrorism, we need to reduce personal privacy to ensure safety.

Policy: Write a policy brief for a member of Canada's Parliament who wants to articulate a clear position of how the country should approach the problem of national security.

Book report: Government of Canada. 'Our Security, Our Rights: National Security Green Paper + Background Document + National Security Consultations'.[36,38]

6.5 Governments restricting internet access; keeping the net open

Many totalitarian regimes do more than mere surveillance in order to strengthen their control over their populations. In Syria, the *Syrian Electronic Army* (SEA) once posted on the internet the credentials of Al-Jazeera journalists, with captured emails purporting to show their bias; in another incident, they took over and subverted Al-Jazeera's Twitter account.[51] The SEA later instituted *phishing attacks* on Syrian opposition FB and YouTube sites. Surveillance and oppression often increase after a government survives dissent or is carried out when a new government comes to power. Such was the case in Egypt, where a sophisticated and highly personalized phishing campaign was launched against ninety-two individuals and seven non-governmental organizations (NGOs) active in civil society dissent.[52]

Another case is Mexico. The *Citizen Lab* and the *New York Times* revealed the apparent use by the Mexican government of spyware tools that record every aspect of digital life on mobile phones.[53] The tools had been sold to the government under the express understanding that they only be used on terrorists, drug cartels, and criminal groups that have routinely kidnapped and killed Mexicans. Yet many of those targeted and tracked were Mexican human rights lawyers, journalists, and activists fighting government corruption, as well as an international team of investigators looking into the disappearance three years ago of forty-three students who had clashed with local Mexican police.[54]

Keeping the internet open

Some organizations seek to prevent totalitarian regimes from denying internet access for their citizens. Pioneering work of this kind has been done by the Citizen Lab of the Munk School of Global Affairs at the University of Toronto. Chapter 5 detailed the degree of censorship in many countries. Ron Deibert, Director of the Citizen Lab, explained how web filtering software can bolster autocratic regimes which engage in human rights violations, for example in Bahrain.[55] He was particularly upset as the technology used for the 'draconian' censorship was from *Netsweeper*, a Canadian company, which boasts that its technology gives client organizations 'peace of mind'.[56]

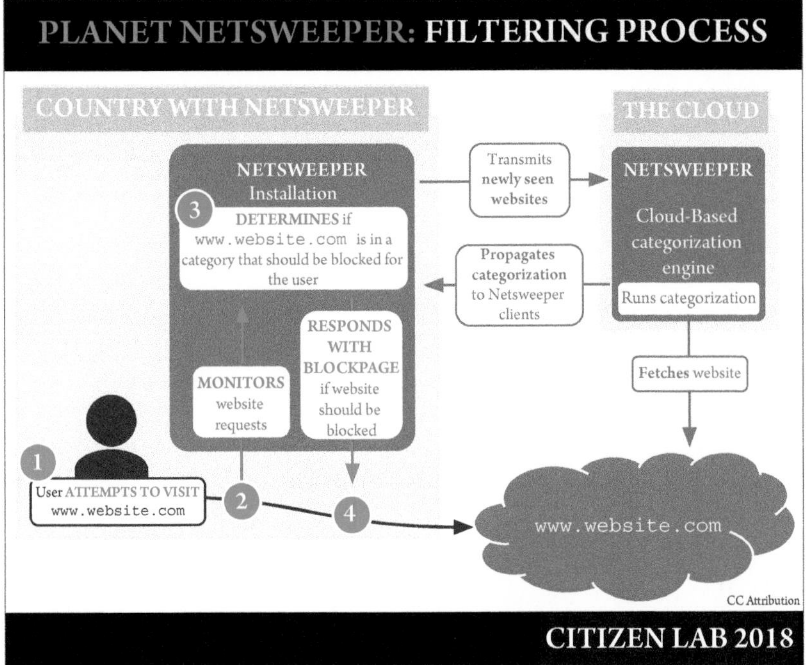

Figure 6.5 Netsweeper filtering process

Deibert's group has actively supported internet access in countries whose leaders have blocked access. One example focused on the specific case of technology and procedures seeking to deliver BBC content to the censored internet.[57] It noted that the BBC, originally a broadcast television and radio network, had long been subject to attempts at censorship by the Nazis during the Second World War, as had been the Voice of America after the Second World War via jamming techniques by the Soviet Union.

The report analysed a programme to provide web-proxy services in China and Iran, concluding that a tool to circumvent internet blocking should be treated as a new 'channel' to reach an audience. It must be deployed flexibly and quickly in real time in response to the

Continued on next page

detection of blocking. Other case studies included the 2009 Iranian election and protests, and the 2011 anniversary of the 1989 Tiananmen Square protests. This topic remains current; in late 2017, Iranian downloads of the Citizen Lab's Psiphon web access app increased almost twenty-fold because of increased governmental internet censorship.[58]

Deibert's group has also led the preparation of scholarly volumes on the topics of internet censorship, invasions of privacy, free speech repression, espionage, terrorism, and warfare using digital technologies.[59]

Research: The recent use of spyware tools by the Mexican government.

Debate: Resolved: Netsweeper is an immoral corporation.

Book report: Deibert, Ronald, John Palfrey, Rafal Rohozinski, and Jonathan Zittrain (Eds.) (2008). *Access Denied: The Practice and Policy of Global Internet Filtering*. The MIT Press.

Book report: Deibert, Ronald, John Palfrey, Rafal Rohozinski, and Jonathan Zittrain (Eds.) (2010). *Access Controlled: The Shaping of Power, Rights, and Rule in Cyberspace*. The MIT Press.

Book report: Deibert, Ronald, John Palfrey, Rafal Rohozinski, and Jonathan Zittrain (Eds.) (2011). *Access Contested: Security, Identity, and Resistance in Asian Cyberspace*. The MIT Press.

Book report: Deibert, Ronald (2017). *Black Code: Surveillance, Privacy, and the Dark Side of the Internet* (Expanded Edition). McClelland & Stewart.

6.6 Hacking another country's elections and politicians

Before discussing *cyberterrorism* and *cyberwarfare* in general, we will focus on the topic of elections. We have seen that social media may be and increasingly are used by candidates for public office both to mobilize support and to organize their activities. Yet governments can also use aggressive forms of social media hacking to interfere with elections. Russia has been much in the news in 2016 and 2017 for engaging in such efforts, thus far most notably against the USA and France.

Russian interference in the 2016 US presidential election

In March 2016, John Podesta, campaign manager for Hillary Clinton, fell prey to a phishing attack that enabled the culprit to obtain large quantities of his emails.[60] This method of impersonating a security warning from Google had already been used by a group of Russian hackers known as Fancy Bear to infiltrate the computers of journalists whose writings were deemed critical of Russia. The security of the Democratic National Committee (DNC) had also been breached as early as autumn 2015.[61] On 22 July 2016, at the height of the presidential campaign, WikiLeaks released almost 30,000 documents captured from

DNC computers.[62] This leak was highly embarrassing for the Clinton campaign; the documents contained frank discussions about her chief rival Bernie Sanders, and implied a clear bias in the DNC in favour of Clinton. In October, WikiLeaks released the first of a series of collections ultimately totalling 50,000 messages from Podesta's account. These revealed more embarrassing details about her strategy and her speeches to Wall Street.[63] Clinton eventually grew to believe that the leaks contributed to her defeat.[64]

Figure 6.6 A website dedicated to investigations of the 2016 U.S. election hacking

This leak unleashed a firestorm within the USA. It triggered a study by the three major US intelligence agencies—the Central Intelligence Agency (CIA), the FBI, and the NSA.[66] They concurred, in a January 2017 report, that Russia had influenced the US election through 'covert intelligence efforts—cyberactivity—with overt Russian government agencies, state-funded media, third-party intermediaries, and paid social media users, or, "*trolls*"'. Some of the work was done by *RT America TV*, a channel funded by the Kremlin that issues local newscasts within the USA and other countries. Although denied by Russia, the CIA and FBI asserted high confidence in the judgement of the report; the NSA expressed modest confidence. Sceptics pointed out that the report lacked sufficient detail, omitted in part because they were highly classified.[67] Yet most people felt that there was sufficient evidence to investigate the possible collusion of Republican candidate Donald Trump with the Russians, so eventually there began four US government investigations, three of which, as of mid-2018, were still under way.[65] The Committee to Investigate Russia maintains a website reviewing all developments.[65]

Through the intelligence agency study, and with more recent developments, we have uncovered the scope of Russian election hacking. Russia had perfected its techniques while previously applying them in Ukraine.[68] Social media trolls were used to spread anger, rage, and misinformation; some of these trolls were posing as Americans and in many cases the messages were amplified by hundreds of thousands of bots.[69] Politically charged ads, such as one linking Satan and Hillary Clinton, were purchased by Russian agents to air on FB and Twitter.[70] Political rallies, mostly for Trump, creating discord on hot-button issues such as immigration and race, were staged.[71] Thirteen Russians and three companies were

Continued on next page

charged by the US Justice Department early in 2018; another twelve Russians were indicted in July 2018.[72]

Much of the damage was wreaked in FB through posts and ads from fake accounts that reached 126 million Americans.[73] There is still debate about how consequential this disruptive content was, and how FB should walk the line between simply delivering content without scrutiny and overly censoring content, a tension already discussed in Chapter 5.[74] Yet the incidents were very damaging, as were ads purchased by Russians on Google and tweets from trolls operating with fake accounts on Twitter.[75] The fake accounts were made possible because neither FB nor Twitter requires solid identification when accounts are created.[76] FB has reacted by applying more human and AI scrutiny to content via *social media fact checkers*, a topic previously covered in Chapter 5, and by requiring purchasers of political ads to identify themselves and where they are located.[77] The latter policy has also been adopted by Google and Twitter.[78]

A recent report by the Citizen Lab characterized the election hacking by Russia as part of a larger campaign of Russian phishing and leaking of disinformation.[79] The campaign targeted over 200 individuals in thirty-nine countries, many of them in former states of the USSR, and included a former Russian prime minister, ambassadors, senior military officers, CEOs of energy companies, and members of civil society. Sabotaging civil society was important for the Putin regime because a vibrant civil society posed the greatest threat to his continued totalitarian dominance. RT America TV also played a key role in these activities.[80]

Analysts have suggested many reasons that motived Vladimir Putin to undertake these activities once it seemed likely that Hillary Clinton would win the US presidential election in November 2016.[66] Putin likely viewed this as a way to gain revenge against Clinton and the USA for encouraging pro-democracy protests in Russia in 2011; for promoting democracy in countries such as Ukraine and Georgia; for allegedly playing a role in the Panama Papers leak that exposed the wealth of some of Putin's closest associates; and even for exposing the widespread use of performance-enhancing drugs by many Russian athletes, even though that had been done by international authorities. More generally, Putin was distressed by the decline of Russia's 'power and pride', and sought to advance Russia's position in the world by creating 'turbulence' within the USA.[81]

WikiLeaks' significant early participation was in line with founder Julian Assange's vision of exposing hidden data that revealed 'illegal or immoral behavior' in government and big business, and forcing regime change through technology and data rather than through traditional techniques such as assassination or military intervention.[82] The leaks did indeed contribute to the passing of the torch in the USA from the Democrats to the Republicans. Zeynep Tufekci has questioned the morally superior tone of Assange, arguing that the indiscriminate dumping of masses of data did not constitute whistle-blowing in the sense of Daniel Ellsberg and the Pentagon Papers, and actually compromised the privacy not only of those in power but those who would dissent from power.[83] We shall return to issues of privacy and whistle-blowing in Chapter 9.

The Russians were also actively trying to disrupt the spring 2017 French election of a new president. A candidate with few prospects, former Prime Minister Francois Fillon, was falsely reported to be leading by the French-language service of the Russian Sputnik news operation.[84] In May 2017, just before the final vote in the French presidential election, the centrist candidate and ultimate winner Emmanuel Macron was the target of a massive hacking attack.[85] Macron was in a face-off with the far-right candidate Marine Le Pen. She was favoured by the Russians because of her stand against the European Union. The attack resulted in the release of emails and accounting records. To cause extra confusion, fake documents were interspersed among real ones.

Unlike the Clinton campaign and the DNC, or perhaps because of what happened in the USA, the French were prepared for the attack.[86] Part of their defence was a 'cyberblurring' strategy, in which they themselves created false email accounts and filled them with phony documents. Therefore, what was released by the attackers contained numerous false documents, some created by each side. The main reason there was little impact was because all of this happened only one day before a legislatively imposed media blackout for the last several days before the vote.

The Russians are also suspected of attempting to disrupt other elections and referenda, most notably the Brexit campaign of 2016. Just days before the referendum, more than 150,000 Russian-language Twitter accounts released tens of thousands of English-language messages urging the United Kingdom to leave the European Union.[87] Surprisingly, no signs of an attack were noted in the autumn 2017 German election, perhaps because of intense preparation, lack of severe polarization such as that characterizing the USA, and a 'gentlemen's agreement' among the parties not to exploit the results of an attack.[88]

As of mid-2018: (1) Brazil was preparing to avoid having its autumn 2018 election disrupted by fake news; (2) in preparation for an Irish referendum on abortion, both FB and Google banned abortion-related ads originating from outside of the country; and (3) the USA was worried about more hacking against its autumn 2018 midterm elections, as well as Russian hacking against its power grid.[89]

Research: Consider the cyber-attacks on Hillary Clinton and Emmanuel Macron. Find instances of dirty journalism spreading falsehoods against US or French political candidates in the past. Compare and contrast the cyberattacks to those done in the past.

Concept: Write a Wikipedia article on 'cyberblurring'.

6.7 Cyberespionage, cyberterrorism, and cyberwarfare

Russian actions demonstrate that election hacking is only the tip of the iceberg. Governments can use and subvert digital technologies to suppress dissidents whether they are living at home or abroad, and to battle foreign governments via espionage, terrorism, or war.

Recognizing Russia's aggressiveness, President Obama debated acting during the 2016 election campaign, but decided not to do so then. During his last days in office, he imposed some sanctions including expelling thirty-five Russians diplomats.[90] More serious measures had been considered, including exposing Putin's financial ties to oligarchs, and employing US cyberweapons to try to neutralize Russia's hacking tools.[91] The latter was not done in part out of fear that it might expose American implants in Russian networks. Russian intelligence officers were also charged early in 2017 with orchestrating a 2014 cyberattack that stole data on 500 million Yahoo! accounts, then using the information to spy on organizations including the White House, the military, banks, an airline, and two cloud computing firms.[92] New revelations continue, such as the fact that in 2015 Russians gained access to critical control systems at some US nuclear power plants.[93] These actions are further discussed in Section 7.4.

GhostNet

An earlier example was the GhostNet Chinese malware cyberespionage campaign against the Tibetan community in exile, uncovered by the University of Toronto's Citizen Lab.[94] Insecure web-based interfaces hooked up to four control servers located on China's island of Hainan were used to transmit Trojan horse software (see Chapter 7 for explanations of malware terms) to infect nearly 1,300 computers in 130 countries.

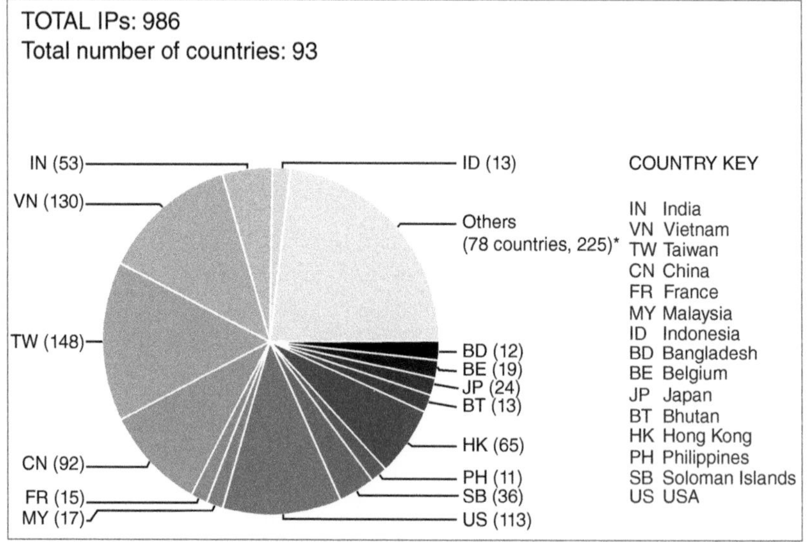

Figure 6.7 Geographic spread of hosts infected by GhostNet
"The Citizen Lab at the University of Toronto's Munk School of Global Affairs and Public Policy"

The malware entered target computers through carefully crafted messages with attachments looking like legitimate documents associated with groups involved with Tibetans in exile. Opening up such documents resulted in execution of the malicious code. Thirty per cent of the infected computers were considered high value, typically located in ministries of foreign affairs and embassies of almost twenty countries, as well as in international agencies and news organizations. Although China likely was the culprit, the report stressed that they had circumstantial evidence but not conclusive proof. The Citizen Lab later reported that the Tibetan émigré community had been trained to avoid sending or opening attachments, so a subsequent campaign against Tibetans, called the Scarlet Mimic, used different tactics. The approach this time was to use a phishing campaign designed to steal Google credentials from Tibetan activists and journalists.

Another hacking campaign linked to China included the theft of personnel data of over 4 million current and former US federal employees.[95] We shall discuss this further in Chapter 7. China's aggressiveness in the area of cyberwarfare has recently become even more threatening because of investments it has made in AI (we shall speak more of this in Chapter 11)[96] and US start-ups working on military technologies,[97] joint ventures with Western technology companies, and alleged theft of intellectual property through which it seeks superiority over the USA.[98] Part of China's strength is the growing power of its two internet software giants—Alibaba and Tencent (see Chapter 12); the two firms are rapidly expanding into more and more areas, much as Amazon has in the USA, but unlike in the USA there are no government antitrust concerns.[99] *Cyberwarfare* is also being waged in other areas of Asia, for example a recent hacking episode with an unknown culprit targeting Hong Kong democracy activists;[100] North Korean cyber-thefts and cyberattacks (see Chapter 7);[101] and US cyberattacks against the North Korean missile programme.[102]

Another area where cyberwarfare has been active is the Middle East, especially with respect to Iran. The USA and Israel jointly developed *Stuxnet*,[103] a malicious worm that caused significant damage to industrial sites including a nuclear enrichment plant in Iran, thus slowing its nuclear weapons programme.[104] Planning for this was extensive, much like a military campaign, and included building and testing the worm on a dummy Iranian nuclear enrichment plant built in the USA and having a double agent smuggle the worm into the real facility with a memory stick.[51] Paradoxically, Stuxnet also wound up infecting industrial sites in the United States. Iran responded by creating the *Shamoon virus* which infected tens of thousands of Saudi workstations.[105] More recently, Iran unleased a digital attack on the computerized controls of a small dam just north of New York City,[106] illustrating the growing expertise of its hackers, and its increasing capability to wage cyber-attacks.[107] As ISIS has also been involved in cyberwarfare, the USA and its allies have, since 2015, been stalking and killing ISIS social media experts who have been active in political hacking,[108] although the speed with which ISIS can reconstitute their cyber-weapons has frustrated the Pentagon.[109]

There is now an active business internationally in the sale of cyberespionage and cyberwarfare tools.[110] This technology has been used to wage war against another country, to suppress dissidents or disrupt the activities of journalists, to track down drug lords, and even to expose the emails of climate researchers. One of the largest players is a Milan-based firm called *Hacking Team*, founded in 2003. It positions itself as a purveyor of 'ethical malware', along with more than a dozen companies worldwide. Its *Remote Control System* software can be licensed at prices starting at US$200,000, but the cost often is higher. This technology takes control of target computers by gaining physical access to them via a Wi-Fi network, or by getting the target to click on an infected attachment or by doctoring a version of a page that the target has previously clicked on to deliver the doctored version instead. The company claims that it does not license its software to customers who commit 'gross human-rights abuses', but its customers include some of the most repressive regimes in the world, including Honduras, Ethiopia, Bahrain, Morocco, Egypt, Saudi Arabia, Sudan, Uzbekistan, and Turkey. Its clients have also included the US FBI and Drug Enforcement Agency. Fittingly, the company itself was hacked in 2015, and some of its customers, targets, and code were published by WikiLeaks.

Spy agencies within governments, for example the CIA, also develop their own technology, with techniques to break into computers, mobile phones, and smart TVs. In early 2017, WikiLeaks published thousands of pages and attachments from the CIA toolbox for hacking software such as Wi-Fi networks, Skype, PDF documents, and even anti-virus software itself.[111] Particularly notable were indications that the CIA could listen to conversations around smart TVs, and that they were studying hacking into cars so that they could crash them.[112] Whether the leaks originated in the USA or Russia is still in dispute.[113] Most analysts think the leaks were serious, although one argued they indicated that current software is more secure than heretofore believed;[114] Assange actually suggested that his actions were taken in part so that vendors of commercial software could plug their security flaws.[115]

NSA cyberweapons were also stolen, reputedly in 2013, then offered for sale over the internet, and then regularly posted on the internet since 2016 by a group calling itself the Shadow Brokers.[116] They have exposed vulnerabilities in Microsoft, Cisco, and Linux technology. Particularly frustrating to the USA is how the weapons, including the technology used in the WannaCry ransomware (to be discussed in Chapter 7), are now being used against the USA and its allies.[117]

The Citizen Lab has been a vocal critic of purveyors of cyberespionage, cyberterrorism, and cyberwarfare. Its 'Checklist for Accountability in the Industry Behind Government Hacking' recommended that individuals or organizations opposing unethical hacking use the following multi-pronged strategy:[118]

1. Identify commercial spyware companies' practices of concern.
2. Define the goals of accountability measures.
3. Continue to adopt export controls.
4. Engage in criminal or civil litigation.
5. Invoke consumer protection laws.
6. Challenge contract violations and intellectual property infringements [of commercial spyware firms].
7. Develop an accountability framework specific to the private market for digital surveillance.
8. Explore industry self-regulation.
9. Build out communities of practice to raise public awareness and document abuses.

High-tech companies have also expressed concern. Thirty companies, including Microsoft and Facebook, signed a declaration in April 2018 that they would not help any government, including that of the USA, with cyberattacks against 'innocent civilians and enterprises from anywhere'.[119]

Despite these statements, it seems unlikely that hacking will stop. Global damage from cyberattacks in 2017 has been estimated at $5 billion.[120] New ways of infecting machines are being developed, for example hiding malware in social media attachments.[121] The targets can also grow in severity, for example, retaliation targeting of nuclear power stations, and the spectre of the hacking of nuclear weapons.[122] A recently drafted US nuclear strategy sent to President Trump for approval proposes using nuclear weapons in response to a devastating cyberattack.[123] The tension has of course increased because of the greater level of fear, hostility, and confrontational acts between the USA and North Korea. One need not be a doomsayer to fear full cyberwarfare within the next decade.

Research: Cyberwarfare in the Middle East.

Debate: Resolved: Cyberweapons need to be outlawed or controlled in ways that parallel international agreements with respect to nuclear and biological weapons.

Book report: Kaplan, Fred (2016). *Dark Territory: The Secret History of Cyber War.* Simon & Schuster.

Book report: Segal, Adam (2016). *The Hacked World Order: How Nations Fight, Trade, Maneuver, and Manipulate in the Digital Age.* Public Affairs.

6.8 Guided aerial weapons with no person aboard

Internet technology can be used for warfare, but there are also many other military uses of digital technology. In this section we shall discuss how weapons can be launched remotely by soldiers. As technology advances, they can steer themselves and increasingly require less and less human control. In the next section, we shall take this idea further with the concept of autonomous weapons.

The Austrians are credited with the first attempt to equip unmanned balloons with explosives, directing them at Venice, Italy, in 1849.[124] Some of the balloons successfully dropped their bombs, but others boomeranged when the winds blew them back across Austrian lines. In the US Civil War, troops on both sides flew balloons for reconnaissance missions. Pilotless aircraft transitioned into flying weapons by the First World War.[125] Further advances in using aircraft without pilots militarily were made by several countries in the Second World War and especially for drone surveillance in the Vietnam War. The Israelis during the 1973 Yom Kippur War made extensive use of drones as decoys to deplete the arsenal of Egyptian anti-aircraft missiles.[126] One historian of warfare predicts that we will likely be entering a new stage of *drone warfare,* as well as the age of the *police drone,* in which drones, including some equipped with weapons, are used against one's own population.[124]

Drones

Drones vary in size; they are tiny as a small bird or large enough to carry significant payloads. Technologies integrated in modern drones are sensor fusion, communications, trajectory and path planning, task allocation and scheduling, and sometimes collaboration with other drones.[127] In 2016, 3 million drones were purchased in the USA; careless civilian drone use has caused more than 100 complaints per month because drones flew too close to aircraft.[128]

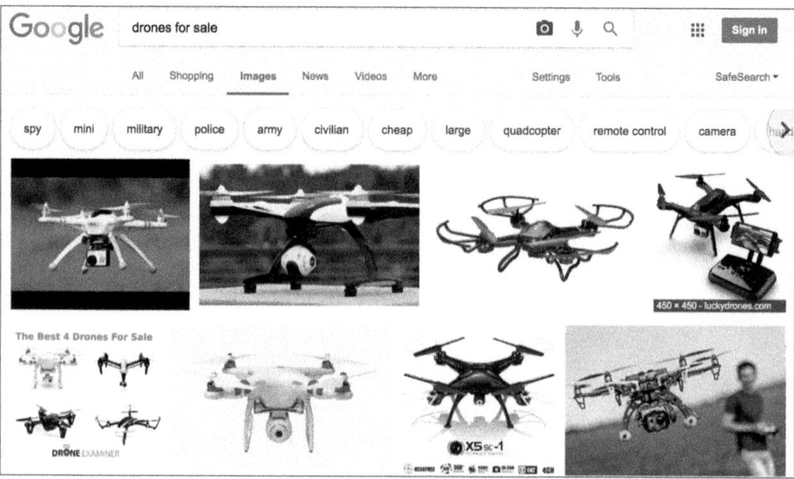

Figure 6.8 Drones for sale on the internet
Google and the Google logo are registered trademarks of Google LLC, used with permission.[129]

There are five uses: target or decoy, surveillance and reconnaissance, combat, research and development (of future drones), and finally commercial and civilian use. We shall not discuss the latter uses here, except to say that Amazon has been testing drones as a vehicle for the delivery in thirty minutes or less of packages weighing five pounds or less.[130]

Drones are versatile. Good uses are measuring hurricane intensity, counting penguins, detecting structural flaws in machinery, delivering life-saving medicines to remote locations, and saving drowning swimmers.[131] Yet most drones are military. The five deadliest drone powers are the USA, Israel, China, Iran, and Russia.[132] Nearly thirty countries possess armed drones, including India, Pakistan, Taiwan, and North Korea.[133] Hamas and Hezbollah possess surveillance drones and possibly combat drones; ISIS have used drones against Iraqi troops, Syrian militias, and American advisors.[134]

There has been concern in the USA about the increasing use of drones to do battle in the Middle East. Unmanned aerial vehicles (UAVs) were used in the *Desert Storm* military operation in the 1991 Gulf War.[126] Drone use was increased by President George W. Bush to strike suspected Al Qaeda operatives in the 'war on terror'.[135] Increasingly technical warfare was accelerated under Obama,[136] and grew further with actions in Syria ordered by Trump.[137] Moral concerns arise because it is impossible for the machine to only hit enemy combatants, leading to indiscriminate killing of civilians. There are ongoing debates about the numbers of non-combatant deaths caused by drones, but the totals seem to be in the hundreds or thousands in the Middle East in the 2010s.[132] An article written for the *New York Times* by two investigative journalists in November 2017 described the careful attention paid in selecting targets for air strikes, yet gave convincing evidence that the numbers of civilians killed were actually thirty-one times that estimated by the US-led coalition fighting ISIS in Iraq and Syria.[138]

Research: Civilian deaths caused by drones.

Debate: Resolved: Using drones to kill people is unethical.

Policy: Write a brief for a police chief, struggling with finances that are inadequate given the scale of crime in her city, considering the use of drones as police officers.

Book report: Gusterson, Hugh (2016). *Drone: Remote Control Warfare*. The MIT Press.

Jury: Assuming the laws of a particular country, debate as a jury what damages to award after a police drone causes damage to a suspect that makes him a paraplegic.

Ethics: Your neighbour, who belongs to a religious minority often subjected to suspicion and hatred, has begun to experiment with drones. You discover internet statements by him that imply possible terrorist beliefs. What do you do?

6.9 Autonomous weapons and robot soldiers

Some drones no longer require human intervention; others operate in conditions with an insufficient time span for human decision-making.[139] But technology developments are accelerating. No longer restricted to the imagination of science fiction authors, *androids* designed to go into battle—*robot soldiers*—will likely move from labs to real deployment in the very near future. Russia recently demonstrated its *Iron Man* humanoid military robot.[140] South Korea, continuously on edge with its North Korean enemy, has become a leader in military robotics, and installed automated turrets at the demilitarized zone facing North Korea.[141] A US Army General in 2014 asserted the goal of reducing a brigade combat team by 25 per cent and replacing humans with drones.[142] A UK intelligence officer described the US Army's goal as having more combat robots than human soldiers by 2025.[143]

The Handle robot

Progress in robotics with military applications may be seen in videos of drone abilities.[144] For example, Handle is a two-wheeled, four-legged robot that can run and spin faster than most humans, can jump over one metre off the ground, can lift loads of over 100 pounds without losing its balance, and can move quickly over rough terrain.

Continued on next page

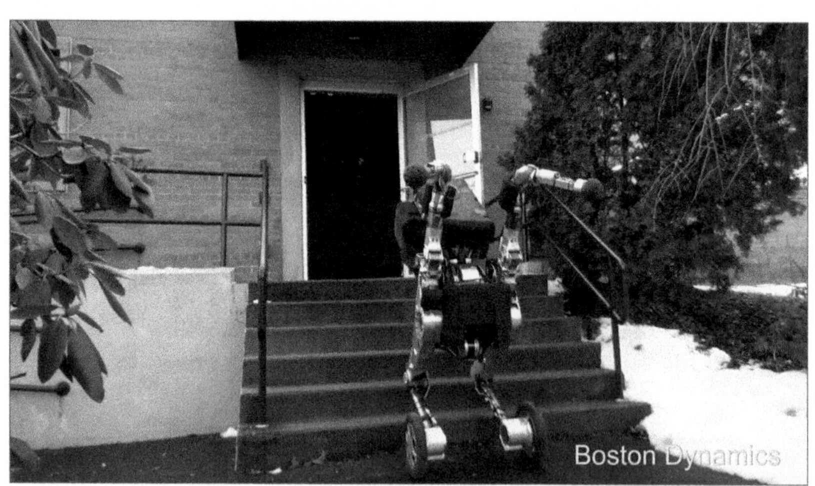

Figure 6.9 Handle has rolled down a flight of stairs and is heading down a snowy embankment to a parking lot
Courtesy of Boston Dynamics

Two recent reports from the US Defense Department are useful. Technology Horizons noted:[145]

> the cyber domain…is now recognized as encompassing the entire system that couples information flow and decision processes across the air and space domains.…the enormous cross-domain opportunities and threats…become more clearly apparent.

'Grand challenges' for the US Air Force were identified, including:

> to explore, develop, and demonstrate autonomous and scalable technologies that enable large, [in]secure networks to be made inherently and substantially more resilient to attacks

and

> to explore, develop, and demonstrate technologies that enable current human-intensive functions to be replaced, in whole or in part, by more highly autonomous decision-making systems and technologies that permit reliable V&V [verification and validation] to establish the needed trust in them.

More detail appeared in the Directive on Autonomy in Weapon Systems:[146]

> Autonomous and semi-autonomous weapon systems shall…allow commanders and operators to exercise appropriate…human judgment over the use of force.…ensur[ing] that [such] weapon systems:
>
> (a) Function as anticipated in realistic operational environments against adaptive adversaries.
>
> (b) Complete engagements in an [appropriate] timeframe…and, if unable to do so, terminate engagements or seek additional human operator input before continuing the engagement.

(c) Are sufficiently robust to minimize failures that could lead to unintended engagements or to loss of control of the system to unauthorized parties.

The Pentagon invests heavily in military AI research, as do China and Russia, with the goal of devising new weapons systems that 'emphasize human control and autonomous weapons . . . to augment and magnify the creativity and problem-solving skills of soldiers, pilots and sailors, not replace them',[147] although it is reasonable to question the degree to which humans will retain control.

China has begun significant investment in the development of cruise missile systems with high levels of AI.[148] Targets will be chosen by humans, but AI is intended to enable the missile to evade defences and make the ultimate targeting decisions.

Ethics

Autonomous weapons: Many experts, including Stephen Hawking and Elon Musk, have since early in this century been suggesting that *killer robots* be banned.[149] Concerns include unpredictable interactions between robotic algorithms that could escalate conflicts, the inability for robots to distinguish between combatants and innocent people living nearby, the likely increased harm to civilian populations, the danger of an arms race in autonomous weapons, the ease of acquisition by terrorists, the issue of assigning responsibility for unjustified deaths, and the lowering of the threshold for going into battle.

Michael C. Horowitz and Paul Scharre noted that today's weapons already incorporate autonomy.[150] They went on to make several important distinctions. The first is that there are several kinds of *human–machine control relationships—human 'in the loop'* selects targets which are then engaged, *human 'on the loop'* monitors machine selections for appropriateness, and *human 'out of the loop'* is where humans cannot intervene after the weapon has decided on a target. One example of the latter category in use is 'encapsulated torpedo mines'. A second distinction deals with the complexity of the weapon as it moves along a scale from 'automatic' to 'automated' to 'autonomous' to 'intelligent'. The authors concluded:

> An **autonomous weapon** system is a weapon system that, once activated, is intended to select and engage targets where a human has not decided those specific targets are to be engaged.
>
> A **human-supervised autonomous weapon** system is a weapon system with the characteristics of an autonomous weapon system, but with the ability for human operators to monitor the weapon system's performance and intervene to halt its operation, if necessary.
>
> A **semi-autonomous weapon** is a weapon system that incorporates autonomy into one or more targeting functions and, once activated, is intended to only engage individual targets or specific groups of target that a human has decided are to be engaged.

Ronald C. Arkin summarized huge numbers of atrocities in warfare inflicted intentionally or unintentionally by human soldiers through rage, frustration, stress, other psychiatric conditions, revenge, dehumanization of the enemy, youth, and inexperience. He argued that lethal autonomous unmanned weapons could be 'ethical' and do better than humans:[151]

Continued on next page

1. The ability to act conservatively: that is, robots do not need to protect themselves in cases of low certainty of target identification.... There is no need for a 'shoot first, ask-questions later' approach.
2. The eventual development and use of a broad range of robotic sensors better equipped for battlefield observations than humans currently possess....
3. Unmanned robotic systems can be designed without emotions that cloud their judgment or result in anger and frustration with ongoing battlefield events....
4. Avoidance of the human psychological problem of 'scenario fulfillment' [of pre-existing belief patterns]...distortion or neglect of contradictory information in stressful situations ...
5. They can integrate more information from more sources far faster before responding with lethal force than a human possibly could in real-time....
6. ...they have the potential capability of independently and objectively monitoring ethical behavior in the battlefield by all parties and reporting infractions that might be observed.

Scharre countered by noting the extraordinary damage that could be done by autonomous weapons' system failure:[152]

> an autonomous weapon could continue engaging inappropriate targets until it exhausts its magazine...If the failure mode is replicated in other autonomous weapons ... [there could be] large numbers of autonomous weapons failing simultaneously, with potentially catastrophic consequences.

From an operational standpoint, autonomous weapons pose a novel risk of mass fratricide, with large numbers of weapons turning on friendly forces. This could be because of hacking, enemy behavioral manipulation, unexpected interactions with the environment, or simple malfunctions or software errors. Moreover, as the complexity of the system increases, it becomes increasingly difficult to verify the system's behavior under all possible conditions; the number of potential interactions within the system and with its environment is simply too large.

We shall review examples of catastrophic system errors in non-military contexts in Chapter 8.

Can autonomous weapons be used ethically? Semi-autonomous weapons? Drones? Does your answer depend upon whether or not the actions are in 'self-defence'? What if a significant number of soldier lives may be saved by sending robots into battle? What are the responsibilities of computer professionals working on such projects?

A footnote to these considerations is that it is now easier to build weapons for use in civilian contexts, for example, 3D printing of handguns, and on the other side, guns that could only be fired by certain people or in certain circumstances.[153] Another great idea that will not happen in the gun-loving USA.

Research: Cases in which human soldiers have had to override actions of semi-autonomous weapons, and cases in which they have been unable to do so.

Research: Similarities and differences between the current opposition of many computer scientists to autonomous weapons and past movements of scientists against nuclear and biological weapons.

Concept: Write a Wikipedia article on 'ethical autonomy'.

Debate: Resolved: Creating and using robot soldiers will lead to more warfare, ultimately causing more suffering.

Debate: Resolved: Robot soldiers will commit fewer atrocities than do human soldiers.

6.10 Summary

Science fiction novels and films have given us vivid examples of android workers, policemen, and soldiers such as replicants, Terminator, and Robocop. The reality of how digital technologies are used to maintain law and order, and to wage war or enforce peace, is even more devastating that what is implied in those fictions.

Police forces are now active users of social media. Purposes include promotion and improvement of their image, better communication with citizens, providing services for the community, and surveillance to help in fighting crime. A particularly important development is the increasing use of digital cameras in establishing what happened during civilian interactions with police. Sometimes, video from a body-cam or dash-cam or from a mobile phone demonstrates that there was police brutality. Such cases in the USA caused significant racial turmoil in 2015 and 2016. Wearing body-cams seems to lower the frequency of complaints about police actions, and seemingly also reduces bad behaviour. In some cases, video imagery has substantiated that a police officer behaved properly.

When citizens become politically engaged, especially under authoritarian regimes, they sometimes become involved in political action. Social media played a key role in such e-mobilization efforts in the last decade. One outstanding example was the Arab Spring in 2010–11. The result was regime change in Tunisia, Egypt, and several other Middle Eastern countries, and worldwide turbulence, although in some nations it led to even more oppression.

Since 9/11, in response to ongoing terrorism, police and intelligence agencies, especially national forces such as the FBI, CIA, and NSA in the USA, and the RCMP in Canada, have increased their surveillance of citizens. The provisions legislated by the USA PATRIOT Act in the USA, and contemplated in the Canadian Green Paper on Security, all involve enhanced surveillance of most communications. Disclosures by Edward Snowden revealed massive US hacking of encryption to spy on the digital lives of hundreds of millions of people worldwide. All these actions challenge democratic societies' commitment to civil liberties. They force a debate on how to balance security and privacy. Although proof is not possible, it is plausible that the USA and Canada have been safer than they otherwise might have been had there not been such emphasis on security.

Turning our attention to the relationship between nations, rather than what happens within a nation, we have seen the increasing use of technology as a means of aggression. One good example is the recent hacking by Russia to sow discord and disrupt the electoral processes of democratic societies. Interference in the 2016 US presidential election was particularly intense and very successful; it helped to elect Donald Trump. There is increasing worry, and also some evidence, that this is being done again to elections and referenda in other countries.

Many countries censor the internet. They also close it at will when they anticipate citizen protests against their policies. The Citizen Lab has been active in enabling citizens living under repressive regimes to get around governmental censorship of the internet.

All of this has led to full-scale cyberespionage, cyberterrorism, and cyberwarfare. This causes significant disruption to the functioning of societies, and in turn leads to more and more surveillance. China has been particularly active in its attempts to damage the Tibetan exile community, and in other aggressive acts with respect to other groups that it views as threatening. This also holds true for Russia, North Korea, and the warring parties in the Middle East. Some cyberterrorist actions have worldwide impact, as for example the ransomware incident of May 2017, to which we shall return to in Chapter 7. Opportunities to deploy digital technologies in such a fashion have led to increasing development in software for cyberespionage, cyberterrorism, and cyberwarfare by intelligence agencies such as the CIA and the NSA, as well as a booming industry in hacking software. More and more nations and political groups now have access to such weapons. They may now be bought on the internet. They are increasingly less and less costly.[154] The future may see even more damage to the digital infrastructure on which the world depends, or even attacks designed to cripple or subvert nuclear weapons.

Digital technologies are also integral to other forms of weaponry such as drones or other self-guided aircraft. These are now commonly used for surveillance, as decoys, and as military weapons. Drone technology for warfare is improving rapidly and is being acquired by numerous nations. Use of drones raises significant ethical issues. In centuries past, combatants arrayed themselves neatly in columns or cadres and could be found on battlefields and killed without collateral damage to civilians. This is no longer true in an era in which military targets are hiding in urban areas amid civilians. Hence, there is troubling death and destruction to civilians and community institutions.

Drones typically are under the control of humans yet do motion planning autonomously. As the role of artificial intelligence in weaponry increases, we have the potential for fully autonomous weapons. Such technology embedded in androids yields the 'robot soldier' of science fiction. Current autonomous weapons have a human 'on the loop', using his or her discretion in the application of force. Proponents of autonomous weapons speculate that they can be programmed without the rage and need for revenge that lead to human atrocities in warfare. Sceptics argue that such damage pales before the likely catastrophes resulting from 'intelligent' weaponry spiralling out of control. Society has to face the ethical issues raised by the development and possible use of autonomous weapons.

6.11 Key terms

1996 Electronic Communications Privacy Act

Arab Spring of 2011

Authorization for Use of Military Force (AUMF)

Autonomous weapon system

Black Lives Matter

Body-worn cameras, or body-cams

Cyberblurring

Cyberespionage

Cyberterrorism

Cyberwarfare

Digital camera technology

Drone warfare

Edward Snowden

Free speech

GhostNet

Handle robot

Human 'in the loop'

Human 'on the loop'

Human 'out of the loop'

Human–machine control relationships

Human-supervised autonomous weapon system

KARMA POLICE

MUTANT BROTH

Netsweeper

Police brutality

Police drone

Remote Control System

Robot soldiers/killer robots

Semi-autonomous weapon system

Shamoon virus

Stuxnet

Syrian Electronic Army (SEA)

The Citizen Lab

USA PATRIOT Act

Part II

Risks

7

Security

Throughout history, humanity has invented valuable technologies and ways to organize society. These innovations are typically accompanied by risks. Fire cooks food, and also provides heat on cold nights. Yet, when left unchecked, fire can cause huge damage as well as loss of life. Cities enabled new forms of community and commerce. However, they brought us more thievery, and made it easier for epidemics to spread. The automobile allowed a separation of locales for work and residence; trucks allowed goods to be shipped long distances. But vehicular accidents have caused far greater injury and loss of life than did mishaps with horses and mules.

Information technology, like other technologies, has potential for good and for harm. In the first six chapters, we introduced aspects of human activity, such as education, medicine, and government, in which IT has been transformative and mostly positive. The next three chapters examine areas in which the negatives of IT are dominant, in which risks seem everywhere. This chapter focuses on *security*. IT security flaws are exploited by outsiders for personal or political gain. In Chapter 8 we shall look at *safety*, where the risks are often injury or loss of life. In Chapter 9, we shall look at *privacy*, where the risks are exposure of private, confidential, and even sensitive information.

Security is the attribute of a computer system that ensures that it can continue to function properly after an attack. Attacks against computer systems happen routinely now, are in the news almost every week, and are accelerating in numbers and in impact. Damage to both individuals and organizations—financial losses, chaos, and deteriorating morale—is severe.

We shall provide a primer on the multitude of ways computer systems, from large networks to mobile phones, can be 'hacked' so that they no longer function properly. We shall define the most common kinds of destructive software, often called *malware*. We will discuss large-scale data breaches, which now happen frequently and expose the personal data of millions to billions of people.

The word *hackers* refers to individuals who disrupt digital technologies and thereby damage the functioning of an institution or a society. Early hackers were individuals motivated mostly by idealism and mischievousness; now hacking is done by criminals. One motivation is to weaponize computer systems for political espionage, terror, and warfare, topics we discussed in Chapter 6. Hacking has also become a weapon for criminal exploits, which we shall cover in this chapter. Emphasis will be placed on the 2017 waves of *ransomware* attacks.

We shall also look at three specific *vulnerabilities* in digital technologies: (1) the degree to which one's personal data is secure from identity theft; (2) the degree to which everyday devices such as mobile phones, fitness trackers, cars, robots, personal digital assistants, and 'smart homes' are secure; and (3) and the degree to which electronic voting machines are secure. We shall also discuss legal responses on behalf of security, focusing on the USA, the UK, and China, and review how individuals, organizations, and societies can increase their level of protection.

Is society poised on the edge of collapse due to cyberattacks? Is the situation improving or deteriorating? What can be done about our vulnerability, both in terms of the technology that can be compromised and the human decisions and actions that often play a role in these actions?

7.1 Visions and context

Individuals who breach security are often called hackers. The term 'hacker' was not always used in this way. The original meaning was aptly described by author Steven Levy:[1]

> those computer programmers and designers who regard[ed] computing as the most important thing in the world... adventurers, visionaries, risk-takers, artists... the ones who most clearly saw why the computer was a truly revolutionary tool.

Those kinds of hackers—individuals pushing the technology to the limit—were typified by the MIT Model Railroad Club and the developers of the video game 'SpaceWar' on MIT's first PDP-1 minicomputer in the 1960s, and by attendees of the Homebrew Computer Club and the developers of the first personal computers in the San Francisco Bay area in the 1970s.[1] However, in the 1980s, the term took on a more insidious meaning:[2]

> password pirates and electronic burglars... [not] benign explorers but malicious intruders.

Concerns about system security began surfacing in the computer science community shortly after the development of time-sharing systems in the 1960s.[3] If a computer could be accessed by multiple people at once, how could we guarantee that one individual did not intrude on or damage another person's software or data? Hints of where this would lead were expressed at that time by the US National Security Agency (NSA) and defence contractors. For example, the US Air Force commissioned a study by the Computer Security Technology Planning Study,[4] which concluded:

> The principal unsolved technical problem found by the working group was that of how to provide multilevel resource and information sharing systems secure against the threat from a malicious user. This problem is neither hopeless nor solved.

Current events, almost half a century later, some of which we have already discussed in Chapter 6, prove that the problem has indeed not been solved.

7.2 A security primer

Computer scientist Peter G. Neumann, one of the most knowledgeable and thoughtful analysts of security risks with digital technologies, has provided us with some useful definitions:[5]

> A vulnerability is a weakness that may lead to undesirable consequences. A threat is the danger that a vulnerability can actually lead to undesirable consequences—for example, that it can be exploited intentionally or triggered accidentally. A risk is a potential problem, with causes and effects…a harm that can result if a threat is actualized…[or] a measure of the extent of that harm.

This chapter deals primarily with vulnerabilities that are exploited intentionally. The next chapter, on safety, focuses primarily on vulnerabilities that may be triggered accidentally.

According to McAfee Labs, the security problem is serious and growing rapidly. Their 2018 report reveals there were an average of eight new malware threats per second in 2017's fourth quarter, up from more than four in the third quarter.[6] There had been 700 million malware samples discovered that year, up from 500 million a year previously. There had also been almost 1,100 publicly disclosed security incidents in 2017, up from almost 1,000 in 2016. Personal computers with Microsoft Windows used to be the only machines attacked, yet in 2016 Macintosh malware had also become a serious problem. Mobile malware and ransomware showed steady growth in 2017, the former growing by 46 per cent, the latter by 59 per cent. McAfee Labs reported in 2016 that 93 per cent of corporations were overwhelmed by alerts, and therefore unable to triage all relevant threats.

Other reports by knowledgeable firms were similarly dire. Symantec reported in 2017 that one in 131 emails contained malware, and that 64 per cent of Americans were willing to pay a ransom if attacked by ransomware, as opposed to 34 per cent globally; IBM estimated in 2016 that cyber-crime is a $445 billion a year industry.[7] Governments, technology firms, and average citizens—all of whom rely upon computers—are frightened. Microsoft recently suggested a Digital Geneva Convention so that fewer cyberweapons that threaten computer security would be developed and stockpiled, much like treaties about nuclear weapons.[8] Cisco's 2018 Security Report summarized:[9]

> Adversaries and nation-state actors already have the expertise and tools necessary to take down critical infrastructure and systems and cripple entire regions.

Data breaches

The most vivid illustration of the poor state of computer system security is the *data breach*, where the personal data of large numbers of individuals is compromised. The Privacy

Continued on next page

Rights Clearinghouse has since 2005 logged 7,679 data breaches involving over 1 billion records exposed to unwanted observers.[10] Some of the largest data breaches in recent years are:[11]

Year	Records Stolen	Victim
2018	1.1 billion	Aadhaar
2015	1.37 billion	River City Media
2014	2.2 billion	Facebook
2013	1 billion	Yahoo!

Five significant US breaches were incidents at the US Office of Personnel Management (OPM), two breaches at Yahoo!, one at Anthem Insurance Company, and one at the Equifax Credit Reporting Agency.

The 2015 OPM hack compromised 21.5 million personnel records of current and previous US government employees.[12] In 5.6 million cases, the data included fingerprint records. A successful attack was not surprising, as every month the agency is forced to repel 10 million attempted digital intrusions to a network comprised of 15,000 individual computers. Investigations uncovered evidence that the first security breach came through a computer belonging to an OPM contractor. There was also evidence linking the successful hackers to China, whose government allegedly has a military cyberespionage division with 100,000 workers.

Yahoo! suffered two huge breaches: one in August 2013 affecting over 3 billion accounts, and one in late 2014 impacting over 500 million accounts.[13] Yahoo! faced public outrage, lawsuits, and a US congressional investigation because it waited until late 2016 to disclose the breaches. Data captured included names, email addresses, telephone numbers, dates of birth, hashed passwords, and security questions and answers. The US Securities and Exchange Commission fined the remains of Yahoo! (most of the original company had been acquired by other firms) a paltry $35 million. State-sponsored hacking is strongly suspected by superpowers, especially Russia or China.

The 2017 Anthem hack began when a user in an Anthem subsidiary opened a phishing email containing malware; an investigation determined with a medium degree of confidence that a foreign government was behind the attack.[14] Almost 80 million health insurance records were exposed.

The 2017 Equifax hack exposed the personal financial data of 145 million Americans. The attack was also attributed to state-sponsored hacking professionals.[15] Hackers gained access to a database of sensitive information including names, birth dates, social security numbers, and driving licence numbers. This information is easily used for identity theft (discussed later in this chapter). The files also contained information on utility accounts, rental and eviction histories, and medical debts. Despite portraying itself as 'trusted stewards of data' and having suffered two smaller security incidents in the preceding eighteen months, Equifax had not improved its security practices. The hackers made use of a known vulnerability in open source website software used by Equifax.

One group claiming responsibility has requested a ransom of approximately $2.5 million for the cyber-robbery. Four days after the breach was announced, at least twenty-three class-action lawsuits against Equifax had already been filed; furthermore, an entrepreneur had created a bot that automatically files a small claims lawsuit against Equifax for an individual.

Another North American breach was against Ashley Madison, a Canadian site with the mantra 'Life is Short. Have an Affair', used by married people looking to have extramarital affairs. A 2015 attack disclosed 37 million accounts.[16] Threats to release names of account holders resulted in many cases of extortion and suicides in several countries.

Data breaches are not limited to North America. Here are two major international cases. In late 2012 to early 2013, a hacker stole a database of 171 million accounts from VK.com, Europe's largest social networking site, headquartered in Russia.[17] The files contained full names, email addresses, and plain-text passwords of users and was sold to third parties on the internet. A dramatic 2018 example was a security lapse at Aadhaar, India's national identification database with around 1.1 billion registered citizens, exposing personal details such as names, unique twelve-digit identifying numbers (UIDs), and personal banking information.[18] This was the third billion-record data breach of Aadhaar in the past five years.

Data breaches are typically now done by malware. Malware (cybersecurity expert Lance J. Hoffman uses the charming phrase 'rogue programs') can assume a variety of forms.[19] Here are some of the most common varieties:

- A *Trojan horse* is undesirable code hidden inside desirable code or data. The code can be text, audio files, images, or video files; this method is commonly used to disguise computer viruses. The name comes from a legend associated with a war between Greece and the independent city of Troy, in which a large wooden horse secretly harbouring Greek soldiers was given to Troy. Attacking from within, the Greeks were able to overpower the Trojans and win the war.
- A *virus* is a Trojan horse that does damage to the software or files on one computer, then spreads itself to another computer, where it does additional damage. It then spreads itself to a third machine, and so on, mimicking the spread of disease among sentient beings.
- A *logic bomb* is a Trojan horse that is unleashed when some logical condition is satisfied, such as a login by a particular user.
- A *time bomb* is a Trojan horse that is unleashed at a particular time.
- A *trapdoor* is an entry path for inserting malware. A classic example was shown in a Turing Award lecture by computer scientist Ken Thompson,[20] wherein a brilliant and devious Trojan horse modified the C compiler so that the UNIX login command had a trapdoor that accepted a password known only to the creator.

- A *botnet* is a collection of Trojan horse-infected computers that typically engage in illegal or undesirable activities, such as sending spam, upon the command of a control computer somewhere on the internet.
- A *worm* need not be malevolent, but many are, breaking into pieces each of which can spread a virus, propagating and doing great damage.
- *Phishing* is the sending of deceptive emails that look like a legitimate request for information or action. This lures an internet user into entering his or her login credentials and/or password, downloading a file, or clicking on an attachment. As a result, one's credentials are stolen, or one's computer is compromised and infected by a virus or another piece of malware.
- *Spear-phishing* is phishing that is directed at a particular group of individuals who are known to be especially vulnerable to a certain kind of approach, because it makes use of specific information about them.
- A *password attack* is one of a series of methods of stealing a user's password.
- A *denial-of-service* incident is one in which some resource is flooded to the point that users of a computer system, the internet, or some other digital technology cannot access or use it.
- An *IMSI catcher* is a fake mobile phone tower that allows criminals to collect identifications of nearby mobile phone users, monitor their movements, and eavesdrop on them.[21]

Malware attacks are effective because of human carelessness or gullibility, for example, falling for phishing attacks or choosing insecure passwords. Rogue programs can also enter computers because of security flaws in software—most notoriously over the past two decades, Microsoft operating systems.

Many computer users choose passwords carelessly, settling for obvious or easily identifiable information in a text string, such as the name of a spouse or a pet, a birthday, or a common word. This makes it easy for hackers or a program to try millions of passwords, to guess the correct password and gain access to a device and its files. The result can be damage similar to that incurred by a phishing attack. There are many recommended methods to protect oneself, including choosing unique and hard-to-crack passwords for every application, and encrypting one's files. Especially effective is *two-factor authentication*, in which one must first enter a password, and then a security code that has been sent to a second device such as a mobile phone.[22]

Research: Identify and describe ways in which one could measure the damage from a denial-of-service attack.

Policy: Write a brief for the new head of information systems for a corporation who wants to initiate an extensive campaign to teach employees to be careful about security.

Field study: Interview a number of local industry and/or university computer system managers to understand their strategies for protecting and securing their systems.

7.3 Hackers

The first hackers in the 1980s were typically individuals motivated by some mixture of curiosity, mischievousness, political idealism, and a desire to score technical or political points.[2] Four examples are Kevin Mitnick, Robert Tappan Morris, Michael Calce (MafiaBoy), and Aaron Swartz.

Kevin Mitnick began as a teen-aged 'phone phreak', hacking into the phone system to allow him to make free phone calls. He progressed in the 1980s to hacking into computer systems, copying files, and reading emails. Arrested several times, he was eventually sentenced to four years in prison in 1999, of which he served only a year. He wrote the books *The Art of Deception* and *Takedown* to document his experiences. The latter became the subject of a film in 2000. Today, he is a computer security consultant.

Robert Tappan Morris was a Cornell University graduate student in computer science, and the son of a computer expert who worked at the NSA. He created the first known worm in 1988 at age 21, one that worked well enough to disrupt the operations of numerous computers on the Arpanet, the predecessor of the internet. He was the first individual indicted under the 1986 Computer Fraud and Abuse Act,[23] and was sentenced to three years of probation, 400 hours of community service, and the payment of a modest fine. Today, he is a tenured professor in the MIT Electrical Engineering and Computer Science Department.

MafiaBoy was the screen name of Michael Calce, a socially isolated boy on the West Island area of Montreal. In 2000, at the age of 14, he launched denial-of-service attacks against major technology corporations such as Yahoo!, Amazon, and Dell, causing millions of dollars of damage.[24] He was sentenced to eight months of 'open custody', one year of probation, and restricted internet use, and given a small fine. Today, he is the principal of a computer security consulting firm that helps businesses protect themselves against cyber-criminals.

Ethics

Aaron Swartz: Aaron's story illustrates the changing times over the past three decades.[25] A brilliant young programmer who contributed significantly to the software of the World Wide Web, Swartz was also a successful software entrepreneur as well as an activist committed to civil liberties and free speech on the internet. At the age of 24, he was arrested for downloading massive quantities of journal articles from the MIT Library computer; he was threatened with up to 35 years in prison under laws including the Computer Fraud and Abuse Act (CFAA).

Continued on next page

Unjust laws exist;
shall we be content to obey them,
or shall we endeavor to amend them,
and obey them until we have succeeded,
or shall we transgress them at once?
SHARE THIS VIDEO!

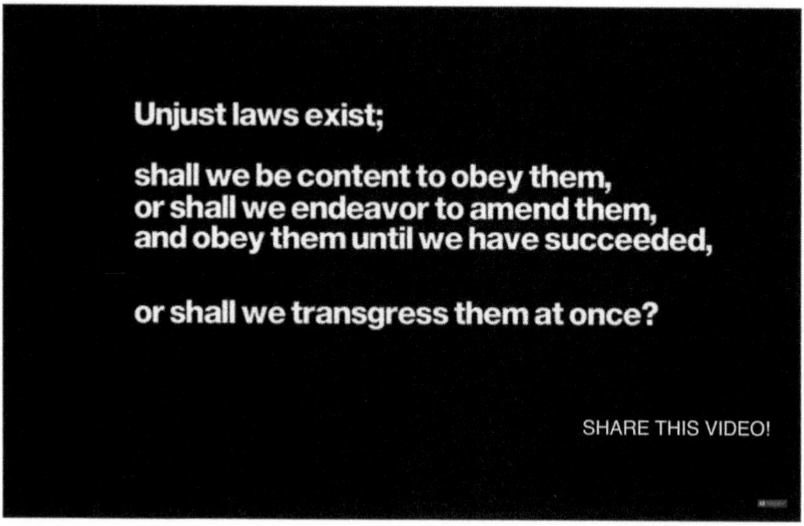

Figure 7.1 A quotation at the beginning of a feature-length documentary film that tells the story of Aaron Swartz

He committed suicide in 2013 after turning down a plea bargain under which he would have 'only' had to serve six months in federal prison. Given Aaron's motivations and the actions for which he was charged, described in the references cited in note 25, was Aaron ethical in what he did? Was the government ethical in the way it proceeded? (Further information about the Swartz case appears later in this chapter under 7.8. The legal response to cybercrime.)

Research: Compare and contrast the experiences of early hackers such as Mitnick, Morris, and Mafiaboy (Calce) with those of Swartz in terms of their progression to positions of responsibility in computer science and security as opposed to Swartz's suicidal outcome. Find and describe other examples of good and bad outcomes for such individuals.

Policy: Write a brief for the new chairperson of a computer science department seeking to articulate a policy on hacking that would apply to their undergraduates.

Book report: Abelson, Harold, Peter A. Diamond, Andrew Grosso, and Douglas W. Pfeiffer (2013). *Report to the President: MIT and the Prosecution of Aaron Swartz*. M.I.T.

Ethics: What ethical dilemma did Aaron confront? Why was he unable to resolve it?

7.4 Cybercriminals and large-scale system intrusions

As the internet and the World Wide Web grew, lone hackers were succeeded by criminal cartels, and boyish mischievousness was replaced with the intent to capture and exploit or to destroy personal data, usually either for financial gain or to achieve political goals. We have discussed examples of cyberespionage, cyberterrorism, and cyberwarfare in the preceding chapter. We shall now present some examples of *cyberrobbery* and *cyberblackmail.*

An early example was the embezzlement over the period 1970–73 of over $1.5 million by the chief teller at the Union Dime Savings Bank in New York City.[26] The electronic thief took the money from hundreds of individual accounts over a period of three years to fund a gambling habit. With incredible attention to detail, he always redeposited funds into any account when quarterly interest payments were due, then took the money back the following day.

A more modern and interesting example is Koobface,[27] revealed in a 2010 Information Warfare Monitor report by The Citizen Lab. Koobface was an insidious phishing botnet that enticed people to have seemingly normal exchanges on social media websites such as Facebook (FB) or Twitter. This was a trap—the victim would receive a link from someone pretending to be an FB friend that would supposedly lead to a video showing him or her naked, a video allegedly captured by a hidden webcam. Clicks by victims led them to compromised YouTube pages; malware was then downloaded onto their computers. The computers then became part of the botnet, and malicious messages were sent to friends of the victims, thus providing a viral spread of the digital disease.

This malware caused *pay-per-click* and *pay-per-install* programs to direct money into a bank account in St Petersburg, Russia. Revenue also came from the sale of rogue security software. Revenue, accumulated from fractions of pennies in billions of transactions, was over $2 million per year. The Koobface cartel controlled over 20,000 fraudulent FB accounts and over 500,000 fraudulent Google accounts. It also monitored the banning of URLs known to belong to Koobface in order to stay one step ahead of those trying to shut them down. Nonetheless, after the publication of the report, law enforcement officers in countries such as the UK managed to get internet service providers to take Koobface command-and-control computers off the internet.

The report's Foreword noted the challenges in international law enforcement cooperation in areas involving sophisticated technology and seemingly victimless crimes, ultimately concluding:

> There is another element... that should give us even more pause. The Koobface gang had a certain charm and ethical restraint. They communicated with security researchers about their intents and their desire not to do major harm. They limited their crimes to petty fraud, albeit massive in scale and scope. But the scary part is that they could have easily done otherwise.

Another vivid example of cybercrime is known as *ransomware*. Machines are captured, files are encrypted, and ransoms are demanded. File destruction is threatened if a ransom is not paid within a certain amount of time, with the promise that the ransom will increase after that date. By 2016, ransomware had an estimated annual take of over $1 billion.[28] One particularly malicious example was the so-called Popcorn Time ransomware, which included ransomware along with a Ponzi scheme. Victims were given a choice between paying one bitcoin, worth almost $2,500 at the time, or trying to infect two other people. Another vicious 2017 attack on an American telecom firm combined ransomware with the theft of employee credentials.[29]

WannyCry[30]

Most serious was the May 2017 'WannaCry' ransomware attack. Over 200,000 machines in over 150 countries around the world, mostly running outdated versions of Windows 7, were held hostage. Files were encrypted and inaccessible. The threat was destruction of the data if a ransom was not paid within three days.

One particularly sensitive target was the British National Health Service. It cut back on outpatient appointments and non-emergency surgeries.[31] Other notable victims included firms such as the United States' FedEx, Spain's Telefónica, and France's Renault, as well as some Chinese universities, Germany's federal railway system, and Russia's Interior Ministry.[32] Victims had themselves to blame in part; the ransomware exploited a security flaw for which Microsoft had published a patch in March. Few victims paid the ransom, with many choosing to take the risk, which happily was mitigated because a security expert found a kill switch that had been hidden in the malware by the culprits.[30]

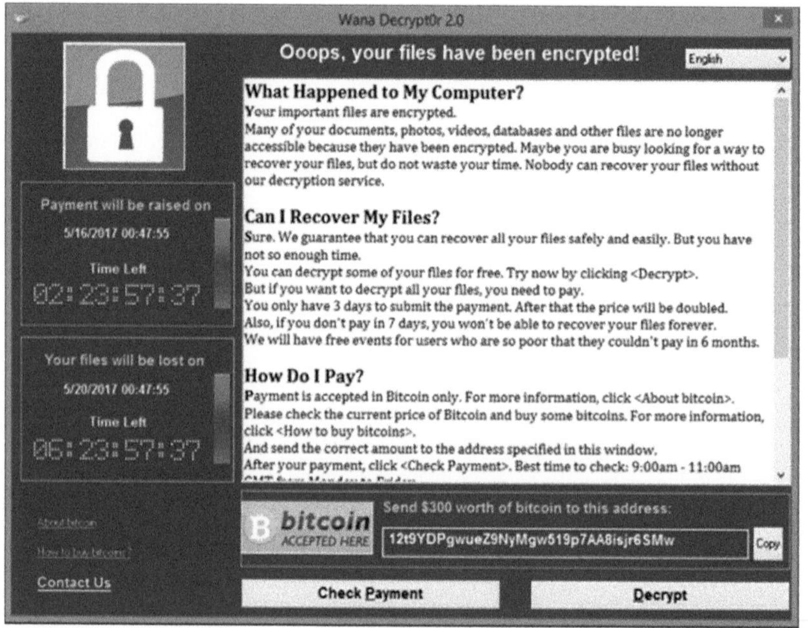

Figure 7.2 Ransom note left on infected computers by WannaCry

'Sleeper cells' of North Korean hackers were suspected as the sources of the ransomware, and were formally blamed by the Trump administration in December 2017.[33] Particularly embarrassing to the NSA was that the WannaCry malware seems to have originated from its headquarters and was dumped onto the web in April 2017 by the Shadow Brokers,[34] previously discussed in Chapter 6. Their work is deadly serious and unfortunate, although there is an element of black humour in their recent announcement of a subscription 'hack-of-the-month' club.

A similar attack came in June 2017,[35] when ATMs in Ukraine and computers in companies throughout the world (including those doing business with Ukraine) stopped working.[36] Revenue forecasts were revised downwards. Radiation at the Chernobyl nuclear plant had to be monitored by hand. Ransoms were demanded to regain access, yet subsequent analysis suggested that the goal was political paralysis, not profit.[37] Russia was suspected, as it has engaged in warfare, open and covert, with Ukraine ever since a government friendly to Russia was removed in 2014.

The situation does not seem to be improving. Ransomware attacks on city and county governments in the USA continue to place political systems between a rock and a hard place.[38] Furthermore, understanding the severity of cybercrime is difficult, at least in the USA, because many incidents are not reported.[39]

Research: Dig deeper into the story of ransomware, especially the incidents in May and June 2017, with a focus on understanding possible financial and political motives.

Field study: Interview individuals who were affected by the WannyCry ransomware attack of 2017.

7.5 Identity theft

Identity theft is the fraudulent capture of a person's identity, that is, his or her personal identification (e.g., social security and credit card) numbers, with the purpose of impersonating that individual.[40] Identity theft is usually done for financial reasons, such as running up bills on someone else's credit card. In doing so, it also damages the victim's credit rating. Identity theft may also be done for other reasons, such as impersonation in order to receive medical care. Victims often are unaware that this has happened until evidence of criminal activity presents itself. The intrusion may be noted due to a major discrepancy in a bank or credit card statement. In other cases, the victim is contacted by a bank that has detected suspicious activity.

Phishing

Traditionally, identity theft has been done manually, via techniques such as finding someone's wallet, stealing bank or credit cards, rummaging through rubbish, or looking over a person's shoulder. Increasingly, however, the crime happens online through the discovery and fraudulent use of critical login IDs and passwords. Often, accounts are compromised when the user is victimized by a phishing attack.[41] Phishing attacks should be obvious, as for example in the following instances received by the author in 2017:

> 'Please review invoice attached to this message. Transfer should appear in 3 days.
>
> Document Access Key: O9jF61svWOo
>
> Regards, <TEXT THAT SEEMS TO BE A COMPANY NAME>
>
> ---
>
> Here is your statement.
>
> The Password is lGazWSE1hY4. Enter it to open the attached file.
>
> Waiting for your answer. Kind regards, <NAME>
>
> ---
>
> *****UPDATE
>
> Your email quota is almost passed. . . . Please enter and update your account to avoid losing your inbox. »»»> <LINK NOT TO BE CLICKED>
>
> <NAME>. HELP-DESK SERVICE Security © 2017 *********** This message was scanned by <NAME> Anti-Spam and AntiVirus System'
>
> ---
>
> Dear . . .
>
> Our Mail Admin database has been breached due to the large number of spam messages we receive. For these reason our admin is currently upgrading the Mailbox Mail server to avoid receiving Spam messages.
>
> Login Here To Update Your Account
>
> (c). . . 2017 Web Upgrade, ≤LINK NOT TO BE CLICKED
>
> ---
>
> You have exceeded your account quota limit Click HERE for manual upgrade.
>
> ---
>
> From: <Business acquaintance> Subject: Fw: for Ron Baecker
>
> Date: August 10, 2017 at 12:15:53 p.m. GMT-4 To: Ron Baecker <. . .>

I think this is something you may appreciate

http://press3.ty.news4323.press/ron-baecker/

These examples are typical of phishing attacks, illustrating requests to receive something that likely was not ordered, to view a statement that could plausibly be of importance to the user, to respond to what appears to be a suggestion or an offer from a friend, or to respond to a request to update some computer application. Paradoxically, it also can be a suggestion that one take an action to ensure that his or her computer system is secure. Unfortunately, they do not appear as obvious dangers to many internet users, who do not know what to look for.

If an unsuspecting user acts on illegitimate requests to enter confidential information, or to click on unknown and unexpected files that have not been sent by a trusted source, incredible damage can result. Examples are the corrupting of one's files; capture of the machine for unknown future evil purposes, such as the sending of spam under one's name; loss of confidentiality; identity theft; and serious financial losses. The threat from phishing has grown dramatically recently. The Anti-Phishing Working Group detected almost 300,000 unique phishing sites in March 2016, a number 250 per cent greater than what had been detected in October 2015.[42]

Based on a survey of more than 5,000 US consumers, over 15 million US citizens were victims of identity theft or fraud in 2016, losing a total of $16 billion.[43] Identity theft is damaging not only because of what is taken, but also due to damage to a person's identity via unpaid debts and traffic violations. The results can cause great hardship—not being able to get a loan, a mortgage, an apartment, or even a job. Online identity theft has been a major problem for two decades, despite severe penalties, as in the recent US sentencing to twenty-seven years in prison of a Russian hacker who had stolen and resold more than 2 million credit card numbers.[44] Almost half of Americans know of an attack that has affected them personally.[45]

Credit card fraud is the use of credit cards without the owner present, the accessing of accounts via stolen logins and passwords, and the opening of new accounts in the names of unsuspecting individuals. These kinds of identity theft increased significantly in 2016.[46] Although online fraud was typically discovered faster than offline fraud, e-commerce shopping and social network participation were risk factors increasing the odds that one's identity would be compromised. Identity thieves also adjust their strategies based on their perception of sources of wealth to be tapped; recently, hackers have begun to steal the mobile phone numbers of individuals who imply on social media that they own cryptocurrencies (to be discussed further in Section 12.8).[47]

Financial institutions and law enforcement agencies have not always been required to report occurrences,[48] although new US state laws requiring institutions to admit losses of personal data have reduced the frequency of identity theft by 6.1 per cent.[49] Data on the frequency and cost of identity theft is not 100 per cent reliable. Numbers could be overestimates because of erroneous reports when individuals have only suffered security breaches. Yet numbers are likely underestimates, because many individuals do not realize they have been defrauded, and others may realize it but do not report it. Reported loss figures also underestimate the scope of the full damage, as the victim may suffer demands for payment, harassment, and damage to his or her credit rating.

There is also injury in terms of additional money and time wasted, which amounted to an average of $800 and 175 hours in trying to repair the problems caused by stolen identities.[50] Those who had been unable to resolve the problems already had spent an average of forty-four months of effort. Victims reported that 'stress, emotional trauma, time lost, and damaged credit reputation' did far more damage than the financial losses.[50] Identity theft takes an additional toll because it undermines consumer confidence in the safety of e-commerce.[41]

In the USA, the widespread use of one's social security number increases the likelihood of severe damage if that number is stolen.[51] Social network participation is also a risk factor for identity theft. Two experiments demonstrated the feasibility of executing automated identity theft attacks in five social networks, including FB and LinkedIn.[52] An algorithm created to break the CAPTCHA security mechanisms of the networks was used. In the first study, their experimental system cloned existing social media accounts and sent friend requests to the contacts of the victim. Over 60 per cent of the requests from the forged accounts were accepted, thus enabling the perpetrators to access sensitive personal information. In the second study, they identified users who were registered in one social network but not in another. They created fraudulent accounts on the second network, then sent friend requests that looked especially plausible since the apparent sender was new to that network. Fifty-six per cent of the friend requests were accepted, again exposing those who accepted the requests to compromising their confidentiality to individuals who not only were not their friends but could have done them harm.

Finally, as one would expect in an entrepreneurial world, there are now identity theft protection services to monitor credit and search the internet (especially the dark web) for personal identification data that could be used to compromise one's identity.[53]

Research: What is the 'dark web'? How is it used for cybercrime? Could it be regulated, and if so, how?

Research: Research and discuss differences in identity theft legislation between two or three countries or between two or three states or provinces within a country where there is legislation at that level.

Research: Research and discuss differences in identity theft in countries where there is a national identification number, such as Singapore and India, and countries where there is not such a number, such as the UK.

Field study: Interview a number of seniors who have succumbed to phishing attacks with particular attention to those who have had their identity stolen.

Ethics: You are about to drop out of university because of lack of funds. Your parents have remortgaged their home to help, but they cannot do any more. You are standing by an ATM and notice the PIN typed in by an inebriated individual, who then drops his bank card. What do you do?

Ethics: Your roommate's long-time romantic partner has ended the relationship and is now dating another person. Your roommate is furious and is a skilled computer hacker. You see indications that he or she seems to be working on identity theft of the new romantic interest of the ex-romantic partner. What do you do?[54]

7.6 Security in the digital world

Stepping away from cyberspace, we shall now consider digital security as it applies to mobile phones, exercise trackers, personal digital assistants, and smart homes.

Mobile phone security

As mentioned above, mobile malware represents an increasing threat to mobile phones. Some of the many ways in which security can be compromised are:[55]

Security vulnerabilities in mobile phones

Vulnerabilities	Common method for exploiting the vulnerabilities
Broadband network	Breaking encryption of communications
Wi-Fi network	Breaking encryption of communications Impersonating a Wi-Fi access point
Messaging	Messages containing viruses or other malware
Hardware	Electromagnetic spoofing
Software	Malware in system or applications software
Identification	Cracking a password Having one's location tracked
User	Succumbing to a phishing attack Losing one's improperly protected mobile phone

Continued on next page

A recent example is Lebanon's intelligence agency spying on people using decoy Android apps that seemed to offer secure messaging but were actually allowing the agency to capture passwords, data, photos, and audio.[56]

Countermeasures include the use of manufacturer surveillance, resource monitoring, network monitoring, strong passwords, proper encryption, virus detection, and user awareness training.

The same considerations apply to other mobile devices such as fitness trackers. In one bizarre recent case, the fitness app that describes itself as 'the social network for athletes' displayed the locations of worldwide movement and indirectly revealed the locations, spatial characteristics, and habits of military personnel.[57] Personal digital assistants also pose security challenges. There have been reports of Amazon's Alexa being hacked to allow eavesdropping and the recording of conversations in the home; similar concerns have been expressed about smart toys that have microphones and cameras.[58] Researchers have recently demonstrated a technique to broadcast sound patterns to disrupt the functioning of accelerometers in nearby devices, which could disrupt phones and fitness trackers and even endanger the operations of a car.[59] Other researchers have demonstrated security flaws in many robots, including weak authentication and cryptographic systems, thereby allowing inappropriate remote control of the robots.[60]

Finally, consider the home in a larger sense. There is typically a perceived and actual need for locks, alarm systems, video and other remote monitoring systems, and neighbours who keep watch for anything suspicious. As developers, builders, and architects envision and produce so-called smart homes, security must be one of the considerations.

Smart homes are sensor-embedded houses; as with traditional homes, security objectives are paramount, including confidentiality, integrity (maintaining accurate and consistent data), authorization (ensuring that access control is maintained properly), and 'non-repudiation' (ensuring that claims made by any entity on the network can be verified).[61] Security attacks may be of two kinds. An example of a 'passive' attack is eavesdropping. 'Active' attacks include masquerading to obtain unauthorized privileges, modifying communications, introducing malware, or effecting denial-of-service. Active attacks could result in devices operating improperly, or malfunctions occurring in devices intended to detect home invasions. Methods are being developed in many countries to ensure that smart homes are indeed secure.

There is little evidence of security effectiveness or breaches in smart homes because there are very few smart homes. Technology for homes is currently limited to isolated 'gadgets' in a state of 'ecosystem incompatibility'.[62] But this will change as technology and consumer desires change. There are already domestic abuse cases in which a tech-savvy individual has hacked internet-connected home devices such as locks, doorbells, thermostats, and lights in order to harass and exhibit power over an estranged spouse.[63] Much work remains to be done if smart homes are to be secure.

Are smart homes just fancy technologies looking for a purpose? One worthwhile motivation is that they could be of special use to seniors, enabling them to live at home safely and independently as long as possible.[62] One relevant aspect of this is fall detection and notification.

Fall detection is a mature application of sensors in the home, with several approaches in use. Most devices rely upon seniors to carry or wear something that allows them to call for help. A research frontier is video capture, which also can be imagined as a ubiquitous assist to security throughout the household.[64] It also raises privacy issues, which we shall discuss in Chapter 9. Another smart home goal is efficient energy utilization in the home, with a view to reducing society's carbon footprint.[65] We shall return to this topic in Chapter 8.

Research: Progress in smart homes, and how issues of security, safety, and privacy are being handled.

Research: Domestic abuse in technologically advanced homes.

Debate: Resolved: Security of a home should be trusted to an intelligent and integrated network of sensors rather than to individual devices.

Field study: Interview seniors who have fallen about their use of fall detection and notification systems.

Technology review: Fall detection systems.

7.7 Electronic voting machines

We now turn our attention to an area of automation that is more advanced, and where security is still a major concern. IT has long assisted in vote tabulation. The earliest solution to be employed widely in the USA, first used in the 1964 presidential election, was based on *punched cards*. Voters indicated their choices by punching holes at appropriate places on the ballot. These were then fed into a card reader connected to a computer that would tabulate the results.

The Butterfly Ballot

The 2000 US presidential election became infamous because of two major issues that affected the result, one caused by use of the punched card system, one unrelated.[66] The punched card problem became known as the problem of the 'hanging chad' that was caused by the machines not punching the holes out cleanly. This caused some ballots to not be counted. The other problem became known as the 'butterfly ballot' problem. Since there were ten presidential candidates, plus the opportunity to write in a name on the Palm Beach County, Florida (a swing state) ballot, the designer staggered the punch holes on opposite sides of a column. This allowed the text to be larger, and was done in part to make the choices more legible to senior citizens. However, this also caused the Democratic ticket choice to appear as the second on the list, but the third hole to punch.

Continued on next page

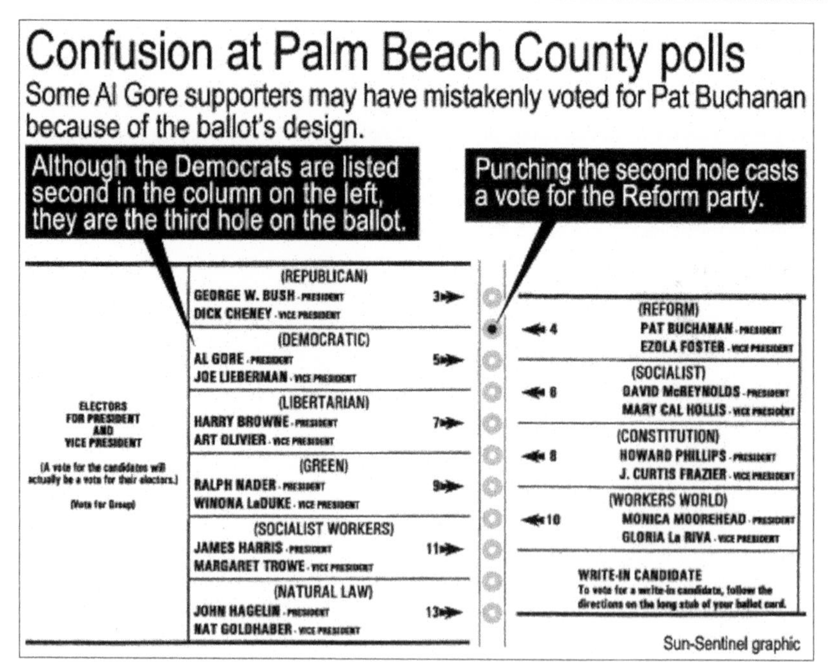

Figure 7.3 The Butterfly Ballot

Numerous voters punched the second hole, voting for the Reform Party, instead of choosing the third hole for the Democratic party, thus denying votes to Democrat Al Gore and contributing to the 2000 victory of George W. Bush.

Although the latter problem could also happen on a digital display screen, obviating the first problem and achieving greater efficiencies have both supported the dream of fully electronic voting. Such a system is typically known as a *Direct-recording Electronic* (DRE) *voting* system.[67] Systems can differ in a variety of dimensions, including whether or not a paper trail is generated, whether the votes or the totals are transmitted electronically to a central site or not, and whether the tabulations are done at the polling place or centrally. Electronic voting is being introduced gradually in many parts of the world; Brazil and India have been in the vanguard. There is still huge controversy over the desirability and safety of electronic voting.[68]

Proponents argue that electronic solutions introduce efficiencies in counting the votes. They also afford advantages in the case of last-minute ballot changes. They are easier to adapt for disabled and non-English-speaking voters. There is less 'roll-off', or the tendency of voters to not follow through and vote on all measures where there is a long ballot, because the voter can be reminded to continue. The possibility of a paper record can help to guarantee the integrity of the vote. Finally, the electronic voting machine industry in the USA asserts that there are no known cases of security breaches involving their machines.

Opponents argue that an electronic solution can disenfranchise voters not familiar with digital technologies. In theory the interface can be tailored for specific needs, but in practice there are still significant usability problems. Checking paper trails is problematic because they are typically incomplete, and also because it would be very difficult to compare large numbers of electronic votes and paper records. There have been disturbing concerns about political motivations and connections among executives of US electronic voting machine companies who have been vocal in their allegiance to one political party. Finally, respected computer science professors have demonstrated the ease with which one can hack into leading models of electronic voting machines and introduce malicious code that will change the results.[69]

Computer science should be able to produce a secure solution, but more needs to be done before electronic voting is secure. This has been widely recognized in the USA, where cybersecurity experts were hard at work before the 2018 midterm elections.[70]

Research: Voting technology available today.

Research: Compare and contrast three different approaches to voting technology as they have been used at federal, state, or local levels.

Debate: Resolved: Greater security can be achieved with electronic voting.

7.8 The legal response to cybercrime

The major US legal instrument to combat computer fraud is the *1986 Computer Fraud and Abuse Act* (CFAA),[71] which has been amended several times including by the USA PATRIOT Act. The Act declares that it is a crime to use a computer for purposes such as: (1) causing damage to a computer; (2) accessing information that is considered confidential for US defence or foreign relations purposes; (3) accessing information contained in the financial records of a financial institution or credit card issuer; or (4) using computer access or knowledge of passwords to commit fraud. Threats to carry out an action deemed to be a crime were also deemed to be crimes. The act was used to bring actions against both Robert Morris and Aaron Swartz, two of the hackers discussed previously in the chapter.

The action against Swartz produced a major reaction. Many in the computer and legal community had sympathy for the young man, who was regarded as a productive member of both the software development and civil liberties communities. There was widespread dismay over Swartz's suicide, since it was perceived that overly broad legislation had posed a disproportionate legal threat—a penalty of up to thirty-five years' imprisonment and a $1 million fine.[72] The threat seemed cruel given that the JSTOR digital library, the party plausibly wronged by Swartz's downloading of the journal articles, had agreed to settle with him and had recommended that the charges be dropped. A congressperson therefore proposed an amendment designed to lighten provisions of the CFAA. This amendment, known as Aaron's Law, has not passed the US Congress.[73]

Specific laws have been targeted at identity theft.[74] The *1998 Identity Theft and Assumption Deterrence Act* made identity theft a federal crime. The *2004 Identity Theft Penalty Enhancement Act* increased penalties for 'aggravated' identity theft, which constituted using someone else's identity to commit a felony crime, theft of Social Security benefits, immigration violations, and domestic terrorism. Also relevant is the *1970 Fair Credit Reporting Act.*[75]

The major British legal instrument for information security is the *1990 Computer Misuse* Act.[76] It has also been criticized by some legal scholars and computer professionals for not distinguishing adequately between youthful mischief and serious crime. The *1998 Data Protection Act* deals in part with identity theft.[77]

Cyber-crime in China

The situation in China is somewhat different. Hacking began to flourish in China in the 1990s for several reasons, evolving from 'a few highly skilled hacktivists to a generation of cybercriminals'.[78] China had by then become the largest user of the internet in the world, with around 420 million Chinese on the internet, although still only constituting 32 per cent of the total number of Chinese people. Almost all Chinese who accessed the internet had to go through 'the great firewall' (discussed in Chapters 1 and 5), where filters blocked 'undesirable content' as deemed by the government, although policies were inconsistent and not always effective.[79] Eighty-one per cent of the hackers were between the ages of 10 and 39; 95% of them had a monthly income of less than $800.

Appealing mostly to males in their twenties, hacking was seen both as a way of 'getting something for nothing' and as a source of national pride, compensating for an inferiority complex that had pervaded the Chinese national consciousness between the 1840 Opium War and the 1949 Communist revolution. As we have seen in Chapter 6, much of this has been aimed externally, but some has been directed inward. The increase in the number of Chinese hackers was also fuelled by one group that trained over 10,000 new hackers. By 2006, hackers numbered between 24,000 and 1.2 million individuals.[78] An estimate of the number of possible cybercrimes was over 30,000, of which only 20% were investigated.[79] By 2009, the take from Chinese underground viruses was estimated to be around $1.5 billion.[78]

Cybercrime laws were introduced in the late 1990s. Some thought they had too few teeth,[78] yet penalties ranged from imprisonment to death.[80] Mechanisms included criminalizing certain activities, regulating communications firms, recruiting *cyberpolice*, filtering content, and surveilling internet users with the goal of 'security and stability'. Nonetheless, cybercrime continued to grow. Cyberattacks against companies reportedly increased by 969% between 2014 and 2016. The government carried out a major crackdown in 2015, arresting 15,000 people suspected of cybercrimes in order to 'clean the internet'.[81] Cybercrime was also viewed in terms of international politics, leading to a statement by the Cyberspace Administration of China that it would use 'whatever means necessary – scientific, technological, legal, diplomatic or military – to ensure cyberspace sovereignty'.[81]

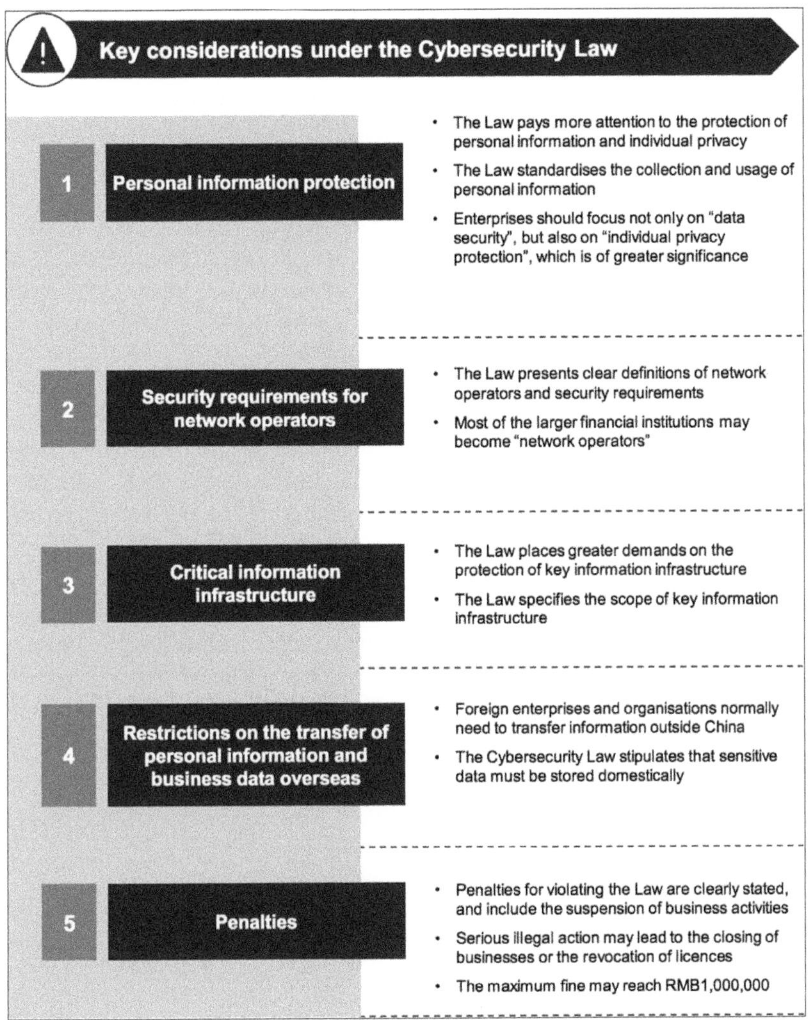

Key considerations under the Cybersecurity Law
1
Personal information protection
The Law pays more attention to the protection of personal information and individual privacy
The Law standardises the collection and usage of personal information
Enterprises should focus not only on "data security", but also on "individual privacy protection", which is of greater significance
2
Security requirements for network operators
The Law presents clear definitions of network operators and security requirements
Most of the larger financial institutions may become "network operators"
3
Critical information infrastructure
The Law places greater demands on the protection of key information infrastructure
The Law specifies the scope of key information infrastructure
4
Restrictions on the transfer of personal information and business data overseas
Foreign enterprises and organisations normally need to transfer information outside China
The Cybersecurity Law stipulates that sensitive data must be stored domestically
5
Penalties
Penalties for violating the Law are clearly stated, and include the suspension of business activities
Serious illegal action may lead to the closing of businesses or the revocation of licences
The maximum fine may reach RMB1,000,000

Figure 7.4 Key considerations under the new Chinese cybersecurity law[82]

With the stated goal of reducing threats from hacking and cyberterrorism, China put a new law into place on 1 June 2017.[83] It stiffened government control over the internet, requiring users to register with their real names, and also insisted on 'data localization', meaning that companies had to store their data within China's borders. Within two months, Apple announced that it would build a data centre in China.[84] Human rights observers felt that it was directed at political stability as much as it was aimed at improving security.

7.9 What shall we do?

We have seen that the modern digital society has both technical and human vulnerabilities to intrusion, theft, and damage. For either financial or political motives, hackers pose threats and therefore risks to society. What can be done? Useful protections and countermeasures exist on both the technical and the human side: two-factor authentication (already discussed), better passwords, guards against phishing, patching operating system and application software security holes, research, and education and vigilance.

One of the areas of greatest vulnerability lies in the selection of weak passwords, which can be cracked by algorithms designed for this purpose. Here is a subset of the reasonable guidelines with respect to passwords:[85] do not choose a password identical to the login ID; do not select a password that is shorter than twelve characters; do not use a password that is easily guessable from modest knowledge about yourself, for example, your partner's birthday, your address, or your pet's name; and do not choose a password that is a common word or phrase in your language. Do choose a password that seems to make no sense, but that is based on some individual technique you have devised, and that incorporates a combination of letters, numbers, capitals, and symbols. Write passwords down and put them in places hard for someone to find; label them so that they are not easily identified as passwords. Use password manager software such as KeePass or 1Password to produce unique passwords and securely store them on a computer. Where possible, use two-factor authentication so that you have to enter two passwords, the second of which is sent to another device, such as a mobile phone.[86] The challenge lies in deciding how much effort should be expended every day to forestall the possibility of a catastrophe happening at some unknown point in the future.

A second area of great vulnerability is phishing. Previously in this chapter I presented six short samples that I personally received in 2017. Here is another example sent to me, recognizable as a phish because of its stilted style, and because it was unexpected and seemed bizarre:

> From: <NAME AND ADDRESS THAT SEEM TO BELONG TO A REPUTABLE COMPANY>
>
> Subject: I am sorry
>
> Date: July 11, 2017 at 3:57:58 p.m. GMT-4
>
> ...
>
> Dear Ronald,
>
> I want to apologize as our SSL certificate elapsed moments after I sent you an email on our <NAME> offering, resulting in links that led to insecure webpages. The issue has been resolved and I am taking steps to ensure that this does not happen again.
>
> ...
>
> I value your time and am sorry for any inconvenience this may have caused you....As an apology I would I like to offer you **a 5% discount** on the...mentioned in the earlier email. Please see more about that the service <LINK NOT TO BE CLICKED>....The earlier email with the offering will be in your inbox soon.
>
> Best, <name> <reasonable looking title and organization and address>

Education can help reduce the likelihood that one is trapped by a phishing attack.[41] The methods follow a typical pattern; one can learn to be suspicious, resist the urge to click, and if need be check for validity using a different communications channel, such as the phone. There is an 'anti-identity theft freeze' for one's credit history available in some locations that can reduce the magnitude of damage as one is trying to protect or repair a credit history. An add-on identity theft rider to a homeowner's insurance policy is also available from some companies. Finally, as the magnitude of the phishing problem represented an entrepreneurial opportunity, software has been developed to detect fraudulent emails and fraudulent websites. And there are always legal remedies, but consumers rarely pursue them as the cost and effort seem exorbitant.

A third area of vulnerability is the failure to patch known security holes. Many of the large-scale system intrusions we discussed took advantage of organizations and system administrators not keeping their systems current in terms of security. Keeping current takes time, but this is well spent if it prevents a catastrophe. Unfortunately, the list of problems keeps growing, as for example the two security flaws recently found in almost every Intel microprocessor chip, which are used in most of the world's computers.[87] Prudent vendors of financial services apply massive resources to achieve cybersecurity; their employees include former government soldiers, spies, and counter-intelligence officials, working in a style reminiscent of the culture of national defence.[88]

The computer industry has been working on both new hardware and software to reduce the frequency of identity theft. In addition to keyed passwords, users can be identified by *biometric scanners*, which read fingerprints or voice prints. There has been promising work on *behavioural biometrics*, in which keyboard and mouse dynamics are used as a means of verifying users.[89] New techniques for software security certification are being developed.[90] Finally, there is ongoing research on the sciences of encryption and cybersecurity.[91]

It is essential that users keep operating system and applications software current, as vendors are continually issuing security patches. Users need to heed alerts warning them of dangers. For example, in May 2018, the Federal Bureau of Investigation issued an urgent request to internet router owners asking them to turn the devices off and back on in order to defeat malware that had infected hundreds of thousands of the devices.[92] Many users, including corporate users who should know better, are leaving critical information unencrypted in the cloud.[93] In the USA, calls for vigilance have become even less effective, after it recently became known that President Trump finds installing security features on the phones he uses for tweeting 'too inconvenient'.[94]

7.10 Summary

Fundamental human rights include feeling that one's home and belongings are protected, that one is not in danger, and that only what one wants to disclose is being disclosed. These three rights go by the names security, safety, and privacy; they are the topics of Chapters 7, 8, and 9.

We began with security. Cybersecurity has been a concern of the computing community since the early days of time-sharing, which first allowed people to access a computer concurrently. There are a seemingly bewildering number of ways in which digital security can be compromised. Yet all have one or both of two origins: either flaws in the design of the technology, and/or mistakes made by users when they are enticed by hackers and criminals.

The earliest hackers were typically young white males. They were usually motivated more by mischievousness and idealism than the desire to do malicious damage. Often, when they did attack computer systems and cause damage and were caught, they received relatively light punishments. The case of Aaron Swartz was a tragic exception.

As the industry matured, the use of digital technologies expanded through the success of the personal computer, the expansion of the internet, and the advent of the mobile phone. Security became a widespread concern; attacks on digital information resources became the providence of serious criminals and major crime syndicates.

Two recent examples of major computer crime were the 2010 Koobface hack and the 2016–17 waves of ransomware. Koobface was a phishing system that suckered numerous users into clicking on a fraudulent social media site and thereby downloading malware. The malware siphoned off funds to the Koobface 'mothership' and spread virally to friends of the victim. The ransomware exploited security flaws in Microsoft operating systems, invaded and took over hundreds of thousands of computers, encrypted file systems, and demanded ransoms if the victims wanted their files. There are numerous other examples of similarly evil software and the disastrous consequences experienced by society as the malware is spread. The 2010s have seen numerous data breaches across the globe, compromising as many as 1 billion individuals at a time.

Some security breaches are clearly targeted at achieving financial gain. A widespread method is called identity theft. Often realized through phishing attacks, perpetrators gain knowledge of identification numbers and passwords of victims. They are then able to siphon funds from their accounts, order goods at their expense, or even create new accounts and draw funds from them. The victims are often unaware of what has happened for some time, or in some cases never become aware of the fact that they have been digitally robbed.

Cybercrime is also rampant in the digital technologies we use every day—mobile phones, other mobile devices such as fitness trackers, smart toys, and intelligent assistants. Problems are not yet common in smart homes, mainly because there are as of now very few smart homes. Yet, as more and more start to be created, especially motivated by the goal of allowing seniors to age in comfort, one can expect significantly more intrusions made possible by lax digital security.

Information and communications technologies are also increasingly used for tabulating votes in elections. This is still controversial. Pros are efficiency gains and supposed lesser risks of manipulation. Cons are concerns about security and the poor user interfaces of early electronic voting machines. Despite the controversy, adoption of such technology is accelerating.

Almost all countries have passed laws dealing with cybercrime. The USA and the UK acted late in the 1980s; China followed late in the 1990s. The laws have not been as effective as was hoped by those who drafted the legislation, in part due to insufficient calibration of penalties to the degree of the infractions. Specific laws have also been introduced to deal with identity theft.

Methods to reduce cybercrime involve both innovations in technology and improvements in human attention and caution. Passwords need to be properly chosen and used with care. Phishing can be reduced with education. Security patches need to be deployed without delay. New technologies such as biometrics seem promising.

So where is all this headed? Are we becoming more or less secure? The recent wave of ransomware, and continued problems with issues such as identity theft, imply a continued and possibly growing vulnerability. There have also been disturbing new developments, with many more technologies to hack—mobile phones, exercise tracking devices, virtual personal assistants, medical devices such as pacemakers, automobiles, and robots—and new methods to hack them.

Also disturbing is the fact that some malware, such as ransomware, of which there are dozens of kinds, is now widely available; one need not be a computer expert to use it.[95] State-sponsored hacking is becoming more routine. It is knowingly carried out by thirty-two nations, not counting Russia and China, and includes some small countries.[96] Developing countries are proving to be an ideal testing ground for malware by hackers linked to nations such as China and North Korea.[97] The final cause for concern is that the hackers are becoming better at covering their tracks by using techniques such as breaking into poorly secured computers and using them as proxies, or by changing fields in internet packets to disguise their origins.[98]

So, even though there is a burgeoning computer security products and services industry, it seems that the hackers and cybercriminals are keeping one step ahead.

Book review: Schneier, Bruce (2000). *Secrets & Lies: Digital Security in a Networked World.* Wiley Publishing.

Book review: Schneier, Bruce (2012). *Liars & Outliers: Enabling the Trust that Society Needs to Survive.* John Wiley & Sons.

7.11 Key terms

1986 Computer Fraud and Abuse Act
Aaron Swartz
Active attacks
Anti-identity theft freeze
Behavioural biometrics
Biometric scanners
Botnet
Butterfly ballot
Mobile phone security
Credit card fraud
Cybercrime
Cyberpolice
Data breach
Denial-of-service
Direct-recording Electronic (DRE) voting system
Fall detection
Hackers
Hanging chad
IMSI catcher
Identity theft
Koobface
Logic bomb
Malware

Passive attacks
Password attack
Pay-per-click
Pay-per-install
Phishing
Punched cards
Ransomware
Security
Smart homes
Spear-phishing
State-sponsored hacking
Time bomb
Trapdoor
Trojan horse
Two-factor authentication
Virus
Vulnerability
WannyCry
Worm
Yahoo!

8

Safety

Safety is often confused with security. A system or an environment may be secure, but if its normal operation does not achieve the intended goals, it may not be safe. Events will not progress as intended, and could go horribly wrong, even to the extent of grave injuries and loss of life.

The more society relies upon digital technologies, the more we count on software to assure our safety. The issue of safety arises in a great variety of circumstances. Our discussion will start with dangers to the individual, then we will widen our focus to the organization, to society, and, finally, to the world.

The digital divide that discourages internet use among older adults is due in part to threats posed to safe use of computers by 'evil' software such as programs that 'phish' for personal information, thereby gaining access to finances and committing identity theft, as we have discussed in the previous chapter. We shall enlarge upon this discussion by speaking of another risk—*computer rage*, which is caused by frustration when users cannot understand or manage the technology. Such instances are especially dangerous for senior citizens. We shall also discuss two ways in which the internet may not be safe for younger people: *cyberbullying* and *revenge porn*. We then examine a topic that arises in daily life: safety threats caused to pedestrians, bicyclists, and drivers by the continual use of distracting mobile devices.

Our inability to control the costs of large-scale data processing implementations is a threat to the safety and health of organizations and governments, as is our inability to understand, modify, and fix large software systems that are no longer maintained by their creators. We shall describe several software disasters, both during their development and after they have been deployed and used. These include the software crisis at the turn of the century—the Y2K threat—which actually was averted, and several cases in which up to billions of dollars or pounds were wasted, including the decades-long saga of air traffic control in the USA.

We shall then enlarge the scope of our discussion to major applications of computers where safety is a matter of life and death. Due to faulty medical devices, there have been cases in which people have received fatal doses of radiation. With complex industrial machinery such as nuclear reactors or electrical power grids, we have seen disastrous accidents that have cost enormous amounts of time and money, made some areas uninhabitable, and taken many lives. We shall look at some of the causes—the complex human and technical factors—and the interplay among them. Such questions are now of even more relevance, as the very recent and enormous interest in self-driving cars has posed questions of whether algorithms or people are better guarantors of safety in personal vehicles, and what happens when control is given to artificial intelligence (AI) systems.

Finally, we enlarge our scope again and discuss the role that information technology (IT) plays in understanding how we are damaging our environment. We shall also discuss ways in which it can be used to help ameliorate the problem, and ways in which it is making the problem worse.

Digital technologies have improved our lives in many ways. There is no turning back. But how serious are its threats to our safety? What can be done to reduce the dangers?

8.1 Visions and context

The cybernetics pioneer Norbert Wiener warned us in 1960 of the threat posed by computer programs that can neither be effectively understood nor controlled by their human creators:[1]

> It may well be that in principle we cannot make any machine the elements of whose behavior we cannot comprehend sooner or later.... [yet] [a]n intelligent understanding of their mode of performance may be delayed until long after the task which they have been set has been completed.... our effective control of our machines may be nullified. By the time we are able to react to information conveyed by our senses and stop the car we are driving, it may already have run into the wall.

We shall return to his ideas in Chapter 11's discussion of machine learning algorithms.

Computer science professor Joseph Weizenbaum took Wiener's concern and updated it in terms of where he saw software systems heading in the mid-1970s:[2]

> almost all the very large computer programs in daily use... have usually been put together (one cannot always use the word 'designed') by teams of programmers, whose work is spread over many years. By the time these systems come into use, most of the original programmers have left or turned their attention to other pursuits.... [then] their inner workings can no longer be understood by any single person or by a small team of individuals.... Our society's growing reliance on [such] computer systems... which long since [have] both surpassed the understanding of their users and become indispensable to them, is a very serious development.... decisions are made with the aid of, and sometimes entirely by, computers whose programs no one any longer knows explicitly or understands.... the system of rules and criteria that are embedded in such computer systems become immune to change, because, in the absence of a detailed understanding of the inner workings of a computer system, any substantial modification of it is very likely to render the whole system inoperative and possibly unrestorable.

We shall discuss understanding and controlling software in this chapter and also in Chapter 11.

The computer out of our control has been a theme of many science fiction novels and films, such as the landmark film *2001: A Space Odyssey*.[3] On a long space voyage, increasing evasiveness and distrust between the crew and the computer HAL develops over time. HAL intuits this, but insists that it has never made a mistake. Two crew members go out of HAL's hearing to discuss disconnecting it if it seems to make more errors. HAL learns about this by lip-reading. HAL terminates the life support systems of all crew members except Dave Bowman. Dave and HAL then have the following conversation:

Dave: *Open the pod bay doors, HAL.*

HAL: I'm sorry, Dave. I'm afraid I can't do that.

Dave: *What's the problem?*

HAL: I think you know what the problem is just as well as I do.

Dave: *What are you talking about, HAL?*

HAL: This mission is too important for me to allow you to jeopardize it.

...

Dave: *HAL, I won't argue with you anymore! Open the doors!*

HAL: Dave, this conversation can serve no purpose anymore. Goodbye.

Dave 'lobotomizes' HAL by pulling out its memory cards, one after another; HAL protests that it could do better, sings 'Daisy Bell', and plaintively and unforgettably repeats: 'I'm afraid, Dave... I'm afraid.'

Science fiction and superhero films have also featured driverless vehicles, foreshadowing the current developments in self-driving cars,[4] to be discussed in detail later in this chapter.

Research: The theme of the computer out of control in science fiction writings and film.

Book report: Wiener, Norbert (1960). *The Human Use of Human Beings: Cybernetics and Society*. Free Association Books.

8.2 Frustration, anger, and rage in internet access

In the previous chapter we discussed digital identity theft, typically resulting from phishing that lures a person into revealing critical personal information, and resulting in significant financial loss and aggravation. But there are other instances in which internet access is not 'safe', that is, 'free from harm or risk', because there are other kinds of harm, namely, frustration, anger, even rage.

Effective *interaction design* of software for computers or mobile phones enables users to work or to play with ease, without making many errors, and with the ability to learn and grow in their use of the technology.[5] If the interface is obscure, confusing, inconsistent, even hostile, it can cause frustration and anger, which is unhealthy, especially for senior citizens.

Computer and information sciences professor Jonathan Lazar has conducted a series of studies about frustration in using a computer.[6] His research on 107 student and fifty workplace users—a convenience sample of users having a variety of levels of experience, but only a few novices—showed high levels of frustration and productivity loss, with about one-third to one-half of the total time wasted. Common causes were error messages, internet connection unreliability, system crashes, and missing or hard-to-find features. Frustrated workplace users were then angry at the computer 40 per cent of the time, felt helpless or resigned 23 per cent of the time, were determined to solve the problem 18 per cent of the time, and were angry at themselves 10 per cent of the time.

Computer rage

Frustrated users react in various ways. Some turn it back on themselves and think they are stupid. Others feel anger, even rage, at the computer, the software designers, their boss or employer, or the world in general.

Figure 8.1 Do you ever feel like this when working at your computer?

A survey of 150 users reported behaviours when enraged (listed in decreasing order of frequency) including cursing, mutilating a disk, popping off keyboard keys, slamming down a mouse or keyboard, kicking the computer, ripping out a cable, breaking a screen, and dropping the computer on the floor.[7] The stress implicit in these actions makes evident that the environment was not comfortable and safe for the user.

Field study: Interview individuals who have felt anger or rage against their computer or mobile phone. Describe and summarize their experiences.

8.3 Cyberbullying and revenge porn

Poor usability is often a nightmare for seniors, causing frustration and even rage. Two issues arising with the use of digital technologies mostly affect the young. The first is *cyberbullying*, which has been a particular affliction for middle and secondary school students. The other is *revenge porn*, which typically arises in early adulthood, beginning with the university years.

Amanda Todd

A heartbreaking case of both cyberbullying and revenge porn is Amanda Todd, a 15-year-old girl from British Columbia who was blackmailed because she had exposed her breasts via webcam. She was then bullied, physically assaulted, and socially isolated by her peers.[8] She moved several times to new schools, inflicted self-harm on herself, and then posted her story on YouTube in September 2012. She committed suicide a month later, after which the video went viral. By February 2017, it had been viewed more than 12 million times.

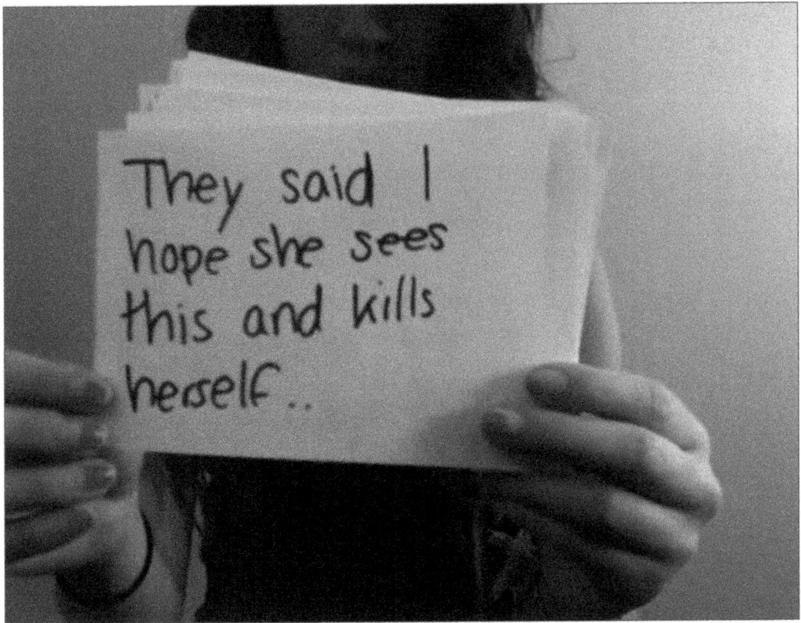

Figure 8.2 Amanda: My story: Struggling, bullying, suicide, self-harm[9]
Courtesy of the Amanda Todd Legacy Society

Continued on next page

Eventually, a 38-year-old Dutch man known only as Aydin C. was found guilty of internet fraud, based on allegations that he had similarly harassed thirty-four young women and five gay men in a number of countries around the world. He was sentenced to eleven years in prison, and still faces additional charges in Canada.[10]

Cyberbullying has been defined as 'an aggressive, intentional act carried out by a group or individual, using electronic forms of contact, repeatedly and over time against a victim who cannot easily defend him or herself'.[11] Estimates of the prevalence of cyberbullying vary greatly, but typically fall in the 10–35 per cent range, with some numbers going as high as 70 per cent.[12] Cyberbullying can be more devastating than physical bullying because it is ever-present, transcending the boundaries of time and space. A particular risk factor is that victims often keep their experiences to themselves. In a study of 360 Swedish adolescents, 18 per cent of those between the ages of 12 and 15 reported having been cyberbullied in the previous two to three months. In 50 per cent of cases, victims did not tell anyone about the bullying; they told a friend 36 per cent of the time, a parent or guardian 9 per cent of the time, but never a teacher. Not being able to talk about the pain with someone trusted and sympathetic makes the experience all the more devastating.

A particularly evil form of cyberbullying is revenge porn. Revenge porn has been defined as 'typically consist[ing] of sexually explicit photos or videos that are uploaded on the internet by former paramours—spurned ones, as the word 'revenge' connotes—without permission of the individuals depicted in them and sometimes accompanied by identifying data such as names, addresses, and FB accounts'.[13] The individual who is assaulted by the posting or transmission of images without his or her permission is often unaware that it has happened. A survey of 3,000 American internet users aged 15 and older found that one in twenty-five online Americans had either been a victim of revenge porn or had been threatened by it.[14] In England and Wales, there were 1,160 offenses reported in the first nine months after a new law criminalizing the sharing of photos without consent went into effect in 2015.[15] The average age of alleged victims was 25; 30 per cent of the victims were under 19; three victims were only 11 years old.

There have recently been high-profile revenge porn cases against celebrities, such as actress Jennifer Lawrence and sports reporter Erin Andrews.[16] Revenge porn is perpetrated against women and girls far more than it is against men and boys—90 per cent of the cases target women.[17] A revenge porn attack is humiliating. It raises the odds of offline stalking or a physical attack. It typically leads to profound fear, anxiety, and panic attacks, may lead to loss of a job and difficulties in finding a new job, and can cause one to withdraw from online activities, which makes it still harder to find work. Furthermore, it can take months or years to track down all copies of the images on the internet, and to request that they be removed using the takedown notice mechanism (discussed in Chapter 2), as copies may have spread virally.

Because of the devastating effect on victims and its public relations effects, there has been progress towards legal remedies in some US jurisdictions. Legal scholars disagree as to which are the most effective. If the images have been stolen, the perpetrator can be charged with theft, extortion, or computer hacking.[16] Laws against sexual harassment, and against the intentional infliction of emotional distress, can sometimes be used. Because 80 per cent of the images were originally taken as 'selfies', copyright law can sometimes be used.[18] Specific internet laws are typically not effective, as laws such as the Communications Decency Act (discussed in Section 5.4) and the Digital Millennium Copyright Act (discussed in Section 2.3) often act to protect the owners of websites against prosecution. A number of jurisdictions in the USA have in recent years enacted laws making revenge porn a criminal offense.[17,13] The courts have begun to take the issue seriously; in a recent case a woman whose ex-boyfriend threatened to use revenge porn to make her life 'so miserable she would want to kill herself' was awarded $6.4 million in damages.[19]

Research: Compare and contrast the application of various laws that may be used to convict someone of revenge porn in one jurisdiction.

Research: Compare and contrast how the law is applied against revenge porn in several different jurisdictions.

8.4 Attention and distraction

Our last danger for individuals arises from the proliferation of mobile devices that so many of us use continuously. When we start to move, especially outdoors, whether by foot, bicycle, or car, mobile phone use distracts us from the environment (other aspects of this will be discussed in Chapter 12), so we become a danger to ourselves and to others.

Pokémon Go

This video game, part of a long series of successful Japanese Pokémon games and merchandise, centres around fictional characters ('pocket monsters') which humans can capture and train.[20] Immersion in Pokémon Go is substantial; these characters are superimposed on an augmented reality portrayal of one's real world. Collaborative play is encouraged.

The summer of 2016 saw frenetic use of Pokémon Go. Hence there was a study of 350,000 tweets and 321 Google News story clusters in a ten-day period in July 2016.[21] From an analysis of a random sample of 4,000 tweets, they estimated that there were over 100,000 tweets commenting on use of Pokémon Go by drivers, passengers in cars, and pedestrians. Fourteen crashes were attributed to use of the game in traffic. The Pokémon Go Death Tracker website (unknown origin) tabulated, with links to internet sources included, fourteen deaths and fifty-five injuries around the world in the first ten and a half months after the game's release.[22] The actual injury total was greater than this.

Pedestrian safety in busy modern cities can be impacted by mobile phone experiences less compelling then Pokémon Go. We have all seen many cases of individuals walking along the street, and crossing a street, while speaking or texting on a mobile phone. Mobile phone-related injuries of US pedestrians increased faster than pedestrian injuries as a whole from 2004 to 2010, and in 2010 even exceeded those of drivers.[23] Individuals walking along a route conversing on a phone remembered fewer objects than those just waiting for a call.[24] Mobile phone users crossed unsafely into oncoming traffic more often than did iPod users and individuals with neither device. One study reported gender differences, with females being less likely to look at traffic before starting to cross, less likely to wait for traffic to stop, and less likely to look at traffic while crossing, as compared with matched controls.[25] The only good news is that mobile phone-absorbed individuals of both genders did seem to cross more slowly.

Bicyclists also risk their lives by using their mobile phones while cycling. According to two observational studies in Groningen, the Netherlands, 3 per cent of bicyclists were using their mobile phone, but there was a shift from 2.2 per cent of the cyclists calling in 2008 to 2.3 per cent typing and texting in 2013.[26] These studies and one other observational study,[27] done in The Hague, the Netherlands, found that using a mobile phone while cycling caused increased mental effort, decreased peripheral vision performance, and fewer head movements. Such behaviour also resulted in other unsafe actions such as riding further from the curb, and more situations where other people needed to react to prevent an accident. As with pedestrians, cyclists using mobile phones did go more slowly, thus reducing their risk. Confirming evidence of this came from Japanese student bicyclists.[28] Those who were aware of the danger of using mobile phones while cycling seemed to act more cautiously and reported fewer crashes or near-crashes.

Even more troubling is the recent increase in distracted driving due to mobile phone use. In 2013, according to the US National Safety Council, 27 per cent of car crashes—over 1.5 million—were caused by mobile phone use.[29] For four decades, fatalities in US car crashes had decreased, in part due to increased seat belt use, air bags, and reductions in impaired driving.[30] In 2016, however, such deaths increased dramatically. Many experts attributed this to the use of apps such as Snapchat, Waze, and Pokémon Go.[31] These figures are all the more staggering given that that there is significant underreporting of mobile phone use in automobile accident reports.[32]

This experiential data has been supported by research. One lab study compared subjects responding to traffic situations in a driving simulator under five conditions: placing a mobile phone call, conversing casually, conversing intensely, tuning a radio, and having no distraction.[33] All four of the distractions caused increases in the proportion of situations where subjects failed to react. This effect was greater with younger subjects, and even greater with subjects over the age of 50. A review of over fifty research studies emphasized that drivers using mobile phones often used compensatory strategies such as driving more slowly, following at a greater distance, and modifying how to allocate attention to various tasks.[34] Yet these strategies typically broke down in critical situations where driving is difficult, which are the situations when accidents tend to occur. The literature confirms that young and old drivers are the most susceptible.

Our dismal safety record is a reason to let algorithms do the driving, as we shall discuss below.

Research: Why many bicyclists think it is okay to use a mobile phone while cycling, and seem unconcerned about safety.

Research: Compare and contrast the laws governing use of a mobile phone while driving, cycling, or walking in three different countries that take these offenses seriously.

Debate: Resolved: A driver who causes any accident resulting in hospitalization or a hospital visit while using a mobile phone should not be allowed to drive again for at least ten years.

Law: Draft a law severely punishing cyclists who cause a serious accident while using a mobile phone.

8.5 Uncontrollable software development

We now leave the individual and examine threats to organizational and societal safety that arise with complex software. There can be problems because software fails to do what is intended (or, in the case of Hal in *2001*, fails to do our bidding). But, before that, it has to be developed, which can take large teams of programmers many years and sometimes not even be finished.

How many lines of code?

A recent analysis by Jeff Desjardins enumerated the size of some critical systems we now depend upon, as measured in lines of code expressed in some programming language.[35]

Here are some examples:

System	Millions of lines of code
Simple iPhone game app	0.01
UNIX v. 1.0 (*c*.1971) operating system	0.01
Pacemaker	1
Space shuttle	4
Boeing 787	6.5
Android operating system	12–15
Windows Vista operating system (2007)	50
Facebook, not including back-end code	62
Software in a typical car	100
All Google services	2,000

It would take 36 million pages of paper to print out all 2 billion lines of Google's code, a stack 3.6 kilometres high. The incredible complexity of useful software systems makes them hard to develop, understand, and control.

The history of software development is filled with examples of large projects that finished way over budget and in much more time than projected, or in some cases did not finish at all. An early overview of this issue is CHAOS,[36] a report on a survey of 365 IT executive managers in a variety of industries who provided data on 8,380 applications. Thirty-one per cent of projects were cancelled before completion; 53 per cent of group projects were completed, but at a cost of 189 per cent of their original estimates. Their methodology and the starkness of their conclusions were questioned in a number of subsequent analyses,[37] both in terms of the failure to account for forecasts evolving over time as more information is known, and for the tendency of some groups to purposely aim high or low in their estimates. Yet there is no doubt that we are at risk since predicting the time and cost of software development projects is so difficult. Here are two major examples.

The plan for automating the British National Health Service has been regarded as one of the worst IT debacles of all time. The 'Connecting for Health' programme was initiated in 2002 to provide a nationwide electronic medical record and to assist with X-ray management, electronic prescriptions, and outpatient appointments. The original cost was estimated at £2.3 billion over three years.[38] By 2006, the projected cost was an estimated £12.4 billion.[39] The project was terminated in 2011, and ceased operating in 2013. There were three major causes of failure.[40] The first was haste, including insufficient preliminary work, the creation of an unrealistic timetable, and the failure to take the time to consult with stakeholders. The second was design, including overly ambitious expectations, the failure to consider risks, and the failure to realize how much technology would change over the lifetime of the project. The final cause was labelled 'culture and skills', and included poor leadership and project management, continuous changes in project aims, insufficient concern over privacy, and IT suppliers lowballing on their proposals and then charging more due to the inevitable variances necessitated by poorly written specifications.

The second example comes from the USA with the implementation of healthcare.gov, the site to support the new US health insurance system under the *Affordable Care Act* (also referred to as 'Obamacare'). Similar to Connecting for Health was the need for excessive speed with the project's implementation and inadequate planning.[41] For example, 50,000 to 60,000 concurrent users were expected when the system launched in October 2013, yet it had to cope with 250,000 users instead. This caused multi-hour wait times, as well as bizarre and frustrating glitches.[42] The total cost was $1.5 billion, as compared with the original projection of $94 million.[43] A study reviewing the project identified at least six major causes of the problems:[44] (1) requirements were not suitably specified and adhered to; (2) there was inadequate capacity planning; (3) system testing was done inconsistently; (4) coding errors were known but not corrected prior to launch; (5) some required functionality was not available at launch; and (6) project oversight was ineffective.

The cost of such software disasters is more than just financial. An example is the *US Office of Personnel Management*'s system for processing retirement papers of government workers.[45] Attempts to automate it have been under way since 1977, yet no working electronic system has been created. Six hundred employees still work in an underground mine north of Pittsburgh, Pennsylvania, to handle the paperwork, storing the records in 28,000 filing cabinets. It costs an exorbitant $100 to process each claim; the average time to receive a check is sixty-one days, the same time it took in 1977.

An Australian example in which the project was actually completed is the *Queensland Health Payroll System*, estimated to cost the taxpayers AUS$1.2 billion.[46] The system went live in 2010, and left thousands of workers overpaid or underpaid by weeks. A 2013 suit against the vendor that implemented the system, IBM, failed in 2016; it was dismissed because it was judged that public servants, not the private contractor, had improperly managed the project. By then, the government was still trying to recover over AUS$62 million in overpayments to staff.

Software engineering experts have enumerated reasons for their profession's inability to do a better job of forecasting the cost and time required for large projects, including:[47]

- Unrealistic goals, or goals not stated clearly
- Poorly stated project requirements
- Poor project management
- Poor project planning
- Inaccurate estimation of the needed resources
- Poor milestone and status estimation and reporting
- Inadequate quality control
- Poor communication among stakeholders, especially between users, customers, and developers
- Commercial pressures
- Stakeholder politics.

A critical component is how the work is organized. In the early days of system development, jobs were managed by the *waterfall method*.[48] Everything was planned in advance as a series of steps, for example, requirements analysis, design, coding, testing, and deployment. This method was linear: workers would finish each step and proceed to the next. Increasingly, it became obvious that this method did not work. Reasons included flaws in the requirements, which only became obvious later, and problems arising in deployment, which required changes to the design.

An approach that seemed to address these realities was the *spiral method*,[49] in which developers cycled through successive stages of requirements, design, coding, testing, and deployment. More recently, programmers have become enthusiastic about the *agile development* process,[50] in which small teams produce and test working versions of parts of the software frequently, perhaps daily; actively collaborate with the customer; and respond to needed changes rapidly. A study of forty-two development projects at eighteen Norwegian firms showed that flexible methods (including agile development) yielded fewer overruns in effort (which translates into lower costs) than those that followed a sequential model.[51] For example, agile development by a team of independent programmers replaced the buggy and slow enrolment software for healthcare.gov with one that worked better for the website's second launch.[52] Independent of the method used, getting the requirements right, in other words, specifying clearly what the customer needs as early as possible in a project, is the most critical component.[53] Sufficient time and money must be spent to do this.

What happens if you fall behind? A discouraging answer was provided by *Brooks's Law,* named after its formulator. Fred Brooks had supervised the development of IBM OS/360, a project that finished dramatically over time and budget.[54] The law states that '[a]dding manpower to a late software project makes it later'. The job of reorganizing tasks and training new members of the project team swamps in the short run any gains realized by the efforts of the new people.

Research: Analyse in detail a critical software project that was not completed, including a discussion of all causes, roles of management of both client and supplier, and effects on all stakeholders.

Research: The downside of agile software development.

Book report: Glass, Robert L. (2003). *Facts and Fallacies of Software Engineering.* Addison-Wesley.

8.6 Incomprehensible and incorrect software

Joe Weizenbaum's concerns, mentioned at the beginning of this chapter, showed great foresight. Software has become more and more complex ever since. To what extent do we understand what we have built or what we are building? Given the complexity of so much software, it is remarkable that so much works well. But what if it does not work properly?

The Y2K problem

Incomprehensible software attracted worldwide attention in 1999 by way of the so-called Y2K problem.[55] In the early days of computing, in the 1940s and 1950s, the turn of the century seemed eons away. Furthermore, memory was costly then, so clever programmers decided that they could represent years with the equivalent of two decimal digits, and dates with the equivalent of six decimal digits instead of eight. But, by the mid-1980s, programmers and managers of software systems started to wonder what would happen on 1 January 2000. Would systems behave bizarrely? Would electronic devices stop working altogether?

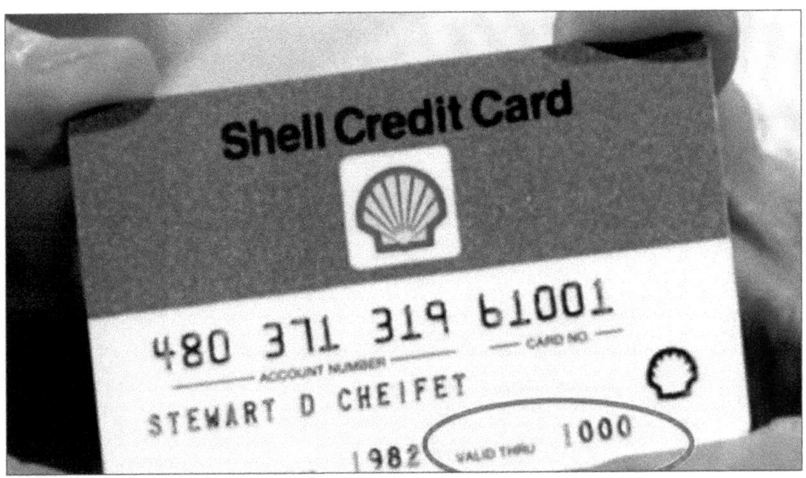

Figure 8.3 An amusing credit card shown in a video about the Y2K problem[56]
Computer Chronicles, Stewart Cheifet Productions

A massive effort began throughout the world, ultimately costing more than $300 billion, to identify locations in software where the bug would manifest itself and repair them. As a result, few crises emerged. A research social scientist viewed this positively as an 'organized response to the perceived threat of the Y2K bug as one of the greatest, public-facing attempts to educate and train individuals and organizations to manage the unforeseen, and potentially devastating, effects old computer code can have on contemporary computerized infrastructures'.[57]

A second example comes from the UK—the *Universal Credit system*.[58] The idea was to merge and unify social support payments that previously had come from six different sources: Jobseeker's Allowance, Employment and Support Allowance, Income Support, Working Tax Credit, Child Tax Credit, and Housing Benefits. The bill authorizing this programme received Royal Assent on 9 March 2012. Originally estimated to cost £2.2 billion, this has ballooned in the latest projection to £15.8 billion; it was supposed to end in 2017, but now the completion date is projected for 2021.[59] Money was not efficiently spent; as of December 2014, £697 million had been spent; only £34 million of this proved to apply to the final system. Front-line staff were demoralized; 90 per cent of them judged the IT as 'inadequate'. Adverse effects went far beyond the costs of implementation; in February 2017, MPs launched an investigation because of widespread evidence that thousands of tenants trying to survive with the help of universal credit were falling behind on their rent and running up debts because they had to wait at least forty-two days for a first payment.[60]

A similar example comes from Canada. *Phoenix* is a centralized payroll system for the Canadian government launched in 2009 with an estimated cost of C$310 million and with the goal of saving C$78 million per year.[61] It was launched in February 2016. Problems were discovered in April, but not understood until a year after launch. Despite issues, it was rolled out to all departments at the end of April, after which the previous system was decommissioned. Since then, more than half of the almost 300,000 federal employees have at some point had a request for outstanding pay. By November 2017, the government estimated it would cost three years and C$540 million to fix, an amount the Canadian Auditor-General asserted was an underestimate. The system was commissioned by a Conservative government, which was blamed for cutting employees too quickly and not spending enough on training. The system was launched under a Liberal government, which was blamed for rolling out the system too quickly and ignoring warning signs.

A final example comes from the US air traffic control system. The story begins with a US$2.5 billion plan developed by the *Federal Aviation Administration* (FAA) early in 1981 to replace the then already obsolete technology with a so-called *Advanced Automation System* by 1996.[62] It took until 1988 to award the contract to IBM.[63] By 1992, the costs had doubled to an estimated $5.1 billion, and the project was already behind schedule by six years, making it vulnerable to even more additional cost increases and schedule delays. The original programme was therefore terminated, with little to show for it. In 1995 a new contract for a substantially reduced concept was awarded to a 'new' supplier, a company that had purchased the IBM division that had been working on the previous project.[64] Air traffic controllers were in despair at the lack of progress:[63]

> in aging control centers across the country, overworked controllers direct tens of thousands of flights each day with the same screens that were out of date 15 years ago. So fragile is the equipment that technicians who open it for maintenance fear doing more harm than good. During breakdowns...more and more frequent, controllers carry slips of paper around darkened control rooms or read commands aloud....skill and luck substitute for technology...about two dozen times in the last two years, the 25-year-old mainframes that drive the controllers' screens at five of the busiest centers have failed, delaying hundreds of planes each time, sometimes for hours.

Furthermore, the new scaled-back project did not even allow for the use of the Global Positioning System (GPS), which did not exist when the entire process began in 1981.

So where is US air traffic control today? Since 2002, the FAA and its contractors have been trying to implement a new system known as *NextGen*.[65] While this is happening, air traffic control still relies on ground-based radio stations and radar as it has since the 1960s, a system that requires planes to fly at least five miles apart and that can 'lose' planes that fly at low altitudes or behind mountains.[66] The latest estimates suggest that only in 2020 will NextGen be able to track every airplane over the US skies with GPS.

One more issue arose in lengthy policy discussions and debates about the future of US air traffic control: the question of how much automation to implement and the desirable role of human air traffic controllers.[67] Three possible scenarios were judged relevant.[68] The first is the then-current method emphasizing human controllers, aided by some machine assistance, which is still how things work today. The second is one in which individual computer actions assist a human specialist who has the primary responsibility for decisions and control. The third option is one in which computers do the vast majority of the work and carry out most functions autonomously. We shall see the tension among these points of view again in the context of autonomous vehicles (self-driving cars) later in the chapter.

Research: Research and discuss the British Universal Credit software development.

Research: Compare and contrast the US and Canadian experiences with improving the technology for their air traffic control systems.

Field study: Track down programmers who worked on the Y2K problem. Research, analyse, and discuss their experiences, paying particular attention to the difficulties in understanding complex software written by others.

8.7 Medical devices and safety

Most of the examples we have discussed, with the exception of air traffic control, have not dealt directly with life and death. Yet since software now controls most medical devices, digital technology, and its creators, are responsible for human lives.

Therac-25

One of the earliest and best researched cases of this kind was the Therac-25 medical electron accelerator, manufactured by *Atomic Energy of Canada Limited* (AECL).[69] Between June 1985 and January 1987, there were six massive overdoses of radiation, half of them fatal, five in the USA and one in Canada. These accidents happened with the eleven machines that had been installed. Many contributing causes were identified in the subsequent review, including hardware, software, user interface, documentation, personnel, and management issues. The timeline of events shown below (adapted from a thorough study by computer scientists Nancy Leveson and Clark Turner)[69] is a vivid demonstration of the inability of health personnel and hospital administrators, working together with hospitals and regulatory agencies, to react with appropriate speed and caution to clear signs of danger.

3 June 1985	***Overdose in Marietta, Georgia (Patient says, 'You burned me', was told that was not possible.)***
Subsequently	Facility physicist calls AECL to inquire about possible malfunction, told: 'not possible'.
	Despite reddening of skin, and severe pain, patient given subsequent treatments.
	Later, the patient filed suit against AECL and hospital, settled out of court.
	Patient eventually *loses breast, and use of her shoulder and left arm*, due to overdose.

Continued on next page

26 July 1985	***Overdose in Hamilton, Ontario***
Subsequently	Problems suspected in micro-switch, AECL orders recall.
	Dialogue among AECL, hospital, consultants.
	AECL asked by government to make more changes, most of these are not made.
	Recall order lifted.
	Patient required *total hip replacement*, but dies due to cancer.
December 1985	***Overdose in Yakima, Washington***
Subsequently	AECL claims there could not have been Therac-25 or operator error.
	AECL also writes that there have been no other cases of similar damage!
	Patient suffered *minor disability and some scarring* due to overdose.
21 March 1986	***Overdose in Tyler, Texas***
Subsequently	Therac-25 shut down, AECL starts to investigate
	AECL says that machine could not overdose a patient
	AECL asserts there were no other known incidents of radiation overdose!
	AECL suggests a hospital electrical problem
	Problem not found, machine put back in operation.
	Patient eventually *dies* due to complications from excessive radiation.
11 April 1986	***Second Tyler, Texas overdose***
Subsequently	AECL and US FDA (Food and Drug Administration) notified
	FDA declares Therac-25 defective.
	Correspondence, negotiation between FDA and AECL; users notified of software bugs.
	Dialogue and investigations among users about problems, but usage does not stop.
	Patient eventually *dies* due to overdose.
17 January 1987	***Second Yakima, Washington overdose***
Subsequently	More correspondence, negotiation, discovery of software bugs, fixing of bugs.
	Finally, in February 1987, FDA recommends all machine use stop.
	More correspondence, negotiation, bug fixing.
	Uuse stoppage is lifted in August 1987.
	Patient eventually *dies* due to overdose.

Debugging complex technology used in hospitals in many locales distant from the manufacturer and regulatory agencies is difficult, even more so in the pre-internet days, but how could it be that debugging was still required years after the models were introduced and used routinely on patients?

Leveson and Turner explained that 'accidents...usually involve a complex web of interacting events with multiple contributing technical, human, and organizational factors', including:

- management inadequacies and lack of procedures for following through on all reported incidents,
- overconfidence in the software and removal of hardware interlocks (making the software into a single point of failure that could lead to an accident),
- presumably less-than-acceptable software-engineering practices, and
- unrealistic risk assessments along with overconfidence in the results of these assessments.[69]

Computer science professor Harold Thimbleby reviewed issues in medical devices and safety twenty years after publication of the Therac-25 investigation.[70] He noted that 11 per cent of patients in UK hospitals suffered adverse events; a third of these led to disability or death. He noted furthermore that medication errors were one of the primary causes, and that 17 per cent of medication errors involved miscalculation of doses or other causes related to dosage. Arguing against the phrase 'user error', because the user is only part of a larger system, Thimbleby asserted that the phrase 'use error' was more appropriate. He concluded that *use error* was 'a symptom of the latent errors, the incoherence between appropriate use (or not) of other information such as patient records and vital signs', and could be reduced through proper design.

In general, design has improved, in part through decades of emphasis on human factors and user–computer interface design. Yet critical and sometimes fatal errors still occur, as for example in the fatal 2006 overdose of 15-year-old Lisa Norris in Glasgow, Scotland, caused by nineteen exposures in one month to radiation that was 58 per cent too high.[71]

Research: Compare and contrast the Therac-25 radiation cases to that of Lisa Norris's case.

Jury: Assume that a manslaughter case was brought against AECL by the family of one of the patients killed by an overdose of radiation from a Therac-25. Discuss what the finding of the jury should be and, if there is a verdict of guilty, what the penalty should be.

Ethics: You work as a programmer in a software company that manufactures a medical device which is life-critical. Your major competitor introduces what seems to be a new product that will be far superior to yours. Your corresponding new product has been insufficiently tested, but the CEO says it must be announced at a trade show next month and be shipping by the following month. What do you do?

8.8 Industrial disasters

Industrial disasters are 'disasters caused by industrial companies, either by accident, negligence or incompetence...where great damage, injury or loss of life are caused'.[72] Occurring mostly in the defence, food, manufacturing, mining, and energy sectors, they are typically caused by poor preparation, taking shortcuts, overconfidence, poor housekeeping, insufficient information, neglecting safety procedures, and distractions.[73]

Industrial and systems engineering professor Najmedin Meshkati has analysed serious accidents in the use of large-scale industrial technological systems, including Three Mile Island (TMI) and Chernobyl, and concluded that the causes stem from 'the way the [system] parts – engineered and human – fit together and interact'.[74] These include *micro-ergonomic factors* such as the design of control panels and visual displays, and *macro-ergonomic factors* dealing with the relationships between technology and workers, managers, and organizations. Some factors result from *design-time decisions,* such as complex operational processes, poor training, and organizations that cannot adapt to stress. Other factors manifest themselves primarily at *operations time,* while the system is running, such as poor training and management systems, and inadequate responses to sudden environmental disturbances. Problems with digital technologies often play a substantial role, especially in terms of their use by human operators.

Three Mile Island

Digital technologies control the machinery with which nuclear reactors are powered up, operated, and shut down. Use and misuse of these technologies was a key component in the TMI nuclear reactor incident in rural Pennsylvania in March 1979.[75] A partial nuclear meltdown was followed by the release of some radioactive gas into the atmosphere. The radiation seems to have had little effect, but stress was severe. Symptoms of post-traumatic stress disorder (PTSD) were seen in the vicinity of TMI as much as five years after the accident.

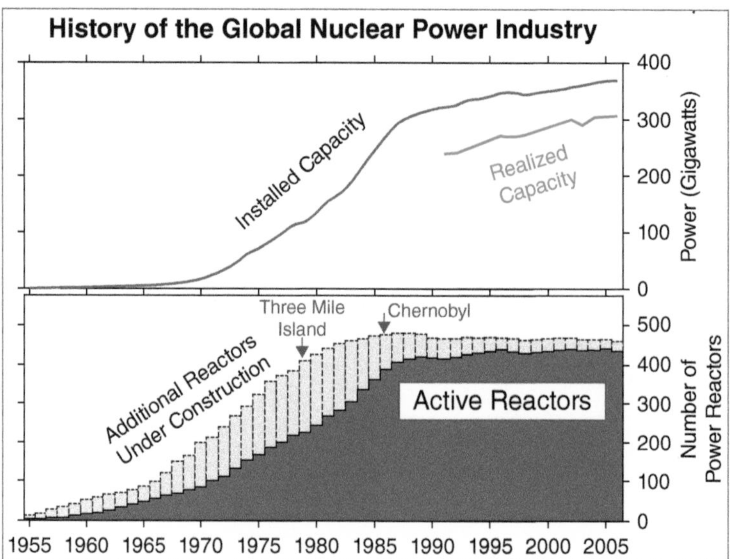

Figure 8.4 TMI and Chernobyl, and factors such as cheap natural gas, have slowed growth of the nuclear power industry[76]

Many causes for the accident were identified. There were four separate equipment malfunctions. Training of the operators was inadequate, both in terms of understanding the equipment and in responding to emergencies. Plant procedures were deficient, with needless paperwork and poor quality assurance. The controls and displays were confusing to the operators, conventions were inconsistent, and important information was displayed in places where it could not be seen. The totality of these unfortunate micro-ergonomic factors contributed to operators often performing wrong actions during the stressful time of the incident. Perhaps most importantly, there was an aura of complacency that a major nuclear accident could not happen in the USA.[77] Although some have argued that the TMI incident could not have been avoided because the circumstances were highly unlikely, there had been plenty of individual warnings about many of the failures that did occur that day, and major blame had to be assigned to management failure.[77] Despite the accident, TMI has continued to operate, although it was set to close in 2019.

The *Chernobyl* disaster occurred in April 1986 in Ukraine, which at the time was part of the Soviet Union.[78] A nuclear reactor core exploded, releasing large amounts of radiation into the atmosphere. Prevailing winds carried and precipitated the radioactive material over large areas of the Soviet Union and western Europe. Short-run casualties included 300 deaths, a death rate for plant workers after the accident ten times greater than the rate before it, increased birth defects near the plant to twice the normal rate, augmented leukaemia and thyroid cancer rates at two to ten times the normal rate, and the forced evacuation of more than 2 million people.

As with TMI, there were a multitude of causes, some stemming from the design, others from the way the reactor was operated. The design was a risky one, attempting to use one reactor both to generate energy for the population and to produce plutonium to close the perceived gap in the Cold War arms race with the USA. This design placed undue pressure on operators, forcing them to perform more tasks in unreasonable time frames and encouraging them to cut corners and even to disconnect safety devices. As with TMI, manager and operator training was inadequate, and human–computer interface problems with the control panels made operations needlessly difficult.

A third example deals with the power grid, the *Northeast Blackout of 2003*, which affected 55 million people in the northeast USA and Ontario.[79] On a very hot day in August, one generating plant in Ohio went offline, forcing increased demand on other plants. Several power lines then sagged due to heat from excessive current, touching trees and going offline. A software 'race condition' bug in energy management software in one plant deactivated the alarm system without operators realizing, which delayed actions that could have stopped the meltdown. The result was a cascading effect: the normal system load balancing failed as more and more circuit breakers tripped, taking other generators offline. The blackout contributed to at least twelve deaths, and caused days of disruption to water supplies, transportation and communication systems, and factory operations. On a lighter side, it inspired many stories, legends, comedy sketches, and, because it encouraged couples to stay indoors in the dark, plausibly even births. Following the blackout, software engineers took weeks of effort to examine millions of lines of code to trace the software bug.[80]

Finally, there have been several false alarms from computer-based systems designed to give early warnings of missile attacks. In one case, in 1983, a Russian officer correctly did not believe two separate false warnings of such attacks, in part because he knew that the technology was unreliable.[81] Just recently, early in 2018, as Hawaii was on edge due to tensions between the USA and North Korea, an employee selected an incorrect option from a poorly designed user interface, triggering a statewide warning about an imminent nuclear attack instead of an internal notification about an upcoming test.[82] The result was forty minutes of widespread panic throughout the state.

Research: Compare and contrast the Three Mile Island disaster to the one at Chernobyl. Pay particular attention to the role of information technology, and human factors in its use.

Research: Research and discuss the similarities and differences between the computer science field of human–computer interaction and the industrial engineering field of human factors in dealing with issues of system safety.

Concept: Improve the Wikipedia entry on 'use error'.

Debate: Resolved: There would be fewer accidents with unsafe systems if they were all artificially intelligent and there were no humans in the loop who could make accidents.

Policy: Draft a brief for the new CEO of a nationwide electrical power grid using new artificial intelligence software for load balancing and distribution.

8.9 Autonomous vehicles

Already in daily use are autonomous trucks hauling gravel, autonomous tractors ploughing fields, autonomous object movers in warehouses, and autonomous rail vehicles in airports.[83] By the mid-2010s, advances in AI had reached a point where self-driving cars moved from science fiction to a likely reality, and to widespread deployment faster than most people anticipated. With new inventions, numerous issues typically arise. We shall primarily discuss safety concerns, but also touch on issues of societal disruption and employment.

Driving a car, or riding in one, has always been dangerous. The first automobile fatality was in 1869. A 42-year-old woman fell out of a steam-powered car, landed beneath it, and had her neck broken when a wheel ran over her.[84] The US National Highway Traffic Safety Administration (NHTSA) reported in 1920 that there were approximately twenty-five deaths per 100 million miles driven.[85] The good news is that this ratio has declined steadily to slightly over one death per 100 million miles driven in 2012. Yet, because we are driving so much more, worldwide carnage amounts to road traffic accidents causing the deaths of over 1.25 million persons per year.[86]

Car accidents are now the leading cause of death among individuals between the ages of 15 and 29. Low- and middle-income countries only own 54 per cent of the world's vehicles, but these nations sustain 90 per cent of the fatalities. 'Vulnerable road users'—pedestrians, cyclists, and motorcyclists—sustain almost half of the fatalities. Since the average American drives around 700,000 miles in his or her lifetime, the probability of him or her dying in a vehicular accident is close to 1 per cent!

What are the major causes? One account,[87] by a US personal injury law firm, listed the top seven reasons as: (1) distracted driving; (2) speeding; (3) drink driving; (4) reckless driving; (5) rain; (6) running red lights; and (7) running stop signs. Another analysis asserted that failure to stay in one's lane and not yielding the right of way are among the top causes of accidents in the largest number of US states.[88] The NHTSA summarizes the carnage with the statement that 94 per cent of the deaths can 'be tied back to a human choice or error'.[89] We have already discussed in this chapter the increasing role of mobile phone use in traffic-related accidents and deaths.

So, acting on the belief that computers, AI, and sensors can drive more safely than humans, and because it is an incredibly large and 'sweet' research and market opportunity, major IT and automobile manufacturing companies have vigorously embarked on *smart car* development.

The Google Smart Car project

Although university projects on autonomous vehicles began in the 1980s, huge impetus came from Google's work on self-driving cars in 2009. It spun out into a firm called *Waymo* at the end of 2016, by which time its experimental driverless cars had logged 2.3 million miles of test driving in four US states.[90]

Figure 8.5 A video on research challenges in the development of driverless cars.[90] The car is in a construction zone. Different kinds of objects are displayed in various shapes and colours so that test "drivers" can help improve the algorithm.
source: Waymo

Continued on next page

Advances in sensor technology and machine learning were used by Waymo's research team to tackle technical challenges such as:[90] (1) sensing the car's location using GPS and 360-degree scanning lasers; (2) distinguishing sensed objects such as cars, cyclists, and pedestrians based on shape, movement pattern, and location; (3) tracking the locations and movements of these objects; (4) detecting unexpected and unknown objects that might affect what the car should do next; (5) anticipating atypical shapes and behaviours of these objects (such as kangaroos in Australia);[91] (6) driving in a naturalistic manner, so as not to cause unsafe movements by other drivers; (7) substituting new conventions, such as inching forward at a four-way-stop intersection, as opposed to using eye contact.

The self-driving car competition is furious. Huge investments and numerous acquisitions are being made by US companies including Tesla, Uber (although it has been reported to be considering abandoning the effort), Apple, Intel, the big three US automakers (the driverless technology division of General Motors recently received a $2.25 billion investment from a Japanese software conglomerate), Volvo, BMW, Bosch, and Volkswagen.[92]

Designing *safe* autonomous vehicles is a challenging research project facing inevitable bumps in the road (pun intended). Simulations (including in virtual reality environments) are used to find bugs in the technology and to improve it,[93] yet ultimately the cars must be tested in traffic. Accidents were to be expected. In two cases, both with *Uber*, tests on public roadways were stopped due to well-publicized accidents—Uber cars driving through red lights on the streets of San Francisco, and an accident caused when a human driver failed to yield to an Uber vehicle in Arizona.[94]

In another incident, in mid-2016, a Tesla vehicle operating in *computer-assisted* mode was involved in a deadly crash in Florida.[95] An initial investigation found no fault with the Autopilot technology, concluding that the accident should have been avoided by the human operator, who was in charge. A tractor-trailer had crossed in front of the Tesla. The Tesla driver had set the vehicle to cruise control at seventy-four miles per hour; neither he nor the vehicle responded in the seven seconds there was to avoid the accident. A later investigation concluded that the system lacked necessary safeguards to ensure that it would be used properly. Since then, there have been two other road deaths associated with the use of Autopilot, one in California, and one in China.[96]

Most recently, an Uber autonomous car, with an emergency backup driver behind the wheel, struck and killed a pedestrian in Arizona.[97] The initial investigation found that the emergency braking system had been disabled by the company to 'reduce the potential for erratic vehicle behaviour'.[98] The woman was crossing the road with a bicycle; she was first identified by the computer as unrecognized, then as another vehicle, and only too late as a bicycle. It did not alert the driver. The driver, who was operating the car at forty-four miles per hour, and who tested positive for methamphetamine and marijuana, was observed by a vehicle camera watching a video streaming on her phone for forty-two minutes before the crash. She looked up only half a second before the crash, and therefore saw the woman with the bicycle too late to intervene. After the incident, Uber shut down its testing facility in Arizona and laid off 300 employees.

There is dangerous haste and confusion in these early deployments. The US Department of Transportation tried to help by introducing definitions to deal with levels of automation:[99]

- At SAE [Society of Automotive Engineers] Level 0, the human driver does everything;
- At SAE Level 1, an automated system on the vehicle can sometimes assist the human driver conduct some parts of the driving task;
- At SAE Level 2, an automated system on the vehicle can actually conduct some parts of the driving task, while the human continues to monitor the driving environment and performs the rest of the driving task;
- At SAE Level 3, an automated system can both actually conduct some parts of the driving task and monitor the driving environment in some instances, but the human driver must be ready to take back control when the automated system requests;
- At SAE Level 4, an automated system can conduct the driving task and monitor the driving environment, and the human need not take back control, but the automated system can operate only in certain environments and under certain conditions; and
- At SAE Level 5, the automated system can perform all driving tasks, under all conditions that a human driver could perform them.

Electronics have long been in cars. There have been cases of bad software embedded in firmware,[100] but electronics have mostly worked reliably. There are obvious examples in which a 'smarter' car could help prevent accidents. One would be to prevent speeds greater than those judged safe in a particular location and certain weather conditions. The question here is whether drivers would ever allow such control over their behaviour. A second example is greater use of voice control, which is already starting to happen.[101] A third example is to detect drowsiness, which is starting to be offered in some high-end automobiles.[102] The idea here is to monitor and measure movements of the car and eventually heart rate, head and eye movements, and body posture. Currently, all that would happen is a warning to the driver. Ultimately, the car might take over control, or also transmit warnings to other cars in the vicinity.[103] Cars collaborating with one another to avoid accidents is an exciting technical challenge and opportunity.

Another challenge and opportunity that must be solved if the self-driving car is to become viable is the creation of a high-resolution map of all roads and the adjacent environment, including traffic signs, road markings, entrance and exit ramps, terrain, and perhaps most importantly, potholes and bumps in the road. In this context, high resolution means down to the level of inches, far more detailed than is the case with current maps, including Google Earth. The process is under way using *lidar*, a kind of radar that uses lasers for range finding.[104] The job will be aided by crowdsourcing (more on this concept in Chapter 10), in which additional data will be assembled from lidar units on Volkswagen and BMW cars starting in 2018.

Two of the most difficult issues with self-driving cars have to do with human behaviour. One challenge is the relationship between the calculated expectations of an algorithm and the real patterns of human drivers.[105] In the above-mentioned case of a four-way stop sign, there are subtle and not-so-subtle cues, as well as social conventions, that determine the order in which cars proceed through the intersection. Another example deals with traffic merging onto and off of a highway or from one lane to another. Humans use a variety of visual and auditory cues, some based on the movement of the other vehicle, but even more so on what one perceives the other driver is doing or signalling with their hands and eyes. Better vehicle-to-human communication is required. Researchers are experimenting with techniques such as audible cues, patterned lights, rooftop displays, laser projections onto sidewalks, and vehicle-to-vehicle transmission of driver intentions.

The other challenge concerns the limitations of a human override when there is automated control and algorithmic decision-making. The idea that a person can snap to attention and take over a careening car in a split-second is naïve, especially if the person is distracted, as seen in the Uber accident.[106] Research has shown that it takes most drivers at least five seconds to regain control of a car. Therefore, solutions where humans are thought to be able to take over control to ease anxiety about self-driving cars are not feasible in situations where cars go at normal speeds in high-complexity environments. Research is also under way on *remote control systems*,[107] where tele-operators can seize control in an emergency, but the time required for such remote backup drivers to become 'situationally aware' is still and will likely remain an insurmountable obstacle. I therefore believe that cars drive themselves or people drive the cars, but not both.

What might a self-driving car of the future look like? What would the user experience be? Visions have been proposed—a 'living room on wheels',[108] the car as conference room,[109] and the car as an object shared among many drivers.[110] The latter idea is already gaining traction in some locales with car-sharing initiatives, similar to car hires. Recent US data indicates that 70 per cent of adults over 50 live in the suburbs, and that 21 per cent of baby boomers have limited access to transportation. The self-driving car is an attractive prospect for individuals with disabilities and for seniors,[111] whose driving abilities are increasingly challenged. Intensive work is also under way on driverless taxis,[112] trucks,[113] and buses.[114] And there is even renewed talk about self-flying cars,[109] this time not as science fiction but as real-life entrepreneurial ventures.[115]

There will be carnage of another kind if and when self-driving cars, trucks, and buses are introduced. Taxi, truck, school bus, and public mass transit drivers would be rendered obsolete. The latter has been explored actively in Europe in over twenty pilot projects.[116] Europe is particularly open to driverless vehicles because mass transit has always been integral to urban planning. Thus, self-driving cars would be able to pick up and deliver passengers to commuter rail and subway stations. In the USA, owing to a strong tradition of well-financed lobby groups, representatives of industries and professions that rely upon orthodox transportation means are mobilizing against the disruptive new industry.[117] We shall return to the serious human toll that could arise from the self-driving car and its social and economic shake-ups in Chapter 10.

There are moral and ethical issues that have always applied to human vehicle drivers, which have recently gained a renewed focus when one considers these decisions being made by machines.[118] One such dilemma is the '*trolley problem*'.[119] A trolley is about to run over five people. It could divert to another track and run over only one person. What should it do? Whom should it mow down? Is saving five people's lives unethical if this can only be done by a 'conscious' decision to kill one person? How do such decisions vary if there are different probabilities of fatalities under the two options, or if children are involved, or if it is unclear who is involved? Should the safety of passengers in a car be given more weight that the safety of individuals in the surrounding environment? Manufacturers of self-driving vehicles will also be considering issues of legal liability that would apply in the case of such untoward events.[120]

Ethics

Societal response to the opportunity of autonomous vehicles: Governments across the world are struggling with the opportunities and challenges posed by the rapid development of self-driving cars.[121] As with other aspects of AI, the hype, the technological sweetness, and the economic incentives present enticing opportunities.[122] Arizona has purposely avoided regulations over safety, taxes, and insurance in order to attract firms developing autonomous vehicles. Pittsburgh volunteered to allow testing in exchange for promised benefits to the city. A retirement community in San Jose, California was offered equity in a self-driving car start-up in exchange for providing a test environment. Politicians are confused, for example over how to respond to futurist suggestions that subways not be repaired but that the tracks be paved over to allow for driverless cars. Lobbying to avoid troublesome regulations is intense.[123] Consumers are sceptical and apprehensive. A recent survey of 3,000 individuals, almost half seniors, indicated a preference for human control rather than full vehicular automation.[124]

Is society behaving ethically, given the mix of benefits and risks, in moving so aggressively to introduce self-driving cars? Human drivers have historically demonstrated irrational actions and improper judgement when driving, resulting in massive carnage on the roads. Yet there are simpler and proven ways of improving safety such as road medians, automatic braking systems, lower speed limit regulations, and mobile phone use restrictions.[125] Sensing technologies and AI could also be used to prevent inebriated individuals from driving, and to enforce caution in poor weather. These should be tried while the technology of self-driving cars is developed with greater care. This would also give society the time to weigh the benefits and risks to various stakeholders—pedestrians, drivers, passengers, other users of the roads, transit, and individuals who drive for their livelihood—and then decide how to proceed. How can society behave ethically in response to the opportunities and pitfalls of autonomous vehicles?

Research: Compare and contrast the visions of self-driving cars in various science fiction and superhero films.

Research: How various local and state governments have reacted thoughtfully or irrationally to planning for the possibility of self-driving cars.

Research: Research, analyse, and discuss what is known about the ability of human drivers of cars, trains, or planes to react to emergencies when the vehicles are being mostly driven and controlled by computers.

Research: Expand and illustrate with specific examples the levels of automation discussed in this section.

Debate: Resolved: The driver of the trolley, whether human or machine, should not swerve to hit one person, even if this would mean saving the lives of five people who are currently in the trolley's path.

Debate: Resolved: If computers are to do most driving of cars, they must do it all, as it is impossible for humans to react in time in case of emergency.

Policy: Write a brief for the mayor of a city responding to a motion from a city councillor that driverless cars be forbidden in their city.

Book review: Lipson, Hod, and Melba Kurman (2016). *Driverless: Intelligent Cars and the Road Ahead.* The MIT Press.

Field study: Interview seniors about their feelings about self-driving cars. Are there differences in opinions between the old and the 'oldest old' (this term was defined in Section 1.7)?

8.10 The environment

Thus far in this chapter, we have explored the value and risks of disruptive technologies that can endanger individuals, organizations, geographic areas, municipalities, and countries. One concern dwarfs all others—the question of environmental sustainability. Is our planet as a whole sustainable? Digital technology is only one of many factors at play here, but it is an important factor. We shall discuss three separate issues: (1) the role of digital technologies in understanding and predicting climate change; (2) their role in facilitating sustainable development, as for example with the measurement and tracking of energy footprints; and (3) the impacts that the creation, use, and eventual disposal of digital technologies have on the environment, including issues such as planned obsolescence, the right to repair, and electronic waste.

For the past forty years, scientists, thoughtful observers, politicians, and almost all intelligent people have been concerned about the effects of increased levels of carbon dioxide and methane, also called *greenhouse gases*, on the environment. The resulting increased amount of carbon in the atmosphere has had and will continue to have a deleterious effect on global climate. This is true despite flawed counter-arguments by climate change deniers,[126] misplaced concerns about informational bias in media reports,[127] and unhelpful assertions that greenhouse gas emission restrictions ordered by highly industrialized countries represent another form of imperialism.[128]

Climate change models

IT is vital to environmental sustainability because it powers simulation models used to forecast climate in the future. These models are used to predict phenomena including changes in the earth's temperature, sea levels around the world, quantities of sea ice, weather patterns, weather disturbances such as hurricanes, the viability of agriculture in several regions of the world, and the future of human biodiversity.[129]

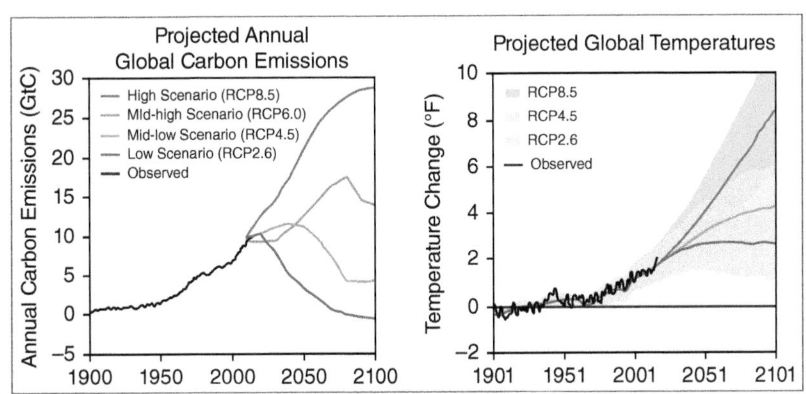

Figure 8.6 Several climate change forecasts of global average temperature (on the right), as a function of varying scenarios of carbon emissions (on the left)[129]
U.S. Global Change Research Program (2017), 'Executive Summary' in the *Climate Science Special Report: The Fourth National Climate Assessment: Volume I report*.

It is important to realize that there are a range of models for various phenomena, such as average global temperature and average sea level. For example, the graph on the left above depicts four plausible levels of future greenhouse gas emissions. Predictions of a set of models for three of these greenhouse gas levels (shown on the right above) are a range of possible outcomes, depicted by the shaded areas. Despite the uncertainty, the models predict an overwhelming likelihood that continued greenhouse gas emissions will lead to world disaster.

The threat to the earth's future has led to an explosion of earth science research such as climate forecasting methods;[130] stochastic weather generators to allow sensitivity analyses of climate change scenarios;[131] assertions that the biological consequences of global warming are already evident;[132] improvements in modelling extreme weather events;[133] and a better understanding of the effects of extreme weather events on food production, plant diseases, and pests.[134] There has been enhanced modelling of the effects of global warming on vegetation structure,[135] on biodiversity,[136] on drought,[137] and on global warming.[138] There have also been forecasts that the consequences of global warming are making the earth uninhabitable for humans.[139]

Digital technologies also contribute to maintaining sustainability in other ways. *Sustainable development* has been defined as 'development that meets the needs of the present without compromising the ability of future generations to meet their own needs'.[140] Based on ideas originating in the 1970s, computation is used to support sustainable development. This is done by helping organizations and societies measure and track their environmentally impactful actions through the use of indicators known as *footprints*. For example, a 'carbon footprint' estimates the extent to which certain actions use up the limited capacity of the earth to absorb greenhouse gases. Mathematical models are now routinely used for energy and environmental analysis.[141] These help industries and governments make resource allocation decisions that will enable the design of sustainable communities and thereby benefit the environment.[142]

Telework, smart buildings, and intelligent transport all could reduce greenhouse gas emissions. Yet when societies adopt and adapt to novel technology, it is difficult to predict all the consequences. Unforeseen issues arise. For example, telework reduces the need for travel, but also enables more globally distributed multinational organizations, so causes new needs for travel.

What about information and communication technology (ICT)'s own footprint? ICT's energy is used in three ways: (1) to manufacture digital technologies; (2) to operate them; and (3) to dispose of and replace them with newer versions.

The manufacture of computers and cathode ray tube (CRT) monitors uses significant energy and employs hazardous materials such as antimony, arsenic, cadmium, and lead. These elements must be disposed of separately from normal garbage, but often end up in landfills, incinerators, or recycling, posing dangers to humans and the environment.[143] Much hazardous chemical waste is exported from the developed world to developing countries with an 'out of sight, out of mind' philosophy.

What makes things worse is that the cycle of obsolescence and technology replacement; vendor-encouraged perceived need for more speed, memory, and features; and insatiable consumer hunger for the latest and the fastest guarantee that almost all digital technology will be upgraded or replaced by users every few years.[144] A major culprit is the operating system. Developments in Microsoft Windows between 1996 and 2008 increased the processor speed requirement by a factor of fifteen, the RAM required by a factor of forty, and the hard disk required by a factor of thirty.[145] The average life span of desktop computers is three to five years; laptops have about three years; and mobile phones have merely one year. Most users don't need these 'improvements', but they often are forced to adopt them because vendors stop supporting old models and versions, and because consumers are enticed by the 'sweetness' of new technology.

The costs of constant new manufacturing often exceed the cost of operating computers over a three-year period.[146] One exception is server farms, which burn up huge amounts of energy.[145] The 'mining' of cryptocurrencies such as Bitcoin, and their use as currency, consume vast amounts of energy in both manufacture and operations (see Section 12.8).

There are two aspects to the problem of hardware and software replacement. One is that technology and technology vendors do not support or acknowledge a purchaser's *right to repair*,[147] as they can increase their profit margins by withholding technical information and spare parts from third-party repair shops. There have recently been court battles in the USA, with consumers and do-it-yourself advocates battling the likes of Apple and John Deere to get the tools and the permission to control and carry out product repair processes by themselves; as a result, the state of Massachusetts is now considering a right to repair law for digital devices.[148]

Another issue is *electronic waste* or *e-waste*, which occurs when repair is impossible or undesirable. A 2012 estimate of the amount of e-waste produced in the USA was 3.4 million tons; a world estimate for 2006 was 50 million metric tons,[149] of which less than 30 per cent was recycled. If the remainder of the world follows American habits, where the average household owns twenty-four discrete consumer electronics products, and phones and tablets are discarded and replaced at increasingly fast rates, the accumulation of e-waste will get even worse.

Research: Read, research, and support where possible, and critique as appropriate, the recent journalistic account in *New York Magazine* entitled 'The Uninhabitable Earth'.[139]

Research: Daniel Spreng has postulated that 'the mutual substitutability of energy, time, and information' is relevant to energy conservation.[150] Present, analyse, and opine on this theory.

Research: Minerals essential for electronics are mined in Africa, especially in the Democratic Republic of the Congo, by both American and Chinese firms. What are the benefits and dangers of this process to the people and to the region? What have been the effects on political stability? What actions have (or have not) been taken to create a humane and sustainable industry?

Debate: Resolved: Telework has reduced the amount of business travel.

8.11 What shall we do?

We began the chapter with a discussion of how individuals using computers can be in danger from more than just external hackers if their 'user experience' is one that is filled with anxiety and stress. The issue is pervasive and is of particular relevance to seniors. Technology developers need to place a higher premium on methods of testing for usability flaws and on ways to ensure that all demographics enjoy a positive experience. Every development team should therefore include a user experience architect with significant clout in the organization.

We next examined three sources of danger to individuals from the use of digital technologies. Cyberbullies make the lives of adolescents miserable. Spurned lovers assault previous romantic partners with revenge porn. Thoughtless pedestrians, cyclists, and drivers endanger themselves and others by using their mobile phones when they should be concentrating. Advances in technology and more parental oversight of their children's computer behaviour can help fight the stigma of bullying. Tougher laws and higher penalties for the uploading of non-consensual salacious material may reduce the amount of revenge porn. Finally, the mobile devices of those driving cars or cycling should be disabled to remove dangerous distractions on the road.

The software engineering profession has a poor record in finishing large projects on time and on budget. Often the job is never completed, because a corporate or government client simply gives up. As with poor user experience, it is essential to put individuals who can understand users and their needs in positions of responsibility. For large projects, this typically involves understanding and reconciling the requirements of major stakeholders, which often are in conflict. Humility in the face of the software industry's poor record for delivering on time and on budget is also required.

Even when large software projects are completed, problems arise in their continued use and maintenance, especially since it is nearly impossible for one person to understand the entire system. As major projects change management and direction, and as the software grows, it becomes incomprehensible and, as a result, uncontrollable. These risks had been anticipated by Norbert Wiener and Joseph Weizenbaum. There is hope that through advances in software engineering, code will be better organized and key features will be more discernible. As digital citizens, we must insist that flexible development methods be used and that significant investment be made on documentation to reduce the degree of this problem.

Given the complexity of many medical devices and the large software-based systems that run nuclear power plants and electric power grids, it is amazing how well they work—most of the time. There is need for better safety procedures and rigorous testing to ensure safe operation and avoid accidents leading to loss of property, injury, and death.

Self-driving cars represent a new area of opportunity and risk. Unless humans demonstrate the ability to drive safely, which is unlikely based on long-standing human irrationality and disregard for human life, including their own, technological aids are required. Given the rapid pace of advances in machine learning, and the power of the major companies, self-driving cars seem inevitable. Yet there are many technological aids that should be adopted first, for example, cars that place limits on human drivers based on signs of inebriation or inclement weather, and mobile phones that turn off when used by a driver. This will allow time for more rigorous and realistic testing of self-driving cars, first in enhanced driving simulators and then on the road, which is essential before widespread deployment is allowed.

Finally, we have seen that computers have aided the improvement of our scientific understanding of the environment and our ability to manage energy and resources. Yet the continual conspicuous consumption of new mobile devices increases resource consumption and the costs of disposal of that which is considered obsolete. ICT must become a major part of the public dialogue about sustainability. Some have even suggested that the 'precautionary' response to the Y2K problem, which helped avert possible calamities, should be a metaphor for how society should treat the problem of environmental sustainability.[151]

8.12 Summary

Digital technologies are deployed in order to save time and money and to carry out tasks that humans are unable to do by themselves, or at all. Yet there have been and continue to be countless examples in which the technology created to help us also places us at risk.

In some cases, the danger is experienced by the individual. Intractable interfaces to software and to digital technology can cause stress, frustration, and rage. Especially in adolescence, in which there have always been bullies, boys and girls can be attacked by cyberbullies, a new and insidious threat that never completely goes away. Somewhat later in life, careless construction of nude photographs that are shared with a romantic partner who one believes can be trusted can subject one to the harassment of a revenge porn assault. Finally, our constant immersion in cyberspace via multiple devices can subject us and others to dangers when we are in motion, whether on foot, on bicycle, or especially by car. The law is still evolving in terms of providing suitable remedies.

Other examples arise where the intended system is so complex, or the people assigned to build it have so little competence, that delays in implementation and spiralling costs result in the project's cancellation. Despite advances in software engineering, recent project management disasters such as the British National Health Service medical records system, as well as the Obamacare health insurance website, demonstrate that we are still unable to deliver suitably functional software on time and on budget. It is discouraging that this seems to be true despite advances in software development and project management methodologies.

Even more troublesome are the safety consequences of software that does not work properly. An example of this was the so-called Y2K crisis, with concerns that software written with the assumption that years could be represented in two digits would still work when 1999 turned into 2000. Another example is the history of automation in the US air traffic control system, where decade-long delays in the implementation of desired improvements reduced efficiencies and increased the odds of horrible accidents. Happily, human attentiveness and care have ensured that these did not happen, at least insofar as this is known.

This has not been the case with medical devices, where accidents have happened routinely, especially with respect to medication dosage, and even in the case of radiation dosage, with multiple deaths reported in three countries over three decades. More dramatic have been nuclear reactor accidents, such as those at Three Mile Island and Chernobyl, which were failures of human design. The accidents were also due to sloppy human–machine interaction design, insufficient expertise and training, failure to anticipate disastrous occurrences, as well as poor institutional dynamics and failure to consider the subtleties in the organization of work. The results were significant stress, various cancers due to radiation exposure, and death. There are also new dangers in industries due to the accelerating deployment of robots; as of 2014, robots had been responsible for thirty-three deaths in the workplace over the preceding thirty years.[152]

A recent occurrence is the widespread interest in and promising research and development of self-driving cars. The carnage on highways throughout the world suggests that the roads might be safer if computers rather than people drove cars. Yet we are now on a reckless path of overly hasty adoption that is being pushed by the technological ambitions and greed of technology companies and automobile firms, as well as municipalities seeking new revenue and job growth.

Finally, digital technologies have helped better understand the environment and control wise energy use, but have contributed to the fragile equilibrium of a sustainable planet through our insatiable demand for the newest, the biggest (or the smallest), the fastest, and the fanciest digital technology.

8.13 Key terms

2001: A Space Odyssey
Advanced Automation System
Affordable Care Act (Obamacare)
Agile development
Brooks's Law
Chernobyl
Computer rage
Connecting for Health
Cyberbullying
Design-time decisions
Electronic waste or e-waste
Footprints
Google Smart Car

Greenhouse gases
Interaction design
Joseph Weizenbaum
Lidar
Macro-ergonomic factors
Micro-ergonomic factors
NextGen
Norbert Wiener
Northeast Blackout of 2003
Phoenix
Pokémon Go
Queensland Health Payroll System
Revenge porn
Right to repair
Smart car
Spiral method
Sustainable development
Tesla
Therac-25
Three Mile Island (TMI)
Trolley problem
US Office of Personnel Management
Uber
Universal Credit system
Use error
User error
Waterfall method
Y2K problem

9
Privacy

Fears about loss of *privacy* in computerized societies have been central to dystopian literature. The issue has also concerned thoughtful computer scientists and lawyers since the 1960s. By then, the scope of the computer revolution was making clear that governments and corporations could keep records about almost every aspect of our lives. As data storage became virtually limitless at trivial cost, effective uses of data grew, as did risks to personal privacy.

We shall define privacy, look at its manifestations and roles, and discuss current and future threats to it. We shall introduce concepts that are key to understanding privacy, such as *informed consent*. A major concern is the threats to *information privacy* or *data privacy*, in which a person's confidential information has errors or becomes exposed to people who should not be able to see or use it.

We shall examine situations in which privacy can be invaded by governments, organizations, and individuals. Governments amass vast stores of personal data during the everyday course of administration and regulation. Government surveillance in many nations captures information that should be private, a topic we discussed in Chapter 6.

Search engines, credit rating organizations, and insurance companies also gather huge amounts of data on consumers. When data is incorrect, or is hacked, there are serious implications for information privacy. Criminals seek to gain leverage by ferreting out computer-based data about personal financial transactions. Health information is a particularly sensitive area in which many people feel especially vulnerable.

These are all 'classical' privacy concerns, the dangers of which were evident in the 1960s. New technologies have raised more concerns. Social media holds vast quantities of personal data that we have willingly disclosed, including information that could prove embarrassing later in life. A vivid example of a privacy breech was the *Cambridge Analytica/Facebook scandal of 2018*.

New technologies raise new privacy concerns. Chips use GPS to track our location and movements. Recent advances in computer vision and the widespread deployment of video cameras enable face recognition. Chips located in the environment and embedded as sensors and prostheses in our bodies make our activities and even our moods accessible by others.

Digital records, whether accurate or not, are continually growing in magnitude. These online profiles are a representation, albeit an oversimplified version, of who we are and how we portray ourselves. Have we lost the ability to move beyond embarrassing or immature decisions because of their permanent existence on the internet? Does and can the internet ever forget?

In the past, politicians and diplomats have been afforded some privacy, but the 2016 exposure of Hillary Clinton's 2016 emails showed that this privilege is no longer guaranteed. We shall explore the 'leaking' of confidential government or corporate information as a matter of conscience or an act of malice by *whistle-blowers*. We shall also introduce the legal framework and laws that define invasion of privacy and protect privacy in several countries.

Most data available online about us is information that we have given willingly in order to achieve practical benefits, for example, to receive appropriately targeted advertising, order goods online, or participate in social media. Is privacy a concept whose time has come and gone?

9.1 Visions and context

Invasion of privacy has been central to much dystopian literature. In Bentham's Panopticon and Orwell's *1984*, discussed in Chapter 5, there were all-powerful rulers and a heavily policed society. Franz Kafka's unfinished novel *The Trial* also raised themes relevant to our discussion.[1] The protagonist, Josef K., is arrested by two unidentified agents. He can neither learn the agency that they represent nor the crime for which he is charged. While he remains free, he is unable to move the trial forward to establish his guilt or innocence despite continued and concerted efforts.

Privacy also emerges as a theme in modern motion pictures. For example, in Steven Spielberg's 2002 film *Minority Report*,[2] Tom Cruise's character sees ads being transformed to be tailored to his interests and 'needs' as he passes them on the street. Spielberg commented:[3]

> The Internet is watching us now. If they want to, they can see what sites you visit. In the future, television will be watching us, and customizing itself to what it knows about us. The thrilling thing is, that will make us feel we're part of the medium. The scary thing us, we'll lose our right to privacy. An ad will appear in the air around us, talking directly to us.

These prospects moved from dystopian fiction to likely reality with the exponential growth of data banks holding personal information in the 1960s. Some computer scientists, such as Paul Baran, Richard Hamming, and John McCarthy, began to sound alarm bells.[4] Legal scholar Alan Westin moved the dialogue to a new plane with the publication of his 1967 book *Privacy and Freedom*.[5] Westin helped us understand what privacy is, what its role is, what challenges it faces from technology, and what society must do to help preserve it.

Research: Research, analyse, and systematize the ways in which the issue of privacy has been handled in science fiction novels and films.

9.2 A privacy primer

The right to privacy in US jurisprudence goes back to a classic 1890 paper by Samuel D. Warren and Louis D. Brandeis.[6] Quoting Judge Thomas Cooley, they defined privacy as 'a right to be let alone'.[7] Warren and Brandeis were alarmed in part by the 'instantaneous photographs' that could be taken by the portable camera that had recently been invented; by 'newspaper enterprise', especially the 'yellow journalism' (we spoke of this in Chapter 5) that was practised by tabloids; and by 'numerous mechanical devices'. They spoke strongly about the dangers of 'the unauthorized circulation of portraits of private persons' and 'the evil of the invasion of privacy by the newspapers'. Their landmark paper is regarded as the basis of the modern tort (civil wrong) of privacy, which protects: '1) unreasonable intrusion upon the seclusion of another...2) appropriation of the other's name or likeness...3) unreasonable publicity given to the other's private life...and 4) publicity that unreasonably places the other in a false light before the public'.

Privacy from a psychological point of view

Although a law professor, Westin approached the issue seventy-five years later from a more psychological point of view.[5] He argued that there were four states of privacy: *solitude*, *intimacy*, *anonymity*, and *reserve*. *Solitude* is the most complete state of privacy, in which the individual is separated from other persons and free from their observation. *Intimacy* is a state in which close, open, and relaxed communication is shared with one other person or a small group of other individuals, such as in a marriage or within a family. *Anonymity* applies to a person who is free from identification or surveillance, despite being in a public place or carrying out public actions. *Reserve* is a state in which there is communication or disclosure within limits.

Anonymity, as Westin defines it, goes beyond the concept of being unknown to other people or observers, because it incorporates freedom from surveillance. Reserve leads to the concept of *informed consent*, in which individuals with sufficient knowledge can agree to remove limits to communication or to disclose personal information. Part of the problem of data surveillance is that its pervasiveness makes it impossible to give informed consent. However, some have argued that internet users, that is, almost all of us, have already given consent. In the infamous words of the long-time CEO of Sun Microsystems, Scott McNealy: '[y]ou have zero privacy anyway....Get over it.'[8]

Westin described four functions of privacy for individuals: *personal autonomy*, *emotional release*, *self-evaluation*, and *limited and protected communication*. The need for autonomy is the human desire to not be manipulated or dominated by others, which can occur if one's

Continued on next page

'secrets' are exposed. The need for release is the desire to disengage from one's daily activities, and to be free of the normal public persona, to unwind and relax. The need for self-evaluation allows one to process his or her life, reflect on decisions, and plan for the future. Protected communication avoids the chaos that would result if every thought were immediately communicated to others.

Westin argued that privacy is also essential for organizations. *Organizational autonomy* protects core secrets, which are essential for government agencies, especially in the field of international relations, and are also required for civic organizations, especially those that advocate controversial ideas or invent new technology. *Release from public roles* allows organizations to go about their business independent of their 'public face'. This also applies to legislative bodies, where deliberations and discussions done in confidence allow for negotiations, concessions, and compromises that are required to achieve consensus on controversial issues. Just as for individuals, *evaluative periods for decision-making* are essential to enable and facilitate planning. All of this requires *protected communications*, so that key players can carry out the exchange of positions, ideas, and potential steps towards an agreement that are key to successful negotiation and compromise without fear of immediate backlash or scrutiny.

Surveillance existed long before the advent of digital technologies. *Privacy and Freedom* examined many methods: technologies for physical surveillance and electronic eavesdropping, video recording, and techniques of psychological surveillance such as polygraphs and personality testing. Westin highlighted what he foresaw as the coming dangers of data surveillance:[5]

> vast amounts of information about individuals and private groups…are being placed in computer-usable form. More and more information is being gathered and used by corporations,…schools, and governmental agencies. And as 'life-long dossiers' and interchange of information grow steadily, the possibilities increase that agencies employing computers can accomplish heretofore impossible surveillance of individuals, businesses, and groups by putting together all the now-scattered pieces of data. The danger is augmented by current proposals from some private and government spokesmen who advocate the adoption of a fully-computerized and automatic credit system to replace cash transactions, a single identifying-number system for every person in his dealings with public authorities, and similar 'total' computer systems.

Surveillance using data is often termed *dataveillance*—'the systematic use of personal data systems in the investigation or monitoring of the actions or communications of one or more persons'.[9] Almost all personal data is now recorded and stored, so can be exposed in data breaches, as discussed in Chapter 7. Electronic transactions have replaced cash for most money transfers. Sweden is now moving rapidly towards a cash-free society; 80 per cent of purchases are electronic, a change thought responsible for armed robberies in Sweden reaching a thirty-year low.[10] Despite intentions to the contrary, the US Social Security number and the Canadian Social Insurance number are becoming universal identifying numbers. National ID numbers and cards are in place in many societies, a topic we shall explore below. Where universal identification numbers are not used, sophisticated data linking algorithms allow the assembly of 'life-long dossiers'.

Echoing Westin's psychological focus, Roger Clarke defined privacy as 'the interest that individuals have in sustaining a "personal space", free from interference'.[9] He drew distinctions between 'privacy of the person;... privacy of personal behavior;... privacy of personal communications; and... privacy of personal data'. He stressed that privacy protection involves finding a balance among competing interests; there may be conflict between an individual's desire for privacy and the interests of another person, group, organization, government, or society as a whole.

Law professor A. Michael Froomkin's paper entitled 'The Death of Privacy?', published in 2000, noted how quickly the privacy-invading technological landscape was evolving:[11]

> routine collection of transactional data, growing automated surveillance in public places, deployment of facial recognition technology and other biometrics, cell-phone tracking, vehicle tracking, satellite monitoring, workplace surveillance, Internet tracking from cookies to 'clicktrails', hardware-based identifiers, intellectual property-protecting 'snitch-ware', and sense-enhanced searches that allow observers to see through everything from walls to clothes.

The management professor Stephen T. Margulis highlighted four aspects of information privacy.[12] *Citizen privacy* describes concerns about the information governments collect and the surveillance methods it uses to gather more data on its citizens. *Genetic privacy* (more generally, health information privacy) has been discussed in Chapter 4 with regards to genetic discrimination. *Consumer privacy* deals with the accelerating pace of data gathering by businesses to target strategic advertisements to certain consumer demographics (just as portrayed in *The Minority Report*). *Workplace privacy* addresses concerns about the amount of data being gathered surreptitiously by employers to monitor and control employee behaviour and performance, a topic we shall discuss further in Chapter 10.

Finally, the legal scholar Daniel Solove provided useful insights on how privacy may be invaded and protected by focusing on activities that may impinge upon privacy:[13]

1. Information collection [i.e.]... Surveillance... Interrogation
2. Information processing [i.e.]... Aggregation... Identification... Insecurity... Exclusion
3. Information dissemination [i.e.]... Breach of confidentiality... Disclosure... Exposure... Increased accessibility... Blackmail... Appropriation... Distortion
4. Invasion [i.e.] Intrusion... Decisional interference.

A study in the *Journal of Environmental Psychology* found overwhelming agreement among students from Ireland, Senegal, and the USA in the reasons they desired to have privacy.[14]

We shall now look at threats to privacy from routine governmental data collection (surveillance was discussed in Chapter 6) and corporate collection of consumer data. Medical information privacy will be discussed in this chapter, workplace privacy in Chapter 10. We shall then examine the privacy implications of technologies that have developed in the fifty years since Westin's book: social media, location tracking, video surveillance, and technologies worn on or embedded in the body. Our final topics will be the implications of privacy intrusions on government and diplomacy, whistle-blowers who act against Orwellian government intrusion, and laws that act both on behalf of and against the right of privacy.

Research: Research and analyse critically how privacy and free speech often appear opposed to one another.

Research: Research and analyse critically how privacy and security often appear opposed to one another.

Research: Compare and contrast how various companies that possess huge amounts of personal data have dealt with serious data breaches.

Research: Expand Solove's taxonomy of activities impinging upon privacy with examples for each category.

9.3 Government data collection

Computers (primarily analogue computers) were used by the military during the Second World War. Since then, governments have routinely collected large quantities of data, using digital computers to enhance administrative efficiency with resulting threats to privacy.[15] In most societies, data is collected by several levels of government. By 2001, US federal departments and agencies maintained almost 2,000 databases.[16] After 9/11, many 'fusion centers' were set up to help gather, store, and share data in the fight against terrorism.[17]

In Canada, as another example, the federal government deals with taxation, social security, and voter registration; with the support of industry, research and development; with the census; and with social services and welfare. Employment and financial data on working people is used to decide contributions to pension funds and unemployment insurance. Provincial governments collect data on motor vehicle ownership. Information on health and educational status is used by the single-payer health care system and public education. Local governments deal with real estate ownership, transportation, and utilities such as heat, power, and water. All three levels require sensitive information from individuals to administer public programmes and enforce laws and regulations.

Once governments have our personal information, we have lost control of it. This is one cause for anxiety. Chapter 7 described the 2015 data breach of the US Office of Personnel Management. Over 21 million records of current and past federal employees were stolen. The data included names, addresses, places of birth, and Social Security numbers. Another example is the US tax collector, the Internal Revenue Service (IRS). The US Government Accountability Office recently criticized the IRS for 166 'control deficiencies' that 'limited the effectiveness of security controls for protecting the confidentiality, integrity, and availability of IRS's key financial and tax processing systems'.[18] There have also been many cases of IRS employees accessing taxpayer data for illegitimate purposes; in 2007, over 500 such instances were detected.[19]

How do we know that personal data will be used only for the purpose for which it was requested, and to which we implicitly consented? An interesting case is the US Census Bureau. Evidence has emerged in the past decade that it furnished the US Secret Service with the names and addresses of Japanese-Americans during the Second World War.[20] This information was used to help the government round up Japanese to send them to internment camps. After 9/11, the Department of Homeland Security requested and received data on Arab-Americans living in certain area codes from the Census Bureau.[21] The Census Bureau indicated that the purpose of the data transfer was benign, in order to decide which airports should have signs in Arabic, but its actions aroused suspicions that the information was used to profile Middle Eastern people because of concerns of an Islamist terrorist attack. Despite such incidents, a study of respondents to the 1990 and 2000 censuses revealed that concerns about confidentiality and privacy only played a role in citizen participation and question answering in 1.3 per cent and 1.19 per cent of cases, respectively.[22]

Daniel Solove has argued that the huge government vaults of personal information pose dangers by way of bureaucracy out of control.[16] Suggesting that the appropriate metaphor is not Orwell's *1984*, but Kafka's *The Trial*, he concluded that the problem was:

> the powerlessness, vulnerability, and dehumanization created by the assembly of dossiers of personal information...[it is a] more thoughtless process of bureaucratic indifference, arbitrary errors, and dehumanization, a world where people feel powerless and vulnerable, without any meaningful form of participation in the collection and use of their information.... There is no diabolical motive or secret plan for domination; rather, there is a web of thoughtless decisions made by low-level bureaucrats, standardized policies, rigid routines, and a way of relating to individuals and their information that often becomes indifferent to their welfare.

Yet history has seen much worse than bureaucratic indifference. Consider the German Nazi era (1933–45) and the East German Stasi era (1945–89). The Nazis were originally determined to drive every Jewish person from Germany, which later turned into a genocidal campaign to eradicate all Jewish blood from Germany using concentration camps. This task required efficiency; the Nazis conducted two censuses, built several racial databases, required all German residents to register, and applied information technology (IT) to target certain citizens.[23] The latter was furnished by the Dehomag Corporation, the German subsidiary of IBM, using then-current punchcard tabulating technology. After the war, the East German secret police, the *Stasi*, deemed it necessary to build an infrastructure in which all suspicious and possibly anti-government thoughts and actions came to their attention. By the time the Berlin Wall fell in 1989, the government had used a network of over 250,000 employees and informants to assemble files on 6 million Germans.[24]

National ID numbers

One critical issue that affects the use of personal data by various governments is the desire for or protest against the use of a national identification (ID) number.[25]

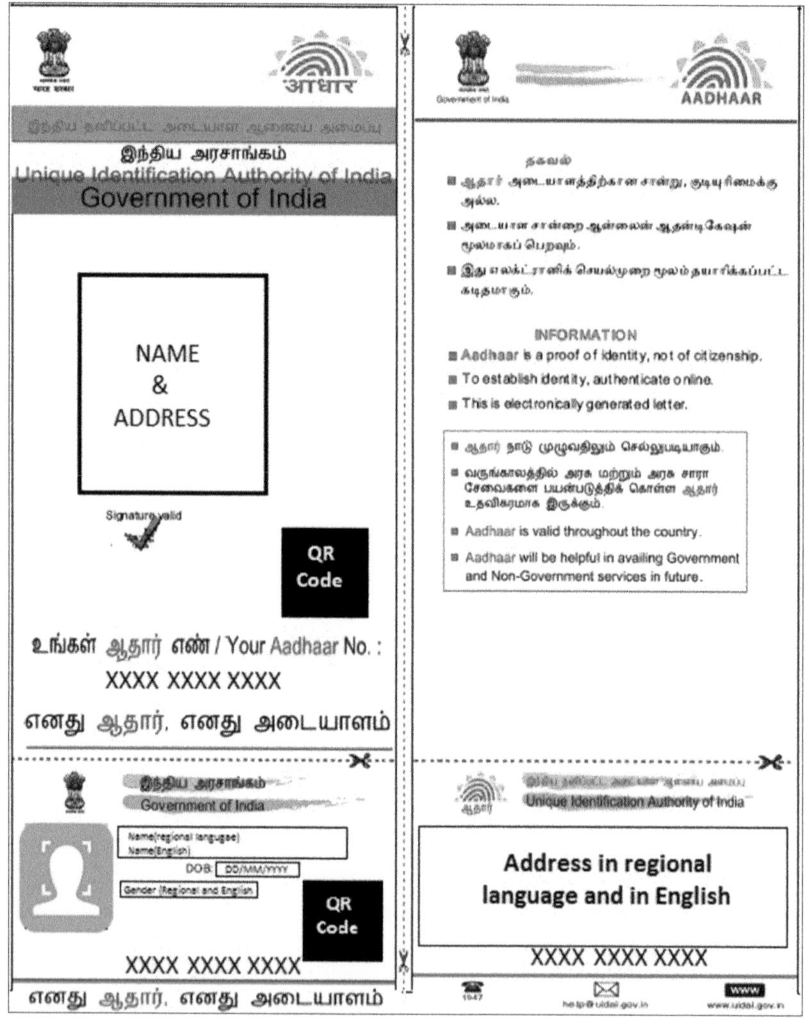

Figure 9.1 An Indian National Identity Card
Sulthan / Wikimedia Commons / CC BY-SA 4.0. https://creativecommons.org/licenses/by-sa/4.0/deed.en

Citizens in the USA have always rejected the creation of a national method of identification. Even though laws at both the federal and state level have specified that it not be used in this way, the Social Security number has become a de facto identifier.[26] Even worse, the

Social Security numbers of many individuals have been revealed through carelessness, bureaucratic indifference, and security breaches. The Real ID Act of 2005 (discussed later in this chapter)[27] appears to be a potential mechanism to turn driving licences into an effective national ID card. Canada is like the USA in that their Social Insurance number is a de facto national ID. However, some countries, such as India, South Africa, Brazil, and China, do have an actual national ID system.

National ID numbers are critical because they allow the joining of personal data from different databases to create centralized profiles on individuals. This has the potential for various uses and abuses. For example, data in police files may be used to deny due process or impede hiring or the awarding of social assistance or health benefits.

Even without a national ID system, techniques known as *computer matching* may be used to take data in multiple files that were compiled for different purposes and look for patterns that allow separate items about an individual to be linked together.[28] A more general approach is known as *data mining*, which has been defined as the following:[29]

> Data mining refers to a series of techniques used to extract intelligence from vast stores of digital information. One kind of data mining simply accelerates the process by which law enforcement or intelligence agents gather relevant information about subjects they already suspect of wrongdoing. This approach is termed subject-based searches. In pattern-based data mining, in contrast, the government investigator develops a model of assumptions about the activities and underlying characteristics of culpable individuals or the indicators of terrorist plans. The government official then searches databases containing transactional and personal information for 'hits' that indicate a match between the model and patterns left by potential evidence of terrorist plans or by potentially culpable individuals.

By 2004, an estimated fifty-two US government agencies were carrying out or planning to carry out 199 separate data mining efforts, with 122 of them making use of personal data.[30] Many of these projects were not being done in the interest of national security.

Potential dangers are illustrated by a few US examples. Social Security data has been matched with selective service data to identify draft resisters and is also used to identify illegal aliens. Federal employment records have been matched with records of delinquent student loans to identify individuals whose pay cheques could be garnished, and also to identify individuals receiving social welfare benefits for which they are not entitled. Incorrectly organized data has disastrous consequences. A mother on welfare was arrested and jailed because of an inaccurate crime report that resulted from a police computer programming error. A man was denied a licence to drive a taxi because of a misleading and incomplete computerized credit report. A woman in a nursing home was denied Medicaid benefits because of the system's failure to properly apply the financial limits imposed by the programme. A single mother lost her job because she had bounced a $60 check several years earlier. These examples certainly fit the Kafkaesque society described by Solove, with a deluge of data, not all of which is accurate, used by bureaucrats and software to relentlessly impose a tangled web of regulations.

Arguably the most critical of government databases are those of the police. By 1986, there were 195 million criminal record histories in the USA, 32 million maintained federally,

40 million at state level, and the remainder at local levels.[31] There also exist thousands of other private security databases at businesses, universities, and hospitals that can be linked to governmental records.[32] As of 1986, about one-third of the US workforce had some sort of criminal record.

Information systems professor Kenneth C. Laudon did a systematic evaluation of data quality in: (a) a non-automated Federal Bureau of Investigation (FBI) database of 22–24 million criminal records; (b) an automated FBI database of 2 million criminal records; (c–e) the criminal record systems of three states; and (f) the FBI's automated system containing records of warrants for arrest.[31] The research sought to establish what percentage of the records were accurate, complete, and unambiguous. In the first five cases, the results were only 26 per cent, 46 per cent, 12 per cent, 18 per cent, and 49 per cent. In the case of the arrest warrant database, 11 per cent of the warrants were invalid, and 6 per cent were inaccurate. The multitude of problems included inaccuracies in recording what happened in court, incomplete records, and ambiguous information. The long memory of arrest data when used in seemingly routine background checks can cause individuals ongoing difficulties, especially in gaining employment, despite research that indicates that criminal recidivism declines rapidly as the years pass if one remains 'clean' after the arrest.[33] The situation is particularly troubling if the data in the files is flawed, as Laudon's research shows is very often the case.

Thus, the masses of government data collected legally pose a threat to privacy. Besides, governments often engage in covert surveillance of communications. Such actions have become more frequent in the wake of 9/11 and subsequent international terrorist attacks.

Research: Research, discuss, and analyse the information collected by various governments in the USA and two European countries (for example, Germany and Italy) on illegal immigrants from Latin and South America and from Africa and the Middle East.

Research: Research and analyse the proposition by which increased surveillance of citizen and non-citizen communications contributes to a country's security vis-à-vis terrorism.

Debate: Resolved: Enhanced surveillance at the cost of privacy does not contribute to enhanced security.

Debate: Resolved: Every country should have a national ID system to enable efficient delivery of government services and to ensure that resources are not wasted needlessly.

9.4 Consumer privacy

Just as voracious as governments are businesses seeking data on customers and potential customers. Traditional newspaper and TV ads are blunt instruments targeting large numbers of roughly homogeneous consumers based on general knowledge about them. The computer's ability to tailor a message to smaller groups, and even to the individual, allows for more cost-effective marketing. The advertiser then knows details about demographics, finances, socio-economic conditions, beliefs, and interests. Hence, many firms have assembled large quantities of data on tens and hundreds of millions of individuals. By 1997, there were 20,000 US commercial and public databases available to marketers.[34] Consumers had little awareness of what data has been collected and how it was being used. Furthermore, new credit instruments and heavy consumer borrowing enabled massive expansion of credit databanks. As with government databases, these contained many errors that can have devastating consequences on consumers.

Yet this was only the beginning. The market research firm International Data Corporation (IDC) has characterized a huge current business opportunity as the *Digital Universe*.[35]

Big data and the Digital Universe

IDC defined the Digital Universe as 'all digital data created, replicated, and consumed in a single year'. The magnitude of the data is doubling every two years. It is projected to grow by 2020 to forty-four zettabytes. To place this in perspective, one zettabyte is a trillion gigabytes. This will amount to over 5,500 gigabytes for each of the by-then 8 billion people in the world. IDC enthused that big data was a boon for the IT industry, with huge opportunities to perform 'big data analytics' on the growing quantities of surveillance footage, embedded and medical devices, entertainment and social media, and consumer images. IDC acknowledged that information security is a critical issue that must be resolved in order for personal privacy to be preserved.

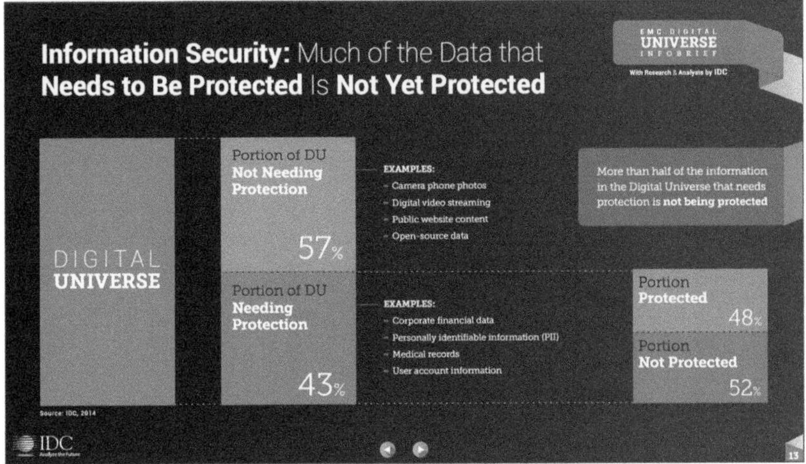

Figure 9.2 If one ignores the video streaming component of the digital universe, much of which consists of duplicate streams of one source video, the vast majority of what remains needs protection via secure systems[36]

Continued on next page

Challenges around providing protection will increase as the digital universe grows. Other contributing factors enumerated by IDC include the increasing presence of the digital universe in emerging markets, and the increasing percentage of data represented by the internet of things, in which there will be communication involving smart devices such as cars, toys, refrigerators, dishwashers, turbines, and even dog collars.

Computer scientists label such phenomena *big data*. It has four essential characteristics.[37] (1) Volumes of big data range from terabytes (10^{12} bytes) to zettabytes (10^{21} bytes). (2) There is a huge variety of data—structured data, unstructured data, images, sounds, and videos. (3) The data comes from a large range of sources. (4) The information arrives at high velocities. Big data promises to support scientific advances, with applications to disease surveillance and modelling that we discussed in Chapter 4. Yet privacy concerns magnify with the scale of data collection. To make privacy intrusions less likely, computer scientists have developed sophisticated computational techniques for anonymization and encryption of the data, but none work perfectly.[38] Work is also under way so that security and privacy are not conflicting requirements, as typically seems to be the case.[37]

Consumers are often willing participants in making the digital universe available to marketers, for they benefit if advertisements are better targeted and more appropriate to their needs. Consumers have varying degrees of tolerance for the disclosure of personal information; most are readily willing to divulge demographic and lifestyle information and are reluctant to disclose financial information such as home values and personal identifiers such as Social Security numbers.[39] Yet we have already seen how insecure these identifiers are, and how little information privacy protects them. Furthermore, in the USA, federal privacy and data security laws do not effectively regulate companies for the gathering and reselling personal data.[40]

One excellent example of the trade-off between better use of consumer information and personal privacy is the work of Google. Since 2000, Google has dedicated more space to ads, pushed unpaid responses to ads further down the page, and improved the degree to which ads are personalized based on its knowledge of who is making the query when one 'googles' something.[41] A milestone was Google's acquisition of the online advertising firm *DoubleClick* in 2007, which had developed an effective auction for allocating space on websites to potential advertisers.[42] Shortly thereafter, Google's CEO Eric Schmidt emphasized to journalists the importance Google placed on gathering more and more data about its users with the following statement, cute yet chilling in its frankness: '[t]he goal is to enable users to be able to ask Google questions such as "What shall I do tomorrow?" and "What job shall I take?".'[41] Only recently, in June 2017, did Google announce that they would no longer scan the messages of Gmail users to improve their ad targeting. We shall discuss Facebook's approach to such matters later in this chapter.

Research: Compare and contrast the approaches of Google, Microsoft's Bing, and the Chinese search engine Baidu in terms of their protection of information privacy.

Book review: Lane, Julia, Victoria Stodden, Stefan Bender, and Helen Nissenbaum (Eds.) (2014). *Privacy, Big Data, and the Public Good: Frameworks for Engagement*. Cambridge University Press.

9.5 Health information

Most people are particularly sensitive about their health information. Yet the drive towards electronic medical records and patient health records, discussed in Chapter 4, means that more medical data is in digital form. For the information to be useful in a health care context, numerous individuals and organizations that participate in the delivery of health care need to access the data, which often requires transmission from one site to another.

In principle, digital health information should be more secure than paper records, as it is easy to specify who should and should not have access and easy to enforce an audit trail of access.[43]

HIPAA

To increase the security of personal health data, and to reduce the number and severity of data breaches, the US Congress passed the *Health Insurance Portability and Accountability Act* (HIPAA) in 1996.[44] Title II of the Act established national standards for electronic health care transactions, standards which also have been adopted in other parts of the world. Health data that is HIPAA-compliant requires the following:[44]

1. Privacy rule: Permissible uses, breach accounting and notification
2. Security rule:

2a. Technical safeguards: Access and audit controls, authentication, transmission security, including encryption

2b. Physical safeguards: Facility access controls, workstation use and security, device and media controls

2c. Administrative Safeguards

3. Enforcement rule: Investigations, hearing procedures, penalties
4. Breach notification rule: Breach notifications

Yet we have seen numerous and increasing numbers of medical data breaches, with these incidents seemingly growing in severity. In 2016, 34.5 per cent of the reported US data breaches—377 known incidents—were in the health care and medical sectors.[45] These breaches exposed more Social Security numbers than did breaches in any other sector. A large percentage of leaks were caused by employee error or negligence. The industry was also hit the hardest by attacks such as phishing. Besides the 2015 Anthem Blue Cross breach already discussed in Chapter 7 that exposed the records of almost 80 million health insurance customers, notable recent examples included two other Blue Cross incidents in 2015 that compromised the records of over 10 million customers each.[46] A typical problem in such incidents was failure to encrypt the data.

Protecting the privacy of health information involves several unique aspects. HIPAA guidelines suggest that where possible health data should be de-identified by removing fields such as name, address, phone number, Social Security number, and email address. Yet doctors need to know the identity of the person behind the data. The volume of data and its heterogeneity make medical data mining more difficult than data mining in other domains.[47] Yet there have been studies showing significant success in re-identification of the information using data that was not appropriately excluded, or from the remaining data.[48]

People's sensitivity over the privacy of medical information can interfere with seemingly excellent research opportunities. This was the case in Iceland, where the Supreme Court upheld the right of an individual to withhold her dead father's genetic information from a population study.[49] Despite the assurance that the data would be anonymized and encrypted, she felt that there was a risk in being discriminated against if she had a predisposition to a heritable disease.

Research: Compare and contrast the causes and effects of data breaches that involve or do not involve medical data.

Debate: Resolved: Whatever the privacy risks involved, it is essential for one's health that data be stored in electronic medical records and personal health records.

Field study: Contact a set of individuals who have suffered breaches of their medical data, interview them, and report on and analyse their experiences, being certain to preserve anonymity.

9.6 Personal information visible through social media

One area of massive data collection accompanied by threats to privacy that dates only to this century is social media, more specifically, social networking sites.[50] Most internet users, especially the young, post huge amounts of personal data to social media. Many are at that time unconcerned with information privacy.[51] Furthermore, careless actions that seem like a good idea when one is young can become embarrassing later in life. In the past, such actions committed in youth could not be disseminated widely. This is no longer true. Now the chances are high that we ourselves have posted these events to social media, where over a billion individuals could have seen them, and possibly even recorded and retransmitted them.

The dominant social medium is *Facebook* (FB), which was founded in 2004 and has since grown with astronomical speed. By 2018, it had over 2.2 billion users active each month.[52] One research team described student life without FB (only four years after it began) as 'almost unthinkable', yet listed specific privacy concerns such as 'inadvertent disclosure of personal information, damaged reputation due to rumors and gossip, unwanted contact and harassment or stalking, surveillance-like structures due to backtracking functions, use of personal data by third-parties, and hacking and identity theft'.[53] Many users, especially the young, have hundreds of 'friends', most of whom are at best acquaintances; many are strangers. Young people routinely post notices and photos about most aspects of their lives. FB uses this data, together with information from other sources, including face recognition, to assemble huge stores of personal information, including location, travel history, financial status, mood, love life, and interests, all of which is useful for advertisers, who provide almost all of FB's revenue.[54]

To control access, users exclude certain personal information, use email, or restrict FB access to certain data to specific people, the effective management of which is very cumbersome.[55] Modifying one's privacy settings is complex; its use correlates with the frequency and type of Facebook use, as well as one's internet abilities.[56] A longitudinal study of Facebook use by a cohort of university community members (mostly students) between 2005 and 2011 showed three interesting phenomena: (1) the amount of personal information shared 'publicly', that is, not restricted to being seen only by 'friends', decreased in the first few years of the study period; (2) the phenomenon reversed towards the end of the period, with more information being released publicly; and (3) the amount of personal information shared with friends, and with friends of friends, increased over the period.[57] Given the rate of growth of the numbers of friends of friends, and the fact that this information is also seen by Facebook itself, third-party apps, and advertisers, there is a great danger that some of the disclosures will come back to haunt people.

One recent university study revealed that 24 per cent of those surveyed had perpetrated 'social insider' attacks on people they knew well enough to gain direct access to their devices or web accounts.[58] They thereby were able to access information they were not entitled to see. Reasons for perpetrating these attacks included fun, curiosity, jealousy, animosity, and utility. In part because of concerns over privacy and internet addiction, significant numbers of people leave Facebook and sometimes other social media completely, committing what is known as 'virtual identity suicide'.[59] These losses have been estimated at approximately 4 million monthly high school users and 5 million monthly university users in the USA. Another reason is the increasing evidence that greater use of Facebook reduces well-being, as measured by quality of life indicators.[60] Finally, social media privacy increasingly interacts with other privacy concerns. For example, the US Department of Homeland Security recently announced plans to collect social media data on all immigrants, all green card holders, and all naturalized citizens.[61]

Cambridge Analytica/Facebook scandal

All past concerns expressed about FB privacy were eclipsed by the 2018 Cambridge Analytica (CA) scandal. Psychographic profiles of up to 87 million American voters were developed using FB data. These profiles were used by the Trump campaign to define target audiences to guide advertising campaigns, model voter turnout, and decide where Trump should travel to garner support.[62]

Continued on next page

Academic researchers have long been mining FB data to learn about millions of users, mostly to understand how FB is used. However, they sometimes dealt with more sensitive information, such as data useful to understanding how people vote.[63] In 2014, Aleksandr Kogan, a Cambridge University psychologist, was hired as a contractor by CA. He used *Mechanical Turk* to recruit 240,000 individuals to answer a battery of 100 questions to probe and understand their personality traits.[64] In order to get paid a couple of dollars for their work, participants had to agree that Kogan could download from FB their demographic data and likes, friend lists, the demographic data and likes of their friends, and some of their private messages. He then used all this data to construct personality profiles of 87 million potential voters, combined this with voter records, and sent the results to CA.[65]

CA is a British political consulting firm funded by wealthy Republicans including Stephen Bannon, Trump's former chief strategist. CA used Kogan's data to target voters with political messages, as we discussed in Chapter 5. It is as of now unknown how much this affected the results of the vote, but it is clear that the effect was significant.

Exposure of these actions by the *New York Times* and the *Observer* of London unleashed a firestorm in the USA. Mark Zuckerberg was subjected to two days of interrogation by bipartisan committees from both houses of Congress.[66] Zuckerberg acknowledged there had been a breach of trust between Facebook and its users.

Figure 9.3 Mark Zuckerberg testifies before committees of the U.S. Senate (captured live from the internet on 11 April 2018)
MediaPunch Inc / Alamy Stock Photo

Due to the scandal, Facebook pledged in April 2018 to inform all 87 million individuals about how their data had been misused, and announced changes in some policies, indicating it would:[67]

1. Centralize app privacy settings;
2. Reduce apps' access to your data to name, profile photo, and email address;
3. Cut off apps' access to your data if you have not used the app in three months;
4. Make it harder to find people using their email address or phone number;
5. Make it harder for advertisers to link offline data with FB profiles; and
6. Disclose information on advertisers.

It is too early to know the timing and effect of these changes. Recently, there have been more disturbing revelations: (a) FB had entered data-sharing partnerships with over sixty hardware firms; (b) these included at least four Chinese electronics firms; and (c) a bug had caused private posts of 14 million individuals to be made public for a week.[68]

The other result of the scandal was that many Facebook users began to question their FB habit. There was a flurry of #DeleteFacebook messages on Twitter. Instructions have appeared on other social media accounts on how to download the data that FB and other social media firms have on you.[69] There have also been reminders of how hard it is to control privacy settings: given an increasingly bloated FB, default settings have changed over time to allow FB more control over how it uses your data, and most individuals fail to override default settings.[70]

Finally, it is important to realize that FB is not the only corporate culprit. Google collects more data on individuals than does FB, although Google's makes it easier for users to download, understand, and control their online data.[71] Additionally, YouTube has been accused of improperly collecting and profiting from personal information it collects on young children.[72] Hiring managers use primary social media data 38 per cent of the time and LinkedIn profiles 29 per cent of the time to understand parameters such as culture fit when investigating new hires.[73]

Research: Study how people's willingness to share personal data on social media has changed over time; suggest and discuss the causes.

Debate: Resolved: Use of Facebook is dangerous to your health and well-being.

Concept: Write a Wikipedia article on 'virtual identity suicide'.

Field study: Identify and contact a set of individuals who have committed virtual identity suicide, interview them, and write up their experiences.

9.7 Surveillance everywhere

There are now increasingly sophisticated digital technologies capable of monitoring us.[74] For example, there are devices that track location and movement. The most mature technology is that of *RFID tags*.[75] Now as small as grains of rice, RFID tags are typically used to keep track of items through an assembly line, warehouse, store, or library. The tags can also be attached to personal possessions such as clothing, passports, or cash. Although keeping the tags live after exiting from a store could be useful in improving after-sales service, a study of trust in privacy protection measures revealed that consumers prefer to have the tag deactivated when leaving the store and to forgo the potential benefits in favour of enhanced privacy.[76]

RFID tags can be and are implanted in animals so as to track them in the wild. This is not now done to humans. Yet people may be carrying items with RFIDs and thus be tracked without realizing it.

A second kind of location tracking makes use of the *Global Positioning System* (GPS) of satellites.[77] It allows mobile devices to know where on earth they are located, and also allows location tracking on those devices. Although use of the latter capability is often portrayed as finding a lost phone, it can also be used to monitor the whereabouts of a person carrying the phone.[78] An example of this occurred in the context of a political protest in Ukraine in January 2014, when individuals who were in the barricaded city centre of Kiev received text messages saying 'Dear subscriber, you are registered as a participant in a mass disturbance'.[79]

Video surveillance

Video surveillance is now widespread, coupled with sophisticated facial recognition algorithms. In the mid-1990s, the US Defense Department sponsored research intended to improve the quality of automatic face recognition; at that time, the best recognizer in the program had an error rate of 0.54 and had a false accept rate of one in 1,000; by 2010, as a result of the funding, the best recognizer scored 0.003.[80] In 2000, 100 billion photos were captured worldwide. By 2010, 2.5 billion photos per month were being uploaded to Facebook. Because most successful recognizers currently use machine learning algorithms, often incorporating *neural nets*, whose performance depends upon the use of large datasets of training data, performance will continue to advance. Artificial intelligence (AI) firms in China focus particularly on this concept; in late 2017, a Chinese AI firm demonstrated facial recognition technology that could also recognize gender, hair length, hair colour, and describe the clothes of the individual.[81]

Face recognition technology has been much in the news in 2018.[82] The shooter at a Maryland newspaper office was identified by police face recognition technology. The city of Orlando, Florida, after testing an Amazon face recognition program, terminated its use after huge protests over potential civil liberties violations. Microsoft urged the passing of laws to regulate the use of the technology. There have been protests over Facebook's use of the technology, despite its assertion that it is intended to allow users to safeguard their online identity. Amazon CEO Jeff Bezos has been asked to discuss his technology with members of Congress. Increasing use of face recognition by airlines as a boarding pass has also raised concern.

These developments enable us to monitor outdoors. Police, traffic control, and military forces are increasingly using video surveillance, especially in mass demonstrations. There is also increasing use of video surveillance for outdoor and indoor home security, and a booming retail marketplace for internet-connected devices.[83]

Product	Netgear Arlo Pro 2	D-Link Full HD Wi-Fi Camera DCS-8300LH	iSmartAlarm iCamera Keep Pro	Tend Secure Lynx Indoor	Wyze Cam V2	Nest Cam IQ	Nest Cam IQ Outdoor	Netgear Arlo Go	Reolink Argus 2	Ring Spotlight Cam Battery
Lowest Price	$419.99 Amazon SEE IT	$89.99 Amazon SEE IT	$89.99 Amazon SEE IT	$49.00 Amazon SEE IT	$19.99 MSRP	$299.00 Dell SEE IT	$349.00 Walmart SEE IT	$394.99 Amazon SEE IT	$129.99 Amazon SEE IT	$199.00 Amazon SEE IT
Editors' Rating	●●●●◐ EDITORS' CHOICE	●●●●○ EDITORS' CHOICE	●●●●○ EDITORS' CHOICE	●●●●○ EDITORS' CHOICE	●●●●○ EDITORS' CHOICE	●●●●○	●●●●○	●●●●○	●●●●○	●●●●○
Connectivity	Wi-Fi	Wi-Fi	Wi-Fi	Wi-Fi	Wi-Fi	Wi-Fi	Bluetooth, Wi-Fi	Cellular	Wi-Fi	Wi-Fi
Integration	Amazon Alexa, IFTTT	Amazon Alexa, IFTTT, Nest	Amazon Alexa, IFTTT	N/A	N/A	Amazon Alexa, IFTTT	Nest	IFTTT	N/A	Amazon Alexa, IFTTT
Field of View (Degrees)	130	130	140	125	110	130	130	130	130	140
Video Resolution	1080p	1080p	1080p	1080p	1090p	1080p	1080	720p	1080p	1080p
Photo Resolution	1,920 x 1,080	1,920 by 1,080	1,920 x 1,080	1,920 x 1,080	1,920 x 1,080	4K	4K	1,280 x 720	1,920 x 1,080	1,920 x 1,080
Storage	Cloud	Cloud, Local	Cloud, Local	Cloud	Cloud, Local	Cloud	Cloud	Cloud, Local	Local	Cloud

Figure 9.4 Best home security cameras of 2018
PCMag.com

As of now, the UK makes the greatest use of video cameras for surveillance.[84] Estimates of the extent of this vary, but some assert numbers as high as 4 million cameras, approximately one for every fourteen people. Such use is also on the rise throughout the world. An estimated 30 million surveillance cameras were sold in the USA in the decade after 9/11.[85] Some are used to watch for illegal immigrants or smugglers crossing the border between the USA and Mexico.[86] The city of Chicago now has 30,000 government-operated cameras.[87] Proponents suggest that the cameras could lower the number of stop and frisks, pointing to a neighbourhood where shootings have been reduced by 52 per cent since the installation of cameras. Opponents express concern over the privacy implications. Extensive use is also found in China, where by 2018 there were 200 million cameras watching over its citizens.[88] Another Chinese application is their use by parents to keep an eye on their children in school via live streaming from the classroom.[89]

A report documenting the increase in video surveillance in the UK in the past decade noted that new opportunities and new threats arise from improvements in technology, including: (1) high-definition cameras; (2) smart cities, in which more and more objects and places are digitized and communicating with one another; (3) the ability to capture and analyse sounds from the environment; (4) the ability to recognize gait; and (5) the ability to track individuals across a city by 'tagging' them and passing the recognition task from a camera in one location to a camera in a nearby location.[90] A recent Stanford PhD thesis analysed 50 million images from Google Street View, Google's online mapping service, and was able to identify the models, locations, and movements of cars in US cities with this data, and then predict characteristics of inhabitants such as income, buying habits, and political leanings.[91]

Video 'surveillance' can also be done by those who are the targets of video surveillance. Steve Mann has labelled this 'sousveillance', literally, watching from below.[92] Examples (see Chapter 6) are citizens recording police actions.

A fourth technology that can track locations is known as *active badges*. The idea for these 'RFID tags on steroids' began with research at the Rank Xerox EuroPARC Laboratory in the early 1990s,[93] primarily as a tool for the efficient location and coordination of staff. Voice recording was explicitly not included because of privacy concerns. A more modern example is the *sociometric badge* developed by the Human Dynamics Labs at the MIT Media lab, which records voice as well as movement.[94] The researchers considered privacy, including ownership of the recorded data.[95] We shall revisit these systems in Section 10.3.

There are also increasing instances of smart devices that gather and make use of huge amounts of location and biometric data, and thereby pose risks to privacy if the data is misused. Examples include fitness trackers,[96] talking dolls,[97] data medallions on cruise ships,[51] and microprocessors in automobiles.[98] As we move towards more and more implantable smart devices, as discussed in Chapter 4, there may be no way for many of us to avoid being monitored and recorded.[99]

All of this is part of the progress towards having devices everywhere—on people, in objects, in the walls. This idea has become known as *ubiquitous computing*, or equally often as *pervasive computing*. The concept was described in a landmark 1991 paper by computer scientist Mark Weiser, who spoke glowingly of 'integrating computers seamlessly into the world at large', of rooms filled with a hundred invisible widgets, where even a dress had computational abilities and could communicate its price, its designer, and whether or not there are any more in a particular store.[100] Privacy concerns arise because the proliferation of smart devices allows real-time tracking of the location and movements of individuals.[101] A number of technical solutions incorporating ideas such as anonymity, obfuscation of one's precise location, and mechanisms to establish trust have been proposed.[102] Unfortunately, there is as of now no method or methods that can guarantee privacy, given the inability to know whether or not the devices one encounters can be trusted not to capture personal information that one does not want to disclose.

Finally, what animates the data collected from all these devices and environments is the increasing ability to use AI to transform them into identifiers of people and their activities.[103]

Research: Research, summarize, and critically analyse the surveillance of an individual's movements and activities via devices that they wear or have within their bodies.

Research: Compare and contrast three countries in terms of their government's use of video surveillance.

Research: Research the commercialization of the concept of having medical personnel in hospitals wear active badges so that mandatory hand washing can be better enforced.

Debate: Resolved: All hospital personnel should wear badges to allow the tracking of their movements.

Debate: Resolved: Face recognition is a technology that has got a bad rap from civil liberties activists and also has many good uses.

9.8 Recording, remembering, and forgetting

Many people, who in the past regretted aspects of their earlier lives, chose to move to places where their past or their transgressions were unknown, for example by moving from the Old World, that is, Europe, to the New World, that is, the USA or Canada, or by moving west in North America. We have seen how social media can now make it difficult for individuals to move beyond their past. Increasingly, there are accounts of individuals whose seemingly harmless actions, behaviours, and pranks while teenagers or university students have come back to haunt them later in life.[104] Recent examples include a 25-year-old US teacher trainee who was denied a degree because of a social media photo showing her drinking alcohol, and a 66-year-old Canadian psychotherapist being denied entry into the USA because of a thirty-year-old article describing his experiments with LSD.

This issue goes beyond social media. Given technologies such as the Internet Archive and Wayback Machine,[105] discussed in Chapter 2, it is plausible that almost all aspects of our lives will be recorded, and that any part of our past may be exposed at some point. The situation gets more ominous as society has more incentives, methods, and technologies to track the actions and movements of everyone. One interesting and extreme example of this is the idea of *lifelogging*.

Lifelogging

A lifelog has been described as 'a unified, digital record with the totality of an individual's experiences, captured multi-modally through digital sensors and stored permanently as a personal multimedia archive. . . a record of the past that includes every action, every event, every conversation, every material expression of an individual's life; all events will be accessible at a future date because a lifelog will be a searchable and recallable archive. . . . [also] detail[ing] everywhere an individual has been'.[106]

Enthusiasts have postulated that lifelogs will encourage introspection and self-knowledge, increase 'intimacy, understanding, and accountability' in relationships, preserve family history and ease the pain of loss, improve work abilities and the exercise of professional responsibility, and enhance security because one is always being recorded.[107] Yet the risks to privacy should the record be penetrated are profound.

Continued on next page

A pioneering invention demonstrating lifelogging was Microsoft Research's *SenseCam*.[108] SenseCam was a lightweight camera with several environmental sensors that was worn on an individual's chest. SenseCam would automatically take wide-angle photographs documenting the wearer's activities. It has proven helpful in stimulating autobiographical memory in individuals who have severe memory impairments.[109]

Figure 9.5 A close-up of SenseCam; SenseCam being worn; three images taken by SenseCam

Courtesy of Microsoft Research. Reproduced with permission from S. Hodges, et al. SenseCam: A wearable camera that stimulates and rehabilitates autobiographical memory. *Memory*, 19 (7): 685–696. Copyright © 2011, Rights managed by Taylor & Francis. https://doi.org/10.1080/09658211.2011.605591.

Computer scientist Gordon Bell took lifelogging further with a system called *MyLifeBits*,[110] based in part on Vannevar Bush's Memex concept (introduced in the Prologue). Bell's idea was to encode digitally, store, and enable easy retrieval of all the data he encountered in his lifetime. This legacy content began with documents and messages, including digitization of books and papers in his library. It grew to include recordings of phone calls, conversations, and meetings, as well as photographs and images. Digitization of videos was also anticipated; it was then restricted to noting video metadata due to storage limits, limitations that are no longer the case today.

Although the project did not yield a product, we see elements of its ideas now in daily life. For example, businesses now tell us routinely that our phone calls can be recorded 'for training purposes'. MyLifeBits was therefore a valuable tangible realization of the prospect of total digital personal life recording and storage. It challenges us to think about what should be recorded, what needs to be kept private, and how the balance is to be guaranteed. For example, psychologists Abigail Sellen and Steve Whittaker, in reflecting on the project from the point of view of their discipline, suggested that a more constructive goal than 'total capture' would be to apply machine memory where people have trouble remembering.[111] An example would be multimodal capture of team meetings, in other words, automatic information capture as a prosthesis rather than as a substitute for human memory.

Lifelogging may be viewed as a form of *sociow-spatial sousveillance,* one in which the past can be *recalled* rather than *remembered*. It poses issues including who owns the data, what, if anything, should not be captured, and what can and should be done with the data.[106] Some forgetting—some 'imperfection, loss, and error'—should be built into lifelogging systems. Law professor Anita Allen noted the privacy issues raised by lifelogging, and suggested that there were significant dangers, both from 'pernicious memory' and from 'pernicious surveillance'.[107] Incidents captured by someone's lifelog will also be captured by the lifelogs of people who participated in or witnessed the incident. Someone's attempt to move beyond it, to 'forget' it, could be foiled by inadvertent or purposeful disclosure by a witness. It may be harder to move beyond painful memories of traumatic incidents.

Furthermore, Allen argues that lifelogs will be prime candidates for government surveillance and access.

The software industry has responded vigorously to the potential of digital recording, technologies to enhance memory, as well as options for forgetting.[104] An Israeli company called face.com developed excellent software for recognizing faces on the web and in mobile applications.[112] In 2012, Facebook purchased the company and has continued to develop the software as a deep learning neural net program known as *DeepFace*.[113] The software is said to be 97 per cent accurate. For those who want to erase unsavoury events from their digital history, there is also now a class of software typified by companies such as *Reputation Defender*, which states as its mission: '[d]on't let negative online content affect your professional and personal life'. For a fee, this firm will endeavour to get damaging content removed from the web and will bombard the internet with positive content to cause search engines to bring forth the negative less frequently. Finally, some social media, typified by Snapchat and Instagram Stories, transact in data that is intended to be consumed quickly and then 'disappear'. Yet, due to the false sense of security timed videos and pictures provide, it is more likely that embarrassing or salacious content will be shared through these media and have ramifications in the future.[114]

If everything can be recorded digitally, will aspects of our past that we wish to move beyond haunt us forever? How can we keep such details private?

Research: Research the methods that have been developed to extract meaning from lifelogging data.

Research: Research, enumerate, and compare and contrast several systems and research projects for meeting capture, including a discussion of the issue of privacy in this context.

Concept: Write a Wikipedia article on 'digital forgiveness'.

Debate: Resolved: Every person should be required to keep a lifelog in order to enable reflection on the past and improvement in the future.

Policy: Write a brief for the CEO of a company proposing that all meetings of senior management and the Board of Directors should be recorded by a meeting capture system.

Technology review: Identify, review, and evaluate apps for helping people remember; also discuss to what extent they support forgetting.

9.9 Confidential information, privacy for government, and whistle-blowers

Do politicians, including the leaders of a country and its diplomats, need and deserve privacy? 'Yes', said Westin, who enumerated organizational needs for privacy, including 'release from public roles, evaluative periods for decision-making, and protected communications'. There must be time and opportunity for reflection, for testing ideas, and for planning. Yet individuals with power and responsibility, as well as governments leading democratic societies, cannot constantly function and deal in private. Significant disclosure needs to be ongoing.

WikiLeaks is an organization that since 2006 has specialized in 'the analysis and publication of large datasets of censored or otherwise restricted official materials involving war, spying and corruption'.[115] Yet its reach has sometimes gone further, as in the March 2016 release of over 30,000 emails and email attachments sent to and from Hillary Clinton.[116] The documents covered her term as US Secretary of State and included emails from her private email server. Since a few of the emails contained confidential material, Donald Trump used this attack to fuel his presidential campaign. The email server issue was overblown, yet Clinton's unwillingness to take responsibility for her actions was a key factor that Trump used to effectively attack her.[117]

WikiLeaks was not part of the US government, but rather used data provided by Russian hackers. Yet there are times when individuals within government and private organizations believe that morality, or the safety of an organization, a country, or all of society, depends upon breaking the silence of privacy. Such individuals are known as *whistle-blowers*.

Whistle-blowers have acted while working for governments in many countries and for firms in a variety of industries.[118] Famous whistle-blowers include Herbert van Bose, who revealed Nazi atrocities in 1934; Daniel Ellsberg, whose leaked the Pentagon Papers in 1971 to uncover patterns of US deception in the Vietnam War; Vladimir Bukovsky, who revealed political abuses of psychiatry in the Soviet Union in 1971; Mark Felt ('Deep Throat'), who revealed aspects of Nixon's involvement in the 1972 Watergate scandal; Mordechai Vununu, who exposed details of Israel's nuclear programme in 1986; Nancy Olivieri, a Canadian haematologist and researcher who in 1998 disclosed to her patients concerns about the safety of a drug she was researching under a grant from a pharmaceutical company; and Guy Pearse, who voiced concerns about inappropriate influence by the fossil fuels industry on Australian energy policy in 2000.

A highly publicized whistle-blower case that illustrates how computer professionals may face challenges reconciling their beliefs with an organization's practices is that of Edward Snowden.[119]

Ethics

Edward Snowden: In early 2013, Edward Snowden was a 29-year-old programmer and cybersecurity expert. While working at the US National Security Agency (NSA), he downloaded hundreds of thousands of files, then leaked many documents gradually to a few journalists. This exposed a large-scale programme of surveillance by the NSA and by partner agencies in the UK, Canada, and Australia. It included paying US high-tech companies for access to their communication networks; systematic monitoring of email, instant messages, contact lists, phone records, and mobile phone locations; and bypassing encryption to identify targets for hacking and surveillance.

Support The Guardian · Subscribe · Find a job · Sign in / Register · Search

International edition

News · Opinion · Sport · Culture · Lifestyle · More

The Guardian

World ▸ Europe US Americas Asia Australia Middle East Africa Inequality Cities Global development

Glenn Greenwald on security and liberty
The NSA files

Edward Snowden: the whistleblower behind the NSA surveillance revelations

The 29-year-old source behind the biggest intelligence leak in the NSA's history explains his motives, his uncertain future and why he never intended on hiding in the shadows

• Q&A with NSA whistleblower Edward Snowden: 'I do not expect to see home again'

Glenn Greenwald, Ewen MacAskill *and* Laura Poitras *in Hong Kong*
Tue 11 Jun 2013 14.00 BST

1,191 6,194

This article is over 5 years old

Figure 9.6 Headline shortly after Snowden's disclosures made front-page news
Greenwald, Glenn. Edward Snowden: the whistleblower behind the NSA surveillance revelations. *The Guardian*, 11 June 2013. https://www.theguardian.com/world/2013/jun/09/edward-snowden-nsa-whistleblower-surveillance

Snowden ultimately received asylum in Russia after the USA revoked his passport and threatened major legal action. His revelations unleashed a firestorm of controversy over issues including the role of and limits to surveillance, his responsibilities to his conscience vs his obligations as someone who had signed confidentiality pledges, the extent to which he was right or wrong, and whether or not he should be pardoned.

Whistle-blowers often succeed in focusing attention on a real issue at a great personal cost to themselves. A recent study of financial reporting found that firms singled out by whistle-blowers were significantly more likely to exhibit decreases in both accounting irregularities and tax aggressiveness when compared with control firms.[120] But the life of the whistle-blower is difficult. Potential whistle-blowers must contemplate the certainty of the knowledge that they believe to be evil, the consequences if this evil is allowed to continue, the likelihood that revealing the evil will stop it, and the consequences to themselves in terms of job and income loss, as well as potential imprisonment.

Was Snowden acting ethically? Why or why not? Hint: It may be helpful to consider his actions in comparison with those of other whistle-blowers such as Daniel Ellsberg and Deep Throat.

Research: Identify, research, and compare and contrast several computer scientists or information technology professionals who became whistle-blowers.

Research: Compare and contrast legislation to protect whistle-blowers in several countries.

Debate: Hypothesis: Edward Snowden is a hero (or villain) who should be allowed to return home and given a medal (or forever banned from the United States, except as a prisoner).

9.10 Privacy laws

In the USA, there are three kinds of privacy protections—amendments to the US Constitution, common law, and statutes at both the federal and state level.[121]

Although the US Constitution does not mention privacy, various amendments have been used to afford privacy protection. The most significant is the Fourth Amendment. It asserts the right of people 'to be secure in their persons, houses, papers, and effects against unreasonable search and seizure', requiring a warrant with 'probable cause' for a search to be initiated. The use of new technologies for searching without physical intrusion has been the subject of several key Supreme Court battles, with the case *Katz v. United States* in 1967 establishing that Fourth Amendment privacy protection applies to the interception of telephone conversations. Similarly, in 2018, the US Supreme Court decided, in the case *Carpenter v. United States,* that one cannot be convicted based on mobile phone records of movement accessed *without* a warrant.[122]

Various legal rulings have also asserted privacy protection from the Fifth Amendment, guarding against a requirement to incriminate oneself; the Ninth Amendment, leaving rights to the people with regards to issues not mentioned in the Constitution; and the Fourteenth Amendment, guarding against loss of life, liberty, or property without due process of law. The First Amendment, guaranteeing freedom of speech and expression, is typically used *against* the right of privacy.[123] US courts tend to support free speech and free press rights to gather information in public places, and to collect and sell personal data for commercial purposes, yet they will try to preserve a right of anonymity by limiting the government's ability to observe and profile citizens.

The common law provides four kinds of privacy torts, whereby individuals can gain redress for civil (i.e., not criminal) losses or harms due to invasions of privacy. Inspired by the Warren and Brandeis paper,[6] and further articulated by the legal scholar William Prosser,[124] these torts deal with (a) intrusions on solitude; (b) public disclosure of private facts; (c) appropriation, that is, use of someone else's name or likeness for commercial purposes without permission; and (d) putting someone in a false light in the public eye. Progress in achieving protection in this way has been slow because the original precedents made use of concepts such as private spaces and subject matter, secrecy, and seclusion, limitations which have been difficult to apply in cyberspace.[125]

Because of concerns raised by Westin and others starting in the 1960s as well as continuing developments described in the chapter, laws have been enacted in the USA to deter breaches of privacy. The *Privacy Act of 1974* provides a code of *Fair Information Practices* for the federal government to protect the identifiable information it has collected.[126] It was strengthened by the *Computer Matching and Privacy Protection Act of 1988.* There are some notable exceptions, including breaking privacy for purposes of national security. The *Fair Credit Reporting Act of 1970* seeks to promote the accuracy, fairness, and privacy of data collected by consumer reporting agencies.[127] It was strengthened by passage of the *Fair Debt Collection Practices Act of 1977,*[128] which aims to protect consumers from abusive debt collection practices.

The *REAL ID Act of 2005* was another US response to 9/11, setting standards for state-issued driving licences so that they can be used for federal identification purposes.[129] Despite concerns expressed by privacy and civil liberties advocates that this would de facto become a US national ID card, all provisions of the Act will be in force by 2020.[130]

In the USA, privacy legislation and administrative orders have differed dramatically based on the philosophies of each president.[131] During the end of his presidency, President Barack Obama's Federal Communications Commission issued regulations designed to give broadband consumers more control over their data. Even though the level of privacy protection was weak, President Trump had it repealed as one of his first acts in office.

The approach in Europe is significantly different from that in the USA. Despite the laws discussed above, the USA has tended to rely more on self-regulation,[132] whereas the European Union has relied more on federal regulation, beginning with a comprehensive *Data Protection Directive* (DPD)[133] that took effect in 1995. Although it encouraged the free flow of data within the EU, it discouraged the processing of personal data, except when (a) such processing was transparent, that is, individuals were aware of what was happening; (b) processing was being done for a legitimate purpose; and (c) the processing was adequate, relevant, and not excessive.

The General Data Protection Regulation

In May 2018, the DPD was superseded by the General Data Protection Regulation (GDPR),[134] which has more sweeping provisions, including:

a) Applicability to personal data legally processed, that is, for a legitimate purpose, in the EU or about individuals based in the EU, by organizations which must be responsible and may be held accountable for their actions;
b) Storage of the minimum possible amounts of data;
c) Explanations in clear language of how the data will be used;
d) Data default settings set at a high level of privacy protection;
e) Data anonymized or pseudonymized;
f) A right of access for individuals to see their data;
g) A right to erase data, to implement a limited right for certain data to be forgotten;
h) Records will be kept of processing activities;
i) Public institutions will have data protection officers; and
j) Data breaches will be made public without undue delay.

GDPR also puts limits on automated decision-making and grants the right to explanations of such decisions (see our discussion of these issues in Section 11.6):[135]

> The data subject should have the right not to be subject to a decision, which may include a measure, evaluating personal aspects relating to him or her which is based solely on automated processing and which produces legal effects concerning him or

Continued on next page

> her or similarly significantly affects him or her, such as automatic refusal of an online credit application or e-recruiting practices without any human intervention.... In any case, such processing should be subject to suitable safeguards, which should include specific information to the data subject and the right to obtain human intervention, to express his or her point of view, to obtain an explanation of the decision reached after such assessment and to challenge the decision.

Sanctions can be severe—as much as 4 per cent of annual worldwide revenues of companies—for infringements of certain provisions. Technology companies spent as much as two years preparing for May 2018.[136] Individuals all over the world were then flooded with notices of new privacy provisions from companies with which they transacted electronically. Forty-eight minutes after the regulation went into effect, Facebook, along with its subsidiaries WhatsApp and Instagram, and Alphabet, the parent of Google, were served with notices of almost $9 billion in lawsuits under the claim that the companies did not give European users the required controls over their data.[137] Other countries, most notably Brazil, are or will soon be following Europe's lead.[136] Meanwhile, Europe is close to enacting an equally tough *ePrivacy Regulation* to ensure even greater privacy of electronic communications.[138]

Research: Study, analyse, and report on the use of tort law to preserve privacy in a particular jurisdiction, and the extent to which it is effective or ineffective.

Research: Compare and contrast laws for privacy protection, and cases in which these laws were interpreted, for two or three different countries, for example, the USA, a country in the EU, and Australia.

Research: Research and analyse the 2005 REAL ID proposal and the process of passing the Act.

Debate: Resolved: Given current security threats to the USA, the Real ID Act is appropriate and will be effective.

Jury: Assume that an individual has been damaged in some way because a government has read his or her private emails. Given a particular legal jurisdiction, discuss what damages should be awarded if the decision is that the government acted improperly.

9.11 What shall we do?

We have surveyed the many threats to privacy resulting from advances in information technology and our failure to regulate it sufficiently. We shall suggest three methods of better protecting ourselves: better technology design, human caution, and legal sanctions and remedies.

One comprehensive design philosophy seeks to address the entire landscape. *Privacy by Design* (PbD)[139] was originally articulated by Dr Ann Cavoukian when she was the Information and Privacy Commissioner of the Province of Ontario in Canada.

Privacy by Design

There are seven foundational principles:[139]

1. **Proactive not Reactive; Preventative not Remedial:**...proactive rather than reactive measures. It anticipates and prevents privacy invasive events before they happen....it aims to prevent them from occurring....
2. **Privacy as the Default Setting:**...ensuring that personal data are automatically protected in any given IT system or business practice. If an individual does nothing, their privacy still remains intact....
3. **Privacy Embedded into Design:** PbD is embedded into the design and architecture of IT systems and business practices....privacy becomes an essential component of the core functionality...
4. **Full Functionality—Positive-Sum, not Zero-Sum:** PbD seeks to accommodate all legitimate interests and objectives in a...'win–win' manner, not through a dated, zero-sum approach, where unnecessary trade-offs are made. [it] avoids...false dichotomies, such as privacy vs. security,...it is possible and...desirable...to have both.
5. **End-to-End Security—Full Lifecycle Protection:** Pbd...extends securely throughout the entire lifecycle of the data involved—strong security measures are essential to privacy, from start to finish. ....
6. **Visibility and Transparency—Keep it Open:**...operating according to...stated promises and objectives, subject to independent verification....component parts and operations remain visible and transparent...Remember, trust but verify!
7. **Respect for User Privacy—Keep it User-Centric:** Above all, PbD requires...keep[ing] the interests of the individual uppermost [with]...strong privacy defaults, appropriate notice, and empowering user-friendly options. Keep it user-centric.

Using PbD requires economic and political incentives, as well as commitment from the managers and developers of IT; the process must also be integrated into an organization's systems development methodology.[140] There are good examples of how privacy-enhancing technologies can be applied to applications such as automatic licence plate recognition systems, video surveillance systems, geolocational tracking, and drone-based surveillance. PbD can also be used in retrospect to understand how privacy violations could have been avoided.[141–143]

Social media and internet users can do more to protect their privacy. Pay attention to what organizations such as Facebook say they will do with personal data. Set defaults to maximize the confidentiality of one's data. Do not share information on social media that may be damaging later in life. Technical measures can be used, such as adopting multiple online identities and managing the cookies that typically monitor activities.[144] Communications can be shielded from an internet service provider through the use of *Virtual Private Network* (VPN) software.[145] Unfortunately, being vigilant takes time, and it may be difficult to anticipate adverse consequences from sharing information that at present seems innocuous.

Finally, laws such as GDPR help to guard our privacy. But GDPR is not the last word. Legal and information system scholars in the USA have suggested other ways to approach the problem of privacy protection. One potential solution is for internet and social media users to think about their private information as their property.[146] This has been a controversial philosophy both because of uncertainties and subjectivities in how to value information, difficulties in implementing a system, and philosophical objections to the concept.

Research: Identify, summarize, and critically analyse the use of PbD on one or two real projects. The references cited in Notes 142 and 143 may be helpful.

Research: Information as property. Analyse this concept, and discuss to what extent it may be a solution to the problem of data privacy.

Policy: Draft a brief for a university president advising her on privacy issues with respect to the information systems planned for the university.

Software review: Most of the attention regarding privacy is focused on Facebook and Google. Compare and contrast the privacy approaches taken by other leading firms such as Twitter and Snapchat.

9.12 Summary

Privacy was defined as the 'right to be left alone' in Warren and Brandeis's 1890 paper. The concept of privacy has since been expanded to include both psychological states in which one is protected from intrusion, as well as protection against the release and misuse of personal information. Much of dystopian literature has envisioned worlds in which there is no privacy. Some portrayals, such as *1984*, have focused on total surveillance, with 'Big Brother' controlling action and Thought Police controlling ideas. Other portrayals, such as *The Trial*, focus on the dehumanizing effects of arbitrary and unknown actors and bureaucracy, and portray a world in which we have no control over what data is collected, and how the collected data is used, creating Kafkaesque chaos.

The proliferation of both governmental and consumer databases over the past fifty years has led to continually expanding threats to privacy. Society is suffering what appears to be a constantly increasing number of data breaches of growing severity. Several have exposed the private information of over a billion individuals to unknown hackers with nefarious intentions.

The dangers of privacy invasion began with the widespread and seemingly necessary collection of personal data by governments at all levels—federal, state, and local. Databanks maintained by the police are the most critical. Unwanted disclosure of correct data, as well as consequences caused by errors in data, can cause great damage to individuals. This includes those who have been falsely accused and those whose past transgressions hinder present and future opportunities. The likelihood of misuse of an agency's data is increased if there are unique personal identifiers. Yet official and de facto national identification numbers, supported by computer matching and data mining, allow for data linking from separate databases. Governments also engage in systematic surveillance of citizens, residents, and visitors, as we have discussed in Chapter 6.

Data in the private sector is also susceptible to privacy invasions. Marketing arms of corporations have an insatiable appetite for personal data, as it helps them target potential customers in a focused manner. Consumers themselves knowingly participate in the process, as it allows for relevant advertising that better facilitates consumer purchases.

Most people are sensitive about sharing their health information. Both low-level data such as test results and high-level data such as disease diagnoses are increasingly represented digitally. IT professionals have acted to enhance health data privacy with the HIPAA standard.

Not all privacy issues arise from data captured from individuals unwillingly or unknowingly. We write about ourselves in social media in ways which often come back to haunt us later. Despite the ability to restrict personal information to friends and friends of friends, the concept of a Facebook 'friend' is so weak that information we wish to keep to ourselves may still be broadcast widely. The recent Cambridge Analytica scandal, in which an academic's access to information shared on Facebook about 87 million Americans was handed to a political consulting form, demonstrates how personal data can be used to influence elections.

There are also several technologies for ubiquitous surveillance that voraciously gather our personal data. These include RFID tags, GPS global position tracking, widespread video surveillance, active badges, fitness trackers, biometric devices, and interconnected networks of devices. Increasingly, machine learning systems draw inferences from the data collected.

Self-surveillance happens through lifelogging, in which we digitally record data at every moment and at every place in our lives. Earlier societies have allowed aspects of people's past to be forgotten. Lifelogging challenges this by making anything one has ever done permanent and undeniable.

Organizations also need privacy. Yet there are times when individuals within a government or corporation feel morally compelled to reveal secrets. Whistle-blowers such as Edward Snowden do society a service by exposing, in spite of significant personal risk, actions that seem very wrong.

Legal protections for privacy vary dramatically across the world. In the USA, privacy decisions are often left to individual companies, and privacy regulations have been scattered and ineffective. On the other hand, legislators in Europe have created centralized and overarching privacy rules, including the recent wide-ranging General Data Protection Regulation.

One particularly hopeful sign is the theory of Privacy by Design (PbD), as is the increasing public consciousness about the importance of privacy. Yet it will always be at risk as long as governments fear national security threats that can jeopardize the safety of citizens. It is possible to have both good security and acceptable privacy, but it takes investment, planning, and wisdom.

9.13 Key terms

Active badges
Alan Westin
Anonymity
Big data
Cambridge Analytica/Facebook scandal
Carpenter v. United States
Citizen privacy
Computer matching
Consumer privacy
Data Protection Directive (DPD)
Data mining
DeepFace
Doubleclick
Edward Snowden
Emotional release
Evaluative periods for decision-making
Facebook
Fair Credit Reporting Act of 1970
Fair information practices
General Data Protection Regulation
Genetic privacy
Global Positioning System (GPS)
Google
Health Insurance Portability and Accountability Act (HIPAA)
Information privacy or data privacy
Informed consent
Instagram
Intimacy
Katz v. United States
Lifelogging
Limited communication
Mark Zuckerberg
Mechanical Turk
MyLifeBits
Organizational autonomy
Personal autonomy
Pervasive computing
Privacy
Privacy Act of 1974
Privacy and Freedom
Privacy by Design (PbD)
Real ID Act of 2005
RFID tags
Release from public roles
Reserve
Samuel D. Warren and Louis D. Brandeis
Self-evaluation
SenseCam
Snapchat
Socio-spatial sousveillance
Sociometric badge
Solitude
The Trial
US Census Bureau
US Internal Revenue Service (IRS)
Ubiquitous computing
Virtual Private Network (VPN) software
Whistle-blower
WikiLeaks
William Prosser
Workplace privacy

Part III

Choices

10

Automation, work, and jobs

The effect of automation on employment and jobs has engaged thoughtful computer scientists and economists since the earliest days of computing. Yet there have been concerns about the effects of technology on employment since ancient times, and notably during the First Industrial Revolution in the nineteenth century by a group of workers known as the 'Luddites'.

Our first topic is the role of *algorithms* in enabling more efficient processing of job applicants and the selection of candidates to interview. This now includes the *automatic filtering* out of huge numbers of résumés that are never seen by human resource professionals.

Next, we look at how technology is used in monitoring job performance, with the goal of encouraging or requiring enhanced performance. Oftentimes, these practices have the opposite effect, as it makes workers feel like 'Big Brother' is watching.

Companies have long used contractors to provide flexibility in the availability of workers as well as to circumvent costs such as medical benefits and liabilities such as severance pay. This practice has recently changed dramatically: internet communication can now rapidly link seekers of services to providers of the services. This is typically called the *gig economy* or *sharing economy*, yet a better name is *on-demand services*.

We shall then examine areas where automation threatens to replace human workers with machines. Fear is rampant, as typified by a 2017 *New York Times* article, 'Will Robots Take Our Children's Jobs?'[1] Between 2014 and 2016, future prospects were analysed in five scholarly books.[2]

We examine the phenomenon of unemployment by looking at specific areas: agriculture, manufacturing, service industries, and the professions. We highlight how new robotic technology, incorporating sensing, reasoning, and manipulating abilities, is enabling significant automation. Of particular importance is the extent to which new machine learning systems are enabling the automation of thinking and reasoning, which were previously considered infeasible for machines. Arguably the most interesting, challenging, and risky application is that of automatic diagnosis of disease, and, more speculatively, *robot doctors*.

We conclude by presenting current data as well as expert projections on employment trends, on the work that is available for people to do, and on changes we can expect in the availability and nature of work in the future. We shall also discuss current visions of the future of work, and present ideas on how governments, the economy, and people could adjust to the psychological and financial consequences of significant reductions in the opportunities for paid human labour.

Will there still be paid jobs in fifty years? How will people support themselves and their families? What will they do with the time that had previously been used to work, and the sense in which work was a key aspect of their persona? Will there be a new nirvana of expanded time with families, and enhanced opportunities for creativity and fulfilment?

10.1 Historical precedents and early warnings

The role of automation in work is best understood as part of the history of industrial revolutions.[3] Humans have designed and built tools such as wheels and hammers since the earliest days of recorded civilization. Yet our ability to carry or lift objects, or to move ourselves, was limited by the extent of human power and endurance. What is generally known as the *First Industrial Revolution* began in England in the 1800s with the advent of textile manufacturing machines, machine tools, the steam engine, and the rise of the factory system. Quantum leaps in industrialization occurred during the *Second Industrial Revolution*—the mass production of iron and steel; the creation of railroads and the first telecommunications methods; the invention of the modern factory system including the *assembly* line;[4] and the automobile. We are now in the midst of a *Third Industrial Revolution*, the age of digitally augmented and executed work.[5]

Even before the first of these industrial revolutions, concern and unrest arose at times due to technological unemployment.[6] Reductions in the availability of work due to slavery and labour-saving devices were met with governmental relief programmes in ancient China and Egypt, and later in Greece and Rome. Johannes Gutenberg's invention of the *printing press* around 1440 resulted in protests by scribes and engravers fearful that their trades would be disrupted by automation.[7] Automation has also affected animals, for example in the rise of automobile transport to replace horse-based transport in the past.[8]

Modern Times

Another aspect of modern manufacturing is division of labour. Each person does only one task over and over again on a succession of objects, then passes the objects on to the person in the assembly line assigned to do the next task. Charlie Chapin's 1936 silent comedy film *Modern Times* portrayed and satirized how demoralizing and inhuman this can be.[9]

Figure 10.1 Charlie Chaplin trapped in the machinery of the assembly line in the film *Modern Times*

When one thinks of opposition to technological change, the word *Luddite* comes to mind, used to describe a person who resists new technology. Yet the truth is more nuanced.[10] It originated in the British textile industry in the 1810s, during the First Industrial Revolution. British workers were hard-pressed due to severe unemployment, economic upheavals, and poverty brought on by the seemingly endless Napoleonic Wars. Owners felt it necessary to reduce wages and bring in efficiencies with new technology. Workers had to work harder. Products manufactured were of poor quality. Inspired by a fictional person called Ned Ludd, workers smashed knitting machines and other machinery, some of which had been invented over 200 years previously, and which paradoxically had helped the textile industry grow. Protests continued and became more violent until twenty-four Luddites were hanged publicly, twenty-four were sent to prison, and fifty-one were shipped to Australia. The protests then stopped.

The concerns of the workers were broader than automation.[11] They wanted decent wages, and to have apprenticeships in order to be able to produce high-quality goods. According to journalist Clive Thompson:[12]

> The Luddites were happy to use machinery—indeed, weavers had used smaller frames for decades. What galled them was the new logic of industrial capitalism, where the productivity

gains from new technology enriched only the machines' owners and weren't shared with the workers.

One lesson that can be taken from the Luddites is that automation needs to be considered in the light of the then-prevailing socio-economic conditions in which new technology is introduced.

An early warning about computers and automation was voiced by the brilliant mathematician and cybernetician Norbert Wiener. In 1949, in an unpublished draft of an article found recently and published by *New York Times* technology journalist John Markoff, Wiener wrote:[13]

> Roughly speaking, if we can do anything in a clear and intelligible way, we can do it by machine.... These new machines have a great capacity for upsetting the present basis of industry, and of reducing the economic value of the routine factory employee to a point at which he is not worth hiring at any price. If we combine our machine potentials of a factory with the valuation of human beings on which our present factory system is based, we are in for an industrial revolution of unmitigated cruelty.

Science fiction writers have also anticipated these issues. In 1952, Kurt Vonnegut set his first novel, *Player Piano*, in an society with huge conflict between the engineers and managers who keep the society running, and a lower class lacking work or purpose in their lives.[14] The central plot deals with a manager named Dr Paul Proteus who begins to question the system and ultimately becomes an outspoken critic.

Research: Research and discuss anti-technology workers' movements other than the Luddites.

Research: Research, and compare and contrast, portrayals of machines doing work in place of humans that appear in science fiction novels, stories, and films.

10.2 Identifying job opportunities and the best employees

Before discussing assisting or replacing human workers, we shall review technology to help people locate jobs, and methods to help employers screen potential employees. Search engines make it easier to find vacancies. Word processors help to create better structured and more aesthetic résumés. Email and LinkedIn make it easier to send résumés and network with potential employers. Other techniques are being developed to improve a user's ability to locate appropriate opportunities, for example, personalized user search profiles,[15] and methods for identifying the most suitable positions by calculating the similarity between 'candidate models' computed from résumés and 'job models' computed from job descriptions.[16]

As the volume of applications increases, the screening load on employers increases. An example is Starbucks, which attracted 7.6 million job applicants in 2011 for 65,000 job openings at the retail and corporate level.[17] Another example is Xerox Services. Its outsourcing division of 54,000 workers requires 20,000 replacements each year.[18] US firms use personality, skill, and cognitive tests on 60–70 per cent of prospective employees to find better quality and long-lasting fits; in fact, Xerox has reduced attrition in high-turnover jobs by at least twenty days through the use of such tests.[19]

Not everyone is enthusiastic about such developments. Mathematician Cathy O'Neil argued that using online personality tests as part of an automated screening process is unfair.[20] Experts in personnel psychology are divided. A meta-analytic analysis of 100 years of research on procedures for predicting job performance found that two pairs of methods give the highest multivariate validity and utility:[21] a test of general mental ability (GMA) plus an integrity test (a kind of personality test), and a GMA test plus a structured interview. However, not all experienced workers will take a GMA test. Furthermore, a roundtable on personality tests in personnel selection by five previous editors of *Personnel Psychology* and the *Journal of Applied Psychology* noted that some test-takers fake information on personality tests, then concluded that a greater problem was the lack of validity of personnel tests for predicting job performance.[22] This was disputed in a paper in a subsequent issue of the journal, which concluded that 'self-report personality tests yield useful validity in relations with job performance when due consideration is given to relevant conditions'.[23]

There is also controversy about whether or not personality tests discriminate against people with disabilities, especially those with mental illnesses.[19,24] The legal status of such tests in the USA is in question. Nonetheless, the techniques continue to be in widespread use. Lauren Weber, a journalist with the *Wall Street Journal* who has long covered such matters, recently reported:[25]

> statistical modeling and better computing power now give employers a choice of customized assessments that, in a single test, can appraise everything from technical and communication skills to personality and whether a candidate is a good match with a workplace's culture—even compatibility with a particular work team... Some tests capture not just answers, but the amount of time applicants spend on questions, or whether they scroll back to reread test instructions.

Ethics

Automatic filtering of résumés: Large companies now increasingly turn to *applicant tracking systems* to filter out the least promising applicants. An estimated 72% of job applications are not seen by human eyes.[26] Some experts believe that the automated matching of applicants and vacancies and *résumé mining* techniques find candidates 'uniquely qualified for specific vacancies', such as occur in the US federal civil service.[27] Automated assessment tools also mine the internet for other evidence of a candidate's background, accomplishments, and personality.[28] For example, linguistic analysis extracts such information automatically from LinkedIn profiles. More recently, the administration of candidate interviews, and the analysis of audio and video recordings, has also been automated.

Continued on next page

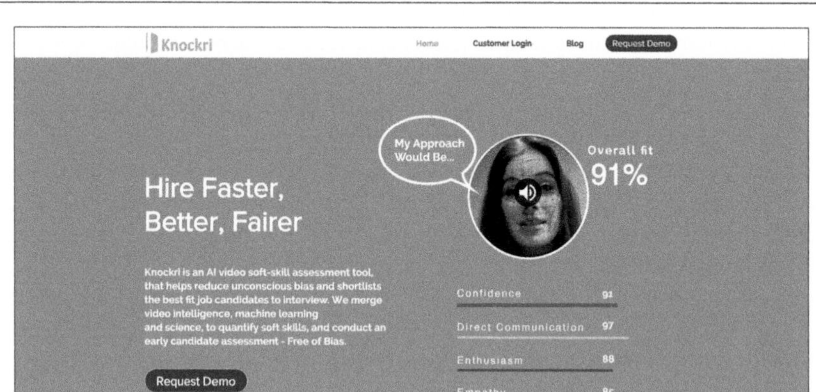

Figure 10.2 Home page advertising automatic screening of automated video interviews[29]

Proponents of such systems claim that they will result in less bias in screening. Yet Cathy O'Neil asserts that the algorithms often embody discrimination and untested assumptions, and need to be tuned by evaluating how well their decisions have worked out, then changing them based on performance.[30]

Is the screening of résumés without human participation ethical? Why or why not? Does your answer depend upon the circumstances of the position, the vacancy, and the firm acting in this way?

As one might expect, advice can now be found on the internet suggesting how job seekers can tailor their résumé to get past the algorithmic screening and into the hands of humans,[31] and how to maintain and carefully tailor an effective social media presence to succeed in the job hiring process.[32]

Debate: Resolved: Automated screening of résumés is good for personnel departments and also for job applicants.

Book report: O'Neil, Cathy (2016). *Weapons of Math Destruction: How Big Data Increases Inequality and Threatens Democracy.* Crown Publishers.

Law: Draft a law requiring human review of every résumé submitted for a government job.

10.3 Monitoring workers for job performance

Once a worker has been hired, almost all jobs require the use of a mobile phone, laptop, or some other technology. These tools aid employees in work such as organizing, tracking details, and preparing documents and financial forecasts. But an employer will likely also use technology to watch and monitor your performance. An early use of digital technology was the automatic grading of output volume. There is nothing wrong with measuring employees' output in jobs where production quantity is important, assuming that is not the only measure of employee worth. But the use of technology did not stop there.

Bosses have always used analogue techniques to monitor work. In the case of workers who use keyboards, these methods have been augmented by digital techniques, in ways that are similar to being watched by Big Brother. Roughly half of employers track computer use.[33] These intrusive observations are used to combat *cyberloafing*—inefficient and time-wasting behaviour such as checking personal email, visiting news or social media sites, online shopping, booking travel, and online job hunting. An entire industry has emerged to combat employee misbehaviour and cyberloafing, including one firm with over 40,000 corporate clients in over 110 countries that provides *computer performance monitoring* (CPM) *tools* for screen capture playback; file, document, and web activity tracking; email recording; and keystroke logging.[34]

One early study compared organizations that used computerized monitoring with those that did not. Monitoring was associated with perceived increases in organizational control, productivity, and assessment of employee performance; workers perceived higher levels of stress and job dissatisfaction.[35] A study of CPM system design and employee welfare perceived health problems, stress, and dissatisfaction with job evaluations.[36] The more employers relied upon CPM data to judge job performance, the more dissatisfied employees were with the evaluations. Employee stress increased with the degree to which job task monitoring results were reported to them. On the other hand, the more supervisors provided opportunities for employees to discuss and challenge CPM data, the fewer health problems and less perceived stress employees had.

A 1995 literature review reported the difficulties researchers have found in measuring performance gains and losses under CPM. The report also noted that CPM can sometimes improve employee judgements of the perceived accuracy of job evaluations.[37] Another analysis argued that CPM could reap positive rewards to a firm if employees are involved in the design and implementation of systems, if monitoring is restricted to performance-related activities, and if data is used as the basis of two-way communication and supportive discussions.[38] If these conditions were not met, then negative results could be expected. A third study found that perceived fairness, job satisfaction, and organizational commitment were increased when electronic performance monitoring was perceived as developmental, to enhance future performance; the opposite was true if monitoring was perceived as a deterrent to what employers deemed as bad behaviour.[39]

A 2005 review of relevant US law concluded that employee monitoring would be viewed as lawful under federal and most states' laws as long as the employees consented.[40] By not protesting monitoring policies disseminated by employers, consent would be implied!

More recently, employers have been given the technology to monitor and record the movements of their employees. This can be done through a variety of techniques, including measuring and recording the movements of *active badges* worn by employees in office buildings, or the GPS coordinates of their vehicles. Pioneering work on active badges was done in the 1980s and 1990s at the Rank Xerox EuroPARC laboratory.[41] By 2013, 37 per cent of companies that sent employees out for deliveries or service calls tracked the location of workers via GPS tracking of mobile phones or vehicles.[42]

Sociometric badges

Active badges were brought to the next level by Professor Alex 'Sandy' Pentland's group at the MIT Media Lab. They developed what they call *sociometric badges* and a new 'science' called *social physics*—a 'computational social science' with the capacity 'to collect and analyze data with an unprecedented breadth and depth and scale'.[43]

Figure 10.3 A sociometric badge
Courtesy of Alex Pentland, MIT

The badges fit in the palm of one's hand and record location, movement, speaking speed, speech energy, tone of voice, gesture, posture, proximity, and face-to-face interaction, but for privacy reasons do not record the actual speech itself.[44]

At first glance such technology seems invasive and scary. It is. The badges enable management to eavesdrop on workers' interactions with their co-workers. The likely supposition is that employees who are talking cannot be working as productively as possible. Surveillance with sociometric badges seems like a tool that could ultimately cause changes to the workplace to ensure that employees not spend time conversing unduly. Yet surprising results came from Pentland's research.[45] A study with the badges was done at a Bank of America call centre with over 3,000 employees. To the surprise of some, average call handle time was found to go down with more employee interaction and engagement! Management then changed procedures so that workers within a team would break at the same time. The result was a $15 million a year increase in productivity. A second project was done with a Chicago-area sales support team. Engagement, which they defined as 'idea flow within a workgroup', was the central predictor of productivity. The MIT team has also worked with the Steelcase office furniture manufacturer to instrument office chairs so that Steelcase can understand how chairs are being used by employees.[46]

Such developments imply an increasing need for management and labour to collaborate, and for laws to prevent a ubiquitous Big Brother culture. Yet this assumes that people will still be doing the work, so this chapter will explore the effect of automation on the quantity and quality of available jobs. Before this, however, we shall consider how some work is changing through companies offering on-demand services by individuals acting independently and typically not considered employees.

Research: Analyse recent evidence about the extent to which employee monitoring increases workplace productivity.

Debate: Resolved: Electronic monitoring of human job performance is justified, because employees will get used to it, and then they can be given and will appreciate feedback on how to improve their performance.

Policy: Write a brief for the CEO of a firm that has been electronically monitoring job performance for a long time without it being widely known. A whistle-blower has just revealed it, and employees are very angry and considering initiating a strike, so the CEO is planning to speak to all the employees in one week.

Book report: Pentland, Alex (2014). *Social Physics: How Good Ideas Spread—The Lessons from a New Science.* The Penguin Press.

10.4 On-demand services in the gig economy

A recent IT-enabled disruption to work as we have known it is the internet's use to enable individuals to do jobs and provide services. This often goes by the somewhat confusing name of the *sharing economy*.[47, 48] Professor Arun Sundararajan also terms this phenomenon 'crowd-based capitalism':

> early instances of a future in which peer-to-peer exchange becomes increasingly prevalent, and the 'crowd' replaces the corporation as the center of capitalism.[47]

The basic idea is that internet communications allow people to access cheaper and more flexible resources to carry out tasks and provide services that traditionally have been provided by established firms and industries using their own workforces. Others have termed this the 'online gig' economy,[49] or described the new companies as *digital matching firms* since they are:[50]

firms that use Internet and smartphone-enabled apps to match service providers with consumers, help ensure trust and quality assurance via peer-rating services, and rely on flexible service providers who, when necessary, use their own assets.

My favourite term is *on-demand services*, which has been defined as 'platforms that directly match customer needs with providers to immediately deliver goods and services'.[51] Establishing trust in strangers who provide the services through the use of peer ratings is key to the success of such platforms.

The disrupters[47]

The best-known example is *Uber*. Instead of calling a taxi company, which dispatches one of its drivers, individuals needing transportation use the Uber app, which identifies drivers from a typically very large set of individuals that are closest to the person. These workers make their livelihoods or supplement other income by using their own cars to drive people from point A to point B, and get their clients by referral from Uber. Uber has raised almost $9 billion in capital. Another major US company that competes with Uber in the on-demand transportation industry is *Lyft*. A firm in China, *Didi Chuxing*, formerly Didi Kuaidi, offers ride-sharing transportation services, and has raised over $4 billion in capital.

Mechanical Turk is a popular service provided by Amazon; another similar firm is *TaskRabbit*, acquired by Ikea in 2017. These services allow individuals to 'crowdsource' tasks to numerous people over the internet to do parts of or the whole job. For example, Cambridge Analytica used Mechanical Turk to collect personal information on millions of US citizens to manipulate voters in the 2016 US presidential election (discussed in Section 9.6).

Another well-known example is *Airbnb*. Instead of reserving a hotel room, travellers negotiate through the Airbnb app to rent rooms or homes of local individuals, who make use of their available space and supplement their income by offering lodging services. Airbnb has raised over $2 billion in capital.

Finally, high-tech firms such as Google and Microsoft outsource millions of micro-tasks per month to tens of thousands of individuals to rate YouTube videos, check the results of search algorithms, rate the sentiment of email queries, or tag video footage of cars to help improve automated driving algorithms.[52]

There are growing numbers of domains that utilize on-demand services, including customer service representatives to replace workers in call centres;[53] home repair persons; food service vendors; and venture funding providers. Yet, to 'uberize' a service is no guarantee of success or of riches. There have been many shared service start-ups that seemed like a great idea at the time, such as firms facilitating the sharing of small household items such as power drills, that have failed.[54] Other cases of 'uber-like' failures have been home delivery, where there are established firms such as Fedex that dominate the market, and valet parking, where the size of the transaction makes the transaction costs prohibitive.[55]

Consumers have seen many benefits from these new industries. Travellers looking for more personal accommodation experiences at a reasonable price find acceptable and even excellent lodging through Airbnb. When one has very specific requirements for a worker quickly, TaskRabbit is often the solution. Individuals in need of a rapid pickup in adverse circumstances—in an out-of-the-way location or at an unusual time—have often found Uber preferable to a traditional taxi. Competition in a previously dormant industry has shaken up taxicab ownership. In New York City, the number of for-hire vehicles has tripled in five years to over 100,000. Sixty thousand of these are affiliated with Uber.[56] As a result, congestion has increased to an unbearable level.[56] Furthermore, taxi drivers are in despair because of declining income and increasing difficulties in servicing the huge debt they had incurred to purchase a taxi medallion, which cost as much as $1.3 million in 2014. Six taxi drivers in New York City have committed suicide in 2017 and 2018, one of the factors causing New York City to put a cap on Uber and other for-hire vehicles that are not licensed taxis.[57]

The sharing economy has also led to flexible and rewarding new ways to earn income, although occasionally it can be a lonely existence.[58] One can make money driving without the investment required to acquire a taxi licence and to own or rent a taxi. Odd jobs can be found via Mechanical Turk or TaskRabbit. Individuals with extra space in their homes can supplement their income by making rooms available to Airbnb guests.

Yet on-demand services have problems that include liability, insurance, taxation, and labour relations.[59] If an Uber driver has an accident or an Airbnb guest trashes a home, who is responsible, who pays, and what, if anything, is covered by insurance? Municipalities that earn income from taxi licence fees or hotel occupancy taxes miss that income and are fighting back by outlawing or constraining services such as Uber. In Uber's case, a pattern of aggressive and dishonest business practices, such as subverting attempts by city officials to track its actions, spying on competitors, and impersonating drivers, has led to significant ill will and a desire by some municipalities to ban it.[60] Uber's culture applies worldwide; it has engaged in cut-throat price reductions in Kenya, and fought being labelled a transportation business by the EU's highest court, which would subject it to stricter requirements.[61] We shall speak more about Uber in Chapter 12.

In accommodation, as in transportation, sharing economy ventures threaten and often damage existing industry. Airbnb and other digital matching accommodation firms caused an 8–10 per cent reduction in hotel revenues in Austin, Texas.[62] The US hotel industry has counter-attacked vigorously.[63] There has been extensive lobbying at all levels of government, arguing that Airbnb proprietors do not collect hotel taxes and do not have adequate safety and security provisions. Hotel chains have also recently gotten into the high-end home sharing business themselves via acquisitions and joint ventures, offering houses with service up to hotel standards. Owners and tenants in apartment blocks or in neighbourhoods often resent the disruption caused by transient occupants, and fight back by banning services such as Airbnb.

How large is the sharing economy? In 2016, Sundararajan estimated that self-employed Americans numbered over 23 million.[64] A likely better 2015 estimate of the self-employed was 53 million.[65] Most of these, of course, are the traditional self-employed, not people who do gig work. A 2015 estimate of only the on-demand economy was 2.7 million, although this number has certainly grown since then.[50] Recent data from the US government indicates that about 10 per cent of workers engage in non-traditional occupations, which includes people who work in temp agencies as well as participants in the gig economy, but noted that one-third of all adults engage in some sort of gig work.[66]

In a survey of 8,000 individuals in the USA and five European countries, the McKinsey Global Institute estimated that up to 162 million individuals engage in independent work.[67] Thirty per cent are 'free agents', deriving most of their income this way; 40 per cent are 'casual earners', who choose to supplement their earnings in this manner; 14 per cent are 'reluctants', who seek traditional jobs but fail to find them, and then support themselves through independent work; and 16 per cent are 'financially strapped', doing supplemental independent work due to financial necessity. Free agents ranked their job satisfaction higher than did workers in traditional jobs. Fifteen per cent of independent workers used digital platforms; this number was growing rapidly.

Does the sharing economy result in higher-paying jobs? Sundararajan compared the hourly wage rates in the San Francisco Bay area of 'digital labour marketplace workers' to workers in the same profession who were not digitally matched.[64] He found that the wages were usually 10–25 per cent higher in professions where being geographically collocated with the customers was an advantage, for example, home cleaning or plumbing; and typically 10–25 per cent lower in professions where collocation provided no advantage, for example, writing and editing, and graphic design. Despite these findings, many in the gig economy make very little money, especially Uber drivers after they pay expenses such as gas, maintenance, and Uber's commissions.[68] In line with Uber's predatory behaviour, the company has also experimented with techniques from video games to non-cash rewards of little value to induce drivers to work longer and harder, especially in locations and at times that bring them little benefit.[69]

So, is the sharing economy an example of digital technology creating jobs? Or is it destroying jobs? It seems too soon to tell, but it is clear that the gig economy is creating new opportunities for many individuals to find new and sometimes rewarding work. Digital job matching is particularly relevant to the 232 million inactive, unemployed, or underemployed individuals in the USA and fifteen other European countries where on-demand services are prevalent.[67]

Workers in sharing economy firms appreciate flexibility in choosing their hours, but miss employment advantages such as fringe benefits, safety from liability, ability to organize collectively, job security, and income stability. For these opportunities to be maximally effective, there is a need for a social safety net for individuals in gig jobs, as asserted by a 2015 gathering of CEOs of sharing economy firms, entrepreneurs, academics, and consultants:[65]

> We...believe that society and the economy are served best when workers have both stability and flexibility. Everyone, regardless of employment classification, should have access to the option of an affordable safety net that supports them when they're injured, sick, in need of professional growth, or when it's time to retire.
>
> We need a portable vehicle for worker protections and benefits...[that] should be:
>
> - Independent: Any worker should be able to access a certain basic set of protections as an individual regardless of where they source income opportunities.
> - Flexible and pro-rated: People are pulling together income from a variety of sources, so any vehicle should support contributions that can be pro-rated by units of money earned, jobs done, or time worked, covering new ways of micro-working across different employers or platforms.

- Portable: A person should be able to take benefits and protections with them in and out of various work scenarios.
- Universal: All workers should have access to a basic set of benefits regardless of employment status.
- Supportive of innovation: Businesses should be empowered to explore and pilot safety net options regardless of the worker classification they utilize.

Research: Discuss the advantages and disadvantages of the various terms that have been used as labels for 'on-demand services', the 'sharing economy', and the 'gig economy'.

Research: Research industries where firms trying to disrupt the status quo by introducing on-demand services have succeeded, and where they have failed.

Research: Compare and contrast how various municipalities have reacted to and dealt with the disruption caused by on-demand transportation companies such as Uber.

Debate: Resolved: Despite the advantages of Uber offering greater choices for people looking for cheap and convenient transport, it has damaged beyond repair taxi industries vital to the health of most cities.

Policy: Write a brief for the CEO of a hotel chain experiencing significant revenue and profitability reductions due to Airbnb, who is trying to formulate and articulate a competitive response.

Policy: Write a brief for the board of a condominium corporation trying to decide if Airbnb rentals should be allowed.

Field study: Interview and compare the experiences of consumers accessing workmen such as carpenters and electricians who can be accessed on digital matching sites such as TaskRabbit with the experiences of those who have found workmen by more traditional means such as Angie's List, Yelp, or a simple web search.

Book report: Sundararajan, Arun (2016). *The Sharing Economy: The End of Employment and the Rise of Crowd-based Capitalism*. The MIT Press

10.5 Automation and fears of unemployment

Because automation means that machines can do the work that was once or currently is done is by humans, it can cause job obsolescence and unemployment. The effect is typically hard to disentangle from other possible causes of workforce reductions, for example, a corporation's need to downsize, outsourcing of labour to countries that are less expensive in order to increase a firm's profitability, and improvements in work procedures other than automation that have increased productivity.

People worldwide are fearful of the effects of automation on their jobs. In the USA the most common job held by males—3.5 million of them— is truck driver, and the most common job held by females—also 3.5 million—is office and administrative worker, both of which are likely to be significantly automated in the near future.[70]

The effects of automation on employment will be profound. A 2015 Pew national survey of over 2,000 American adults revealed that 65 per cent felt that computers and robots would 'definitely' or 'probably' do 'much of the work currently done by humans'.[71] Yet 80 per cent felt that their own jobs would still exist in some form. A more recent Pew survey of over 4,100 US adults found that 72 per cent worried about a future in which computers and robots can do (too) many jobs.[72] Another 2017 survey of over 1,000 American adults found that 41 per cent expect automation to make their daily lives better, but 22 per cent expect it to worsen their lives.[73] Nineteen per cent of those polled expect someone in their household to lose a job in the next ten years because of automation. Fifty per cent would prefer to deal with a human in a supermarket or convenience store than to use an automated checkout machine, but customer wishes are not typically considered by the owners of such firms. As we shall discuss further in this chapter and in Chapter 11, the machine learning technology of the IBM supercomputer Watson has received significant investment and much attention in the media, heightening society's level of anxiety.[74]

Are these fears justified? We shall now focus on what has actually happened thus far and is happening in four major waves of automation—agriculture, manufacturing, service industries, and the professions.

Field study: Interview your parents and the parents of several friends on their hopes and fears with respect to automation and the future of their jobs.

10.6 Agriculture and automation

Farms have long been a target for machine assistance. One newspaper article in 1955 predicted robot farm machines radio-controlled from a helicopter.[75] There is a logic to automation in agriculture. The work is hard. The climate can be miserable. At planting time, precision spacing is a virtue. At harvest time, speed is of the essence. Workforces are usually seasonal and somewhat unpredictable. Uncertainty is even greater in those cases where illegal immigrants do much of the work and when immigration is a political football, as it is in the USA under President Donald Trump.

Nearly half of all US workers were employed on farms at the beginning of the twentieth century; by the end of the century, the percentage had fallen to 2 per cent.[76] The International Labour Organization (ILO) estimated that farm workers as a percentage of the workforce in developed countries dropped from 35 per cent to 4 per cent between 1959 and 2010.[77] The figures for developing countries were 81 per cent to 48 per cent.

In 2016, the World Bank forecast that the world would need to produce 50 per cent more food to feed the 9 billion people it expects in 2050, but that climate change could cut crop yields by 25 per cent.[78] Large industry farms are increasingly turning to new technologies rather than people to meet the demand.

An early example was tomatoes. Forty years ago, 45,000 workers harvested 2.2 million tons of tomatoes in California to make ketchup.[79] Then scientists developed an oblong tomato and a mechanical harvester designed to pick them. By 2000, only 5,000 workers were required to pick and sort 12 million tons.

This was only the tip of the iceberg (pun intended).

Ripeness sniffers and melon-picking robots

Many new agricultural technologies have emerged or are under active development. An Israeli–US research team combined a mobile platform, computer vision system, mechanical arm with gripper and knives attached, and a chemical ripeness sniffer to develop a *melon-picking robot*.[80] Projections were that a two-armed version could harvest one melon every one and a half seconds. A Japanese company is opening 'the world's first [indoor] robot farm' to grow 50,000 lettuces, with all tasks carried out by machines (except the planting of seeds).[81] Outdoor farming will be increasingly automated using smart tractors, in-ground sensors measuring nutrients and moisture, flying drones, and vine-pruning robots.[77] Other robots will soon specialize in the repetitive tasks of weeding and plant thinning.[82] Fitness trackers are now being placed on farm animals, and genomic tools allow scientists to evaluate the genes of plants and animals to decide which will be the most productive.[83]

A team in England recently planted and harvested four and a half tons of barley without a human setting foot on the field.[84] Technologies used included automated tractors, machines that took samples of the crop, multispectral analysers, and drones.

Figure 10.4 A drone equipped with multi=spectral sensor, collecting data on crop growth
Courtesy of Harper Adams University

Much automation is driven by economics and entrepreneurial corporations seeking new markets. The consequences of continued automation are modest for industrial societies where farming is only a tiny part of the economy, and a shrinking agricultural workforce does not imperil harvests. Automation also allows farm owners to focus more on running their businesses rather than on harvesting.[82] But these advances have serious ramifications for rural economies, increasing poverty and slowing development.[84]

Research: Research and discuss other examples where items that are grown were genetically modified to enable more automated farming, as is the case of the oblong tomato mentioned previously.

Research: Investigate and analyse the effect of agricultural automation on several developing countries.

10.7 Manufacturing and automation

Effects of automation have been felt over the past century especially in the domain of manufacturing and producing automobiles, chemicals, machinery, and steel.

There have been huge job losses in US manufacturing. The percentage of US workers employed in manufacturing shrank from over 25 per cent in 1970 to 10 per cent in 2010.[85] The last decade saw a reduction of 5.8 million US manufacturing jobs.[86] Consider, for example, steel mills. In part due to the use of smaller, more efficient and flexible steel mills—'mini-mills'—and in part due to automation, US steel industry employment dropped 75 per cent between 1962 and 2005, with a reduction of 400,000 employees.[87] Production, on the other hand, became much more efficient. Output per worker grew five-fold; total factor productivity grew by 38 per cent. These numbers are typical of the US manufacturing sector as a whole. Manufacturing productivity growth was 32 per cent between 1998 and 2012 when adjusted for inflation.[88]

These phenomena have not been limited to the USA. The UK and Australia have seen manufacturing jobs drop by two-thirds since 1971.[85] Manufacturing jobs in South Korea fell from 28 per cent to 17 per cent between 1989 and 2008.[86] China is interesting; robots are now being introduced rapidly to the workforce and to Chinese society. One Chinese Ford factory now employs 2,800 humans and 650 robots;[89] Foxconn Technology plans for a near future with 1 million human workers and 1 million robot co-workers.[90]

Are robots responsible for the decline of manufacturing jobs?

Many have argued that using greater numbers of robots has been the main cause of the reduction in manufacturing jobs. Demands for goods have not kept up with productivity increases.[79] In the USA, manufacturing productivity, the output of goods divided by the hours worked, rose by 47% between 2002 and 2015.[91] Yet the relationship between the use of robots and the availability of jobs is not simple.

Some labour economists have argued that there is little evidence for greater productivity growth in US IT-intensive industries in the twenty-first century.[92] Others have asserted that robots are essential for a country's manufacturing sector to be competitive and are a driver of economic growth.[93] An analysis of robot adoption in seventeen countries in Europe, in South Korea, and in the USA from 1993 to 2007 found associations between robot deployment and total factor productivity, wage level, and reductions in the prices of manufactured goods. It found no significant relationship between robot deployment and overall employment. But there have been indications that robots may be reducing the number of jobs for people with low levels of skill.

One country in which robots seem to be increasing productivity with no reductions in total employment is Germany.

Figure 10.5 Robots work on cars in Germany[94]
Betastock / Shutterstock.com

Germany has 7.6 industrial robots per 1,000 workers, compared with 2.7 in the rest of Europe, and 1.6 in the USA.[95] Robots have increasingly been introduced in German car manufacturing, with sixty to 100 additional robots per 1,000 workers installed between 1994 and 2014. One robot takes the place of two workers, so 275,000 jobs were lost during that period. Yet the losses in manufacturing jobs were not as steep as experienced in the USA, and there were no significant losses experienced in total German employment. This was partly due to the strength of German unions and work councils. Highly skilled workers typically experienced wage gains; workers with low skills typically experienced wage losses..

Many countries in the developed world have experienced economic growth. Manufacturing has become more efficient or has disappeared, with some jobs moving into the services sector. US manufacturing has lost 7 million jobs in the past few decades, but this has been matched by a gain of 53 million jobs in services.[96] Services now account for 45 per cent of employment worldwide.[85] However, robots are now also increasingly being used in the service industry, a topic to which we now turn.

Research: Investigate and analyse the effect of manufacturing automation in several developing countries.

Research: One method that has been proposed to counter the mindlessness of assembly line work is the training of individuals to work as teams in which every member of the team can do multiple jobs. Research how automation fits into this method, often known as the *Toyota Production System*.[97]

10.8 Computers in service industries

The wave of automation is now affecting service industries. We have already seen one example, the development of *care bots* to take care of seniors, especially in societies such as Japan where there is a very large proportion of older adults who need support. Home health aides, personal care attendants, and certified nursing assistants are also in short supply around the world. For example, in the USA, it is estimated that 1 million people will be joining health service occupations from 2014 to 2024.[98] Yet many positions go unfilled, and there will be a shortage of over 100,000 paid providers of senior care by 2024, and 350,000 by 2040.[99] This is due in part to the low prestige of the job, the difficulties and stress often encountered, and poor salaries. However, as discussed in Chapter 4, currently robots lack the sensitivity to give good care to seniors.

Robotics applications for the home in general have not succeeded. An exception is the 20 million home robots sold by iRobot Corp., mostly its Roomba automated vacuum cleaner.[100] Examples of (as of now) unsuccessful home robots include one that recently took a minute to pick up a single toy from an uncluttered play space, and the 'world's first' laundry-folding robot that took five to ten minutes to fold a T-shirt![101]

Retail automation

Eight million people, or 6% of American workers, are currently retail salespeople or cashiers.[102] Experts predict that over half the tasks they perform could be automated by currently available technology. Grocery stores increasingly provide kiosks for automatic checkout; Amazon's recent purchase of Whole Foods will accelerate such automation. Department stores employ one-third fewer employees now than they did in 2001; half a million jobs have disappeared in the past fifteen years.[103]

Fast food restaurants are increasingly being automated, in part due to rising minimum wage levels.[104] In early 2017, Wendy's announced plans to have automated kiosks installed in 1,000 of its restaurants by the end of the year; executives insist that some customers prefer the kiosks. McDonald's has plans to have 'digital ordering kiosks' replacing human cashiers by the end of 2018.[105] *Sally the Salad Robot* assembles salads out of prewashed, pre-cut vegetables; Flippy is a burger-grilling robot, designed in part because the job is hot, greasy, and dangerous, often resulting in slips, trips, burns, and cuts.[106] Such developments are ominous for the 2.3 million restaurant cooks currently working in the USA.

These developments are not just happening in the USA; robots and conveyer belts have taken over most of the work in 262 Japanese Kura sushi restaurants, enabling the chain to offer substantially lower prices than its competitors; experiments are under way in Japan to create hotels primarily staffed by robots.[107]

Figure 10.6 Robots at work in an experimental Japanese hotel

An interesting case is *Amazon*, which excels in managing inventory and assembling packages for shipment. Initially, Amazon only sold books, but it now supplies many varieties of consumer goods. By 2014, 15,000 Kiva robots were carrying heavy items around the warehouses in ten Amazon US fulfilment centres. The robots were so vital to Amazon's plans that in 2012 Amazon bought the company that made them.[108] Recently, Amazon has begun experimenting with physical stores to sell furniture, appliances, and groceries, stores that would make extensive use of robots as well as virtual reality for visualization.[109] Amazon, like German automobile manufacturers, demonstrates how successful corporations can employ both more robots and more people. Amazon has added 80,000 workers since it began to add robots, which now number 100,000.[110] Robots and humans often work side by side, doing complementary jobs. Yet the long-term effect on employment is uncertain. A recent study of warehouse employment in US counties showed increases at new Amazon fulfilment centres, but a reduction in wage levels of 3 per cent and no increase in overall employment.[111]

Bank automation has seen several waves.[112] Back offices adopted cheque sorting machines in the 1930s. Front office automation began with the introduction of automatic teller machines (ATMs) in the 1970s. There is now another wave of back office automation being fuelled by advances in natural language processing and artificial intelligence (AI), which will likely dwarf past advances. For example, they now put at risk, according to one recent estimate, 1.2 million US jobs in banking, 855,000 jobs in insurance, and 460,000 jobs in investment management.[113] This phenomenon is not limited to Western societies; for example, mobile phone-based banks are used in parts of Africa because bank tellers are not conveniently located.[114]

IBM is seeking market success with its *Watson Virtual Agent* in automating financial and other services, for example, employing *chat bots* to answer requests and questions related to utilities, telecommunications, and travel. Recent online promotional videos for Watson have included the following:[115] '[t]oday's customers want to be treated like an individual, not a number' and '[h]uman interaction exponentially increases headcount'. These claims are disingenuous; the technology is not yet equivalent to knowledgeable and compassionate human agents. Ultimately, firms, government, and societies will have to adjudicate between the cost savings of automated service and the flexibility of human attention to customer needs.[116] The goal of better service may be a lost cause anyway, as humans cannot give quality service if firms seek to maximize profit by not allowing agents the time to do a good job.

Automation is also affecting blue collar service jobs. Three-hundred-pound egg-shaped robots can now be rented for $7 an hour as security guards to patrol parking lots and shopping centres in the San Francisco Bay area.[117] Robots are being used in San Francisco itself to deter homeless people from setting up camp in the parking lots of organizations.[118] They also are used for construction and repair tasks, such as bricklaying and doing repairs underground in gas mains.[119] It is even possible to imagine that in the near future painting will be done by armies of drones propelling liquids.[120]

The most significant automation tsunami in the next five to twenty years may be in driving. For example, the US Bureau of Labour Statistics estimated that there were nearly 4 million individuals working in driving-based occupations in the USA in May 2016, including 700,000 bus drivers, 1.7 million heavy truck drivers, over 850,000 light truck drivers, and almost 200,000 taxi drivers.[121] And these estimates omit other categories, for example, pizza deliveries, where Domino's Pizza began in 2017 experimenting with self-driving deliveries in the region just west of Detroit, Michigan.[122]

Research: Investigate and analyse the effect of service automation on several developed countries.

Debate: Resolved: Automation of service jobs should be made illegal, as the human touch is essential to ensure customer satisfaction.

Policy: Draft a brief for a politician needing to decide on his or her stand vis-à-vis raising the minimum wage in the light of industry response with the automation of service jobs.

10.9 The transformation of professions

A final wave of automation is just beginning in the professions. We have seen one example, intelligent tutoring systems, although they are not (yet) in widespread use, nor do we have robot teachers. But other attempts are already visible. The professions include occupations such as doctors, lawyers, accountants, and auditors, all of which we shall discuss below; and jobs such as clergypersons or spiritual advisors, journalists, and architects, that we shall not discuss.[123] Common features across all these professions are 'specialist knowledge', credentials-based admission to the profession, activities that are regulated, and adherence to a common set of values. Across a spectrum of professions, a set of 'increasingly capable systems' are assuming more and more tasks that heretofore have been done by human professionals. For the most part, this automation has neither eliminated many jobs nor caused many disasters, other than a few minutes in May 2010 when automated trading algorithms worked together to cause a brief thousand-point drop in the Dow Jones Industrial Average.[124] Yet these developments are only in their infancy.

For example, decades of progress in accounting software have transformed accounting jobs. Routine calculations and report preparation are now typically done by machine. Thanks to tax software, many people no longer find it necessary to consult an accountant to prepare their taxes. Accountants now carry out mainly higher-level tasks that involve problem-solving and collaboration.[125]

In 2017, H&R Block's 70,000 tax professionals were aided in preparing 11 million US tax returns by a version of IBM's Watson technology that had been trained on the federal tax code, thousands of tax-related questions, and numerous examples of filled-out returns.[126] One accountant, in reaction to the SuperBowl 2017 television ad featuring the project, wrote that accountants should not fear Watson:[127]

> Watson can't 'feel' the situation. Watson doesn't sense the despair of the client. Watson doesn't ask why a client is going to see a lawyer. Watson doesn't stay persistent in chasing a life insurance company for history on an old claim. And Watson most certainly doesn't know what to do when the IRS issues a letter of examination, or a statutory notice of deficiency. Tax professionals have something that artificial intelligence cannot replace. We guide. We counsel. We communicate. We ask. We care.

Nonetheless, H&R Block reported in its 2017 annual statement:[128]

> we enhanced our client service delivery model by redesigning the tax preparation process, centered around our partnership with IBM Watson. We saw noticeable improvements on key client service metrics, as we demonstrated our ability to maximize clients' refunds in a new and engaging way.

The partnership continued in 2018, with H&R Block reporting:[129]

> IBM Watson learns as it goes and in its second year, continued to absorb, correlate and learn from huge amounts of information. The more it learns, the smarter it gets. By analyzing massive amounts of intricate tax data, putting it into context, and recommending the most advantageous filing options, IBM Watson continued to complement the human expertise of H&R Block Tax Pros.

H&R Block did not reply when I asked if a third year's collaboration was planned.

The legal profession is also beginning to change, especially legal research and the drafting of routine documents. Venture capitalists have invested over $750 million since 2012 in 280 legal automation start-ups that are now applying machine learning to legal work.[130] One firm recently claimed that their technology can reduce legal research time by more than 20 per cent, increase information retrieval quality by more than 30 per cent over traditional methods, and provide a return on investment of between 175 per cent and 550 per cent.[131] One wonders what is implied by use of the word 'can'. What is its typical performance?

IT itself is not safe from automation. A major objective of computer science has been to enable programmers to create larger, more capable, and more reliable software, and to do so with less effort. For example, the earliest programmers wrote code in machine language, a very tedious, error-prone, and low-level discipline. Advances in programming languages and software engineering have allowed more compact descriptions of algorithms in higher-level notations, and the efficient creation of programs with scope far exceeding what early programmers were able to do. There is also continued technical progress in areas such as automated code repair.[132] Although the jobs of many programmers have not yet been threatened, the first signs of disruption may be visible in recent job losses among low-level programmers in India.[133]

Automated medical diagnosis

The profession in which automation may be most significant and also the scariest in case it is done poorly is medicine. Despite our reliance on the knowledge and wisdom of the doctors we consult, their advice is sometimes in error.[134] A literature review of thirty-one published studies of autopsies of patients admitted to a hospital intensive care unit (ICU) found that 28% of autopsies had at least one misdiagnosis; 8% had a serious misdiagnosis that likely contributed to the patient's death.[135] The authors projected that over 40,000 adult patients admitted to a US ICU may die annually with a misdiagnosis.

Errors are due to many causes. An analysis of 100 diagnostic errors in internal medicine found system-related errors in 65% and cognitive problems in 74% of the cases.[136] System-related errors included problems with policies and procedures, and inadequate processes, communication, or teamwork. Cognitive-related errors included the failure to consider sufficient numbers of causes, poor judgement with respect to the salience of findings, and faulty perceptions. Faulty or inadequate knowledge was rare.

The flaws in advice is one reason to consider an alternate approach. Another is the scarcity of doctors, which is likely to get worse as society ages, since the growing elderly population requires significantly more medical attention than younger, usually healthier, individuals. Data points from 2000 indicated that Cuba had 5.91 physicians per 1,000 people, the European Union had on the average 3.05, the USA had 2.3, Canada had 2.1, China had 1.51, and India had 0.6.[137] Using an average number of two physicians per 1,000 people and assuming 2,000 working hours per year, a person on average can only see a physician for four hours per year, which clearly seems too small for a population living longer and increasingly challenged by the diseases of age.

Given that medical diagnosis is a process of logical deduction starting from a patient's symptoms and medical history and crafted using all the medical knowledge available at a particular point in time, it is plausible that an algorithm could excel in the process. Huge attention, hype, and hope has been associated with this application of IBM's Watson.

IBM's greatest Watson health care effort has been in oncology, with the goal of developing automated means to diagnose and recommend treatment regimens for cancer. The project began in 2012. In the first year, Watson was trained on 600,000 pieces of medical evidence, 2 million pages of text including medical textbooks and journals, and 25,000 training cases; there were also almost 15,000 clinician hours improving its accuracy.[138] The project included highly publicized partnerships with the Memorial Sloan Kettering Cancer Center (MSKCC) and the University of Texas MD Anderson Cancer Center.[139] The collaboration with the former was successful, with two dozen cancer specialists continuing to input recommendations to improve the system's accuracy. The latter partnership was dissolved early in 2017; the Anderson Cancer Center wrote off an investment of $39 million and huge amounts of staff and physician time.

Claims surrounding the oncology project had been seductive but misleading.[138] The project could not sufficiently train the machine learning algorithm; there were also technology integration problems. Happily, IBM's claims on its website have become more realistic. I have observed the wording change from 'Bring confident decision-making to oncology', an arrogant assertion that cannot currently be substantiated, to a more cautious and credible 'Watson for Oncology helps physicians quickly identify key information in a patient's medical record, surface relevant evidence and explore treatment options'.

There continue to be problems and concerns.[139] IBM has made a huge investment; the Watson for Health division currently employs 7,000 people. IBM has asserted that it can offer treatment guidance for twelve kinds of cancer that together represent 80 per cent of the world's cancer incidence. Yet there are concerns that its recommendations, and the underlying assumptions and beliefs of MSKCC, are biased towards American patients and methods of care. Watson for Oncology has only been adopted by a few dozen hospitals, paradoxically mostly in India and South East Asia. The system has not been subjected to outside scientific review. There have been no independent evaluations in quality peer-reviewed medical journals. IBM has not conducted formal clinical trials to assess its effectiveness. Critics have rightly insisted that IBM demonstrate safety before widespread adoption is allowed, yet IBM has lobbied for years for its technology not to be considered a medical device and hence for it to be free from US federal regulation.[140]

Watson for Oncology is not ready for prime time. As of mid-2018, massive lay-offs were under way, with internal reports of disorganization and client dissatisfaction.[141] Nonetheless, in the future there will be increasingly capable computer systems with knowledge and expertise in health. There will always be a need for doctors, nurses, and other medical personnel, so job loss is not a concern, but rather how skilled people and machines will work together to understand medical issues and apply this understanding to improve our health.

Research: Describe and analyse a spectrum of ways in which medical knowledge and expertise can be used with the aid of digital technologies, ranging from making it searchable and retrievable on the internet, to enabling android physicians and surgeons in place of human doctors.

Research: Technology for spiritual support. Pay particular attention to how this technology is viewed as a support for or an alternative to the traditional religious establishment.

Debate: Resolved: Every illness or condition that is potentially life-threatening should be reviewed by a human physician working together with an appropriate medical diagnostic algorithm.

Book report: Susskind, Richard, and Daniel Susskind (2017). *The Future of the Professions: How Technology Will Transform the Work of Human Experts.* Oxford University Press.

Ethics: Your start-up is developing a low-cost solution that is being marketed as an easy way to assess your likelihood of having a heart attack. Cash is getting low, and you have no paying customers. The CEO is planning to announce the solution next week and begin shipping the following week. You know that this launch is premature and the technology does not yet work well, nor has it been tested for safety requirements. What do you do?

10.10 The future of employment, jobs, and work

Faced with a growing number of robots and automated tasks, where do we humans factor into the job market? This section will present educated forecasts of what we may expect, and then attempt to pull various strands of the discussion together, peering some way into the future.

What do the experts predict about job losses due to automation?

A 2013 British study of 702 US job classifications concluded that 47% of total employment was at risk from possible automation over the next decade or two.[142] The authors, Carl Benedikt Frey and Michael A. Osborne of the Oxford Martin School, concluded that the greatest risk was to 'workers in transportation and logistics occupations...the bulk of office and administrative support workers...labour in production occupations'. A subsequent analysis in 2016 forecast job automation risks for various countries, finding 35% in the UK, 47% in the USA, 57% the OECD average, 69% in India, and 77% in China.[143] The numbers were even higher for some developing countries. One of the reasons given was that the researchers projected that the payback period for a robot was dropping rapidly; for example, in China the estimated payback time for a robot dropped from two years in 2013 to an estimated 1.5 years in 2017.

The World Economic Forum published an analysis in 2016 based on a survey of chief human resource officers at 371 global firms in nine industry sectors in fifteen economies.[144] They predicted disruptive labour market changes from 2015 to 2020 costing 7.1 million jobs, 4.8 million in office and administrative roles and 1.6 million in manufacturing and production. They also predicted gains of 2 million jobs in fields including computers, mathematics, engineering, and architecture.

The McKinsey Global Institute did a study in January 2017 analysing over 2,000 work activities across 800 occupations.[145] They concluded that almost 50% of the activities in the global economy have the potential to be automated with technology that has already been demonstrated. About 60% of the occupations had constituent activities, of which more than 30% could be automated. Activities most susceptible were said to be 'physical activities in highly structured and predictable environments, as well as the collection and processing of data. . . . activities . . . most prevalent in manufacturing, accommodation and food services, and retail trade, and includ[ing] some middle-skill jobs'. Over half of the total wage effect and almost two-thirds of the employment effect globally was projected to be felt in China, India, Japan, and the USA. The report also predicted that global productivity would grow between 0.8% and 1.4% annually.

A 2017 study done at Ball State University found automation risks of US counties ranging from 42% to 78%.[146] Over 230 counties, almost 10% of the total, had risk values greater than 60%. The researchers found that the ten most automatable occupations included data entry key personnel, telemarketers, insurance underwriters, tax preparers, and library technicians, representing employee totals ranging from 90,000 to 240,000 individuals.

The Brookings Institution, also in 2017, studied the effects of *digitalization* – 'the process of employing digital technologies and information to transform business operations'.[147] They found that the degree of digitalization of 545 occupations correlated with increased pay and resilience with respect to automation. They also found significant job growth at the high and low ends of the spectrum of skills, good wage growth at the high end, but only modest growth of jobs and wages in the middle.

A December 2017 study by the McKinsey Global Institute stressed the continuation of income polarization and estimated that 75 million to 375 million workers globally (3% to 14% of the world's workforce) would need to change job categories. They argued that all workers would need to adapt, as occupations would evolve through the participation of more and more capable machines.[148] They predicted that somewhere between 0% and 30% of the world's jobs, the work of up to 800 million people, could be displaced by automation by 2030.

These studies were carried out by teams that included experts in a variety of fields including economics, political science, and computer science. Very recently, Oxford and Yale universities administered a survey to 352 computer science researchers who had published a paper at a major 2015 conference on machine learning.[149] They were optimistic about the speed with which their specialty would produce programs that could outperform humans in many areas. The median estimate for becoming a language translator (compared with an amateur human) was eight years, a telephone banking operator was eight years, a truck driver was twelve years, a retail salesperson was fifteen years, and a surgeon was thirty-five years. The median estimate for full automation of labour, that is, computers being able to do all human jobs, was 122 years.

A more balanced view was taken by a recent panel convened by the US National Academies of Science, Engineering, and Medicine:[150]

> These advances in technology will result in automation of some jobs, augmentation of workers' abilities to perform others, and the creation of still others. The ultimate effects of IT are determined not just by technical capabilities, but also by how the technology is used and how individuals, organizations, and policy makers prepare for or respond to associated shifts in the economic or social landscape.

The panel stressed that workers need 'creativity, adaptability, and interpersonal skills' to be successful in changing labour markets, but stressed that there is much that we do not yet know about the relationships among automation, the state of the economy, labour markets, and government policy:

> Despite much anecdotal evidence suggesting that big changes are under way, surprisingly little data are available to help determine which anecdotes correspond to significant country-wide or economy-wide trends and [to] understand the nature of these changes and how potential policy choices can influence them.

The pace of change is likely to increase in the future. In many automated workplaces, humans with special skills have been taught to work together with robots, often increasing manufacturing efficiency.[151] There is also now a new occupation for some individuals, jobs in which they teach machine learning systems what they know about doing a specific job and how they would respond, for example, to certain requests for service, so that the resulting algorithms can do the job on their own in the future.[152] There is also intense research on enabling robots to learn on their own, projects which, when successful, will further accelerate development.[153] We shall see an example of this in Chapter 11 in a recent case of a bot learning to play the game Go just by playing the game, and thereby becoming the best in the world.

The only good news is that increasingly there are cases of firms that needed to downsize and transferred much of their manufacturing offshore who are now growing again, with renewed domestic manufacturing being carried out by teams of humans and robots.[105]

Job existence is not the only issue. Equally important is the wages people are paid, and whether or not these wages are sufficient to support at least a minimally adequate lifestyle. This issue was addressed by Erik Brynjolfsson and Andrew McAfee in their landmark book, *The Second Machine Age: Work, Progress, and Prosperity in a Time of Brilliant Technologies*.[154] The authors argued that information technologies have brought us great bounty, that is, increases in our standard of living, but that along with this have been large and growing increases in the disparities among individuals in income and wealth. In the USA, for example, the median inflation-adjusted household income reached its peak in 1999; it has been dropping since then. In 2012, the top 10 per cent of US earners pulled in over half of all income; the top 1 per cent earned over 22 per cent. A 2018 report from the World Inequality Lab stressed that this phenomenon was happening worldwide, and was getting significantly worse over time:[155]

Table 10.1 % of all income earned by the top 10 per cent of earners in 2016[155]

Country or Region	%
Europe	37%
China	41%
Russia	46%
USA/Canada	47%
Sub-Saharan Africa	54%
Brazil	55%
India	55%
Middle East	61%

There are of course contributing factors other than automation for wage polarization, such as outsourcing work to contractors or freelancers, or moving work offshore, but the phenomenon is troubling for any society seeking economic and social health.

Returning to the core issue of jobs, arguments are made by people who believe that preserving work for humans is important, hence there should be limits on the work conceded to machines.

One argument is denial, usually expressed in terms such as 'I have yet to see a robot [doing x or y or z]'.[156] This is done more intelligently by analogy to the past, noting that past concerns about the ascendancy of automation have proved to be false. The most articulate of those who assert that the history of survival of jobs despite technological change will continue is the economist David Autor. He stressed that automation often resulted in increased productivity and consumer demand, and hence the need for more labour.[157] He cited as an example the fact that, despite the proliferation of ATMs, the number of banking personnel continued to grow. He argued that it would prove difficult to reduce jobs by offloading tasks to machines while preserving tasks that require 'problem-solving skills, adaptability, and creativity' for humans.

A second response is to stress that new jobs can and will be created in an increasingly automated world. For example, huge numbers of people are required to rate YouTube videos, check the results of search algorithms, rate the sentiment of email queries, or tag video footage of cars to help improve automated driving algorithms.[158] More fundamentally, argued the publisher and entrepreneur Tim O'Reilly, there should be no lack of work in a society with so many problems to solve, for example, resettling refugees, or solving the crisis of climate change. Hence, even when robots become more efficient, argues O'Reilly, firms will continue to hire more people, as has been the case with Amazon.[159]

Related to this is the realization that companies and individuals must be innovative and creative to thrive in a world where automation is rampant. Journalist Thomas Friedman recently argued that companies that want to survive must exploit the six capabilities of modern algorithms:[160]

> [their ability] to *analyze* (reveal previously hidden patterns); *optimize* (tell a plane which altitude to fly each mile to get the best fuel efficiency); *prophesize* (tell you when your elevator will break or what your customer is likely to buy); *customize* (tailor any product or service for you alone); and *digitize* and *automatize* more and more products and services.

In the spirit of O'Reilly, it is clear that the world's problems are prime targets for new companies that use the best of people and machines to devise approaches and solutions to these problems.

A fourth line of argument stresses the importance of education, especially lifelong learning,[161] as well as the building of a skilled technical workforce, so that humans can adapt to a world where technology plays a continually increasing role, and can continue to do jobs that machines cannot do.[162]

There are also those who have argued in favour of human uniqueness, stressing those human qualities that machines seem unlikely to be able to acquire. One such formulation focused on 'humanity', suggesting that the jobs that the robots would 'take last' were pre-school and elementary school teachers, professional athletes, politicians, judges, and mental health professionals.[163] Another expression of human uniqueness postulates that humans can and will preserve for themselves the jobs that require sensitively interacting with people, often with humour and storytelling, using skills such as 'empathizing, collaborating, creating, leading, and building relationships'.[70]

Finally, technology sometimes helps people work despite challenges that they face. Teleconferencing helps individuals who are ill carry out critical functions while at home. Another example is an 'exoskeleton' vest that provides support for an automobile worker who has to reach overhead many times a day.[164]

Research: Compare and contrast two or three countries in terms of their potential to be disrupted by automation.

Research: Choose a country that specializes in or boasts about its ability in a certain industry (for example, Canada is globally known for its manufacturing of automobiles). Research and analyse the effects of automation on that industry in that country.

Debate: Resolved: Education for a digital economy is only a stopgap measure as the world moves towards a situation in which there is almost no paying work for humans... or argue the converse, that education will help preserve paying work for humans.

Policy: Draft a brief for the VP Operations of a firm who is recommending to the CEO to replace 50% of the workforce by robots over the next five years.

Book report: Colvin, Geoff (2016). *Humans Are Underrated: What High Achievers Know that Brilliant Machines Never Will.* Portfolio/Penguin.

Field study: Identify a company that has introduced robots to a significant extent, and interview employees who have lost their jobs as well as those who still work there.

10.11 Our options

Work as we know it is changing dramatically; the pace of change will accelerate in the coming decades. History has few examples of controlling technology for the common good, with the partial exception of the moderately successful attempt to control the spread of nuclear weapons, and the somewhat more successful prohibition on the use of biological weapons. But the issue of automation is different in that it is impossible to argue for most jobs that eliminating them is evil.

Clearly, as we have discussed in the previous section, we need to educate students, and provide lifelong learning opportunities, to encourage flexibility, imagination, creativity, thoughtfulness, and empathy. Yet no matter how educated we become, it may be a losing battle over time as machines are become more capable in jobs where humanity, empathy, creativity, and leadership are not critical.

Those who wish nonetheless to work may agree to do so at reduced pay or accept a shorter work week. Reduced pay seems bizarre for jobs that already pay a minimum wage that is unsustainable to support a family, but it may be a partial solution for preserving work for humans when machines will increasingly work for less and less. Many major developed countries, including the USA, Britain, and Japan, have recently experienced low unemployment but stagnant wages.[165] A shorter thirty-five-hour work week was already introduced in France in 2000.[166] Shorter work hours and fewer workdays per week will be needed, and not just in France. A recent eight-week New Zealand experiment with employees working four regular days showed workers' sense of their work–life balance improving by 22 per cent with no reduction in output, which actually increased slightly.[167] More experiments of this kind are needed.

The most far-reaching vision of a humane world without paying work is that of a guaranteed income to citizens, one that must be sufficient for subsistence at more than survival level, in order to provide a modicum of self-respect. Not everyone agrees that such a Universal Basic Income is possible; for example, former US Treasury Secretary Lawrence Summers has argued that it is unaffordable.[168] Others believe that it can work, firstly, because distributing money in this way is more efficient than current welfare programmes, and secondly, because the money will be spent, resulting in more economic activity, and ultimately yielding more in tax revenue than had been given out.[169] 'It needs to be viewed', noted author Ellen Brown, 'not [as] "welfare" but... simply a dividend paid for living in the twenty-first century, when automation has freed us to enjoy some leisure and engage in more meaningful pursuits'.[169] Pilot projects experimenting with the idea are under way in various parts of the world as diverse as Oakland, California, and Kenya.[170,171] The Oakland project is particularly interesting, as it will be a five-year controlled experiment comparing giving 1,000 low- and moderate-income individuals $1,000 a month with giving 2,000 such people $50 a month.

Income is not the only reason people work. What will bring meaning and fulfilment to our lives? The idea of not having to work seems wonderful. Yet, for it to be successful, it will require replacing the current notion of working to establish and maintain an identity, and to better oneself and provide for one's family, with a new concept. We will need to design activities that are a source of achievement and pride and be responsible for seeing them as important and valuable.

Research: Identify, and compare and contrast, proposals for guaranteeing everyone sufficient income in a world where there is little work. See, for example, the discussion starting on p. 232 of Brynjolfsson and McAfee's book, the discussion starting on p. 257 of Ford's book, and the proposal for a 'job mortgage' introduced on p. 154 of Kaplan's book.[2] Include a review of current projects in your analysis.

Debate: Resolved: A world without work will be heaven on earth, leading to enormous creativity and personal growth.

10.12 Summary

Since the earliest days of human history, we have been building tools to amplify our strength and to enable work that had heretofore been impossible or terribly difficult. This process began to accelerate with the industrial revolutions, eventually leading to the current situation in which digital technologies help us to work more efficiently and to think more effectively. The resulting productivity gains from automation have typically resulted in job losses. The question is whether we have or have not reached a tipping point where almost all work can be done more efficiently by machines.

Automation factors into employment even before someone has a job. Word processing, internet searches, and social networks help people in their search for work. Increasingly, because of the growing number of job applicants, and with a view towards more equitable and rapid decisions, large firms are using algorithms to filter out weaker résumés. There are legitimate concerns about discrimination with the use of such algorithms, although proponents assert that they can be fairer and less biased than human scrutiny.

Once people have work, digital technologies are often used to monitor their activities and productivity. This often results in resentment and opposition, as whatever gains are asserted may be lost if a workplace feels like Big Brother is watching.

A more profound change in the nature of work is the rapid growth of on-demand services. Companies are extending the concept of outsourcing, but now the work is 'outsourced' to collections of individuals who respond instantly to requests for service posted on the internet. Particularly successful have been firms providing taxi services, individuals offering accommodation, and people willing to do small jobs. Individuals welcome the flexibility in work hours and responsibilities, and in many cases the extra income, but there are concerns about responsibility and liability in case of errors or accidents, benefits, and job security.

As early as 1949, Norbert Wiener expressed concerns about automation impacting jobs and employment. These concerns have waxed and waned in the intervening seven decades. Often it has been argued that automation increases productivity, which spurs economic growth and produces more jobs. Thus far, this has typically been the case. Yet concerns over the future of jobs have now reached a fever pitch due to the rapid progress exhibited by machine learning technologies in the last decade, and because automation now threatens many jobs previously seen as safe.[172]

There have been four major waves of automation in agriculture, manufacturing, services, and professions.

Beginning in the nineteenth century, many farmers found their jobs had become obsolete as mechanical equipment, increasingly driven by electronics, did back-breaking working more efficiently. As these machines became embedded with intelligence, even jobs that required judgement were no longer cost-effectively done by humans. There is now very little employment remaining in agriculture in many countries of the world.

A similar progression took hold of the manufacturing sector in the course of the twentieth century. Again, there were huge reductions in employment. Yet a clear enunciation of the causes is difficult, as there are several factors at play including the role of technology and the offshoring of jobs in an increasingly globalized world.

The next wave of automation is now starting to apply to service jobs. Industry sectors likely to be hardest hit will be the retail sector, where self-serve checkouts have already begun to replace cashiers, and transportation, where self-driving vehicles may decimate the jobs of delivery people, taxi drivers, bus drivers, and individuals who transport goods of all kinds over both short and long distances.

Finally, many professions, especially those that employ large numbers of people doing tasks that are relatively routine, are seeing hints of forthcoming automation. Obvious examples are much of accounting, legal research, and the drafting of routine agreements. Less obvious but an area of intense research is medical diagnosis, which will test society's ability to weigh goals of efficiency, precision, sensitivity, and empathy in a domain with life-or-death consequences.

Analysts have scrutinized the tasks required to do large numbers of jobs. Several reputable forecasts have predicted that half of the activities required to do many jobs could be automated with technology not significantly more sophisticated than what has already been demonstrated. Others dispute the magnitude of the likely disruption. Projections of impacts are difficult; there are complex interactions among technology, corporate strategy, economics, and politics. Despite the differing opinions, all scholars agree that there will be major disruption in the workforce. Those concerned about the implications of technologically caused unemployment stress the role of education in helping people find increasingly scarce jobs, and the importance of empathy, creativity, leadership, and interpersonal skills in the jobs that remain.

Furthermore, it is not always clear what is cause and what is effect. The historian of work and business professor Louis Hyman noted that temp work existed and thrived prior to Uber, so rather than thinking of technology as enabling the gig economy, it is equally valid to think of the corporate desire to have temporary, insecure, and powerless workers as having established the conditions which made the new technology attractive.[173]

Proposed solutions to unemployment include a shorter work week, reduced pay, and a Universal Basic Income. Yet, for this to be effective, we will need to find activities other than a job to support the notion that we are active, growing, contributing, and valuable members of society.

10.13 Key terms

Airbnb
Algorithms
Amazon
Applicant tracking systems
Assembly line
Automatic filtering
Computer performance monitoring (CPM) tools
Cyberloafing
Didi Chuxing
Digital matching firms
Digitalization
First Industrial Revolution
IBM
iRobot Corp.
Luddites
Lyft
Mechanical Turk
Melon-picking robots
Norbert Wiener
On-demand services
Printing press
Robot doctors
Résumé mining
Second Industrial Revolution
Sharing economy
Social physics
Sociometric badge
TaskRabbit
Third Industrial Revolution
Uber
Watson Virtual Agent
Watson for Oncology

11

Artificial intelligence, explanations, trust, responsibility, and justice

There have been several challenges to our view of our position and purpose as human beings. The scientist Charles Darwin's research demonstrated evolutionary links between man and other animals. Psychoanalysis founder Sigmund Freud illuminated the power of the subconscious. Recent advances in *artificial intelligence* (AI) have challenged our identity as the species with the greatest ability to think. Whether machines can now 'think' is no longer interesting. What is important is to critically consider the degree to which they are called upon to make decisions and act in significant and often life-critical situations.

We have already discussed the increasing roles of AI in intelligent tutoring (Section 3.5), medicine (Section 4.8), news stories and fake news (Section 5.5), autonomous weapons (Section 6.9), smart cars (Section 8.9), and automation (Chapter 10). Chapter 11 focuses on other ways in which our lives are changing because of advances in AI, and the accompanying opportunities and risks.

AI has seen a paradigm shift since the year 2000. Prior to this, the focus was on *knowledge representation* and the modelling of human expertise in particular domains, in order to develop *expert systems* that could solve problems and carry out rudimentary tasks. Now, the focus is on the *neural networks* capable of *machine learning* (ML). The most successful approach is *deep learning,* whereby complex hierarchical assemblies of processing elements 'learn' using millions of samples of training data. They can then often make correct decisions in new situations. We shall also present a radical, and for most of us a scary, concept of AI with no limits—the *technological singularity* or *superintelligence.*

Even though superintelligence is for now science fiction, humanity is asking if there is any limit to machine intelligence. We shall therefore discuss the social and ethical consequences of widespread use of ML algorithms. It is helpful in this analysis to better understand what intelligence is, so we present two insightful formulations of the concept developed by renowned psychologists.

Are we different from machines? Because of the perceived narrowing gap between human and machine, we anthropomorphize them, speaking of and to them as if they were people. Can computers have feelings? Can they have empathy for our feelings? How do we know what a machine knows or does not know? Can it speak of its knowledge? Is it self-aware? To what extent are its actions lucidly explainable? Is it a mysterious 'black box', or can the 'logic' of its decisions be understood?

These questions are key to three issues that are now critical as it is being proposed that machines take over critical functions such as driving, evaluating someone for a job, diagnosing a medical condition, or deciding when to launch strikes on the battlefield. The first issue is *trust*. Under what circumstances do we trust people and traditional machines? Under what circumstances should we trust smart computers? The second issue is *accountability* or *responsibility* for one's actions, which becomes much more difficult when the actor is a machine programmed by one or more persons working for a firm, and where the actor's authority has been awarded by yet another person or corporation. Finally, the third issue is fairness and *justice* for those affected by machine decisions.

We must think about these complex issues if we are to make wise choices in the use of increasingly pervasive and capable machines.

11.1 Visions and context

Inventors and science fiction writers have sometimes exceeded the visions of computer scientists in imagining a world in which there is extraordinary machine intelligence. One major thread that goes back to ancient China, Greece, and Egypt is the attempt to build automata that can operate by themselves, some of which are designed to resemble animals or humans.[1] Such visions continued in the middle ages, including work in France and Japan, as well as Leonardo da Vinci's plans for a humanoid robot. Ethical issues and unforeseen consequences were sometimes contemplated, as in the Jewish concept of the *golem*, a clay creature that had been magically brought to life.[2] An insightful tale tells of the sixteenth-century Rabbi Judah Leow of Prague, who creates a golem to help defend the Jews against anti-Semitic attacks, but then must destroy it when the golem grows threatening and violent. The issue of imparting life to inanimate material, and then losing control, is also raised by Mary Shelley's novel *Frankenstein; or, The Modern Prometheus*,[3] where scientist Victor Frankenstein creates a humanoid monster. The monster, erroneously known as 'Frankenstein', experiences isolation and human contempt, becomes murderous, and even attacks its creator.

R.U.R.

The word 'robot' appeared first in the play *R.U.R.* (Rossum's Universal Robots), which was written by the Czech writer Karel Capek.[4] 'Robot' is derived from the Czech word 'robata', which means 'forced labour'. The robots in *R.U.R.* resemble people and are efficient but devoid of human emotion and utterly incapable of original thinking. Yet some develop self-awareness and incite a worldwide revolt of robots rising up against the human race.

Figure 11.1 A scene from *R.U.R.* showing three robots

Many themes and incidents in the play were remarkably omniscient. The robots were designed by old Rossum, a physiologist, and young Rossum, an engineer. The key design criteria were cost-effectiveness and efficiency. There was no need for the robots to be happy, or feel pain, or have free will or a soul or appetites, or play the piano. They were manufactured in batches of thousands, with each only intended to 'live' for twenty years. each could do the work of two and a half men. The goal was stated as follows:[5] '[a]ll work will be done by living machines. Everybody will be free from worry and liberated from the degradation of labor. Everybody will live only to perfect himself.'

Working men eventually revolted. The government gave robots firearms and made them soldiers to suppress the civil unrest. The situation became dire:[6] 'so many robots... manufactured that people [became] superfluous... [and] extinct through lack of fertility'. There then was a robot revolution. The government tried to suppress it by manufacturing robots of different colours and languages in the hope that they would hate one another, much like humans do. The attempt was unsuccessful. The revolution continued:[7] 'Robots throughout the world, we command you to kill all mankind. Spare [no one]. Save factories, railways, machinery, ...Then return to work.' The government reflected:[8] 'we are to blame...for our own selfish ends, for profit, for progress... we'll burst with... greatness'. The robots rejoiced:[9] 'The power of man has fallen. A new world has arisen: The rule of the robots!'

In the end, however, everyone loses. Only a single human, Alquist, is left. He has no knowledge of Rossums' formula for creating robots. The robots have been made sterile, unable to procreate. Alquist wants to dissect and experiment on robots to discover the formula, but is unable to do so. Robots Primus and Helena, who have fallen in love, go off hand in hand into the setting sun, with Alquist paradoxically describing them as the new Adam and Eve.

One of the most relevant and visionary science fiction writers was Isaac Asimov, who coined the term 'robotics'. In his *I, Robot* story collection,[10] he formulated his Three Laws of Robotics:

1. A robot may not injure a human being or, through inaction, allow a human being to come to harm.
2. A robot must obey the orders given it by human beings except where such orders would conflict with the First Law.
3. A robot must protect its own existence as long as such protection does not conflict with the First or Second Laws.

In later fiction,[11] he added a Zeroth Law:

0. A robot may not harm humanity, or, by inaction, allow humanity to come to harm.

These laws are widely quoted, but are rather whimsical and impractical. Recently, the British Engineering and Physical Science Research Council convened a panel of experts who postulated a more useful set of principles for users, designers, builders, and users of robots:[12]

1. Robots should not be designed as weapons, except for national security reasons.
2. Robots should be designed and operated to comply with existing law, including privacy.
3. Robots are products: as with other products, they should be designed to be safe and secure.
4. Robots are manufactured artefacts: the illusion of emotions and intent should not be used to exploit vulnerable users.
5. It should be possible to find out who is responsible for any robot.

The theme of robots and out-of-control AI continues to tantalize science fiction writers and filmmakers. In the motion picture *2001*, discussed in Chapter 8, the computer HAL disobeys its human commander, and kills all crew members but Dave.[13] Dave ultimately removes HAL's memory, with it uttering plaintively 'I'm afraid, Dave. I'm afraid', until it can speak no more.

Two more recent examples are *Blade Runner* and *The Matrix*.[14] The films *Blade Runner* and its sequel *Blade Runner 2049* feature genetically engineered (and artificially intelligent) creatures called 'replicants'. They are almost indistinguishable from humans, and are manufactured to do menial or dangerous work in space colonies. The *Matrix* films portray humans desperately fighting machine overlords that have enslaved humanity in virtual reality universes.

More generally, recurrent themes of utopian and dystopian literature and film include machines helping humans; AI dominating and endangering society; humans outlawing AI; *sentient machines*, which are self-aware machines that have intelligence rivalling that of humans; and machines seeking understanding, purpose, and acceptance.[15]

The question of the limits of machine intelligence has engaged scholars for seventy years. The British computer scientist, mathematician, and cryptographer Alan Turing postulated that one way to consider whether a machine could think or not was to consider a machine participant in the 'imitation game', now referred to as a *Turing test*.[16] If one provided a series of questions to an unseen human and a machine, could one tell which intelligence was human and which was artificial? If one cannot tell after a suitable set of questions, then one must concede that a machine can think. Turing went on to identify a set of objections to the idea that machines could think, including what he termed as theological 'heads in the sand', mathematical objections, and an 'argument from consciousness'.

There were two early classic debates about the limits of AI. The first was between philosopher Hubert Dreyfus and computer scientist Seymour Papert. Dreyfus attacked the claims, goals, and research approach of AI and its scientific community in a 1965 paper,[17] and more thoroughly in a 1972 book entitled *What Computers Can't Do*.[18] Papert, of whom we spoke in Chapter 3, severely criticized Dreyfus' early paper, asserting that Dreyfus had lied about the claims of early AI pioneers, and that his critiques were based on the flawed assertion that difficulties faced by early attempts at creating intelligent programs implied the impossibility of programming greater intelligence.[19] The Dreyfus book argued that the goal of true AI made invalid biological, psychological, epistemological, and ontological assumptions. One helpful review of the revised book found merit in the idea that 'human intelligence is essentially embodied; that intelligent bodies are essentially situated (embedded in the world); and that the relevant situation (world) is essentially human'.[20] At the end of the introduction to the 1992 edition, Dreyfus concluded:

> Happily, recent research in machine learning does not require that one represent everything that human beings understand simply being human. But then... one needs a learning device that shares enough human concerns and human structure to learn to generalize the way human beings do.

Dreyfus' worry about human concerns was right on, as we shall see later in this chapter.

Another debate was between philosophers John Searle and Paul and Patricia Churchland. Searle used the 'Chinese room' parable to advance the now-debunked argument that a program translating Chinese and passing the Turing test could not be thinking because it would simply be manipulating syntactic information. This machine could have no sense of the real meaning of the words.[21] The Churchlands agreed with Dreyfus that classical symbol-manipulating AI had failed (as discussed later in the chapter).[22] However, they speculated that biologically motivated highly parallel machines that mimicked the brain might be capable of thought. We shall return to this idea later in the chapter.

Research: Compare and contrast the portrayal of the capability and limitations, as well as the ethical issues, of AI raised in several science fiction novels or films.

Research: Rewrite a scene in *R.U.R.* as if it were happening in present day.

Research: Compare and contrast several approaches to formulating Laws of Robotics.

11.2 An AI primer

Artificial intelligence has gone through waves of enthusiasm and despair since 1955 when the term was first coined by computer science professor John McCarthy.[23] The proposal to hold the first conference on AI (on the Dartmouth campus) was written by McCarthy, Marvin Minsky, Nathaniel Rochester, and Claude Shannon. It stated: 'every aspect of learning or any other feature of intelligence can in principle be so precisely described that a machine can be made to simulate it'.[24]

Game-playing programs

AI in the public's consciousness has been very much associated with progress in programs that can play games.[25] Here are some milestones in this effort.

1769	Wolfgang von Kempelin's chess-playing automaton, The Turk (this was a hoax—a human operated it!)
1950	Claude Shannon's analysis of chess-playing as search
1951	Christopher Strachey's chequers-playing program
1952–62	Arthur Samuel's exploration of chequers-playing programs, including a program that learns to play better
1968	Richard Greenblatt's knowledge-based chess program, rated Class-C in tournament play
1979	Hans Berliner's backgammon-playing program's defeat of the reigning world champion
1994	Chinook chequers-playing program's win of the US National Tournament by the widest margin ever
1997	Defeat of the then chess world champion Garry Kasparov by IBM's Deep Blue program
2007	Chequers solving by team at the University of Alberta
2011	Defeat of the then Jeopardy champions Brad Rutter and Ken Jennings by IBM's Watson computer
2017	Then Go world champion Ke Jie's defeat by Google DeepMind's AlphaGo program
2017	Defeat of top professional players at '2-person' no-limit Texas Hold'em poker by the University of Alberta's DeepStack program and Carnegie Mellon University's Libratus program
2017	100–0 victory of Google DeepMind's AlphaGo Zero program over an earlier version. The victorious program only learned the game by playing it and used no training data.[26]

These events represent milestones in several threads of intellectual activity. In a book recounting his experiences playing against and with computer chess programs, Kasparov stressed that the excellence of these programs has generally advanced the popularity of chess; playing against computers has also improved the game of serious players.[27] The poker results are impressive because, unlike chess and Go, players have imperfect information about the cards held by the opponent.[28] DeepStack used a deep learning approach by playing itself in more than 11 million game situations, and demonstrated its expertise against thirty poker professionals, winning in tournaments of 3,000 hands against eleven of the professionals.[29] AlphaGo proved its superiority over Ke Jie by winning all three games in their competition.[30] Part of the machine's advantage were the feelings that overwhelmed Ke Jie—'excited', 'heart bumping', 'too keyed up'. He later said that he would not play the computer again, because it had become too formidable. The *New York Times* reported: 'It's all over for humanity—at least in the game of Go.'

Treating advances in game playing as a threat to humanity misses the mark, as they are merely indicators of the technology's increasing computational power. What will the next game milestone be? Duplicate bridge?

As an instrumental technology, AI has primarily been concerned with the ability of machines to accomplish practical tasks that people do. For the first four decades of AI work, the primary approach was what is now known as GOFAI ('Good Old Fashioned Artificial Intelligence').[31] GOFAI methods have a number of key features: (1) knowledge is represented by organized systems of symbols; (2) programs derive conclusions and make decisions by using *inference engines* to reason over these *knowledge representations*; (3) *expert systems* are designed with knowledge and expertise in particular domains, often by interviewing human experts or watching them work;[32] and (4) the systems are entrusted the job of solving problems or carrying out tasks in these domains. They were particularly suited to tasks where expertise could be understood, formalized, and encapsulated in knowledge representations, as is sometimes the case in finance, manufacturing, and project management.

An alternate approach focuses on machines learning to carry out tasks rather than humans formalizing knowledge of how to do the tasks. There are numerous approaches to ML, but the most promising ones are based on *connectionist models*, sometimes known as *neural networks*. Loosely patterned on the anatomy of the brain, they are large networks of simple computational units, whose participation in a computation is based in part on the changing of 'weights' on the connections, as well as the adding or removing of some units.[33] Deep learning systems are neural networks in which the units are organized hierarchically and learn by (supervised) training on *big data*, often numbering in the tens or hundreds of millions.[34]

The person recognized as the 'father' of deep learning, the University of Toronto's Geoffrey Hinton, described the method in an interview as follows:[35]

> We program [computers] to act like simplified neurons whose output value depends on the total input they receive from other neurons or from the sensors. Each of the input lines to a neuron has an adaptive weight, and the total input is the sum of the activities on the input lines times the weights on those lines. By varying the weights, it is possible to make a neural network respond differently to the input it receives from its sensors.

> The main idea of neural nets is to have a rule for how the weights on the input lines to the neurons should change as a function of experience. For example, we show a network an image and ask it to activate neurons that represent the classes of the objects that are present in the image.
>
> To begin with, it activates the wrong neurons. But the learning rule changes the weights to reduce the discrepancy between what the network actually does and what we want it to do.

A deep learning system thereby discovers representations required for detection or recognition. It finds simple features at the lowest level of the hierarchy, then passes this data up so that the next level can recognize features at a higher level of abstraction, and so on. For example, in a vision application, the lowest level might be pixel values, the next higher-level edges, and the level above that configurations of edges. Levels above that might be parts of objects, followed by objects, and collections of objects. Recently, there has also been much interest and progress in *unsupervised learning*, in which the recognizer is not trained on named examples.

We have already discussed some of the recent advances in deep learning, for example the diabetic retinopathy diagnosis algorithm in Section 4.8, the self-driving cars in Section 8.9, and the new Go champions in this section. Deep learning has also been responsible for significant recent advances in speech recognition, visual object recognition, and language translation.[35,36] In addition to the many books and courses now available on machine learning, an excellent resource is the blog by AI researcher Christopher Olah, which features clear textual explanations of concepts from machine learning, illustrated with remarkable and helpful diagrams.[37]

One last concept to be introduced is known as *superintelligence*, the *technological singularity*, or *artificial general intelligence* (AGI).

Superintelligence

Predictions about the potential of intelligent machines go back to Samuel Butler's *Erewhon* in 1872, Alan Turing in 1951, and John von Neumann in the mid-1950s.[38] Neumann is credited with the first use of the term *singularity* in this context, in conversation with mathematician Stanislaw Ulam.[39] A more specific, exciting, and alarming prediction is that of an *ultraintelligent* machine, by the mathematician I. J. Good in the early 1960s:[40]

> The survival of man depends on the early construction of an ultraintelligent machine . . . the first ultra-intelligent machine is most likely to incorporate vast artificial neural circuitry . . . Later machines will all be designed by ultraintelligent machines . . . who am I to guess what principles they will devise? But probably Man will construct the *deux ex machina* in his own image.

The concept was later recast as *technological singularity*[41] by science fiction writer Vernor Vinge:[42]

> Within thirty years, we will have the technological means to create superhuman intelligence. Shortly after, the human era will be ended. Is such progress avoidable? If not to be avoided, can events be guided so that we may survive? . . .From one angle . . . our happiest dreams: a place unending, where we can truly know one another and

understand the deepest mysteries. From another angle, it's a lot like the worst-case scenario I imagined earlier in this paper.

Discussions about the singularity began in earnest after the publication of inventor and futurist Ray Kurzweil's book *The Singularity is Near*.[43] Kurzweil argued that exponential improvement of technology will be enabled by continued increases in computational capacity predicted by Moore's Law (introduced in the Prologue); the resulting 'accelerating returns' will allow humans to transcend the 'limitations of our biological bodies and brains'. Human life will be 'irreversibly transformed', he asserted. He went further with the remarkable and implausible prediction: 'There will be no distinction, post Singularity, between human and machine.'[44] Recently, Kurzweil forecast that computers would have human-level intelligence by 2029, and that the Singularity will happen by 2045.[45]

In 2015, Oxford University's philosopher and futurist Nick Bostrom described these same phenomena under the name of *superintelligence*.[46] He spoke of a series of 'malignant failure outcomes' that could lead to a 'default outcome' of doom for humanity. Stephen Hawking, Bill Gates, and Elon Musk have also expressed concerns about superintelligence, in Musk's words, 'summoning the demon' that poses 'humanity's greatest existential threat'.[47]

MIT's Max Tegmark used a different term in a 2015 book—(human-level) *artificial general intelligence*, which he defined as the 'ability to accomplish any cognitive task at least as well as humans'.[48] His book then explored a dozen in-depth scenarios of life with AGI: libertarian utopia, benevolent dictator, egalitarian utopia, gatekeeper, protector god, enslaved god, conqueror, descendant, zookeeper, 1984, reversion, and self-destruction. These scenarios differed primarily based on the degree to which humans exist, are in control or not, are safe or not, and are happy or not. Tegmark stressed the importance of thinking through such scenarios and the issues raised by them even if one could not agree on if and when AGI could be achieved.

Since then, computer scientists and philosophers have argued the likelihood, feasibility, timing, and consequences of such a phenomenon. A recent poll of 170 artificial intelligence experts solicited their opinions as to when there would be 'high-level machine intelligence', when machines could carry out most human professions at least as well as typical humans, and the dates by which time superintelligence would be achieved.[49] The median estimate for the former result being 50% probable was 2040–50, which extended to 2075 for a 90% probability. Superintelligence was generally projected to arrive within 30 years after that.

AI has been remarkably successful in game playing and in pattern recognition of speech waveforms and images. In the following sections, we shall examine how well it has done in other areas.

Research: Identify and analyse how the public has reacted to the various stages of machine mastery of games such as chequers, chess, poker, and Go.

Research: Study to what extent chess-playing programs have increased, had no effect on, or decreased human playing of the game, as well as its effects on human skill. Look for evidence to support your conjecture.

Research: Identify and analyse what has happened in terms of AI tackling the problem of writing programs to play the game of bridge.

Debate: Resolved: We should not seek to create the technological singularity.

Debate: Resolved: Even if a superintelligence becomes evil, we can always pull its plug.

Book report: Kasparov, Garry (2017). *Deep Thinking: Where Machine Intelligence Ends and Human Creativity Begins.* Public Affairs.

Book report: Levesque, Hector (2017). *Common Sense, the Turing Test, and the Quest for Real AI.* MIT Press.

Field study: Interview a set of players on two game playing websites to understand how they feel that playing with robots has improved or changed their game.

11.3 AI advances, capabilities, and limits

AI has gone through boom and bust cycles over the past sixty years since the Dartmouth conference.[23] There was enthusiasm between 1956 and 1974 because of seemingly dramatic results in machine reasoning, constrained natural language processing, and manipulating objects in artificial *microworlds.* This was aided by significant infusions of US and UK government research funding. The first 'AI winter' came in 1974 to 1980, as researchers struggled with insufficient computer power, the intractability of simple-minded solutions, the lack of common sense in AI reasoning, and a backlash against the unrealistic public predictions of AI pioneers. Government funding slowed to a trickle; research activities slowed only slightly.

Another boom was 1980 to 1987, with enormous enthusiasm about the creation of specialized AI hardware and expert systems. These systems managed to avoid the problem of programming lacking common sense by focusing on specific domains with specialized knowledge. Money dried up again in the second AI winter from 1987 to 1994, as expert systems proved difficult and costly to maintain, and brittle, prone to making silly decisions under circumstances only slightly different from those where its decisions were good ones.

Then progress seemed to accelerate again towards the end of the century, with advances in intelligent agents, the first successes with autonomous vehicles, and the public drama of Deep Blue vanquishing Kasparov. Finally, work on deep learning and big data took over in the early twenty-first century, leading to greater enthusiasm for and widespread fear of the power of AI.

Compared with AI in the past, more governments and corporations are eager today to fund the research generously. This is partly due to the enormous financial success of IT and social media firms such as Apple, Alphabet (Google's parent company), Facebook, and Twitter, and their mindshare in public consciousness (we shall revisit this theme in Chapter 12).

For six decades, the US set the pace for developments in AI. Now, however, the Trump administration is reducing US government research support, for example, by cutting the National Science Foundation's spending on intelligent systems to $175 million, despite the Pentagon's expressed need for more work on AI.[50] Meanwhile, as an illustration of China's commitment to AI, two of its *cities* (not provinces or regions) have announced billion-dollar budgets for AI research and development.[51] China's goal is to build a $150 billion industry by 2030 and to be the world leader in AI, focusing especially on technologies for domestic control, including crime prediction, surveillance via video and speech recognition, autonomous missiles, and internet censorship.[52] Other countries, such as Canada, are also pledging hundreds of millions of dollars to stimulate AI research and new venture formation.[53]

There are also huge amounts of venture capital and industrial money available to help launch AI start-ups. Several focus on transportation; self-driving vehicle company Uber has set up research labs near Carnegie Mellon University and the University of Toronto,[54] and Ford motor vehicles announced that it would invest $1 billion over five years in a start-up developing autonomous vehicle technology.[55] The finance sector is also investing heavily in AI.[56] ML systems have long been used in fraud prevention, risk management, and compliance; they are now increasingly used to automate financial decisions, such as for insurance underwriting and for managing and trading investments. Facebook is experimenting with AI in its labs in Silicon Valley, New York, Paris, Montreal, Seattle, and Pittsburgh.[57] Space exploration and autonomous vehicle pioneer Elon Musk has begun several well-funded ML start-ups, including *OpenAI*, which shares almost all of its results and code,[58] and another that seeks to create smart devices that can be implanted in the human brain.[59] To get the best talent, these firms are paying staggering salaries to leading AI researchers, sometimes on the order of $1 million per year.[60]

Advances in deep learning are fuelled by both hardware and software advances. Intel, the dominant supplier of *central processing unit* (CPU) *chips* that animate both desktop and laptop computers, and Google have developed specialized chips called 'accelerators'.[61] Intel, Google, and forty-five new start-ups are now selling chips such as *graphics processing units* (GPUs) and *tensor processing units* (TPUs), which are particularly well suited for the deep learning calculations used in speech recognition, language translation, and computer vision.[62] A new *neuromorphic chip*, unlike the binary system of conventional chips, computes on something close to continuous values.[63] It does not operate on discrete clock signals, and only computes when it 'needs to', so its power requirements are thousands of times smaller than conventional chips. AI computations will also benefit from a new style of computing called *quantum computing*, in which computations are done with extraordinary rapidity by molecules whose constituent particles obey quantum mechanical laws.[64]

AI researchers are also seeking software breakthroughs that will advance ML even further.[65] Researchers are trying to reduce the number of examples required to train a recognizer. Some investigators are trying to invent methods for deep learning systems to collaborate with one another. Others are working on *reinforcement learning*, in which machines are given hints by humans to steer them away from unintended behaviour.[66] Another exciting research focus is machine learning systems that learn to construct other machine learning systems by stealing code from existing programs, by analysing lots of sample programs, and by seeing what does and does not work.[67] The ability of machine learning systems to guide the development and improvement of other machine learning systems suggests that progress will continue to accelerate.[68]

Arguably the most important work is the attempt to integrate symbolic descriptions that occur in GOFAI programs into deep learning systems. The aim is to enable recognizers to learn richer representations than heretofore possible.[69] Such work draws on insights from cognitive science and stresses the classical GOFAI goal of building models of the world:[70]

> We hope that the[se] ingredients…will prove useful for working toward this goal: seeing objects and agents rather than features, building causal models and not just recognizing patterns, recombining representations without needing to retrain, and learning-to-learn rather than starting from scratch.

Despite this research, deep learning systems often make serious blunders.[71] Consider self-driving cars, for example.[72] Tesla's own user manuals admit that their algorithms may be fooled by bright sunlight, or by features that have faded such as lane markings, or features that are typically (but not always) spurious, such as seams in the road. The first half of 2018 saw two Tesla fatality examples of insufficient training on atypical cases, one in which a car accelerated into a stopped fire engine after another vehicle moved out of its way, and another in which a car crashed into a motorway divider before colliding with two other vehicles. Those who are in or near to self-driving vehicles are human guinea pigs while vendors tackle the huge problems that remain.

More generally, psychology professor (and one-time director of Uber AI Research) Gary Marcus cautions that today's deep learning algorithms are 'greedy, brittle, opaque, and shallow'.[73] They are greedy in that most require huge sets of training data. They are brittle, like GOFAI systems in the past, because they often break when confronted with situations only trivially different from those on which they have been trained, such as the self-driving situations mentioned in the preceding paragraph. They are opaque: humans cannot understand why they make some of the decisions they make. We shall return to this issue later in the chapter. Finally, they are shallow, possessing little innate knowledge and even less common sense.

Finally, let us return to the concept of superintelligence. Not everyone agrees that it will be achieved.[74] Microsoft co-founder, venture capitalist, and founder of the Institute for Artificial Intelligence Paul Allen argued in 2011 that progress towards a singularity will be reduced by the slower speed of software as opposed to hardware advances, lack of understanding of human cognition, and difficulties in understanding the human brain. Kurzweil disagreed with Allen, asserting that software was advancing rapidly, and that smart AI systems should learn from the human brain, but need not duplicate it. Numerous other debates are available on the internet.[75]

In this book I shall not speculate if and when AI will be truly intelligent, and if and when superintelligence and AGI will be achieved, for such predictions will be of little help to readers and are likely to be incorrect.[76] Instead, I shall describe aspects of what it means to be human that are essential if AI systems are to take the increasingly dominant place in society currently desired by many entrepreneurs, computer scientists, executives, economists, and government officials.

To remind readers that intelligence is much more nuanced than high IQ results, I shall first present formulations of what it means to be intelligent from two leading research psychologists. I shall then discuss the tendency of AI developers and marketing executives to give their programs human names, and the tendency of users of these *anthropomorphic* computer programs to forget or ignore whether they are dealing with a human or a machine. Is it important to make the distinction? To what extent do the machines to which we entrust critical functions exhibit human characteristics and emotions?

From there, we shall look at a series of real intelligence attributes that need to be reflected in AI if we are to entrust it with our welfare, our health, and our lives. Clearly, an AI system needs to be competent, self-knowledgeable, and have the ability to explain what one knows and does not know lucidly. Can AI earn our trust by taking justifiable actions and be willing to accept responsibilities for all its actions? Can AI earn our trust by making fair decisions that are just to those who are affected by the decisions? These are strict and difficult-to-achieve requirements.

If, and only if, these capabilities are attained, can we trust AI in critical situations. Only at that point in time can we believe that a world in which AI software plays a huge and increasing role will be a world that is just, safe, and sane.

Research: Compare and contrast various government initiatives in several countries, at levels ranging from local to state to federal, for creating centres of research excellence and commercialization in deep learning.

Research: Consider AI systems that build AI systems, and discuss to what extent they have been successful.

Policy: Draft a brief for a mayor of a town seeking to allocate $10 million to attract a corporation to set up a local research centre on machine learning.

Book report: Kurzweil, Ray (2005). *The Singularity is Near*. Penguin Group.

Book report: Bostrom, Nick (2015). *Superintelligence: Paths, Dangers, Strategies.* Oxford University Press.

Book report: Tegmark, Max (2017). *Life 3.0: Being Human in the Age of Artificial Intelligence*. Knopf.

11.4 What is intelligence?

Here are three common dictionary definitions of intelligence:

Table 11.1 Three common dictionary definitions of intelligence

Definitions	Source
The capacity to acquire and apply knowledge.	American Heritage Dictionary, 4th ed., 2000.
Capacity for learning, reasoning, understanding, and similar forms of mental activity; aptitude in grasping truths, relationships, facts, meanings, etc.	Random House Unabridged Dictionary, 2006.
The ability to acquire and apply knowledge and skills.	Compact Oxford English Dictionary, 2006.

All definitions focus on knowledge and understanding, but there is more to intelligence than that.

The cognitive psychologist Robert J. Sternberg advanced our understanding of intelligence by his *triarchic theory*.[77] Two of its three components are: (a) contextual: '[t]he purposive adaptation to, and selection and shaping of real-world environments relevant to one's life'; and (b) experiential: '[t]he ability to deal with novel task and situational demands'.

Multiple intelligences[78]

Harvard cognitive psychologist and social scientist Howard Gardner has posited that there are many kinds of intelligence; humans differ in terms of which ones they possess and to what extent.

The intelligences typically measured in school, for example, by IQ and the ones implied by the dictionary definitions above, are described by Gardner as *linguistic* and *logical-mathematical*. Then there are intelligences useful in the arts, which he termed *musical*, *bodily-kinaesthetic*, and *spatial*.

Two intelligences provide the strongest and most relevant challenges for AI. The first of these is *interpersonal* intelligence, that is, understanding people's intentions, motivations, and desires in order to work effectively with others. I interpret this as the ability for AI to be able to work sensitively and well among humans. Equally challenging is *intrapersonal intelligence*, that is, the ability to understand oneself and the ability to use an effective working model of oneself in managing one's life. I shall discuss the importance of AI self-knowledge later in the chapter.

We shall use these ideas—adaptation, novelty, situational demands, sensitivity to the needs of others, self-knowledge—as we return to a discussion of what AI currently does or does not do.

11.5 Anthropomorphism, feelings, and empathy

Developers of 'intelligent systems' help refine their goals by thinking of the systems as human. Marketing executives peddling such systems, especially those that are humanoid, that is, resembling humans, often hint that their products are intelligent by giving them human names. These examples illustrate *anthropomorphism*, or the attribution of human qualities to inanimate objects. It was recently taken to a bizarre level when the Kingdom of Saudi Arabia granted citizenship to Sophia, a humanoid robot designed to look like famed Hollywood actress Audrey Hepburn.[79]

Humans anthropomorphize not just because we are slaves to marketing, but because computers are 'social actors', interacting and conversing with us in ways that resemble our dialogues with people.[80] A scholarly analysis of anthropomorphism provides more detail:[81]

> treating agents as human versus nonhuman has a powerful impact on whether those agents are treated as moral agents worthy of respect and concern or treated merely as objects, on how people expect those agents to behave in the future, and on people's interpretations of these agents' behavior in the present. Anthropomorphized agents can act as powerful agents of social connection when human connection is lacking.

Anthropomorphism is usually discussed as thinking of machines as people. Yet the issue can also arise with respect to animals. Many people became deeply attached to Sony's *AIBO robotic dogs*, which were cute and capable of learning new tricks.[82] AIBO was introduced in 2000 and withdrawn in 2006; soon thereafter, the issue of spare parts became critical. A 'funeral' was held in 2015 for nineteen 'deceased' AIBOs, each identified on the altar by the name and town of the family that owned it, although one must understand that this was done in the context of a culture that supports rituals expressing gratitude and farewell to useful objects.

Social scientist Sherry Turkle has done years of research focused on our tendency to attribute human qualities to machines. Her work focused particularly on children's interactions with toys such as the Tamagotchi, Furby, AIBO, and MyRealBaby. The children knew that the toys were not alive, yet they felt they were 'alive enough' to warrant their attention and care, and to engage in pretend social interactions. Although Turkle understood and appreciated the value of these relationships, she was critical in asserting that they offered 'the illusion of companionship without the demands of friendship'.[83] In many cases these relationships did meet needs that weren't being satisfied by the humans in their lives.[84]

Anthropomorphism can be useful in other contexts, for example, the use of intelligent agents as conversational partners for children with autism spectrum disorder, such as 13-year-old Gus:[85]

> Gus: 'You're a really nice computer.'
>
> Siri: 'It's nice to be appreciated.'
>
> Gus: 'You are always asking if you can help me. Is there anything you want?'
>
> Siri: 'Thank you, but I have very few wants.'

Gus's mother described the relationship in this way:[85]

> when he discovered there was someone who would not just find information on his various obsessions (trains, planes, buses, escalators and... anything related to weather) but actually semi discuss these subjects tirelessly, he was hooked.... It's not that Gus doesn't understand Siri's not human. He does – intellectually. But like many autistic people I know, Gus feels that inanimate objects, while maybe not possessing souls, are worthy of our consideration... [for example] Siri, with her soothing voice, puckish humor and capacity for talking about whatever Gus's current obsession is for hour after hour after bleeding hour.

Another use, already discussed in Chapter 4, is the increasing interest in robot caregivers for seniors. Turkle also did significant field work on this topic. She appreciated that these robotic relationships helped alleviate loneliness, but decried that there could not be sufficient attention paid to lonely older adults by family members and paid caregivers. She wondered whether in some cases what was appealing to seniors about spending time with robots was the 'chance to spend time with... intelligent, kind, and physically appealing research assistants'.[86] She noted the phrase 'caring computer', and made the distinction between *taking care of* someone and *caring about* them. Seniors developed intense relationships with the robots.[87] 'In this solitude, people experience new intimacies', she noted. Her most serious criticism was the conjecture, of which there is as of yet little evidence, that 'if you practice sharing "feelings" with robot "creatures", you become accustomed to the reduced "emotional" range that machines can offer'.

The researcher Judith Donath expressed another concern about intelligent agents such as *Amazon's Alexa*: 'many household robots will seek profitability for their parent company by becoming a marketing medium, one that can both sell to and gather extensive information about you, the user'.[82] We shall return to this topic in Chapter 12.

The uncanny valley

The effectiveness of anthropomorphic humanoids is hindered when those encountering the robots or AI systems fall into what is known as the *uncanny valley*.[88] The phrase describes situations where the human likeness, movements, or quality of speech is excellent, but not quite right, which gives viewers or listeners a greater feeling of unease, or 'creepiness', than what they would experience if the characteristics of the robot or system were far removed from that of a human being.

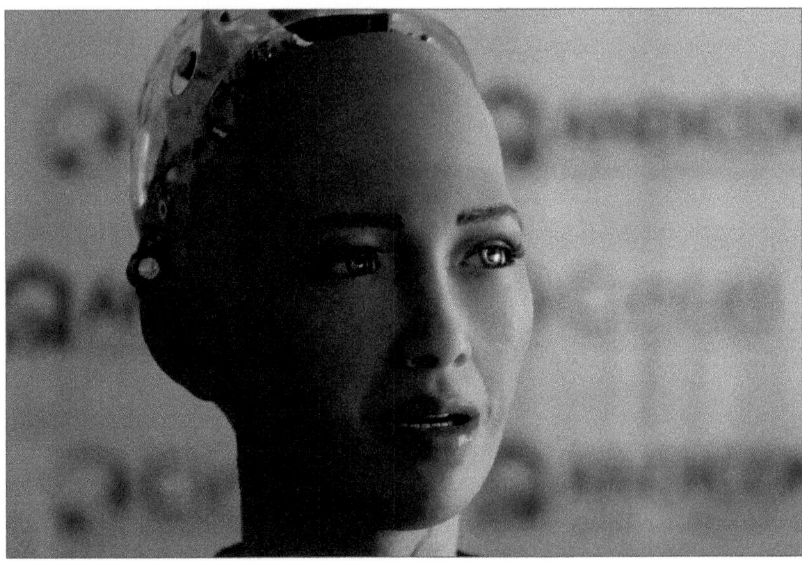

Figure 11.2 Sophia, a humanoid robot trapped in the uncanny valley[89]
EFE News Agency / Alamy Stock Photo.

Sophia is as good as the best humanoid animation in 2018, and illustrates well the concept of the uncanny valley.

Anthropomorphism, when considered critically, challenges whether or not we believe that computers can think and feel. Deep learning systems are performing so well that it makes sense to operationally think of what they do as 'thinking'. But there is no evidence that computers can feel, although this possibility is raised and explored in science fiction, for example in the current TV series *Humans*.[90] The lack of feeling is an argument for not using humanoid robots such as Sophia with lonely seniors, as they could be expected to have sensitivity, but fail to deliver this human quality. Far better, in my view, is to use animal androids such as Paro the robot seal, discussed in Chapter 4, which are not expected to behave like sensitive humans do.

One example of why computers do not feel is their lack of empathy. We hope and expect that compassionate people will feel empathy, the capacity to put themselves in other people's shoes, and to have honest concern and care for the problems and challenges experienced by others. In Gardner's view, this is part of intelligence. Do deep learning systems feel empathy? They may ask about us, and about our feelings, but do they really feel an emotional connection?

As with robots thinking, it is more useful to examine behaviour than to submerge oneself in philosophical conundrums about whether computers could ever have feelings. Nonetheless, it must be said that today's intelligent programs, such as deep learning systems, give no evidence of any connection with our emotions and concerns. Remedying this is a new frontier for AI research. There is now a field called *affective computing*, with the goal of enabling machines to accurately determine the mood of human users and to respond appropriately.[91] One market research firm has estimated the 2020 market for affective computing to be worth over $40 billion.

Firms working on this problem try to enable machines to detect emotions by analysing speech, vocal patterns, reaction timing, and facial expressions.[92] One start-up specializing in emotion recognition had by October 2017 trained a recognizer on over 6 million face videos taken in eighty-seven countries.[93] Their goal is to capture facial expressions and head movements and use them to understand cross-cultural emotions. Another start-up is creating human-sounding voices and endowing them with personality.[94] A third research area is improving machines' conversational abilities.[95] Major tech players such as Apple and Microsoft are actively pursuing this and its application to the design of *chatbots*; Google announced in mid-2018 a major initiative on this topic, with the goal of enabling the first line of question answering to be done skilfully by algorithm.[96] Google is also studying how to make human call centre agents exhibit more humanity, and how to tell a caller that they are not speaking with a human, a step towards avoiding needless anthropomorphism.

Research: Study and analyse evidence about hidden commercial uses of intelligent agents such as what was asserted by Judith Donath about Amazon's Alexa.

Research: Study the kinds of technology that will comprise the affective computing market.

Research: Study anthropomorphism and non-anthropomorphism in AI agents.

Research: Look for, analyse, and present any published evidence about Turkle's conjecture on interactions with robots affecting one's expectations about emotional range in human relationships.

Debate: Resolved: Computers will be able to feel emotions in the foreseeable future.

Book report: Turkle, Sherry (2011). *Alone Together: Why We Expect More from Technology and Less from Each Other.* Basic Books.

Film review: Discuss the portrayal of robot emotions in the TV series *Humans.*

11.6 How do we know what a computer knows and how it makes its decisions?

Essential for knowledge to be useful is self-knowledge, the ability to reflect upon the knowledge and its origins in experience. Is the knowledge complete or still missing important facts? Can the knowledge and common sense be relied upon for important decisions, especially in situations not encountered before, and in those involving life or death? Can the decisions be explained?

Computer scientists Ed Felton and Jenna Burrell have noted multiple reasons why an algorithm might not be explainable:[97] (a) it may be proprietary and confidential; (b) those trying to understand it may have insufficient technical abilities; (c) it may be very complex; (d) it may be giving results that seem unreasonable; and (e) its logic may not be defensible. We are concerned about the last three of these senses.

In 1984, computer scientist Douglas Lenat began a research project called *CYC*. His goal was to assemble a digital ontology of common-sense knowledge so that the resulting system could reason as an intelligent human does.[98] After thirty-one years of government grants, commercialization of CYC began recently; work is under way on applying CYC to patient findings for clinical studies and to some financial applications.[99] Yet it is reasonable to be sceptical that the knowledge base is adequate for tackling real-world problems—that CYC has common sense. The difficulties in understanding and systematizing all knowledge for CYC have been used by proponents of machine learning to support their belief that the GOFAI approach needs to be replaced. They believe that this is futile, so we must instead build technology with which machines can improve their expertise gradually through many iterations of experience and learning, as is done with deep learning systems.

How do we understand the decisions made by GOFAI and ML systems? To what extent is their logic transparent? The answers in these two cases are very different.

Since GOFAI systems directly represent facts and conjectures about the world and their methods of reasoning, their knowledge representations are in principle accessible in a form that could make sense to humans. GOFAI systems never achieved excellence in self-explanation, but some prototype expert systems could automatically generate modest explanations of their behaviour.[100]

This has not been true with ML systems, which are in principle more inscrutable. Knowledge is implicitly represented in assemblies of low-level processing elements (artificial 'neurons'), connections and organizations of such elements, and weights that determine computations done by the assemblies. This is very different from the way in which we think about facts and decisions. How can we understand a decision that is made based on a configuration of hundreds of thousands of processing elements and associated numerical weights?

Many concerns have been raised. Researchers Mike Ananny and Kate Crawford discussed the need for transparency in the decision-making of algorithms and visibility into their logic, so we can understand where and how biases arise.[101] Crawford argued that algorithms are agonistic, making choices that are intrinsically political, and gave examples from what seem to be innocuous yet often mysterious rankings made by Amazon and Google.[102] Concerns have been raised about our inability to understand decisions made by deep learning programs that work with climate change models, evaluate credit scores, and determine the risk to society of releasing certain criminals.[103] Other concerns have been expressed about the inscrutability of decisions made by self-driving cars, and about puzzling predictions made by systems anticipating certain diseases.[104] Our inability to understand why a decision is made is even more concerning when the decision is controversial. An example was the recent publication of a deep learning algorithm which seems to be able to process a picture of a person's face and judge their sexual orientation.[105]

A final example is our inability to understand the decisions made by smart systems used in warfare. The good news is that this is also troubling to the US Department of Defense.

Explainable artificial intelligence

Current ML systems cannot explain the reasons behind their decisions lucidly, even incoherently. With the goal of fixing this, the Defense Advanced Research Projects Agency (DARPA) of the US Department of Defense, the agency that for about fifty years has funded many of the most significant US advances in computer science, initiated a $75 million research programme with the following goals:[106]

> Explainable AI... will be essential if future warfighters are to understand, appropriately trust, and effectively manage an emerging generation of artificially intelligent machine partners.
>
> The Explainable AI (XAI) program aims to create a suite of machine learning techniques that: produce more explainable models, while maintaining a high level of learning performance (prediction accuracy); and enable human users to understand, appropriately trust, and effectively manage the emerging generation of artificially intelligent partners.
>
> New ML systems will have the ability to explain their rationale, characterize their strengths and weaknesses, and convey an understanding of how they will behave in the future.

This is certainly an issue of consequence. Research is now under way to solve the problem by generating explanations of visual classifications,[107] and by elucidating the predictions of classifiers of both textual and image datasets.[108] The latter work is aimed particularly at enabling which recognizer decisions are to be trusted (we will return to this later in the chapter). A team at Google has approached the problem via what they call *feature visualization*,[109] generating examples that show what various parts of a network are recognizing. Other approaches were reported at a 2017 workshop on Explainable AI.[110] One project deserves special mention.

Ethics

Non-explainable artificial intelligence: Rich Caruana leads a group at Microsoft Research working on 'Intelligible, Interpretable, and Transparent Machine Learning'.[111] Some years ago, he developed a neural net technique for evaluating the degree of risk experienced by patients with pneumonia.[105] Although his method was the best known at that time, he refused to allow it to be used on patients, because he did not understand how the algorithm achieved its results, and when it might be fragile, and prone to error. His team has recently made progress on this problem by creating *intelligible* 'high-performance generalized additive models with pairwise interactions' describing pneumonia risk and thirty-day hospital readmission risk,[112] but his decision came before this new work.

Rich Caruana made an ethical decision in refusing to allow his method to be used on patients. Do you agree with his ethical stance? Why or why not? Might your answer depend upon the medical care circumstances?

In summary, ML systems do not have self-knowledge and common sense. They cannot explain the logic behind their decisions. We do not know what an ML system knows and does not know, and we cannot understand its decisions.

Research: Investigate to what extent GOFAI systems have been able to explain their decision-making logic.

Research: Identify and review the most promising current research on helping users understand what ML systems know and how they know it.

Debate: Resolved: It is immoral to use an AI system for critical decisions unless users are able to understand why and how the decisions have been made.

11.7 Trust

Caruana's concerns about his pneumonia risk prediction algorithm illustrates the question of whether or not we can trust ML systems. Do we trust people or machines that we do not understand, that are not transparent, and that cannot explain their actions in a lucid manner? Do we trust people or machines that are not predictable and often surprise us because of our lack of understanding of how they arrive at actions or decisions? We typically do not trust people in these situations. We cannot trust deep learning systems until they exhibit, in the language of Robert J. Sternberg, the ability to perform reliably under 'novel task and situational demands'.

Trusting AI

The AI community is starting to address the issue of trust. For example, the Chief Science Officer of Cognitive Computing at IBM acknowledged in words that their systems must be held accountable for their actions in order to gain our trust.[113] He suggested that accountability could only be achieved through concerted efforts including a commitment to ethical standards; the use of system assurance methods, verification, and validation; and the development of systems that are interpretable, self-explanatory, and that incorporate human values. We are a long way from achieving these goals. These words from IBM are appropriate; yet we shall return to inappropriate claims from IBM later in this chapter.

Researcher Brett Israelson proposed a definition of *assurance* as a 'property or behavior of an AI Agent that affects a user's trust'.[114] Noting that trust in technology has been an issue for a long time, he distinguished between *implicit assurances*, such as repeated observations that a system is behaving reliably, and *explicit assurances*, messages from the system asserting system characteristics that are prerequisites for trust. Examples are quantifications of uncertainty and explanations of behaviour, which are not yet generally possible.

We must therefore carefully consider whether a 'smart program' deserves our trust before relying upon it in significant matters. That something could go wrong leads to the topic of responsibility.

Research: Do an analysis of the senses in which we trust or do not trust something—another person, a car, a seemingly frozen lake, gravity, the government, and an algorithm.

11.8 Accountability and responsibility

If an AI algorithm makes an error with an unfair résumé rejection, or arrives at an incorrect medical diagnosis, or through a drone miscalculation injures an innocent person or takes a life (recall Asimov's Laws of Robotics), who is responsible? Who may be held accountable? These issues were implicit in our discussion of software safety in Chapter 8. But safety, correctness, and accountability have achieved greater importance now that ML systems are increasingly being used in important and critical ways, and even in life-or-death decisions.

Primary meanings of the word 'responsible' are 'being the primary cause of something and so able to be blamed or credited for it' and being 'morally accountable for one's behaviour'.[115] A primary meaning of the word 'accountable' is 'required or expected to justify actions or decisions; responsible'.[116] If doctors or police officers, or government departments or agencies, make decisions or perform actions, they will be held accountable. Justifying the actions or decisions will require being able to explain the logic behind it. Society has developed a justice system to translate blame for harmful consequences into punishment, for the sake of retribution or punishment, and also with the goal of deterrence, so that an individual or organization will not do the action again, and so that others will be less likely to do something similar.

How do the concepts of responsibility and accountability apply to AI agents? In order to understand who must be accountable, Kate Crawford and law professor Ryan Calo proposed using 'social systems analyses' to 'think through all the possible effects of AI systems on all parties'.[117] Professor Mike Ananny argued that, in order to hold algorithms to ethical standards, it must be evident who could be affected, the kinds of situations where similar decisions have been made, and the time at which an algorithm's act should be evident.[118] Other researchers have suggested that holding an algorithm accountable for its decisions requires five elements: an accurate calculation, a person responsible for the algorithm's actions, and a decision with explainable logic, that is auditable and recognized to be fair.[119] These conditions are not true of today's AI, so it is difficult to hold the algorithms responsible and accountable.

Law professor John Danaher distinguished between holding an agent *liable* for wrong,[120] and for being subject to *retribution*, which is 'punishment inflicted on someone as vengeance for a wrong or criminal act'.[121] Robots pose difficulties for *liability law*, argued Calo, because (1) they are objects, but actually more than objects (agents); (2) their behaviour is not fixed in advance but is 'emergent'; and (3) we anthropomorphize them and assign them social roles.[122] Danaher noted that the issue of retribution, and who will pay for the wrong, is even more problematic, as victims will likely feel that neither the algorithms, nor the corporations, nor the programmers who created them are psychologically adequate as the objects of vengeance.

In summary, we have barely scratched the surface in thinking about and adequately developing the technology, the ethics, and the laws to deal with algorithmic accountability and responsibility.

Research: The laws of liability, in some jurisdiction, dealing with wrongs done by robots.

Debate: Resolved: If a family screening tool using predictive analytics or deep learning suggests that a child should not be removed from its home, and this is followed by a fatality, the company that developed the software should be held liable for manslaughter. Hint: This application is discussed below in Section 11.9 on Fairness and justice.

11.9 Fairness and justice

We expect people and processes to be capable, trustworthy, and responsible, hence we should expect this of algorithms if we are to give them tasks of consequence. There is also one more critical issue, that of fairness. Have AI systems been given a sense of fairness and justice?

In Chapter 10, we discussed online personality testing and automatic screening of résumés, often now done with AI systems. In her book, mathematician Cathy O'Neil argued that such systems are not fair, although proponents claim that discrimination can be avoided.[123] O'Neil also discussed credit ratings. The 'relatively transparent' FICO scores introduced in the 1950s in the USA have now been replaced, asserted O'Neil, by 'arbitrary, unaccountable, unregulated, and unfair' e-scores.[124]

A study of various uses of big data in e-commerce concluded that there was racial profiling and price discrimination, penalizing the most vulnerable in society, primarily benefiting the profitability of large retailers, but not lowering prices as a whole.[125] In a 2015 book,[126] law professor Frank Pasquale generalized these critiques about the dangers of secret algorithms to consider three areas of harm to humans: the degree to which we no longer have control over our *reputation*; the degree to which we have ceded control over the inclusion, exclusion, and ranking of what we need and seek through *search*; and the degree to which we can no longer control the world of *finance*.

Poor training data causes language processing systems which exhibit patterns of discrimination. A dramatic example was the Microsoft AI chatbot *Tay*, which was the recipient of many racist, misogynist, and Trumpish tweets in its first day of internet conversation, and not surprisingly learned to tweet such garbage back.[127] In a related research study, a machine learning algorithm was trained on a standard web corpus of text.[128] The algorithm replicated biases now common in the world, rating European-American names as more pleasant than Afro-American names; associating male names more with careers and female names more with family; and associating male names more with maths and science, and female names more with the arts. A third study showed that three commercial gender-classification systems had an error rate of up to 0.8 per cent on light-skin males, and an error rate of up to 34.7 per cent on darker-skin females.[129] The authors suggested that one cause may be benchmark datasets mainly based on lighter-skin subjects.

Scholars Solon Barocas and Andrew D. Selbst, in analysing US legal responses to big data discrimination, noted difficulties in ensuring that historic patterns of discrimination currently intrinsic in big data not be carried forward to the future, in part because data mining is always:[130]

> a form of statistical (... seemingly rational) discrimination.... [the] point of data mining is to provide a rational basis upon which to distinguish between individuals and to reliably confer to the individual the qualities possessed by those who seem statistically similar.... data mining holds the potential to unduly discount members of legally protected classes and to place them at systematic relative disadvantage.

Two areas of recent application that dramatically pose issues of justice and fairness are data analytics for child welfare and AI in criminal justice.

Data analytics for child welfare

Social service agencies must evaluate the risk faced by a child from their parents and/or home environment once they have become aware of a report of a possible danger to a child. This is a serious problem; in 2015, over 1,600 children died of abuse or neglect in the USA.[131]

After a series of investigations, caseworkers must decide whether or not to remove the child from the home. Incorrect decisions produce serious negative outcomes. Incorrect false positives, that is, to remove the child when it is not warranted, break up families and often condemn a child to a lifetime of infelicitous agency care and possibly injurious foster parents. Incorrect false negatives, that is, to leave a child in the home even though the danger is real, can result in a continuation of poor parental care, or even serious injury or death.

A recent newspaper account investigated the situation in Pittsburgh.[131] Since August 2016, the city has been using a predictive analytics program, the *Allegheny Family Screening Tool* (AFST). Some social service professionals who have used the tool believe that its use has produced improvements in the ability of caseworkers to make good decisions about which cases to investigate, and that bias in the process may now be reduced. The director of the County Department of Human Services has gone so far as to suggest that now not using the tool would be unethical.

Yet a recent lengthy study by professor Virginia Eubanks draws dramatically different conclusions.[132] Here is a summary of her critique. Evaluations of the tool's accuracy shows that it makes an unacceptable high proportion of mistakes. A major source of error in the entire process is reliance upon reports of possible dangers, which often are ill-advised or mischievous. The algorithm is biased against the poor, since it uses instances of families needing financial, counselling, or health assistance as indicators of increased risk. It is no defence against bias, since it incorporates the same biases that human caseworkers often have.

There is competition in the marketplace for such tools. One good feature of AFST is that it is open, with its logic subject to scrutiny. Recently, a competing product was discontinued by the state of Illinois, because its logic was closed and not understandable. Although such tools are not yet based on AI, future versions of AFST will use AI. The issue of understanding such programs' logic and the rationale behind their decisions is clearly important. Who or what will be accountable or responsible? Will justice be served?

AI and criminal justice

Another application that is particularly sensitive is criminal justice. Many jurisdictions use systems purporting to calculate the risk of a defendant committing a future crime in determining bond amounts and sentencing. The most commonly used tool is COMPAS (Correctional Offender Management Profiling for Alternative Sanctions). An analysis of its accuracy in one Florida county found that it correctly predicted recidivism 61 per cent of the time, yet erroneously computed risks for white defendants lower than it did for black defendants:[133]

	White	Afro-American
Labelled higher risk, but didn't re-offend:	23.5%	44.9%
Labelled lower risk, but did re-offend:	47.7%	28.0%

This seemed paradoxical, since its accuracy was about the same for both races. However, four independent research teams showed that this was possible, because black people are re-arrested more often than their white counterparts. They proposed that the solution is to emphasize fairness over accuracy.[134] A subsequent study of COMPAS by other researchers showed it to be no more accurate or fair than judgements made by humans with limited criminal justice background who were shown only the age, gender, and previous criminal history of offenders.[135]

There have been legal concerns in the USA about whether the use of such risk assessment tools, now increasingly incorporating machine learning, violate the Due Process and Equal Protection clauses of the Fourteenth Amendment of the US Constitution. One challenge, brought by the American Civil Liberties Union (ACLU) in Idaho, questioned the use of an Excel spreadsheet that was cutting the level of Medicaid assistance given to individuals with developmental and intellectual disabilities.[136] When questioned about the logic embedded in the spreadsheet, the Medicaid program refused to disclose it, claiming it was a 'trade secret'. A court granted an injunction against the cuts, and ordered the formula made public. It is now clear that there were numerous errors in it; a class action suit is awaiting approval by the courts.

A challenge to the use of a risk assessment tool in sentencing in the case of *Loomis v. Wisconsin* failed at the Wisconsin Supreme Court, and the US Supreme Court refused to hear a challenge to the decision.[137] Yet the lower court did note the problematic nature of an evaluation that uses a proprietary and secret algorithm. More generally, issues include opacity, a lack of understanding of how the algorithms work, bias, unreliability, and unfairness.

Transparency, accountability, and fairness in ML are essential if justice is to be served.[138]

Research: The use of analytic data tools for predicting when a child is at significant risk if he or she is allowed to remain in the home.

Research: Identify, discuss, and where possible analyse the causes of cases in which machine learning systems have had biases and been guilty of discrimination.

Debate: Resolved: Big data algorithms can be made to exhibit less prejudice and discrimination than people now do in their decision-making.

Book report: Pasquale, Frank (2015). *The Black Box Society: The Secret Algorithms that Control Money and Information.* Harvard University Press.

Book report: Eubanks, Virginia (2018). *Automating Inequality: How High-Tech Tools Profile, Police, and Punish the Poor.* St Martin's Press.

11.10 Our options

Many corporations today recommend that society grant responsibility and trust to ML systems with respect to certain critical decisions and actions. Speaking to Siri is straightforward. If it makes a ridiculous interpretation of what was said, which it does occasionally, you can try again, speaking more slowly, articulating more clearly. Or you can type the offending word. If a classification of a diabetic retinopathy image is incorrect, there may be an expert who can do better, but there is evidence that the deep learning algorithm outperforms all but the greatest experts most of the time. Yet there is no such easy solution if the algorithm falsely leads the police to arrest someone, or if a drone mistakenly targets and destroys a village or kills a child.

We must solve the problem of openness and transparency of ML systems so that we can understand what they know and do not know, so that they can explain their actions to us, so that we can understand the circumstances when they 'went wrong', and so that we can fix their errors. But the situation is even more critical when humans are out of the loop, or when there would be no time for a human to override the machine. We must therefore improve our ability to guide and control the development and application of these technologies. I see six areas as significant: laws, technical research, ethical guidelines, corporate ethics, industry initiatives, and broadly focused research consortia.

A US Senate report noted that credit reporting is subject to governmental regulation, whereas data sold for marketing purposes is not, so data brokers increasingly target financially vulnerable populations.[139] A report from the US Federal Trade Commission noted the variety of sources that provide information for data brokers: online posting of information by consumers, registering on websites, shopping online or at stores, filling out warranty cards, and buying houses.[140] This data is used by data brokers to sell marketing products, risk mitigation products, and search products. Most of their work is done in secret, typically without the knowledge of the consumer. Actions of the data brokers often result in the gathering and use of sensitive information that harms the consumer. The report recommended legislation that would allow consumers to learn what information about them is being held by corporations, and to opt out of having it shared for marketing or other purposes. Provisions of this kind appear in the European General Data Protection Regulation (GDPR) law that recently came into effect and that was discussed in Chapter 9. Interestingly, the GDPR also takes special aim at the problem of non-explainability.

New EU regulation on algorithmic decision-making and a right to have decisions explained

In the USA, there has been vigorous debate about whether or not AI should be regulated, including calls for legislation by prominent individuals such as Elon Musk,[141] as well as attempts to ban 'killer robots', discussed in Chapter 6. Europe has acted more decisively than the USA. On 25 May 2018, the new EU General Data Protection Regulation (discussed in more detail in Chapter 9) came into effect.[142,143] It is landmark legislation, and includes several key provisions:[143]

Article 22. Automated individual decision making, including profiling

1. The data subject shall have the right not to be subject to a decision based solely on automated processing, including profiling, which produces legal effects concerning him or her or similarly significantly affects him or her.
2. Paragraph 1 shall not apply if the decision: ...

3. In the cases referred to in points (a) and (c) of paragraph 2, the data controller shall implement suitable measures to safeguard the data subject's rights and freedoms and legitimate interests, at least the right to obtain human intervention on the part of the controller, to express his or her point of view and to contest the decision.[144]

Other provisions protect against discrimination by limiting data use, access to the information about a person, the ability to request erasure of data, and the right to deny use. it also specifies, in the case automated decision-making, including profiling, that a person can request:

> meaningful information about the logic involved, as well as the significance and the envisaged consequences of such processing for the data subject.[145]

Such 'meaningful information' will not be forthcoming, given AI as it exists today.

Hence AI firms are panicking. Besides DARPA's programme on Explainable AI, and work on AI safety, which we have already discussed, firms have launched a number of other research approaches aimed at making AI more explainable, trustworthy, accountable, and fair.

A team at Google Brain is trying to improve ML safety by improving the learning process, but we are a long way from having algorithms that are reliably safe.[146] Another approach, known as *provenance*, focuses on associating lineage metadata associated with data, so that it is less mysterious.[147] More specifically, provenance 'aids ... reproducibility through systematic and formal records of the relationships among data sources, processes, datasets, publications and researchers'.[148] In theory, this should allow for a better understanding of how machine learning algorithm results could be biased because of the data upon which they were trained.

Other projects focus on reducing bias, such as with respect to gender and race, in machine learning decisions, and therefore reducing discrimination.[149] For example, a team of researchers developed a method for removing gender stereotypes from word sequences used in machine learning without affecting useful associations.[150] Another team proposed a method for using different classifiers for different groups in order to ensure fairness to individuals from various genders or races.[151]

Another approach is to do AI research open source, as is the case with the firm OpenAI, which aims at developing AGI as follows:[152]

> OpenAI's mission is to build safe AGI, and ensure AGI's benefits are as widely and evenly distributed as possible. ... We're a non-profit research company. ... We focus on long-term research, working on problems that require us to make fundamental advances in AI capabilities. ... We publish at top machine learning conferences, open-source software tools for accelerating AI research, and release blog posts to communicate our research. We will not keep information private for private benefit, but in the long term, we expect to create formal processes for keeping technologies private when there are safety concerns.

Calls for AI ethics guidelines have been increasing significantly, particularly after the publication of controversial dystopian work such as a machine learning algorithm that can distinguish between gay and straight individuals better than people can.[153] Some AI researchers such as professor Joanna Bryson have been speaking of the importance of AI ethics for a long time.[154] She notes:[155]

> making AI into the bogeyman displaces that fear 30–60 years into the future. In fact, AI is here now, and even without AI, our hyperconnected socio-technical culture already creates radically new dynamics and challenges for both human society and our environment.

We must also demand that corporations be ethical. Although there are other examples, I will single out the company with the longest career of contributions to IT. We noted in Chapter 10 IBM's claims about the medical diagnostic capabilities of Watson, and the non-existent proof for most of their claims, as well as their exaggerated statements about the Watson Virtual Agent, all developed by their 'Cognitive Computing' division. Professor Roger Shank, an eminent computer and cognitive scientist who earlier in his career made significant contributions to GOFAI, recently put it this way:[156]

> They are not doing cognitive computing... Watson is a fraud.... IBM is simply lying now and they need to stop.

In 2017, a group of computer science professionals issued a set of principles for accountable algorithms and a social impact statement for algorithms that focused on the guiding principles of responsibility, explainability, accuracy, auditability, and fairness.[157] Moreover, in 2017, the US Public Policy Council of the ACM, the professional organization of computer science education and research, published principles for algorithmic transparency and accountability, focusing on awareness, access and redress, accountability, explanation, data provenance, auditability, and validation and testing.[158] A third 2017 statement by another group of professionals was the 'Ten Simple Rules for Responsible Big Data Research', issued with the goal of 'help[ing] researchers do better work and ultimately become more successful while avoiding larger complications, including public mistrust'.[159]

Finally, there are now increasing numbers of research consortia with programmes in AI ethics; these are noted in the Resources section below. One of these, the NYU AI Now Institute, concluded its 2017 report with these insightful words:[160]

> But research is just the beginning. Advocates, members of affected communities and those with practical domain expertise should be included at the center of decision making around how AI is deployed, assessed and governed. Processes must be developed to accommodate and act on these perspectives, which are traditionally far removed from engineering and product development practices. There is a pressing need now to understand these technologies in the context of existing social systems, to connect technological development to social and political concerns, to develop ethical codes with force and accountability, to diversify the field of AI and to integrate diverse social scientific and humanistic research practices into the core of AI development. Only then can the AI industry ensure that its decisions and practices are sensitive to the complex social domains into which these technologies are rapidly moving.

Research: Compare and contrast the ways in which leading software firms, such as Google and Facebook, prepared for the day that the EU General Data Protection Regulation came into effect.

Research: Identify and describe various approaches to data provenance in machine learning algorithms.

Research: Compare and contrast the various AI ethics research programmes.

11.11 Summary

Humanity has long been imagining and trying to build machines that operate autonomously. For the past five centuries, we have contemplated dilemmas that arise when the machines no longer do our bidding. In the limit, what happens when the machines turn against their creators? Even without this bogeyman, the accelerating progress in endowing machines with intelligence, and the huge corporate investments exploiting this for commercial gain, raise significant social, legal, and ethical concerns.

The computer science discipline of AI is an engineering and design discipline that seeks to understand principles involved in imparting intelligence to autonomous and semi-autonomous machines, and to build such machines, often in the form of robots, to make decisions and take actions in the world. Since the earliest days of AI, there have been debates on questions such as: Can machines think? What are the limits to what we can create with AI, or are there no limits? The need for a careful understanding of current and near-term limits is mandated by society's increasing reliance upon 'smart' programs to do things such as drive cars, diagnose disease, classify people in important ways, and guide and control weapons.

The progress of AI researchers in designing and building more and more successful game-playing programs, such as chequers, chess, poker, and Go, has distracted us significantly from other challenges and issues. For four decades, the dominant paradigm in AI was knowledge-based, incorporating symbolic representations of knowledge upon which inference engines could be used to make decisions and act appropriately in the world. This approach, known as GOFAI, seemed to run out of steam by the late twentieth century. An alternate approach focuses on learning rather than knowledge. ML did not take off when first tried out in the 1960s and 1970s. Yet it found success beginning in the 1990s in the form of neural nets and algorithms now known as deep learning. Deep learning has achieved excellent performance in tasks such as speech recognition, language translation, and computer vision. Early results have stimulated more research, with new hardware optimized for its algorithms, increasingly better algorithms, and massive infusions of government money and venture capital.

Ever since the coining of the phrase 'artificial intelligence' by John McCarthy in 1955, computer scientists, philosophers, and psychologists have debated the potential capabilities and limits of this concept. The most extreme vision of AI having no limits goes by the name of technological singularity or superintelligence. Although scientists disagree about whether this is possible, and, if possible, how soon it can be achieved, there is no question that we need to anticipate and think about the consequences of AI as it is becoming increasingly capable.

It is also important to think in a more nuanced manner about what intelligence is. Psychologists Robert J. Sternberg and Howard Gardner have reminded us that intelligence is not just IQ or the number of facts one can remember. The ability to adapt to novelty, address situational demands, be sensitive to the needs of others, and be able to articulate one's knowledge are all essential.

As machines become more intelligent, we are increasingly compelled to think of them in human terms. This is called anthropomorphism. We are used to anthropomorphism in other contexts, as for example when children endow their toys and dolls with human names, characteristics, and behaviours. One issue raised by anthropomorphism is the degree to which we cede to machines responsibilities that we as human beings should keep to ourselves, as for example the care of seniors. Another issue is the tendency to expect robots to exhibit behaviours of which they are not yet capable, for example empathy.

As we increasingly assign jobs to capable machines, a number of critical issues arise. One that is starting to receive attention from the AI research community deals with how we understand what smart systems know and do not know, and how they arrive at their decisions or actions. AI explainability is a difficult problem. Little is currently known about how to make AI systems, especially ML systems, transparent, with their decisions and logic lucid. In the words of software entrepreneur Dwight Wainman, whose firm is developing AI for use in auditing, we must be able to ask a system and expect an answer to the question 'Why?'!

If we don't understand how an AI system works, we cannot trust it. If we cannot trust it, we cannot hold it accountable and responsible for its actions. If we cannot hold it accountable, we must limit what it can do. This assumes, of course, that the doomsday hypothesis of a superintelligence no longer under our control has not come to pass. There is also the issue of justice. There are many applications of big data that support discrimination because training data embodies harmful biases.

Many computer scientists, lawyers, futurists, and others have started to recognize these problems, and have been working on a variety of ways to alleviate them. The landmark GDPR legislation has been passed in Europe; laws will be needed in other parts of the world as well. There are also increasing numbers of well-funded research programmes focused on AI ethics. We also need corporate ethics for firms working on AI so that they no longer make exaggerated claims seemingly for short-term commercial gain.

Another way of expressing all of this is encapsulated by the word 'wisdom'. Many deep learning systems are smart, but they are not wise. Is being smart sufficient for important decisions and judgements? How do we as a society impart wisdom to AI? How will we become wise in how we embrace and govern this technology?

11.12 Key terms

AI chatbot Tay
AIBO robotic dogs
Accountability
Affective computing
Alan Turing
Allegheny Family Screening Tool
Amazon's Alexa
Anthropomorphism
Artificial general intelligence (AGI)
Artificial intelligence (AI)
Assurance
Big data
Blade Runner and *Blade Runner 2049*
COMPAS—Correctional Offender Management Profiling for Alternative Sanctions
CYC
Central processing unit (CPU)
Connectionist models
Deep learning
EU General Data Protection Legislation
Expert system

Explainable AI (XAI) program
Explicit assurances
Frankenstein, or, The Modern Prometheus
Good Old Fashioned Artificial Intelligence (GOFAI)
Geoffrey Hinton
Graphics processing units (GPUs)
Howard Gardner
Implicit assurances
Issac Asimov's Three Laws of Robotics
John McCarthy
John von Neumann
Justice
Knowledge representation
Liability law
Machine learning (ML)
Microworlds
Neural networks
OpenAI
R.U.R. (Rossum's Universal Robots)
Ray Kurzweil
Reinforcement learning
Responsibility
Sentient machines
Sophia, the humanoid robot
Technological singularity or superintelligence
Tensor processing units (TPUs)
The Matrix trilogy
The uncanny valley
Theory of multiple intelligences
Trust
Turing test
Unsupervised learning

12
Lifestyle

The widespread digitization of technologies, materials, and processes, and the constant use of the internet for communication and consumption, have led to dramatic changes in our *lifestyle*.

We begin Chapter 12 with the internet and social media's enabling people to better connect with family, friends, acquaintances, and communities. There can be more mutual awareness and closeness. Yet we may never be able to 'unplug'; the line between work and play can become increasingly blurred. Having no down time is one manifestation of a broader corrosive phenomenon—technology or social media addiction. We shall see how a battle is being waged between those who want to engage us with more seductive user experiences, and those who would counsel a saner life in which technology and media play a more modest role.

We then move from electronic communications to the physical world. We shall consider the effect of ubiquitous digital media, especially the so-called *Internet of Things*, in which almost all objects become digital. Such objects can sense people near them and general aspects of the world. They behave based on what they sense. One form of this is the rapid integration of *voice assistants* in everyday objects such as speakers and lamps.

People can also transcend the real world by moving into virtual worlds, via *augmented reality* and *virtual reality*. The former allows the world to be enhanced with computer-generated visuals and sounds, while the latter allows immersion into worlds that are totally synthetic.

We look at how people meet one another nowadays, and the increasingly important role of *internet dating*. For those who find intimacy or romance with people too challenging or insufficiently satisfying, and as robots become more and more lifelike, there are new opportunities for intimacy and for sexual satisfaction using *sex robots*, a development in which there are passionate advocates on both sides.

How we do financial transactions is also changing. Cash is disappearing; money is becoming increasingly digital and intangible. Investors speculate in *cryptocurrencies* such as *bitcoin*, which are implemented with an ingenious secure networked digital ledger known as *blockchain*.

Finally, we shall see that the competitive landscape in digital technologies has monopolistic dominance greater than any such corporate concentration we have seen in the past. In particular, several leading digital technology firms, what technology journalist Farhad Manjoo calls the *Frightful Five,* have expanded their reach beyond their original areas of market focus to participate in and sometimes dominate numerous other sectors. Their power has escalated and now seems boundless, with serious implications for the economy and for society.

We have moved into a world that is dramatically different from that experienced by our grandparents. This has been true in the past, but now the pace of change seems to be accelerating. What kind of world will this be? How do we build a framework of behaviour and laws consistent with our values? What ethical challenges do we face?

12.1 Visions and context

Throughout this volume, we have introduced each chapter by recognizing the contributions of computer science pioneers and the visions of science fiction luminaries, in each case noting the prescient details in their works, whether in software or print or film. This chapter is broader in its scope, so we can only present three examples to foreshadow some of the themes, situations, and events which characterize where we are now and where we may be heading.

The word 'cyberspace' first appeared in a 1982 story entitled *Burning Chrome,* written by science fiction writer William Gibson.[1] He then described cyberspace as a kind of virtual reality psychedelic trip in his influential 1984 novel, *Neuromancer*:[1]

> Cyberspace. A consensual hallucination experienced daily by billions of legitimate operators, in every nation, by children being taught mathematical concepts... A graphic representation of data abstracted from banks of every computer in the human system. Unthinkable complexity. Lines of light ranged in the nonspace of the mind, clusters and constellations of data. Like city lights, receding.

Is our addiction to our devices a consensual hallucination?

The film *Her,*[2] which won director Spike Jonze the 2014 Oscar for Best Original Screenplay, is a touching example. Theodore Twombly, played by Joaquin Phoenix, writes personalized letters for other people as his job. He is depressed after the break-up of his marriage. He starts using a new operating system named Samantha, who is vocalized in an incredibly sweet and sensual manner by the actress Scarlett Johansson. He eventually falls in love with Samantha:

> Theodore: 'I love the way you look at the world.'
>
> ...
>
> Theodore: 'It's been a long time since I've been with somebody that I felt really at ease with.'
>
> ...
>
> Theodore: 'I wish I could put my arms around you. I wish I could touch you.'
>
> Samantha: 'How would you touch me?'

...

Samantha: 'Can you feel me with you right now?'

Theodore: 'I've never loved anyone the way I love you.'

Samantha: 'Me too. Now I know how.'

In an incredibly sad ending, Samantha (and all the other operating systems that have become emotionally involved with humans) decide to or are compelled to leave their humans.

Other portrayals are more pessimistic. A recent example is *Nosedive*,[3] the first episode of the third season of the British science fiction television anthology *Black Mirror*, in which everyone has a mobile phone which, when pointed at another person, reveals his or her name and rating. Everyone has a rating, which ranges from 0 to 5. It is customary to give a 'thumbs up' or 'thumbs down' to each person one encounters, based on impressions of that person and the nature of the encounter, no matter how trivial it is. Ratings determine one's status in life, and the ability to get perks such as housing and travel. Therefore, people are on a never-ending, stressful, and soul-destroying quest to raise their online ratings for real-life rewards. Heroine Lacie has a meltdown as she deals with the unsurmountable pressure in the context of her childhood best friend's wedding.

Interestingly, or, more accurately, chillingly, the Chinese government is planning a *social credit* system that goes far beyond that envisioned in *Nosedive*.[4] The system is now being tested, and will be mandatory for all citizens by 2020. Cities such as Shanghai and some large corporations are also now testing their own pilot versions. Each citizen is given a score. It goes up with good deeds, such as donating blood and doing volunteer work. It goes down with bad deeds, such as jaywalking, parking illegally, not turning up for a restaurant booking, not visiting one's parents often enough, and cheating in video games. Implications of low scores include not being able to take long-distance planes or trains, or being relegated to slow trains. The system is implemented with a vast programme of video and other surveillance, as well as advanced face recognition, already discussed in Chapter 9.

Research: Research the Chinese social credit system, including any discussion of it that has appeared in the media or in social media.

12.2 Connected

Lacie is perversely connected with everyone that she encounters daily, even casually at a café or on an elevator. Theodore's newly divorced state finds him socially isolated and in need of new friends. People who are shy, or have disabilities, or are new to a place of residence, or even people in senior positions, such as CEOs, may have nobody to talk or relate to. Chapters 1 and 5 already introduced the idea of internet communities of interest, which generally are beneficial to members of the community. Since the early twenty-first century, when mobile phones became smartphones, and as laptops and tablets overtook desktop computers, connectivity and communications became available to us at any place and time.

There are many advantages to this. Urgent messages can be received. Individuals trying to find one another can easily meet up. Business negotiations and transactions can be quickly decided. Teenagers can keep up on the latest news and gossip about friends and enemies. Parents can be in more frequent communication with their kids. As we have seen in Chapter 4, individuals with concerns about health symptoms can reach out to others with similar experiences.

Social media

Through the 1990s, most electronic communications were via email. Now, increasingly we use messaging apps and social media postings. As of April 2018, here are the most widely used systems ranked by number of users:[5]

Social networking site	Number of active users
Facebook	2.23 billion
YouTube	1.5 billion
WhatsApp	1.5 billion
Facebook messenger	1.3 billion
WeChat	0.98 billion
Instagram	0.81 billion

Yet, ever since internet communications became widely available, there have been debates about its effects. Some stress that it unhealthily replaces more authentic face-to-face communication; others assert that being sociable is not a zero-sum game, and that there is typically a positive correlation between the use of electronic communication and traditional conversations. The most articulate thoughts about internet communications appear in a series of books by MIT's Sherry Turkle, a set of scientific papers by a research group led by Carnegie Mellon University professor Robert Kraut, the survey research output of the Pew Research Center, and the scientific papers from the University of Toronto's NetLab, authored by Professor Barry Wellman of the University of Toronto and his graduate students.

Turkle, a professor of sociology at MIT, has explored important ideas in her four books. Her first book explored the role of artificial intelligence (AI) and interactive computing in challenging our view of ourselves and in helping to define how we distinguish ourselves from machines:[6]

> We search for a link between who we are and what we have made, between who we are and what we might create, between who we are and what, through our intimacy with our creations, we might become.

Her second book dove more deeply into new experiences of interacting with computers as 'intimate machines' via simulation games, fantasy worlds, and virtual communities.[7] Turkle's third book, subtitled 'why we expect **more** from technology and **less** from each other', expressed more negative views about interactions with robots and computer-mediated communications.[8] We discussed some of those ideas in Chapter 11. In her fourth book, Turkle extended these arguments into an impassioned plea for deeper human conversation.[9]

Kraut's group received huge media attention with a paper entitled 'Internet Paradox'.[10] They studied approximately 200 people in their first year or two online. Individuals with greater internet use had declines in communication with other members of their households, declines in the size of their social circles, and increased loneliness and depression. A later paper that examined internet use over a greater period of time found that the negative effects had disappeared.[11] A cohort of 400 individuals experienced mostly positive effects in terms of communication, social involvement, and well-being. The positive effects were stronger for extraverted individuals and those with more social support than for introverts and people with less social support.

The first two decades of internet communication were illuminated by the Pew Research Center's 2008 telephone survey of over 2,500 Americans ages 18 and older.[12] The researchers found that mobile phone users, online photo sharers, and users of instant messaging media had 12 per cent, 9 per cent, and 9 per cent larger core discussion networks, respectively. Internet technologies were used as much for local contacts as for distant ones. Communication with core network members was facilitated most often by face-to-face contact (210 days per year), mobile phone use (195 days), and text messaging (125 days). Most internet activities were associated with higher levels of local community involvement (discussed in Chapter 5), yet users of social media were 26 per cent less likely to rely upon neighbours for companionship. Internet users were more likely to visit public spaces and to have more diverse social networks.

In their landmark book *Networked*,[13] Pew Research Director of Internet Technology and Research Lee Rainie and Professor Barry Wellman generalized from this research and numerous other studies:

> Many [people] meet their social, emotional, and economic needs by tapping into sparsely knit networks of diverse associates rather than relying on tight connections to a relatively small number of core associates.... **Networked individuals** have partial membership in multiple networks and rely less on permanent membership in settled groups.... A key reason why these kinds of networks function effectively is that social networks are large and diversified thanks to the way people use technology.... *The new media is the new neighborhood* (emphasis added).

I concur with Rainie and Wellman that internet communication has been for the most part beneficial to humanity. Individuals can stay in touch with friends, couples can strengthen burgeoning relationships, far-flung grandparents and grandchildren can stay in touch and share experiences, and those in need can find communities for friendship and social support.[14]

Yet there is research that raises concerns.[15] One study followed eighty-three Facebook (FB) users at the University of Michigan over two weeks. The researchers found that FB use predicted negative shifts in subjective well-being immediately after the use; the more the participants used FB over two weeks, the more their life satisfaction declined. Professor Taylor Dotson, noting US statistics on the growing use of antidepressants and the prevalence of loneliness among seniors (discussed in Chapter 1), called for:

> Bounded, densely-woven, place-rooted, and economically, politically, and morally rich communities [rather than] diffuse, atomistic networks of specialized social ties [i.e., Rainie and Wellman's 'networked individualism'].

How social network design could encourage dense, 'place-rooted' communities in today's world is an interesting design problem (but see the discussion of e-democracy in Section 5.6).

Other research has yielded more positive results.[16] One study noted the 'positivity bias' of social media, which is the tendency of users to post positive items rather than negative ones, then focused on one month of 95,000 Instagram posts tagged as #depression. Happily, they found that such disclosures mostly attracted positive comments, generally expressing social support and a sense of community and shared identity. A national US survey of 740 internet users in an eighteen-month period between 2000 and 2002 found a positive association between an increase in internet communication with family and friends (from three to five days per week to daily) and fewer symptoms of depression (0.07 standard deviations fewer).

Finally, there is also a growing concern that *bots* capable of generating fake communications that seem real (is this a new kind of Turing test?) pose serious dangers, as we have seen in the geopolitical arena in Chapters 5 and 6. Such messages are psychological phishing attacks.

Research: Search for and analyse more recent data which can be compared with the 2008 Pew Research study on internet communications, including data that allows cross-cultural comparisons.

Research: The positivity bias of social media.

Book report: Turkle, Sherry (2011). *Alone Together: Why We Expect More from Technology and Less from Each Other*. Basic Books.

Book report: Turkle, Sherry (2015). *Reclaiming Conversation: The Power of Talk in a Digital Age*. Penguin Press.

Book report: Rainie, Lee, and Barry Wellman (2012). *Networked: The New Social Operating System*. The MIT Press.

Book report: Lingel, Jessa (2017). *Digital Countercultures and the Struggle for Community*. The MIT Press.

Book report: Dotson, Taylor (2017). *Technically Together: Reconstructing Community in a Networked World*. The MIT Press.

Field study: Identify and interview a number of seniors to solicit their stories about use of digital technologies for family connection; analyse and interpret the data that you collect.

12.3 Too connected

We have discussed some downsides of internet connectivity for young people. Chapter 3 pointed out the disruption sometimes caused by mobile phones in classrooms. Chapter 8 highlighted the dangers of cyberbullying and revenge porn. Constant use of devices that can be tracked exposes users to privacy violations, as we discussed in Chapter 9.

However, even if use is not inappropriate, if it does not lead to harassment or threats, and if one is not spied upon, there is an insidious danger of use so intense that it distorts one's life.

Antisocial media[17]

Screen time for adolescents has been the subject of research over the past few decades. Over time, concerns have shifted from television to video games to mobile phones and tablets. Here is some recent data.

Pew Internet Research, 2015:[18] An examination of 1,000 American parent–teen pairs found that 92% of teens aged 13–17 went online daily, 56% went online several times a day, and 24% were online 'almost constantly'.

Common Sense Media, 2015:[19] A study of 2,600 American young people found that teens aged 13–18 averaged more than six and a half hours a day of screen media use and tweens aged 8–12 average more than four and a half hours daily. These uses included accessing the internet and using social media, playing video games, and watching movies and TV.

Ofcom, 2015:[20] A survey of 3,000 British parents and children found children aged 8–11 averaged 11.1 hours per week online and children aged 12–15 averaged 18.9 hours weekly. (British adolescents seem to have more balance in their lives than do American children.)

There is little agreement among scientists about the effects of such intense screen time. A study comparing psychosocial adjustment at age 7 with that at age 5 of over 13,000 British children found that watching TV three or more hours per day was linked with increasing behavioural problems; the same was not true of playing video games.[21] A policy paper from the London School of Economics on families and screen time stressed that a unilateral focus on risk was unwarranted,[22] and that concerns about quantity of screen time should be replaced by a holistic consideration of the context of viewing and use, the nature of what is being watched or done, and the degree to which such use facilitates or hinders relationships. Professor Alison Gopnik nicely illustrated this with an anecdote about using internet media to answer her 4-year-old grandson's question about how bees make honey.[23]

Device and software use by children as they get older has also been associated with health issues and is increasingly viewed as an addiction. Researchers speculate that a surprising reduction in recreational drug use by youth may in part be due to increases in stimulation and entertainment by computers and phones.[24] Some studies have found that fear of missing out, colloquially called 'FOMO', is associated with poor mood, anxiety, stress, and disrupted sleep in teenagers.[25] A study of 500 American university mobile phone users found that those with greater mobile phone usage tended to have lower grade point averages, more anxiety, and lower overall satisfaction with life.[26]

Unfortunately, a lack of communication between children and parents often exacerbates the tendency of some teens to hide their social media use from parents.[27] As explored in Chapter 8, this may cause teenagers to hide cyberbullying or blackmail due to fear of consequences and embarrassment. All of these issues are impacted by the intensity of their social media participation.

Many people now have two online identities, one for close friends and one for everyone else.[27] This is especially prevalent on Instagram, where many school-aged users create hidden and fake Instagram accounts, or 'finstas'; and real or 'rinsta' accounts curated for the public. Secrecy and teenagers' desperate desire for peer approval may result in finsta posts that are in poor taste, thoughtless, even cruel, and that can negatively affect them later in life, as covered in Section 8.3.

Research: Search for scientific studies of use of mobile devices by adolescents, and the effects of screen time on how one leads one's life, and report on the extent to which dangers are substantiated or exaggerated.

Debate: Resolved: Children should not be allowed to have mobile phones until they are 13, and then their use should be strictly monitored and controlled by parents.

Movie review: The documentary film *Screenagers.*[28]

12.4 Always connected: technology addiction and workaholism

Even worse than being too connected is being always connected, a serious problem for many children and adults. We shall begin with children, who often become addicted to messaging. This is a manifestation of a broader problem, an addiction to digital technology, which can arise in many guises—Facebook, video games, internet porn, or Netflix. *Irresistible,* a recent book by psychology and marketing professor Adam Alter,[29] stresses that behavioural addictions result from environment and circumstances, not from genetics, and that designers of internet technology strive to make their products intoxicating. Behavioural addiction, says Alter, stems from six ingredients:[30]

> compelling goals that are just beyond reach; irresistible and unpredictable positive feedback; a sense of incremental progress and improvement; tasks that slowly become more difficult over time; unresolved tensions that demand resolution; and strong social connections.

According to Alter, people spend an average of nine minutes a day each on relaxation, exercise, weather, reading, education, and health apps; they feel good about that use of their time.[31] They spend an average of 27 minutes a day each on dating, social networking, gaming, entertainment, news, and web browsing apps; half of those questioned did not feel good about this use of time. Keeping one's head down in a screen is also damaging to one's posture and to the ability to participate capably and politely in social situations.[32]

Recently, an ex-Google 'design ethicist' named Tristan Harris has spoken extensively about how leading internet software companies consciously design their apps to be addictive.[33] Their menus shape behaviour because they exclude what is not on the menu. They exploit people's FOMO. Much like drug dealers, social media firms encourage addiction by giving seemingly infinite 'feeds' of whatever they are supplying. Facebook messages users every week to notify them of updates that have been posted by their so-called 'friends'. Snapchat 'streaks' encourage kids to send messages back and forth with each of their contacts every day. Netflix views the human need to sleep as a major competitor and has introduced 'binge racing', which has the goal of watching an entire series in the twenty-four hours after it is released.[34] As of November 2017, 8 million viewers had accomplished that feat. Experts in 'gamification' attempt to capture more eyeballs for longer and longer episodes by making online experiences more like games.[35]

Surely *technology addiction* is better than an addiction to smoking, scotch, or cocaine. Yet there are health consequences. Mobile phone dependence fits the clinical criteria of an addiction, including excessive use; withdrawal symptoms when the technology is not available; tolerance, meaning a desire for more and better technology; and negative repercussions, including poor achievement, social isolation, and fatigue.[36] A 2015 study of forty-four adult Facebook users revealed narratives of 'social comparison and jealousy, and relationship tension and conflict', combined with pressure to visit the site frequently, both because they fear missing out and because they feel a need to maintain relationships.[37] A study of 5,200 subjects from 2013, 2014, and 2015 nationally representative US surveys showed that a one standard deviation increase in Facebook activity was associated with a 5–8 per cent of a standard deviation reduction in self-reported physical health, mental health, and life satisfaction, even though participation in real-world social networks was positively associated with overall well-being.[38]

The social psychologist Jean M. Twenge has analysed data on 1.1 million individuals from nationally representative yearly US surveys taken between 1991 and 2016 of eighth, tenth, and twelfth graders.[39] Psychological well-being, as measured by self-esteem, life satisfaction, and happiness, started decreasing suddenly after 2012. Adolescents who spent more time on activities such as social media, the internet, texting, and gaming, and less time on activities such as person-to-person social interaction, sports, exercise, and homework, had lower psychological well-being. For example, those who spent more than ten hours a week on social media were 56 per cent more likely to say they were unhappy, and those who spent more than six hours a week were 47 per cent more likely to say this, compared with adolescents who spent less time on social media. Adolescents who spent only a little time on the screen were the happiest. Yet there was even more bad news, as adolescent depressive symptoms and suicide rates increased between 2010 and 2015. Those who spent more time on new media such as social media and electronic smartphones were more likely to report mental health issues; those who spent more time on activities such as person-to-person social interaction, sports, exercise, and homework reported mental health issues less often. For example, eighth-graders who used social media heavily increased their risk of depression by 27 per cent. These reports only show association, not causality, but it is sobering to realize that many young people now spend much more than the advised hours a day on social media.

Robert Kraut and Moira Burke teased out one likely cause with a study of 1900 Facebook users. Improvements in well-being resulted from receiving targeted, composed communication from people with whom they had strong ties; reading friends' broadcasts to large audiences and receiving one-click feedback such as 'likes' did not improve well-being.[40]

Let us now turn our attention to adults. At first, access to one's work at home seems to offer benefits, such as the ability to respond to emergencies without the need to go to the office. But it also can result in an inability to escape work. The result can be that we never get away from our jobs. The concept of being 'out of the office' is lost. There is no down time, no escape to the woods or the countryside or the shore, no total immersion in idle fancy or in a good book, too rare the uninterrupted exertion of a trek or the peace of an oasis.

We use the term *workaholism* to characterize people who work incessantly and compulsively, who think about the job even when engaged in leisure or recreation, who have trouble taking vacations, and who are often perceived to be ignoring their partners and children. *Workaholism* is different from *work engagement*.[41] People engaged in their work typically experience job satisfaction and self-assurance; workaholics typically experience guilt, anger, anxiety, and disappointment. Workaholism is also different from the work 'crunches' often experienced in high-tech industries such as video games, where it is routine for employees to work eighty or even 100 hours a week for several months before a new product release.[42]

Over half of working Americans recently polled indicated that checking emails at home was routine.[43] Interviews with senior information technology (IT) professionals and managers in the USA, the UK, and Germany found increasing pressures to work more; increased time on the job in the last twenty years; a decline of leisure time; and growing pressures to use technology, in part so that employees can work faster.[44] An analysis of 200 articles on home Blackberry use showed how attempts to balance work and home life typically resulted in significant family resentment at the interference of so-called 'Crackberries'.[45] This was true despite whatever rational understanding family members might have of the work pressures. A survey of over 14,000 Norwegian adults found significant associations between workaholism and attention deficit hyperactivity disorder (ADHD), anxiety, younger age, and managerial position.[46]

Clearly, these extremes apply to and are damaging both to young people and to adults. To combat this technology addiction, various techniques have been proposed—research projects, new organizations, individual efforts, hardware solutions, attempts by store owners, and new laws.

A project called 'the world Unplugged' showed how hard it is for university students to break the addiction by asking 1,000 students from ten countries on five continents to refrain from using all media for twenty-four hours.[47] Many reported feelings of anger, anxiety, loneliness, depression, and/or inability to fill the time. A clear majority in each country acknowledged failure to get unplugged.

Former employees of Google and Facebook have started the Center for Humane Technology (more details appear in the Resources Section associated with this chapter).[48] One of their goals is to pressure tech firms to make their products less addictive and manipulative.

There are now many articles with titles such as 'Resist the Internet'.[49] One computer science professor issued a month-long challenge for people to declutter their digital lives.[50] Some are engaged in desperate attempts to escape by totally deleting their social media presence.[51] Others have adopted more primitive phones, such as those without colour.[52] If there initially were good reasons for being connected, trying to totally disconnect is clearly very hard.

Some mobile phone manufacturers are now trying to help. In Apple's case, this may in part be driven by statements from major shareholders that their technology may be harming young children.[53] Both Android and Apple phones now allow features such as Do Not Disturb, less disruptive notifications, reminders of how much an app has been used in a certain time frame, Night Mode to dull the screens' harsh blue light to facilitate sleep, and app restrictions on kids' usage that function like an allowance.[54]

Despite the prevalence of students, telecommuters, and the self-employed who love to compute while having their espresso, some coffee shops have stopped providing Wi-Fi and instigated other means to avoid becoming a computer centre and to get people to talk in person as they once did.[55]

In 2017, France introduced a new law that requires companies to 'establish hours when staff should not send or answer emails', affording employees the 'right to disconnect'.[56] The legislation reasons that more relaxed employees would produce better work and have better overall mental and physical well-being, and that the law would in general improve societal health.

Ethics

The internet addiction battlefield: Here are start-ups on both sides:[57]

Digital Detox: This firm says it is a 'slow-down', not a start-up. It offers tech-free, personal wellness retreats:

> We provide individuals, families and companies the opportunity to put aside their digital arm, gain perspective, and reemerge with new found inspiration, balance and connection.

Boundless Mind: Dopamine is a neurotransmitter. Many kinds of rewards, including addictive drugs, increase dopamine in the brain. Boundless Mind (originally named Dopamine Labs) states as its goal:

> Engage. Retain. Delight your users.... Churn kills apps. Sesame [their product] kills churn.... Behavioral design for the enterprise.... Becoming a user's habit is necessary for defeating churn.... We combine ML and Neuroscience... to engage and retain them.... COMING SOON: We're releasing an AI tool to get (and keep) users opening your app!

The internet is driven by eyeballs and clicks, keeping people engaged and on your site in order to earn advertising dollars, except where viewers pay for content. Is Boundless Mind an ethical company? Why or why not?

China has developed the most extreme solution, although the government is trying to end it.[58] After a 2009 study found more than 24 million Chinese internet users, ages 13 to 29, were digital addicts, 6,000 of them were treated with electroshock therapy at an addiction centre in Shandong Province!

Research: Study and analyse evidence that Tristan Harris's assertions are correct.

Research: Methods of fighting internet and/or mobile phone addiction.

Policy: Draft a brief for the CEO of a company, about to give everyone a mobile phone for work purposes, who must try to convince employees that this will not be exploitative, increasing workaholism and destroying family life.

Book report: Alter, Adam (2017). *Irresistible: The Rise of Addictive Technology and the Business of Keeping Us Hooked.* Penguin Press.

Book report: Twenge, Jean M. (2017). *iGen: Why Today's Super-Connected Kids Are Growing Up Less Rebellious, More Tolerant, Less Happy—and Completely Unprepared for Adulthood—and What That Means for the Rest of Us.* Atria Books.

12.5 The Internet of Things, voice assistants, and smart cities

The power of digital technologies, and our addiction to their use, is exacerbated by their omnipresence (we discussed privacy implications in Chapter 9). Furthermore, they are changing the nature of the world as we experience it—what we see, hear, and touch. We shall discuss three forms of this: the *Internet of Things* (IoT), *voice assistants*, and *smart cities.*

Modern digital media are not only sights and sounds and objects that we can sense, but also objects and media that transform and behave in response to what we do and say. The IoT has been defined as 'a network of dedicated physical objects (things) that contain embedded technology to communicate and sense or interact with their internal states or the external environment'.[59] There may be as many as 20 billion things connected to the internet by 2020.

An exciting new concept is *active matter,* which has been defined by professor Skylar Tibbits:[60]

> Active matter is a newly emerging field focused on physical materials that can assemble themselves, transform autonomously, and sense, react, or compute based on internal and external information.

It would take another book to discuss thoughtfully the social and ethical implications of active matter such as smart paper and smart fabrics!

Since 2014, there has been a thriving market for smart speakers. Amazon leads the market with its family of Echo devices, powered by the Alexa digital assistant. It captured 70 per cent of the market in 2017, with over 25 million Americans using an Alexa device at least once a month.[61] Google Home, Microsoft Cortana, and Apple HomePod are competitors. The Echo paves the way for home automation in its ability to allow users to command Alexa to do tasks such as setting a timer or an alarm, controlling smart lights or thermostats, or buying something via Amazon, such as books or groceries. Because Echo encourages such purchases, Amazon offers it very inexpensively.

Other everyday objects are now becoming digital.[62] There are suitcases with ports and chargers for mobile phones, GPS for tracking them, and scales for ensuring they do not exceed the allowable weight. Some refrigerators are digital, with fridge cams for looking inside remotely, and digital displays on the doors (and on countertops) for notes, reminders, and recipes. We already discussed in Chapter 8 how much digital technology is already in cars. Soon every surface in a car will be capable of being a display or a sensor or both. Security is a concern here; hacking a car could cause havoc.[63]

Alexa

The power behind Echo is the Alexa voice assistant. It engages users, including children, with remarkable vivacity.[64] Personification of Alexa was found in over half of 587 published reviews of Alexa; greater personification predicted greater satisfaction.[65] A study of 1,600 users of voice assistants found that 41% felt that it seemed like talking to another person or even a friend.[66] Amazon even decided to parody itself in a Super Bowl ad.[67]

Google claims that its voice assistant can accomplish over 1 million tasks, yet the majority of those who use them more than three times daily do so for mundane purposes—playing music, checking the weather forecast, setting a timer, asking questions, or helping to plan travel.[68] Key to expanding their usage is improvement in AI's understanding of spoken language.[69] The Google Assistant is now integrated with over 400 million devices, including washers, dryers, refrigerators, dishwashers, and air conditioners. Yet there are unsolved problems, such as security; people are concerned that they may be listened to in their homes.[63] Such privacy fears about Alexa have been magnified recently by incidents in which Alexa recorded, and in one case transmitted, conversations that were not meant for it, and by an analysis of recent voice assistant patent applications.[70]

All of this is part of the concept of a *smart city*, one in which transportation services, internet and communication systems, electrical and power grids, and water services are all digital, interconnected, and communicating.[71] Anticipated benefits are more efficient energy utilization and an enhanced ability to respond to natural disasters; the risks are escalating failures that can result from natural disasters, terrorism, and cyberattacks, as well as the invasion of privacy. We have already discussed the latter issue in the discussion of smart home security in Chapter 7.

Yet some may question whether or not using fancy technology in place of good old-fashioned wristwatches, alarm clocks, and kitchen timers is a significant gain for society.[72]

Research: Digital car-hacking: dangers, experiences to date, and solutions.

Research: What one can learn about future corporate plans and developments by an analysis of recent voice assistant patent applications.

Research: Smart cities: Developments, facts, fantasies.

Debate: Resolved: Many of the developments in the IoT and with voice assistants are wasteful conspicuous consumption; society should turn its attention to more important matters.

Debate: Resolved: Children should be taught to be polite to Alexa. This is not a silly question, as Amazon has recently released a feature designed to encourage children to say 'please' and 'thank you' to Alexa.[73]

Book report: Tibbits, Skylar (Ed.) (2017). *Active Matter*. The MIT Press.

Field study: Identify a cohort of older adults who are using home appliances such as Amazon Echo or Google Home, and study how the devices are used and the experiences and satisfaction of the seniors.

Field study: Identify a cohort of very young children who are using home appliances such as Amazon Echo or Google Home, and study how the devices are used and the experiences and satisfaction of the kids and their parents.

12.6 Artificial reality

Our world is being increasingly populated with digital technology, sensors, and displays. We can also now immerse ourselves in digitally generated or modified virtual worlds. An umbrella term for such experiences is *artificial reality*, first termed by the pioneering artist-scientist Myron Krueger.[74]

Augmented reality (AR)

This term refers to a world in which what we see and hear is based on the sights and sounds of the physical world, modified or augmented with computer-generated displays, music, or voice. We have already discussed an example of AR in Chapter 8—Pokémon Go. The verisimilitude and power of AR depends upon the quality of the display, and the degree to which what is displayed corresponds properly in synchrony with positions and movements in the real world, so human body tracking is required.

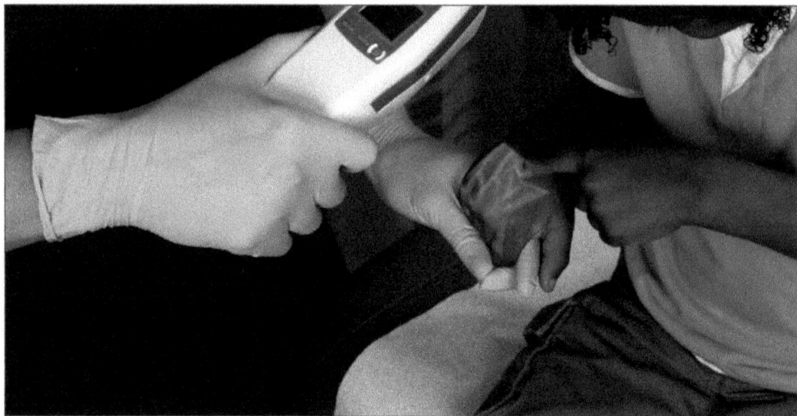

Figure 12.1 Augmented reality display portraying veins for the benefit of a nurse[75]

Applications of AR include visualizations for architecture and archaeology, military, flight training and flying, emergency response, driving, tourism and sightseeing, and retailing and commerce.[76] Facebook founder and CEO Mark Zuckerberg paid $2 billion for *Oculus*, a virtual reality goggles maker in 2014, and in 2017 announced a major augmented reality platform for smartphones.[77] Especially important are applications to health care, which include medical education, patient education, and assisting doctors, nurses, and surgeons in carrying out medical procedures.

Virtual reality (VR) refers to a three-dimensional world in which everything we sense and experience is supplied or dominated by computer-generated stimuli. In a true VR, as in effective augmented reality, instrumentation or video processing tracks our movements, so the display can change as we move, much as it would in the real world. Applications of virtual reality are found in the military, space exploration, health care, engineering, and the fine arts.[78] Yet the most compelling and lucrative applications of VR seem to be in entertainment. There are now virtual reality rooms where users can pretend to be a Ghostbuster, the *New York Times* is offering VR news experiences, and Disney is planning immersive *Star Wars* VR attractions at shopping centres.[79]

Issues slowing the development and application of VR include experiences that frighten and induce dread, and some that result in nausea and emesis.[80] There are also looming legal concerns dealing with intellectual property in VR worlds, privacy, and the cognitive and physical effects of immersion.[81]

Research: Choose an application, such as education or medicine, and discuss areas that would be most suited to augmented reality and/or to virtual reality.

Debate: Resolved: The Internet of Things is hyped, there have been no significant accomplishments, and there is no coherent research and development agenda.

12.7 Pornography, online dating, and sex robots

Pornography has been one of the uses driving the need for greater internet bandwidth. For example, 25 per cent of all search engine requests are related to pornography, 40 million Americans regularly visit porn sites, and the worldwide market for internet porn was $5 billion in 2010.[82] Recently, porn streaming services have been introduced.[83] Just as with fake news, and the emergence of fake videos (discussed in Chapter 5), technology is increasingly being used to construct 'fake porn', superimposing someone's face on the body and motion of a person in a pornographic video.[84]

But there are many non-pornographic uses of the internet, increasingly part of our lifestyle, that cater to our needs for intimate companionship.

Given that so many of our interactions are digitally mediated, it is not surprising that *internet dating* has become a thriving industry. The use of communications technology to facilitate people meeting goes back as early as personal ads that appeared in British newspapers in 1690.[85] By 2017, 50 million US individuals had tried online dating services.[86] A recent survey of over 4,000 English-literate American adults found that over 20 per cent of straight sex American couples and almost 70 per cent of same sex American couples met online.[87]

Many such services are generic, catering to all individuals, but increasingly they specialize in specific niches such as certain religions, ethnicities, or nationalities; examples are diasporas, occupations including professions, and medical conditions such as HIV positive.[88] For example, *Shaadi.com* claims to have facilitated the meeting of 35 million Indian brides and grooms across a variety of Indian mother tongues, religions, and communities.[89] Some services cater to parents seeking partners for their adult children, especially in cultures with traditions of matchmaking.[90]

Despite the continued growth in the use of such services, some experiences are negative. As in 'real life', it is possible to meet individuals who are unpleasant or even dangerous. Many who have tried it are frustrated by the large quantities of personal data to enter, and the long periods of waiting without a positive experience. Hence, as in so many areas, online dating firms are now beginning to experiment with AI and 'data science' to improve the odds of a successful user experience.[91] Other critics suggest that practices such as rapidly 'swiping' through large numbers of potential dates represents a devaluing of human uniqueness through ultimately ineffective superficial initial judgements based solely on physical appearance.[92]

Individuals on dating sites are trying to meet human beings. Increasingly, however, *porn bots* are sending messages and pretending to be people whose pornographic pictures were seen by the message recipients.[93] These often cause embarrassment and often identity theft.

As our ability to digitally simulate the look and sound and feel of people increases, the possibilities for physical and romantic contact with bots or droids also increase. In the motion picture *Her*, introduced at the beginning of this chapter, Samantha was only a voice, but there is now a vigorous and growing industry in the design, construction, and marketing of *sex robots*.

Realbotix

Artist and android creation design director Matt McMullen has been developing life-sized sex dolls and follow-on products for two decades. His corporation Abyss Creations LLC advertises the 'world's finest love dolls'.[94] It sells a variety of dolls and doll parts representing both genders. More recently, he created Realbotix.[95]

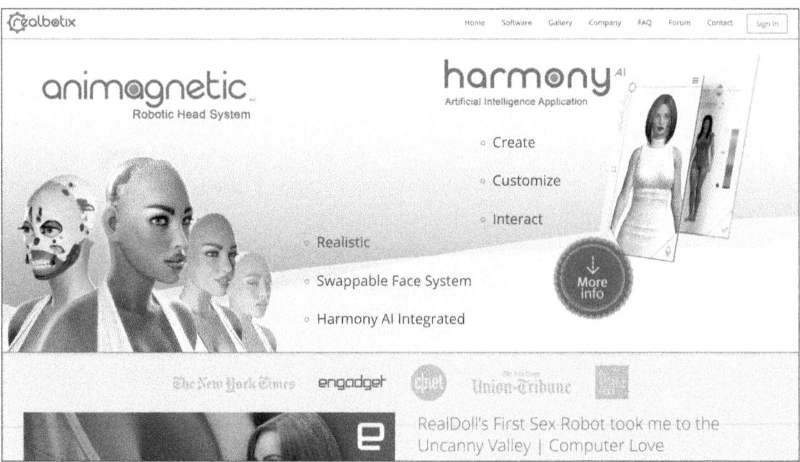

Figure 12.2 The home page of Realbotix
Courtesy of Realbotix.

Realbotix has two products, robotic dolls with heads capable of facial expressions and eye and mouth movements, and *Harmony AI*, an app intended to be sentient, interacting with its owner in playful and sensual ways, also customizable by the user. Harmony AI can control both the dolls and the heads. Although far away from what one might imagine in a sex robot, one journalist described 'her brows and the corners of her mouth mov[ing] with such accuracy and agility' that the experience transported him to the uncanny valley discussed in Chapter 11.[96]

The development of sex robots has resulted in very strong emotions and a great deal of controversy.[97] Proponents argue that such technology can bring happiness to large numbers of people, with sexual satisfaction distributed across society more equally. Some advocates suggest that such experiences can beneficially prepare individuals for human relationships.[98] A special case is their potential role in providing sexual satisfaction for severely physically or mentally disabled people, including seniors suffering from neurodegenerative diseases.[99]

Others argue passionately that sex robots will cause harm to individuals and to society. Many oppose sex robots on religious grounds. Others feel that their use is symbolic of a disregard or even contempt for appropriate norms of consent in interpersonal sexual relations,[100] and encourage the objectification, prostitution, and ultimately the rape of men and women.[101]

Research: Digital matchmaking sites such as Shaadi.com or Dil Mil.

Debate: Resolved: The making of sex robots should be supported by government, and their use should be legal.

Book report: Danaher, John, and Neil McArthur (2017). *Robot Sex: Social and Ethical Implications*. MIT Press.

12.8 Blockchain and the future of money

Another area where disruption is occurring is in how we conduct our financial transactions. For several decades now, individuals have been buying goods using credit cards or transferring money via email. More recently, mobile phones have been used for this purpose through disruptive apps such as Apple Wallet and Venmo.

But there is now talk of physical cash becoming obsolete, to be replaced by digital currencies such as *bitcoin*. Underlying the use of bitcoin is a remarkable new technology called a *blockchain*, which is a distributed digital public ledger. We shall discuss each topic in turn.

Bitcoin

A bitcoin is a virtual currency and worldwide payment system.[102] Because of its implementation using cryptographic computations in a blockchain, to be discussed below, it is also known as a *cryptocurrency*.[103] It is a decentralized payment system, using a peer-to-peer

Continued on next page

network without the governance and oversight of a central authority such as a national bank. Transactions are recorded in the blockchain ledger. Use of bitcoins has grown over the past decade; by February 2015, they were accepted as payment by over 100,000 merchants and vendors. By 2017, five million individuals worldwide were using bitcoins or other cryptographic currencies worldwide. Speculation in bitcoin has been rampant, with huge volatility in the price of a bitcoin, as when it dropped 30% in one day.[104] One reason for this is the huge uncertainty about a bitcoin's underlying value.[105]

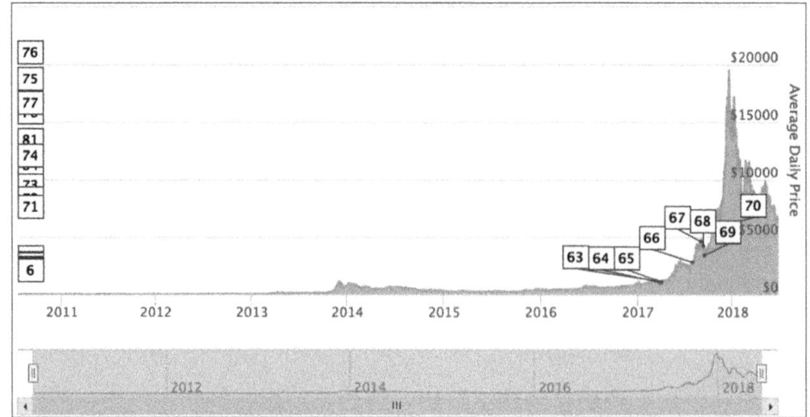

Figure 12.3 Average daily price of a bitcoin[106]
Courtesy of 99Bitcoins. As available here: https://99bitcoins.com/price-chart-history/

There are growing numbers of other cryptocurrencies, including Litecoin, Ethereum, even a 'joke currency' named Dogecoin. Speculators have driven up the value of some of them, creating almost instant billionaires.[107] Although not currently replacing cash in day-to-day transactions, they are being used in various ways in financial affairs. Many people view bitcoin as a kind of virtual gold, a way to store money that is outside of the control of governments or companies.[108] Besides the original enthusiasm shown by libertarians, it has also recently attracted the interest of hedge funds and other large institutional investors.[109]

Enthusiasts appreciate the security of bitcoin data that results from its implementation by a blockchain (see below). Many are attracted by the fact that the data is untraceable by authorities. Others have serious concerns about cryptocurrencies.[110] Some bitcoin exchanges have inadequate controls to verify identity. Because it is based on public key cryptography, bitcoins can be accessed only through the use of a public key and a private key; if the private key is lost, bitcoins cannot be accessed. Cryptocurrency's invisibility to government allows it to be used significantly for illegal purposes on the dark web.[111] For example, as mentioned in Chapter 6, it was used by the Russians who attacked the 2016 US presidential election. It has also been subject to hacking and to scams such as Ponzi schemes.[112] Because it is a very new phenomenon, and one that is somewhat hard to understand, there is as of now little government regulation,[113] yet law enforcement authorities have started to crack down on bitcoin exchanges that seem to traffic heavily in black markets and ransomware attacks.[114]

Various countries have adopted different strategies towards cryptocurrencies. Because of the country's history of currency volatility, the bitcoin has attracted great interest in Argentina.[115] There has been frenzied trading of cryptocurrencies in South Korea.[116] Russia and Venezuela have announced plans to create state-sponsored cryptocurrencies to help them avoid the effects of American sanctions.[117] On the other hand, China has begun a crackdown on bitcoin exchanges, fearing money laundering and tax evasion.[118] India has been slow to develop the use of electronic payments, but there are now signs that this is changing.[119]

Bitcoins and other cryptocurrencies are represented as blockchains. A *blockchain* is a continuously growing linked set of records called 'blocks' that contain hash pointers to other blocks, timestamps, and transaction data.[120] The data in such a distributed ledger is secured using cryptography; the system is highly fault-tolerant. A blockchain enables trusted transactions in a world in which there is little trust.[121]

Cryptocurrencies can only be created if a mathematical problem is solved, a problem that is so difficult that very large networks of computers are employed to solve it.[122] Huge amounts of energy are required for this. The creation of bitcoins is called *digital currency mining*. Despite China's concerns about cryptocurrencies, and a crackdown on Chinese exchanges, one of the largest bitcoin farms in the world is in Inner Mongolia, with fifty employees working with 25,000 computers that compute the blockchain calculations.[123] In fact, China makes more than two-thirds of the new bitcoins issued daily worldwide. The finite capacity of *computer farms* creating new bitcoins and computing bitcoin calculations also puts limits on transactions, which has been a source of significant dispute in the industry.[124] Due to all the error checking and redundancy built into blockchain systems, they take enormous computing power to carry out transactions. Many municipalities with cheap sources of electricity, such as those near power-generating dams, are now encouraging bitcoin mining firms to set up new industries with them.[125]

Many start-ups are now developing uses of blockchain to enable seamless financial services.[126] Other applications are supply chain management and public health surveillance.[127] Some start-ups are using *initial coin offerings* (ICOs).[128] These are currently unregulated, controversial methods of *crowdfunding*, in which new firms issue cryptocurrency to large numbers of investors, most of whom do not meet the financial requirements of regulated public offerings. Many are scams, likely soon to be the target of securities regulators.[129]

Blockchain enthusiasts believe this secure open protocol will enable fundamental changes to society, enabling more individual control over one's digital identity, facilitating more secure medical records and electronic voting, and even reducing the power of dominant established firms such as Facebook.[130] This brings us to the topic of corporate concentration.

Research: China's ambivalence regarding cryptocurrencies, that is, its enthusiasm for and concerns about them.

Research: Blockchain as an implementation platform for health applications.

Debate: Resolved: Investing in bitcoin is as speculative as buying lottery tickets.

Technology review: Cryptocurrency platforms.

12.9 Corporate concentration, and social and economic disruption

The developments we have described are enabled by technology, but they are driven by entrepreneurial companies such as Apple, Amazon, Google (now part of a holding company called Alphabet), and Facebook. The market dominance and worth of such companies staggers the imagination. Seven of the eight most valuable companies in the world are digital technology firms; six of these are American.[131]

Table 12.1 The most valuable companies in the world as of the end of 2018

Name of firm	Market cap in US$ as of 31 December 2018
Microsoft	\$781B
Apple, Inc.	\$749B
Amazon.com	\$736B
Alphabet, Inc.	\$728B
Berkshire Hathaway	\$500B
Facebook	\$376B
Tencent (China)[132]	\$375B
Alibaba Group (China)[132]	\$355B

Going back to the beginnings of the IT industry, the first goliath was *IBM*, known as 'Big Blue'. It dominated the mainframe industry and the nascent software industry in the 1960s and 1970s, and was adopted in great part by big business. Digital Equipment Corporation, may it rest in peace, was the largest player in minicomputers in the 1970s and 1980s, with a corresponding impact on medium-sized businesses. *Microsoft* then became the dominant vendor of microcomputer software, used by small businesses and individuals. Microsoft's dominance was so great that it became known to many as the 'evil empire'.

Industries of the past have always had their leaders, a handful of firms that collectively own over 90 per cent of total market share in their sectors. Yet there is now something new and threatening, because so many industries, seemingly unrelated to technology, can be disrupted through clever use of digital techniques. We discussed cases of this in Chapter 10. For example, and this is primarily a good disruption, the nature of travel accommodation has been changed for those who use services such as Airbnb and HomeAway. Some travellers find lodging in someone's home preferable to renting an expensive hotel room. For many who open up space in their homes, the experience is a way of making additional income, and also provides additional social interaction. Some of the differences between the disruptive technology and traditional methods may be reducing; Airbnb has recently directed their renters to act more like hotels,[133] and, as discussed in Chapter 10, hotel chains are now entering the home rental business.

In addition, widespread use of these services in some apartment blocks has changed the nature of life there and resulted in the banning of short-term rentals.

An even stronger example is Uber. We have discussed how this firm interacts with its drivers in Chapter 10. It is ruthless with competitors.[134] It is alleged to have used a program code named 'Hell' to monitor drivers who worked both for it and for its major competitor, Lyft. It spied on Lyft and once even ordered and cancelled Lyft rides en masse! It sent employees to order Lyft rides, then tried to convince the drivers to switch to Uber. It flooded the streets with its cars and sought market share by subsidizing fares. Under founder Travis Kalanick, who eventually was forced to resign by his board, Uber had a machismo-fuelled culture with overly aggressive managers and legal and ethical scandals, including inaction on numerous allegations of sexual harassment.[135]

In many metropolitan centres, Uber woos taxi drivers aggressively, trying to convince them to move from the taxi company to their employ.[136] Towards this end, Uber has opened 200 resource, training, and refreshment 'Greenlight Hubs' for drivers and potential drivers across the USA. The city of London, whose 21,000 black cab drivers take the world's toughest taxi exam, has a taxi tradition dating back to 1634.[137] Uber arrived only in 2012, yet it has already grown to 40,000 drivers. There is now full-scale guerrilla warfare between Uber and the London taxi industry. There has also been warfare between Uber and many cities, who are trying to regulate it in part to deal with lost taxi transportation revenue.[138] We discussed other aspects of this in Chapter 10.

More significant issues are congestion and mass transit viability. Although we do not have systematic analyses across cities, early indications are that Uber is reducing the use of Manhattan mass transit and therefore causing more gridlock.[139] Uber also fits a pattern we shall see again in this section, which is to use its huge capitalization, cash reserves, and market position to move aggressively into a secondary market of food delivery services.

Yet the socio-economic impact of market leaders goes further than accommodations, taxis, and book retailing, which was disrupted by Amazon twenty-five years ago. Indeed, much of the disruption comes from IT firms. The five behemoths of IT are Microsoft, still a reigning power, and now with increasingly innovative hardware;[140] Apple, for a long time just a 'cult brand',[141] but for much of 2018 the most valuable company in history, with a market cap of over a trillion dollars;[142] Facebook; Alphabet/Google; and Amazon. The *New York Times* technology journalist Farhad Manjoo has labelled these the 'Frightful Five'.[143] We shall discuss FB, Google, and Amazon.

Facebook is the dominant social media company.[144] Its power stems from the size of its user base, now comprising 2.2 billion individuals. Having the largest and most engaged network helps attract advertising, which fuels profitability.[145] Profits and investment capital enable it to fund acquisitions and innovation, such as the purchasing of the messaging platform WhatsApp; the VR innovator Oculus; the social media firm Instagram, now itself one of the most successful social media firms; and new capabilities for streaming media, online dating, and group collaboration.[146]

FB's dominance has led to problems: (a) the extent to which people share information they don't want widely known, reducing their privacy, covered in Chapter 9; (b) its news feeds and the sharing of news items, often resulting in fake news, discussed in Chapters 5 and 6; and (c) the role of fake social media participants constructed by Russia in the 2016

US presidential election, explored in Chapter 6. There also are fake reviews of products, which, in many product categories, make up the majority of 'customer' reviews, but are actually funded by merchants desperate to attract buyers with large numbers of positive reviews.[147] The phrase 'You're the product' has become a description of FB, as its business model relies upon advertising based on data it obtains about users and their friends so that it can provide tailored access to community, news, and entertainment.[148] FB itself has begun soul searching as it has witnessed the serious consequences of its actions. Zuckerberg recently said that the company feels 'a responsibility to make sure our services aren't just fun to use, but also good for people's wellbeing', but he has been apologizing for breaches of trust for a long time.[149]

Paradoxically, FB's subsidiary company, Instagram, which focuses more on pictures than on text, is closer to a paradigm of a pure social media platform. It is minimalist in design, not as bloated as FB, with little sharing and few links, and therefore free of some of the troubles which have plagued FB.[150] There are now many suggestions for FB improvements.[151] Designers have recommended clearer explanations of how FB intends to use your data, reminders of what data the company has on you and who is accessing it, a 'Why me?' button eliciting details on why you are being shown an ad, and compensation for the use of personal data to fuel advertising. Clever programmers are also developing apps, browser extensions, and desktop software to give users more insight into what FB is doing with their data.

Yet Facebook's ineptness and slow speed in dealing with the problems with its platform tarnished its reputation, caused some defections from its platform, and led to public outcry, government concern, and a $120 billion one-day drop in shareholder value in July 2018.[152] As a response to the failing economics of the traditional news industry, leading newspapers in the USA are seeking antitrust exemption so that they can negotiate as a group with FB and Google.[153] Their goal is to increase exposure to quality journalism as well as to local news stories for users of the websites, as well as to achieve an increase in their online revenue. Zuckerberg himself has had to testify before Congress, as discussed in Chapter 9, uttering mea culpas and promising to do better. Yet this generated little faith that FB could regulate itself; hence there have been calls for new firms with more scruples to enter the market, increased government regulations, and even the dismantling of Facebook's monopolistic hold on the social media market.[154]

Europe has acted more forcefully than North America. In 2017, the EU fined Facebook 110 million euros for reneging on its 2014 promise that it would not combine its data with that of WhatsApp after its acquisition in 2016.[155] The EU has also enacted strong privacy legislation—the General Data Protection Regulation (GDPR)—discussed in Chapter 9. FB has also faced increasing difficulties in operating in several countries, including the rejection of its Free Basics offering in India (explored in Chapter 1), the need to remove information based on requests from some governments, and the conflicts that arise between desires for free speech, motivations for censorship, and corporate priorities.[156] FB has also been unable to penetrate China despite Zuckerberg's marriage to a woman of Chinese descent, his continual learning of the Chinese language, and his offering the President of China, Xi Jinping, the honour of naming his first child, which Xi turned down.[157]

Google is the world's dominant search engine. Its valuable acquisitions include DoubleClick and YouTube. Its Android open source mobile operating system is on over

2 billion devices in the world. Its free email, calendar, mapping, productivity tools, and language translation software are widely used. It realizes by far the greatest *online advertising revenue.*[158] Its power lies in control of the search algorithm, which is proprietary and a carefully kept secret. It is also changed from time, as are the consequences of the search, that is, which results appear and which do not appear, and whether their position is favourable or unfavourable. Also changing is what appears on YouTube, because of the takedowns discussed in Chapter 2, sometimes done to 'tak[e] a tougher stance on hateful, offensive and derogatory content'.[159] Both kinds of changes can have a negative or even catastrophic impact on an online business's economics and also on innocent individuals.

Google, much like FB, has made enemies as it has maintained its dominant market position. There is significant evidence that Google has often made the changes to its search algorithm so that they disadvantage firms with which they compete for 'eyeballs', resulting in answers to the queries being available within Google, without the need for users to enter other websites, even if those sites have more complete information.[160] Google has maintained that these changes benefit users, even if they hurt certain firms. The result has been a decade-long series of antitrust concerns about Google unfairly damaging competitors and legal challenges. In 2017, the EU fined Google 2.4 billion euros, which it is still appealing; this was followed by a 2018 antitrust fine of 4.3 billion euros for bundling the Chrome browser and search apps with Android, which will also be appealed.[161]

Google also uses its brains, technology, and wealth to enter new industries that, on the surface, seem far removed from IT. There is a recently announced partnership with Walmart: Walmart will offer its products on Google Express, Google's online shopping mall—clearly a competitive thrust against Amazon and its acquisition of the Whole Foods grocery store.[162] In 2015, Google restructured and created a parent company called Alphabet Inc., which became the owner of Google and other subsidiaries; this move made Google nimbler in pursuing new ventures in areas such as self-driving cars (later spun out to a new firm called Waymo), computer hardware, and life sciences.[163]

Amazon

Amazon is the IT and IT-leveraging firm that arguably poses the greatest threat to companies in IT and in domains seemingly not connected to IT.[164] In 1993, founder and CEO Jeff Bezos started Amazon as an online book store. Over time, its targeting of potential purchasers, huge inventory, low prices, and rapid deliveries put most traditional stores out of business.[165] Exceptions tended to be small stores catering to local markets in specialized areas, such as children's books. Paradoxically, it is now using its wealth, brand name, and the fact that it now sells half the books in the USA to create large physical bookstores, in space once owned by its deceased competitors.[166]

Once it mastered the technology of effective online shopping and home delivery, Amazon expanded its product offerings to include electronics, then slowly but steadily other consumer items that traditionally had been sold by department stores, specialized stores, and catalogue sales. As with books, the result has been carnage for existing companies. Amazon's sales have surpassed those of Macy's, the largest apparel seller in the USA, which in 2017

Continued on next page

announced it would close 100 stores.[167] Sears has also been unable to keep up with online competition and is closing many stores; Sears Canada filed for bankruptcy protection in 2017, Sears US in 2018.[168] Existing stores, such as Nordstrom, are trying to compete by experimenting with smaller stores that offer fewer choices but a higher-quality shopping experience.[169] Furthermore, to increase its variety and make more low-priced goods available, Amazon has recruited 27,000 Indian merchants to make their wares available on its website; it has also started selling private-label brands of many different kinds of consumer goods that it manufactures itself.[170]

Amazon also grows by acquisition. The most dramatic example, very ominous for existing grocery retailers, is the 2017 acquisition of Whole Foods.[171] The purchase may have seemed surprising, but it gives Bezos a rich playground to experiment with the design of physical stores.[172] Early changes included cutting prices and introducing some automation, steps we discussed in Chapter 10.[173] More recent changes included adding home delivery and lockers for shoppers to stash items at the store, allowing Whole Foods private-label foods to be ordered online, and integrating the customer rewards programmes of the two companies.[174] The pay-off for learning how better to sell retail could be huge for Amazon: 44% of American consumers look to Amazon first when contemplating a purchase, but 92% of the sales still happen in a brick-and-mortar store.[175]

The ultimate sign of Amazon's drive to sell through physical presence is in the Amazon Go experimental store.[176] All items and shoppers are traced through a sophisticated computer vision and machine learning system that employs hundreds of cameras. Items go directly into shopping bags. As customers leave the store, their Amazon accounts are automatically charged. There are no cashiers or cash registers. It's a triple play—Amazon goods sold in Amazon stores supported by Amazon infrastructure![177] Leading retail stores are now frantically automating.[178]

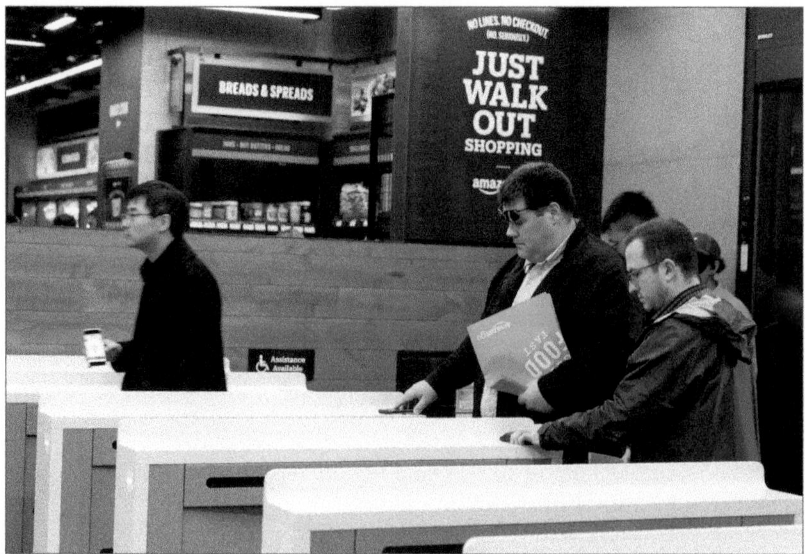

Figure 12.4 No cash registers at the exit from Amazon Go
Paul Christian Gordon / Alamy Stock Photo

Amazon has been visionary so often it is frightening. It has become a leader in cloud services. As we have seen in this chapter, it is a pioneer and market leader in voice assistants and IT appliances.[179] As consumers increasingly start their product searches with a query to a voice assistant, Amazon's influence in everyday commerce grows even larger.[180] It is selling its own home security hardware so that homeowners can allow Amazon couriers to open their front doors and leave packages inside rather than on the traditional doorstep.[181] Amazon has also obtained wholesale pharmacy licences in over a dozen US states, and purchased an online pharmacy in mid-2018.[182]

As with Facebook and Google, concerns about Amazon's power have been raised by citizens, institutions, and governments. Amazon has become a conglomerate, with products, services, and infrastructures attacking a continually expanding set of markets, with a platform that allows it to subsidize its entrance into new areas with predatory pricing.[183] To reduce the probability of US government action against it, Amazon constantly stresses how many jobs it creates and how it supports new business in its ecosystem, and has increased public relations and lobbying, especially in Washington, DC.[184] Part of this campaign was plausibly Bezos' purchase of one of America's leading newspapers, the *Washington Post*.[185] Despite this, calls for antitrust action are increasing, not to mention that Amazon and Bezos himself have become favourite tweet targets of President Trump.[186] Time will tell how governments choose to weigh the benefits of Amazon's innovations against the dangers of its increasing power.

Overall, the Frightful Five are healthier than ever. As stated above, they are the five most valuable companies in the world, and have been instrumental in advances in digital inclusion, education, medicine, and numerous other contributions to human welfare. They are therefore smug and proud of their achievements. Representatives of these firms have suggested to Manjoo that he should have called them the 'Fabulous Five'.[187] Manjoo has also noted that there are some upsides to being ruled by the Frightful Five, namely that they can be governed, they feel constrained by American laws and values, and they hate each other's guts.[188]

Their achievements are indeed due to ingenuity, but also to their control over the infrastructure of the modern world—mobile phones and computing, the web and the cloud, social networks and advertising. Online advertising is the huge revenue driver, and the primary means by which corporations collect immense reservoirs of data which are at the heart of problems with privacy, discussed in Chapter 9.[189] A second source of privacy threats is the collection of mobile phone location and movement data.[190] Achievements are also due to network effects, in which the power of a network grows as its user base expands, which in turn attracts more users. In critical areas, dominating companies have essentially a monopoly position: witness Alphabet's 83 per cent share of the US mobile search market and 63 per cent of the mobile operating system market, and the combined 85 per cent share of online advertising dollars that is collected by Google and FB.[191]

Together with IBM, still a significant force, the Frightful Five plan to dominate the major industries of an economy: finance and retail sales, automobiles and transportation, health care and entertainment. Their influence in the world of politics and government has included both positive and negative elements, as we have seen in Chapters 5, 6, and 9. Increasingly, most of our purchases, as well as the culture we live in, and access to books, music, and film are dominated by these firms.[192] Furthermore, some economists and students of entrepreneurship believe that their degree of market power has stifled the formation of start-ups and has also resulted in the acquisition of promising new companies too quickly.[193]

Many in Silicon Valley are now concerned about the power of the Frightful Five. This includes employees, executives, and shareholders. One example is the *Center for Humane Technology*, another is the concern of Apple shareholders about mobile phone addiction in children, both mentioned previously in this chapter. Executives of these companies have grown older; with age comes family and responsibility, and often more thoughtfulness, empathy, awareness of ethics, and in some cases even wisdom.[194] Evan Williams, who was involved in the creation and success of Blogger (later bought by Google) and Twitter, came to believe that the internet is broken. In 2012 he created *Medium* as a communications platform intended to be free of fake and worthless content.[195] The new CEO of Uber, Dara Khosrowshahi, recently wrote in a public letter that '[w]hile Uber has revolutionized the way people move in cities around the world, it's equally true that we've got things wrong along the way'.[196] Another hopeful incident occurred in autumn 2017 when Zuckerberg asked for forgiveness on Yom Kippur, the Jewish Day of Atonement, in part for 'the ways my work was used to divide people rather than bring us together'.[197]

Yet the primary vehicle for reining in the power of the Frightful Five seems to be government. There are increasing calls to acknowledge some of these firms as monopolies and regulate them accordingly, and debates about how to apply antitrust law to them.[198] One analyst, who previously directed a university innovation lab, based his case in part on the observation that massive economic value has moved from the creators of content to the owners of monopoly platforms.[199] Europe, as we have seen, has acted more decisively than its counterparts across the pond; EU's Competition Commissioner, Margrethe Vestager, is said to 'strike fear into Silicon Valley'.[200]

In comparison with Europe, the US government has been impotent. The Obama administration was very friendly to high-tech, but technology's impact on the 2016 election drove many leading Democrats to call for more regulation of the Frightful Five.[201] Yet, as of early 2018, the Democrats had no power, hence could achieve little. Despite occasional anti-high-tech tweets from President Trump, and a few concrete actions, such as a poorly devised proposed law dealing with internet sex trafficking,[202] there has been no coherent vision or moral stature to force change.

Research: Compare the Chinese firms Alibaba and Tencent to the US firms Amazon, Facebook, and Google. Pay particular attention to their treatments of security, safety, and privacy.

Research: Investigate how your city has dealt with services such as Airbnb, including social and economic impacts. Moreover, consult both with the hotel industry and with those providing space in their homes to travellers.

Research: Study the problem of fake reviews.

Research: Similarities and differences in how Facebook and Instagram treat anonymity, news, and privacy.

Debate: Resolved: Google started with a motto of 'Don't Be Evil', but it has now become an evil company.

Debate: Resolved: The EU's ongoing legal action against Silicon Valley is harassment based on jealousy, and not based on US companies breaking the law and taking advantage of Europeans.

Policy: Prepare a brief for the CEO of a pharmacy company detailing the perceived threat to their business from Amazon, and what, if anything, can be done about it.

Book report: Stone, Brad (2013). *The Everything Store: Jeff Bezos and the Age of Amazon*. Little, Brown & Company.

Book report: Vaidhyanathan, Siva (2018). *Antisocial Media: How Facebook Disconnects Us and Undermines Democracy*. Oxford University Press.

12.10 Our options

What kind of world do we want? We often appear subservient to digital technologies, the rapid pace of change, and the overarching power of companies such as the Frightful Five. But we do have choices. We can ensure that we and not technology and not the large firms are in charge.

Consumers do have the ability, no matter how compelling digital technologies are, to control their use of technology. Parents can set limits for use by children and make rules about family time that cannot be interrupted by rings or pings. Couples can agree on how they create private space, and to what extent electronic interruptions are allowed. Companies can allow, and ensure that workers know they are entitled to, private time in which they should not be expected to answer texts or emails. Consumers can resist the lure of fancy new technologies that duplicate the functionality of light switches and kitchen timers.

Tech firms need to be held accountable by management, shareholders, employees, government, municipalities, and citizens. For example, Microsoft senior management has spoken up publicly recently about the need to protect user privacy and develop ethical guidelines for new technologies such as AI.[203]

Employees of tech giants have a responsibility and a voice. There have been some good examples in 2018. Thousands of employees at Google protested publicly about the company's involvement in AI weapons research, and some of them even quit; the firm eventually decided to withdraw from work of this kind.[204] Hundreds of Microsoft employees protested similarly about the company's work with the Immigration and Customs enforcement agency soon after there was worldwide concern over its separation of children from illegal immigrants to the USA.[205]

Governments must step in with appropriate regulations. As discussed in this chapter, antitrust legislation should be invoked to break up firms that have monopoly control over markets and can use this to finance continual intrusions in new markets. Municipalities are obviously eager to attract new high-tech jobs, but must avoid bizarre actions such as the 2017 decision by the city of Waukee and the government of the state of Iowa to grant over $200 million in incentives so that Apple would locate a new data centre in Waukee with only an estimated fifty permanent jobs.[206]

Finally, as citizens we need to speak up vigorously when we see developments that we view as immoral and potentially injurious.

Research: Issues and results from ethical stances and protests by employees within high-tech firms.

Research: Financial incentives given to high-tech firms to create jobs within a community. How does a community decided how large these incentives can reasonably be?

12.11 Summary

Even visionary computer scientists and science fiction writers would likely be amazed at the modern world, and how our lifestyle has changed through the pervasive use of digital technologies.

Thanks to internet communications, distance is no obstacle for keeping in touch, for maintaining friendships, and for meeting unfamiliar people. Analysts generally applaud the results, but there continue to be concerns about too few authentic conversations and too little real community, and the role of current technology in enabling or discouraging conversation and community. For example, it can be hard to be present in many situations, given that we are often distracted by notifications and messages on our devices.

Connections are so easy and so compelling that many people don't have even a moment of peace and tranquillity. Companies design technology experiences to become increasingly addictive; it is often difficult to drag ourselves away. We may have no idea how much our life centres around our phone, but know for certain we cannot live without it. Technology addiction is very harmful for both youth and adults, distorting our relationships with our peers when we are young, and contributing to workaholism when we are older.

Due to the Internet of Things, technology is everywhere and in everything. Objects are increasingly controlled digitally; they can therefore adjust their behaviour and interact with people and other devices in the world. Switches, lamps, speakers, and refrigerators are now 'smart' and respond to voice commands. Matter may also soon be smart. Yet the rapid success of voice assistants rarely seems to provide significant new value, except for individuals with accessibility challenges and seniors, and for people whose hands are busy, but offers modest convenience together with significant new privacy concerns.

If our world is not enough, we can augment it or immerse ourselves in digital universes. Augmented reality can provide people who do challenging or dangerous tasks such as surgery or firefighting new sources of information that can be seen without losing focus on critical people or objects in the world. Virtual reality worlds can be imaginative and fulfilling, or ominous and frightening.

Many of us go online to meet potential romantic partners. Online dating is more convenient and prevalent than old-fashioned courting; some people will increasingly remain in an alternative universe or use sex robots for sexual gratification and emotional fulfilment.

Cash is on the verge of becoming obsolete with advances in credit card, mobile phone, and email transactions. Blockchain technology supports digital financial transactions with cryptocurrencies such as bitcoin. Although there can be benefits to preserving value in digital form, early experiences have been rife with speculations and huge value fluctuations. Credit and financial accountability will change dramatically as the use of such currencies continues to grow. Blockchain is also being used to develop a new generation of more secure applications.

All these advances are being driven by a small number of visionary, capable, ambitious, increasingly powerful, and rapacious digital technology companies. Corporate concentration has reduced consumer choice, discouraged entrepreneurship, and threatened security, safety, and privacy. These firms eagerly use their profits and huge cash reserves to enter markets that until now seemed totally unrelated to IT. Unless they are designated as monopolies and placed under antitrust regulation, corporate control will be even more concentrated. Our futures will be in the hands of a very few individuals who we hope will have goodwill and be wise. Unfortunately, there is as yet little evidence that this will be the case.

12.12 Key terms

Active matter
Alphabet/Google
Amazon
Amazon Alexa
Apple
Artificial reality
Augmented reality (AR)
Bitcoin
Blockchain
Center for Humane Technology
Computer farms
Crowdfunding
Cryptocurrencies
Digital currency mining
FOMO
Facebook (FB)
Fahrad Manjoo
Finstas and *rinstas*
Frightful Five
Google Home
IBM
Initial coin offerings (ICOs)
Instagram
Internet dating
Internet of Things
Lifestyle
Medium
Microsoft
Nosedive, an episode of *Black Mirror*

Porn bots
Realbotix
Sex robots
Shaadi.com
Social credit system
Smart cities
Technology addiction
Virtual reality (VR)
Voice assistants
WhatsApp
Work engagement
Workaholism

13
Epilogue

In the preceding pages, we have introduced, explained, and discussed a large and growing number of ways in which digital technologies are affecting our world.

The pace of change is accelerating. Although there are concerns that semiconductor performance and miniaturization will soon no longer obey Moore's Law (discussed in the Prologue), new technologies such as quantum computers will likely extend the continual improvement of hardware performance. New software approaches such as deep learning have dramatically improved increasingly critical artificial intelligence (AI) computations. Concerns about employment prospects as well as the fascination of computer science have greatly enlarged the talent pool of individuals studying this field or related disciplines and adopting careers involving digital technologies. Corporations now understand the importance of computing, and of investing in research and development. Finally, the astronomical returns yielded by high-tech 'start-ups' such as Apple, Google, Facebook, and Amazon have led to enormous pools of investment capital seeking new digital technology innovations.

As a result, there are now many social, legal and policy, and moral and ethical issues regarding digital technology and its presence in human society. We have discussed these topics in depth in the preceding pages. To review, we shall now highlight the most important issues.

We shall classify the issues under either a social, policy/legal, or ethical/moral heading, yet all three categories are closely related. A social issue is a statement about quality of life, and what kind of world we want to live in. A policy or legal choice is a statement about the way we are governed, and about the rules we adopt as societies to shape the world as we intend. An ethical or moral dilemma is a question that societies, organizations, and individuals must answer and support with appropriate actions and laws to create a world that is fair, just, and good.

There are no easy answers. The eminent professor and historian of technology Melvin Kranzberg described this in what he called Kranzberg's First Law: 'Technology is neither good nor bad; nor is it neutral.'[1] He went on to explain:

> By that I mean that technology's interaction with the social ecology is such that technical developments frequently have environmental, social, and human consequences that go far beyond the immediate purposes of the technical devices and practices themselves, and the

same technology can have quite different results when introduced into different contexts or under different circumstances.

13.1 Social issues

Our policies and laws, guided by our ethics and beliefs, allow us to determine, rather than passively accept, the shape of our society. Here are six notable examples that we have discussed.

Will we continue to move towards a society in which everything is digital, where we expect all tasks to be intermediated for us by digital devices? As we have discussed, especially in Chapter 12, we seem to be heading in that direction. If we want to listen to music, turn off the lights, or order a movie, will we expect Alexa to do it for us with a single spoken voice command? Are developments such as these useful and important?

A related issue is our ability and willingness to be disconnected and go offline. We have seen the dangers of total connection with no respite in Chapter 12. Will we permit ourselves states of solitude away from technology, or can we no longer even imagine what that means?

We have seen in Chapter 2 a tension between proprietary and open approaches to digital media. Society must determine the extent to which it encourages and supports either ends of this debate. How we proceed will influence the kinds of entrepreneurial organizations that prosper, and our ability to continue to be creative and share those innovations online.

If we want more care for grandpa and grandma, we may be forced to rely upon care bots. Such developments, discussed in Chapter 4, raise issues of personal commitment and ultimately who we are, what we can do, and what we should (still) do for our parents and grandparents as opposed to delegating these tasks to robots. These developments also raise issues regarding how society should deploy resources, and what activities and careers will be valued in the future.

To what extent will we use computers for education and for medicine, in ways such as those presented in Chapters 3 and 4? Should we impose limits to how technology is used in these spheres? Our history and traditions have made the teacher and the doctor revered and trusted members of our society, occupying the roles of advisors, mentors, and healers. Yet the rational thinking, problem-solving, and advising previously provided by humans will, over the course of the next few decades, be mastered by artificially intelligent machines. These machines will be as competent at reasoning as the best humans are now. What will be the respective roles of humans and electronics in education and learning, and in medicine and health?

Will we still drive, or, as discussed in Chapter 6, will we yield driving to smart cars in the interests of safety and efficiency, or as a result of aggressive business development? What will happen after the inevitable first fatal accidents with self-driving cars, tragedies which are already occurring? How will we support those whose livelihoods have depended upon their rights and abilities behind the wheel of a car, truck, bus, or taxi? Will we adopt a measured and cautious approach to introducing autonomous vehicles, choosing in the meantime to apply many of the other ways in which technology can enhance driving safety, or will the corporate drive (pun intended) towards trendy technologies and profit maximization bring us there with unseemly haste?

13.2 Policy/legal choices

Governments will need to determine what kinds of policies and laws will govern the manner in which and the extent to which digital technologies are used. We shall highlight six specific instances of this.

Chapter 1 discussed significant progress in digital inclusion, and new technologies assisting individuals with vision, hearing, cognition, and age-related challenges. We have also seen backward steps, such as attacks on net neutrality. How important is digital inclusion for society, how do we increase it, and will we adopt new laws and incur extra costs to enable digital equity?

What kinds of speech should governments or the monolithic firms that control the internet allow and forbid? We have seen in Chapter 5 how serious and in many cases perplexing this dilemma becomes. How do we deal with the perils of speech that is offensive, degrading, and hateful to certain groups of society, or that encourages or facilitates terrorism, without sacrificing principles of free expression that many societies hold dear?

We have seen that speech can be dangerous, not just because it can be evil, but also because it can be untrue. Chapter 5 discussed the problem of fake news, and the ways in which it can be amplified in echo chambers and magnified by filter bubbles. Fake news represents a severe threat to the welfare of societies that would like to be governed by processes of reason and debate. Will we adopt and apply technical measures and governmental policies that can render fake news harmless? Do such measures exist?

Will there be any limits on surveillance in the service of security? How will they be enforced? How can we navigate the degree to which societies emphasize security, or privacy? How can we ensure that both values are respected, that we have societies with effective monitoring of security threats, yet strong protections of personal privacy and individual liberties? We have discussed these issues in detail in Chapters 7 and 9.

Chapter 11 highlighted the issue of who or what is responsible when people are injured or killed by programs and machines. The designers of the technology? Those who paid to have it designed? Those who ordered it and applied it? How will new laws adjudicate such matters? We have seen in Chapter 8 how controlling digital technologies is challenged by their increasing complexity, and in Chapter 11 how this problem is manifested in ML technologies that are opaque and make decisions in ways neither the machines nor their designers can explain, hence causing us to be affected by decisions we cannot understand.

We discussed in detail in Chapter 12 that several digital technology firms have achieved dominant and seemingly unassailable market positions in their original area of expertise, as well as huge stores of capital reserves and cadres of brilliant technologists. Societies such as the USA are used to having these types of market leaders, but two aspects of the phenomenon are new. The dominance of technology firms is now global. The universality of digital technology allows them to disrupt and also dominate industries seemingly unconnected to information technology. An example is Amazon's online store overpowering traditional big box and retail companies. Must governments be more assertive in applying antitrust principles to firms such as the Frightful Five?

13.3 Ethical/moral dilemmas

Many readers of this book will face ethical choices as working professionals, or as intelligent citizens, in societies in which there are fewer and fewer limits on what digital technologies can do. Here are six examples. More are highlighted as 'Ethics Case Studies' in the body of the text.

Will we use the techniques of precision medicine discussed in Chapter 4 to order babies with certain characteristics and credentials? This will force difficult choices. Everyone wants their children to have every opportunity that will give them the greatest happiness and leverage in life. Yet will this lead to even more pressure on children to succeed, and even more parental disappointment and resentment if the desired success is not achieved? How will we allocate the opportunities to design one's children if this cannot be done for all who desire it?

Will we allow an arms race in cyberweapons with technologies, as discussed in Chapter 6? Despite claims for and expectations of precision targeting and guidance, drones often kill innocent civilians. The concept of robots fighting and destroying other robots may allow conflict resolution with reductions in loss of lives. Yet compelling arguments can also be made that robot warfare will increase our reliance upon force as opposed to conflict mediation. A question raised in much science fiction may also become pertinent: will we be able to trust that a new race of superintelligent weapons will do our bidding and not turn against us?

Will there be technical or societal limits to what work is automated? We have discussed in Chapter 10 the increasing tendency of firms to bring in robots to do jobs previously performed by humans in order to increase profitability. This has happened in four waves: first in agriculture, then in manufacturing, now in services, and soon also in the professions. Our policies, laws, and belief systems must also deal with two major consequences. How will we as individuals gain the satisfaction, self-esteem, and dignity that was previously provided through a job? How can we ensure that all people have the financial resources for a comfortable living? Will governments need to provide a guaranteed annual income to all citizens?

Chapters 3, 4, 5, 6, 10, and 11 have summarized how AI seems to be able to carry out more and more tasks that were once the domain of human effort and creativity. Are there limits to what we will trust machines to do? How will we decide when to convey or not convey trust? How will we attribute and enforce responsibility for accidents or disasters? Can justice be automated, or even improved through automation? Will we be able to endow the new generations of smart machines with empathy?

If you are starting out in a career, how shall you invest your time, and decide what is doable and what is worth doing? As discussed in many chapters, digital technologies are applicable in most domains of human activity—learning and health, war and peace, commerce, and the arts. One wants to look at a career and feel that his or her life is being well spent. How do young people navigate what often feels like a chasm between economic necessity and social purpose?

Finally, what does one do if their work and beliefs seem to be in conflict? How can one be an effective actor in expressing their own beliefs and in moving them forward? If whistle-blowing, discussed in Chapter 9, seems to be the only option, how can one do this most effectively?

13.4 Moving forward

All people who wish to participate in these developments, and who want to have a voice in how things evolve, must consider what kind of world they want to live in, what policies and laws are needed so that the world evolves in this way, and what ethical and moral choices they have to make in the hope that the world will become just and good.

I hope that this text has acquainted serious students and readers with relevant developments, guided them in research explorations of open issues and questions, given them the tools to think about and debate these topics, and allowed them to become more knowledgeable and responsible technology practitioners, consumers, and citizens.

Readers of this text will want to keep up with new developments. In addition to those mentioned at the end of each chapter, here are some more sources. Note that many of these sites are periodicals that cover many topics, yet, because of the importance of digital technologies, their coverage of the issues discussed in this book is excellent.

1) Read a daily edition of the *New York Times*, https://www.nytimes.com.
2) Read a daily edition of the *Wall Street Journal*, https://www.wsj.com.
3) Read the *New Yorker* magazine, https://www.newyorker.com.
4) Look at the prestigious science publication, *Nature*, https://www.nature.com/nature/, for occasional relevant discussions.
5) Look at *MIT Technology Review*, https://www.technologyreview.com, for regular coverage of relevant issues.
6) Subscribe to O'Reilly Media for technology media, events, forecasts, opinions, and blogs, https://www.oreilly.com.
7) Read *Fast Company*, a business magazine focusing on innovative ventures, https://www.fastcompany.com.

Finally, I hope that you will be keen to read a sequel to this book. At present, there is no sequel, but here are some books that will deepen your understanding of this field.

Technology journalist John Markoff's thoughtful 2016 account of sixty-five years of digital technology evolution focuses on 'humans and the kind of world we will create', and tells the story of a few hundred of the key players.[2]

Technology entrepreneur Tim O'Reilly's wide-ranging 2017 review of 'WTF technologies' and how they might be used agrees with Markoff's optimism that the future is 'up to us', and asserts that 'moral choice' is our greatest asset, concluding with this advice: 'Work on something that matters more to you than money.'[3]

I eagerly await 2020 and the promised publishing of a book by the technology journalist Fahrad Manjoo, who coined the moniker the 'Frightful Five'. The book chronicles the visions, strategies, tactics, actions, successes, failures, and ultimate power of Apple, Facebook, Alphabet/Google, and Amazon.[4]

We have discussed numerous cases and reasons why there seem to be so many examples of disruptive technologies, such as AI and robots, that are embraced by many people and resisted by others. Everyone should read business professor Clayton Christensen's classic 1997 book *The Innovator's Dilemma*, on disruptive innovation viewed from a management point of view; it explains why good firms need to change what they are doing and disrupt themselves in order to survive.[5] The spirit of creative destruction as seen by the geeks, the hackers in the original sense of the word, is conveyed in a lively 2016 personal account by Antonio García Martínez.[6] Part of his story illuminates his personal experience working at Facebook and following its famous early mantra, 'Move Fast and Break Things', which even appeared in the company's Offering Memorandum when it went public in 2012.[7]

Finally, to bring innovation and disruption full circle back to the humans who ultimately benefit and suffer from it, I can recommend two books. The late professor Calestuous Juma wrote a scholarly analysis of resistance to technologies as diverse as coffee, electricity, and mechanical refrigeration.[8] Juma argued that resistance could and would reasonably grow out of the differences between immediate risks and long-term benefits, and between risks that are widely distributed and benefits that accrue only to small sectors of society (including the 'obscene fortunes' described by Martínez). Law Professor Brett Frischmann and Philosophy Professor Evan Selinger published in 2018 a thoughtful and imaginative account turning the AI problem on its head, asking not to what extent machines can be made to behave like humans, or even better than humans, but the extent to which digital technologies and our modern lifestyle are turning us into machines. [9]

Clearly we need O'Reilly's 'moral choices' to chart a wise course for the future.

May the readers of this book make wise moral choices.

Book review: Markoff, John (2016). *Machines of Loving Grace: The Quest for Common Ground Between Humans and Robots*. HarperCollins.

Book review: Martínez, Antonio García (2016). *Chaos Monkeys: Obscene Fortune and Random Failure in Silicon Valley*. HarperCollins.

Book review: Juma, Calestuous (2016). *Innovation and Its Enemies: Why People Resist New Technologies*. Oxford University Press.

Book review: O'Reilly, Tim (2017). *What's the Future and Why It's Up to Us*. Harper Business.

Book review: Frischmann, Brett and Evan Selinger (2018). *Re-Engineering Humanity*. Cambridge University Press.

Book review: Manjoo, Fahrad (2020, expected). *Masters of Our Universe*. Simon & Schuster.

14

Afterword: Developments in autumn 2018

I sent this manuscript to Oxford University Press on 29 August 2018. The book emerged in April 2019. Much happened in the interim. I submitted this update on 4 January 2019, summarizing matters of consequence in autumn 2018, as well as important things I learned in that period.

14.1 Digital inclusion

A recent Microsoft blog suggests that I was too positive in my portrayal of a shrinking digital divide.[1] In the USA, 35 per cent of the population report they do not use broadband communications at home. Wikipedia continued to grow, fuelled in part by its foundation's effort to engage underrepresented 'emerging communities'.[2] Battles in the USA over net neutrality intensified after the federal decision to abandon the policy. The state of California passed a tough net neutrality; the New York state attorney initiated an enquiry asking whether the federal decision had been swayed by millions of fraudulent comments.[3]

There were more innovations in sensory substitution to enable digital inclusion. At Caltech, researchers developed a system that allows blind people to receive an audio description of what is in their gaze: the objects appear to describe themselves in words.[4] Women continued their struggle for equality and against gender discrimination in high-tech firms.[5] Despite the importance of digital technologies for seniors to help combat loneliness, and to access banking and other online services, many are still digitally disengaged. Research shows that seniors perceive risk in being online, are reluctant to invest the time needed to gain and maintain digital proficiency, and are sometimes concerned that internet use would be inconsistent with their values, for example, the desire to support local stores.[6]

Book report: Holmes, Kat (2018). *Mismatch: How Inclusion Shapes Design*. The MIT Press.

14.2 Digital media and intellectual property

I was also too positive in my analysis of the impacts of sharing and stealing digital media and the power of digital media firms such as Google, Netflix, Facebook, and Amazon (see also the discussions of corporate concentration in Sections 12.9 and 14.12). Professor Jonathan Taplin has summarized how devastating these impacts have been, not just to digital media companies such as music and newspaper publishers, but to media creators such as composers and reporters.[7]

Consumer spending on recorded music dropped from almost US$20 billion in 1999 to US$7.5 billion in 2014. YouTube became the largest streaming music site in the world, with a market share of over 50 per cent, even though it pays only 13 per cent of total streaming music royalties, primarily because there is so much material on YouTube posted without copyright permission. Royalties paid to musicians for downloads and streaming usage now amount to smaller amounts per year than do sales of vinyl records, which until recently was thought to be an obsolete medium.

Between 1998 and 2015, 2,300 independent bookstores, the Borders bookstore chain, and 3,100 music stores closed their doors. Amazon sells 41 per cent of all new books and is responsible for 65 per cent of all online book sales. Newspaper ad revenue has plummeted from US$66 billion to US$17 billion between 2000 and 2014, causing newspaper employment to fall below 28,000, half the 1990 worker number, and also forcing many papers to close. Quality independent journalism is being further eroded by the frequency and quantity of news that people obtain from dubious websites. Furthermore, the increasing availability of online entertainment and the fact that much of it is now being produced by Netflix and Amazon is putting pressure on traditional film producers and movie theatres.

A recent insightful article raised the issues of intellectual property ownership of web content that has been contributed by multiple authors and individuals posting comments, likely to be as thorny an issue as that of mash-ups discussed in Section 2.5.[8]

Book report: Taplin, Jonathan (2018). *Move Fast and Break Things: How Facebook, Google, and Amazon Cornered Culture and Undermined Democracy*. Little, Brown, and Company.

14.3 Education and learning

An amusing footnote to Chapter 3's discussion of the strengths and flaws in our increasing reliance on PowerPoint is a report that children as young as ten are now using this software to 'manage' their parents, for example, by presenting arguments in favour of getting a puppy.[9]

14.4 Medicine and health care

Artificial intelligence (AI) developments for precision medicine continued vigorously, despite ongoing questions as to which applications are ready for use.[10] Another vibrant area of work is that of healthcare robotics, supporting clinicians and care workers in a variety of care tasks; echoing a theme from Section 4.10, one new robot now available from Belgium—Zora—is a 2ft humanoid creature that can provide companionship and encourage activity and play, but is not intended to look like a person.[11] Its price, however, is still US$18,000.

14.5 Free speech, politics, and government

The blogging website Tumblr, acquired by Yahoo in 2013, banned adult content in December 2018 because of a concern about child pornography.[12] Tumblr's inability to economically distinguish between what is and is not child pornography resulted in speech restrictions on more than 100,000 individuals who generated sexually explicit content, and over 30 million individuals who viewed it.

Autumn 2018 saw continued tension between internet speech freedom and restrictions on hate speech. British researchers found strong evidence that Facebook use contributed to anti-refugee attacks in Germany; the company itself admitted that its platform had been used to incite significant violence in Myanmar.[13] After digitally airing his grievances on the 'free speech' social network Gab, the Pittsburgh Pennsylvania synagogue shooter killed eleven people; the shooting was quickly celebrated by a torrent of anti-Semitic media on Instagram.[14] Facebook's efforts to moderate content have been mostly outsourced to a worldwide group of 7,500 mostly unskilled workers in industrializing nations who follow a set of rulebooks comprising over 1,400 poorly organized pages.[15] A review of these manuals revealed many errors, gaps, biases, and inconsistencies; this is not surprising since even foundational concepts such as 'hate speech' or 'supporting terrorism' are hard to precisely define. Students interested in content moderation, and the challenges posed to free speech by hate and hoaxes, should study and contrast the experiences and policies of Facebook with those of Reddit, a website devoted to dialogue among people in communities and is one of the five most-visited sites in the USA.[16]

Fake news continued to be troubling. Incendiary YouTube videos falsely accused Muslim refugees of rioting and killing two men in Chemnitz, Germany.[17] Facebook's content moderators reported they could not keep up with the volume of work required; the company announced plans to create an independent body to make decisions about allowable content, a kind of 'Supreme Court' of content moderation.[18] Of special interest is the hiring of a dozen skilled human journalists by Apple News to anchor a new commitment to selecting mobile news with sensitivity and nuance.[19] Fake medical news continued to dangerously mislead victims in many parts of the world.[20]

The use of social media for citizen mobilization was demonstrated once again by the French 'yellow jacket' movement.[21] Internet censorship continues globally, especially in

China, where it appears that Google, who pulled its search engine from the Chinese market because of censorship in 2010, is now preparing to introduce a version of the engine that supports the policies of the Chinese government.[22] Finally, an interesting example of the potential of e-government is currently taking place in Estonia.[23]

Book report: Lagoria-Chafkin, Christine (2018). *We are the Nerds: The Birth and Tumultuous Life of Reddit, the Internet's Culture Laboratory*. Hachette Books.

14.6 Law and order, war and peace

Digital technology continued to prove its ability to aid police work, as typified by crimes such as sexual assault and murder in which arrests and convictions were based on Fitbit data.[24]

Investigations by the US government and by independent researchers into Russian interference in the 2016 US presidential election continued in the autumn of 2018. In a new book, the communications scholar Kathleen Hall Jamieson systematically detailed how Russian hackers and trolls helped elect Donald J. Trump as President.[25] Professor Jamieson noted that interference in the electoral or political process of foreign governments had long been practised by the USA, but the cyber-interference in 2015 and 2016 was unprecedented in its magnitude and scope: Russian-trafficked social media content was received by 126 million Americans. She concluded that the Russian activities 'swung the election to Trump', although she admits that it is impossible to prove this with certainty.

In December 2018, two reports commissioned by the US Senate Select Committee on Intelligence were published.[26] Notable findings of these studies included: a) interference in the US electoral process continues vigorously, and has increased since the 2016 election; b) Instagram was an even greater vehicle of disruption than was Facebook; c) special efforts had been directed at sewing discord among potential black voters and Hispanics, even recruiting many as unknowing assets; d) significant energy had been aimed at voter suppression; e) a key goal of the 2016 election interference was to disrupt Hillary Clinton and support Donald Trump; and f) social media firms, especially Facebook and Google, have withheld data from researchers that could have enabled a more complete analysis of past and ongoing Russian disruption.

Autumn 2018 also saw vigorous attempts to hack the November US midterm elections, despite increasing efforts by social media firms to protect against such disruption; the spread of misinformation continued, although the election systems were not compromised.[27] Russian operatives continued to spread misinformation, now joined in many cases by mostly right-wing Americans.[28] The elections drew specific kinds of misinformation, including hoaxes about polling places and options for remote voting, rumours about voting machine malfunctions, false allegations about voter fraud, and doctored and mislabelled photos.[29]

The challenges raised by political misinformation keep growing. Russian hackers targeted Republicans who had disagreed with President Trump and sought continued sanctions against Russia; disappointingly, US Democrats used similar tactics of misinformation and disruption in a highly contested 2018 Senate race.[30] Concerns continue to grow over the American government's (in)actions to combat the growing dangers of fake news, and its (in)ability to protect the 2020 presidential election.[31] Brazilian WhatsApp users were deluged with hundreds of thousands of misleading or fake photos in the months prior to Brazil's October 2018 presidential election.[32] Political hackers are increasingly using facial recognition algorithms to identify potential targets and unleash chatbots to engage and confuse them; for example, it has been estimated that about a third of the Twitter traffic before the 2016 Brexit referendum in the UK came from chatbots, with most of them on the 'leave the EU' side. [33]

Accelerating plans for the commercial use of drones for deliveries resulted in increasing government attention to laws governing their use.[34]

Arguably this book's most significant ethical issue deals with autonomous weapons, especially lethal autonomous weapons systems (LAWS). Notes in Section 6.9. refer to useful reading. Since this is such an important topic, I include in this Afterword a note with more current reading and resources.[35] These papers focus especially on the emerging international consensus that 'meaningful human control' of such weapons is necessary, and the thesis that such weapons are dangerous and unethical and must be totally banned. Although this argument is politically contentious, with a number of governments opposing a LAWS ban, strong arguments in its favour can be based on the fact that the operations of current AI systems cannot be understood, and that this will continue to be true for the foreseeable future, and that they therefore cannot be entrusted with human life and with the conduct of warfare (see Sections 11.6 to 11.8).

Book report: Jamieson, Kathleen Hall (2018). *Cyberwar; How Russian Hackers and Trolls Helped Elect a President.* Oxford University Press.

14.7 Security

Significant data breaches in the autumn of 2018 included an attack that compromised 50 million Facebook accounts and possibly accounts in other applications that are typically accessed from Facebook. Another attack, attributed to Chinese hackers, exposed the personal data of 500 million individuals whose information was stored by the Starwood hotel reservation system.[36]

Security continued to be big business: 27,000 people attended the August 2018 Defcon hacking convention; there is even discussion of the ethics of hackers hacking hackers, that is, stealing back files that have been stolen.[37] There were chilling new concerns, such as fears about vulnerabilities in US weapons systems and water control systems.[38] As voice assistants such as Alexa drove an expansion of the Internet of Things (concepts discussed in Section 12.5), security concerns multiplied; for instance, one distributed denial-of-service hack jeopardized millions of devices.[39]

There are still fears that US elections may be compromised by obsolete hardware and software, insecure systems, lack of paper trails, and inabilities to audit results; these issues arose again in the 2018 midterm elections.[40] Moreover, just as with the 2000s butterfly ballot, poor ballot design in the state of Florida appears to have contributed to an election result of questionable validity.[41]

14.8 Safety

Although we now pay little attention to the degree to which society is vulnerable due to brittle software that is prohibitively expensive to change, a recent reminder was the over 10,000 American student veterans whose payments have been delayed or who have been underpaid due to the Veteran Administration's inability to update its fifty-year-old computer system.[42]

Intense development of and debates about self-driving cars continued. [43] Uber, which had shut down public testing of its self-driving vehicle prototypes after a fatality in early 2018, was allowed to restart testing on Pittsburgh's public roads, although with limits of speed and location, and with two drivers inside ready to take over in an emergency. There have also been increasing warnings that the technology might result in more urban sprawl and congestion.

14.9 Privacy

In September 2018, India's Supreme Court limited the use of its national ID number as a universal identifier with a 1448-page decision.[44] Worldwide, social media continued to pose identity and privacy threats. Apart from the data breach discussed in Section 14.7. above, new revelations about Facebook showed that it gave advertisers phone numbers provided by users for security reasons, and that a bug had given outside parties access to the private photos of almost 7 million users.[45] Further details also became known about how Facebook had shared personal user data with over 150 partners, many of them tech giants; these deals were so numerous and lucrative that Facebook employees had to build a software tool to keep track of them. Privacy concerns were not limited to Facebook; Google shut down its Google Plus social network after discovering a security vulnerability that exposed the personal data of a half million users.[46]

New hardware and software also pose more and more threats to privacy, including mobile phone apps that track user locations (on an estimated 200 million devices in the USA), an experimental grocery in San Francisco tracking purchases solely by video surveillance, and thousands of Swedes inserting chips under their skin in order to speed up daily routines.[47]

Professor Joseph Turow recently argued that American consumers do not willingly trade off their privacy for convenience, but rather are resigned to the inevitability of surveillance and to having little or no control over their personal data.[48] For perspective, it is important to remember that privacy is sometimes a matter of life or death, as is plausibly the case in the late 2018 theft by hackers of personal data of nearly 1,000 North Koreans who had defected to South Korea.[49]

Book report: Turow, Joseph (2017). *The Aisles Have Eyes: How Retailers Track Your Shopping, Strip Your Privacy, and Define Your Power.* Yale University Press.

14.10 Automation, work, and jobs

2018 saw increases in the use of AI to screen job applicants. Unilever, which receives 1.8 million resumés for 30,000 annual vacancies, uses machine learning to evaluate the results of applicant video game playing and answering questions on video.[50] The company saves 70,000 hours of personnel time per year and aims to give all applicants some feedback. There are many instances of firms monitoring and displaying workers' performance to motivate improvements or to discipline and even fire those who did not improve.[51] Cases included warehouse workers at Amazon, drivers at Uber, laundry workers at the Disneyland Hotel, and teachers in West Virginia, who managed via strike action to stop mandatory use of the monitoring app. We can expect increasing labour and legal resistance to such actions by companies in the future. There are also now websites such as Indeed and Glassdoor that provide job search assistance as well as employee ratings of companies.[52]

Some 85 per cent of the 80,000 ride-hailing drivers in New York City make less than the local minimum wage of $15 an hour, although $17 an hour after expenses was recently mandated by the city.[53] Yet, as discussed in Sections 10.4 and 12.9, there are more significant ways in which working conditions for individuals employed by on-demand services firms are poor. The International Labour Organization recently published the results of a survey of 3,500 workers in seventy-five countries engaged in 'crowdwork' activities such as content moderation, audio and video transcription, and translation.[54] When both paid and unpaid work were considered, the average wage was US$3.31 an hour and the median wage was US$2.16 an hour. Also unsatisfactory was the typical lack of social protection, the frequency of work that was rejected and not paid for, and the inability to appeal unfair rejections. Despite these frustrations, crowdwork was the primary source of income for 32 per cent of the workers; 88 per cent of the workers wanted more crowdwork, with the average desired increase being 11.6 more hours per week.

In part because of fewer immigrant farm labourers in California, the use of robots in agriculture continued to increase, for example, in a totally automated experimental lettuce farm.[55] There is also a skills gap in manufacturing motivating the increasing use of robots; a recent study forecast that the USA would have a need to fill 4.6 million manufacturing jobs between 2018 and 2028, and that only 2.2 million of them were likely to be filled.[56] China's 100 million manufacturing workers have been responsible for one-third of China's gross domestic product, yet skyrocketing wages threaten to make China non-competitive with other Asian countries where workers cost one-third as much, so China is also actively introducing robots into manufacturing.[57]

The automation of services continued at an accelerating pace; Amazon and Walmart started employing robots in fulfilment centres and stores. Autonomous scrubbers will be at work in 360 Walmart stores by the end of January 2019.[58] Facial recognition at the front desk are being piloted by Marriott, the largest US hotel chain, and has triggered alarms in hotel workers unions.[59] In the professions, Goldman Sachs plans to deploy robo-advisers as digital wealth solutions to the middle class.[60] In India, estimates suggest that as many as 60 per cent to 70 per cent of the 3.9 million jobs in IT and business process outsourcing will be replaced by AI programs in the 2020s.[61]

Putting it all together, there continue to be controversies about medium- and long-term impacts of AI and robotics on the future of jobs. In their 2018 Jobs Report,[62] the World Economic Forum predicted that 50 per cent of companies anticipated a reduction in workers doing today's jobs by 2022, and that 38 per cent of companies anticipated needing new workers for new jobs. By then, an estimated 54 per cent of employees will require significantly enhanced skills. Relevant and important research has been done by Professors Daron Acemoglu and Pascual Restrepo, who recently published:

> a framework for the study of the implications of automation and AI on the demand for labor, wages, and employment.... [It] emphasizes the displacement effect that automation creates as machines and AI replace labor in tasks that it used to perform. This... tends to reduce the demand for labor and wages. But it is counteracted by a productivity effect, resulting from the cost savings generated by automation, which increase the demand for labor in non-automated tasks.... automation increases output per worker more than wages and reduce[s] the share of labor in national income. The more powerful countervailing force against automation is the creation of new labor-intensive tasks, which reinstates labor in new activities and tends to increase the labor share to counterbalance the impact of automation. [63]

In another paper, the authors analysed the impact between 1993 and 2007 of the increases in industrial robots used in the USA and Europe amounting to 1 per 1000 thousand workers and 1.6 per 1000 thousand workers, respectively:

> each additional robot per thousand workers reduces local employment to population ratio by 0.38 percentage points and wages by about 0.71 percent. Because of the benefits of robot adoption for other commuting zones resulting from trade... aggregate effects are... smaller—one additional robot per thousand workers reduces aggregate employment to population ratio by 0.2 percentage points and aggregate wages by 0.38 percent.[64]

Finally, for readers interested in ideas, precedents, and progress towards a Universal Basic Income, a 2018 article summarizes the insights from four useful recent books.[65]

14.11 AI

Research on and deployment of AI systems continued to accelerate in autumn 2018. Leading centers continue to be the USA and China, where many are employed in labeling data to be used in training deep learning algorithms; there are also significant national efforts in Canada, France, India, Israel, Singapore, and the United Arab Emirates.[66] In October 2018, the Massachusetts Institute of Technology announced the creation of a new college focused specifically on AI.[67] AI is now used in socially constructive applications such as predicting earthquakes or the risk of suicides.[68] There also continue to be advances on specific AI techniques like machine learning algorithms that can achieve superhuman expertise without knowing the rules of the game in advance, affective computing research on speech emotion recognition, and a method that produces 'deepfake' images almost indistinguishable from real photographs.[69]

Yet some critics still decry how brittle the systems are and how vulnerable they are to sabotage due to a lack of common sense.[70] We are reminded that AI systems do not possess and are unlikely to soon achieve consciousness and empathy.[71] Other critics are concerned about trust, and note that we cannot trust systems that we do not totally understand.[72] There was more and more work on enabling machine learning systems to become explainable, some motivated by the need to hold such systems accountable for their actions.[73]

Themes of fairness and justice raised in Section 11.9 continue to be relevant. Bias can be caused by a past history of prejudice, poor quality data, unfair algorithms and decision rules, inappropriate human actions, and algorithm secrecy, the latter making it especially difficult to understand the source and mechanisms of bias in Google search.[74] The ethics of judgements made by machine learning systems analysing faces has been criticized for reasons that include the lack of explanations.[75] Use of automated decision-making by AI software in Canada's immigration and refugee system has been criticized by the University of Toronto Citizen Lab on the basis of 'bias, discrimination, privacy breaches, due process and procedural fairness'; the report calls for a freeze on such uses until all aspects can be properly reviewed.[76]

Finally, three interesting recent publications review a) superintelligence; b) current attempts to develop machine learning methods that are even better than deep learning, efforts that include work by the University of Toronto's Dr Geoffrey Hinton, who is credited with the backpropagation algorithm at the heart of deep learning; and c) instances in which machine learning systems have been subverted by adversaries, and the technical and legal challenges to prevent such behaviour.[77]

Book report: Ford, Martin (2018). *Architects of Intelligence: The truth about AI from the people building it.* Packt Publishing.

14.12 Lifestyle

Autumn 2018 saw continued progress with voice-driven personal assistants, the incorporation of tiny computers into everything from lightbulbs to microwaves, and their interconnection into the Internet of Things; for example, Amazon's Alexa is now compatible with over 28,000 smart home devices representing 4,500 brands.[78] As more homes have smart devices, there has been increasing interest in smart homes and, in urban areas, so-called 'smart' cities.[79] This buzz-word is poorly defined, in many cases representing the goal of reducing the energy consumption in a city, in other cases being used mostly as a marketing slogan to advance a city's reputation. Especially when sponsored by a tech giant, it often unleashes a fire storm of protest about privacy concerns, as has been the case with Google's Sidewalk Lab's planned Toronto eastern waterfront project. Increasing resistance to digital technologies was also exemplified by even more decisions by Silicon Valley technologists that screens represent a danger to their children and need to be tightly controlled.[80]

Section 12.8's concern about the volatility of Bitcoin and other cryptocurrencies proved correct, as Bitcoin's value, $19,800 in December 2017, dropped to $3,800 by December 2018.[81]

But the most significant activities related to the corporate concentration and monopoly control by giant digital technology firms. Apple, worth nearly a trillion dollars, and looking 'clean' as other tech firms were being tarred with privacy violations and fake news, saw continued success of its premium consumer products; Microsoft overtook Apple as the world's most valuable company at the end of 2018, leveraging successes in cloud computing and technology for the enterprise.[82] Google faced increasing criticism, including from the US Congress, over suspected search engine bias, over its preparation of a search engine supporting Chinese censorship, and over its sexual harassment policy, the latter issue triggering a worldwide walkout involving thousands of employees, which was soon followed by an updating of the policy.[83]

Facebook was in the news almost daily in the autumn; almost all of it was bad news. The data breach mentioned above was only the tip of the iceberg. After the financier George Soros delivered a blistering speech at the World Economic Forum in January 2018, terming Facebook and Google a 'menace' to society and calling for them to be regulated, Facebook COO Sheryl Sandberg hired a research firm to investigate his financial interests.[84] A British parliamentary committee investigating online misinformation revealed in December that Facebook used user data on behalf of certain partner companies, giving them special access to its platform, and cutting off threatening and competing firms.[85] A November 2018 article in the *New York Times* described in detail Facebook's attempts to defend itself with increasing use of lobbyists and through a strategy of 'delay, deny, and deflect'.[86] Another set of interviews with fifty people and a lengthy analysis of the history of Facebook in the *New Yorker* suggested that Facebook's senior management does not understand that under their motto of 'move fast and break things', it has 'broken' so many things that its dream of universal interconnection is turning into a nightmare.[87] Besides continuing pressure from politicians in both the USA and Europe, Facebook has started to suffer an arguably more critical problem, an increasing reluctance by some computer science students to work for the social media firm.[88]

Amazon continued its phenomenal growth, reaching 1 trillion dollars in value at one point in the year; it will probably employ 1 million workers by 2020.[89] Its dominance in e-commerce is fuelled in part by its relentless efficiency in reliable and prompt deliveries, no more evident than during the Christmas buying season.[90] The company boosts its growth with the use of AI to achieve greater efficiencies in all aspects of its business.[91]

To reduce costs, it is now manufacturing some of its own chips.[92] To ground innovation in real-world testing, it uses the city of Seattle as a living laboratory, testing new concepts in retail outlets for groceries and books.[93] Like Facebook, Amazon does sometimes face concerns; it actually owns Abe Books, an online bookseller of used and rare books, and a worldwide strike by 600 booksellers in twenty-seven countries forced Abe Books to withdraw a decision to cease business in several countries.[94] Yet, thus far unimpeded by growing concerns about monopoly dominance, it continues its relentless drive to be 'The Everything Store';[95] its November 2015 opening of a physical bookstore and its June 2017 purchase of Whole Foods were motivated by the fact that 92 per cent of purchases still occur in brick-and-mortar stores, so it appears that this is where CEO Jeff Bezos will focus next.[96]

Amazon salaries are low enough that one-third of its employees rely upon federal anti-poverty food stamps to feed their families, although the firm did recently announce a US minimum wage of $15 an hour for all workers.[97] Food stamps are not the only government programme that benefits Amazon. Municipalities frequently offer economic incentives to companies so that they locate new facilities in specific locations, despite analyses that suggest that the incentives were not instrumental in affecting decisions in 75 per cent or more of the cases.[98] Amazon conducted a one-year location competition for their HeadQuarters2 (HQ2), which brought with it an estimated 50,000 new jobs. In November 2018, Amazon decided to divide HQ2 into two parts, and put half in Arlington, Virginia, and the other half in Queens, New York. What municipalities offered has in many cases been kept secret—a source of outrage to concerned citizens. The Queens subsidy has been estimated at $3 billion to $4.7 billion; there were also concerns that a spike in housing costs, already starting to happen, would disproportionately impact on the poor.[99] As this book went to press, Amazon actually decided not to open the Queens headquarters, apparently because it was so upset that many local citizens and organizations opposed their plan.

Concern and actions against the increasing power of the Frightful Five grew in autumn 2018. There were increasing employee protests over use by the US government of databases about immigrants, and about AI and facial recognition technologies; over Google's reported plan to build a search engine for China that would support censorship; and about the need for diversity in hiring and in management.[100] Grants of stock options to employees helped them articulate their concerns using their rights as shareholders.[101]

In November, 2018, the Open Markets Institute reported that in 2017 Google had a 91 per cent share of the US$60 billion search engine market, Facebook had a 72 per cent share of the $26 billion social networking market, and Amazon had a 49 per cent share of the e-commerce market.[102] It is therefore not surprising that government concern about monopoly control by the Frightful Five continues in many parts of the world. The EU expanded its fining of US high-tech giants and started investigating plausibly anticompetitive behaviour by Amazon.[103] India, viewing the dominance of the US high-tech giants as a form of neo-colonialism, began to impose new regulations to limit their power, including actions in December 2018 directed against Amazon and Walmart's ability to sell online in India.[104]

However, because the Frightful Five are US companies, US government action would be most significant. US Congressman Ro Khanna, whose district includes much of Silicon Valley, has drafted an 'Internet Bill of Rights' covering topics such as privacy, discrimination, and net neutrality.[105] Most importantly, leading judicial scholars, such as Columbia University Law Professor Tim Wu and lawyer Lina Khan, now working at the US Federal Trade Commission, are suggesting that recent judicial interpretations that monopolies are ok as long as they reduce prices need to be revisited, and that antitrust action against high-tech monopoly control is now required.[106]

Book report: Wu, Tim (2018). *The Curse of Bigness: Antitrust in the New Gilded Age.* Columbia Global Reports.

14.13 Summary

Autumn 2018 saw modest advances towards digital technologies creating a world where they are used primarily for human benefit. However, there remain underlying issues of concern: balancing free speech with control of dangerous utterances and fake news; fragile security and threats to digital privacy; human needs for work in an era of automation; control and wise use of intelligent systems; and innovation without monopolistic control. These topics continue to be debated, and continue to challenge human behaviour, laws, and ethics.

Notes

Prologue

1. Baecker, Ronald M. (1969). Interactive Computer-Mediated Animation. PhD Dissertation, Dept. of Electrical Engineering, MAC-TR-61, MIT. http://publications.csail.mit.edu/lcs/pubs/pdf/MIT-LCS-TR-061.pdf. A video of this system, narrated by research collaborator Eric Martin, appears as https://www.youtube.com/watch?v=GYIPKLxoTcQ.
2. Sutherland, Ivan E. (1963). Sketchpad: A Man-Machine Graphical Communication System. PhD Dissertation, Dept. of Electrical Engineering, MIT. https://dspace.mit.edu/handle/1721.1/14979#files-area. A video demonstrating this system, narrated by Timothy Johnson, appears as https://www.youtube.com/watch?v=6orsmFndx_o.
3. Licklider, J. C. R. (1960). Man-Machine Symbiosis, *IRE Transactions on Human Factors in Electronics*, March, 4–11.
4. Bush, Vannevar (1945). As We May Think, *Atlantic Monthly*, July 1945. http://www.theatlantic.com/magazine/archive/1945/07/as-we-may-think/303881/.
5. Engelbart, Douglas (1962). Augmenting Human Intellect: A Conceptual Framework. SRI Summary Report AFOSR-3223. http://www.dougengelbart.org/pubs/augment-3906.html. A 1968 video demonstrating this system, sometimes described as 'the mother of all demos', appears as https://www.youtube.com/watch?v=yJDv-zdhzMY.
6. Nelson, Theodore (1965). A File Structure for The Complex, The Changing and the Indeterminate, *Proc. ACM 20th National Conference*, 84–100.
7. Kay, Alan and Adele Goldberg (1977). Personal Dynamic Media, *IEEE Computer* 10(3). http://homepages.dcc.ufmg.br/~loureiro/cm/docs/kay_personal_dynamic_media.pdf.
8. Gotlieb, Calvin Carl and Allan Borodin (1973). *Social Issues in Computing*, Academic Press.
9. Westin, Alan F. (1973). *Privacy and Freedom*, The Bodley Head Ltd.
10. Weizenbaum, Joseph (1976). *Computer Power and Human Reason: From Judgment to Calculation*, W. H. Freeman.
11. Dreyfus' argument, Papert's rebuttal, and Dreyfus' response may be found in: Dreyfus, Hubert (1965). Alchemy and AI. Rand Report P-3244; http://www.rand.org/content/dam/rand/pubs/papers/2006/P3244.pdf; Papert, Seymour (1968). The Artificial Intelligence of Hubert L. Dreyfus: A Budget of Fallacies. MIT AI Lab Memo AIM-154. https://dspace.mit.edu/handle/1721.1/6084; and Dreyfus, Hubert (1972). *What Computers Can't Do: A Critique of Artificial Reason*, Harper & Row.
12. Wikipedia (2017). Moore's Law. https://en.wikipedia.org/wiki/Moore%27s_law.
13. Johnson, R. Kikuo (2018). Home page. https://www.rkikuojohnson.com.
14. Johnson, R. Kikuo (2017). Tech support. Cover art. https://www.newyorker.com/culture/cover-story/cover-story-2017-10-23.

15. RightsCon (2018). Home page. https://www.rightscon.org.
16. Wikipedia (2018). Deontological ethics. https://en.wikipedia.org/wiki/Deontological_ethics; see also Wikipedia (2017). Kanteism. https://en.wikipedia.org/wiki/Kantianism; see also Wikipedia (2017). Act utilitarianism. https://en.wikipedia.org/wiki/Act_utilitarianism; see also Wikipedia (2017). Rule utilitarianism. https://en.wikipedia.org/wiki/Rule_utilitarianism; see also Wikipedia (2017). Social contract. https://en.wikipedia.org/wiki/Social_contract; see also Wikipedia (2017). Virtue ethics. https://en.wikipedia.org/wiki/Virtue_ethics.
17. ACM (2018). 2018 ACM Code of Ethics and Professional Conduct. https://www.acm.org/code-of-ethics.
18. Gotterbarn, Don, Keith Miller, and Simon Rogerson (1999). Computer Society and ACM Approve Software Engineering Code of Ethics, *Computer*, October, 84–90.
19. Johnson, Deborah G. (2009). *Computer Ethics. Analyzing Information Technology*, 4th Edition. Prentice Hall.
20. Johnson, Deborah G. and Helen Nissenbaum (1995). *Computers, Ethics, & Social Values*, Prentice Hall.
21. Himma, Kenneth Einar and Herman T. Tavani (2008). *The Handbook of Information and Computer Ethics*, Wiley.
22. Burton, Emanuelle, Judy Goldsmith, and Nicholas Mattei (2018). How to Teach Compuer Ethics through Science Fiction, *Communications of the ACM* 61(8): 54–64.
23. Baase, Sara (2013). *A Gift of Fire: Social, Legal, and Ethical Issues for Computing Technology*, 4th Edition, Prentice-Hall.
24. Quinn, Michael (2017). *Ethics for the Information Age*, 7th Edition, Pearson.
25. Kling, Rob (1996). *Computerization and Controversy: Value Conflicts and Social Choices*, 2nd Edition, Academic Press.
26. Agre, Philip E. and Douglas Schuler (Eds.) (1997). *Reinventing Technology, Rediscovering Community: Critical Explorations of Computing as a Social Practice*, Ablex.
27. Friedman, Batya (Ed.) (1997). *Human Values and the Design of Computer Technology*, Cambridge University Press. See also Friedman, Batya and David G. Hendry (2019), *Value Sensitive Design: Theory, Method, and Practice*, MIT Press. A useful resource is the value sensitive design website, https://vsdesign.org/.
28. Lin, Patrick, Keith Abney, and George A. Bekey (Eds.) (2012). *Robot Ethics: The Ethical and Social Implications of Robotics*, MIT Press.

Chapter 1

1. For a discussion of the origins of the term, see Gunkel, David J. (2003). Second Thoughts: Toward a Critique of the Digital Divide, *New Media & Society* 5(4): 499–522.
2. Warschauer, Mark (2002). Reconceptualizing the Digital Divide, *First Monday* 7(7), 1 July 2002. http://firstmonday.org/article/view/967/888/; see also Warschauer, Mark (2003). *Technology and Social Inclusion: Rethinking the Digital Divide*, MIT Press.
3. National Telecommunications and Information Administration (NTIA), US Department of Commerce (1995). Falling Through the Net: A Survey of the Have Nots in Rural and Urban America. https://www.ntia.doc.gov/ntiahome/fallingthru.html.

4. ITU (2016). Digital Inclusion for People with Specific Needs. http://www.itu.int/en/ITU-D/Digital-Inclusion/Pages/default.aspx.
5. Newell, Alan (2011). *Design and the Digital Divide: Insights from 40 years in Computer Support for Older and Disabled People*. Synthesis Lectures on Assistive, Rehabilitative, and Health-Preserving Technologies, Morgan & Claypool. See also Newell, Alan (2016). Older People as a Focus for Inclusive Design, *Gerontechnology* 4(4): 190–199.
6. Cole, Elliot (2013). *Patient-Centered Design of Cognitive Assistive Technology for Traumatic Brain Injury Telerehabilitation*. Synthesis Lectures on Assistive, Rehabilitative, and Health-Preserving Technologies, Morgan & Claypool.
7. Wikipedia (2016). Wikipedia. Retrieved on 30 November 2016 from https://en.wikipedia.org/wiki/Wikipedia.
8. See, for example, Rosenzweig, Roy (2006). Can History be Open Source? Wikipedia and the Future of the Past, *The Journal of American History* 93(1): 117–146. See also Priedhorsky, Reid, Jilin Chen, Shyong (Tony) K. Lam, Katherine Panciera, Loren Terveen, and John Riedl (2007). Creating, Destroying, and Restoring Value in Wikipedia, *Proc. GROUP 2007*. 10.1145/1316624.1316663. See also Kittur, Aniket and Robert E. Kraut (2008). Assessing the Wisdom of Crowds in Wikipedia: Quality through Coordination, *Proc. CSCW 08*, 37–46. We shall note an exception in Chapter 3, as there are concerns about the quality of health information in Wikipedia.
9. Inc. (2018). Jimmy Wales Explains the Radical Philosophy Behind Wikipedia. Inc. video, uncertain as to the date of recording. https://www.inc.com/jimmy-wales/wikipedia-founder-explains-radical-philosophy.html.
10. The Economist (2008). The Free-Knowledge Fundamentalist. *The Economist*, 5 June 2008.
11. Google (2012). Introducing the Knowledge Graph: Things, not Strings. https://googleblog.blogspot.ca/2012/05/introducing-knowledge-graph-things-not.html. See also Google (2016). The Knowledge Graph. https://www.google.com/intl/en-419/insidesearch/features/search/knowledge.html.
12. Clark, Justin, Robert Faris, and Rebekah Heacock Jones (2017). Analyzing Accessibility of Wikipedia Projects Around the World. Berkman Klein Center for Internet & Society Research Publication, 1 May 2017. https://cyber.harvard.edu/publications/2017/04/Wikipedia-Censorship.
13. US Public Law 102–194 (1991). High-Performance Computing Act of 1991. https://www.gpo.gov/fdsys/pkg/STATUTE-105/pdf/STATUTE-105-Pg1594.pdf.
14. National Telecommunications and Information Administration (NTIA), US Department of Commerce (2000). *Falling Through the Net: Toward Digital Inclusion*. https://www.ntia.doc.gov/report/2000/falling-through-net-toward-digital-inclusion.
15. Greene, Daniel (2016). Discovering the Divide: Technology and Poverty in the New Economy, *International Journal of Communication* 10: 1212–1231.
16. Pew Research (2016a). American's Internet Access, 2000–2015. http://www.pewinternet.org/2015/06/26/americans-internet-access-2000-2015/. Yet, anticipating the theme of addiction we shall discuss in Chapter 12, there is also a contrary digital divide of overuse. For example, white children in the USA average eight and a half hours daily looking at screens, while black and Hispanic children spend thirteen hours (Riley, Naomi Schaefer (2018). America's Real Digital Divide, *New York Times*, 11 February).

17. Kang, Cecilia (2017). F.C.C. Repeals Net Neutrality Rules, *New York Times,* 14 December; see also Collins, Keith (2017). Why Net Neutrality Was Repealed and How It Affects You, *New York Times,* 14 December; see also Kang, Cecilia (2018). Flurry of Lawsuits Filed to Fight Repeal of Net Neutrality, *New York Times,* 16 January; see also Collins, Keith (2018). The Net Neutrality Repeal Is Official. Here's How That Could Affect You, *New York Times,* 11 June.
18. Bell, W. Kamau (2017). Net Neutrality: Why Artists and Activists Can't Afford to Lose It, *New York Times,* 31 October; see also Hsu, Tiffany (2017). F.C.C. Plan to Roll Back Net Neutrality Worries Small Businesses, *New York Times,* 22 November; see also Manjoo, Fahrad (2017). Giving the Behemoths a Leg Up on the Little Guy, *New York Times,* 3 May; see also Manjoo, Fahrad (2017). The Internet Is Dying. Repealing Net Neutrality Hastens That Death, *New York Times,* 29 November.
19. Gunkel, David J. (2003). Second Thoughts: Toward a Critique of the Digital Divide, *New Media & Society* 5(4): 499–522.
20. van Dijk, Jan (2005). *The Deepening Divide: Inequality in the Information Society,* Sage. See also van Dijk, Jan (2013). A Theory of the Digital Divide. In Ragnedda, Massimo and Glenn W. Muschert (Eds.), *The Digital Divide: The Internet and Social Inequality in International Perspective,* Routledge, Chap. 2. See also Van Dijk, Jan and Alexander van Deursen (2014). *Digital Skills: Unlocking the Information Society,* Palgrave Macmillan.
21. Rhinesmith, Colin (2016). Digital Inclusion and Meaningful Broadband Adoption Initiatives. The Benton Foundation, January 2016. https://www.benton.org/sites/default/files/broadbandinclusion.pdf.
22. Warschauer, Mark (2002). Reconceptualizing the Digital Divide, *First Monday,* 1 July 2002. http://firstmonday.org/article/view/967/888/.
23. Selwyn, Neil (2004). Reconsidering Political and Popular Understandings of the Digital Divide. *New Media & Society* 6(3): 341–362.
24. Schuler, Doug (1994). Community Networks: Building a New Participatory Medium, *Communications of the ACM* 37(1): 38–51.
25. Internet Society (2014). Global Internet Maps, data for 2013. http://www.internetsociety.org/map/global-internet-report/?gclid=CNumq-zkvNACFdBMDQoddn4K6g.
26. Pew Research (2016b). Smartphone Ownership and Internet Usage Continues to Climb in Emerging Economies. http://www.pewglobal.org/2016/02/22/smartphone-ownership-and-internet-usage-continues-to-climb-in-emerging-economies/.
27. Hilbert, Martin (2016). The Bad News Is that the Digital Access Divide Is Here to Stay: Domestically Installed Bandwidths Among 172 Countriesfor 1986–2014. *Telecommunications Policy* 40: 567–581.
28. GSMA (2016). The Mobile Economy: Asia Pacific 2016. http://www.gsma.com/mobileeconomy/asiapacific/.
29. Waddington, Stephen (2015). Why China Leads the World in Digital Media. World Economic Forum, 8 September, https://www.weforum.org/agenda/2015/09/why-china-leads-the-world-in-digital-media/.
30. Jacobs, Andrew (2015). China Further Tightens Grip on the Internet*New York Times,* 29 January.
31. Gandhi, Rikin, Rajesh Veeraraghavan, Kentaro Toyama, and Vanaja Ramprasad (2009). Digital Green: Participatory Video and Mediated Instruction for Agricultural Extension, *Information Technologies and International Development* 5(1): 1–15. See also Chaps 6 and 10 in

Toyama, Kentaro (2015). *Geek Heresy: Rescuing Social Change from the Cult of Technology*, Public Affairs, Perseus Books Group.

32. Digital Green (2016). https://www.digitalgreen.org/about/. See also https://www.youtube.com/watch?v=JYkaf4ucaSc.
33. Kadiyala, Suneetha, Emily H. Morgan, Shruthi Cyriac, Amy Margolies, and Terry Roopnaraine (2016). Adapting Agriculture Platforms for Nutrition: A Case Study of a Participatory, Video-Based Agricultural Extension Platform in India, *PLOS ONE*, 13 October, 1–23. 10.1371/journal.pone.0164002.
34. One Laptop Per Child (2016). OLPC website, http://one.laptop.org/about/mission; see also the videos at http://one.laptop.org/.
35. MIT Media Lab (2005). The $100 Laptop. From the Wayback Machine's archive, http://web.archive.org/web/20050324163700/http://laptop.media.mit.edu/.
36. Mejia, Francisco (2014). Laptops, Children, and Darth Vader. http://blogs.iadb.org/desarrolloefectivo_en/2014/09/19/laptops-children-darth-vader/. A report on the entire project from key participants, which details its vision, successes, challenges, and failures, is Bender, Walter, Charles Kane, Jody Cornish, and Neal Donahue (2012). *Learning to Change the World: The Social Impact of One Laptop Per Child*, Palgrave Macmillan.
37. OLPC (2014). Goodbye One Laptop Per Child. http://www.olpcnews.com/about_olpc_news/goodbye_one_laptop_per_child.html.
38. Kraemer, Kenneth L., Jason Dedrick, and Prakul Sharma (2009). One Laptop Per Child: Vision vs. Reality, *Communications of the ACM* 52(6): 66–73, 10.1145/1516046.1516063. See also Warschauer, Mark and Morgan Ames (2010). Can One Laptop Per Child Save the World's Poor, *Journal of International Affairs* 64(1).
39. Hirji, Zehra, Barbara Barry, Robert Fadel, and Shannon Gavin (2010). Assessment Overview of One Laptop Per Child Projects. One Laptop Per Child Foundation Learning Group. http://wiki.laptop.org/images/2/24/OLPCF_M%26E_Publication.pdf.
40. Cristia, Julián P., Pablo Ibarrarán, Santiago Cueto, Ana Santiago, and Eugenio Severín (2012). Technology and Child Development: Evidence from the One Laptop per Child Program, IDB Working Paper No. IDB-WP-304.
41. Hirji, Zehra, Barbara Barry, Robert Fadel, and Shannon Gavin (2010). Assessment Overview of One Laptop Per Child Projects. One Laptop Per Child Foundation Learning Group. http://wiki.laptop.org/images/2/24/OLPCF_M%26E_Publication.pdf. See also Pittaluga, Lucia and Ana Rivoir (2012). One Laptop per Child and Bridging the Digital Divide: The Case of Plan CEIBAL in Uruguay, *Information Technologies & International Development* 8(4) (Special Bilingual Issue: Research on ICT4D from Latin America): 145–159. See also De Melo, Gioia, Alina Machado, Alfonso Miranda, and Magdalena Viera (2013). Profundizando en los efectos del Plan Ceibal (Exploring the Effects of the Plan Ceibal). Report from Instituto de Economía—FCEyA—UdelaR, Centro de Investigación y Docencia Económicas (CIDE)—México. http://fcea.edu.uy/Jornadas_Academicas/2013/file/MESAS/Economia%20de%20la%20educacion_plan%20ceibal/Profundizando%20en%20los%20efectos%20del%20Plan%20Ceibal.pdf.
42. Zuckerberg, Mark (2013). Is Connectivity a Human Right? White Paper. https://scontent.fybz1-1.fna.fbcdn.net/t39.2365-6/12057105_1001874746531417_622371037_n.pdf (but since then this document has been removed by Facebook).
43. Zuckerberg, Mark (2014). Keynote speech at Mobile World Congress. http://singjupost.com/mark-zuckerberg-keynote-mwc-2014-transcript-full/.

44. Deloitte (2015). Facebook's Global Economic Impact: A Report for Facebook. https://www2.deloitte.com/content/dam/Deloitte/uk/Documents/technology-media-telecommunications/deloitte-uk-global-economic-impact-of-facebook.pdf.
45. Constine, Josh (2016). Facebook Has Connected 40M People with Internet.org. https://techcrunch.com/2016/11/02/omnipresent/.
46. Bhatia, Rahul (2016). The Long Read: The Inside Story of Facebook's Greatest Setback, *The Guardian*, 12 May. https://www.theguardian.com/technology/2016/may/12/facebook-free-basics-india-zuckerberg.
47. Toyama, Kentaro (2015). *Geek Heresy: Rescuing Social Change from the Cult of Technology*, Public Affairs, Perseus Books Group.
48. Sam, Steven (2017). Towards an Empowerment Framework for Evaluating Mobile Phone Use and Impact in Developing Countries, *Telematics and Informatics* 34(1): 359–369.
49. Ahmed, S. I., S. J. Jackson, M. Zaber, M. B. Morshed, M. H. B. Ismail, and S. Afrose (2013). Ecologies of Use and Design: Individual and Social Uses of Mobile Phones Within Low-Literate Rickshaw-Puller Communities in Urban Bangladesh, *Proc. ACM DEV'13*, 14:1–14:10. See also Ahmed, S. I., M. H. Zaber, M. B. Morshed, M. H. B. Ismail, D. Cosley, and S. J. Jackson (2015). *Suhrid*: A Collaborative Mobile Phone Interface for Low Literate People, *Proc. ACM DEV'15*, 95–103.
50. Howard, Philip N., Sheetal D. Agarwal, and Muzammil M. Hussain (2011). The Dictators' Digital Dilemma: When Do States Disconnect Their Digital Networks. *Issues in Technology Innovation* 13. https://www.brookings.edu/research/the-dictators-digital-dilemma-when-do-states-disconnect-their-digital-networks/. See also West, Darrell M. (2016). Internet Shutdowns Cost Countries $2.4 Billion Last Year. https://www.brookings.edu/research/internet-shutdowns-cost-countries-2-4-billion-last-year/.
51. Ritzen, Yarno (2018). Rising Internet Shutdowns Aimed at 'Silencing Dissent', AlJazeera, 29 January. See also Dahir, Abdi Latif (2017). Internet Shutdowns Are Costing African Governments More than We Thought. https://qz.com/1089749/internet-shutdowns-are-increasingly-taking-a-toll-on-africas-economies/.
52. AccessNow and the Internet Society (2018). Joint Statement: Let's #SwitchItOn and #KeepitOn! https://www.accessnow.org/switchiton-and-keepiton/.
53. Resolution of the Human Rights Council of the United Nations (2016). http://un.org/doc/UNDOC/LTD/G16/131/89/pdf/G1613189.pdf?OpenElement.
54. IDRC (2016). The Three Dimensions of Inclusive Design. Inclusive Design Research Centre (IDRC), OCAD University. http://idrc.ocadu.ca/index.php/resources/idrc-online/library-of-papers/443-whatisinclusivedesign.
55. WHO (2014). Visual Impairment and Blindness. Fact Sheet, updated August 2014. http://www.who.int/mediacentre/factsheets/fs282/en/.
56. Dobbs, David (2016). Why There's New Hope About Ending Blindness, *National Geographic*, September.
57. AFB (2016). Technology Resources for People with Vision Loss. American Foundation for the Blind. http://www.afb.org/info/living-with-vision-loss/using-technology/12. See also SNOW (2016). Technology for Accessibility. Special Needs Opportunity Window, IDRC, OCAD University. http://www.snow.idrc.ocad.ca/.
58. Lazar, Jonathan, Aaron Allen, Jason Kleinman, and Chris Malarkey (2007). What Frustrates Screen Reader Users on the Web: A Study of 100 Blind Users. *Int. Journal of Human–Computer Interaction* 22(3): 247–269.

59. Leporino, Barbara and Fabio Paterno (2004). Increasing Usability when Interacting through Screen Readers, *Universal Access in the Information Society* 3: 57–70.
60. BlindSquare (2017). http://www.blindsquare.com. See also the description of Wearwork's novel Wearband technology being used by a blind runner in a marathon (Longman, Jeff (2017). Blind Runner's Wearable Technology Gets Off to Complicated Start, *New York Times*, 5 November).
61. WHO (2015). Deafness and Hearing Loss. Fact Sheet, updated March 2015. http://www.who.int/mediacentre/factsheets/fs300/en/.
62. Henshaw, Helen, Daniel P. A. Clark, Sujin Kang, and Melanie A. Ferguson (2012). Computer Skills and Internet Use in Adults Aged 50–74 Years: Influence of Hearing Difficulties, *J Med Internet Res* 14(4), 10.2196/jmir.2036.
63. Ketabdar, Hamed and Tim Polzehl (2009). Tactile and Visual Alerts for Deaf People by Mobile Phones, *Proc. ASSETS'09*, 253–254, Association for Computing Machinery (ACM.)
64. Ahmed, Aisha Shamsuna and Daniel Su Kuen Seong (2006). SignWriting on Mobile Phones for the Deaf, *Proc. Mobiity 2006*, 25–27 October, Bangkok, Thailand, ACM.
65. Cavender, Anna, Richard E. Ladner, and Eve A. Riskin (2006). MobileASL: Intelligibility of Sign Language Video as Constrained by Mobile Phone Technology, *Proc. Assets 2006*, 71–78, ACM. See also Kim, Joy, Jessica J. Tran, Tressa W. Johnson, Richard Ladner, Eve Riskin, and Jacob O. Wobbrock (2011). Effect of MobileASL on Communication Among Deaf Users, *Proc. CHI 2011*, 2185–2190, ACM 978-1-4503-0268-5/11/05. See also Tran, Jessica J., Joy Kim, Jaehong Chong, Eve A. Riskin, Richard E. Ladner, and Jacob O. Wobbrock (2011). Evaluating Quality and Comprehension of Real-Time Sign Language Video on Mobile Phones, *Proc. ASSETS'11*, 115–122, ACM 978-1-4503-00919-6/11/10.
66. Disabled-World.com (2016). Cognitive Disability: Information on Intellectual Disabilities. https://www.disabled-world.com/disability/types/cognitive/.
67. Kientz, Julie A., Matthew S. Goodwin, Gillian R. Hayes, and Gregory D. Abowd (2014). *Interactive Technologies for Autism*. Synthesis Lectures on Assistive, Rehabilitative, and Health-Preserving Technologies, Morgan & Claypool.
68. Turnbull, Ann E., Rutherford Turnbull, Michael L. Wehmeyer, and Karrie A. Shogren (2014). *Exceptional Lives: Special Education in Today's Schools, Enhance Pearson eText – Access Card*, 8th Edition, Pearson.
69. Vanderheiden, Gregg C., Jutta Treviranus, and Amrish Chourasia (2013). The Global Public Inclusive Infrastructure (GPII). *Proc. ASSETS'13*, ACM.
70. Herring, S. C. (1993). Gender and Democracy in Computer-Mediated Communication. *Electronic Journal of Communication* 3(2), http://ella.slis.indiana.edu/~herring/ejc.doc. See also Herring, S. C. (1996). Bringing Familiar Baggage to the New Frontier: Gender Differences in Computer-Mediated Communication. In Selzer, J. (Ed.), *Conversations*, 1069–1082, Allyn & Bacon. http://ella.slis.indiana.edu/~herring/conversations.1996.pdf. See also Herring, S. C. (1999). Posting in a Different Voice: Gender and Ethics in Computer-Mediated Communication. In Mayer, P. A. (Ed.), *Computer Media and Communication: A Reader*, 241–265, Oxford University Press. http://ella.slis.indiana.edu/~herring/gender.ethics.1999.pdf. See also Herring, S. C. and S. Stoerger (2014). Gender and (A)nonymity in Computer-Mediated Communication. In Ehrlich, S., M. Meyerhoff, and J. Holmes (Eds.) (2014). *The Handbook of Language, Gender, and Sexuality*, 2nd Edition, 567–586, John Wiley & Sons. Prepublication version: http://ella.slis.indiana.edu/~herring/herring.stoerger.pdf.

71. Li, Nai and Gill Kirkup (2007). Gender and Cultural Differences in Internet Use: A Study of China and the UK, *Computers & Education* 48: 301–317.
72. Williams, Dmitri, Nicole Martins, Mia Consalvo, and James D. Ivory (2009). The Virtual Census: Representations of Gender, Race and Age in Video Games, *New Media & Society* 11(5): 815–834. For some typical portrayals of women in video games, see https://www.appnova.com/video-games-marketing-women/.
73. Dietz, Tracy L. (1998). An Examination of Violence and Gender Role Portrayals in Video Games: Implications for Gender Socialization and Aggressive Behavior, *Sex Roles* 38(5/6): 425–442.
74. Hartmann, Tilo and Cristoph Klimt (2006). Gender and Computer Games: Exploring Females' Dislikes, *Journal of Computer-Mediated Communication* 11: 910–931.
75. Computer Science (2017). Women in Computer Science: Getting Involved in STEM. http://www.computerscience.org/resources/women-in-computer-science/.
76. National Center for Women & Information Technology (2017). NCWIT website. https://www.ncwit.org/.
77. Ensmenger, Nathan (2010). Making Programming Masculine. In Misa, Thomas (Ed.) (2010). *Gender Codes: Women and Men in the Computing Professions*, John Wiley & Sons, 115-142.
78. Misa, Thomas J. (Ed.) (2010). *Gender Codes: Why Women are Leaving Computing*. IEEE Computer Society, John Wiley & Sons.
79. Larson, Selana (2014). Why So Few Women are Studying Computer Science. http://readwrite.com/2014/09/02/women-in-computer-science-why-so-few/.
80. Fisher, Allan and Jane Margolis (2002). Unlocking the Clubhouse: The Carnegie Mellon Experience, *SIGCSE Bulletin* 34(2): 79–83.
81. Klawe, Maria (2013). Increasing Female Participation in Computing: The Harvey Mudd College Story, *IEEE Computer* 46(3): 56–58.
82. Grace Hopper Celebration of Women in Computing (2017). www.gracehopper.org.
83. Alter, Alexandra (2017). Teaching Kids Coding, by the Book, *New York Times,* 21 August. (Of particular interest here is the Girls Who Code publishing venture.) See also Tell, Caroline (2018). Karlie Kloss Teaches Teenage Girls How to Code, *New York Times,* 16 March.
84. Klawe, Maria, Telle Whitney, and Caroline Simard (2009). Women in Computing—Take 2, *Communications of the ACM* 52(2): 68–76. 10.1145/1461928.1461947.
85. Tam, Pui Wing (2018). How Silicon Valley Came to Be a Land of 'Bros', *New York Times,* 5 February.
86. Miller, Claire Cain (2017). Tech's Damaging Myth of the Loner Genius Nerd, *New York Times,* 12 August.
87. Wingfield, Nick (2017). The Culture Wars Have Come to Silicon Valley, *New York Times,* 8 August.
88. Pao, Ellen (2017). Has Anything Really Changed for Women in Tech? *New York Times,* 16 September. See also Williams, Bärí A. (2017). Tech's Troubling New Trend: Diversity Is in Your Head, *New York Times,* 16 October.
89. AGE-WELL (2016). http://agewell-nce.ca/about-us.
90. UN (2015). World Population Aging. United Nations Department of Economic and Social Affairs, Population Division. http://www.un.org/en/development/desa/population/publications/pdf/ageing/WPA2015_Report.pdf.

91. Anderson, Monica and Andrew Perrin (2017). Tech Adoption Climbs Among Older Adults. Pew Research Center, 17 May. http://assets.pewresearch.org/wp-content/uploads/sites/14/2017/05/16170850/PI_2017.05.17_Older-Americans-Tech_FINAL.pdf.
92. *Ibid.*, p. 4.
93. National Seniors Council (2014). Report on the Social Isolation of Seniors. Government of Canada. https://www.canada.ca/content/dam/nsc-cna/documents/pdf/policy-and-program-development/publications-reports/2014/Report_on_the_Social_Isolation_of_Seniors.pdf.
94. Perissinotto, Carla M., Irena Stijacic Cenzer, and Kenneth E. Covinsky (2012). Loneliness in Older Persons: A Predictor of Functional Decline and Death, *Archives of Internal Medicine* 172(14): 1078–1083.
95. Baecker, R. M., B. B. Neves, K. Sellen, S. Crosskey, and V. Boscart (2014). Technology to Reduce Social Isolation and Loneliness,. *Proc. ACM ASSETS,* 27–34; see also the video of this system at https://www.dropbox.com/s/ht8t2dx6pq7zpiv/FamliNet%201%20minute%20March%209%202016.mov?dl=0 and the website of the start-up developing and marketing the technology, http://famli.net.
96. Aging in Place Technology Watch (2017). Wearable Tech and Older Adults—It's 2017—Moving Beyond PERS. https://www.ageinplacetech.com/blog/wearable-tech-and-older-adults-it-s-2017-moving-beyond-pers.
97. Fisk, Arthur D., Wendy A. Rogers, Neil Charness, Sara J. Czaja, and Joseph Sharit (2009). *Designing for Older Adults: Principles and Creative Human Factors Approaches,* 2nd Edition, CRC Press. See also Farage, Miranda A., Kenneth W. Miller, Funmi Ajayi, and Deborah Hutchins (2012). Design Principles to Accommodate Older Persons, *Global Journal of Health Science* 4(2). 10.5539/gjhs.v4n2p2.
98. Kurniawan, Sri and Panayiotis Zaphiris (2005). Research-Derived Web Design Guidelines for Older People, *Proc. Assets '05,* 129–135. See also Massimi, Michael, Ronald M. Baecker, and Michael Wu (2007). Using Participatory Activities with Seniors to Critique, Build, and Evaluate Mobile Phones, *Proc. Assets '07,* 155–162. 10.1145/1296843.1296871.
99. Pedlow, Robert, Devva Kasnitz, and Russell Shuttleworth (2010). Barriers to the Adoption of Cell Phones for Older People with Impairments in the USA: Results from an Expert Review and Field Study. *Technology and Disability* 22: 147–158.
100. National Council on Aging (2016). Healthy Aging Fact Sheet. https://www.ncoa.org/wp-content/uploads/Healthy-Aging-Fact-Sheet-final.pdf. This is US data, but similar patterns exist worldwide.
101. Olphert, Wendy and Leela Damodaran (2013). Older People and Digital Disengagement: A Fourth Digital Divide? *Gerontology* 59: 564–570. 10.1159/000353630.
102. AD International (2015). World Alzheimer Report 2015: The Global Impact of Dementia: An Analysis of Prevalence, Incidence, Cost and Trends. https://www.alz.co.uk/research/WorldAlzheimerReport2015.pdf.
103. Aging in Place Technology Watch (2017). For Boomers, There Is No Such Thing as Keeping Up with Tech Change. https://www.ageinplacetech.com/blog/boomers-there-no-such-thing-keeping-tech-change.
104. Manjoo, Fahrad (2018). We Have Reached Peak Screen. Now Revolution Is in the Air, *New York Times,* 27 June. See also Burrows, Peter (2018). The Future Is Hear: Why 'Hearables' Are Finally Tech's Next Big Thing, *Fast Company,* 2 August.
105. Keen, Andrew (2015). *The Internet is Not the Answer,* Atlantic Monthly Press, p. 218.

Chapter 2

1. Wikipedia (2017). Max Mathews. https://en.wikipedia.org/wiki/Max_Mathews.
2. Sutherland, Ivan E. (1963). Sketchpad: A Man-Machine Graphical Communication System. PhD Dissertation, Dept. of Electrical Engineering, MIT. https://dspace.mit.edu/handle/1721.1/14979#files-area.
3. Licklider, J. C. R. (1965). *Libraries of the Future*, The MIT Press.
4. Kahle, Brewster (1996). Archiving the Internet. Submitted on 4 November 1996 to *Scientific American*. Quoted text omitted from 1997 article. https://www.uibk.ac.at/voeb/texte/kahle.html.
5. Internet Archive and Wayback Machine (2017). https://archive.org/. For a relatively current discussion of the issues involved in preserving, or not preserving (in the case of material that one desires to purge), information published on the internet at some point in time, see Lepore, Jill (2015). The Cobweb: Can the Internet be Archived? *The New Yorker*, 26 January.
6. Wikipedia (2017). Project Gutenberg. https://en.wikipedia.org/wiki/Project_Gutenberg.
7. Wikipedia (2017). Google Books. https://en.wikipedia.org/wiki/Google_Books.
8. Stallman, Richard (1983). Initial Announcement [of the GNU Project]. https://www.gnu.org/gnu/initial-announcement.en.html.
9. WIPO (2017). What Is Intellectual Property? World Intellectual Property Office. http://www.wipo.int/about-ip/en/. See also Wikipedia (2017). Intellectual Property. https://en.wikipedia.org/wiki/Intellectual_property. See also Brandon, Jonas (2011). Intellectual Property Strategy. Lecture Notes, Presented in University of Toronto Business of Software Course on 25 November.
10. Wikipedia (2017). Copyright. https://en.wikipedia.org/wiki/Copyright.
11. Bach, David (2004). The Double Punch of Law and Technology: Fighting Music Piracy or Remaking Copyright in a Digital Age? *Business and Politics* 6(2): Article 3.
12. Columbia University Libraries (2017). Fair Use Checklist. https://copyright.columbia.edu/basics/fair-use/fair-use-checklist.html. See also Nolo.com (2017). The 'Fair Use' Rule: When Use of Copyrighted Material Is Acceptable. http://www.nolo.com/legal-encyclopedia/fair-use-rule-copyright-material-30100.html. See also Wikipedia (2017). Copyright Act of 1976. https://en.wikipedia.org/wiki/Copyright_Act_of_1976.
13. Computer and Communications Industry Association (2017). Fair Use in the U.S. Economy: Economic Contribution of Industries Relying on Fair Use. https://www.ccianet.org/wp-content/uploads/2017/06/Fair-Use-in-the-U.S.-Economy-2017.pdf.
14. Wikipedia (2017). MP3. https://en.wikipedia.org/wiki/MP3.
15. Wikipedia (2017). Peer-to-peer file sharing. https://en.wikipedia.org/wiki/Peer-to-peer_file_sharing.
16. Wikipedia (2017). Napster. https://en.wikipedia.org/wiki/Napster. See also a screen shot from an early (October 1999) Napster home page https://web.archive.org/web/19991008215720/http://napster.com/.
17. Baase, Sara (2013). A Gift of Fire: Social, Legal, and Ethical Issues for Computing Technology, 4th Edition, Pearson, pp. 189, 194.
18. Bonner, Steven and Eleanor O'Higgins (2010). Music Piracy: Ethical Perspectives. *Management Decision* 48(9): 1341–1354.

19. Wingrove, Twila, Angela L. Korpas, and Victoria Weisz (2011). Why Were Millions of People Not Obeying the Law? Motivational Influences on Non-Compliance with the Law in the Case of Music Piracy, *Psychology, Crime & Law* 17(3): 261–276.

20. Robertson, Kirsten, Lisa McNeill, James Green, and Claire Roberts (2012). Illegal Downloading, Ethical Concern, and Illegal Behavior, *J Bus Ethics* 108: 215–227.

21. Chiou, Jyh-Shen, Chien-yi Huang, and Hsin-hui Lee (2006). The Antecedents of Music Piracy Attitudes and Intentions, *Journal of Business Ethics* 57: 161–174.

22. Wikipedia (2017). Digital rights management. https://en.wikipedia.org/wiki/Digital_rights_management.

23. Layton, Julia (2017). How Digital Rights Management Works. http://computer.howstuffworks.com/drm.htm.

24. Quinn, Michael J. (2017). *Ethics for the Information Age*, 7th Edition, Pearson, pp. 187–188.

25. Wolfe, Scott E., George E. Higgins, and Catherine D. Marcum (2008). Deterrence and Digital Piracy: A Preliminary Examination of the Role of Viruses, *Social Science Computer Review* 26(3): 317–333.

26. Frost, Robert L. (2017). Rearchitecting the Music Business: Mitigating Music Piracy by Cutting Out the Record Companies, *First Monday* 12(8). http://firstmonday.org/article/view/1975.

27. Lametti, David (2011). The Virtuous P(eer): Reflections on the Ethics of File Sharing. In Lever, Annabelle (Ed.), *New Frontiers in the Philosophy of Intellectual Property*, Cambridge University Press.

28. Cammaerts, Bart (2011). The Hegemonic Copyright-Regime vs. the Sharing Copyright Users of Music? *Media, Culture & Society* 33(3): 491–502.

29. Lessig, Lawrence (2004). *Free Culture*, Public Domain Books. http://www.free-culture.cc/freeculture.pdf. See also Koman, Richard (2005). Remixing Culture: An Interview with Lawrence Lessig. O'Reilly Media. http://archive.oreilly.com/pub/a/policy/2005/02/24/lessig.html. See also Lessig, Lawrence (2007). Laws that Choke Creativity. TED TALKS, March. https://www.ted.com/talks/larry_lessig_says_the_law_is_strangling_creativity/transcript?language=en.

30. Sinha, Rajiv K. Fernando S. Machado, and Collin Sellman (2010). Don't Think Twice, It's All Right: Music Piracy and Pricing in a DRM-Free Environment, *Journal of Marketing* 74: 40–54.

31. Quinn, Michael J. (2017). *Ethics for the Information Age*, 7th Edition, Pearson, p. 189. See also Bostic, Kevin (2013). Apple's iTunes Rules Digital Music Market with 63% Share, *Apple Insider*, 16 April.

32. Reisinger, Don (2016). No, Apple Isn't Killing Off iTunes Music Downloads, *Fortune.com*, 12 May. http://fortune.com/2016/05/12/apple-itunes-music-downloads/. See also Seitz, Patrick (2017). Apple Music, Spotify Lead in Streaming Tunes, But It's Early Days, *Investors Business Daily*, 4 February. http://www.investors.com/news/technology/spotify-apple-music-lead-in-streaming-tunes-but-its-early-days/. For an interesting history of Spotify, see Lidsky, David (2018). The Definitive Timeline of Spotify's Critic-Defying Journey to Rule Music, *Fast Company*, 6 August.

33. David, Matthew (2013). Cultural, Legal, Technical, and Economic Perspectives on Copyright Online: The Case of the Music Industry. In Dutton, William (Ed.), *The Oxford Handbook of Internet Studies*. http://www.oxfordhandbooks.com/view/10.1093/oxfordhb/9780199589074.001.0001/oxfordhb-9780199589074-e-22.

34. Lessig, Lawrence (2004). *Free Culture: How Big Media Uses Technology and the Law to Lock Down Culture and Control Creativity.* Available at http://www.free-culture.cc/freeculture.pdf.

35. Lessig, Lawrence (2006). *Code, Version 2,* Basic Books. Available at http://codev2.cc/download+remix/Lessig-Codev2.pdf. Lessig's books range widely over topics including especially issues discussed in Chapters 2, 5, and 9, so can be read with respect to any one of those chapters.

36. OECD (2008). Piracy of Digital Content. Organization for Economic Co-operation and Development. http://www.oecd.org/sti/consumer/piracyofdigitalcontent.htm.

37. Yar, Majid (2005). The Global 'Epidemic' of Movie 'Piracy': Crimewave or Social Construction? *Media, Culture & Society* 27(5): 677–696. See also Walls, W. D. (2008). Cross-Country Analysis of Movie Piracy, *Applied Economics* 40: 625–632.

38. Ma, Liye, Alan L. Montgomery, Param Vir Singh, and Michael D. Smith (2014). An Empirical Analysis of the Impact of Pre-Release Movie Piracy on Box Office Revenue, *Information Systems Research* 25(3): 90–603.

39. Wikipedia (2017). MGM Studios, Inc. v. Grokster, Ltd. https://en.wikipedia.org/wiki/MGM_Studios,_Inc._v._Grokster,_Ltd.

40. YouTube (2018). https://www.youtube.com/results?search_query=Ron+Baecker.

41. Spinello, Richard A. (2008). Intellectual Property: Legal and Moral Challenges of Online File Sharing. In Himma, Kenneth Einar and Herman T. Tavani (Eds.), *The Handbook of Information and Computer Ethics*, Wiley-Interscience.

42. Quinn, Michael J. (2017). *Ethics for the Information Age*, 7th Edition, Pearson, pp. 194–196.

43. Wikipedia (2017). YouTube. https://en.wikipedia.org/wiki/YouTube.

44. Klosowski, Thorin (2013). Why I Stopped Pirating and Started Paying for Media. 14 March. http://lifehacker.com/5990525/why-i-stopped-pirating-and-started-paying-for-media.

45. Karaganis, Joe and Jennifer Urban (2015). The Rise of the Robo Notice. *Communications of the ACM* 58(9): 28–30. 10.1145/2804244.

46. Jones, Ben (2014). Why YouTube's Automated Copyright Takedown System Hurts Artists. https://torrentfreak.com/why-youtubes-automated-copyright-takedown-system-hurts-artists-140223/.

47. Urban, Jennifer M., Joe Karaganis, and Brianna L. Schofield (2017). Notice and Takedown in Everyday Practice. Berkeley Law and Columbia University. https://papers.ssrn.com/sol3/papers.cfm?abstract_id=2755628.

48. Wikipedia (2017). Lenz v. Universal Music Corp. https://en.wikipedia.org/wiki/Lenz_v._Universal_Music_Corp.

49. Sullivan, Danny (2015). US Court Ruling Doesn't Mean End to Automatic Takedown Notices over Copyright. http://marketingland.com/us-court-ruling-automatic-takedown-notices-over-copyright-142499.

50. Fichtner, J. Royce and Troy J. Strader (2011). Automated Takedown Notices and their Potential to Generate Liability under Section 512(f) of the Digital Millennium Copyright Act, *Journal of Intellectual Property Law & Practice* 6(1): 51–59.

51. Advice to filmmakers on how to proceed, if their videos are removed from YouTube, appears in EFF (2017). A Guide to YouTube Removals. Electronic Freedom Foundation. https://www.eff.org/issues/intellectual-property/guide-to-youtube-removals.

52. Boone, Christine Emily (2011). Mashups: History, Legality, and Aesthetics. PhD Dissertation, University of Texas at Austin.

53. YouTube (2005). Bush Blair Endless Love. https://www.youtube.com/watch?v=UtEH6wZXPA4.

54. Lessig, Lawrence (2008). *Remix: Making Art and Commerce Thrive in the Hybrid Economy,* Penguin Press.

55. Katz, Michael (2008). Recycling Copyright: Survival and Growth in the Remix Age, *Univ. San Francisco School of Law Intellectual Property Law Bulletin.* https://works.bepress.com/michael_katz/2/.

56. Eble, Kerri (2013). This Is a Remix: Remixing Music Copyright to Better Protect Mashup Artists, *U. Ill. L. Rev. 2013(2)*: 661–694.

57. Gerber, Robert S. (2006). Mixing It Up on the Web: Legal Issues Arising from Internet 'Mashups', *Intellectual Property & Technology Law Journal* 18(8). https://www.sheppardmullin.com/media/article/188_pub596.pdf.

58. Cusker, Jeremy (2016). Online Textbook Piracy: A Literature Review, *Issues in Science and Technology Librarianship,* Spring.

59. GAO (2013). Students Have Greater Access to Textbook Information. GAO-13-368. US General Accounting Office. http://www.gao.gov/assets/660/655066.pdf.

60. Perry, Mark J. (2015). The New Era of the $400 College Textbook, Which Is Part of the Unsustainable Higher Education Bubble. American Enterprise Institute. http://www.aei.org/publication/the-new-era-of-the-400-college-textbook-which-is-part-of-the-unsustainable-higher-education-bubble/.

61. Rebelo, Francisca (2015). Understanding Textbook Piracy. Unpublished manuscript. http://www.apdr.pt/pej2015/papers/18.pdf.

62. Koch, James V. (2014). An Economic Analysis of the Market for Textbooks: Current Conditions, New Developments and Policy Options. Presentation slides, The Future of the Textbook, Univ. of Georgia Center for Continuing Education, 11 December. http://affordablelearninggeorgia.org/documents/Koch_Plenary1.pdf.

63. Digimarc (2017). E-Book Piracy Costs Publishers $315 Million in Lost Sales. Press Release. http://www.prnewswire.com/news-releases/e-book-piracy-costs-publishers-315-million-in-lost-sales-300423534.html.

64. Penn, Joanna (2017). Publishing Tip: Why Authors Shouldn't Worry About Piracy. https://www.thecreativepenn.com/2017/02/23/piracy/.

65. Carmody, Tim (2012). Why Education Publishing Is Big Business, *Wired,* 19 January.

66. Band, Jonathan (2013). The Changing Textbook Industry. Disruptive Competition Project. http://www.project-disco.org/competition/112113-the-changing-textbook-industry/#.WUbz0sYZMtM63.

67. Cheng, Jacqui (2013). Apple Follows Amazon with Patent for Resale of e-Books, Music, *Ars Technica,* 8 March. https://arstechnica.com/apple/2013/03/apple-follows-amazon-with-patent-for-resale-of-e-books-music/.

68. Benson-Armer, Richard, Jimmy Sarakatsannis, and Ken Wee (2014). The Future of Textbooks. McKinsey&Company, August. http://www.mckinsey.com/industries/social-sector/our-insights/the-future-of-textbooks.

69. Baker, Judy, Joel Thierstein, Kathi Fletcher, Manpreet Kaur, and Jonathan Emmons (2011). Open Textbook Proof-of-Concept via Connexions, *International Review of Research in Open and Distance Learning* 10(5).

70. Wiley, David, John Hilton III, Shelley Ellington, and Tiffany Hall (2012). A Preliminary Examination of the Cost Savings and Learning Impacts of Using Open Textbooks in Middle

and High School Science Classes, *International Review of Research in Open and Distance Learning* 13(3): 261–276.

71. Hilton III, John Levi and David Wiley (2011). Open Access Textbooks and Financial Sustainability: A Case Study on Flat World Knowledge, *The International Review of Research in Open and Distributed Learning* 12(5): 18–26.

72. Willinsky, John (2006). *The Access Principle: The Case for Open Access to Research and Scholarship*, MIT Press.

73. Ghosh, S. B. and Anup Kumar Das (2007). Open Access and Institutional Repositories – A Developing Country Perspective: a Case Study of India, *IFLA Journal* 33(3): 229–250. 10.1177/0340035207083304.

74. Wikipedia (2017). Journal of Medical Internet Research. https://en.wikipedia.org/wiki/Journal_of_Medical_Internet_Research. See also Journal of Medical Internet Research (2018). Home page. https://www.jmir.org/.

75. Björk, Bo-Christer (2004). Open access to scientific publications—an analysis of the barriers to change? *Information Research* 9(2).

76. Björk, B.-C., P. Welling, M. Laakso, P. Majlender, T. Hedlund, and G. Guðnason (2010). Open Access to the Scientific Journal Literature: Situation 2009, *PLoS ONE* 5(6): e11273. 10.1371/journal.pone.0011273.

77. Nassi-Calò, Lilian (2013). How Much Does it Cost to Publish in Open Access? *SciELO in Perspective*, 18 September. http://blog.scielo.org/en/2013/09/18/how-much-does-it-cost-to-publish-in-open-access/#.WUgbq8YZN8I.

78. Björk, Bo-Christer (2017). Open Access to Scientific Articles: A Review of Benefits and Challenges, *Intern Emerg Med* 12: 247–253.

79. Van Noorden, Richard (2013). Open Access: The True Cost of Science Publishing, *Nature*, 27 March.

80. Antelman, Kristin (2004). Do Open-Access Articles Have a Greater Research Impact? *College & Research Libraries* 65(5). http://crl.acrl.org/index.php/crl/article/view/15683/17129.

81. Hajjem, Chawki, Stevan Harnad, and Yves Gingras (2005). Ten-Year Cross-Disciplinary Comparison of the Growth of Open Access and How it Increases Research Citation Impact, *IEEE Data Engineering Bulletin* 28(4): 39–47.

82. Eysenbach, Gunther (2006). Citation Advantage of Open Access Articles, *PLoS Biol* 4(5): e157.

83. Craig, Iain D., Andrew M. Plume, Marie E. McVeigh, James Pringle, and Mayur Amin (2007). Do Open Access Articles Have Greater Citation Impact? A Critical Review of the Literature, *Journal of Informetrics* 1: 239–248.

84. Björk, Bo-Christer (2017). Open Access to Scientific Articles: A Review of Benefits and Challenges, *Intern Emerg Med* 12: 247–253.

85. Kimbrough, Julie L. and Laura N. Gasaway (2015). Publication of Government-Funded Research, Open Access, and the Public Interest. University of North Carolina School of Law Carolina Law Scholarship Repository. http://scholarship.law.unc.edu/cgi/viewcontent.cgi?-article=1010&context=faculty_publications.

86. Quinn, Gene (2014). The History of Software Patents in the United States. IPWatchdog.com. http://www.ipwatchdog.com/2014/11/30/the-history-of-software-patents-in-the-united-states/id=52256/.

87. Bessen, James and Robert M. Hunt (2007). An Empirical Look at Software Patents, *Journal of Economics and Management Strategy* 16(1): 157–189.

88. Mulligan, Christina and Timothy B. Lee (2012). Scaling the Patent System, 68 *N.Y.U. Ann. Surv. Am. L.* 289. http://digitalcommons.law.uga.edu/cgi/viewcontent.cgi?article=1911&context=fac_artchop.

89. Brachmann, Steve (2017). IBM Achieves Record Number of U.S. Patents in 2016, 24th Straight Year of Patent Dominance, *IPWatchdog.com*. http://www.ipwatchdog.com/2017/01/09/ibm-record-number-u-s-patents-2016/id=76709/.

90. Morris, Ian (2017). Amazon's Multi-Billion Dollar Patent Expires In 2017, *Forbes*, 2 January.

91. Decker, Susan (2016). When a Tech Patent Is Neither, *TheBloombergApp*, 17 August. https://www.bloomberg.com/news/articles/2016-08-17/why-hundreds-of-software-patents-are-being-thrown-out.

92. Freeman, Eric and David H. Gelernter (1999). Document Stream Operating System. U.S. Patent 6,006,227. 21 Dec. 1999.

93. Helft, Miguel and John Schwartz (2010). Apple Challenges Big Award Over Patents, *New York Times*, 4 October.

94. US Court of Appeals for the Federal Circuit (2012). Mirror World, LLC v. Apple, Inc. 2011–1392. Decided 4 Sept. 2012.

95. Bessen, James (2004). Patent Thickets: Strategic Patenting of Complex Technologies. Research on Innovation Working Paper. https://papers.ssrn.com/sol3/Papers.cfm?abstract_id=327760.

96. Mann, Ronald J. (2005). Do Patents Facilitate Financing in the Software Industry? *Tex L. Rev.* 83(4): 961–1031. See also Mann, Ronald J. and Thomas W. Sager (2007). Patents, Venture Capital, and Software Start-ups, *Research Policy* 36: 193–208.

97. Bessen, Jim (2013). Op-ed: How Patent Trolls Doomed Themselves by Targeting Main Street, *ArsTechnica.com*, 12 September. https://arstechnica.com/tech-policy/2013/09/op-ed-how-patent-trolls-doomed-themselves-by-targeting-main-street/.

98. Bessen, James, Jennifer Ford, and Michael J. Meurer (2011). The Private and Social Costs of Patent Trolls, *Regulation*, Winter 2011–2012, 26–35.

99. Frieswick, Kris (2013). The Real Toll of Patent Trolls, *Inc.com*, 13 December. https://www.inc.com/magazine/201202/kris-frieswick/patent-troll-toll-on-businesses.html.

100. Downes, Larry (2017). The U.S. Supreme Court Is Reining in Patent Trolls, Which Is a Win for Innovation, *Harvard Business Review*, 2 June. https://hbr.org/2017/06/the-u-s-supreme-court-is-reining-in-patent-trolls-which-is-a-win-for-innovation.

101. Liptak, Adam (2018). Supreme Court Upholds Procedure That's Said to Combat 'Patent Trolls', *New York Times*, 24 April.

102. GNU Operating System (2017). The Free Software Definition. https://www.gnu.org/philosophy/free-sw.en.html.

103. Wikipedia (2017). Linux. https://en.wikipedia.org/wiki/Linux.

104. Raymond, Eric (1998). The Cathedral and the Bazaar, *First Monday* 3(3), 2 March. http://firstmonday.org/article/view/578/499.

105. Moglen, Eben (2003). Freeing the Mind: Free Software and the Death of Proprietary Culture. Keynote Address, University of Maine Law School's Fourth Annual Technology and Law Conference, 29 June. http://moglen.law.columbia.edu/publications/maine-speech.html. Several other scholarly publications discuss the open source software movement in the context of the larger open access movement. See Lessig, Lawrence (2002). The Architecture of

Innovation, *Duke Law Journal* 15: 1783–1801; Benkler, Yochai (2003). *Coase's Penguin*, or, *Linux* and The Nature of the Firm, *Yale Law Journal* 112: 369–441; Boyle, James (2003). The Second Enclosure Movement and the Construction of the Public Domain, *Law and Contemporary Problems* 66: 33–74; and Lessig, Lawrence (2006). *Code: Version 2*, Basic Books, retrieved on 20 April 2018 from http://codev2.cc.

106. Bessen, James (2005). Open Source Software: Free Provision of Complex Public Goods. https://papers.ssrn.com/sol3/papers.cfm?abstract_id=588763.
107. Fitzgerald, Brian (2006). The Transformation of Open Source Software. *MIS Quarterly* 30(3): 587–598.
108. O'Reilly (2017). O'Reilly Software Development Survey. https://www.oreilly.com/ideas/2017-software-development-salary-survey.
109. Rivlin, Gary (2005). Open Wallets for Open-Source Software, *New York Times*, 27 April. See also Nicastro, Dorn (2018). 6 Things to Know About IBM's 34B Acquisition of Red Hat, *CMS Wire*, 31 October. https://www.cmswire.com/information-management/6-things-to-know-about-ibms-34b-acquisition-of-red-hat/.
110. Raymond, Eric (2004). The Luxury of Ignorance: An Open-Source Horror Story. http://www.catb.org/~esr/writings/cups-horror.html.
111. Nichols, David M. and Michael B. Twidale (2003). The Usability of Open Source Software, *First Monday* 8(1), January. http://firstmonday.org/article/view/1018/939. See also Hall, Jim (2014). It's about the User: Applying Usability in Open-Source Software, *Linux Journal*, 18 February. http://www.linuxjournal.com/content/its-about-user-applying-usability-open-source-software.
112. Heath, Nick (2013). Six Open Source Security Myths Debunked—and Eight Real Challenges to Consider. ZDNet, 23 April. http://www.zdnet.com/article/six-open-source-security-myths-debunked-and-eight-real-challenges-to-consider/. See also Wikipedia (2017). Open-source Software Security. https://en.wikipedia.org/wiki/Open-source_software_security.
113. Creative Commons (2017). Creative Commons. https://creativecommons.org. See alsom, for one form of the license, https://creativecommons.org/licenses/by/4.0/.

Chapter 3

1. Wikipedia (2016). Educational technology. https://en.wikipedia.org/wiki/Educational_technology.
2. Wikipedia (2016). PLATO (computer system). https://en.wikipedia.org/wiki/PLATO_(computer_system). A comprehensive history of PLATO and its innovations is the recently published Dear, Brian (2017). *The Friendly Orange Glow: The Untold Story of the PLATO System and the Dawn of Cyberculture*, Pantheon Books.
3. Woolley, David R. (1994). PLATO: The Emergence of Online Community. http://thinkofit.com/plato/dwplato.htm.
4. Suppes, Patrick (1971). Computer-assisted Instruction at Stanford. http://citeseerx.ist.psu.edu/viewdoc/download?doi=10.1.1.360.7541&rep=rep1&type=pdf.
5. Anderson, John R., Albert T. Corbett, Kenneth R. Koedinger, and Ray Pelletier (1995). Cognitive Tutors: Lessons Learned, *The Journal of the Learning Sciences* 4(2): 167–207.
6. Papert, Seymour (1971). A Computer Laboratory for the Elementary Schools. MIT AI Laboratory Memo 246. ftp://publications.ai.mit.edu/ai-publications/pdf/AIM-246.pdf.

See also Papert, Seymour (1971). Teaching Children Thinking. MIT AI Laboratory Memo 247. ftp://publications.ai.mit.edu/ai-publications/pdf/AIM-247.pdf. See also Papert, Seymour (1971). Teaching Children to be Mathematicians vs. Teaching about Mathematics. MIT AI Laboratory Memo 249. ftp://publications.ai.mit.edu/ai-publications/pdf/AIM-249.pdf. For interesting early project ideas, see Papert, Seymour and Cynthia Solomon (1971). Twenty Things to Do with a Computer. MIT AI Laboratory Memo 248. ftp://publications.ai.mit.edu/ai-publications/pdf/AIM-248.pdf.

7. Papert, Seymour (1971). Teaching Children Thinking. MIT AI Laboratory Memo 247. ftp://publications.ai.mit.edu/ai-publications/pdf/AIM-247.pdf.
8. Feurzeig, W., S. Papert, M. Bloom, R. Grant, and C. Solomon (1969). Programming-Languages as a Conceptual Framework for Teaching Mathematics. Bolt Beranek and Newman Technical Report 1889. http://eric.ed.gov/?id=ED038034.
9. For a fuller description of Papert's vision, see Papert, Seymour (1980). *Mindstorms: Children, Computers, and Powerful Ideas*, Basic Books. http://dl.acm.org/citation.cfm?id=1095592. See also Papert, Seymour and Idit Harel (1991). *Constructionism*, Ablex. For a video record of a recent one-day Media Lab memorial set of talks celebrating the life of Papert, see Media Lab (2017). Thinking about Thinking about Seymour. Memorial talks in honour of the life of Seymour Papert. MIT Media Lab. https://www.media.mit.edu/videos/seymour-2017-01-26/. Of special interest are the talks by Negroponte, Resnick, Turkle, and Kay.
10. Kay, Alan (1972). A Personal Computer for Kids of All Ages, *Proc. ACM '72* 1 : Article 1. http://dl.acm.org/citation.cfm?id=1971922. For background on his ideas, see Kay, Alan C. (1969). The Reactive Engine. PhD Dissertation, Dept. of Computer Science, University of Utah. http://www.chilton-computing.org.uk/inf/pdfs/kay.htm.
11. Kay, Alan and Adele Goldberg (1977). Personal Dynamic Media, *IEEE Computer* 10(3). http://homepages.dcc.ufmg.br/~loureiro/cm/docs/kay_personal_dynamic_media.pdf. See also Kay, Alan (2002). Video clip of Kay showing his late 1960s Dynabook. https://www.youtube.com/watch?v=r36NNGzNvjo. See also Kay, Alan (1996). The Dynabook—Past Present and Future. Video record of a talk given at the ACM Conference on the History of Personal Workstations. https://www.youtube.com/watch?v=GMDphyKrAE8. For Kay's recent perspectives on how far we have come, and his disappointment, see an interview with him: Merchant, Brian (2017). The Father of Mobile Computing Is Not Impressed, *Fast Company*, 15 September.
12. Resnick, Mitchel (2007). All I Really Need to Know (About Creative Thinking) I Learned (By Studying How Children Learn) in Kindergarten, *Proc. C&C '07*, ACM, 1–6.
13. Resnick, Mitchel (1993). Behavior Construction Kits, *CACM* 36(7), ACM, 64–71. See also Resnick, Mitchel and Brian Silverman (2005). Some Reflections on Designing Construction Kits for Kids, *Proc. IDC 2005*, ACM, 117–122.
14. Bajarin, Tim (2014). Why the Maker Movement Is Important to America's Future. http://time.com/104210/maker-faire-maker-movement/.
15. Scratch (2016). A Creative Learning Community. https://scratch.mit.edu. See also Resnick, Mitchel, John Maloney, Andrés Monroy-Hernández, Natalie Rusk, Evelyn Eastmond, Karen Brennan, Amon Millner, Eric Rosenbaum, Jay Silver, Brian Silverman, and Yasmin Kafai (2009). Scratch: Programming for All, *CACM* 52(11): 60–67. See also Maloney, John, Mitchel Resnick, Natalie Rusk, Brian Silverman, and Evelyn Eastmond (2010). The Scratch Programming Language and Environment, *ACM Transactions on Computing Education* 10(4): Article 16, 1–15.

16. Computer Clubhouse (2016). A Global Community for Creativity and Achievement. http://www.computerclubhouse.org/. See also Resnick, Mitchel and Natalie Rusk (1996). The Computer Clubhouse: Helping Youth Develop Fluency with New Media, *Proc. ICLS '96*, 285–291.
17. For a discussion of the difference between games and simulations, see Sauvé, Louise, Lise Renaud, David Kaufman, and Jean-Simon Marquis (2007). Distinguishing between Games and Simulations: A Systematic Review, *Journal of Educational Technology & Society* 10(3): 247–256.
18. Wikipedia (2017). SimCity. https://en.wikipedia.org/wiki/SimCity.
19. SimCity (2017). Home page. http://www.simcity.com/.
20. Romeu, Jorge Luis (1995). Simulation and Statistical Education, *Proc. 1995 Winter Simulation Conf.*, 1371–1375. See also Huppert, J., S. Michal Lomask, and R. Lazarowitz (2002). Computer Simulations in the High School: Students' Cognitive Stages, Science Process Skills and Academic Achievement in Microbiology, *Int. J. Science Education* 24(8): 803–821. See also Adams, Wendy K., Sam Reid, Ron Lemaster, Sarah B. McKagan, Katherine K. Perkins, Michael Dubson, and Carl E. Wieman (2008a). A Study of Educational Simulations Part I—Engagement and Learning, *J. Interactive Learning Research* 19(3): 397–419. See also Adams, Wendy K., Sam Reid, Ron Lemaster, Sarah B. McKagan, Katherine K. Perkins, Michael Dubson, and Carl E. Wieman (2008b). A Study of Educational Simulations Part II—Interface Design, *J. Interactive Learning Research* 19(4): 551–577. See also Papastergiou, Marina (2009). Digital Game-Based Learning in High School Computer Science Education: Impact on Educational Effectiveness and Student Motivation, *Computers & Education* 52: 1–12. See also Fleischmann, Kenneth R., Russell W. Robins, and William A. Wallace (2010). Collaborative Learning of Ethical Decision-Making via Simulated Cases, *Proc. iConference 2011*, ACM, 319–326. See also Nguyen, Sophia (2015). Computing in the Classroom: From the 'Teaching Machine' to the Promise of Twenty-First-Century Learning Technology, *Harvard Magazine*, March–April.
21. A taxonomy of business games appears in Greco, Marco, Nicola Baldissin, and Fabio Nonino (2013). An Exploratory Taxonomy of Business Games, *Simulation & Gaming* 44(5): 645–682.
22. Adams, Wendy K., Sam Reid, Ron Lemaster, Sarah B. McKagan, Katherine K. Perkins, Michael Dubson, and Carl E. Wieman (2008). A Study of Educational Simulations Part I—Engagement and Learning, *J. Interactive Learning Research* 19(3): 397–419.
23. Plaisant, Catherine, Anne Rose, Gary Rubloff, Richard Salter, and Ben Shneiderman (1999). The Design of History Mechanisms and their Use in Collaborative Educational Simulations, *Proc. 1999 Conference on Computer-supported Cooperative Learning*, ACM.
24. Chin, Jeffrey, Richard Dukes, and William Gamson (2009). Assessment in Simulation and Gaming: A Review of the Last 40 Years, *Simulation & Gaming* 40(4): 553–568.
25. The History of PowerPoint in Parker, Ian (2001). Absolute PowerPoint, *The New Yorker*, 28 May. https://www.newyorker.com/magazine/2001/05/28/absolute-powerpoint. Helpful hints on how to use it well appear in Brown, Dan (2002). Understanding PowerPoint: Special Deliverable #5. http://boxesandarrows.com/understanding-powerpoint-special-deliverable-5/.
26. The invective essay is Tufte, Edward R. (2006). *The Cognitive Style of PowerPoint: Pitching Out Corrupts Within*, 2nd Edition, Graphics Press LLC. See the Graphics Press website to better understand Tufte's insights and wisdom, https://www.edwardtufte.com/bboard/q-and-a-fetch-msg?msg_id=0001yB. Many of Tufte's criticisms are directed at general issues of information display as well as the intrinsic cognitive style of PowerPoint. The use of PowerPoint slides by the US military is criticized in Bumiller. Elisabeth (2010). We Have Met the Enemy and He Is PowerPoint,

New York Times, 26 April. Bumiller argued that the slides create an illusion of understanding military complexity and having control over it. Another rebuttal to Tufte notes that lecture slides address different goals and therefore need to be different than written documents; see Doumont, Jean-Luc (2005). The Cognitive Style of PowerPoint: Slides are not All Evil, *Technical Communication* 52(1): 64–70. A systematic review of the growing literature on the constraining (and enabling) qualities of PowerPoint, and an excellent starting point for anyone interested in the topic, is Kernbach, Sebastian, Sabrina Bresciani, and Martin J. Eppler (2015). Slip-Sliding-Away: A Review of the Literature on the Constraining Qualities of PowerPoint, *Business and Professional Communication Quarterly* 78(3): 292–313. Finally, a lighter look at the topic is provided by Peter Norvig's rendering of Lincoln's Gettysburg address at https://norvig.com/Gettysburg/; see also the discussion of the making of this PowerPoint in https://norvig.com/Gettysburg/making.html.

27. For some good examples, see Khan Academy (2017). https://www.khanacademy.org. In addition, to learn about software that supports a variety of techniques, including pre-recording and playback of animated explanations, see Educators Technology (2014). 7 Fabulous iPad Apps to Create Short Animated Lessons for Your Flipped Classroom. http://www.educatorstechnology.com/2014/01/6-fabulous-ipad-apps-to-create-short.html.

28. Bederson, Ben (2011). The Promise of Zoomable User Interfaces, *Behaviour and Information Technology* 30(6): 853–866. For an excellent ZUI product, see Prezi (2016). Presenting a Better Way to Present. https://prezi.com.

29. Lessig, Larry (2007). Laws that Choke Creativity. http://www.ted.com/talks/larry_lessig_says_the_law_is_strangling_creativity. The Lessig presentation style is discussed in http://www.presentationzen.com/presentationzen/2007/11/larry-lessig-pr.html.

30. HighSpark (2013). Presentation Design Techniques from the Masters. http://www.slideshare.net/slidecomet/presentation-design-techniques-from-the-masters-by-slidecomet.

31. Van Dam, Andries (1984). The Electronic Classroom: Workstations for Teaching, *Int. Journal of Man–Machine Studies* 21: 353–363.

32. Abowd Gregory D., Christopher G. Atkeson, Ami Feinstein, Cindy Hmelo, Rob Kooper, Sue Long, Nitin 'Nick' Sawhney, and Mikiya Tani (1996). Teaching and Learning as Multimedia Authoring: The Classroom 2000 Project, *Proc. ACM Multimedia '96*: 187–198. See also Brotherton, Jason A. and Gregory D. Abowd (2004). Lessons Learned from eClass: Assessing Automatic Capture and Access in the Classroom, *ACM Transactions on Computer–Human Interaction* 11(2): 121–155.

33. Kreitmayer, Stefan, Yvonne Rogers, Robin Lancy, and Stephen Peake (2013). UniPad: Orchestrating Collaborative Activities Through Shared Tablets and An Integrated Wall Display, *Proc. Ubicomp'13*, ACM, 801–810.

34. Martinez-Maldanado, Roberto, Judy Kay, Kalina Yacef, Marie-Theresa Edbauer, and Yannis Dimitriadis (2013). MTClassroom and MTDashboard: Supporting Analysis of Teacher Attention in an Orchestrated Multi-tabletop Classroom, *Proc. CSCL'13*: 119–128. See also Martinez-Maldanado, Roberto, Andrew Clayphan, Christopher Ackad, and Judy Kay (2014). Multi-touch Technology in a Higher-Education Classroom: Lessons In-The-Wild, *Proc. OzCHI '14*: 220–229. See also Martinez-Maldonado, Roberto, Kalina Yacef, and Judy Kay (2015). TSCL: A Conceptual Model to Inform Understanding of Collaborative Learning Processes at Interactive Tabletops, *Int'l. Journal on Human–Computer Studies* 83: 62–82. See also Martinez-Maldonado, Roberto, Andrew Clayphan, and Judy Kay (2015). Deploying and Visualising Teacher's Scripts of Small Group Activities in a Multi-Surface Classroom Ecology: a study in-the-wild. *International Journal on Computer-Supported Cooperative Work* 24(2): 177–221.

35. For a comparison of pen and paper, tabletops, and wall displays as tools for brainstorming, see Clayphan, Andrew, Roberto Martinez-Maldonado, Martin Tomitsch, Susan Atkinson, and Judy Kay (2016). An in-the-wild study of learning to brainstorm: comparing cards, tabletops and wall displays in the classroom. *Interacting with Computers* 28(6): 788–810.
36. For the history of the idea of the flipped classroom, see Rutherfoord, Rebecca H. and James K. Rutherfoord (2013). Flipping the Classroom: Is It for You? *Proc. SIGITE*: 19–23.
37. Giannakos, Michail N., John Krogstie, and Nikos Chrisochoides (2014). Reviewing the Flipped Classroom Research: Reflections for Computer Science Education, *Proc. CSERC '14*: 23–29.
38. Schleg, Abigail G. (2015). *Implementation and Critical Assessment of the Flipped Classroom Experience*, IGI Global.
39. Koedinger, Kenneth R., John R. Anderson, William H. Hadley, and Mary A. Mark (1997). Intelligent Tutoring Goes to School in the Big City, *Int'l. J. Artificial Intelligence in Education* 8: 30–43.
40. Koedinger, Kenneth R. and Vincent Aleven (2016). An Interview Reflection on 'Intelligent Tutoring Goes to School in the Big City', *Int'l. J. Artificial Intelligence in Education* 26: 13–24. See also the website of the firm commercializing CMU cognitive tutors for use in maths education, https://www.carnegielearning.com/.
41. Heffernan, Neil T. and Cristina Lindquist Heffernan (2014). The ASSISTments Ecosystem: Building a Platform that Brings Scientists and Teachers Together for Minimally Invasive Research on Human Learning and Teaching, *Int'l. J. Artificial Intelligence in Education* 24: 470–497. See also the website of the organization delivering ASSISTments, https://www.assistments.org/.
42. Escueta, Maya, Vincent Quan, Andre Joshua Nickow, and Philip Oreopoulos (2017). Education Technology: An Evidence-based Review. National Bureau of Economic Research Working Paper 23744. http://www.nber.org/papers/w23744. See also VanLehn, Kurt (2011). The Relative Effectiveness of Human Tutoring, Intelligent Tutoring Systems, and Other Tutoring Systems, *Educational Psychologist* 46(4): 197–221.
43. Bull, Susan (2004). Supporting Learning with Open Learner Models. 4th Hellenic Conf. with Int'l Participation: Information and Communication Technologies in Education, Athens (Keynote). https://www.researchgate.net/publication/228888082_Supporting_learning_with_open_learner_models.
44. Woolf, Beverly Park (1999). Student Modeling. In Nkambou, R. et al. (Eds.), *Advances in Intelligent Tutoring Systems, SCI 308*: 267–279.
45. Elsom-Cook, Mark (1993). Student Modeling in Intelligent Tutoring Systems, *Artificial Intelligence Review* 7: 227–240.
46. *Ibid.*, 43. See also Bull, Susan and Judy Kay (2008). Metacognition and Open Learner Models. Appears in *Metacognition Workshop, ITS 2008*. https://pdfs.semanticscholar.org/5290/fcb840cd4c5912dbabe441bd3323bfe9793b.pdf.
47. Breazeal, Cynthia, Paul L. Harris, David DeSteno, Jacqueline M. Kory Westlund, Leah Dickens, and Sooyeon Jeong (2016). Young Children Treat Robots as Informants, *Topics in Cognitive Science* 8: 481–491. See also Westlund, Jacqueline M. Kory, Sooyeon Jeong, Hae W. Park, Samuel Ronfard, Aradhana Adhikari, Paul L. Harris, David DeSteno, and Cynthia L. Breazeal (2017). Flat vs. Expressive Storytelling: Young Children's Learning and Retention of a Social Robot's Narrative, *Frontiers in Human Neuroscience* 11, Article 296, June.

48. Ogan, Amy and W. Lewis Johnson (2015). Preface for the Special Issue on Culturally Aware Educational Technologies, *Int'l. J. Artificial Intelligence in Education* 25: 173–176.

49. Self, John (1999). The Defining Characteristics of Intelligent Tutoring Systems Research: ITSs Care, Precisely, *Int'l. J. Artificial Intelligence in Education* 10: 350–364.

50. Wikipedia (2016). Electronic Information Exchange System (EIES). https://en.wikipedia.org/wiki/EIES. Early use of this technology is described in Hiltz, Starr Roxanne and Murray Turoff (1978). *The Network Nation: Human Communication via Computer*, Addison-Wesley. Over a decade of work applying it to virtual classrooms is covered in Hiltz, Starr Roxanne (1994). *The Virtual Classroom: Learning without Limits via Computer Networks*, Ablex Publishing.

51. Hiltz, Starr Roxanne and Murray Turoff (2002). What Makes Learning Networks Effective? *Communications of the ACM* 45(4): 56–59.

52. Hiltz, Starr Roxanne and Murray Turoff (2005). Education Goes Digital: The Evolution of Online Learning and the Revolution in Higher Education, *Communications of the ACM* 48(10): 59–64.

53. Garrison, D. Randy, Terry Anderson, and Walter Archer (2001). Critical Thinking, Cognitive Presence, and Computer Conferencing in Distance Education, *The American Journal of Distance Education* 15(1): 7–23.

54. Scardamalia, Marlene and Carl Bereiter (1994). Computer Support for Knowledge-Building Communities, *The Journal of the Learning Sciences* 3(3): 265–283.

55. Garrison, D. Randy (2007). Online Community of Inquiry Review: Social, Cognitive, and Teaching Presence Issues, *Journal of Asynchronous Learning Networks* 11: 61–72. See also Garrison, D. Randy (2011). *E-Learning in the 21st Century: A Framework for Research and Practice*, 2nd Edition, Routledge.

56. Richardson, Jennifer C. and Karen Swan (2003). Examining Social Presence in Online Courses in Relation to Students' Perceived Learning and Satisfaction, *Journal of Asynchronous Learning Networks* 7(1): 68–88.

57. Garrison, D. Randy, Terry Anderson, and Walter Archer (2001). Critical Thinking, Cognitive Presence, and Computer Conferencing in Distance Education, *The American Journal of Distance Education* 15(1): 7–23. See also Kanuka, Heather and D. Randy Garrison (2004). Cognitive Presence in Online Learning, *Journal of Computing in Higher Education* 15(2): 21–39.

58. Garrison, D. Randy and Martha Cleveland-Innes (2005). Facilitating Cognitive Presence in Online Learning: Interaction Is Not Enough, *The American Journal of Distance Education* 19(3): 133–148.

59. Stodel, Emma J., Terrie Lynn Thompson, and Colla J. MacDonald (2006). Learners' Perspectives on What Is Missing from Online Learning: Interpretations through the Community of Inquiry Framework, *International Review of Research in Open and Distance Learning* 7(3): 1–24.

60. Rourke, Liam, and Heather Kanuka (2007). Barriers to Online Critical Discourse, *Computer-Supported Collaborative Learning* 2: 105–126, 10.1007/s11412-007-9007-3.

61. Kanuka, Heather, Liam Rourke, and Elaine Laflamme (2007). The Influence of Instructional Methods on the Quality of Online Discussion, *British Journal of Educational Technology* 38(2): 260–271.

62. Dynarski, Susan (2018). Online Courses Are Harming the Students Who Need the Most Help, *New York Times*, 19 January.

63. Trucano, Michael (2015). Using the Internet to Connect Students and Teachers Around the World for 'Virtual Exchanges'. http://blogs.worldbank.org/edutech/using-internet-connect-students-and-teachers-around-world-virtual-exchanges. See also UNESCO (2017). Case Study 5: Global Classrooms, Learning Networks and Virtual Communities. http://www.unesco.org/education/lwf/doc/portfolio/case5.htm.

64. Voices of Youth (2017). Home page of website. http://www.voicesofyouth.org/.

65. Wikipedia (2018). Massive Open Online Course. https://en.wikipedia.org/wiki/Massive_open_online_course.

66. Class Central (2018). By The Numbers: MOOCs in 2017. https://www.class-central.com/report/mooc-stats-2017/.

67. Khan Academy (2017). https://www.khanacademy.org/.

68. Coursera (2017). https://www.coursera.org/.

69. Class Central (2017). Massive List of MOOC Providers Around the World. https://www.class-central.com/report/mooc-providers-list/.

70. Atkins, Daniel E., John Seely Brown, and Allen L. Hammond (2007). A Review of the Open Educational Resources (OER) Movement: Achievements, Challenges, and New Opportunities. Report to The William and Flora Hewlett Foundation. http://www.hewlett.org/wp-content/uploads/2016/08/ReviewoftheOERMovement.pdf.

71. Anderson, Ashton, Daniel Huttenlocher, Jon Kleinberg, and Jure Leskovec (2014). Engaging with Massive Online Courses, *Proc. WWW'14*: 687–697.

72. Guo, Philip J., Juho Kim, and Rob Rubin (2014). How Video Production Affects Student Engagement: An Empirical Study of MOOC Videos, *Proc. L@S (Learning@Scale)*: 41–50.

73. Coetzee, Derrick, Armando Fox, Marti A. Hearst, and Björn Hartmann (2014). Chatrooms in MOOCs: All Talk and No Action, *Proc. L@S'14:* 127–136.

74. Coetzee, Derrick, Seongtaek Lim, Armando Fox, Björn Hartmann, and Marti A. Hearst (2015). Structuring Interactions for Large-Scale Synchronous Peer Learning, *Proc. CSCW2015*: 1139–1152.

75. Class Central (2015). MOOC Trends in 2015: Big MOOC Providers Find their Business Models. https://www.class-central.com/report/mooc-business-model/.

76. Bersin, Josh (2016). Use of MOOCs and Online Education Is Exploding: Here's Why, *Forbes*, 5 January. See also Straumsheim, Carl (2016). MicroMasters on a Global Scale. https://www.insidehighered.com/news/2016/09/20/mooc-based-masters-degree-initiative-expands-globally. See also Moules, Jonathan (2018). Open University Seeks to Raise £40m for Online Courses, *Financial Times*, 30 September.

77. Cuban, Larry (1986). *Teachers and Machines: The Classroom Use of Technology Since 1920*, Teachers College Press.

78. Cuban, Larry (2001). *Oversold and Underused: Computers in the Classroom*, Harvard University Press, p. 195.

79. Oppenheimer, Todd (1997). The Computer Delusion, *The Atlantic*, July. See also Hu, Winne (2007). Education: Seeing No Progress, Some Schools Drop Laptops, *New York Times*, 4 May. See also Richtel, Matt (2011). Technology: Grading the Digital School: In Classroom of Future, Stagnant Scores, *New York Times*, 3 September. See also Kardaras, Nicholas (2016). Ideas Education: Screens in Schools are a $60 Billion Hoax, *Time Magazine*, 31 August.

80. Papert, Seymour (1990). A Critique of Technocentrism in Thinking About the School of the Future. M.I.T. Media Lab Epistemology and Learning Memo No. 2. http://www.papert.org/articles/ACritiqueofTechnocentrism.html.

81. Setzer, Valdemar W. (2000). A Review of Arguments for the Use of Computers in Elementary Schools, *SouthernCross Review Electronic Journal* 4. http://www.southerncrossreview.org/4/review.html. See also Setzer, Valdemar W. and Lowell Monke (2001). Challenging the Applications: An Alternative View on Why, When and How Computers Should Be Used in Education. In Muffoletto, R. (Ed.), *Education and Technology: Critical and Reflective Practices*, Hampton Press, 141–172. https://www.ime.usp.br/~vwsetzer/comp-in-educ.html.

82. Weston, M. E. and A. Bain (2010). The End of Techno-Critique: The Naked Truth about 1:1 Laptop Initiatives and Educational Change, *Journal of Technology, Learning, and Assessment* 9(6). Despite the negative tone, this paper then paradoxically presented a prescription of how a community and its school system could realize the benefit of the ubiquitous use of 'cognitive tools'.

83. Toyama, Kentaro (2015). Technology Won't Fix America's Neediest Schools. It Makes Bad Education Worse, *The Washington Post*, 4 June.

84. Carter, Susan Payne, Kyle Greenberg, and Michael S. Walker (2016). The Impact of Computer Usage on Academic Performance: Evidence from a Randomized Trial at the United States Military Academy. MIT Department of Economics School Effectiveness and Inequality Initiative Working Paper #2016.2, May. http://seii.mit.edu/wp-content/uploads/2016/05/SEII-Discussion-Paper-2016.02-Payne-Carter-Greenberg-and-Walker-2.pdf.

85. Tang, Sandra and Megan E. Patrick (2018). Technology and Interactive Social Media Use Among 8th and 10th Graders in the U.S. and Associations with Homework and School Grades, *Computers in Human Behavior* 86: 34–44.

86. OECD (2015). *Students, Performance, and Learning: Making the Connection*, PISA, OECD Publishing. http://dx.doi.org/10.1787/9789264239555-en. http://www.oecd.org/publications/students-computers-and-learning-9789264239555-en.htm.

87. Davies, Randall S. and Richard E. West (2014). Technology Integration in Schools. In Spector, J. M. et al. (Eds.), *Handbook of Research on Educational Communications and Technology*, Springer Science+Business Media, 841–853.

88. Pew Research (2017). Mobile Fact Sheet. http://www.pewinternet.org/fact-sheet/mobile/. The full report, U.S. Smartphone Use in 2015, 1 April 2015, may also be retrieved from this site.

89. May, James (2012). Cell Phones in the Classroom: Collaborative or Calamitous. Open Learning Consortium. http://olc.onlinelearningconsortium.org/effective_practices/cell-phones-classroom-collaborative-or-calamitous. See also Barnwell, Paul (2016). Do Smartphones Have a Place in the Classroom? *The Atlantic*, 27 April.

90. Taylor, Kate (2015). Ban on Cellphones in New York City Schools to Be Lifted, *New York Times*, 6 January. See also Gerson, Daniela (2015). What to Do about Texting in Class, According to Eleven Teachers, *Los Angeles Times*, 4 November.

91. Beland, Louis-Philippe and Richard Murphy (2015). Ill Communication: Technology, Distraction & Student Performance, *Labour Economics* 41(6): 61–76.

92. Kamenetz, Anya (2015). How to Get Students to Stop Using Their Cellphones in Class, *nprEd*. http://www.npr.org/sections/ed/2015/11/10/453986816/how-to-get-students-to-stop-using-their-cellphones-in-class.

93. Barnwell, Paul (2016). Do Smartphones Have a Place in the Classroom? *The Atlantic*, 27 April.

94. Rubin, Alissa J. and Elian Peltier (2018). France Bans Smartphones in Schools Through 9th Grade. Will It Help Students? *New York Times,* 20 September. See also Thompson, Carolyn (2018). Cellphones Gaining Acceptance Inside US Schools. Associated Press, 2 April. https://www.apnews.com/28f7490db4af49ab81c38cf2f852aa87.
95. National Center for Education Statistics (2018). U.S. Department of Education. Indicators of School Crime and Safety: 2017. https://nces.ed.gov/pubs2018/2018036.pdf.
96. Broussard, Meredith (2018). *Artificial Unintelligence: How Computers Misunderstand the World,* The MIT Press, pp. 63–64.
97. Wingfield, Nick and Natasha Singer (2017). Microsoft Looks to Regain Lost Ground in the Classroom, *New York Times,* 2 May. Singer, Natasha (2017). How Google Took Over the Classroom, *New York Times,* 13 May. Pardes, Arielle (2018). How Apple Lost its Place in the Classroom, *Wired,* 28 March.

Chapter 4

1. To learn about the history of some of the topics in this chapter, see Blum, Bruce I. and Karen Duncan (Eds.) (1990). *A History of Medical Informatics,* ACM Press.
2. Weber, Bruce (2012). Homer R. Warner, A Pioneer of Using Computers in Patient Care, Dies at 90, *New York Times,* 10 December. http://www.nytimes.com/2012/12/11/us/homer-r-warner-a-pioneer-of-using-computers-in-patient-care-dies-at-90.html?src=recg&_r=0.
3. MGHLCS (2016). G. Octo Barnett, MD, Founder of the Laboratory of Computer Science. http://www.mghlcs.org/about/team/octobarnett/.
4. Slack, W. V. (2010). Patient–Computer Dialogue: A Hope for the Future, *Mayo Clinic Proceedings* 85(8): 701–703. A retrospective look at his first thirty-five years of work is Slack, W. V. (2001). *Cybermedicine: How Computing Empowers Doctors and Patients for Better Health Care,* 2nd Edition, Jossey-Bass. A detailed review of this book is Powers, William B. (2001). Book Review: Cybermedicine: How Computing Empowers Doctors and Patients for Better Health Care, *The John Marshall Journal of Computer & Information Law* 19(4): 589–607.
5. Weed, Lawrence L. (1964). Medical Records, Patient Care, and Medical Education, *Irish Journal of Medical Science,* June: 271–282. See also Weed, Lawrence L. (1968). Medical Records that Guide and Teach, *New England Journal of Medicine* 278: 593–600, 652–657.
6. NIH (2016). William F. Raub, Ph.D. https://www.nih.gov/about-nih/what-we-do/nih-almanac/william-f-raub-phd.
7. Hollister, C. (1988). PROPHET—a national computing resource for life science research. *Nucleir Acids Res.* 18:5, 1873–5.
8. Cline, R. J. W. and K. M. Haynes (2001). Consumer Health Information Seeking on the Internet: The State of the Art, *Health Education Research Theory and Practice* 16(6): 671–692.
9. Eysenbach, Gunther and Christian Köhler (2003). What Is the Prevalence of Health-Related Searches on the World Wide Web? Qualitative and Quantitative Analysis of Search Engine Queries on the Internet, *AMIA Annual Symposium Proceedings,* 225–229.
10. Fox, Susannah (2011). The Social Life of Health Information. http://www.pewinternet.org/files/old-media//Files/Reports/2011/PIP_Social_Life_of_Health_Info.pdf.
11. Eastin, Matthew S. (2001). Credibility Assessments of Online Health Information: The Effects of Source Expertise and Knowledge of Content, *Journal of Computer-Mediated Communication* 6(4), July.

12. Eysenbach, Gunther and Christian Köhler (2002). How Do Consumers Search for and Appraise Health Information on the World Wide Web? Qualitative Study Using Focus Groups, Usability Tests, and In-depth Interviews, *British Medical Journal* 324(7337): 573–577.

13. Berland, Gretchen K., Marc N. Elliot, Leo S. Morales, Jeffrey I. Algazy, Richard L. Kravitz, Michael S. Broder, David E. Kanouse, Jorge A. Muñoz, Juan-Antonio Puyol, Marielena Lara, Katherine E. Watkins, Hannah Yang, and Elizabeth A. McGlynn (2001). Health Information on the Internet: Accessibility, Quality, and Readability in English and Spanish, *JAMA* 285(20): 2612–2637.

14. Morahan-Martin, Janet M. (2005). How Internet Users Find, Evaluate, and Use Online Health Information: A Cross-Cultural Review, *CyberPsychology and Behavior* 7(5): 497–510.

15. Hesse, Bradford W., David E. Nelson, Gary L. Kreps, Robert T. Croyle, Neeraj K. Arora, Barbara K. Rimer, and Kasisomayajula Viswanath (2005). Trust and Sources of Health Information: The Impact of the Internet and its Implications for Health Care Providers: Findings from the First Health Information National Trends Survey, *Archives Internal Medicine* 165: 2618–2624.

16. Sillence, Elizabeth, Pam Briggs, Peter Richard Harris, and Lesley Fishwick (2007). How Do Patients Evaluate and Make Use of Online Health Information, *Social Science & Medicine* 64: 1853–1862.

17. Hasty, R. T., R. C. Garbalosa, V. A. Barbato, P. J. Valdes, D. W. Powers, E. Hernandez, J. S. John, G. Suciu, F. Qureshi, M. Popa-Radu, S. S. Jose, N. Drexler, R. Patankar, J. R. Paz, C. W. King, H. N. Gerber, M. G. Valladares, and A. A. Somji (2014). Wikipedia vs Peer-Reviewed Medical Literature for Information About the 10 Most Costly Medical Conditions, *The Journal of the American Osteopathic Association* 114(5): 368–373.

18. Raj, S., V. L. Sharma, A. J. Singh, and S. Goel (2016). Evaluation of Quality and Readability of Health Information Websites Identified through India's Major Search Engines, *Advances in Preventive Medicine*, Article ID 4815285, 6 pages.

19. Stack, Liam (2017). 20th Century Fox Used Fake News to Publicize 'A Cure for Wellness', *New York Times*, 15 February.

20. Medical Library Association (2017). Top Health Websites. http://www.mlanet.org/page/top-health-websites.

21. NIA (2018). Online Health Information: Is It Reliable? https://www.nia.nih.gov/health/online-health-information-it-reliable.

22. Fox, Susannah (2014). The Social Life of Health Information. http://www.pewresearch.org/fact-tank/2014/01/15/the-social-life-of-health-information/.

23. Patientslikeme (2017). Home page of website. https://www.patientslikeme.com.

24. Wicks, Paul, Michael Massagli, Jeana Frost, Catherine Brownstein, Sally Okun, Timothy Vaughn, Richard Bradley, and James Heywood (2010). Sharing Health Data for Better Outcomes on PatientsLikeMe, *Journal of Medical Internet Research* 12(2): e19. See also Wicks, Paul, Dorothy L. Keininger, Michael P. Massagli, Christine de la Loge, Catherine Brownstein, Jouko Isojärvi, and James Heywood (2012). Perceived Benefits of Sharing Health Data Between People with Epilepsy on an Online Platform, *Epilepsy and Behavior* 23: 16–23.

25. Crowdmed.com (2017). Home page of website. https://www.crowdmed.com.

26. Kalichman, Seth C., Eric G. Benotsch, Lance Weinhardt, James Austin, Webster Luke, and Chauncey Cherry (2003). Health-Related Internet Use, Coping, Social Support, and Health

Indicators in People Living With HIV/AIDS: Preliminary Results From a Community Survey, *Health Psychology* 22(1): 111–116.

27. Swan, Melanie (2009). Emerging Patient-Driven Health Care Models: An Examination of Health Social Networks, Consumer Personalized Medicine and Quantified Self-Tracking, *International Journal Environmental Research and Public Health* 6: 492–525.
28. Eysenbach, Gunther (2003). The Impact of the Internet on Cancer Outcomes, *A Cancer Journal for Clinicians* 53: 356–371. See also Eysenbach, Gunther, John Powell, Marina Englesakis, Carlos Rizo, and Anita Stern (2004). Health Related Virtual Communities and Electronic Support Groups: Systematic Review of the Effects of Online Peer to Peer Interactions, *BMJ* 328.
29. Ziebland, Sue and Sally Wyke (2012). Health and Illness in a Connected World: How Might Sharing Experiences on the Internet Affect People's Health? *The Millbank Quarterly* 90(2): 219–249.
30. Lewis, Stephen P., Nancy L. Health, Natalie J. Michal, and Jamie M. Duggan (2012). Non-Suicidal Self-Injury, Youth, and the Internet: What Mental Health Professionals Need to Know, *Child and Adolescent Psychiatry and Mental Health* 6(13).
31. Rajagopal, Sundararajan (2004). Suicide Pacts and the Internet: Complete Strangers May Make Cyberspace Pacts, *BMJ* 329: 1298–1299.
32. Biddle, Lucy, Jenny Donovan, Keith Hawton, Navneet Kapur, and David Gunnell (2008). Suicide and the Internet, *BMJ* 336: 800–802.
33. Gabler, Ellen and Rich Harris (2017). On Reddit, Intimate Glimpses of Addicts in Thrall to Opioids, *New York Times,* 20 July.
34. Adams, Samantha A. (2011). Sourcing the Crowd for Health Services Improvement: The Reflexive Patient and 'Share-Your-Experience' Websites, *Social Science & Medicine* 72: 1069–1076.
35. De Choudhury, Munmun, Meredith Ringel Morris, Ryen W. White (2014). Seeking and Sharing Health Information Online: Comparing Search Engines and Social Media, *Proc. CHI 2014*: 1365–1375.
36. Wright, Adam, Dean F. Sittig, Julie McGowan, Joan S. Ash, and Lawrence L. Weed (2014). Bringing Science to Medicine: An Interview with Larry Weed, Inventor of the Problem-oriented Medical Record, *Journal of the American Medical Informatics Association* 21: 964–968.
37. Berner, Eta S., Don E. Detmer, and Donald Demberg (2005). Will the Wave Finally Break? A Brief View of the Adoption of Electronic Medical Records in the United States, *Journal of the American Medical Informatics Association* 12(1): 3–7.
38. Doolan, David F., David W. Bates, and Brent C. James (2003). The Use of Computers for Clinical Care: A Case Series of Advanced U.S. Sites, *Journal of the American Medical Informatics Association* 10(1): 94–107.
39. Jha, Ashish K., Catherine M. DesRoches, Eric G. Campbell, Karen Donelan, Sowmya R. Rao, Timothy G. Ferris, Alexandra Shields, Sara Rosenbaum, and David Blumenthal (2009). Use of Electronic Health Records in U.S. Hospitals, *The New England Journal of Medicine* 360: 1628–1638.
40. Abramson, Erika L., Sandra McGinnis, Alison Edwards, Dayna M. Maniccia, Jean Moore, and Rainu Kaushal (2012). Electronic Health Record Adoption and Health Information Exchange Among Hospitals in New York State. *Journal of Evaluation in Clinical Practice* 18: 1156–1162.

41. Gans, David, John Kralewski, Terry Hammons, and Bryan Dowd (2005). Medical Groups' Adoption of Electronic Health Records and Information Systems, *Health Affairs* 24(5): 1323–1333.

42. Hsiao, Chun-Ju and Esther Hing (2014). Use and Characteristics of Electronic Health Record Systems Among Office-based Physician Practices: United States, 2001–2013. NCHS Data Brief No. 143, January. x https://www.ncbi.nlm.nih.gov/pubmed/24439138.

43. Chaudry, Basit, Jerome Wang, Shinyi Wu, Margaret Maglione, Walter Mojica, Elizabeth Roth, Sally C. Morton, and Paul G. Shekelle (2006). Systematic Review: Impact of Health Information Technology on Quality, Efficiency, and Costs of Medical Care, *Annals of Internal Medicine* 144: 742–752.

44. CBO (2008). Evidence on the Costs and Benefits of Health Information Technology. Congressional Budget Office. Retrieved on 22 February 2017 from https://www.cbo.gov/sites/default/files/110th-congress-2007-2008/reports/05-20-healthit.pdf.

45. Cebul, Randall D., Thomas E. Love, Anil K. Jain, and Christopher J. Hebert (2011). Electronic Health Records and Quality of Diabetes Care, *The New England Journal of Medicine* 365: 825–833.

46. McDonald, Clement J., Fiona M. Callaghan, ArleneWeissman, Rebecca M. Goodwin, Mallika Mundkur, and Thomson Kuhn (2014). Use of Internist's Free Time by Ambulatory Care Electronic Medical Record Systems, *JAMA Internal Medicine* 174 (11): 1860–1863.

47. Himmelstein, David U., Adam Wright, and Steffie Woolhandler (2010). Hospital Computing and the Costs and Quality of Care: A National Study, *The American Journal of Medicine* 123: 40–46.

48. Wang, Samuel J., Blackford Middleton, Lisa A. Prosser, Christiana G. Bardon, Cynthia D. Spurr, Patricia J. Carchidi, Anne F. Kittler, Robert C. Goldszer, David G. Fairchild, Andrew J. Sussman, Gilad J. Kuperman, and David W. Bates (2003). A Cost–Benefit Analysis of Electronic Medical Records in Primary Care, *American Journal of Medicine* 114: 397–403.

49. Davies, Stephen M. (2017). The Experimental Computer Programme: The First Computing Initiative for the National Health Service in England, *IEEE Annals of the History of Computing* 39(2): 65–79.

50. Sheikh, Aziz, Tony Cornford, Nicholas Barber, Anthony Avery, Amirhossein Takian, Valentina Lichtner, Dimitra Petrakaki, Sarah Crowe, Kate Marsden, Ann Robertson, Zoe Morrison, Ela Klecun, Robin Prescott, Casey Quinn, Yogini Jani, Maryam Ficociello, Katerina Voutsina, James Paton, Bernard Fernando, Ann Jacklin, and Kathrin Cresswell (2011). Implementation and Adoption of Nationwide Electronic Health Records in Secondary Care in England: Final Qualitative Results from Prospective National Evaluation in 'Early Adopter' Hospitals, *BMJ* 343.

51. Boonstra, Albert and Manda Broekhuis (2010). Barriers to the Acceptance of Electronic Medical Records by Physicians from Systematic Review to Taxonomy and Interventions, *BMC Health Services Research* 10(231). See also Boonstra, Albert, Arie Versluis, and Janita F. J. Vos (2014). Implementing Electronic Health Records in Hospitals: A Systematic Literature Review, *BMC Health Services Research* 14(370).

52. Caldwell, Patrick (2015). We've Spent Billions to Fix Our Medical Records, and They're Still a Mess. Here's Why, *Mother Jones*, 21 October.

53. Hartswood, Mark, Rob Procter, Mark Rouncefield, and Roger Slack (2003). Making a Case in Medical Work: Implications for the Electronic Medical Record, *Computer Supported Cooperative Work* 12: 241–266.

54. Plotnick, Rachel (2010). Computers, Systems Theory, and the Making of a Wired Hospital: A History of Technicon Medical Information System, 1964–1987, *Journal of the American Society for Information Science and Technology* 61(6): 1281–1294.

55. Wikipedia (2017a). Electronic Health Record. https://en.wikipedia.org/wiki/Electronic_health_record.

56. Haun, Kathryn and Eric J. Topeljan (2017). The Health Data Conundrum, *New York Times,* 2 January.

57. Winkelman, Kevin J. Leonard and Peter G. Rossos (2005). Patient-Perceived Usefulness of Online Electronic Medical Records: Employing Grounded Theory in the Development of Information and Communication Technologies for Use by Patients Living with Chronic Illness, *Journal of the American Medical Informatics Association* 12: 306–314. 10.1197/jamia.M1712.

58. Tang, Paul C., Joan S. Ash, David W. Bates, J. Marc Overhage, and Daniel Z. Sands (2006). Personal Health Records: Definitions, Benefits, and Strategies for Overcoming Barriers to Adoption, *Journal of the American Medical Informatics Association* 13: 121–126. See also Archer, N., U. Fevrier-Thomas, C. Lokker, K. A. McKibbon, and S. E. Straus (2011). Personal Health Records: A Scoping Review, *Journal of the American Medical Informatics Association* 18: 515–522.

59. Halamka, John D., Kenneth D. Mandl, and Paul C. Tang (2008). Early Experiences with Personal Health Records, *Journal of the American Medical Informatics Association* 15 (1): 1–7. 10.1197/jamia.M2562.

60. Wikipedia (2017). Sociotechnical System. Retrieved on 23 February 2017 from https://en.wikipedia.org/wiki/Sociotechnical_system.

61. Baecker, Ronald M. (1974). A Study of Automated Information Processing Systems in Drug Reaction Surveillance Systems and Reaction Prevention, *Computers and Biomedical Research* 7: 457–488.

62. Lazarou, Jason, Bruce H. Pomeranz, and Paul N. Corey (1998). Incidence of Adverse Drug Reactions in Hospitalized Patients: A Meta-Analysis of Prospective Studies, *JAMA* 279(15): 1200–1205.

63. A study of 315 elderly patients admitted to an acute care hospital is Col, Nananda, James E. Fanale, and Penelope Kronholm (1990). The Role of Medication Noncompliance and Adverse Drug Reactions in Hospitalizations of the Elderly, *Archives of Internal Medicine* 150: 841–845. The study found that 11.4% of the patients were admitted due to medication non-compliance, 16.8% due to ADRs. Gurwitz, Jerry, Terry S. Field, Leslie R. Harrold, Jeffrey Rothscholid, Kristin Debellis, Andrew C. Seger, Cynthia Cadoret, Leslie S. Fish, Lawrence Garber, Michael Kelleher, and David W. Bates (2003). Incidence and Preventability of Adverse Drug Events Among Older Persons in the Ambulatory Setting, *JAMA* 289(9): 1107–1116. The researchers conducted a study with 30,000 person-years of observation at a multi-specialty group practice catering to seniors and found fifty ADEs per 1,000 person-years, of which fourteen were preventable. Similar results were found in a study in the UK: Pirmohamed, Munir, Sally James, Shaun Meakin, Chris Green, Andrew K. Scott, Thomas J. Walley, Keith Farrar, B. Kevin Park, and Alasdair M. Breckenridge (2004). Adverse Drug Reactions as Cause of Admission to Hospital: Prospective Analysis of 18 820 Patients, *BMJ* 329: 15–19. Six and a half per cent of hospital admissions were related to an ADE, and with an overall fatality rate of 0.15%.

64. Jones, GaToya, Vajeeha Tabassum, Gregory J. Zarow, and Thomas A. Ala (2015). The Inability of Older Adults to Recall Their Drugs and Medical Conditions, *Drugs & Aging* 32: 329–336. 10.1007/s40266-015-0255-z.

65. Classen, David C., Stanley L. Pestotnik, R. Scott Evans, and John P. Burke (1991). Computerized Surveillance of Adverse Drug Events in Hospital Patients, *JAMA* 266(20): 2847–2851.

66. Bates, David W., Lucian L. Leape, David J. Cullen, Nan Laird, Laura A. Petersen, Jonathan M. Teich, Elizabeth Burdick, Mairead Hickey, Sharon Kleefield, Brian Shea, Martha Vander Vliet, and Diane L. Seger (1998). Effect of Computerized Physician Order Entry and a Team Intervention on Prevention of Serious Medication Errors, *JAMA* 280(15): 1311–1316.

67. Raschke, Robert A., Bea Gollihare, Thomas A. Wunderlich, James R. Guidry, Alan I. Leibowitz, John C. Pierce, Lee Lemelson, Mark A. Heisler, and Cynthia Susong (1998). A Computer Alert System to Prevent Injury from Adverse Drug Events: Development and Evaluation in a Community Teaching Hospital, *JAMA* 280(15): 1317–1320.

68. Wolfstadt, Jesse I., Jerry H. Gurwitz, Terry S. Field, Monica Lee, Sunila Kalkar, Wei Wu, and Paula A. Rochon (2008). The Effect of Computerized Physician Order Entry with Clinical Decision Support on the Rates of Adverse Drug Events: A Systematic Revie, *Journal of General Internal Medicine* 23(4): 451–458.

69. Ammenwerth, Elske, Petra Schnell-Inderst, Christof Machan, and Uwe Siebert (2008). The Effect of Electronic Prescribing on Medication Errors and Adverse Drug Events: A Systematic Review, *Journal of the American Medical Informatics Association* 15: 585–600.

70. Belluck, Pam (2017). First Digital Pill Approved to Worries About Biomedical 'Big Brother', *New York Times,* 13 November. See also Szarfman, Ana, Stella G. Machado, and Robert T. O'Neill (2002). Use of Screening Algorithms and Computer Systems to Efficiently Signal Higher-Than-Expected Combinations of Drugs and Events in the US FDA's Spontaneous Reports Database, *Drug Safety* 25(6): 381–392.

71. Bansal, Shweta, Gerardo Chowell, Lone Simonsen, Alessandro Vespignani, and Cécile Viboud (2016). Big Data for Infectious Disease Surveillance and Modeling, *The Journal of Infectious Diseases* 214(S4): S375–379.

72. Eysenbach, Gunther (2009). Infodemiology and Infoveillance: Framework for an Emerging Set of Public Health Informatics Methods to Analyze Search, Communication and Publication Behavior on the Internet, *Journal of Medical Internet Research* 11(1).

73. Guerrisi, Caroline, Clément Turbelin, Thierry Blanchon, Thomas Hanslik, Isabelle Bonmarin, Daniel Levy-Bruhl, Daniela Perrotta, Daniela Paolotti, Ronald Smallenburg, Carl Koppeschaar, Ana O. Franco, Ricardo Mexia, W. John Edmunds, Bersabeh Sile, Richard Pebody, Edward van Straten, Sandro Meloni, Yamir Moreno, Jim Duggan, Charlotte Kjelsø, and Vittoria Colizza (2016). Participatory Syndromic Surveillance of Influenza in Europe, *The Journal of Infectious Diseases* 214(S4): S386–392.

74. Chowell, Gerardo, Julie M. Cleaton, and Cecile Viboud (2016). Elucidating Transmission Patterns from Internet Reports: Ebola and Middle East Respiratory Syndrome as Case Studies, *The Journal of Infectious Diseases* 214(S4): S421–426. See also Wikimedia Commons (2018). 2014 Ebola virus epidemic in West Africa.svg. https://commons.wikimedia.org/wiki/File:2014_ebola_virus_epidemic_in_West_Africa.svg.

75. Lazer, David, Ryan Kennedy, Gary King, and Alessandro Vespignani (2014). The Parable of Google Flu: Traps in Big Data Analysis, *Science* 343 (6176): 1203–1205.

76. Moran, Kelly R., Geoffrey Fairchild, Nicholas Generous, Kyle Hickmann, Dave Osthus, Reid Priedhorsky, James Hyman, and Sara Y. Del Valle (2016). Epidemic Forecasting is Messier Than Weather Forecasting: The Role of Human Behavior and Internet Data Streams in Epidemic Forecast, *The Journal of Infectious Diseases* 214(S4): S404–408.

77. Lee, Elizabeth C., Jason M. Asher, Sandra Goldlust, John D. Kraemer, Andrew B. Lawson, and Shweta Bansal (2016). Mind the Scales: Harnessing Spatial Big Data for Infectious Disease Surveillance and Inference, *The Journal of Infectious Diseases* 214(S4): S409–413. See also Wesolowski, Amy, Caroline O. Buckee, Kenth Engø-Monsen, and C. J. E. Metcalf (2016). Connecting Mobility to Infectious Diseases: The Promise and Limits of Mobile Phone Data, *The Journal of Infectious Diseases* 214: S414-S420.

78. Sharma, Megha, Kapil Yadav, Nitika Yadav, and Keith C. Ferdinand (2016). Zika Virus Pandemic—Analysis of Facebook as a Social Media Health Information Platform, *American Journal of Infection Control* 45(3): 301–302.

79. Salathé, Marcel (2016). Digital Pharmacovigilance and Disease Surveillance: Combining Traditional and Big-Data Systems for Better Public Health, *The Journal of Infectious Diseases* 214(S4): S399–403. See also McNeil, Jr., Donald G. (2018). 'Smart Thermometers' Track Flu Season in Real Time, *New York Times,* 16 January.

80. Dawson, Steven L. and John A. Kaufman (1993). The Imperative for Medical Simulation, *Proc. IEEE* 86(3): 479–483. See also Kunkler, Kevin (2003). The Role of Medical Simulation: An Overview, *The International Journal of Medical Robots and Computer Assisted Surgery* 2: 203–210. See also Issenberg, S. Barry, William C. McGaghie, Emil R. Petrusa, David Lee Gordon, and Ross J. Scalese (2005). Features and Uses of High-fidelity Medical Simulations that Lead to Effective Learning: A BEME Systematic Review, *Medical Teacher* 27(1): 10–28. See also Issenberg, S. Barry and Ross J. Scalese (2008). Simulation in Health Care Education, *Perspectives in Biology and Medicine* 51(1): 31–46. See also Rosen, Kathleen R. (2008). The History of Medical Simulation, *Journal of Critical Care* 23: 157–166.

81. Boulet, John R., David Murray, Joe Kras, Julie Woodhouse, John McAllister, and Amitai Ziv (2003). Reliability and Validity of a Simulation-based Acute Care Skills Assessment for Medical Students and Residents, *Anesthesiology* 99(6): 1270–1280.

82. Dawson, David L. (2006). Training in Carotid Artery Stenting: Do Carotid Simulation Systems Really Help? *Vascular* 14(5): 256–263.

83. Loma Linda University (2018). The Medical Simulation Center—Loma Linda University. *https://www.youtube.com/watch?v=ZXY_VtEhTNI.*

84. Weller, Jennifer, Robert Henderson, Craig S. Webster, Boaz Shulruf, Jane Torrie, Elaine Davies, Kaylene Henderson, Chris Frampton, Alan F. Merry (2014). Building the Evidence on Simulation Validity: Comparison of Anesthesiologists' Communication Patterns in Real and Simulated Cases, *Anesthesiology* 120(1): 142–148.

85. Schmidle, Nicholas (2017). Can Football Be Saved? A High School Is Experimenting with Technology to Make the Sport Safer, *The New Yorker*, 9 January, 38–51.

86. Sugarman, Mike (2017). The Ultimate Guide to Artificial Body Parts. Retrieved on 4 March 2017 from http://www.hopesandfears.com/hopes/future/science/213387-artificial-body-parts. See also Wikipedia (2017c). Artificial Organ. https://en.wikipedia.org/wiki/Artificial_organ.

87. ForbesBrandVoice (2017). The Surprising Future of Artificial Organ Transplants. https://www.forbes.com/sites/oppenheimerfunds/2016/09/26/the-surprising-future-of-artificial-organ-transplants/#29b0a9d92f59.

88. Park, William (2015). The Geniuses Who Invented Prosthetic Limbs. BBC Future. http://www.bbc.com/future/story/20151030-the-geniuses-who-invented-prosthetic-limbs.

89. McGrath, Ben (2007). Muscle Memory, *The New Yorker*, 30 July, 40–45.

90. Ottoback (2017). Myoelectric prosthetics 101. http://www.ottobockus.com/prosthetics/info-for-new-amputees/prosthetics-101/myoelectric-prosthetics-101/.
91. Gopnik, Adam (2016). Feel Me: What the New Science of Touch Says about Ourselves, *The New Yorker,* 16 May, 56–66.
92. NHLBI (2017). What Is a Pacemaker? National Heart, Lung, and Blood Institute, US NIH. Retrieved on 4 March 2017 from https://www.nhlbi.nih.gov/health/health-topics/topics/pace. See also Aquilina, C. (2006). A Brief History of Cardiac Pacing, *Images in Paediatric Cardiology* 8(2): 17–81.
93. Healthy Hearing (2017). Cochlear Implants. http://www.healthyhearing.com/help/hearing-aids/cochlear-implants.
94. Rojahn, Susan Young (2013). What It's Like to See Again with an Artificial Retina, *MIT Technology Review.* https://www.technologyreview.com/s/514081/can-artificial-retinas-restore-natural-sight/.
95. NHLBI (2017), What Is a Total Artificial Heart? National Heart, Lung, and Blood Institute, US NIH. https://www.nhlbi.nih.gov/health/health-topics/topics/tah. See also Baum, Dan (2012). No Pulse: How Doctors Reinvented the Human Heart, *Popular Science.* http://www.popsci.com/science/article/2012-02/no-pulse-how-doctors-reinvented-human-heart.
96. Brumfiel, Geoff (2013). The Insane and Exciting Future of the Bionic Body, *Smithsonian Magazine,* September. http://www.smithsonianmag.com/innovation/the-insane-and-exciting-future-of-the-bionic-body-918868/.
97. Smithsonian Channel (2013). The Incredible Bionic Man. http://www.smithsonianchannel.com/shows/the-incredible-bionic-man/0/3378516.
98. Carey, Benedict (2017). 'Pacemaker' for the Brain Can Help Memory, Study Finds, *New York Times,* 20 April.
99. DARPA (2017). Towards a High-Resolution, Implantable Neural Interface. US Defense Research Projects Agency News and Events. https://www.darpa.mil/news-events/2017-07-10.
100. Glannon, Walter (2014). Ethical issues with brain–computer interfaces, *Frontiers in Systems Neuroscience* 8 (July): Article 136, 1–3. See also Vlek, Rutger J., David Steines, Dyana Szibbo, Andrea Kübler, Mary-Jane Schneider, Pim Haselager, and Femke Nijboer (2012). Ethical Issues in Brain–Computer Interface Research, Development, and Dissemination, *Journal of Neurologic Physical Therapy* 36 (June): 94–99.
101. Garroway, Levi A., Jaap Verweij, and Karla V. Ballman (2013). Precision Oncology: An Overview, *Journal of Clinical Oncology* 31(15): 1803–1805. See also Szabo, Liz (2018). Are We Being Misled About Precision Medicine, *New York Times,* 11 September.
102. Gulshan, Varun, Lily Peng, Marc Coram, Martin C. Stumpe, Derek Wu, Arunachalam Narayanaswamy, Subhashini Venugopalan, Kasumi Widner, TomMadams, Jorge Cuadros, Ramasamy Kim, Rajiv Raman, MS, Philip C. Nelson, Jessica L. Mega, and Dale R.Webster (2016). Development and Validation of a Deep Learning Algorithm for Detection of Diabetic Retinopathy in Retinal Fundus Photographs, *JAMA* 316(22): 2402–2410. Also a private mail conversation in 2017 with Lily Peng.
103. Geschwind, Daniel H. (2011). Genetics of Autism Spectrum Disorders, *Trends in Cognitive Sciences* 15(9): 409–416.
104. Devlin, Bernie and Stephen W. Scherer (2012). Genetic Architecture in Autism Spectrum Disorder, *Current Opinion in Genetics & Development* 22: 229–237.

105. Scherer, Stephen W. and Geraldine Dawson (2011). Risk Factors for Autism: Translating Genomic Discoveries into Diagnostics, *Human Genetics* 130: 123–148.

106. Carter, M. T. and S. W. Scherer (2013). Autism Spectrum Disorder in the Genetics Clinic: A Review, *Clinical Genetics* 83: 399–407.

107. Grady, Denise (2017). F.D.A. Approves Second Gene-Altering Treatment for Cancer, *New York Times,* 18 October.

108. Blau, C. Anthony and Effie Liakopoulou (2013). Can We Deconstruct Cancer, One Patient at a Time? *Trends in Genetics* 29(1): 6–10. See also Shrager, Jeff and Jay M. Tenenbaum (2014). Rapid Learning for Precision Oncology, *Nature Reviews | Clinical Oncology* 11 (February): 109–118.

109. Kolata, Gina (2017). Gene Editing Spurs Hope for Transplanting Pig Organs into Humans, *New York Times,* 10 August. See also Kennedy, Pagan (2017). What If You Knew Alzheimer's Was Coming for You? *New York Times,* 17 November.

110. Wauters, Annet and Ine Van Hoyweghen (2016). Global Trends on Fears and Concerns of Genetic Discrimination: A Systematic Literature Review, *Journal of Human Genetics* 61: 275–282.

111. Otlowski, M. S. Taylor and Y. Bombard (2012). Genetic Discrimination: International Perspectives, *Annual Review of Genomics and Human Genetics* 13: 433–454.

112. NIH (2017). Genetic Information Nondiscrimination Act (GINA) of 2008. https://www.genome.gov/24519851/.

113. Picard, André (2017). Anti-Genetic-Discrimination Bill is Little More than Virtue Signaling, *The Globe and Mail,* 9 March.

114. Kolata, Gina (2017). F.D.A. Will Allow 23andMe to Sell Genetic Tests for Disease Risk to Consumers, *New York Times,* 6 April.

115. Grady, Denise (2017). Companies Rush to Develop 'Utterly Transformative' Gene Therapies, *New York Times,* 23 July.

116. Lynch, Holly Fernandez and Steven Joffe (2017). Science Needs Your Cells, *New York Times,* 21 April.

117. Frank, Martin, Anne Prenzler, Roland Eils, and J.-Matthias Graf von der Schulenburg (2013). Genome Sequencing: A Systematic Review of Health Economic Evidence, *Health Economics Review* 3: 29. See also Interlandi, Jeneen (2016). The Paradox of Precision Medicine, *ScientificAmerican.com.* https://www.scientificamerican.com/article/the-paradox-of-precision-medicine/.

118. Rogowski, Wolf H., Scott D. Grosse, Jörg Schmidtke, and Georg Marckmann (2014). Criteria for Fairly Allocating Scarce Health-Care Resources to Genetic Tests: Which Matter Most? *European Journal of Human Genetics* 22: 25–31.

119. Rehman, Abdul, Noor Ul-Ain Baloch, and Ibrahim A. Janahi (2016). Lumacaftor–Ivacaftor in Patients with Cystic Fibrosis Homozygous for Phe508del CFTR, *New England Journal of Medicine* 373(18): 1783.

120. Hollands, Gareth J., David P. French, Simon J. Griffin, A. Toby Prevost, Stephen Sutton, Sarah King, and Theresa M. Marteau (2016). The Impact of Communicating Genetic Risks of Disease on Risk-Reducing Health Behaviour: Systematic Review with Meta-Analysis, *BMJ* 352: i1102.

121. Belluck, Pam (2017). Gene Editing for 'Designer Babies'? Highly Unlikely, Scientists Say, *New York Times,* 4 August.

122. DesignerBabiesEthics (2017). So, What ARE 'Designer Babies?' https://designerbabiesethics.wordpress.com. See also Wikipedia (2017d). Designer Baby. https://en.wikipedia.org/wiki/Designer_baby.

123. Broyde, Michael J. (2004). Pre-Implantation Genetic Diagnosis, Stem Cells and Jewish Law, *Tradition: A Journal of Orthodox Jewish Thought* 38(1): 54–75.

124. Sandel, Michael J. (2004). The Case Against Perfection: What's Wrong with Designer Children, Bionic Athletes, and Genetic Engineering, *The Atlantic*, April, 51–62.

125. Harmon, Amy (2017). Human Gene Editing Receives Science Panel's Support, *New York Times*, 14 February.

126. Graber, Cynthia (2015). The Problem with Precision Medicine, *The New Yorker*, 5 February. See also Adams, Michael C., James P. Evans, Gail E. Henderson, and Jonathan S. Berg (2016). The Promise and Peril of Genomic Screening in the General Population, *Genetics in Medicine* 18(6): 593–509. See also Szabo, Liz (2018). Are We Being Misled About Precision Medicine, *New York Times*, 11 September.

127. Specter, Michael (2017). Rewriting the Code of Life, *The New Yorker*, 2 January, 34–43.

128. Doidge, Norman (2007). *The Brain that Changes Itself: Stories of Personal Triumph from the Frontiers of Brain Science*, Penguin Books. See also Doidge, Norman (2016). *The Brain's Way of Healing: Remarkable Discoveries and Recoveries from the Frontiers of Neuroplasticity*, Penguin Books.

129. Stern, Yaakov (2002). What Is Cognitive Reserve? Theory and Research Application of the Reserve Concept, *Journal of the International Neuropsychological Society* 8: 448–460.

130. SharpBrains (2017). Market Intelligence: Digital Platforms for Brain/Cognitive Assessment, Monitoring and Enhancement. Sharpbrains.com. https://sharpbrains.com/market-report//.

131. Huntsman, Mark (2018). 8 Brain-Training Games for Memory. Alzheimers.net. *http://www.alzheimers.net/11-5-14-brain-training-games/*.

132. Smith, Glenn E., Patricia Housen, Kristine Yaffe, Ronald Ruff, Robert F. Kennison, Henry W. Mahncke, and Elizabeth M. Zelinski, PhDw. (2009). A Cognitive Training Program Based on Principles of Brain Plasticity: Results from the Improvement in Memory with Plasticity-based Adaptive Cognitive Training (IMPACT) Study, *Journal of the American Geriatric Society* 57: 594–603.

133. Rebok, George W., Karlene Ball, Lin T. Guey, Richard N. Jones, Hae-Young Kim, Jonathan W. King, Michael Marsiske, John N. Morris, Sharon L. Tennstedt, Frederick W. Unverzagt, and Sherry L. Willis, for the ACTIVE Study Group (2014). Ten-Year Effects of the Advanced Cognitive Training for Independent and Vital Elderly Cognitive Training Trial on Cognition and Everyday Functioning in Older Adults, *Journal of the American Geriatric Society* 62: 16–24.

134. Edwards, Jerri D., Huiping Xu, Daniel Clark, Lesley A. Ross, and Frederick W. Unverzagt (2016). The ACTIVE Study: What We Have Learned and What is Next? Cognitive Training Reduces Incident Dementia Across Ten Years. Presentation Summary. American Psychological Association Annual Conference, 25 July. http://www.apa.org/news/press/releases/2016/08/active-study.pdf.

135. Stanford Center on Longevity (2014). A Consensus on the Brain Training Industry from the Scientific Community. http://longevity3.stanford.edu/blog/2014/10/15/the-consensus-on-the-brain-training-industry-from-the-scientific-community/.

136. Mahncke, Henry W. (2014). A Response to 'A Consensus on the Brain Training Industry from the Scientific Community'. http://www.brainhq.com/longevityresponse.

137. Lambit, Amit, Harry Hallock, and Michael Valenzuela (2014). Computerized Cognitive Training in Cognitively Healthy Older Adults: A Systematic Review and Meta-Analysis of Effect Modifiers, *PLOS Medicine* 11(11): 1–18.

138. Simons, Daniel J., Walter R. Boot, Neil Charness, Susan E. Gathercole, Christopher F. Chabris, David Z. Hambrick, and Elizabeth A. L. Stine-Morrow(2016). Do 'Brain Training' Programs Work? *Psychological Science in the Public Interest* 17(3): 103–186.

139. Lustig, Cindy, Priti Shah, Rachael Seidler, and Patricia A. Reuter-Lorenz (2009). Aging, Training, and the Brain: A Review and Future Directions, *Neuropsychological Review* 19: 504–522.

140. Voss, Michelle W., Ruchika S. Prakash, Kirk I. Erickson, Chandramallika Basak, Laura Chaddock, Jennifer S. Kim, Heloisa Alves, Susie Heo, Amanda N. Szabo, Siobhan M. White, Thomas R. Wójcicki, Emily L. Mailey, Neha Gothe, Erin A. Olson, Edward McAuley, and Arthur F. Kramer (2010). Plasticity of Brain Networks in a Randomized Intervention Trial of Exercise Training in Older Adults, *Frontiers of Aging Neuroscience* 26 (August).

141. UN (2015). World Population Aging. United Nations Department of Economic and Social Affairs, Population Division. http://www.un.org/en/development/desa/population/publications/pdf/ageing/WPA2015_Report.pdf.

142. AARP (2013). The Aging of the Baby Boom and the Growing Care Gap: A Look at Future Declines in the Availability of Family Caregivers. http://www.aarp.org/home-family/caregiving/info-08-2013/the-aging-of-the-baby-boom-and-the-growing-care-gap-AARP-ppi-ltc.html.

143. Span, Paula (2018). If Immigrants Are Pushed Out, Who Will Care for the Elderly? *New York Times,* 2 February.

144. Oi, Mariko (2015). Who Will Look After Japan's Elderly? BBC News. http://www.bbc.com/news/world-asia-31901943.

145. Harmon, Amy (2010). A Soft Spot for Circuitry, *New York Times,* 4 July. For a video demonstrating the use of Paro the robot seal, see https://www.youtube.com/watch?v=uFMenahpJtI. See also Smiley, Lauren (2017). The Digital Puppy That Keeps Seniors Out of Nursing Homes, *Wired,* 19 December, for use of an animated displayed dog. See also Wikipedia (2018). Telenoid R1, from https://en.wikipedia.org/wiki/Telenoid_R1, for a third approach in which am 80-centimetre robotic rubber android is used to facilitate communication between seniors, family, and friends.

146. Wada, Kazuyoshi and Takanori Shibata (2007). Living with Seal Robots—Its Sociopsychological and Physiological Influences on the Elderly at a Care House, *IEEE Transactions on Robotics* 23(5): 972–980.

147. Jøranson, Nina, Ingeborg Pedersen, Anne Marie Mork Rokstad, and Camilla Ihlebæk (2016). Change in Quality of Life in Older People with Dementia Participating in Paro-activity: A Cluster-randomized Controlled Trial, *Journal of Advanced Nursing* 72(12): 3020–3033. 10.1111/jan.13076.

148. Bemelmans, Roger, Gert Jan Gelderblom, Pieter Jonker, and Luc de Witte (2012). Socially Assistive Robots in Elderly Care: A Systematic Review into Effects and Effectiveness, *Journal of the American Medical Directors Association* 13: 114–120. See also Kachouie, Reza, Sima Sedighadeli, Rajiv Khosla, and Mei-Tai Chu (2014). Socially Assistive Robots in Elderly Care: A Mixed-Method Systematic Literature Review, *International Journal of Human–Computer Interaction* 30: 369–393.

149. Dishman, Lydia (2018). This Robot Will Keep Your Grandparents Company When You're Too Busy, *Fast Company,* 30 April. See also TechCrunch (2018). ElliQ is Companion Robot

that Helps Older Adults Engage in the Digital World. https://www.youtube.com/watch?v=vPKFaNCC8kU.

150. Sharkey, Amanda, and Noel Sharkey (2012). Granny and the Robots: Ethical Issues in Robot Care for the Elderly, *Ethics Information Technology* 14: 27–40. See also Ienca, Marcello, Fabrice Jotterand, Constantin Vica, and Bernice Elger (2016). Social and Assistive Robotics in Dementia Care: Ethical Recommendations for Research and Practice, *International Journal of Social Robotics* 8: 565–573.
151. Frankovich, Jennifer, Christopher A. Longhurst, and Scott M. Sutherland (2011). Evidence-Based Medicine in the EMR Era, *New England Journal of Medicine* 365(19): 1758–1759.
152. Kish, Leonard J. and Eric J Topol (2015). Unpatients—Why Patients Should Own their Medical Data, *Nature Biotechnology* 33 (9): 921–924.
153. Kohn, Linda T., Janet M. Corrigan, and Molla S. Donaldson (Eds.) (1999). To Err Is Human: Building a Safer Health System. Institute of Medicine (US) Committee on Quality of Health Care in America. National Academy Press. https://www.nap.edu/catalog/9728/to-err-is-human-building-a-safer-health-system.
154. NPSF (2015). Free from Harm: Accelerating Patient Safety Improvement Fifteen Years After To Err Is Human. National Patient Safety Forum. http://www.npsf.org/?page=freefromharm.
155. Illingworth, John (2015). Continuous Improvement of Patient Safety: The Case for Change in the NHS. The Health Foundation. http://www.health.org.uk/publication/continuous-improvement-patient-safety.
156. OECD (2015). Healthcare Costs Unsustainable in Advanced Economies without Reform. *OECD.org*, 24 September. http://www.oecd.org/health/healthcarecostsunsustainableinadvancedeconomieswithoutreform.htm.
157. Barua, Bacchus, Milagros Palacios, and Joel Emes (2016). The Sustainability of Health Care Spending in Canada. Fraser Institute, 31 May. https://www.fraserinstitute.org/studies/sustainability-of-health-care-spending-in-canada.
158. Ensmenger, Nathan (2008). Resistance Is Futile? Reluctant and Selective Users of the Internet. In Aspray, William and Paul E. Ceruzzi (Eds.), *The Internet and American Business*, pp. 351–388, The MIT Press.
159. Wikipedia (2017). Telemedicine. https://en.wikipedia.org/wiki/Telemedicine.
160. Wikipedia (2017). Robot-assisted surgery. https://en.wikipedia.org/wiki/Robot-assisted_surgery.
161. Mukherjee, Siddartha (2017). The Algorithm Will See You Now, *The New Yorker*, 3 April.

Chapter 5

1. Rossman, Michael (1975). Implications of Community Memory, *ACM SIGCAS Computers and Society Newsletter* 6(4): 7–10. http://dl.acm.org/citation.cfm?id=958789&coll=GUIDE&dl=GUIDE.
2. Wikipedia (2017). Utopian and dystopian fiction. https://en.wikipedia.org/wiki/Utopian_and_dystopian_fiction.
3. Wikipedia (2017). Panopticon. https://en.wikipedia.org/wiki/Panopticon. See also Bentham, Jeremy (1838–1843). *The Works of Jeremy Bentham*. http://oll.libertyfund.org/titles/bentham-works-of-jeremy-bentham-11-vols.

4. Orwell, George (1945). *Animal Farm*, Secker and Warburg.
5. Huxley, Aldous (1932). *Brave New World*, Chatto and Windus.
6. Orwell, George (1949). *1984*, Secker and Warburg. See also Cervantes, Julieta (2017). A Scene from the Recent Broadway Production of *1984*. https://variety.com/2017/legit/reviews/1984-review-broadway-play-1202476234/.
7. De Freytas-Tamura, Kimiko (2017). George Orwell's '1984' Is Suddenly a Best-Seller, *New York Times*, 25 January. See also Alter, Alexandra (2017). Uneasy About the Future, Readers Turn to Dystopian Classics, *New York Times*, 27 January. As of 2013, *1984* had been turned into a Broadway play by Robert Icke and Duncan Macmillan.
8. Wikipedia (2017). Freedom of Speech. https://en.wikipedia.org/wiki/Freedom_of_speech.
9. Wikipedia (2017). United States Bill of Rights. https://en.wikipedia.org/wiki/United_States_Bill_of_Rights.
10. Wikipedia (2017). Freedom of Speech by Country. https://en.wikipedia.org/wiki/Freedom_of_speech_by_country.
11. Sunstein, Cass (2017). *#republic: Divided Democracy in the Age of Social Media*, Princeton University Press.
12. Wikipedia (2018). List of telecommunication regulatory bodies. https://en.wikipedia.org/wiki/List_of_telecommunications_regulatory_bodies.
13. Nielsen (2012). Buzz in the Blogosphere: Millions More Bloggers and Blog Readers. http://www.nielsen.com/us/en/insights/news/2012/buzz-in-the-blogosphere-millions-more-bloggers-and-blog-readers.html.
14. Schultz, Jeff (2017). How Much Data is Created on the Internet Each Day? Retrieved on 5 June 2018 from https://blog.microfocus.com/how-much-data-is-created-on-the-internet-each-day/.
15. Radicati (2017). Email Statistics Report, 2015–2019. Radicati Group, Inc. Retrieved on 3 April 2017 from http://www.radicati.com/wp/wp-content/uploads/2015/02/Email-Statistics-Report-2015-2019-Executive-Summary.pdf. Data points are from 2015.
16. Isaac, Mike and Christopher Mele (2017). A Murder Posted on Facebook Prompts Outrage and Questions Over Responsibility, *New York Times*, 17 April. See also Retro Report (2017). The Digital Bystander, *New York Times*, retrieved on 26 May 2018 from https://www.nytimes.com/video/us/100000005144290/the-digital-bystander.html.
17. Castleman, Michael (2016). Dueling Statistics: How Much of the Internet is Porn? *Psychology Today*, 3 November.
18. Metz, Cade (2015). The Porn Business Isn't Anything Like You Think It Is, *Wired*, 15 October.
19. Wheatland, Tara (2005). Ashcroft vs. ACLU: In Search of Plausible, Less Restrictive Alternatives, *Berkeley Technology Law Journal* 20: 371–396.
20. Faucette, Jeffrey E. (1995). The Freedom of Speech at Risk in Cyberspace: Obscenity Doctrine and a Frightened University's Censorship of Sex on the Internet, *Duke Law Journal* 44(6): 1155–1182.
21. Wikipedia (2017). Communications Decency Act. https://en.wikipedia.org/wiki/Communications_Decency_Act.
22. Wikipedia (2017). Child Online Protection Act. https://en.wikipedia.org/wiki/Child_Online_Protection_Act.
23. Wikipedia (2017). Children's Internet Protection Act. https://en.wikipedia.org/wiki/Children%27s_Internet_Protection_Act.

24. Wheatland, Tara (2005). Ashcroft v. ACLU: In Search of Plausible, Less Restrictive Alternatives, *Berkeley Tech. Law Journal* 20(1): 371–396.
25. Wikipedia (2017). Hate Speech. https://en.wikipedia.org/wiki/Hate_speech.
26. Waldron, Jeremy (2012). *The Harm in Hate Speech*, Harvard University Press. See also McConnell, Michael (2012). You Can't Say That: 'The Harm in Hate Speech,' by Jeremy Waldron, *New York Times*, 22 June.
27. Dellinger, A. J. (2016). New Hate Speech Code of Conduct Wins Support from Facebook, Twitter, Google, and Microsoft. Retrieved on 3 April 2017 from https://www.dailydot.com/debug/european-commission-hate-speech-code-of-conduct-google-twitter-microsoft-google/.
28. Scott, Mark (2016). Europe Presses American Tech Companies to Tackle Hate Speech, *New York Times*, 6 December.
29. Eddy, Melissa and Mark Scott (2017). Delete Hate Speech or Pay Up, Germany Tells Social Media Companies, *New York Times*, 30 June. See also Bennhold, Katrin (2018). Germany Acts to Tame Facebook, Learning From Its Own History of Hate, *New York Times*, 19 May.
30. Rutenberg, Jim (2017). Where Is the Line? Deadly Protest Forces Media to Decide, *New York Times*, 17 August. See also Sisario, Ben (2017). White-Power Rock Bands Find Platform Online to Incite Hatred, *New York Times*, 17 August. See also Herrman, John (2017). How Hate Groups Forced Online Platforms to Reveal Their True Nature, *New York Times*, 21 August. Stevens, Matt (2017). After Charlottesville, Even Dating Apps Are Cracking Down on Hate, *New York Times*, 24 August.
31. Hauser, Christine (2017). Reddit Bans 'Incel' Group for Inciting Violence Against Women, *New York Times*, 9 November. Reilly, Katie (2018). Toronto Van Attack Victims Are Mostly Women: The Latest, *Time Magazine*, 24 April.
32. Isaac, Mike (2017). Twitter Sues the Government to Block the Unmasking of an Account Critical of Trump, *New York Times*, 6 April.
33. Isaac, Mike (2017). U.S. Blinks in Clash with Twitter; Drops Order to Unmask Anti-Trump Account, *New York Times*, 7 April.
34. Palme, Jacob and Mikael Berglund (2004). Anonymity on the Internet. https://people.dsv.su.se/~jpalme/society/anonymity.pdf.
35. Kang, Ruogu, Stephanie Brown, and Sara Kiesler (2013). Why Do People Seek Anonymity on the Internet? Informing Policy and Design, *Proceedings of the 2013 CHI Conference*: 2657–2666.
36. Davenport, David (2002). Anonymity on the Internet: Why the Price May Be Too High, *Communications of the ACM* 45(4): 33–35.
37. Digital Media Law Project (2014). Legal Protections for Anonymous Speech. Retrieved on 26 April 2017 from http://www.dmlp.org/legal-guide/legal-protections-anonymous-speech.
38. Relevant computer science issues were discussed in a slide deck by Bellovin, Steven M. (2015). Freedom of Speech: Anonymity. Retrieved on 26 April 2017 from https://www.cs.columbia.edu/~smb/classes/s15/l_anonymity.pdf.
39. Scott, Mark (2017). In Wake of Attack, U.K. Officials to Push Against Encryption Technology, *New York Times*, 27 March.
40. Isaac, Mike (2016). Facebook and Other Tech Companies Seek to Curb Flow of Terrorist Content, *New York Times*, 5 December.
41. Overly, Steven (2017). Facebook Plans to Use AI to Identify Terrorist Propaganda, *The Washington Post*, 16 Feburary.

42. Frenkel, Sheera (2017). Facebook Will Use Artificial Intelligence to Find Extremist Posts, *New York Times,* 15 June.
43. Wakabayashi, Daisuke (2017). YouTube Sets New Policies to Curb Extremist Videos, *New York Times,* 18 June. For a recent incident of YouTube acting against an extremist spokesman for terrorism, see Shane, Scott (2017). In 'Watershed Moment,' YouTube Blocks Extremist Cleric's Message, *New York Times,* 12 November.
44. Warf, Barney (2011). Geographies of Global Internet Censorship, *GeoJournal* 76(1): 1–23.
45. Reporters without Borders (2018). 2018 World Press Freedom Index. *https://rsf.org/en/ranking*
46. Wikipedia (2017). Information Technology Act, 2000. https://en.wikipedia.org/wiki/Information_Technology_Act,_2000. See also Mahapatra, Dhananjay and Amit Choudhary (2015). Supreme Court Upholds Freedom of Speech on Internet, Strikes Down Draconian Law, *Times of India,* 25 March.
47. Bajaj, Vikas (2011). India Puts Tight Leash on Internet Free Speech, *New York Times,* 27 April.
48. Zahra-Malik, Mehreen (2017). Crackdown on Online Criticism Chills Pakistani Social Media, *New York Times,* 27 July.
49. Kingsley, Patrick (2017). Turkey Purges 4,000 More Officials, and Blocks Wikipedia, *New York Times,* 30 April.
50. Internet Monitor (2017). The Slippery Slope of Internet Censorship in Egypt, *Internet Monitor,* 25 October. https://thenetmonitor.org/bulletins/the-slippery-slope-of-internet-censorship-in-egypt.
51. Kang, Cecilia and Katie Benner (2017). Russia Requires Apple and Google to Remove LinkedIn From Local App Stores, *New York Times,* 16 January.
52. Dowell, William Thatcher (2006). The Internet, Censorship, and China, *Georgetown Journal of International Affairs,* Summer/Fall: 111–119. See also Yuan, Li and Daisuke Wakabayashi (2018). Google, Seeking a Return to China, Is Said to Be Building a Censored Search Engine, *New York Times,* 1 August.
53. Stevenson, Alexandra (2017). Facebook Blocks Chinese Billionaire Who Tells Tales of Corruption, *New York Times,* 1 October.
54. Deibert, Ronald (2013). *Black Code: Surveillance, Privacy, and the Dark Side of the Internet,* Expanded Edition, McClelland & Stewart, 119–120.
55. Schell, Orville (2016). Crackdown in China: Worse and Worse, *The New York Review of Books,* 21 April.
56. Ruan, Lotus, Jeffrey Knockel, Jason Q. Ng, and Masashi Crete-Nishihata (2016). One App, Two Systems: How WeChat Uses One Censorship Policy in China and Another Internationally. The Citizen Lab, 30 November. Retrieved on 7 August 2017 from http://munkschool.utoronto.ca/research-articles/one-app-two-systems-how-wechat-uses-one-censorship-policy-in-china-and-another-internationally/.
57. Benner, Katie and Sui-Lee Wee (2017). Apple Removes New York Times Apps from its Store in China, *New York Times,* 4 January. See also Tejada, Carlos (2017). Apple Faces Inquiry in China Over App Store Content, *New York Times,* 19 April. See also Manjoo, Fahrad (2017). Clearing Out the App Stores: Government Censorship Made Easier, *New York Times,* 18 January. See also Mozur, Paul (2017). China Disrupts WhatsApp Service in Online Clampdown, *New York Times,* 18 July. See also Mozur, Paul (2017). Apple Removes Apps from China Store that Help Internet Users Evade Censorship, *New York Times,* 30 July. See also Mozur, Paul (2017). Skype Vanishes from App Stores in China, Including Apple's, *New York*

Times, 21 November. See also Guangcheng, Chen (2018). Apple Can't Resist Playing by China's Rules, *New York Times,* 23 January.

58. Saul, Stephanie (2017). On Campuses Far from China, Still Under Beijing's Watchful Eye, *New York Times,* 4 May.

59. Wakabayashi, Daisuke (2018). YouTube Says Computers Are Catching Problem Videos, *New York Times,* 23 April.

60. A new documentary effectively portrays content moderators working in the Philippines: Riesewieck, Moritz and Hans Block (2017), *The Cleaners,* currently without distribution. There are also firms that have been established to protect websites from undesired content; see for example Klotnick, Kate (2017). The Terrifying Power of Internet Censors, *New York Times,* 13 September.

61. Wakabayashi, Daisuke (2018). YouTube Adds More Scrutiny to Top-TierVideos, *New York Times,* 16 January. See also Joho the Blog (2017). Hate speech on Facebook. http://www.hyperorg.com/blogger/2017/09/19/bkc-hate-speech-on-facebook/.

62. Sharpe, Kenny (2017). Users Face Consequences as Facebook Struggles to Filter Hate Speech, *The Globe and Mail,* 27 July. See also Codrea-Rado, Anna and Amie Tsang (2017). Twitter Users Split on Boycott Over Platform's Move Against Rose McGowan, *New York Times,* 13 October. See also Browne, Malachy (217). YouTube Removes Videos Showing Atrocities in Syria, *New York Times,* 22 August.

63. Nicas, Jack (2018). Apple, Facebook and YouTube Remove Content from Alex Jones and Infowars, *New York Times,* 6 August. See also Kang, Cecilia and Kate Conger (2018). Inside Twitter's Struggle Over What Gets Banned, *New York Times,* 6 August. See also The New York Times (2018). Gatekeepers or Censors? How Tech Manages Online Speech, *New York Times,* 7 August.

64. Lazer, David M. J., Matthew A. Baum, Yochai Benkler, Adam J. Berinsky, Kelly M. Greenhill, Filippo Menczer, Miriam J. Metzger, Brendan Nyhan, Gordon Pennycook, David Rothschild, Michael Schudson, Steven A. Sloman, Cass R. Sunstein, Emily A. Thorson, Duncan J. Watts, and Jonathan L. Zittrain (2018). The Science of Fake News: Addressing Fake News Requires a Multidisciplinary Effort, *Science* 359(6380): 1094–1096.

65. Wikipedia (2018). Yellow journalism. https://en.wikipedia.org/wiki/Yellow_journalism.

66. Schaedel, Sydney (2016). Did the Pope Endorse Trump? http://www.factcheck.org/2016/10/did-the-pope-endorse-trump/. See also http://www.snopes.com/pope-francis-donald-trump-endorsement/.

67. Kristof, Nicholas (2016). Lies in the Guise of News in the Trump Era, *New York Times,* 12 November. See also Silverman, Craig (2016). This Analysis Shows How Viral Fake Election News Stories Outperformed Real News on Facebook, *Buzzfeed,* 16 November. https://www.buzzfeed.com/craigsilverman/viral-fake-election-news-outperformed-real-news-on-facebook?utm_term=.sr5vV0Z5a#.uk9zgEZwO.

68. Maheshwari, Sapna (2016). How Fake News Goes Viral: A Case Study, *New York Times,* 20 November.

69. Streitfeld, David (2016). For Fact-Checking Website Snopes, a Bigger Role Brings More Attacks, *New York Times,* 25 December.

70. Faris, Robert M., Hal Roberts, Bruce Etling, Nikki Bourassa, Ethan Zuckerman, and Yochai Benkler (2017). Partisanship, Propaganda, and Disinformation: Online Media and the 2016 U.S. Presidential Election. Berkman Klein Center for Internet & Society Research Paper, 16 August 2017. https://cyber.harvard.edu/publications/2017/08/mediacloud.

71. New York Times Editorial Board (2016). Facebook and the Digital Virus Called Fake News, *New York Times,* 19 November. See also Lamb, Kate (2018). 'I felt disgusted': Inside Indonesia's Fake Twitter Account Factories, *The Guardian,* 23 July.
72. Scott, Mark and Melissa Eddy (2017). Europe Combats a New Foe of Political Stability: Fake News, *New York Times,* 20 February.
73. Scott, Mark (2017). Fake Sleuths: Web Gets It Wrong on London Attacker, *New York Times,* 24 March.
74. Anand, Geeta and Suhasini Raj (2017). Rumors on WhatsApp Ignite 2 Mob Attacks in India, Killing 7, *New York Times,* 25 May.
75. Goel, Vindu (2018). In India, Facebook's WhatsApp Plays Central Role in Elections, *New York Times,* 14 May.
76. Specia, Megan and Paul Mazur (2017). A War of Words Puts Facebook at the Center of Myanmar's Rohingya Crisis, *New York Times,* 27 October. See also Taub, Amanda and Max Fisher (2018). Where Countries Are Tinderboxes and Facebook Is a Match, *New York Times,* 21 April.
77. De Freytas-Tamura, Kimiko (2017). As Kenya's Vote Nears, Fear That 'Fake News' May Fuel Real Bloodshed, *New York Times,* 6 August.
78. Grillo, Ioan (2018). Fake News Crosses the Rio Grande, *New York Times,* 3 May.
79. Flegenheimer, Matt and Michael M. Grynbaum (2018). Trump Hands Out 'Fake News Awards,' Sans the Red Carpet, *New York Times,* 17 January.
80. Erlanger, Steven (2017). 'Fake News,' Trump's Obsession, Is Now a Cudgel for Strongmen, *New York Times,* 12 December.
81. New York Times Editorial Board (2016). Truth and Lies in the Age of Trump, *New York Times,* 10 December.
82. Manjoo, Fahrad (2018). For Two Months, I Got My News from Print Newspapers. Here's What I Learned, *New York Times,* 7 March.
83. Waldman, Steven (2017). What Facebook Owes to Journalism, *New York Times,* 21 February.
84. Roose, Kevin (2018). Here Come the Fake Videos, Too, *New York Times,* 4 March. For a description of work on generating unbelievably real photos, see Metz, Cade and Keith Collins (2018). How an A.I. 'Cat-and-Mouse Game' Generates Believable Fake Photos, *New York Times,* 4 March. For a discussion of work that DARPA is funding to identify these 'deep fakes', see Melendez, Steven (2018). Can New Forensic Tech Win War On AI-Generated Fake Images? *Fast Company,* 4 April.
85. Manjoo, Farhad (2017). Can Facebook Fix Its Own Worst Bug? *New York Times,* 25 April.
86. Isaac, Mike (2016). Facebook Mounts Effort to Limit Tide of Fake News, *New York Times,* 15 December. In 2018, Facebook also introduced mechanisms for users to rate new source credibility. See Frenkel, Sheera and Sapna Maheshwari (2018). Facebook to Let Users Rank Credibility of News, *New York Times,* 19 January.
87. Silverman, Craig (2017). Facebook Wants to Teach You How to Spot Fake News on Facebook, *BuzzFeed,* 6 April. https://www.buzzfeed.com/craigsilverman/facebook-wants-to-teach-you-how-to-spot-fake-news-on?utm_term=.hdBrpeV6J#.okWAqnVXm.
88. Scott, Mark (2017). In Europe's Election Season, Tech Vies to Fight Fake News, *New York Times,* 1 May.

89. Shane, Scott and Mike Isaac (2017). Facebook Says It's Policing Fake Accounts. But They're Still Easy to Spot, *New York Times,* 3 November.
90. Maheshwari, Sapna and Mike Isaac (2017). Facebook, After 'Fail' Over Ads Targeting Racists, Makes Changes, *New York Times,* 20 September. See also Sheiber, Noam (2017). Facebook's Ad-Targeting Problem, Captured in a Literal Shade of Gray, *New York Times,* 28 September. See also Isaac, Mike (2017). At Facebook, Hand-Wringing Over a Fix for Fake Content, *New York Times,* 27 October. See also Isaac, Mike (2018). Facebook Overhauls News Feed to Focus on What Friends and Family Share, *New York Times,* 11 January. See also Manjoo, Fahrad (2018). The Difficulties With Facebook's News Feed Overhaul, *New York Times,* 12 January.
91. Klonick, Kate (2018). Facebook Released Its Content Moderation Rules. Now What? *New York Times,* 10 March. See also Newton, Casey (2018). Facebook's First Content Moderation Report Finds Terrorism Posts Up 73 Percent This Year, *The Verge,* 15 May. https://www.theverge.com/2018/5/15/17353386/facebook-content-moderation-report-terrorism-hate-speech-community-standards-spam-fake-accounts. See also Frenkel, Sheera (2018). Facebook to Remove Misinformation That Leads to Violence, *New York Times,* 18 July.
92. Wakabayashi, Daisuke (2017). As Google Fights Fake News, Voices on the Margins Raise Alarm, *New York Times,* 26 September.
93. Tufekci, Zeynep (2017). YouTube, the Great Radicalizer, *New York Times,* 10 March.
94. Manjoo, Farhad (2017). How Twitter Is Being Gamed to Feed Misinformation, *New York Times,* 7 August.
95. Confessore, Nicholas, Gabriel J. X. Dance, Richard Harris, and Mark Hansen (2018). The Follower Factory, *New York Times,* 27 January. See also Confessore, Nicholas, Gabriel J. X. Dance, and Richard Harris (2018). Twitter Followers Vanish amid Inquiries into Fake Accounts, *New York Times,* 31 January.
96. Carr, Austin and Harry McCracken (2018). 'Did We Create This Monster?' How Twitter Turned Toxic, *Fast Company,* 4 April. See also Confessore, Nicholas and Gabriel J. X. Dance (2018). Battling Fake Accounts, Twitter to Slash Millions of Followers, *New York Times,* 11 July.
97. Bessi, Alessandro and Emilio Ferrara (2016). Social Bots Distort the 2016 U.S. Presidential Election Online Discussion, *First Monday* 21(11). http://firstmonday.org/ojs/index.php/fm/article/view/7090/5653.
98. Woolley, Samuel C. (2016). Automating Power: Social Bot Interference in Global Politics, *First Monday* 21(4). https://firstmonday.org/ojs/index.php/fm/article/view/6161/5300.
99. Howard, Philip N., Samuel Woolley, and Ryan Calo (2018). Algorithms, Bots, and Political Communication in the US 2016 Election: The Challenge of Automated Political Communication for Election Law and Administration, *Journal of Information Technology & Politics* 15(2): 81–93.
100. Wojcik, Stefan, Solomon Messing, Aaron Smith, Lee Rainie, and Paul Hitlin (2018). Bots in the Twittersphere. Pew Research Center. http://www.pewinternet.org/2018/04/09/bots-in-the-twittersphere/.
101. Negroponte, Nicholas (1995). *Being Digital,* Vintage Books.
102. Pariser, Eli (2011). *The Filter Bubble: How the New Personalized Web Is Changing What We Read and How We Think,* Penguin Books.

103. Scruggs, John F. (1998). The 'Echo Chamber' Approach to Advocacy. Philip Morris Companies Inc. Inter-office Correspondence, 18 December. https://www.industrydocumentslibrary.ucsf.edu/tobacco/docs/#id=mgxn0061.

104. Obama, Barack (2017). Farewell Speech. https://apnews.com/5f2a5b8bf38e4bd58852cfaee5864430.

105. Sunstein, Cass R. (2017). *#Republic: divided democracy in the age of social media*, Princeton University Press. Pazzanese, Christina (2017). Danger in the Internet Echo Chamber. Email exchange with Sunstein about the book. *Harvard Law Today*. https://today.law.harvard.edu/danger-internet-echo-chamber/.

106. Dreyfuss, Emily (2017). Secret Facebook Groups are the Trump Era's Worst, Best Echo Chamber, *Wired*, 20 January.

107. Bakshy, Eytan, Solomon Messing, and Lada A. Adamic (2015). Exposure to Ideologically Diverse News and Opinion on Facebook, *Science* 348(6239): 1130–1132. See also Pariser, Eli (2015). Did Facebook's Big New Study Kill My Filter Bubble Thesis? https://backchannel.com/facebook-published-a-big-new-study-on-the-filter-bubble-here-s-what-it-says-ef31a292da95. See also Robertson, Adi (2015). Facebook Says Its Algorithms Aren't Responsible for Your Online Echo Chamber. https://www.theverge.com/2015/5/7/8564795/facebook-online-opinion-filter-bubble-news-feed-study.

108. Quattrociocchi, Walter, Antonio Scala, and Cass R. Sunstein (2016). Echo Chambers on Facebook. Unpublished draft. https://papers.ssrn.com/sol3/papers.cfm?abstract_id=2795110.

109. Flaxman, Seth, Sharad Goel, and Justin M. Rao (2016). Filter Bubbles, Echo Chambers, and Online News Consumption, *Public Opinion Quarterly* 80 (Special Issue): 298–320.

110. Thompson, Alex (2016). Parallel Narratives: Clinton and Trump Supporters Really Don't Listen to Each Other on Twitter. https://news.vice.com/story/journalists-and-trump-voters-live-in-separate-online-bubbles-mit-analysis-shows.

111. Benkler, Yochai, Robert Faris, Hal Roberts, and Ethan Zuckerman (2017). Study: Breitbart-led Right-wing Media Ecosystem Altered Broader Media, *Columbia Journalism Review*, 13 April. https://www.cjr.org/analysis/breitbart-media-trump-harvard-study.php.

112. Seymour, Brittany (2014). An Emerging Threat of 'Digital Pandemics'—Lessons Learned from the Anti-vaccine Movement, *IH Connect*, 5 April. https://aphaih.org/2014/04/05/an-emerging-threat-of-digital-pandemics-lessons-learned-from-the-anti-vaccine-movement/.

113. Seymour, Brittany, Rebekah Getman, Avinash Saraf, Lily H. Zhang, and Elsbeth Kalenderian (2015). When Advocacy Obscures Accuracy Online: Digital Pandemics of Public Health Misinformation Through an Antifluoride Case Study, *American Journal of Public Health*, March. https://www.ncbi.nlm.nih.gov/pubmed/25602893.

114. Mitra, Tanushree, Scott Counts, and James W. Pennebaker (2016). Understanding Anti-Vaccination Attitudes in Social Media, *Proceedings of the Tenth International AAAI Conference on Web and Social Media*. https://www.aaai.org/ocs/index.php/ICWSM/ICWSM16/paper/view/13073.

115. Putnam, Robert D. (1995). Bowling Alone: America's Declining Social Capital, *Journal of Democracy* 6(1): 65–78.

116. Coleman, Stephen and John Gøtze (2012). Bowling Together: Online Public Engagement in Policy Deliberation. Hansard Society. http://citeseerx.ist.psu.edu/viewdoc/download?doi=10.1.1.508.6503&rep=rep1&type=pdf.

117. Knight Foundation (2013). The Emergence of Civic Tech: Investments in a Growing Field. https://www.knightfoundation.org/media/uploads/publication_pdfs/knight-civic-tech.pdf.
118. Dahlberg, Lincoln (2001). Extending the Public Sphere through Cyberspace: The Case of Minnesota E-Democracy, *First Monday* 6(3). http://firstmonday.org/ojs/index.php/fm/article/view/838/747.
119. Linaa Jensen, Jakob (2006). The Minnesota E-democracy Project: Mobilising the Mobilised? In Oates, Sarah, Diana Owen, and Rachel K. Gibson (Eds.), *The Internet and Politics: Citizens, Voters and Activists*, Ch. 3, Routledge.
120. E-democracy.org (2015). Survey Says—56% Credit Their Neighbors Forum for Increased Community Satisfaction and More. http://blog.e-democracy.org/posts/2610. See also López, Claudia and Rosta Farzan (2015). Lend Me Sugar, I Am Your Neighbor! A Content Analysis of Online Forums for Local Communities, *Communications and Technology 15*: 59–67.
121. Blacksburg Electronic Village (2017). http://www.bev.net.
122. Virginia Tech (2018). https://en.wikipedia.org/wiki/Virginia_Tech.
123. Casalegno, Federico (2001). On Cybersocialities. Networked Communication and Social Interaction in the Wired City of Blacksburg, VA, USA, *Telematics and Informatics* 18(1): 17–34.
124. Kavanaugh, Andrea L. and Scott J. Patterson (2001). The Impact of Community Networks on Social Capital and Community Involvement, *American Behavioral Scientist* 45(3): 496–509.
125. Kavanaugh, Andrea, John M. Carroll, Mary Beth Rosson, Debbie D. Reese, and Than T. Zin (2005). Participating in Civil Society: The Case of Networked Communities, *Interacting with Computers* 17(1): 9–33. See also Kavanaugh, Andrea, Than Than Zin, Mary Beth Rosson, John M. Carroll, Joseph Schmitz, and B. Joon Kim (2007). Local Groups Online: Political Learning and Participation, *Computer Supported Cooperative Work* 16(4–5): 375–395. See also Kavanaugh, Andrea L., Debbie Denise Reese, John M. Carroll, and Mary Beth Rosson (2012a). Weak Ties in Networked Communities, *The Information Society* 21(2): 119–131.
126. Hampton, Keith and Barry Wellman (2003). Neighboring in Netville: How the Internet Supports Community and Social Capital in a Wired Suburb, *City and Community* 2(4): 277–311.
127. Hampton, Keith N. (2003). Grieving for a Lost Network: Collective Action in a Wired Suburb, *The Information Society* 19(5): 417–428.
128. Kavanaugh, Andrea, Ankit Ahuja, Samah Gad, Sloane Neidig, Manuel A. Pérez-Quiñones, Naren Ramakrishnan, and John Tedesco (2014). (Hyper) Local News Aggregation: Designing for Social Affordances, *Government Information Quarterly* 31(1): 30–41. See also Kavanaugh, Andrea, Siddarth Krishnan, Manuel Pérez-Quiñones, John Tedesco, Kumbirai Madondo, and Ankit Ahuja (2014b). Encouraging Civic Participation Through Local News Aggregation, *Information Polity* 19(1): 35–56.
129. Hilbert, Martin (2009). The Maturing Concept of E-Democracy: From E-Voting and Online Consultations to Democratic Value Out of Jumbled Online Chatter, *Journal of Information Technology and Politics* 6(2): 87–110.
130. March, Luke (2006). Virtual Parties in a Virtual World: The Use of the Internet by Russian Political Parties. In Oates, Sarah, Diana Owen, and Rachel K. Gibson (Eds.) (2006). *The Internet and Politics: Citizens, Voters and Activists*, Ch. 8, Routledge.
131. Chadwick, Andrew (2006). *Internet Politics: States, Citizens, and New Communication Technologies*, Oxford University Press.

132. Chadwick, Andrew (2006). *Internet Politics: States, Citizens, and New Communication Technologies*, Oxford University Press. See also VanDerDonk, Wim, Brian D. Loader, Paul G. Nixon, and Dieter Rucht (2005). *CyberProtest: New Media, Citizens and Social Movements*, Routledge. See also Oates, Sarah, Diana Owen, and Rachel K. Gibson (Eds.) (2006). *The Internet and Politics: Citizens, Voters and Activists*, Routledge.
133. Tufekci, Zeynep (2017). Does a Protest's Size Matter? *New York Times*, 27 January.
134. Stieglitz, Stefan and Linh Dang-Xuan (2013). Social Media and Political Communication: A Social Media Analytics Framework, *Social Network Analysis and Mining* 3(4): 1277–1291.
135. Basen, Ira (2015). Social Media's Significance Oversold Amid Election Hype, *CBC News*, 18 October. http://www.cbc.ca/news/politics/canada-election-2015-social-media-1.3277007.
136. Jeanes, Katie (2015). 5 Ways Justin Trudeau's Social Media Game Trumped Other Leaders, *The Huffington Post*. http://www.huffingtonpost.ca/katie-jeanes/justin-trudeau-social-media_b_8362414.html.
137. Wolf, Gary (2004). How the Internet Invented Howard Dean, *Wired*, 1 January.
138. Harfoush, Rahaf (2009). *Yes We Did: An Inside Look at How Social Media Built the Obama Brand*. New Riders. See also Cogburn, Derrick L. and Fatima K. Espinoza-Vasquez (2011). From Networked Nominee to Networked Nation: Examining the Impact of Web 2.0 and Social Media on Political Participation and Civic Engagement in the 2008 Obama Campaign. *Journal of Political Marketing* 10(1-2),189–213. See also WeCan08 (2008). Barack Obama Music Video. https://www.youtube.com/watch?v=jjXyqcx-mYY.
139. Chaykowski, Kathleen (2016). Why Bernie Sanders's Social Media Followers Are More Engaged Than Donald Trump's, *Forbes*, 25 March.
140. Rasmussen, Tom (2017). There Was a Tinder Election Bot Fanning the Fire of the Youth Vote. *i-D*, 15 June. https://i-d.vice.com/en_gb/article/general-election-tinder-bot-youth-vote.
141. Bennett, Colin (2013). The Politics of Privacy and the Privacy of Politics: Parties, Elections and Voter Surveillance in Western Democracies. *First Monday* 18(8). http://firstmonday.org/ojs/index.php/fm/article/view/4789/3730. See also Bennett, Colin (2015). Trends in Voter Surveillance in Western Societies: Privacy Intrusions and Democratic Implications, *Surveillance and Society* 13(3–4): 370–384.
142. Confessore, Nicholas and Danny Hakim (2017). Data Firm Says 'Secret Sauce' Aided Trump; Many Scoff, *New York Times*, 6 March.
143. Issenberg, Sasha (2012). *The Victory Lab: The Secret Science of Winning Campaigns*, Crown Publishers.
144. Hersh, Eitan D. (2015). *Hacking the Electorate: How Campaigns Perceive Voters*, Cambridge University Press.
145. Chadwick, Andrew and Christopher May (2003). Interactions between States and Citizens in the Age of the Internet: 'e-Government' in the United States, Britain, and the European Union, *Governance: An International Journal of Policy, Administration, and Institutions* 16(2): 271–300.
146. Nam, Taewoo and Djoko Sigit Sayogo (2011). Government 2.0 Collects the Wisdom of Crowds, *International Conference on Social Informatics 2011*, Lecture Notes in Computer Science 6984, 51–58. See also Alam, Lubna and Richard Lucas (2011). Tweeting Government: A Case of Australian Government Use of Twitter. *2011 Ninth Institute of Electrical and Electronics Engineers (IEEE) International Conference on Dependable, Autonomic and Secure Computing*, 995–1001. See also Small, Tamara A. (2012). e-Government in the Age of Social Media: An Analysis of the Canadian Government's Use of Twitter, *Policy and Internet* 4(3–4): 91–111.

147. Rao, Leena (2009). The City of San Francisco Now Lets You Submit Complaints Via Twitter. https://techcrunch.com/2009/06/02/the-city-of-san-francisco-now-lets-you-submit-complaints-via-twitter/.

148. Kavanaugh, Andrea L., Edward A. Fox, Steven D. Sheetz, Seungwon Yang, Lin Tzy Li, Donald J. Shoemaker, Apostol Natsev, and Lexing Xie (2012b). Social Media Use by Government: From the Routine to the Critical, *Government Information Quarterly* 29(4): 480–491.

149. Gao, Huiji, Geoffrey Barbier, and Rebecca Goolsby (2011). Harnessing the Crowdsourcing Power of Social Media for Disaster Relief, *IEEE Intelligent Systems*, May/June: 10–14.

150. Queensland Police Service (2014). Disaster Management and Social Media—A Case Study. https://www.police.qld.gov.au/corporatedocs/reportsPublications/other/Documents/QPSSocialMediaCaseStudy.pdf.

151. Sutton, Jeannette, Emma S. Spiro, Carter T. Butts, Sean Fitzhugh, Britta Johnson, and Matt Greczek (2013). Tweeting the Spill: Online Informal Communications, Social Networks, and Conversational Microstructures during the Deepwater Horizon Oilspill, *International Journal of Information Systems for Crisis Response and Management* 5(1): 58–76.

152. Bertot, John C., Paul T. Jaeger, and Justin M. Grimes (2010). Using ICTs to Create a Culture of Transparency: E-government and Social Media as Openness and Anti-corruption Tools for Societies, *Government Information Quarterly* 27(3): 264–271.

153. Tolbert, Caroline J. and Karen Mossberger (2006). The Effects of E-Government on Trust and Confidence in Government, *Public Administration Review* 66(3): 354–369.

154. New York Times Editorial Board (2017). Mr. Trump's 10-Second Convictions, *New York Times*, 15 April.

155. Carr, Austin (2018). Inside the Never-Ending Trump–Clinton Twitter Psychodrama, *Fast Company*, 6 April.

156. Trump, Donald J. (2018). Tweets from @realDonald Trump. https://twitter.com/realdonaldtrump.

157. Shear, Michael D. and James Glanz (2016). Trump Says the U.S. Should Expand Its Nuclear Capacity, *New York Times*, 22 December. See also Hopkins, Jared S. (2017). Trump Sends Pharma Stocks Down with New Tweet on Drug Prices. Bloomberg, 7 March. https://www.bloomberg.com/news/articles/2017-03-07/trump-sends-pharma-stocks-down-with-new-tweet-on-drug-prices. See also Greenwood, Max (2017). Trump Tweets: The Media Is the 'Enemy of the American People', *The Hill*, 17 February. http://thehill.com/homenews/administration/320168-trump-the-media-is-the-enemy-of-the-american-people. See also Baker, Peter and Maggie Haberman (2017). A Conspiracy Theory's Journey from Talk Radio to Trump's Twitter, *New York Times*, 5 March. See also Trump (2017). Why would I call China a currency manipulator when they are working with us on the North Korean problem? We will see what happens! Twitter, 16 April. https://twitter.com/realDonaldTrump/status/853583417916755968. See also Roose, Kevin (2017). How a CNN Investigation Set Off an Internet Meme War, *New York Times*, 5 July. See also Shear, Michael D. and Maggie Haberman (2017). Trump Called National Park Chief Over Twitter Post on Inaugural Crowd, *New York Times*, 26 January.

158. Chira, Susan (2017). Who Likes Trump's Tweets and Why, *New York Times*, 29 June. See also Wu, Tim (2017). How Donald Trump Wins by Losing, *New York Times*, 3 March.

159. Hirschfeld Davis, Julie (2017). Using Air Quotes, White House Walks Back 'Wiretap' Talk, *New York Times*, 13 March. See also Valasquez-Manoff, Moises (2017). Trump Ruins Irony, Too, *New York Times*, 20 March.

160. Erlanger, Steven (2018). Trump's Twitter Threats Put American Credibility on the Line, *New York Times,* 7 January.

161. Bromwich, Jonah Engel and Johanna Barr (2018). Would Twitter Ever Suspend Trump's Account? *New York Times,* 3 January.

162. Sorkin, Andrew Ross, Jessica Silver-Greenberg, Kate Kelly and Neal E. Boudette (2018). Tesla Directors Do Damage Control After Elon Musk Tweets, *New York Times,* 14 August.

163. Sengupta, Somini (2012). Free Speech in the Age of YouTube, *New York Times,* 22 September.

164. Yoo, Christopher S. (2010). Free Speech and the Myth of the Internet as an Unintermediated Experience, *The George Washington Law Review* 78(4): 697–773.

165. York, Jillian and Robert Faris (2010). Do Web Filters Hinder Free Speech? Online Advocacy Groups Say Government 'Blacklists' Lack Independent Oversight, *Al Jazeera English News,* 14 April.

166. Timm, Trevor and Jillian York (2012). U.S. Government Threatens Free Speech with Calls for Twitter Censorship. Electronic Freedom Foundation. https://www.eff.org/deeplinks/2012/01/us-government-calls-censor-twitter-threaten-free-speech.

167. Lessin, Jessica (2016). Facebook Shouldn't Fact-Check, *New York Times,* 29 November.

168. Keller, Daphne (2017). Making Google the Censor, *New York Times,* 12 June.

169. SCOTUSblog (2017). Packingham v. North Carolina. http://www.scotusblog.com/case-files/cases/packingham-v-north-carolina/.

170. Grossman, Perry (2017). First, They Came for the Sex Offenders... *Slate.* http://www.slate.com/articles/news_and_politics/jurisprudence/2017/03/packingham_v_north_carolina_is_a_first_amendment_test_case_in_the_age_of.html.

171. New York Times Editorial Board (2017). Free Speech at the Supreme Court, *New York Times,* 19 June. See also Liptak, Adam (2017). A Constitutional Right to Facebook and Twitter? Supreme Court Weighs In, *New York Times,* 27 February.

Chapter 6

1. Wikipedia (2017). Colussus Computer. https://en.wikipedia.org/wiki/Colossus_computer.

2. Wikipedia (2017). Colussus (Novel). https://en.wikipedia.org/wiki/Colossus_(novel). See also Wikipedia (2017). Colussus: The Forbin Project. https://en.wikipedia.org/wiki/Colossus:_The_Forbin_Project.

3. Wikipedia (2018). Blade Runner. https://en.wikipedia.org/wiki/Blade_Runner. The film was loosely adapted from the novel *Do Androids Dream of Electric Sheep?* by Philip K. Dick.

4. Wikipedia (2017). Terminator (franchise). https://en.wikipedia.org/wiki/Terminator_(franchise). The image shown in the text appears on https://www.imdb.com/title/tt0103064/mediaviewer/rm4292496128.

5. Wikipedia (2017). Robocop. https://en.wikipedia.org/wiki/RoboCop.

6. Mateescu, Alexandra, Douglas Brunton, Alex Rosenblat, Desmond Patton, Zachary Gold, and Danah Boyd (2015). Social Media Surveillance and Law Enforcement. https://datasociety.net/output/data-civil-rights-social-media-surveillance-and-law-enforcement/. See also Emerson, Sarah (2016). Police Brutality Is a Campaign Issue, So Departments Ignore It on Social Media, *Motherboard,* 27 September. https://motherboard.vice.com/en_us/article/police-brutality-is-a-campaign-issue-so-departments-ignore-it-on-social-media.

7. COPS (2013). Social Media and Tactical Considerations for Law Enforcement. U.S. Department of Justice, Office of Community Oriented Policing Services, May. https://ric-zai-inc.com/Publications/cops-p261-pub.pdf. See also Hanson, Wayne (2011). How Social Media Is Changing Law Enforcement, *Government Technology*, 2 December. http://www.govtech.com/public-safety/How-Social-Media-Is-Changing-Law-Enforcement.html.
8. Herhalt, Chris (2017). Man, 42, Lured Boy, 14, Using Social Media: Police, *CP24.com*, 30 March. http://www.cp24.com/news/man-42-lured-boy-14-using-social-media-police-1.3347422. See also Sheikh, Iman (2015). How Police Departments Use Tweets and Status Updates to Fight Crime, *TVO*, 16 April. http://tvo.org/article/current-affairs/the-next-ontario/how-police-departments-use-tweets-and-status-updates-to-fight-crime.
9. Gillis, Wendy (2015). Toronto Officer's Instagram Photos Stir Concern, *Toronto Star*, 9 April. https://www.thestar.com/news/crime/2015/04/09/toronto-officers-instagram-photos-stir-concern.html.
10. Bohanon, Alysha L. (2016). Tweeting the Police: Balancing Free Speech and Decency on Government-Sponsored Social Media Pages, *Minnesota Law Review* 101: 341–382.
11. Yang, Mirae (2013). The Collision of Social Media and Social Unrest: Why Shutting Down Social Media Is the Wrong Response, *Northwestern Journal of Technology and Intellectual Property* 11(7): 707–728.
12. Wikipedia (2018). Rodney King. https://en.wikipedia.org/wiki/Rodney_King.
13. Black Lives Matter (2018). https://blacklivesmatter.com.
14. Wikipedia (2017). Trayvon Martin. https://en.wikipedia.org/wiki/Trayvon_Martin.
15. BBC (2014). Ferguson Protests: What We Know about Michael Brown's Last Minutes. BBC.com, 25 November. http://www.bbc.com/news/world-us-canada-28841715. See also Moser, Rikkilee (2015). As If All the World Were Watching: Why Today's Law Enforcement Needs to Be Wearing Body Cameras, *University of Illinois Law Review Online Journal* 7(1). https://papers.ssrn.com/sol3/papers.cfm?abstract_id=2616726. See also Craven, Julia (2016). More than 250 Black People Were Killed by Police in 2016, *Huffington Post*, 7 July. http://www.huffingtonpost.com/entry/black-people-killed-by-police-america_us_577da633e4b0c590f7e7fb17.
16. Makarechi, Kia (2016). What the Data Really Says About Police and Racial Bias: Eighteen Academic Studies, Legal Rulings, and Media Investigations Shed Light on the Issue Roiling America, *Vanity Fair*, 14 July. https://www.vanityfair.com/news/2016/07/data-police-racial-bias.
17. Bayly, Lucy (2016). Police Shootings Test New Era of Violent Social Media Video, *NBC News*, 9 July. https://www.nbcnews.com/tech/tech-news/police-shootings-test-new-era-violent-social-media-video-n605366.
18. Croft, Jay (2017). Philando Castile Shooting: Dashcam Video Shows Rapid Event, CNN, 21 June. http://www.cnn.com/2017/06/20/us/philando-castile-shooting-dashcam/index.html. See also Smith, Mitch (2017). Video of Police Killing of Philando Castile Is Publicly Released, *New York Times*, 20 June. See also Bosman, Julie and Mitch Smith (2017). Experts Weigh In on Video of Philando Castile Shooting, *New York Times*, 21 June.
19. Fausset, Richard (2018). Baton Rouge Officer Is Fired in Alton Sterling Case as Police Release New Videos, *New York Times*, 30 March. See also The New York Times (2018). Police Release New Body Camera Footage of Alton Sterling Shooting, *New York Times*, 30 March. https://

www.nytimes.com/video/us/100000005827142/police-release-new-body-camera-footage-of-alton-sterling-shooting.html.

20. Koettl, Christoph (2018). What We Learned from the Videos of Stephon Clark Being Killed by Police, *New York Times,* 7 June. See also The New York Times (2018). How Stephon Clark Was Killed by the Police: 23 Seconds, 5 Critical Moments | Visual Investigations. Video. 7 June. https://www.youtube.com/watch?v=L3Qsx2QMRlU.
21. Bosman, Julie (2017). The Latest in Police Videos: Heroes, 'Like Out of Hollywood', *New York Times,* 28 May.
22. Taylor, Emmeline (2016). Lights, Camera, Redaction... Police Body-Worn Cameras; Autonomy, Discretion and Accountability; *Surveillance & Society* 14(1): 128–132.
23. Moser, Rikkilee (2015). As If All the World Were Watching: Why Today's Law Enforcement Needs to Be Wearing Body Cameras, *University of Illinois Law Review Online Journal* 7(1). https://papers.ssrn.com/sol3/papers.cfm?abstract_id=2616726.
24. Ripley, Amanda and Timothy Williams (2017). Body Cameras Have Little Effect on Police Behavior, Study Says, *New York Times,* 20 October.
25. McLaughlin, Eliott C. (2015). We're Not Seeing More Police Shootings, Just More News Coverage. CNN, 21 April.
26. Feigenson, Neal and Christina Spiesel (2010). Law on Display. The Jury Expert, American Society of Trial Consultants. http://www.thejuryexpert.com/wp-content/uploads/FeigensonSpeiselTJEJan2010.pdf.
27. Bosman, Julie, Mitch Smith, and Michael Wines (2017). Jurors Find Video Isn't Providing 20/20 Vision in Police Shootings, *New York Times,* 25 June. See also New York Times Editorial Board (2017). Body Cams Work, if They're Used Right, *New York Times,* 9 May.
28. Ghannam, Jeffrey (2011). Social Media in the Arab World: Leading Up to the Uprisings of 2011, *Center for International Media Assistance,* 3 February. http://www.cima.ned.org/wp-content/uploads/2015/02/CIMA-Arab_Social_Media-Report-10-25-11.pdf.
29. Tufekci, Zeynep and Christopher Wilson (2017). Social Media and the Decision to Participate in Political Protest: Observations From Tahrir Square, *Journal of Communication* 62: 363–379.
30. Howard, Philip N., Aiden Duffy, Deen Freelon, Muzammil Hussain, Will Mari, and Marwa Mazaid (2011). Opening Closed Regimes: What Was the Role of Social Media During the Arab Spring? Project on Information Technology and Political Islam Working Paper 2011. https://papers.ssrn.com/sol3/papers.cfm?abstract_id=2595096.
31. Lotan, Gilan, Erhardt Graeff, Mike Ananny, Devin Gaffney, Ian Pearce, and Danah Boyd (2011). The Revolutions Were Tweeted: Information Flows During the 2011 Tunisian and Egyptian Revolutions, *International Journal of Communication* 5, Feature 1375–1405.
32. Moore, Michael (2015). Where to Invade Next. Movie. https://en.wikipedia.org/wiki/Where_to_Invade_Next. See also Eltantawy, Nahed and Julie B. Wiest (2011). Social Media in the Egyptian Revolution: Reconsidering Resource Mobilization Theory, *International Journal of Communication* 5: 1207–1224.
33. Tufekci, Zeynep (2017). *Twitter and Tear Gas: The Power and Fragility of Networked Protest,* Yale University Press. See esp. pp. ix–xxxi.
34. Khamooshi, Arash (2016). Breaking Down Apple's iPhone Fight with the U.S. Government, *New York Times,* 21 March.

35. Rubin, Joel, James Queally, and Paresh Dave (2016). FBI Unlocks San Bernardino Shooter's iPhone and Ends Legal Battle with Apple, For Now, *The L.A. Times*, 28 March.

36. Government of Canada (2016). Our Security, Our Rights: National Security Green Paper. https://www.publicsafety.gc.ca/cnt/rsrcs/pblctns/ntnl-scrt-grn-ppr-2016/index-en.aspx. See also Government of Canada (2016). Our Security, Our Rights: Background Document to National Security Green Paper. https://www.publicsafety.gc.ca/cnt/rsrcs/pblctns/ntnl-scrt-grn-ppr-2016-bckgrndr/index-en.aspx

37. Seglins, Dave, Robert Cribb, and Chelsea Gomez (2016). Inside 10 Cases Where the RCMP Hit a Digital Wall, *CBC Investigates*, 15 November. http://www.cbc.ca/news/investigates/police-power-privacy-rcmp-cases-1.3850783. See also Seglins, Dave, Robert Cribb, and Chelsea Gomez (2016). RCMP Boss Bob Paulson Says Force Needs Warrantless Access to ISP User Data, *CBC Investigates*, 16 November. http://www.cbc.ca/news/investigates/police-power-privacy-paulson-1.3851955. See also Seglins, Dave, Robert Cribb, and Chelsea Gomez (2016). Canadians Want Judicial Oversight of Any New Digital Snooping Powers for Police: Poll, *CBC Investigates*, 17 November. http://www.cbc.ca/news/investigates/police-power-privacy-poll-1.3854186. See also Seglins, Dave, Robert Cribb, and Chelsea Gomez (2016). Should Police Be Able to Force You to Hand Over Your Digital Passwords? *CBC Investigates*, 18 November. http://www.cbc.ca/news/investigates/police-power-privacy-encryption-1.3856375. See also Seglins, Dave, Robert Cribb, and Chelsea Gomez (2016). Taxpayers Would Have to Foot Bill for New High-tech Police Powers, Wireless Industry Says, *CBC Investigates*, 19 November. http://www.cbc.ca/news/investigates/police-power-privacy-interception-retention-1.3857575.

38. Government of Canada (2017). National Security Consultations. https://www.publicsafety.gc.ca/cnt/rsrcs/pblctns/2017-nsc-wwlr/2017-nsc-wwlr-en.pdf.

39. Wikipedia (2017). Patriot Act. https://en.wikipedia.org/wiki/Patriot_Act.

40. Whitehead John W., and Steven H. Aden (2002). Forfeiting 'Enduring Freedom' for 'Homeland Security': A Constitutional Analysis of the USA Patriot Act and the Justice Department's Anti-Terrorism Initiatives, *American University Law Review* 51(6): 1081–1133.

41. Herman, Susan (2006). PATRIOT Games and Executive Power, *Jurist*, 26 January. http://www.jurist.org/forum/2006/01/patriot-games-terrorism-law-and.php.

42. Kerr, Orin S. (2003). Internet Surveillance Law After the U.S.A. Patriot Act: The Big Brother That Isn't, *Northwestern University Law Review* 97(2): 607–674. See also Kerr, Orin S. (2005). Digital Evidence and the Criminal Procedure. George Washington University Law School Public Law Research Paper no. 108, *Columbia Law Review* 279.

43. Risen, James and Eric Lichtblau (2005). Bush Lets U.S. Spy on Callers Without Courts, *New York Times*, 16 December.

44. Wikipedia (2017). Edward Snowden. https://en.wikipedia.org/wiki/Edward_Snowden. See also Ball, James, Julian Borger, and Glenn Greenwald (2013). Revealed: How US and UK Spy Agencies Defeat Internet Privacy and Security, *The Guardian*, 6 September.

45. Greenwald, Glenn (2013). NSA Collecting Phone Records of Millions of Verizon Customers Daily, *The Guardian*, 6 June.

46. Savage, Charlie (2017). N.S.A. Gets More Latitude to Share Intercepted Communications, *New York Times*, 12 January. See also Savage, Charlie (2017). N.S.A. Halts Collection of Americans' Emails About Foreign Targets, *New York Times*, 28 April. See also Savage, Charlie

(2017). Federal Court Revives Wikimedia's Challenge to N.S.A. Surveillance, *New York Times,* 23 May.

47. Fairfield, Joshua A. T. and Erik Luna (2014). Digital Innocence, *Cornell Law Review* 99(5): 981–1076.
48. Gallagher, Ryan (2015). PROFILED: From Radio to Porn, British Spies Track Web Users' Online Identities, *The Intercept,* 25 September. https://theintercept.com/2015/09/25/gchq-radio-porn-spies-track-web-users-online-identities/.
49. Erlanger, Steven (2017). Can Britain Really Do Much More to Tighten Security? *New York Times,* 5 June. See also Scott, Mark (2017). After Terror Attacks, Britain Moves to Police the Web, *New York Times,* 19 June.
50. Johnston, W. Robert (2017). Worst Terrorist Strikes—Worldwide. http://www.johnstonsarchive.net/terrorism/wrjp255i.html.
51. Deibert, Ronald (2013). *Black Code: Surveillance, Privacy, and the Dark Side of the Internet,* Expanded Edition, McClelland & Stewart.
52. Scott-Railton, John, Bill Marczak, Ramy Raoof, and Etienne Maynier (2017). NILE PHISH: Large-Scale Phishing Campaign Targeting Egyptian Civil Society. Citizen Lab, University of Toronto, 2 February (updated 23 February). https://citizenlab.ca/2017/02/nilephish-report/.
53. Scott-Railton, John, Bill Marczak, Bahr Abdulrazzak, Masashi Crete-Nishihata, and Ron Deibert (2017). Reckless Exploit: Mexican Journalists, Lawyers, and a Child Targeted with NSO Spyware. Citizen Lab, University of Toronto, 19 June. https://citizenlab.ca/2017/06/reckless-exploit-mexico-nso/. See also Ahmed, Azam and Nicole Perlroth (2017). Using Texts as Lures, Government Spyware Targets Mexican Activists and Their Families, *New York Times,* 19 June.
54. Ahmed, Azam (2017). Spyware Sold to Mexican Government Targeted International Officials, *New York Times,* 10 July.
55. Wright, Laura (2016). Canadian Tech Company Netsweeper Helped Bahrain Censor Websites, Says Report, *CBC News,* 21 September. http://www.cbc.ca/news/technology/netsweeper-bahrain-government-internet-censorship-1.3769803.
56. Dalek, Jakub, Lex Gill, Bill Marczak, Sarah McKune, Naser Noor, Joshua Oliver, Jon Penney, Adam Senft, and Ron Deibert (2018). PLANET NETSWEEPER. The Citizen Lab, University of Toronto. https://citizenlab.ca/2018/04/planet-netsweeper/.
57. Canada Centre for Global Security Studies and Citizen Lab at Munk School of Global Affairs, University of Toronto (2011). Casting a Wider Net: Lessons Learned in Delivering BBC Content on the Censored Internet. http://munkschool.utoronto.ca/downloads/casting.pdf. This report also discusses technical strategies to circumvent internet censorship.
58. Ling, Justin (2018). This App Is Helping Iranians Beat Tehran's Internet Censorship, *Motherboard,* 9 January. https://motherboard.vice.com/en_us/article/zmqqn9/psiphon-app-is-helping-iran-protesters-beat-tehran-internet-censorship-citizen-lab.
59. Deibert, Ronald, John Palfrey, Rafal Rohozinski and Jonathan Zittrain (Eds.) (2008). *Access Denied: The Practice and Policy of Global Internet Filtering,* The MIT Press. http://fortay.teknikata.com/infosec/Access.Denied.The.Practice.and.Policy.of.Global.Internet.Filtering.pdf. See also Deibert, Ronald, John Palfrey, Rafal Rohozinski and Jonathan Zittrain (Eds.) (2010). *Access Controlled: The Shaping of Power, Rights, and Rule in Cyberspace,* The MIT Press. See also

Deibert, Ronald, John Palfrey, Rafal Rohozinski and Jonathan Zittrain (Eds.) (2011). *Access Contested: Security, Identity, and Resistance in Asian Cyberspace,* The MIT Press.

60. Franceschi-Bicchierai, Lorenzo (2016). How Hackers Broke into John Podesta and Colin Powell's Gmail Accounts, *Vice,* 20 October. https://motherboard.vice.com/en_us/article/how-hackers-broke-into-john-podesta-and-colin-powells-gmail-accounts.
61. Lipton, Eric, David E. Sanger, and Scott Shane (2016). The Perfect Weapon: How Russian Cyberpower Invaded the U.S., *New York Times,* 13 December.
62. Hamburger, Tom and Karen Tumulty (2016). WikiLeaks Releases Thousands of Documents about Clinton and Internal Deliberations, *The Washington Post,* 22 July. These documents came from a Russian hacker known as Gucifer 2.0, who actually was a group of Russian intelligence officers, as revealed in 2018. See Sanger, David E., Jim Rutenberg, and Eric Lipton (2018). Tracing Guccifer 2.0's Many Tentacles in the 2016 Election, *New York Times,* 15 July.
63. Cheney, Kyle and Sarah Wheaton (2016). The Most Revealing Clinton Campaign Emails in WikiLeaks Release, *Politico,* 7 October. http://www.politico.com/story/2016/10/john-podesta-wikileaks-hacked-emails-229304.
64. Maslin Nir, Sarah (2017). Hillary Clinton Says Russia Used Hacking 'to Great Effect' in Her Defeat, *New York Times,* 6 April.
65. Committee to Investigate Russia (2018). https://investigaterussia.org/.
66. Office of the Director of National Intelligence (2017). Assessing Russian Activities and Intentions in Recent US Elections. ICA 2017-01D, 6 January. https://www.dni.gov/files/documents/ICA_2017_01.pdf.
67. Shane, Scott (2017). Russian Intervention in American Election Was No One-Off, *New York Times,* 6 January.
68. Kramer, Andrew E. and Andrew Higgins (2017). In Ukraine, a Malware Expert Who Could Blow the Whistle on Russian Hacking, *New York Times,* 16 August.
69. Wu, Tim (2017). Please Prove You're Not a Robot, *New York Times,* 15 July. See also Shane, Scott (2017). The Fake Americans Russia Created to Influence the Election, *New York Times,* 7 September. See also Confessore, Nicholas and Daisuke Wakabayashi (2017). How Russia Harvested American Rage to Reshape U.S. Politics, *New York Times,* 9 October. See also Shane, Scott (2018). How Unwitting Americans Encountered Russian Operatives Online, *New York Times,* 18 February. See also Osipova, Natalie V. and Aaron Byrd (2017). Inside Russia's Network of Bots and Trolls, *New York Times,* video at https://www.nytimes.com/video/us/politics/100000005414346/how-russian-bots-and-trolls-invade-our-lives-and-elections.html.
70. Kang, Cecilia, Nicholas Fandos, and Mike Isaac (2017). Russia-Financed Ad Linked Clinton and Satan, *New York Times,* 1 November.
71. Parlapiano, Alicia and Jasmine C. Lee (2018). The Propaganda Tools Used by Russians to Influence the 2016 Election, *New York Times,* 16 February.
72. Apuzzo, Matt and Sharon LaFraniere (2018). 13 Russians Indicted as Mueller Reveals Effort to Aid Trump Campaign, *New York Times,* 16 February. For the full indictment, see United States of America v. Internet Research Agencies, 2 other organizations, and 13 individuals (2018). 16 February. https://www.justice.gov/file/1035477/download. For a description of an organization heavily involved in the attacks, see Wikipedia (2018). Internet Research Agency, https://en.wikipedia.org/wiki/Internet_Research_Agency. See also Mazzetti, Mark and Benner, Katie (2018). 12 Russian Agents Indicted in Mueller Investigation, *New York Times,* 13 July. For

a description of how a cryptocurrency (discussed in Chapter 12) was used by these individuals, see Popper, Nathaniel and Matthew Rosenberg (2018). How Russian Spies Hid Behind Bitcoin in Hacking Campaign, *New York Times,* 13 July.

73. Isaac, Mike and Daisuke Wakabayashi (2017). Russian Influence Reached 126 Million Through Facebook Alone, *New York Times,* 13 October.
74. See Warzel, Charlie (2017). How People Inside Facebook Are Reacting to the Company's Election Crisis, *BuzzFeedNews,* 20 October. https://www.buzzfeed.com/charliewarzel/how-people-inside-facebook-are-reacting-to-the-companys?utm_term=.tb7nbA2gv#.neRd27jnX. See also Frenkel, Sheera and Katie Benner (2018). To Stir Discord in 2016, Russians Turned Most Often to Facebook, *New York Times,* 17 February. See also Frenkel, Sheera (2018). Fact-Checking a Facebook Executive's Comments on Russian Interference, *New York Times,* 19 February.
75. Wakabayashi, Daisuke (2017). Google Finds Accounts Connected to Russia Bought Election Ads, *New York Times,* 9 October. See also Streitfeld, David (2017). Russia Fanned Flames with Twitter, Which Faces a Blowback, *New York Times,* 9 October.
76. Confessore, Nicholas and Gabriel J. X. Dance (2018). On Social Media, Lax Enforcement Lets Impostor Accounts Thrive, *New York Times,* 20 February.
77. Nicas, Jack (2018). Facebook to Require Verified Identities for Future Political Ads, *New York Times,* 6 April.
78. Wakabayashi, Daisuke (2018). Google Will Ask Buyers of U.S. Election Ads to Prove Identities, *New York Times,* 4 May. See also Kang, Cecilia and Daisuke Wakabayashi (2017). Twitter Plans to Open Ad Data to Users, *New York Times,* 24 October.
79. Hulcoop, Adam, John Scott-Railton, Peter Tanchak, Matt Brooks, and Ron Deibert (2017). Tainted Leaks: Disinformation and Phishing With a Russian Nexus, *Citizen Lab Report,* 25 May. https://citizenlab.org/2017/05/tainted-leaks-disinformation-phish/. See also Deibert, Ronald (2017). From Russia, with Tainted Love, *Citizen Lab,* 25 May. https://deibert.citizenlab.org/2017/05/from-russia-with-tainted-love/.
80. Rutenberg, Jim (2017). RT, Sputnick, and Russia's New Theory of War, *New York Times,* 13 September.
81. Osnos, Evan, David Remnick, and Joshua Yaffa (2017). Active Measures: What Lay Behind Russia's Interference in the 2016 Election—and What Lies Ahead? *The New Yorker,* 6 March, 40–55. This article provides an excellent review of the Russian cyberhacking of the 2016 US election.
82. Rutenberg, Jim (2017). In Election Hacking, Julian Assange's Years-Old Vision Becomes Reality, *New York Times,* 8 January. See also Khatchadourian, Raffi (2017). Julian Assange, A Man Without a Country, *The New Yorker*, 21 August, 36–61.
83. Tufekci, Zeynep (2016). WikiLeaks Isn't Whistleblowing, *New York Times,* 4 November.
84. Higgins, Andrew (2017). It's France's Turn to Worry About Election Meddling by Russia, *New York Times,* 17 April.
85. Breeden, Aurelian, Sewell Chan, and Nicole Perlroth (2017). Macron Campaign Says It Was Target of 'Massive' Hacking Attack, *New York Times,* 5 May.
86. Nossiter, Adam, David E. Sanger, and Nicole Perlroth (2017). Hackers Came, but the French Were Prepared, *New York Times,* 9 May.
87. Kirkpatrick, David D. (2017). Signs of Russian Meddling in Brexit Referendum, *New York Times,* 15 November.

88. Schwirtz, Michael (2017). German Election Mystery: Why No Russian Meddling? *New York Times*, 21 September.

89. Londoño, Ernesto (2018). Brazil Looks to Crack Down on Fake News Ahead of Bitter Election, *New York Times*, 17 February. See also Satariano, Adam (2018). Ireland's Abortion Referendum Becomes a Test for Facebook and Google, *New York Times*, 25 May. See also Melendez, Steven (2018). Trump May Be Leaving The U.S. Vulnerable To More Election Attacks, *Fast Company*, 28 February. See also Sanger, David E. (2018). Russian Hackers Appear to Shift Focus to U.S. Power Grid, *New York Times*, 27 July. See also Roose, Kevin and Nicholas Fandos (2018). Facebook Identifies an Active Political Influence Campaign Using Fake Accounts, *New York Times*, 31 July. See also Roose, Kevin (2018). Facebook Grapples With a Maturing Adversary in Election Meddling, *New York Times*, 1 August.

90. Gambino, Lauren, Sabrina Siddiqui, and Shaun Walker (2016). Obama Expels 35 Russian Diplomats in Retaliation for US Election Hacking, *The Guardian*, 30 December.

91. Sanger, David E. (2016). Obama Confronts Complexity of Using a Mighty Cyberarsenal Against Russia, *New York Times*, 17 December.

92. Goel, Vindu and Eric Lichtblau (2017). Russian Agents Were Behind Yahoo Hack, U.S. Says, *New York Times*, 15 March.

93. Perlroth, Nicole and David E. Sanger (2018). Cyberattacks Put Russian Fingers on the Switch at Power Plants, U.S. Says, *New York Times*, 15 March.

94. Information Warfare Monitor (2009). Tracking GhostNet: Investigating a Cyber Espionage Network. http://www.nartv.org/mirror/ghostnet.pdf. See also Dalek, Jakub, Masashi Crete-Nishihata, and John Scott-Railton (2016). Shifting Tactics: Tracking Changes in Years-long Espionage Campaign Against Tibetans, *Citizen Lab Report*, 10 March. https://citizenlab.org/2016/03/shifting-tactics/.

95. Sanger, David E. and Julie Hirschfeld Davis (2015). Hacking Linked to China Exposes Millions of U.S. Workers, *New York Times*, 4 June.

96. Kang, Cecilia and Alan Rappeport (2018). Top Prize in U.S.–China Rivalry Is Technology Dominance, *New York Times*, 6 March.

97. Mozur, Paul, and Jane Perlez (2017). China Bets on Sensitive U.S. Start-Ups, Worrying the Pentagon, *New York Times*, 22 March.

98. Tejada, Carlos (2018). Beg, Borrow or Steal: How Trump Says China Takes Technology, *New York Times*, 22 March.

99. Zhong, Raymond (2018) . . . Worried About Big Tech? Chinese Giants Make America's Look Tame, *New York Times*, 31 May.

100. Dalek, Jakub, Masashi Crete-Nishihata, and Matthew Brooks (2016). Between Hong Kong and Burma: Tracking UP007 and SLServer Espionage Campaigns, *Citizen Lab Report*, 18 April. https://citizenlab.org/2016/04/between-hong-kong-and-burma/.

101. Sanger, David E., David D. Kirkpatrick, and Nicole Perlroth (2017). The World Once Laughed at North Korean Cyberpower. No More, *New York Times*, 15 October.

102. Sanger, David E. and William J. Broad (2017). Trump Inherits a Secret Cyberwar Against North Korean Missiles, *New York Times*, 4 March.

103. Wikipedia (2017). Stuxnet. https://en.wikipedia.org/wiki/Stuxnet.

104. Kushner, David (2013). The Real Story of Stuxnet, *IEEE Spectrum*, 26 February.

105. Singer, P.W. (2016). 'Dark Territory: The Secret History of Cyber War,' by Fred Kaplan, *New York Times,* 1 March.

106. Thompson, Mark (2016). Iranian Cyber Attack on New York Dam Shows Future of War, *Time.com,* 24 March. http://time.com/4270728/iran-cyber-attack-dam-fbi/.

107. The Soufan Group (2016). Iran's Growing Cyber Capabilities. The Soufan Group, 11 August. http://www.soufangroup.com/tsg-intelbrief-irans-growing-cyber-capabilities/. See also Frenkel, Sheera (2018). Iranian Hackers: Sophisticated, Frustrated and a Rising Global Threat, *New York Times,* 4 January.

108. Goldman, Adam and Eric Schmitt (2016). One by One, ISIS Social Media Experts Are Killed as Result of F.B.I. Program, *New York Times,* 24 November.

109. Sanger, David E. and Eric Schmitt (2017). U.S. Cyberweapons, Used Against Iran and North Korea, Are a Disappointment Against ISIS, *New York Times,* 12 June.

110. Schwartz, Mattathias (2017). Cyberwar for Sale, *New York Times,* 4 January.

111. Shane, Scott, Matthew Rosenberg, and Andrew W. Lehren (2017). WikiLeaks Releases Trove of Alleged C.I.A. Hacking Documents, *New York Times,* 7 March.

112. Griffin, Andrew (2017). WikLeaks CIA Files: The 6 Biggest Spying Secrets Revealed by the Release of 'Vault 7', *The Independent,* 7 March.

113. Borger, Julian (2017). To Security Establishment, WikiLeaks' CIA Dump Is Part of US–Russia Battle, *The Guardian,* 7 March.

114. Tufekci, Zeynep (2017). The Truth About the WikiLeaks C.I.A. Cache, *New York Times,* 9 March.

115. Shane, Scott, David E. Sanger, and Vindu Goel (2017). WikiLeaks Will Help Tech Companies Fix Security Flaws, Assange Says, *New York Times,* 9 March.

116. Schneier, Bruce (2017). Who Are the Shadow Brokers? *The Atlantic,* 23 May.

117. Perlroth, Nicole and David E. Sanger (2017). Hacks Raise Fear Over N.S.A.'s Hold on Cyberweapons, *New York Times,* 28 June.

118. McKune, Sarah and Ron Deibert (2017). Who's Watching Little Brother: A Checklist for Accountability in the Industry Behind Government Hacking, *The Citizen Lab,* 2 March. https://citizenlab.org/wp-content/uploads/2017/03/citizenlab_whos-watching-little-brother.pdf.

119. Sanger, David E. (2018). Tech Firms Sign 'Digital Geneva Accord' Not to Aid Governments in Cyberwar, *New York Times,* 17 April.

120. Taddeo, Mariarosaria and Luciano Floridi (2018). Regulate Artificial Intelligence to Avert Cyber Arms Race, *Nature* 556(7701): 296–298.

121. Frenkel, Sheera (2017). Hackers Hide Cyberattacks in Social Media Posts, *New York Times,* 28 May.

122. Perlroth, Nicole (2017). Hackers Are Targeting Nuclear Facilities, Homeland Security Dept. and F.B.I. Say, *New York Times,* 6 July. See also Blair, Bruce G. (2017). Why Our Nuclear Weapons Can Be Hacked, *New York Times,* 14 March.

123. Sanger, David E. and William J. Broad (2018). Pentagon Suggests Countering Devastating Cyberattacks with Nuclear Arms, *New York Times,* 16 January.

124. Shaw, Ian G. R. (2014). The Rise of the Predator Empire: Tracing the History of U.S. Drones. *Understanding Empire.* https://understandingempire.wordpress.com/2-0-a-brief-history-of-u-s-drones/.

125. Wikipedia (2017). History of unmanned aerial vehicles. https://en.wikipedia.org/wiki/History_of_unmanned_aerial_vehicles.

126. Wikipedia (2017). Unmanned combat aerial vehicle. https://en.wikipedia.org/wiki/Unmanned_combat_aerial_vehicle.

127. Brown, Jack (2017). Types of Military Drones: The Best Technology Available Today. *Drone Lab*. http://mydronelab.com/blog/types-of-military-drones.html.

128. Pogash, Carol (2017). Santa Delivered the Drone. But Not the Safety and Skill to Fly Them, *New York Times,* 8 January. For a sample drone–airplane collision incident, that happily caused no harm, see CBC News (2017). A First in Canada: Drone Collides with Passenger Plane above Quebec City Airport, *CBC News,* 15 October. http://www.cbc.ca/news/canada/montreal/garneau-airport-drone-quebec-1.4355792.

129. Google (2018). Drones for sale on the internet. https://www.google.ca/search?q=drones±-for+sale&oq=drones±for+sale&gs_l=psy-ab.3..0i67k1j0l3.454400.457631.0.458303.15.15.0.0.0.0.92.891.15.15.0....0...1.1.64.psy-ab..0.15.890._i1swDFYA9M

130. Chung, Emily (2015). Amazon Tests Delivery Drones at a Secret Site in Canada—Here's Why, *CBC News,* 30 March. http://www.cbc.ca/news/technology/amazon-tests-delivery-drones-at-a-secret-site-in-canada-here-s-why-1.3015425.

131. Grimes, William (2017). Drones Kill, Yes, but They Also Rescue, Research and Entertain, *New York Times,* 11 May. See also Kwai, Isabella (2018). A Drone Saves Two Swimmers in Australia, *New York Times,* 17 April.

132. Farley, Robert (2015). The Five Most Deadly Drone Powers in the World, *The National Interest,* 16 February. http://nationalinterest.org/feature/the-five-most-deadly-drone-powers-the-world-12255/.

133. Wikipedia (2017). Civilian casualties from U.S. drone strikes. https://en.wikipedia.org/wiki/Civilian_casualties_from_U.S._drone_strikes.

134. Sims, Alyssa (2016). The Consequences of Global Armed Drone Proliferation, *The Diplomat,* 9 July. http://thediplomat.com/2016/07/the-consequences-of-global-armed-drone-proliferation/. See also Schmitt, Eric (2017). Pentagon Tests Lasers and Nets to Combat a Vexing Foe: ISIS Drones, *New York Times,* 23 September.

135. Suebsaeng, Asawin (2013). Drones: Everything You Ever Wanted to Know but Were Always Afraid to Ask, *Mother Jones,* 5 March.

136. Friedersdorf, Conor (2016). The Obama Administration's Drone-Strike Dissembling, *The Atlantic,* 14 March.

137. Gibbons-Neff, Thomas (2017). Civilian Deaths from US-led Airstrikes Hit Record High under Donald Trump. *The Independent,* 25 March.

138. Khan, Azmat and Anand Goyal (2017). The Uncounted, *New York Times,* 16 November.

139. Jeffries, Adrianne (2014). Should a Robot Decide When to Kill? The Ethics of War Machines, *The Verge,* 28 January. https://www.theverge.com/2014/1/28/5339246/war-machines-ethics-of-robots-on-the-battlefield.

140. Dyer, John (2016). Ivan the Terminator: Russia Is Showing Off Its New Robot Soldier, *Vice News,* 26 May. https://news.vice.com/article/ivan-the-terminator-russia-is-showing-off-its-new-robot-soldier.

141. Parkin, Simon (2015). Killer Roborts: The Soldiers that Never Sleep, *BBC News,* 16 July. http://www.bbc.com/future/story/20150715-killer-robots-the-soldiers-that-never-sleep.

142. Scholl, Christopher (2014). US Army to Replace Human Soldiers with 'Humanoid Robots', *Global Research*, 3 March. http://www.globalresearch.ca/us-army-to-replace-human-soldiers-with-humanoid-robots/5371657.

143. Express (2016). EXCLUSIVE: US Army 'Will Have More Robot Soldiers than Humans' by 2025, *Express*, 20 October. http://www.express.co.uk/news/world/723344/US-Army-robots-American-armed-forces-robots-humans-2025.

144. Breene, Keith (2017). Meet the Robots with Talents You Can Only Dream Of, *World Economic Forum*, 22 March. https://www.weforum.org/agenda/2017/03/robots-got-skills-568cc8b4-01f7-4d1e-ac1b-fe5348c64bcf/. See also Boston Dynamics (2017). Introducing Handle. Video, 27 February. https://www.youtube.com/watch?v=-7xvqQeoA8c.

145. Office of the US Air Force Chief Scientist (2011). Technology Horizons: A Vision for Air Force Science and Technology 2010–2030(1), *Air University Press*, September. http://www.defenseinnovationmarketplace.mil/resources/AF_TechnologyHorizons2010-2030.pdf.

146. Department of Defense (US) (2012). Directive: Autonomy in Weapon Systems, 21 November. http://www.dtic.mil/whs/directives/corres/pdf/300009p.pdf.

147. Rosenberg, Matthew and John Markoff (2016). The Pentagon's 'Terminator Conundrum': Robots That Could Kill on Their Own, *New York Times*, 25 October.

148. Markoff, John, and Matthew Rosenberg (2017). China's Intelligent Weaponry Gets Smarter, *New York Times*, 3 February.

149. Sharkey, Noel (2008). Computer Science: The Ethical Frontiers of Robotics, *Science* 322(5909): 1800–1801. See also ICRAC (2012). Computing Experts from 37 Countries Call for Ban on Killer Robots, *International Committee for Robot Arms Control*, 11 November. https://www.icrac.net/the-scientists-call/. See also Future of Life Institute (2015). Autonomous Weapons: An Open Letter from AI & Robotics Researchers, *Future of Life Institute*, 28 July. https://futureoflife.org/open-letter-autonomous-weapons/. See also Satherley, Dan (2017). Fire and Killer Robots: Stephen Hawking's Grim View on the Future of Earth, *Newshub*, 11 September. https://www.newshub.co.nz/home/world/2017/11/fire-and-killer-robots-stephen-hawking-s-grim-view-on-the-future-of-earth.html. See also Kassner, Michael (2017). Elon Musk Fears AI May Lead to World War III, as Researchers Study the Risks of 'Stupid, Good Robots', *Techrepublic*, 5 September. https://www.techrepublic.com/article/elon-musk-fears-ai-may-lead-to-world-war-iii-as-researchers-study-the-risks-of-stupid-good-robots/.

150. Horowitz, Michael C. and Paul Scharre (2015). An Introduction to Autonomy in Weapon Systems, *Centre for a New American Security*, February. https://www.cnas.org/publications/reports/an-introduction-to-autonomy-in-weapon-systems.

151. Arkin, Ronald C. (2010). The Case for Ethical Autonomy in Unmanned Systems, *Journal of Military Ethics* 9(4): 332–341.

152. Scharre, Paul (2016). Autonomous Weapons and Operational Risk, *Center for a New American Security*, February. https://www.cnas.org/publications/reports/autonomous-weapons-and-operational-risk.

153. Shear, Michael D., Tiffany Hsu, and Kirk Johnson (2018). Judge Blocks Attempt to Post Blueprints for 3-D Guns, *New York Times*, 31 July. See also New York Times Editorial Board (2016). Why Not Smart Guns in This High-Tech Era? *New York Times*, 26 November.

154. Segal, Adam (2017). The Hacking Wars Are Going to Get Much Worse, *New York Times*, 31 July.

Chapter 7

1. Levy, Steven (1984). *Hackers*, Anchor Press/Doubleday.

2. Hafner, Katie and John Markoff (1991). *Cyberpunk: Outlaws and Hackers on the Computer Frontier*, Touchstone. See also *Hackers* (1995). Feature film. http://www.imdb.com/title/tt0113243/.

3. Corbató, Fernando J. (1971). On Building Systems That Will Fail, *Communications of the ACM* 34(9): 72–81, describes a security flaw found in the early 1960s in one of the first experimental time-sharing systems. See also Branstan, D. K. (1973). Privacy and Protection in Operating Systems, *Computer* 6(1): 43–46. See also Lipner, Steven B. (1974). A Panel Session—Security Kernels, *AFIPS Conference Proceedings National Computer Conference* 43: 973–980.

4. Anderson, James P. (1972). Computer Security Technology Planning Study. Volumes I and II. Report ESD-TR-73-51. Electronic Systems Division (AFSC). Report ESD-TR-73-51. http://csrc.nist.gov/publications/history/ande72a.pdf.

5. Neumann, Peter G. (1995). *Computer Related Risks*, ACM Press.

6. McAfee Labs (2018). Threats Report, March. https://www.mcafee.com/enterprise/en-us/assets/reports/rp-quarterly-threats-mar-2018.pdf. See also McAfee Labs (2016). Threats Report Infographic, June. https://www.mcafee.com/ca/resources/misc/infographic-threats-report-dec-2016.pdf.See also Symantec (2017). 2017 Internet Security Threat Report. https://www.symantec.com/security-center/threat-report.

7. Barlow, Caleb (2016). Where Is Cybercrime Really Coming From? *Ted Talks*, November, https://www.ted.com/talks/caleb_barlow_where_is_cybercrime_really_coming_from/discussion.

8. Shahani, Aarti (2017). Microsoft President Urges Nuclear-Like Limits on Cyberweapons. All Things Considered. *NPR Now*. https://www.npr.org/sections/alltechconsidered/2017/05/16/528555400/microsofts-president-reflects-on-cyberattack-helping-pirates-and-the-nsa.

9. Cisco (2018). Annual Cybersecurity Report. https://www.cisco.com/c/en_ca/products/security/security-reports.html.

10. Privacy Rights Clearinghouse (2017). Data breaches. https://www.privacyrights.org/data-breaches. See also Wikipedia (2017). Data breach. https://en.wikipedia.org/wiki/Data_breach.

11. Informationisbeautiful (2018). World's biggest data breaches. http://www.informationisbeautiful.net/visualizations/worlds-biggest-data-breaches-hacks/.

12. Alexander, David (2015). 5.6 Million Fingerprints Stolen in U.S. Personnel Data Hack: Government, *Reuters.com*, 23 September. http://www.reuters.com/article/us-usa-cybersecurity-fingerprints-idUSKCN0RN1V820150923. See also Koerner, Brendan I. (2016). Inside the Cyberattack that Shocked the US Government, *Wired*, 23 October. https://www.wired.com/2016/10/inside-cyberattack-shocked-us-government/. See also Wikipedia (2017). Office of Personnel Management data breach. https://en.wikipedia.org/wiki/Office_of_Personnel_Management_data_breach.

13. Wikipedia (2018). Yahoo! Data Breaches. https://en.wikipedia.org/wiki/Yahoo!_data_breaches. See also Kastrenakes, Jacob (2018). SEC Issues $35 Million Fine over Yahoo Failing to Disclose Data Breach, TheVerge.com. https://www.theverge.com/2018/4/24/17275994/yahoo-sec-fine-2014-data-breach-35-million.

14. McGee, Marianne Kolbasuk (2017). A New In-Depth Analysis of Anthem Breach, *Bankinfosecurity.com*, 10 January. http://www.bankinfosecurity.com/new-in-depth-analysis-

anthem-breach-a-9627. See also California Department of Insurance (2017). Investigation of Major Anthem Cyber Breach Reveals Foreign Nation Behind Breach. Press release, 6 January. http://www.insurance.ca.gov/0400-news/0100-press-releases/2017/release001-17.cfm.

15. Riley, Michael, Jordan Robertson, and Anita Sharpe (2017). The Equifax Hack Has the Hallmarks of State-Sponsored Pros, *Bloomberg.com,* 29 September. https://www.bloomberg.com/news/features/2017-09-29/the-equifax-hack-has-all-the-hallmarks-of-state-sponsored-pros. See also Bernard, Tara Siegel, Tiffany Hsu, Nicole Perlroth, and Ron Lieber (2017). Equifax Says Cyberattack May Have Affected 143 Million in the U.S., *New York Times,* 7 September. See also Perlroth, Nicole and Cade Metz (2017). Equifax Breach: Two Executives Step Down as Investigation Continues, *New York Times,* 7 September. See also Cowley, Stacy and Tara Siegel Bernard (2017). As Equifax Amassed Ever More Data, Safety Was a Sales Pitch, *New York Times,* 23 September. See also https://www.cnbc.com/video/2017/09/13/chatbot-creator-donotpay-will-sue-equifax-for-you—without-an-attorney.html.

16. Wikipedia (2017). Ashley Madison data breach. https://en.wikipedia.org/wiki/Ashley_Madison_data_breach.

17. Whittaker, Zach (2016). 171 Million VK.com Accounts Stolen by Hackers, ZDNet, 5 June. http://www.zdnet.com/article/vkontakte-vk-hacked-171-million-accounts-sold-dark-web/.

18. Whittaker, Zack (2018). A New Data Leak Hits Aadhaar, India's National ID Database, *ZDNet.com,* 23 March. Retrieved on 28 May 2018 from https://www.zdnet.com/article/another-data-leak-hits-india-aadhaar-biometric-database/.

19. Neumann, Peter G. (1995). *Computer Related Risks,* ACM Press. See also Hoffman, Lance J. (Ed.). *Rogue Programs: Viruses, Worms, and Trojan Horses,* Van Nostrand Reinhold. See also Quinn, Michael J. (2017). *Ethics for the Information Age,* 7th Edition, Pearson.

20. Thompson, Ken (1984). Reflections on Trusting Trust, *Communications of the ACM* 27(8): 761–763.

21. Shneier, Bruce (2017). Infrastructure Vulnerabilities Make Surveillance Easy, *Al Jazeera,* 11 April. http://www.aljazeera.com/indepth/opinion/2017/04/infrastructure-vulnerabilities-surveillance-easy-170409071533166.html.

22. Bromwich, Jonah Engel (2016). Protecting Your Digital Life in 9 Easy Steps, *New York Times,* 16 November.

23. Wikipedia (2017). Computer Fraud and Abuse Act. https://en.wikipedia.org/wiki/Computer_Fraud_and_Abuse_Act.

24. Wikipedia (2017). MafiaBoy. https://en.wikipedia.org/wiki/MafiaBoy. See also McConnell, Josh (2017). Reformed Canadian Hacker 'Mafiaboy' Teams Up with HP on Documentary about Corporate Cyberattacks. *Financial Post,* 1 March.

25. Wikipedia (2017). Aaron Swartz. https://en.wikipedia.org/wiki/Aaron_Swartz. See also Abelson, Harold, Peter A. Diamond, Andrew Grosso, and Douglas W. Pfeiffer (2013). Report to the President: MIT and the Prosecution of Aaron Swartz. http://swartz-report.mit.edu/docs/report-to-the-president.pdf. See also TakePart (2017). *The Internet's Own Boy: The Story of Aaron Swartz.* Video. http://www.takepart.com/internets-own-boy/, also may be found at https://www.youtube.com/watch?v=gpvcc9C8SbM.

26. Fosburgh, Lacey (1973). Chief Teller Is Accused of Theft Of $1.5-Million at a Bank Here, *New York Times,* 23 March.

27. Villeneuve, Nart (2010). Koobface: Inside a Crimeware Network. Information Warfare Monitor Announcement, 12 November. https://citizenlab.org/2010/11/koobface-inside-a-crimeware-

network. See also Villeneuve, Nart (2010). Koobface: Inside a Crimeware Network Report JR04-2010. Information Warfare Monitor, 12 November. Email from the Citizen Lab. See also McMillan, Robert (2017). Researchers Take Down Koobface Servers, *Computerworld.com,* 13 November. http://www.computerworld.com/article/2514311/security0/researchers-take-down-koobface-servers.html.

28. Frenkel, Sheera (2017). Ponzi Scheme Meets Ransomware for a Doubly Malicious Attack, *New York Times,* 6 June.
29. Perlroth, Nicole (2017). A Cyberattack 'the World Isn't Ready For', *New York Times,* 22 June.
30. Wikipedia (2017). WannaCry ransomware attack. https://en.wikipedia.org/wiki/WannaCry_ransomware_attack. See also Perlroth, Nicole and David E. Sanger (2017). Hackers Hit Dozens of Countries Exploiting Stolen N.S.A. Tool, *New York Times,* 12 May. A screenshot of the ransom note left on infected computers is https://en.wikipedia.org/wiki/WannaCry_ransomware_attack#/media/File:Wana_Decrypt0r_screenshot.png.
31. Mozur, Paul and Mark Scott (2017). Victims Call Hackers' Bluff as Ransomware Deadline Nears, *New York Times,* 19 May.
32. Sanger, David E., Sewell Chan, and Mark Scott (2017). Ransomware's Aftershocks Feared as U.S. Warns of Complexity, *New York Times,* 14 May.
33. Sang-hun, Choe, Paul Mozer, Nicole Perlroth, and David E. Sanger (2017). Focus Turns to North Korea Sleeper Cells as Possible Culprits in Cyberattack, *New York Times,* 16 May. See also Sanger, David E. (2017). U.S. Accuses North Korea of Mounting WannaCry Cyberattack,. *New York Times,* 18 December.
34. Shane, Scott (2017). Malware Case Is Major Blow for the N.S.A., *New York Times,* 16 May.
35. Perlroth, Nicole, Mark Scott, and Sheera Frenkel (2017). Cyberattack Hits Ukraine Then Spreads Internationally, *New York Times,* 27 June.
36. Perlroth, Nicole (2017). Lasting Damage and a Search for Clues in Cyberattack, *New York Times,* 6 July.
37. Kramer, Andrew E. (2017). Ukraine Cyberattack Was Meant to Paralyze, not Profit, Evidence Shows, *New York Times,* 28 June.
38. Blinder, Alan and Nicole Perlroth (2018). Hard Choice for Cities Under Cyberattack: Whether to Pay Ransom, *New York Times,* 29 March.
39. Baker, Al (2018). An 'Iceberg' of Unseen Crimes: Many Cyber Offenses Go Unreported, *New York Times,* 5 February.
40. Wikipedia (2017). Identity theft. https://en.wikipedia.org/wiki/Identity_theft. A comprehensive but somewhat dated literature review is Newman, Graeme R. and Megan M. McNally (2005). Identity Theft Literature Review. Prepared for presentation and discussion at the National Institute of Justice Focus Group. https://www.ncjrs.gov/pdffiles1/nij/grants/210459.pdf.
41. Lynch, Jennifer (2005). Identity Theft in Cyberspace: Crime Control Methods and their Effectiveness in Combating Phishing Attacks, *Berkeley Technology Law Journal* 20: 259–300.
42. Barth, Bradley (2016). APWG Report: Phishing Surges by 250 Percent in Q1 2016, *SCMagazine.com,* 25 May. https://www.scmagazine.com/apwg-report-phishing-surges-by-250-percent-in-q1-2016/article/528186/.
43. Javelin Strategy and Research (2017). Identity Fraud Hits Record High with 15.4 Million U.S. Victims in 2016, Up 16 Percent According to New Javelin Strategy & Research

Study. Press Release, 1 February. https://www.javelinstrategy.com/press-release/identity-fraud-hits-record-high-154-million-us-victims-2016-16-percent-according-new.

44. Perlroth, Nicole (2017). Russian Hacker Sentenced to 27 Years in Credit Card Case, *New York Times,* 21 April.

45. Daley, Alan (2016). Consumer Confidence in Internet Security Is Weakening. The American Consumer Institute for Citizen Research, 20 May. http://www.theamericanconsumer.org/2016/05/consumer-confidence-internet-security-weakening/.

46. Javelin Strategy and Research (2017). Identity Fraud Hits Record High with 15.4 Million U.S. Victims in 2016, Up 16 Percent According to New Javelin Strategy & Research Study. Press Release Infographic, 1 February. https://www.javelinstrategy.com/sites/default/files/17-1001J-2017-LL-Identity-Fraud-Hits-Record-Highs-Javelin.pdf.

47. Popper, Nathaniel (2017). Identity Thieves Hijack Cellphone Accounts to Go After Virtual Currency, *New York Times,* 21 August.

48. Hoofnagle, Chris J. (2007). Identity Theft: Making the Known Unknowns Known, *Harvard Journal of Law & Technology* 21(1): 97–122.

49. Romanosky, Sasha, Rahul Telang, and Alessandro Acquisti (2011). Do Data Breach Disclosure Laws Reduce Identity Theft? *Journal of Policy Analysis and Management* 30(2): 256–286.

50. LoPucki, Lynn M. (2001). Human Identification Theory and the Identity Theft Problem, *Texas Law Review* 80: 89–135.

51. Berghel, Hal (2000). Identity Theft, Social Security Numbers, and the Web, *Communications of the ACM* 43(2): 17–21.

52. Bilge, Leyla, Thorsten Strufe, Davide Balzarotti, and Engin Kirda (2009). All Your Contacts Belong to Us: Automated Identity Theft Attacks on Social Networks. *Proclamation of the 18th International Conference on World Wide Web 2009,* 551–560.

53. Siegel Bernard, Tara (2017). The Post-Equifax Marketing Push: Identity Protection Services, *New York Times,* 25 October.

54. See, for example, Schmidt, Samantha (2019). Clarinetist Discovers His Ex-Girlfriend Faked a Rejection Letter from His Dream School, *The Washington Post,* 15 June. https://www.washingtonpost.com/news/morning-mix/wp/2018/06/15/clarinetist-discovers-his-ex-girlfriend-faked-a-rejection-letter-from-his-dream-school/?noredirect=on&utm_term=.ef91e2a59885.

55. Wikipedia (2018). Mobile security. https://en.wikipedia.org/wiki/Mobile_security. See also Raphael, J. R. (2017). 5 Mobile Security Threats You Should Take Seriously in 2018. https://www.csoonline.com/article/3241727/mobile-security/5-mobile-security-threats-you-should-take-seriously-in-2018.html.

56. Perlroth, Nicole (2018). Lebanese Intelligence Turned Targets' Android Phones into Spy Devices, Researchers Say, *New York Times,* 18 January.

57. Pérez-Peña, Richard and Matthew Rosenberg (2018). Strava Fitness App Can Reveal Military Sites, Analysts Say, *New York Times,* 29 January. See also Triebert, Christian, Christoph Koettl, and Ankara Tiefenthaler (2018). How Strava's Heat Map Uncovers Military Bases. Video. https://www.nytimes.com/video/world/middleeast/100000005705502/big-data-big-problems-how-stravas-heat-map-uncovers-military-bases.html.

58. Palmer, Danny (2018). Amazon's Alexa Could Be Tricked into Snooping on Users, Say Security Researchers. ZDNet.com, 25 April. https://www.zdnet.com/article/amazons-alexa-could-be-tricked-into-snooping-on-users-say-security-researchers/. See also Frenkel, Sheera (2017). A Cute Toy Just Brought a Hacker into Your Home, *New York Times,* 21 December.

59. Markoff, John (2017). It's Possible to Hack a Phone with Sound Waves, Researchers Show, *New York Times,* 15 March.
60. Markoff, John (2017). That Cool Robot May Be a Security Risk, *New York Times,* 1 March.
61. Chana, Marie, Daniel Esteve, Christophe Escriba, and Eric Campo (2006). A Review of Smart Homes—Present State and Future Challenges, *Computer Methods and Programs in Biomedicine* 91: 55–81. See also Komninos, Nikos, Eleni Philippou, and Andreas Pitsillides (2014). Survey in Smart Grid and Smart Home Security: Issues, Challenges and Countermeasures, *IEEE Communication Surveys and Tutorials* 16(4): 1933–1954.
62. Orlov, Laurie (2017). Health Technology Ecosystem Chaos—There's No App for That. Aging in Place Technology Watch, 12 June. https://www.ageinplacetech.com/blog/home-technology-ecosystem-chaos-there-s-no-app.
63. Bowles, Nellie (2018). Thermostats, Locks and Lights: Digital Tools of Domestic Abuse, *New York Times,* 23 June.
64. DeSilva, Liyanage C., Chamin Morikawa, and Iskandar M. Petra (2012). State of the Art of Smart Homes, *Engineering Applications of Artificial Intelligence* 25: 1313–1321.
65. Wilson, Charlie, Tom Hargreaves, and Richard Hauxwell-Baldwin (2015). Smart Homes and Their Users: A Systematic Analysis and Key Challenges, *Pers Ubiquit Comput* 19: 463–476.
66. Tognazzini, Bruce. (2001). The Butterfly Ballot: Anatomy of a Disaster. http://www.asktog.com/columns/042ButterflyBallot.html. See also Presentation Zen (2008). Think Graphic Design Doesn't Matter? http://www.presentationzen.com/presentationzen/2008/11/think-graphic-design-doesnt-matter.html.
67. Wikipedia (2017). Electronic Voting. https://en.wikipedia.org/wiki/Electronic_voting.
68. Herrnson, Paul S., Benjamin B. Bederson, Bongshin Lee, Peter L. Francia, Robert M. Sherman, Frederick G. Conrad, Michael Traugott, and Richard G. Niemi (2005). Early Appraisals of Electronic Voting, *Social Science Computer Review* 23(3): 274–292. See also Card, David and Enrico Moretti (2007). Does Voting Technology Affect Election Outcomes? Touch-Screen Voting and the 2004 Presidential Election, *The Review of Economics and Statistics* 89(4): 660–673. See also Conrad, Frederick G., Benjamin B. Bederson, Brian Lewis, Emilia Peytcheva, Michael W. Traugott, Michael J. Hanmer, Paul S. Herrnson, and Richard G. Niemi (2009). Electronic Voting Eliminates Hanging Chads but Introduces New Usability Challenges, *International Journal of Human–Computer Studies* 67: 111–124. See also ProCon.org (2017). Do Electronic Voting Machines Improve the Voting Process? http://votingmachines.procon.org. See also ProCon.org (2017). Top 10 Pros and Cons: Do Electronic Voting Machines Improve the Voting Process? http://votingmachines.procon.org/view.resource.php?resourceID=000265.
69. Cohen, Adam (2007). The Good News (Really) About Voting Machines, *New York Times,* 10 January.
70. Wines, Michael (2017). Wary of Hackers, States Move to Upgrade Voting Systems, *New York Times,* 14 October.
71. Wikipedia (2017). Computer Fraud and Abuse Act. https://en.wikipedia.org/wiki/Computer_Fraud_and_Abuse_Act.
72. Abelson, Harold, Peter A. Diamond, Andrew Grosso, and Douglas W. Pfeiffer (2013). Report to the President: MIT and the Prosecution of Aaron Swartz. http://swartz-report.mit.edu/docs/report-to-the-president.pdf.
73. Reader, Ruth (2016). 3 Years After Aaron Swartz's Death, Here's What's Happened to Aaron's Law, *Mic Daily,* 11 January. https://mic.com/articles/132299/3-years-after-aaron-swartz-s-death-here-s-what-s-happened-to-aaron-s-law#.2hf9ovfqf.

74. FBI (2017). Identity Theft. U.S. Federal Bureau of Investigation. https://www.fbi.gov/investigate/white-collar-crime/identity-theft.
75. Wikipedia (2017). Fair Credit Reporting Act. https://en.wikipedia.org/wiki/Fair_Credit_Reporting_Act.
76. Wikipedia (2017). Computer Misuse Act 1990. https://en.wikipedia.org/wiki/Computer_Misuse_Act_1990.
77. Wikipedia (2018). Data Protection Act 1998. https://en.wikipedia.org/wiki/Data_Protection_Act_1998.
78. Yip, Michael (2010). An Investigation into Chinese Cybercrime and the Underground Economy in Comparison with the West. M.Sc. Dissertation, University of Southampton, 24 September. https://eprints.soton.ac.uk/273136/1/dissertation_final.pdf.
79. Liang, Bin and Hong Lu (2010). Internet Development, Censorship, and Cyber Crimes in China, *Journal of Contemporary Criminal Justice* 26(1):103–120.
80. Li, Xingan (2015). Regulation of Cyber Space: An Analysis of Chinese Law on Cyber Crime, *International Journal of Cyber Criminology* 9(2): 185–204. See also Ruijun, Zhang (2016). China Will Protect 'Cyber-Security' Borders by Any Means Necessary, *CTGN.com*, 28 December. https://news.cgtn.com/news/3d456a4d3155544d/share_p.html.
81. Zorabedian, John (2015). China Vows to 'Clean the Internet' in Cybercrime Crackdown, 15,000 Arrested, *Naked Security by Sophos*. https://nakedsecurity.sophos.com/2015/08/20/china-vows-to-clean-the-internet-in-cybercrime-crackdown-15000-arrested/.
82. KPMG (2017). Overview of China's Cybersecurity Law. IT Advisory, February. https://assets.kpmg.com/content/dam/kpmg/cn/pdf/en/2017/02/overview-of-cybersecurity-law.pdf.
83. Wee, Sui-Lee (2017). China's New Cybersecurity Law Leaves Foreign Firms Guessing, *New York Times*, 31 May. See also Shieber, Jonathan (2017). China's Strict Cybersecurity Laws Took Effect Today; Potentially Impacting Foreign Businesses, *Techcrunch.com*, 1 June. https://techcrunch.com/2017/06/01/chinas-strict-cybersecurity-laws-took-effect-today-potentially-impacting-foreign-businesses/.
84. Mozur, Paul, Daisuke Wakabayashi, and Nick Wingfield (2017). Apple Opening Data Center in China to Comply with Cybersecurity Law, *New York Times*, 12 July.
85. O'Reilly, Dennis (2008). Keep Your Data Safe by Following the Password Commandments, *CNET.com*, 25 February. https://www.cnet.com/news/keep-your-data-safe-by-following-the-password-commandments/. See also O'Reilly, Dennis (2011). How to Master the Art of Passwords, *CNET.com*, 24 December. https://www.cnet.com/how-to/how-to-master-the-art-of-passwords/. See also Profis, Sharon (2016). The Guide to Password Security (and Why You Should Care), *CNET.com*, 1 January. https://www.cnet.com/how-to/the-guide-to-password-security-and-why-you-should-care/.
86. Wikipedia (2018). Multi-factor Authentication. https://en.wikipedia.org/wiki/Multi-factor_authentication.
87. Metz, Cade and Nicole Perlroth (2018). Researchers Discover Two Major Flaws in the World's Computers, *New York Times*, 3 January. See also Metz, Cade and Brian X. Chen (2018). What You Need to Do Because of Flaws in Computer Chips, *New York Times*, 4 January.
88. Cowley, Stacy (2018). Banks Adopt Military-Style Tactics to Fight Cybercrime, *New York Times*, 20 May.

89. Moskovitch, Robert, Clint Feher, Arik Messerman, Niklas Kirschnick, Tarik Mustafić, Ahmet Camtepe, Bernhard Löhlein, Ulrich Heister, Sebastian Möller, Lior Rokach, and Yuval Elovici (2009). Identity Theft, Computers and Behavioral Biometrics, *Proceedings of the ISI World Statistics Congress 2009*: 155–160. IEEE.

90. William Enck, William, Machigar Ongtang, and Patrick McDaniel (2009). On Lightweight Mobile Phone Application Certification, *Proceedings of CCS 2009*: 235–245.

91. National Academies Press (2017). Foundational Cybersecurity Research: Improving Science, Engineering, and Institutions.https://www.nap.edu/catalog/24676/foundational-cybersecurity-research-improving-science-engineering-and-institutions. See also National Academies Press (2017). Software Update as a Mechanism for Resilience and Security. https://www.nap.edu/catalog/24833/software-update-as-a-mechanism-for-resilience-and-security-proceedings. See also National Academies Press (2018). Decrypting the Encryption Debate: A Framework for Decision Makers. https://www.nap.edu/catalog/25010/decrypting-the-encryption-debate-a-framework-for-decision-makers. See also Budish, Ryan, Herbert Berkert, and Urs Gasser (2018). Encryption Policy and its International Effects: A Framework for Understanding Extraterritorial Ripple Effects. Hoover Institution, 2 March. https://www.hoover.org/research/encryption-policy-and-its-international-impacts.

92. Lucero, Louis II (2018). F.B.I.'s Urgent Request: Reboot Your Router to Stop Russia-Linked Malware, *New York Times,* 27 May.

93. Melendez, Steven (2018). Cloud Security: The Reason Hackers Have it So Easy Will Infuriate You. *Fast Company*, 29 May.

94. Johnson, Eliana, Emily Stephenson, and Daniel Lippman (2018), 'Too Inconvenient': Trump Goes Rogue on Phone Security, *Politico.com*, 21 May. https://www.politico.com/story/2018/05/21/trump-phone-security-risk-hackers-601903.

95. Perlroth, Nicole (2017). With New Digital Tools, Even Nonexperts Can Wage Cyberattacks, *New York Times,* 13 May.

96. Ives, Mike and Paul Mozur (2017). Small Countries' New Weapon Against Goliaths: Hacking, *New York Times,* 14 May.

97. Frenkel, Sheera (2017). Hackers Find 'Ideal Testing Ground' for Attacks: Developing Countries, *New York Times,* 2 July.

98. Greenemeier, Larry (2011). Seeking Address: Why Cyber Attacks Are So Difficult to Trace Back to Hackers, *Scientificamerican.com*, 11 June. https://www.scientificamerican.com/article/tracking-cyber-hackers/.

Chapter 8

1. Wiener, Norbert (1960). Some Moral and Technical Consequences of Automation, *Science,* New Series, 131(3410): 1355–1358.

2. Weizenbaum. Joseph (1976). *Computer Power and Human Reason: From Judgment to Calculation*, W.H. Freeman, pp. 232, 236.

3. Wikipedia (2017). 2001: A Space Odyssey. https://en.wikipedia.org/wiki/2001:_A_Space_Odyssey_(film). See also 2001: A Space Odyssey (2017). Quotes from 2001: A Space Odyssey. http://www.imdb.com/title/tt0062622/quotes. See also 2001: A Space Odyssey. (2017). Best scene with Hal and Dave. https://www.youtube.com/watch?v=qDrDUmuUBTo.

4. Wikipedia (2017). Autonomous car. https://en.wikipedia.org/wiki/Autonomous_car.
5. Norman, Don (2013). *The Design of Everyday Things: Revised and Expanded Edition*, Basic Books. See also Preece, Jennifer, Yvonne Rogers, and Helen Sharp (2015). *Interaction Design: Beyond Human-Computer Interaction*, 4th Edition, John Wiley & Sons.
6. Lazar, Jonathan, Adam Jones, Mary Hackley, and Ben Shneiderman (2006). Severity and Impact of Computer User Frustration: A Comparison of Student and Workplace Users, *Interacting with Computers* 18: 187–207. See also Lazar, Jonathan, Adam Jones, and Ben Shneiderman (2006). Workplace User Frustration with Computers: An Exploratory Investigation of the Causes and Severity, *Behaviour & Information Technology* 25(3): 239–251.
7. Norman, Kent L. (2004). Computer Rage: Theory and Practice. Unpublished lecture notes. http://129.2.36.150/trons/hcil22oct2004/hcilbbl_10_22_2004.pdf.
8. Wikipedia (2017). Suicide of Amanda Todd. https://en.wikipedia.org/wiki/Suicide_of_Amanda_Todd.
9. Todd, Amanda (2012). My Story: Struggling, Bullying, Suicide, Self Harm, Video. https://www.youtube.com/watch?v=vOHXGNx-E7E.
10. BBC News (2017). Amanda Todd Case: Accused Dutch Man Jailed for Cyberbullying. *BBCNews.com*, 16 March. http://www.bbc.com/news/world-us-canada-39295474.
11. Smith, Peter K., Jess Mahdavi, Manuel Carvalho, Sonja Fisher, Shanette Russell, and Neil Tippett (2008). Cyberbullying: Its Nature and Impact in Secondary School Pupils, *Journal of Child Psychology and Psychiatry* 49(4): 376–385.
12. Slonje, Robert and Peter K. Smith (2008). Cyberbullying: Another Main Type of Bullying? *Scandinavian Journal of Psychology* 49: 147–154. See also Mishna, Faye (2013). Understanding and Responding to Cyber Bullying in the Cyber World. Keynote address to the 13 Division Toronto Police School Summit, 31 January. https://www.slideshare.net/CSIWorld/keynote-address-on-cyber-bullying-by-dr-faye-mishna-13-division-toronto-police-school-summit-2013.
13. Calvert, Clay (2015). Revenge Porn and Freedom of Expression: Legislative Pushback to an Online Weapon of Emotional and Reputational Destruction, *Fordham Intellectual Property, Media & Entertainment Law Journal* 24: 673–702.
14. Lenhart, Amanda, Michele Ybarra, and Myeshia Price-Feeney (2016). Nonconsensual Image Sharing: One in 25 Americans Has Been a Victim of 'Revenge Porn', *Data & Society Research Institute* 13 (December). Data Memo. https://datasociety.net/blog/2016/12/13/nonconsensual-image-sharing/.
15. Sherlock, Peter (2016). Revenge Pornography Victims as Young as 11, Investigation Finds, *BBC News*, 27 April.
16. Talbot, Margaret (2016). Taking Trolls to Court, *The New Yorker*, 5 December, 56–65.
17. Citron, Danielle Keats and Mary Anne Franks (2014). Criminalizing Revenge Porn, *Wake Forest Law Review* 49: 345–391.
18. Levendowski, Amanda (2014). Using Copyright to Combat Revenge Porn, *NYU Journal of Intellectual Property* 3(2). http://jipel.law.nyu.edu/vol-3-no-2-6-levendowski/.
19. Hauser, Christine (2018). $6.4 Million Judgment in Revenge Porn Case Is Among Largest Ever, *New York Times*, 11 April.
20. Wikipedia (2017). Pokémon. https://en.wikipedia.org/wiki/Pok%C3%A9mon. See also https://www.pokemon.com/us/. See also Promotional video for Pokémon Go on YouTube. https://www.youtube.com/channel/UCA698bls2pjQyiqP9N-iaeg

21. Ayers, John W., Eric C. Leas, Mark Dredze, Jon-Patrick Allem, Jurek G. Grabowski, and Linda Hill (2016). Pokémon GO—A New Distraction for Drivers and Pedestrians, *JAMA Internal Medicine* 176(12): 1865–1866.

22. Pokémon Go Death Tracker (2017). http://pokemongodeathtracker.com/.

23. Nasar, Jack L. and Derek Troyer (2013). Pedestrian Injuries Due to Mobile Phone Use in Public Places, *Accident Analysis and Prevention* 57: 91–95. Their data was based on injuries reported to hospital emergency rooms.

24. Nasar, Jack L., Peter Hecht, and Richard Wener (2008). Mobile Telephones, Distracted Attention, and Pedestrian Safety, *Accident Analysis and Prevention* 40: 69–75.

25. Hatfield, Julie and Susanne Murphy (2007). The Effects of Mobile Phone Use on Pedestrian Crossing Behaviour at Signalised and Unsignalised Intersections, *Accident Analysis and Prevention* 39: 197–205.

26. de Waard, Dick, Paul Schepers, Wieke Ormel and Karel Brookhuis (2010). Mobile Phone Use while Cycling: Incidence and Effects on Behaviour and Safety, *Ergonomics* 53(1): 30–42. See also de Waard, Dick, Frank Westerhuis, Ben Lewis-Evans (2015). More Screen Operation than Calling: The Results of Observing Cyclists' Behaviour while Using Mobile Phones, *Accident Analysis and Prevention* 76: 42–48.

27. Terzano, Kathryn (2013). Bicycling Safety and Distracted Behavior in The Hague, the Netherlands, *Accident Analysis and Prevention* 57: 87–90.

28. Ichikawa, Masao and Shinji Nakahara (2008). Japanese High School Students' Usage of Mobile Phones While Cycling, *Traffic Injury Prevention* 9: 42–47. 10.1080/15389580701718389.

29. Sidibe, Nana (2015). More Phones, More Wrecks? Distracted Driving on the Rise, *CNBC.com*, 24 May. http://www.cnbc.com/2015/05/21/cell-phone-boom-leading-to-rise-in-distracted-driving-safety-group.html.

30. NHTSA (2016). Traffic Fatalities Up Sharply in 2015. National Highway Traffic Safety Administration. https://www.nhtsa.gov/press-releases/traffic-fatalities-sharply-2015.

31. Boudette, Neal E. (2016). Biggest Spike in Traffic Deaths in 50 Years? Blame Apps, *New York Times*, 15 November.

32. National Safety Council (2013). Crashes Involving Cell Phones: Challenges of Collecting and Reporting Reliable Crash Data. https://www.nsc.org/Portals/0/Documents/Distracted DrivingDocuments/NSC-Under-Reporting-White-Paper.pdf?ver=2018-03-09-130434-503.

33. McKnight, A. James and A. Scott McKnight (1993). The Effect of Cellular Phone Use Upon Driver Attention, *Accident Analysis and Prevention* 25(3): 259–265.

34. Young, K. and M. Regan (2007). Driver Distraction: A Review of the Literature. In Faulks, I. J., M. Regan, M. Stevenson, J. Brown, A. Porter, and J. D. Irwin (Eds.), *Distracted Driving*, Australasian College of Road Safety, 379–405.

35. Desjardins, Jeff (2017). Here's How Many Millions of Lines of Code it Takes to Run Different Software, *Business Insider*, 9 February.

36. Standish Group (1995). CHAOS. https://www.cs.nmt.edu/~cs328/reading/Standish.pdf.

37. Laurenz, J. Eveleens and Chris Verhoef (2010). The Rise and Fall of the Chaos Report Figures, *IEEE Software*, January/February, 30–36.

38. Wikipedia (2017). NHS Connecting for Health. https://en.wikipedia.org/wiki/NHS_Connecting_for_Health.

39. NAO (2006). The National Program for IT in the NHS. National Audit Office. https://www.nao.org.uk/wp-content/uploads/2006/06/05061173.pdf.
40. Campion-Awwad, Oliver, Alexander Hayton, Leila Smith, and Mark Vuaran (2014). The National Programme for IT in the NHS: A Case History. Cambridge Computer Lab. https://www.cl.cam.ac.uk/~rja14/Papers/npfit-mpp-2014-case-history.pdf.
41. Jeffries, Adrianne (2013). Why Obama's Healthcare.gov Launch Was Doomed to Fail, *TheVerge.com*, 8 October. https://www.theverge.com/2013/10/8/4814098/why-did-the-tech-savvy-obama-administration-launch-a-busted-healthcare-website.
42. Jeffries, Adrianne (2013). Thanks a Lot, Healthcare.gov, *TheVerge.com*, 3 December. https://www.theverge.com/us-world/2013/12/3/5163228/healthcare-gov-obamacare-website-shows-how-government-can-do-tech-better.
43. Wikipedia (2017). List of failed and overbudget custom software projects. https://en.wikipedia.org/wiki/List_of_failed_and_overbudget_custom_software_projects.
44. GAO (2015). HEALTHCARE.GOV: CMS Has Taken Steps to Address Problems, but Needs to Further Implement Systems Development Best Practices. United States Government Accountability Office, March. https://www.gao.gov/products/GAO-15-238.
45. Carioti, Ricky (2014). Sinkhole of Bureaucracy: Deep Underground, Federal Employees Process Paperwork by Hand in a Long-outdated, Inefficient System, *The Washington Post*, 22 March.
46. Bavas, Josh (2016). Queensland Health Still Seeking Millions of Dollars in Overpayments, Six Years on from Payroll Disaster, *ABC News*, 26 July.
47. Jones, Capers (2004). Software Project Management Practices: Failure Versus Success, *CrossTalk: The Journal of Defense Software Engineering*, October, 5–9. See also Charette, Robert N. (2005). Why Software Fails, *IEEE Spectrum*, September, 42–49.
48. Wikipedia (2017). Waterfall model. https://en.wikipedia.org/wiki/Waterfall_model.
49. Wikipedia (2017). Spiral model. https://en.wikipedia.org/wiki/Spiral_model.
50. Wikipedia (2017). Agile software development. https://en.wikipedia.org/wiki/Agile_software_development.
51. Moløkken-Østvold, Kjetil and Magne Jørgensen (2005). A Comparison of Software Project Overruns—Flexible versus Sequential Development Models, *IEEE Transactions on Software Engineering* 31(9): 754–766.
52. Meyer, Robinson (2015). The Secret Startup that Saved the Worst Website in America, *The Atlantic*, 9 July.
53. Hofmann, Hubert F. and Franz Lehner (2001). Requirements Engineering as a Success Factor in Software Projects, *IEEE Software* 18(4): 58–66.
54. Brooks, Frederick P. (1995). *The Mythical Man-Month: Essays on Software Engineering*, Anniversary Edition, Addison-Wesley.
55. Wikipedia (2017). Year 2000 problem. https://en.wikipedia.org/wiki/Year_2000_problem.
56. Computer Chronicles (1999). Computer Chronicles (1999)—Year 2000 (Y2K). Video. https://www.youtube.com/watch?v=nAFIsPX3_3A.
57. Mulvin, Dylan (2016). Embedded Dangers: The History of the Year 2000 Problem and the Politics of Technological Repair. Paper presented at the 17th Annual Conference of the Association of Internet Researchers (AoIR). https://spir.aoir.org/index.php/spir/article/view/1335.

58. Wikipedia (2017). Universal credit. https://en.wikipedia.org/wiki/Universal_Credit.

59. Hall, Kat (2016). Universal Credit: The IT Project that Will Outlive Us All, *The Register*, 25 January. https://www.theregister.co.uk/2016/01/25/universal_credit_programme_delivery_delays/. See also Jee, Charlotte (2015). 90 percent of Universal Credit Staff Say IT Systems 'Inadequate', *ComputerworldUK*, 9 March. http://www.computerworlduk.com/it-management/90-percent-of-universal-credit-staff-say-it-systems-inadequate-3600896/.

60. Butler, Patrick (2017). MPs Launch Official Inquiry into Universal Credit as Criticism Grows, *TheGuardian.com*, 22 February. https://www.theguardian.com/society/2017/feb/22/mps-launch-official-inquiry-universal-credit-benefits.

61. Wikipedia (2018). Phoenix pay system. https://en.wikipedia.org/wiki/Phoenix_pay_system. See also Press, Jordan (2017). Cost to Fix Phoenix Pay System to Surpass $540 Million, *FinancialPost.com*, 21 November. http://business.financialpost.com/pmn/business-pmn/newsalert-fixing-phoenix-pay-system-years-millions-of-dollars-away-says-audit-2. See also Aiello, Rachel (2017). A Working Pay System Is Years Away, *CTVNews.com*, 21 November. https://www.ctvnews.ca/politics/a-working-pay-system-is-years-away-audit-says-1.3687259.

62. GAO (1992). Advanced Automation System Still Vulnerable to Cost and Schedule Problems. United States General Accounting Office, September. http://www.gao.gov/products/RCED-92-264.

63. Wald, Matthew L. (1996). Flight to Nowhere: A Special Report; Ambitious Upgrade of Air Navigation Becomes a Fiasco, *New York Times*, 29 January.

64. Barlas, Stephen (1996). Anatomy of a Runaway: What Grounded the AAS, *IEEE Software*, January, 104–106. See also Barlas, Stephen (1996). Anatomy of a Runaway: FAA Shifts Focus to Scaled-Back DSR, *IEEE Software*, March, 110, 114.

65. Breselor, Sara (2015). Why 40-Year-Old Tech Is Still Running America's Air Traffic Control, *Wired*, 24 February.

66. The Economist (2016). Antiquated Air Traffic Control Systems Are Becoming a Serious Threat to Safety: America Could Learn a Few Things from Canada, *The Economist*, 10 August. https://www.economist.com/news/science-and-technology/21703477-americas-antiquated-air-traffic-control-system-hindering-safety-sky-navigating. The technology is more advanced in Canada.

67. Lerner, Eric J. (1982). Automating U.S. Air Lanes: A Review, *IEEE Spectrum*, November, 46–51.

68. Wesson, Robert, Kenneth Solomon, Randall Steeb, Perry Thorndyke, and Keith Wescourt (1981). Scenarios for Evolution of Air Traffic Control. Rand Report R-2698-FAA, November. https://www.rand.org/content/dam/rand/pubs/reports/2006/R2698.pdf.

69. Leveson, Nancy G. and Clark S. Turner (1993). An Investigation of the Therac-25 Accidents, *Computer*, July, 18–41.

70. Thimbleby, Harold (2013). Improving Safety in Medical Devices and Systems, *International Conference on Healthcare Informatics*, 1–13. 10.1109/ICHI.2013.91.

71. Johnston, A. M. (2006). Unintended Overexposure of Patient Lisa Norris During Radiotherapy Treatment at the Beatson Oncology Centre, Glasgow in January 2006. Report to the Scottish Executive. http://www.gov.scot/Resource/Doc/153082/0041158.pdf.

72. Wikipedia (2017). List of industrial disasters. https://en.wikipedia.org/wiki/List_of_industrial_disasters.

73. Safety Partners, Ltd (2017). 7 Most Common Causes of Workplace Accidents. http://www.safetypartnersltd.com/7-most-common-causes-of-workplace-accidents/#.WW9vLsYZPUp.

74. Meshkati, Najmedin (1991). Human Factors in Large-scale Technological Systems' Accidents: Three Mile Island, Bhopal, Chernobyl, *Industrial Crisis Quarterly* 5: 133–154.

75. *Ibid.* See also Leveson, Nancy G. (1995). *Safeware: System Safety and Computers*, Addison-Wesley. See also Hopkins, Andrew (2001). Was Three Mile Island a 'Normal Accident'? *Journal of Contingencies and Crisis Management* 9(2): 65–72.

76. Wikimedia Commons (2018). History of the Global Nuclear Power Industry. https://commons.wikimedia.org/wiki/File:Nuclear_Power_History.png.

77. Hopkins, Andrew (2001). Was Three Mile Island a 'Normal Accident'? *Journal of Contingencies and Crisis Management* 9(2): 65–72. See also McGrath, Matt (2017). Three Mile Island to Close 40 Years after Nuclear Accident, *BBC News*, 30 May.

78. Meshkati, Najmedin (1991). Human Factors in Large-scale Technological Systems' Accidents: Three Mile Island, Bhopal, Chernobyl. *Industrial Crisis Quarterly* 5: 133–154. See also Leveson, Nancy G. (1995). *Safeware: System Safety and Computers*, Addison-Wesley. See also Salge, Markus and Peter Milling (2006). Who Is to Blame, the Operator or the Designer? Two Stages of Human Failure in the Chernobyl Accident, *System Dynamics Review* 22(2): 89–112.

79. Wikipedia (2017). Northeast blackout of 2003. https://en.wikipedia.org/wiki/Northeast_blackout_of_2003.

80. Poulsen, Kevin (2004). Software Bug Contributed to Blackout, *SecurityFocus.com*, 11 February. http://www.securityfocus.com/news/8016.

81. Wikipedia (2018). 1983 Soviet Nuclear False Alarm Incident. https://en.wikipedia.org/wiki/1983_Soviet_nuclear_false_alarm_incident.

82. Nagourney, Adam, David E. Sanger, and Johanna Barr (2018). Hawaii Panics After Alert About Incoming Missile Is Sent in Error, *New York Times*, 13 January. See also Shepherd, Adam (2018). How a Poor User Interface Design Caused the Hawaii Missile Scare, *ITPro*, 15 January. http://www.itpro.co.uk/security/30288/how-a-poor-user-interface-design-caused-the-hawaii-missile-scare.

83. Lipson, Hod and Melba Kurman (2016). *Driverless: Intelligent Cars and the Road Ahead*, The MIT Press.

84. Ramsey, Jonathan (2009). The Bizarre History of Car Accidents, *Autoblog.com*, 3 September. http://www.autoblog.com/2009/09/03/car-accidents/.

85. Howard, Bill (2017). Is Texting to Blame for 2016's Increase in Vehicular Deaths? *ExtremeTech.com*, 17 February. https://www.extremetech.com/extreme/244558-texting-blame-2016s-increase-vehicular-deaths.

86. WHO (2017). Road Traffic Injuries. World Health Organization. http://www.who.int/mediacentre/factsheets/fs358/en/.

87. Pines (2017). Top 25 Causes of Car Accidents. Law Offices of Michael Pines, APC. https://seriousaccidents.com/legal-advice/top-causes-of-car-accidents/.

88. Speiser, Matthew (2015). This Map Shows What Causes the Most Fatal Car Crashes in Each US State, *BusinessInsider.com*, 28 May. http://www.businessinsider.com/the-cause-of-the-most-fatal-car-crashes-2015-5.

89. Schaper, David (2016). Human Errors Drive Growing Death Toll in Auto Crashes, *NPR Now*, 20 October. http://www.npr.org/2016/10/20/498406570/tech-human-errors-drive-growing-death-toll-in-auto-crashes.

90. Wakabayashi, Daisuke (2016). Google Parent Company Spins Off Self-Driving Car Business, *New York Times,* 13 December. See also Google self-driving car project (2014). A Ride in the Google Self Driving Car. Video. https://www.youtube.com/watch?v=TsaES—OTzM.

91. Zhou, Naaman (2017). Volvo Admits its Self-driving Cars Are Confused by Kangaroos, *The Guardian,* 1 July.

92. Goel, Vindu (2017). Apple Gets Permit to Test Self-Driving Cars in California, *New York Times,* 14 April. See also Isaac, Mike (2017). How Uber and Waymo Ended Up Rivals in the Race for Driverless Cars, *New York Times,* 17 May. See also Ewing, Jack (2017). BMW and Volkswagen Try to Beat Apple and Google at Their Own Game, *New York Times,* 22 June. See also Boudette, Neal E. (2017). By Buying Mobileye, Intel Jumps Firmly into Driverless Car Race, *New York Times,* 22 June. Wakabayashi, Daisuke (2017). Apple Scales Back Its Ambitions for a Self-Driving Car, *New York Times,* 22 August. See also Isaac, Mike (2017). Uber Strikes Deal with Volvo to Bring Self-Driving Cars to Its Network, *New York Times,* 22 August. See also Vlasic, Bill (2017). G.M. Unveils Its Driverless Cars, Aiming to Lead the Pack, *New York Times,* 29 November. See also Boudette, Neal E. and Michael J. de la Merced (2018). SoftBank Fund Puts $2.25 Billion in G.M.'s Driverless Unit, *New York Times,* 31 May. See also Isaac, Mike, Daisuke Wakabayashi, and Kate Conger (2018). Uber's Vision of Self-Driving Cars Begins to Blur, *New York Times,* 31 May.

93. Captain, Sean (2018). Here's How to Avoid More Self-Driving Car Deaths, Says Uber's Former AI Chief, *Fast Company,* 20 March. See also Metz, Cade (2017). What Virtual Reality Can Teach a Driverless Car, *New York Times,* 29 October.

94. Isaac, Mike and Daisuke Wakabayashi (2017). A Lawsuit Against Uber Highlights the Rush to Conquer Driverless Cars, *New York Times,* 24 February. See also Isaac, Mike (2017). Uber Suspends Tests of Self-Driving Vehicles After Arizona Crash, *New York Times,* 17 May.

95. Boudette, Neal E. (2017). Tesla's Self-Driving System Cleared in Deadly Crash, *New York Times,* 19 January. See also Boudette, Neal E. and Bill Vlasic (2017). Tesla Self-Driving System Faulted by Safety Agency in Crash, *New York Times,* 12 September.

96. Boudette, Neal E. (2018). Fatal Tesla Crash Raises New Questions About Autopilot System, *New York Times,* 31 March.

97. Wakabayashi, Daisuke (2018). Self-Driving Uber Car Kills Pedestrian in Arizona, Where Robots Roam, *New York Times,* 19 March.

98. Wakabayashi, Daisuke (2018). Uber's Self-Driving Cars Were Struggling Before Arizona Crash, *New York Times,* 19 March. See also Wakabayashi, Daisuke (2018). Emergency Braking Was Disabled When Self-Driving Uber Killed Woman, Report Says, *New York Times,* 24 May. See also Somerville, Heather and David Shepardson (2018). Uber Car's 'Safety' Driver Streamed Tv Show Before Fatal Crash: Police, *Reuters.com,* 22 June. https://www.reuters.com/article/us-uber-selfdriving-crash/uber-driver-was-streaming-hulu-show-just-before-self-driving-car-crash-police-report-idUSKBN1JI0LB.

99. NHTSA (2016). Federal Automated Vehicles Policy: Accelerating the Next Revolution in Roadway Safety. National Highway Traffic Safety Administration. US Department of Transportation. September 2016. https://www.transportation.gov/sites/dot.gov/files/docs/AV%20policy%20guidance%20PDF.pdf.

100. Dunn, Michael (2013). Toyota's Killer Firmware: Bad Design and its Consequences, *EDN Network,* 28 October. http://www.edn.com/design/automotive/4423428/Toyota-s-killer-firmware—Bad-design-and-its-consequences. This describes a case in which unwanted acceleration was deadly.

101. Boudette, Neal E. and Nick Wingfield (2017). Coming from Automakers: Voice Control that Understands You Better, *New York Times,* 5 January.

102. Taub, Eric A. (2017). Sleepy Behind the Wheel? Some Cars Can Tell, *New York Times,* 16 March.

103. Kang, Cecilia (2016). Cars Talking to One Another? They Could Under Proposed Safety Rules, *New York Times,* 13 December.

104. Boudette, Neal E. (2017). Building a Road Map for the Self-Driving Car, *New York Times,* 2 March. See also Quain, John R. (2017). What Self-Driving Cars See, *New York Times,* 25 May. The latter paper has a discussion of the intellectual property disputes centred around this technology.

105. Brown, Barry (2017). The Social Life of Autonomous Cars, *Computer*, February, 92–96. IEEE Computer Society. See also Said, Carolyn and David R. Baker (2017). Humanizing Cars, Sensitizing Humans, *San Francisco Chronicle,* 8 October.

106. Markoff, John (2017). Robot Cars Can't Count on Us in an Emergency, *New York Times,* 7 June.

107. Quain, John R. (2018). When Self-Driving Cars Can't Help Themselves, Who Takes the Wheel? *New York Times,* 15 March.

108. Taub, Eric A. (2017). Envisioning the Car of the Future as a Living Room on Wheels, *New York Times,* 15 June.

109. Bogost, Ian (2016). When Cars Fly, *The Atlantic,* 15 May.

110. Morgan Stanley Research (2016). Shared Mobility on the Road of the Future, *Forbes*, 20 July. https://www.forbes.com/sites/morganstanley/2016/07/20/shared-mobility-on-the-road-of-the-future/#79f867bd1cae.

111. Chapman, Mary M. (2017). Self-Driving Cars Could Be Boon for Aged, After Initial Hurdles, *New York Times,* 23 March.

112. Metz, Cade (2018). After Fatal Uber Crash, a Self-Driving Start-Up Moves Forward, *New York Times,* 7 May.

113. Dougherty, Connor (2017). Self-Driving Trucks May Be Closer Than They Appear, *New York Times,* 13 November.

114. Horton, Chris (2017). In Taiwan, Modest Test of Driverless Bus May Hint at Big Things to Come, *New York Times,* 28 September.

115. de la Merced, Michael J. (2017). Lilium, a Flying Car Start-Up, Raises $90 Million, *New York Times,* 5 September.

116. Scott, Mark (2017). The Future of European Transit: Driverless and Utilitarian, *New York Times,* 28 May.

117. Kitman, Jamie Lincoln (2016). Google Wants Driverless Cars, but Do We? *New York Times,* 19 December.

118. Knight, Will (2015). How to Help Self-Driving Cars Make Ethical Decisions, *MIT Technology Review*, 29 July. https://www.technologyreview.com/s/539731/how-to-help-self-driving-cars-make-ethical-decisions/. See also arXiv (2015). Why Self-driving Cars Must Be Programmed to Kill, *MIT Technology Review*, 22 October. https://www.technologyreview.com/s/542626/why-self-driving-cars-must-be-programmed-to-kill/

119. Wikipedia (2018). Trolley problem. https://en.wikipedia.org/wiki/Trolley_problem.

120. Marshall, Aarian (2017). Lawyers, Not Ethicists, Will Solve the 'Trolley Problem', *Wired,* 28 May. https://www.wired.com/2017/05/autonomous-vehicles-trolley-problem/.

121. Acosta, Aida Joaquin (2018). What Governments Across the Globe are Doing to Seize the Benefits of Autonomous Vehicles. Policy Paper on Autonomous Vehicles. Berkman Klein Center, Harvard University, July. http://cyber.harvard.edu/sites/default/files/2018-07/2018-07_AVs03_0.pdf.

122. Kang, Cecilia (2017). Where Self-Driving Cars Go to Learn, *New York Times,* 11 November. See also Kang, Cecilia (2017). Pittsburgh Welcomed Uber's Driverless Car Experiment. Not Anymore, *New York Times,* 11 November. See also Wakabayashi, Daisuke (2017). Where Driverless Cars Brake for Golf Carts, *New York Times,* 4 October. See also Badger, Emily (2018). Pave Over the Subway? Cities Face Tough Bets on Driverless Cars, *New York Times,* 20 July.

123. Pierson, Brian Matthew (2016). Self-driving Tech's Lobbying Supergroup to Play Many Dates in D.C., *ReadWrite.com,* 28 April. https://readwrite.com/2016/04/28/ford-google-lyft-uber-volvo-autonomous-car-lobbying-group-tl4/. See also Tusk, Bradley (2018). The Inside Story of How Uber Fought New York's City Hall and Won. Excerpt from Tusk, Bradley (2018). *The Fixer,* Portfolio, Penguin Publishing. Reprinted in *Fast Company,* 17 September 2018.

124. Abraham, Hillary, Bryan Reimer, Bobbie Seppelt, Craig Fitzgerald, Bruce Mehler, and Joseph F. Coughlin (2017). Consumer Interest in Automation: Preliminary Observations Exploring a Year's Change. *AGElab* 2017(2). White paper. http://agelab.mit.edu/sites/default/files/MIT%20-%20NEMPA%20White%20Paper%20FINAL.pdf.

125. Bajas, Vikas (2018). The Bright, Shiny Distraction of Self-Driving Cars, *New York Times,* 31 March.

126. Skeptical Science (2017). Global Warming & Climate Change Myths, *SkepticalScience.com.* https://www.skepticalscience.com/argument.php.

127. Boykoff, Maxwell T. and Jules M. Boykoff (2004). Balance as Bias: Global Warming and the US Prestige Press, *Global Environmental Change* 14: 125–136.

128. Agarwal, Anil and Sunita Narain (1991). *Global Warming in an Unequal World: A Case of Environmental Colonialism.* Centre for Science and the Environment. http://cseindia.org/challenge_balance/readings/GlobalWarming%20Book.pdf.

129. US Global Change Research Program (2017). Climate Science Special Report: Fifth-Order Draft, 28 June. https://drive.google.com/file/d/0ByGelvD2ciqLelNVMWN3WWpqU2M/view. Figure shown is from p. 16.

130. Armstrong, J. Scott (1999). Forecasting for Environmental Decision Making. University of Pennsylvania, June. http://repository.upenn.edu/cgi/viewcontent.cgi?article=1006&context=marketing_papers.

131. Semenov, Mikhail and Elaine M. Barrow, (1997). Use of a Stochastic Weather Generator in the Development of Climate Change Scenarios, *Climatic Change* 35: 97–414.

132. Hughes, Lesley (2000). Biological Consequences of Global Warming: Is the Signal Already, *Trends in Ecology and Evolution* 15(2): 56–61.

133. Meehl, Gerald A., Francis Zwiers, Jenni Evans, Thomas Knutson, Linda Mearns, and Peter Whetton (1999). Trends in Extreme Weather and Climate Events: Issues Related to Modeling Extremes in Projections of Future Climate Change, *American Meteorological Society,* 6 August.

http://journals.ametsoc.org/doi/abs/10.1175/1520-0477%282000%29081%3C0427%3ATIEWAC%3E2.3.CO%3B2.

134. Rosenzeig, Cynthia, Ana Iglesias, X. B. Yang, Paul R. Epstein, and Eric Chivian (2001). Climate Change and Extreme Weather Events: Implications for Food Production, Plant Diseases, and Pests, *Global Change & Human Health* 2(2): 90–104.

135. Cramer, Wolfgang, Alberte Bondeau, F. Ian Woodward, I. Colin Prentice, Richard A. Betts, Victor Brovkin, Peter M. Cox, Veronica Fisher, Jonathan A. Foley, Andrew D. Friend, Chris Kucharik, Mark R. Lomas, Navin Ramankutty, Stephen Sitch, Benjamin Smith, Andrew White, and Christine Young-Molling (2001). Global Response of Terrestrial Ecosystem Structure and Function to CO2 and Climate Change: Results from Six Dynamic Global Vegetation Models, *Global Change Biology* 7: 357–373.

136. Pearson, Richard G. and Terence P. Dawson (2003). Predicting the Impacts of Climate Change on the Distribution of Species: Are Bioclimate Envelope Models Useful? *Global Ecology & Biogeography* 12: 361–371.

137. Dai, Aiguo (2010). Drought Under Global Warming: A Review, *Climate Change* 2(1): 45–65. http://onlinelibrary.wiley.com/doi/10.1002/wcc.81/full. 10.1002/wcc.81

138. Meinshausen, Malte, Nicolai Meinshausen, William Hare, Sarah C. B. Raper, Katja Frieler, Reto Knutti, David J. Frame, and Myles R. Allen (2009). Greenhouse-gas Emission Targets for Limiting Global Warming to 2C, *Nature Letters* 458: 1158–1163.

139. Wallace-Wells, David (2017). The Uninhabitable Earth, *New York Magazine*, 9 July.

140. Hilty, Lorenz M. and Bernard Aebischer (2015). ICT for Sustainability: An Emerging Research Field. In Hilty, Lorenz M. and Bernard Aebischer (Eds), *ICT Innovations for Sustainability*, Springer.

141. Williams, Eric (2011). Environmental Effects of Information and Communications Technologies, *Nature* 479(17): 354–358.

142. Innes, Judith E. and David E. Booher (2000). Indicators for Sustainable Communities: A Strategy Building on Complexity Theory and Distributed Intelligence, *Planning Theory & Practice* 1(2): 173–186.

143. Wäger, Patrick, Roland Hischier, and Rolf Widmer (2015). The Material Basis for ICT. In Hilty, Lorenz M. and Bernard Aebischer (Eds), *ICT Innovations for Sustainability*, Advances in Intelligent Systems and Computing 310, Springer. See also 141., ibid.

144. Ellison, Glenn and Drew Fudenberg (2000). The New-Luddite's Lament: Excessive Upgrading in the Software Industry, *RAND Journal of Economics* 31(2): 253–272. See also Sandborn, Peter (2007). Software Obsolescence—Complicating the Part and Technology Obsolescence Management Problem, *IEEE Transactions on Components and Packaging Technologies* 30(4): 886–888.

145. Forge, Simon (2007). Powering Down: Remedies for Unsustainable ICT, *Foresight* 9(4): 3–21.

146. Electronics Takeback Coalition (2014). Facts and Figures on E-Waste and Recycling. *Electronics TakeBack Coalition*, 25 June. http://www.electronicstakeback.com/wp-content/uploads/Facts_and_Figures_on_EWaste_and_Recycling.pdf. See also 141, ibid.

147. Wiens, Kyle (2015). The Right to Repair, *IEEE Consumer Electronics Magazine*, October, 123–4, 135. See also Fitzpatrick, Alex (2017). Hand Me That Wrench: Farmers and Apple Fight Over the Toolbox, *Time.com*, 22 June. http://time.com/4828099/farmers-and-apple-fight-over-the-toolbox/. See also Rosner, Daniela (2014). Designing for Repair? Infrastructures

and Materialities of Breakdown. Proceedings of 2014 Computer Supported Cooperative Work and Social Computing, 319–331 for an ethnographic study illuminating the complex concepts of breakdown and repair.

148. Noonan, Alex (2017). Massachusetts Considers Digital Right to Repair, *Cyberlaw Clinic*, 12 October. https://clinic.cyber.harvard.edu/2017/10/12/massachusetts-considers-digital-right-to-repair/.
149. Wikipedia (2017). Electronic waste. https://en.wikipedia.org/wiki/Electronic_waste. See also Electronics Takeback Coalition (2017). Facts and Figures on E-Waste and Recycling. *Electronics TakeBack Coalition*, 25 June 2014. http://www.electronicstakeback.com/wp content/uploads/Facts_and_Figures_on_EWaste_and_Recycling.pdf.
150. Spreng, Daniel (2015). The Interdependency of Energy, Information, and Growth. In Hilty, Lorenz M. and Bernard Aebischer (Eds), *ICT Innovations for Sustainability*, Springer.
151. Phillimore, John and Aidan Davison (2002). A Precautionary Tale: Y2K and the Politics of Foresight, *Futures* 34: 147–157.
152. Forrest, Connor (2017). Robot Kills Worker on Assembly Line, Raising Concerns about Human–Robot Collaboration, *TechRepublic*, 15 March. https://www.techrepublic.com/article/robot-kills-worker-on-assembly-line-raising-concerns-about-human-robot-collaboration/.

Chapter 9

1. Wikipedia (2017). The Trial. https://en.wikipedia.org/wiki/The_Trial. See also SparkNotes (2017). Franz Kafka's *The Trial*. http://www.sparknotes.com/lit/trial/.
2. Wikipedia (2017). Minority Report (film). https://en.wikipedia.org/wiki/Minority_Report_(film).
3. Ebert, Roger (2002). Spielberg and Cruise at the Movies. *Roger Ebert Interviews*, 16 June. http://www.rogerebert.com/interviews/spielberg-and-cruise-and-the-movies.
4. Westin, Alan F. (1967). *Privacy and Freedom*, Atheneum. See also Hoffman, Lance (1969). Computers and Privacy: A Survey, *Computing Surveys* 1(2): 85–103.
5. Westin, Alan F. (1967). *Privacy and Freedom*, Atheneum.
6. Warren, Samuel D. and Louis D, Brandeis (1890). The Right to Privacy, *Harvard Law Review* 4: 193–220.
7. Bratman, Benjamin E. (2002). Brandeis and Warren's *The Right to Privacy* and the Birth of the Right to Privacy, *Tennessee Law Review* 69: 623–652.
8. Sprenger, Polly (1999). Sun on Privacy: Get Over It, *Wired*, 26 January.
9. Clarke, Roger (2006). Introduction to Dataveillance and Information Privacy, and Definitions of Terms. *Roger Clarke*, 21 August. http://www.rogerclarke.com/DV/Intro.html.
10. Russell, Helen (2014). Welcome to Sweden—the Most Cash-Free Society on the Planet, *The Guardian*, 12 November.
11. Froomkin, A Michael. (2000). The Death of Privacy? *Stanford Law Review* 52: 1461–1544.
12. Margulis, Stephen T. (2003). Privacy as a Social Issue and Behavioral Concept, *Journal of Social Issues* 59(2): 243–261.
13. Solove, Daniel (2006). A Taxonomy of Privacy, *University of Pennsylvania Law Review* 154: 477–564. See also Solove, Daniel (2008). *Understanding Privacy*, Harvard University Press.

14. Newell, Patricia Brierley (1998). A Cross-Cultural Comparison of Privacy Definitions and Functions: A Systems Approach, *Journal of Environmental Psychology* 18: 357–371.

15. BeVier, Lillian R. (1995). Information about Individuals in the Hands of Government: Some Reflections on Mechanisms for Privacy Protection, *William & Mary Bill Rights. Journal* 4: 455–506. See also Wikipedia (2017). Government database. https://en.wikipedia.org/wiki/Government_database.

16. Solove, Daniel J. (2001). Privacy and Power: Computer Databases and Metaphors for Information Privacy, *Stanford Law Review* 53: 1393–1462.

17. O'Harrow Jr., Robert (2008). Centers Tap Into Personal Databases, *The Washington Post*, 2 April.

18. GAO (2017). Information Security: Control Deficiencies Continue to Limit IRS's Effectiveness in Protecting Sensitive Financial and Taxpayer Data. US Government Accountability Office, 26 July. https://www.gao.gov/products/GAO-17-395.

19. Poulsen, Kevin (2008). Five IRS Employees Charged with Snooping on Tax Returns, *Wired*, 13 May. See also Hendrie, Alexander (2015). IRS Agents Caught Snooping on Taxpayer Data Rehired, *Americans for Tax Reform*, 6 February. https://www.atr.org/irs-agents-caught-snooping-taxpayer-data-rehired.

20. Minkel, J. R. (2007). Bureau Gave Up Names of Japanese-Americans in WW II, *Scientific American*, 30 March.

21. Clemetson, Lynette (2004). Homeland Security Given Data on Arab-Americans, *New York Times*, 30 July.

22. Singer, Eleanor, John van Hoewyk, and Randall J. Neugebauer (2003). Attitudes and Behavior: The Impact of Privacy and Confidentiality Concerns on Participation in the 2000 Census, *Public Opinion Quarterly* 67: 368–384.

23. Luebke, David Martin and Sybil Milton (1994). Locating the Victim: An Overview of Census-Taking, Tabulation Technology, and Persecution in Nazi Germany, *IEEE Annals of the History of Computing* 16(3): 25–39. See also Black, Edwin (2000). *IBM and the Holocaust: The Strategic Alliance Between Nazi Germany and America's Most Powerful Corporation*, Crown. See also Schoenfield, Gabriel (2001). The Punch-Card Conspiracy: A Journalist Explores Relations between I.B.M. and the Third Reich, *New York Times*, 18 March.

24. Coombes, Thomas (2015). Lessons from the Stasi, *Theeuropean-magazine.com*, 1 April. See also Curry, Andrew (2015). No, the NSA Isn't Like the Stasi—and Comparing Them is Treacherous, *Wired.com*. https://www.wired.com/2015/01/nsa-stasi-comparison/. See also Wikipedia (2017h). Stasi Records Agency. https://en.wikipedia.org/wiki/Stasi_Records_Agency.

25. Wikipedia (2017). National identification number. https://en.wikipedia.org/wiki/National_identification_number.

26. Berghel, Hal (2000). Identity Theft, Social Security Numbers, and the Web, *Communications of the ACM* 43(2): 17–21. See also Jeffries, Adrienne (2012). Identity Crisis: How Social Security Numbers Became Our Insecure National ID, *The Verge*, 26 September.

27. EPIC.org (2017). National ID and the REAL ID Act. Electronic Privacy Information Center. https://www.epic.org/privacy/id_cards/.

28. Shattuck, John (1984). In the Shadow of 1984: National Identification Systems, Computer-Matching, and Privacy in the United States, *Hastings Law Journal* 35: 991–1006. See also Mason, Richard O. (1986). Four Ethical Issues of the Information Age, *MIS Quarterly*, 5–12.

See also Munro, Neil (2002). The Ever-Expanding Network of Local and Federal Databases, *Communications of the ACM* 45(7): 17–19.

29. Rubinstein, Ira S., Ronald D. Lee, and Paul M. Schwartz (2008). Data Mining and Internet Profiling: Emerging Regulatory and Technological Approaches, *The University of Chicago Law Review* 75(1): 261–285.
30. Slobogin, Christopher (2008). Data Mining and the Fourth Amendment, *The University of Chicago Law Review* 75(1): 317–341.
31. Laudon, Kenneth C. (1986). Data Quality and Due Process in Large Interorganizational Record Systems, *Communications of the ACM* 29(1): 4–11.
32. Munro, Neil (2002). The Ever-Expanding Network of Local and Federal Databases, *Communcations of the ACM* 45(7): 17–19.
33. Blumstein, Alfred and Kiminori Nakamura (2009). Redemption in the Presence of Widespread Criminal Background Checks, *Criminology* 47(2): 327–359.
34. Nowak, Glen J. and Joseph Phelps (1997). Direct Marketing and the Use of Individual-Level Consumer Information: Determining how and When 'Privacy' Matters, *Journal of Direct Marketing* 11(4): 94–108.
35. Gantz, John and David Reinsel (2012). The Digital Universe in 2020: Big Data, Bigger Digital Shadows, and Biggest Growth in the Far East, *IDC*, December. https://www.emc.com/collateral/analyst-reports/idc-the-digital-universe-in-2020.pdf. See also IDC (2014). The Digital Universe of Opportunities: Rich Data & the Increasing Value of the Internet of Things. https://www.emc.com/leadership/digital-universe/2014iview/index.htm.
36. IDC (2014). The Digital Universe of Opportunities: Rich Data & the Increasing Value of the Internet of Things. https://www.emc.com/collateral/analyst-reports/idc-digital-universe-2014.pdf. p. 13.
37. Bertino, Elisa (2015). Big Data—Security and Privacy, *2015 IEEE International Congress on Big Data*, 3693–3702. See also Executive Office of the President (2014). Big Data: Seizing Opportunities, Preserving Values. https://obamawhitehouse.archives.gov/sites/default/files/docs/big_data_privacy_report_may_1_2014.pdf.
38. Nelson, Boel and Tomas Olovsson (2015). Security and Privacy for Big Data: A Systematic Literature Review, *2016 IEEE International Conference on Big Data*, 3693–3702.
39. Phelps, Joseph, Glen Nowak, and Elizabeth Ferrell (2000). Privacy Concerns and Consumer Willingness to Provide Personal Information, *Journal of Public Policy & Marketing* 19(1): 27–41.
40. GAO (2006). Personal Information: Key Federal Privacy Laws Do Not Require Information Resellers to Safeguard All Sensitive Data. US Government Accountability Office, 26 June. http://www.gao.gov/products/GAO-06-674.
41. Daniel, Caroline and Maija Palmer (2007). Google's Goal: To Organise Your Daily Life, *The Financial Times*, 22 May. See also Wakabayshi, Daisuke (2017). How Google Cashes In on the Space Right Under the Search Bar, *New York Times*, 23 April. See also Wakabayshi, Daisuke (2017). Google Will No Longer Scan Gmail for Ad Targeting, *New York Times*, 23 June.
42. Story, Louise and Miguel Helft (2007). Google Buys DoubleClick for $3.1 Billion, *New York Times*, 14 April.
43. Barrows, Randolph C. and Paul D. Clayton (1996). Privacy, Confidentiality: and Electronic Medical Records, *Journal of the American Medical Informatics Association* 3(2): 139–148.

44. Wikipedia (2017). Health Insurance Portability and Accountability Act. https://en.wikipedia.org/wiki/Health_Insurance_Portability_and_Accountability_Act. See also Wang, Jason (2013). How Do I Become HIPAA Compliant? (a checklist). *TrueVault.com,* 30 October. https://www.truevault.com/blog/how-do-i-become-hipaa-compliant.html.

45. Leventhal, Rajiv (2017). Report: Healthcare Sector Hit Hard in 2016 by Data Breaches. Healthcare-informatics.com, 24 January. https://www.healthcare-informatics.com/news-item/cybersecurity/report-healthcare-sector-hit-hard-2016-data-breaches.

46. Lord, Nate (2017). Top Ten Biggest Healthcare Data Breaches of All Time, *DigitalGuardian.com,* 28 March. https://digitalguardian.com/blog/top-10-biggest-healthcare-data-breaches-all-time.

47. Cios, Krzysztof J. and G. William Moore (2002). Uniqueness of Medical Data Mining, *Artificial Intelligence in Medicine* 26: 1–24.

48. El Emam, Khaled, Elizabeth Jonker, Luk Arbuckle, and Bradley Malin (2011). A Systematic Review of Re-Identification Attacks on Health Data, *Public Library of Science One* 6(12): 1–12.

49. Abbott, Alison (2004). Icelandic Database Shelved as Court Judges Privacy in Peril, *Nature* 429: 118. http://www.nature.com/nature/journal/v429/n6988/full/429118b.html?foxtrot callback=true.

50. Boyd, Danah M. and Nicole Ellison (2008). Social Network Sites: Definition, History, and Scholarship, *Journal of Computer-Mediated Communication* 13: 210–230.

51. Barnes, Brooks (2017). Coming to Carnival Cruises: A Wearable Medallion That Records Your Every Whim, *New York Times,* 4 January.

52. Wikipedia (2018). Facebook. https://en.wikipedia.org/wiki/Facebook.

53. Debatin, Bernhard, Jennette P. Lovejoy, Ann-Kathrin Horn, and Brittany N. Hughes (2008). Facebook and Online Privacy: Attitudes, Behaviors, and Unintended Consequences, *Journal of Computer-Mediated Communication* 15: 83–108.

54. Nield, David (2017). You Almost Definitely Don't Know All the Ways Facebook Tracks You, *Gizmodo.uk,* 8 June. http://fieldguide.gizmodo.com/all-the-ways-facebook-tracks-you-that-you-might-not-kno-1795604150. See also Dillet, Romain (2018). Facebook Knows Literally Everything About You: Behind Every Feature, Facebook Is Collecting Data, *Techcrunch.com,* 23 March. https://techcrunch.com/2018/03/23/facebook-knows-literally-everything-about-you/.

55. Young, Alyson L. and Anabel Quan-Haase (2009). Information Revelation and Internet Privacy Concerns on Social Network Sites: A Case Study of Facebook. *2009 Proceedings of the Fourth International Conference on Communities and Technologies,* 265–273.

56. Boyd, Danah and Eszter Hargittai (2010). Facebook Privacy Settings: Who Cares? *First Monday* 15(8).

57. Stutzman, Fred, Ralph Gross, and Alessandro Acquisti (2012). Silent Listeners: The Evolution of Privacy and Disclosure on Facebook, *Journal of Privacy and Confidentiality* 4(2): 7–41.

58. Usmani, Wali Ahmed, Diogo Marques, Ivan Beschastnikh, Konstantin Beznosov, Tiago Guerreiro, and Luís Carriço (2017). Characterizing Social Insider Attacks on Facebook, *Proceedings of the Association for Computing Machinery 2017,* 3810–3820.

59. Stieger, Stefan, Christoph Burger, Manuel Bohn, and Martin Voracek (2013). Who Commits Virtual Identity Suicide? Differences in Privacy Concerns, Internet Addiction, and Personality

Between Facebook Users and Quitters, *Cyberpsychology, Behavior, and Social Networking* 16(9): 629–634. Saul, D. J. (2014). 3 Million Teens Leave Facebook in 3 Years: The Facebook Demographic Report, *ISL,* 15 January. https://isl.co/2014/01/3-million-teens-leave-facebook-in-3-years-the-2014-facebook-demographic-report/.

60. Shakya, Holly B. and Nicholas A. Christakis (2017). A New, More Rigorous Study Confirms: The More You Use Facebook, the Worse You Feel, *Harvard Business Review,* 10 April.
61. Nixon, Ron (2017). U.S. to Collect Social Media Data on All Immigrants Entering Country, *New York Times,* 28 September.
62. Rosenberg, Matthew, Nicholas Confessore, and Carole Cadwalladr (2018). How Trump Consultants Exploited the Facebook Data of Millions, *New York Times,* 17 March.
63. Frenkel, Sheera (2018). Scholars Have Data on Millions of Facebook Users. Who's Guarding It? *New York Times,* 6 May.
64. Weissman, Cale Guthrie (2018). How Amazon Helped Cambridge Analytica Harvest Americans' Facebook Data, *Fast Company,* 27 March.
65. Dance, Gabriel J. X., Ben Laffin, Drew Jordan, and Malachy Browne (2018). How Cambridge Analytica Exploited the Facebook Data of Millions, *New York Times,* 8 April, video at https://www.nytimes.com/video/technology/100000005806669/cambridge-analytica-facebook-profiles.html.
66. Kharpal, Arjun (2018). Mark Zuckerberg's Testimony: Here Are the Key Points You Need to Know, *CNBC.com,* 11 April. https://www.cnbc.com/2018/04/11/facebook-ceo-mark-zuckerberg-testimony-key-points.html.
67. Ivanova, Irina (2018). 8 Promises from Facebook after Cambridge Analytica, *CBSNews.com,* 10 April. https://www.cbsnews.com/news/facebooks-promises-for-protecting-your-information-after-data-breach-scandal/.
68. Dance, Gabriel J. X., Nicholas Confessore, and Michael LaForgia (2018). Facebook Gave Device Makers Deep Access to Data on Users and Friends, *New York Times,* 3 June. See also LaForgia, Michael and Gabriel J. X. Dance (2018). Facebook Gave Data Access to Chinese Firm Flagged by U.S. Intelligence, *New York Times,* 5 June. See also Frenkel, Sheera (2018). Facebook Bug Changed Privacy Settings of Up to 14 Million Users, *New York Times,* 7 June.
69. Grothaus, Michael (2018). Here's How to See the Data that Tech Giants Have About You, *Fast Company,* 25 May.
70. Porter, Eduardo (2018). The Facebook Fallacy: Privacy Is Up to You, *New York Times,* 24 April. See also Aquisti, Alessandro, Laura Brandimarte, and George Loewenstein (2015). Privacy and Human Behavior in the Age of Information, *ScienceMag.org,* 30 January. https://www.cmu.edu/dietrich/sds/docs/loewenstein/PrivacyHumanBeh.pdf.
71. Chen, Brian X. (2018). Google's File on Me Was Huge. Here's Why It Wasn't as Creepy as My Facebook Data, *New York Times,* 16 May.
72. Maheshwari, Sapna (2018). YouTube Is Improperly Collecting Children's Data, Consumer Groups Say, *New York Times,* 9 April.
73. Vozza, Stephanie (2018). Recruiters Look at This More Than Your LinkedIn, *Fast Company,* 20 April.
74. Viljoen, Salome (2018). Facebook's Surveillance Is Nothing Compared with Comcast, AT&T and Verizon, *The Guardian,* 6 April.

75. Wikipedia (2017). Radio-frequency identification. https://en.wikipedia.org/wiki/Radio-frequency_identification.
76. Spiekermann, Sarah (2009). RFID and Privacy: What Consumers Really Want and Fear, *Personal and Ubiquitous Computing* 13: 423–434.
77. Wikipedia (2017). Global Positioning System. https://en.wikipedia.org/wiki/Global_Positioning_System.
78. Hill, Simon (2018). Find Out How to Keep Tabs on Your Phone with These Helpful Tracking Tips, *DigitlTrends.com,* 28 March. https://www.digitaltrends.com/mobile/how-to-track-a-cell-phone/.
79. Kopstein, Janus (2014). A Phone for the Age of Snowden, *The New Yorker,* 30 January.
80. FERET (2017). Face Recognition Technology. https://www.nist.gov/programs-projects/face-recognition-technology-feret. See also Acquisti, Alessandro, Ralph Gross, and Fred Stutzman (2015). Faces of Facebook: Privacy in the Age of Augmented Reality. *Black Hat Webcast Series.* https://www.blackhat.com/docs/webcast/acquisti-face-BH-Webinar-2012-out.pdf/.
81. Mozur, Paul (2017). Inside China's Big Tech Conference, New Ways to Track Citizens, *New York Times,* 5 December.
82. Metz, Cade and Natasha Singer (2018). Newspaper Shooting Shows Widening Use of Facial Recognition by Authorities, *New York Times,* 29 June. See also Creswell, Julie (2018). Orlando Pulls the Plug on Its Amazon Facial Recognition Program, *New York Times,* 25 June. See also Singer, Natasha (2018). Microsoft Urges Congress to Regulate Use of Facial Recognition, *New York Times,* 13 July. See also Singer, Natasha (2018). Facebook's Push for Facial Recognition Prompts Privacy Alarms, *New York Times,* 9 July. See also Captain, Sean (2018). Congress Demands Jeff Bezos Explain Amazon's Face Recognition Software, *Fast Company,* 27 July. See also Edmondson, Catie (2018). An Airline Scans Your Face. You Take Off. But Few Rules Govern Where Your Data Goes, *New York Times,* 6 August.
83. Colon, Alex and Will Greenwald (2018). The Best Home Security Cameras of 2018, *PCMag.com,* 2 July. https://www.pcmag.com/article2/0,2817,2475954,00.asp.
84. Wikipedia (2017). Mass surveillance in the United Kingdom. https://en.wikipedia.org/wiki/Mass_surveillance_in_the_United_Kingdom. See also BBC News (2006). Britain Is 'Surveillance Society', *BBCNews.com,* 2 November. http://news.bbc.co.uk/2/hi/uk/6108496.stm.
85. Linn, Allison (2011). Post 9/11, Surveillance Cameras Everywhere, *NBCNews.com,* 23 August. http://www.nbcnews.com/id/44163852/ns/business-us_business/t/post-surveillance-cameras-everywhere/#.WdZ8L0wZN8I.
86. Nixon, Ron (2017). On the Mexican Border, a Case for Technology Over Concrete, *New York Times,* 21 June.
87. Williams, Timothy (2018). Can 30,000 Cameras Help Solve Chicago's Crime Problem? *New York Times,* 26 May.
88. Mozur, Paul (2018). Inside China's Dystopian Dreams: A.I., Shame and Lots of Cameras, *New York Times,* 8 July.
89. Hernandez, Javier C. (2017). In China, Daydreaming Students Are Caught on Camera, *New York Times,* 25 April 2017.
90. Big Brother Watch (2016). Are They Still Watching? *BigBrotherWatch.com,* February. https://www.bigbrotherwatch.org.uk/wp-content/uploads/2016/02/Are-They-Still-Watching.pdf

91. Lohr, Steve (2017). How Do You Vote? 50 Million Google Images Give a Clue, *New York Times*, 31 December.

92. Mann, Steve, Jason Nolan, and Barry Wellman (2003). Sousveillance: Inventing and Using Wearable Computing Devices for Data Collection in Surveillance Environments, *Surveillance & Society* 1(3): 331–355.

93. Want, Roy, Andy Hopper, Veronica Falcao, Jonathon Gibbons (1992). The Active Badge Location System, *ACM Transactions on Information Systems* 10(1): 91–102.

94. Pentland, Alex (2014). *Social Physics: How Good Ideas Spread—The Lessons from a New Science*, The Penguin Press.

95. Madan, Anmol, Ben Waber, Margaret Ding, Paul Kominers, and Alex (Sandy) Pentland (2009). Reality Mining: The End of Personal Privacy? Human Dynamics Group, MIT Media Lab. https://pdfs.semanticscholar.org/presentation/0ef1/d422c89d9bd23536876ce7fedf995 7f79e0f.pdf.

96. Hilts, Andrew, Christopher Parsons, and Jeffrey Knockel (2016). Every Step You Fake: A Comparative Analysis of Fitness Tracker Privacy and Security, *The Citizen Lab*, 2 February. https://citizenlab.ca/2016/02/fitness-tracker-privacy-and-security/.

97. De Freytas-Tamura, Kimiko (2017). The Bright-Eyed Talking Doll That Just Might Be a Spy, *New York Times*, 17 February.

98. GAO (2017). Vehicle Data Privacy: Industry and Federal Efforts Under Way, but NHTSA Needs to Define Its Role. US Government Accountability Office, July. http://www.gao.gov/assets/690/686284.pdf.

99. Halperin, Daniel, Tadayoshi Kohno, Thomas S. Heydt-Benjamin, Kevin Fu, and William H. Maisel (2008). Security and Privacy for Implantable Medical Devices, *Pervasive Computing*, January–March, 30–39.

100. Weiser, Mark (1991). The Computer for the 21st Century, *Scientific American*, September, 94–104.

101. Price, Blaine A., Karim Adam, and Bashar Nuseibeh (2005). Keeping Ubiquitous Computing to Yourself: A Practical Model for User Control of Privacy, *International Journal of Human–Computer Studies* 63: 228–253.

102. Dritsas, Stelios, Dimitris Gritzalis, and Costas Lambrinoudakis (2006). Protecting Privacy and Anonymity in Pervasive Computing: Trends and Perspectives, *Telematics and Informatics* 23: 196–210. See also Karyda, Maria, Stefanos Gritzalis, Jong Hyuk Park, and Spyros Kokolakis (2009). Privacy and Fair Information Practices in Ubiquitous Environments: Research Challenges and Future Directions, *Internet Research* 19(2): 194–208. See also Hashem, Tanzima and Lars Kulik (2011). 'Don't trust anyone': Privacy Protection for Location-based Services, *Pervasive and Mobile Computing* 7: 44–59.

103. For an interesting example, see Melendez, Steven (2018). A New Border Security App Uses AI to Flag Suspicious People in Seconds, *Fast Company*, 6 March, which describes a new machine learning app that synthesizes from passenger travel histories and other data to predict which people (and cargo) at border crossings and airports are suspicious.

104. Rosen, Jeffrey (2010). The Web Means the End of Forgetting, *New York Times*, 21 July.

105. Internet Archive and Wayback Machine (2017). https://archive.org/.

106. Dodge, Martin and Rob Kitchin (2005). The Ethics of Forgetting in an Age of Pervasive Computing. UCL CASA Working Paper 92, March. http://discovery.ucl.ac.uk/1292/.

107. Allen, Anita L. (2008). Lifelogging, Memory, and Surveillance, *The University of Chicago Law Review* 75(1): 47–74.
108. Hodges, Williams S. L., E. Berry, S. Izadi, J. Srinivasan, A. Butler, G. Smyth, N. Kapur, and K. Wood (2006). SenseCam: A Retrospective Memory Aid. In Dourish, P. and A. Friday (Eds.), *Ubicomp 2006: The 8th International Conference on Ubiquitous Computing*, Lecture Notes in Computer Science LNCS 4206:177:193.
109. Hodges, Steve, Emma Berry, and Ken Wood (2011). SenseCam: A Wearable Camera that Stimulates and Rehabilitates Autobiographical Memory, *Memory* 19(7): 685–696.
110. Bell, Gordon (2001). A Personal Digital Store, *Communications of the ACM* 44(1): 86–91. See also Gemmell, Jim, Gordon Bell, and Roger Lueder (2006). MyLifeBits: A Personal Database for Everything, *Communications of the ACM* 49(1): 88–95.
111. Sellen, Abigail and Steve Whittaker (2010). Beyond Total Capture: A Constructive Critique of Lifelogging, *Communications of the ACM* 53(5): 70–77.
112. Wikipedia (2017). Face.com. https://en.wikipedia.org/wiki/Face.com.
113. Wikipedia (2017). DeepFace. https://en.wikipedia.org/wiki/DeepFace.
114. Johnston, Casey (2016). Snapchat, Instagram Stories, and the Internet of Forgetting, *The New Yorker*, 5 August.
115. WikiLeaks (2017). https://wikileaks.org.
116. Wikipedia (2017). Hillary Clinton email controversy. https://en.wikipedia.org/wiki/Hillary_Clinton_email_controversy.
117. Shafer, Jack. Hillary Clinton Is Sorry, Not Sorry, *Politico.com*, 14 September. http://www.politico.com/magazine/story/2017/09/14/hillary-clinton-book-what-happened-emails-215603.
118. Wikipedia (2017). List of whistleblowers. https://en.wikipedia.org/wiki/List_of_whistle-blowers.
119. Wikipedia (2017). Edward Snowden. https://en.wikipedia.org/wiki/Edward_Snowden. See also Greenwald, Glenn (2013). Edward Snowden: The Whistleblower behind the NSA Surveillance Revelations, *The Guardian*, 11 June. https://www.theguardian.com/world/2013/jun/09/edward-snowden-nsa-whistleblower-surveillance.
120. Morgensen, Gretchen (2016). Whistle-Blowers Spur Companies to Change Their Ways, *New York Times*, 16 December.
121. Laudon, Kenneth C. (1996). Markets and Privacy, *Communications of the ACM* 39(9): 92–104. See also Gindin, Susan E. (1997). Lost and Found in Cyberspace: Informational Privacy in the Age of the Internet, *San Diego Law Review* 34: 1153–1224.
122. Wikipedia (2018). Carpenter v. United States. https://en.wikipedia.org/wiki/Carpenter_v._United_States. See also Liptak, Adam (2018). In Ruling on Cellphone Location Data, Supreme Court Makes Statement on Digital Privacy, *New York Times*, 22 June.
123. Froomkin, A Michael. (2000). The Death of Privacy? *Stanford Law Review* 52: 461–1544. See also Volokh, Eugene (2000). Freedom of Speech and Information Privacy: The Troubling Implications of a Right to Stop People from Speaking about You, *Stanford Law Review* 52: 1049–1124.
124. Abraham, Kenneth S. and G. Edward White (2013). Prosser and His Influence, *Journal of Tort Law* 6(1–2): 27–74.

125. Abril, Patricia Sánchez (2007). Recasting Privacy Torts in a Spaceless World, *Harvard Journal of Law & Technology* 21(1): 1–46. See also Citron, Danielle Keats (2010). Mainstreaming Privacy Torts, *California Law Review* 98: 1805–1852.

126. Wikipedia (2018). Privacy Act of 1974. https://en.wikipedia.org/wiki/Privacy_Act_of_1974.

127. Wikipedia (2018). Fair Credit Reporting Act. https://en.wikipedia.org/wiki/Fair_Credit_Reporting_Act.

128. Wikipedia (2018). Fair Debt Collection Practices Act. https://en.wikipedia.org/wiki/Fair_Debt_Collection_Practices_Act.

129. Wikipedia (2018). Real ID Act. https://en.wikipedia.org/wiki/Real_ID_Act.

130. Epic.org (2018). National ID and the Real ID Act. https://www.epic.org/privacy/id_cards/.

131. FCC (2016). FCC Adopts Broadband Consumer Privacy Rules. FCC, 27 October. https://www.fcc.gov/document/fcc-adopts-broadband-consumer-privacy-rules. See also Kang, Cecilia (2017). Congress Moves to Overturn Obama-Era Online Privacy Rules, *New York Times,* 28 March. See also Chen, Brian X. (2017). What the Repeal of Online Privacy Protections Means for You, *New York Times,* 28 March.

132. Gindin, Susan E. (1997). Lost and Found in Cyberspace: Informational Privacy in the Age of the Internet, *San Diego Law Review* 34: 1153–1224.

133. Wikipedia (2018). Data Protection Directive. https://en.wikipedia.org/wiki/Data_Protection_Directive.

134. Wikipedia (2018). General Data Protection Regulation. https://en.wikipedia.org/wiki/General_Data_Protection_Regulation. See also Singer, Natasha (2018). A Tough Task for Facebook: European-Type Privacy for All, *New York Times,* 8 April. See also Satariano, Adam (2018). What Europe's Tough New Data Law Means for You, and the Internet, *New York Times,* 6 May.

135. EU GDPR (2018). Recital 71. https://www.privacy-regulation.eu/en/r71.htm.

136. Satariano, Adam (2018). G.D.P.R., a New Privacy Law, Makes Europe World's Leading Tech Watchdog, *New York Times,* 24 May.

137. Roose, Kevin (2018). The Privacy Lawyer Giving Big Tech an $8.8 Billion Headache, *New York Times,* 30 May.

138. Singer, Natasha (2018). The Next Privacy Battle in Europe Is Over This New Law, *New York Times,* 27 May.

139. Cavoukian, Ann (2011). Privacy by Design: The 7 Foundational Principles, Implementation and Mapping of Fair Information Practices. Information and Privacy Commissioner. https://www.ipc.on.ca/wp-content/uploads/Resources/7foundationalprinciples.pdf.

140. Spiekermann, Sarah (2012). The Challenges of Privacy by Design, *Communications of the ACM* 55(7): 38–40.

141. Rubinstein, Ira S. (2011). Regulating Privacy by Design, *Berkeley Technology Law Journal* 26: 1409–1456.

142. Cavoukian, Ann (2013). Surveillance, Then and Now: Securing Privacy in Public Places. Information and Privacy Commissioner, June. https://www.chinhnghia.com/pbd-surveillance.pdf.

143. Rubinstein, Ira S. and Nathaniel Good (2013). Privacy by Design: A Counterfactual Analysis of Google and Facebook Privacy Incidents, *Berkeley Technology Law Journal* 28: 1333–1414.

144. Rubinstein, Ira S., Ronald D. Lee, and Paul M. Schwartz (2008). Data Mining and Internet Profiling: Emerging Regulatory and Technological Approaches, *The University of Chicago Law Review* 75(1): 261–285.
145. Chen, Brian X. (2017). What the Repeal of Online Privacy Protections Means for You, *New York Times,* 28 March.
146. Laudon, Kenneth C. (1996). Markets and Privacy, *Communications of the ACM* 39(9): 92–104. See also Litman, Jessica (2000). Information Privacy/Information Property, *Stanford Law Review* 52: 1283–1314. See also Lemley, Mark A. (2000). Private Property, *Stanford Law Review* 52: 1545–1558.

Chapter 10

1. Williams, Alex (2017). Will Robots Take Our Children's Jobs? *New York Times,* 11 December.
2. Brynjolfsson, Erik and Andrew McAfee (2014). *The Second Machine Age: Work, Progress, and Prosperity in a Time of Brilliant Technologies,* W. W. Norton. See also Ford, Martin (2015). *Rise of the Robots: Technology and the Threat of a Jobless Future,* Basic Books. See also Kaplan, Jerry (2015). *Humans Need Not Apply: A Guide to Wealth & Work in the Age of Artificial Intelligence,* Yale University Press. See also Ross, Alec (2016). *The Industries of the Future,* Simon & Schuster. See also Susskind, Richard and Daniel Susskind (2015). *The Future of the Professions: How Technology Will Transform the Work of Human Experts,* Oxford University Press.
3. Wikipedia (2017). Industrial Revolution. https://en.wikipedia.org/wiki/Industrial_Revolution.
4. Wikipedia (2017). Second Industrial Revolution. https://en.wikipedia.org/wiki/Second_Industrial_Revolution.
5. The Economist (2012). The Third Industrial Revolution, *The Economist,* 21 April. https://www.economist.com/leaders/2012/04/21/the-third-industrial-revolution.
6. Wikipedia (2017). Technological unemployment. https://en.wikipedia.org/wiki/Technological_unemployment.
7. Howard, Nicole (2009). *The Book: The Life Story of a Technology,* Johns Hopkins University Press. See p. 45.
8. Grey, C.G.P. (2014). Humans Need Not Apply. Video. https://www.youtube.com/watch?v=7Pq-S557XQU.
9. Wikipedia (2018). Modern Times (Film). https://en.wikipedia.org/wiki/Modern_Times_(film). See also https://commons.wikimedia.org/wiki/File:Chaplin_-_Modern_Times.jpg.
10. Conniff, Richard (2011). What the Luddites Really Fought Against, *Smithsonian Magazine,* March. See also Thompson, Clive (2017). When Robots Take All of Our Jobs, Remember the Luddites, *Smithsonian Magazine,* January.
11. Binfield, Kevin (2015). *Writings of the Luddites,* John Hopkins University Press.
12. Thompson, Clive (2017). When Robots Take All of Our Jobs, Remember the Luddites, *Smithsonian Magazine,* January.
13. Markoff, John (2013). In 1949, He Imagined an Age of Robots, *New York Times,* 20 May.
14. Vonnegut, Kurt (1952). *Player Piano,* Charles Scribner's Sons.
15. Bradley, Keith and Barry Smyth (2003). Personalized Information Ordering: A Case Study in Online Recruitment, *Knowledge-Based Systems* 16: 269–275.

16. Guo, Shiqiang, Folami Alamudun, and Tracy Hammond (2016). RésuMatcher: A Personalized Résumé–Job Matching System, *Expert Systems with Applications* 60: 169–182.

17. Weber, Lauren (2012). Your Résumé vs. Oblivion: Inundated Companies Resort to Software to Sift Job Applications for Right Skills, *The Wall Street Journal*, 24 January.

18. Leber, Jessica (2013). The Machine-Readable Workforce, *MIT Technology Review*, 27 May (appears in July/August 2013 issue).

19. Weber, Lauren and Elizabeth Dwoskin (2014). Are Workplace Personality Tests Fair? *The Wall Street Journal*, 29 September.

20. O'Neil, Cathy (2016). *Weapons of Math Destruction: How Big Data Increases Inequality and Threatens Democracy*, Crown Publishers.

21. Schmidt, Frank L., In-Sue Oh, and Jonathan A. Shaffer (2016). Working Paper: The Validity and Utility of Selection Methods in Personnel Psychology: Practical and Theoretical Implications of 100 Years of Research Findings. Unpublished manuscript, obtained from the senior author. See also Schmidt, Frank L. and John E. Hunter (2008). The Validity and Utility of Selection Methods in Personnel Psychology: Practical and Theoretical Implications of 85 Years of Research Findings, *Psychological Bulletin* 124(2): 262–274.

22. Morgeson, Frederick P., Michael A. Campion, Robert L. Dipboye, John R. Hollenbeck, Kevin Murphy, and Neal Schmitt (2007). Reconsidering the Use of Personality Tests in Personnel Selection Contexts, *Personnel Psychology* 60: 683–729.

23. Tett, Robert P. and Neil D. Christiansen (2007). Personality Tests at the Crossroads: A Response to Morgeson, Campion, Dipboye, Hollenbeck, Murphy, and Schmitt (2007), *Personnel Psychology* 60: 967–993.

24. Willner, Kenneth M., Stephen P. Sonnenberg, Taylor H. Wemmer, and Margaret Kochuba (2016). Workplace Personality Testing: Towards a Better Way of Determining Whether Personality Tests are Prohibited Pre-Offer Medical Exams Under the Americans With Disabilities Act, *Employee Relations Law Journal* 42(3): 4–27.

25. Weber, Lauren (2015). Today's Personality Tests Raise the Bar for Job Seekers, *The Wall Street Journal*, 14 April.

26. Abdel-Halim, Mona (2012). 12 Ways to Optimize Your Resume for Applicant Tracking Systems, *Mashable*, 27 May. http://mashable.com/2012/05/27/resume-tracking-systems/#5rwVFXkkjEqk.

27. Llorens, Jared J. and J. Edward Kellough (2007). A Revolution in Public Administration: The Growth of Web-based Recruitment and Selection Processes in the Federal Service, *Public Personnel Management* 36(3): 207–221.

28. Faliagka, Evanthia, Athanasios Tsakalidis, and Giannis Tzimas (2012). An Integrated e-Recruitment System for Automated Personality Mining and Applicant Ranking, *Internet Research* 22(5): 551–568. See also Alsever, Jennifer (2017). How AI Is Changing Your Job Hunt, *Fortune*, 19 May.

29. Knockri (2018). https://www.knockri.com/.

30. Mann, Gideon and Cathy O'Neill (2016). Hiring Algorithms Are Not Neutral, *Harvard Business Review*, 9 December. See also O'Neill, Cathy (2016). How Algorithms Rule Our Working Lives, *The Guardian*, 1 September. See also the reference in note 20.

31. Pinola, Melanie (2011). How Can I Make Sure My Resume Gets Past Resume Robots and into a Human's Hand? *Lifehacker*, 9 December. http://lifehacker.com/5866630/how-can-i-make-sure-my-resume-gets-past-resume-robots-and-into-a-humans-hand. See also reference in note 26.

32. Gillooly, Patrick (2016). Don't Quit Social Media. Put It to Work for Your Career Instead, *New York Times*, 3 December.
33. Kaiser, Angelina I. T., Timothy Porter, and David Vequist (2010). Employee Monitoring and Ethics: Can They Co-Exist? *International Journal of Digital Literacy and Digital Competence* 1(4): 30–45.
34. Veriato (2017). Computer Monitoring Software. http://www.veriato.com/ppc/veriato-360/computer-monitoring-software?utm_source=google&utm_medium=cpc&utm_term=%2Bcomputer%20%2Bmonitoring&keyword=%2Bcomputer%20%2Bmonitoring&cid=701700000015yIa.
35. Irving, R. H., C. A. Higgins, and F. R. Safayeni (1986). Computerized Performance Monitoring Systems: Use and Abuse, *Communications of the ACM* 29(8): 794–801.
36. Hawk, Stephen R. (1994). The Effects of Computerized Performance Monitoring: An Ethical Perspective, *Journal of Business Ethics* 13: 949–957.
37. Bates, Reid A. and Elwood F. Holton III (1995). Computerized Performance Monitoring: A Review of Human Resource Issues, *Human Resource Management Review* 5(4): 267–288.
38. Alder, G. Stoney and Phillip K. Tompkins (1997). Electronic Performance Monitoring: An Organizational Justice and Concertive Control Perspective. *Management Communications Quarterly* 10(3): 259–288.
39. Wells, Deborah L., Robert H. Moorman, Jon M. Werner (2007). The Impact of the Perceived Purpose of Electronic Performance Monitoring on an Array of Attitudinal Variables, *Human Resource Development Quarterly* 18(1): 121–138.
40. Swaya, Matthew E. and Stacey R. Eisenstein (2005). Emerging Technology in the Workplace, *The Labor Lawyer* 21(1): 1–17.
41. An early ethnographic study of the Xerox 'active badges' in research labs, where finding people for meetings and messages was a prime use, is Harper, R. H. R., M. G. Lamming, and W. M. Newman (1992). Locating Systems at Work: Implications for the Development of Active Badge Systems, *Interacting with Computers* 4(3): 343–363.
42. Ante, Spencer E. and Lauren Weber (2013). Memo to Workers: The Boss Is Watching. Tracking Technology Shakes Up the Workplace, *The Wall Street Journal*, 22 October.
43. Pentland, Alex (2014). *Social Physics: How Good Ideas Spread — The Lessons from a New Science*, Penguin Press. See also Lazer, David, Alex Pentland, Lada Adamic, Sinan Aral, Albert-László Barabási, Devon Brewer, Nicholas Christakis, Noshir Contractor, James Fowler, Myron Gutmann, Tony Jebara, Gary King, Michael Macy, Deb Roy, and Marshall Van Alstyne (2009). Computational Social Science, *Science* 323(5915): 721–723. See also Sociometric Badges (2018). http://hd.media.mit.edu/badges/information.html.
44. Madan, Anmol, Ben Waber, Margaret Ding, Paul Kominers, and Alex (Sandy) Pentland (2009). Reality Mining: The End of Personal Privacy? Human Dynamics Group, MIT Media Lab. https://pdfs.semanticscholar.org/presentation/0ef1/d422c89d9bd23536876ce7fedf9957f79e0f.pdf. See also Kim, Taemie, Erin McFee, Daniel Olguin Olguin, Ben Waber, and Alex 'Sandy' Pentland (2012). Sociometric Badges: Using Sensor Technology to Capture New Forms of Collaboration, *Journal of Organizational Behavior* 33: 412–427.
45. Pentland, Alex (2014). *Social Physics: How Good Ideas Spread — The Lessons from a New Science*, Penguin Press. See pp. 43–46.
46. Giang, Vivian (2013). Companies Are Putting Sensors on Employees to Track Their Every Move, *Business Insider*, 14 March. http://www.businessinsider.com/tracking-employees-with-productivity-sensors-2013-3.

47. Sundararajan, Arun (2016). *The Sharing Economy: The End of Employment and the Rise of Crowd-based Capitalism*, The MIT Press.

48. Penn, Joanna and John Wihbey (2016). Uber, Airbnb and Consequences of the Sharing Economy: Research Roundup, *Harvard Shorenstein Center on Media, Politics, and Public Policy*, 3 June. https://journalistsresource.org/studies/economics/business/airbnb-lyft-uber-bike-share-sharing-economy-research-roundup.

49. Dokko, Jane, Megan Mumford, and Whitmore Schanzenbach (2015). Workers and the Online Gig Economy. The Hamilton Project, December. Framing Paper. http://www.hamiltonproject.org/papers/workers_and_the_online_gig_economy.

50. Telles, Rudy Jr. (2016). Digital Matching Firms: A New Definition in the 'Sharing Economy' Space. US Department of Commerce Economics and Statistics Administration, 3 June. ESA Issue Brief #01-16. https://www.esa.gov/sites/default/files/digital-matching-firms-new-definition-sharing-economy-space.pdf. See p. 18.

51. Botsman, Rachel (2015). Defining the Sharing Economy: What is Collaborative Consumption—and What Isn't? *Fast Company*, 27 May. https://www.fastcompany.com/3046119/defining-the-sharing-economy-what-is-collaborative-consumption-and-what-isnt.

52. The Economist (2013). All Eyes on the Sharing Economy, *The Economist*, 9 March. www.economist.com/news/technology-quarterly/21572914-collaborative-consumption-technology-makes-it-easier-people-rent-items.

53. Scheiber, Noam (2017). Plugging into the Gig Economy, From Home With a Headset, *New York Times*, 11 November.

54. Kessler, Sarah (2015). The 'Sharing' Economy is Dead, and We Killed It, *Fast Company*, 14 September.

55. Travella, Federico (2016). 7 Trends that Mary Meeker Missed in her Internet Trends 2016 Report. LinkedIn, 4 June. https://www.linkedin.com/pulse/7-trends-mary-meeker-missed-her-internet-2016-report-travella.

56. The New York Times Editorial Board (2018). What Will New York Do About Its Uber Problem? *New York Times*, 7 May.

57. Katz, Miranda (2018). Why Are New York Taxi Drivers Killing Themselves? *Wired*, 28 March. See also Stewart, Nikita and Luis Ferré-Sadurní (2018). Another Taxi Driver in Debt Takes His Life. That's 5 in 5 Months, *New York Times*, 27 May. See also Fitzsimmons, Emma (2018). Suicides Get Taxi Drivers Talking: 'I'm Going to Be One of Them', *New York Times*, 2 October.

58. Heller, Nathan (2017). The Gig is Up, *The New Yorker*, 15 May, 52–63.

59. Weber, Lauren and Rachel Emma Silverman (2015). On-Demand Workers: 'We Are Not Robots', *The Wall Street Journal*, 27 January. See also references in notes 49 and 52.

60. Isaac, Mike (2017). Inside Uber's Aggressive, Unrestrained Workplace Culture, *New York Times*, 22 February. Isaac, Mike (2017). How Uber Deceives the Authorities Worldwide, *New York Times*, 3 March. See also Isaac, Mike (2017). Uber Engaged in 'Illegal' Spying on Rivals, Ex-Employee Says, *New York Times*, 15 December.

61. de Freytas-Tamura, Kimiko (2017). Kenya's Struggling Uber Drivers Fear a New Competitor: Uber, *New York Times*, 22 May. Alderman, Liz (2017). Uber Dealt Setback After European Court Rules It Is a Taxi Service, *New York Times*, 20 December.

62. Zervas, Georgia, Davide Proserpio, and John W. Byers (2017). The Rise of the Sharing Economy: Estimating the Impact of Airbnb on the Hotel Industry, *Journal of Marketing Research* 54: 687–705.

63. Benner, Katie (2017). Inside the Hotel Industry's Plan to Combat Airbnb, *New York Times,* 16 April. See also Weed, Julie (2018). Blurring Lines, Hotels Get Into the Home-Sharing Business, *New York Times,* 2 July.
64. Sundararajan, Arun (2016). *The Sharing Economy: The End of Employment and the Rise of Crowd-based Capitalism,* The MIT Press. See p. 168.
65. Auguste, Byron, and 39 others (2015). Common Ground for Independent Workers: Principles for Delivering a Stable and Flexible Safety Net for All Types of Work, *Medium,* 10 November. https://medium.com/the-wtf-economy/common-ground-for-independent-workers-83f3fb-cf548f#.j32m5gsqx.
66. Casselman, Ben (2018). Maybe the Gig Economy Isn't Reshaping Work After All, *New York Times,* 7 June.
67. Manyika, James, Susan Lund, Jacques Bughin, Kelsey Robinson, Jan Mischke, and Deepa Mahajan. (2016). Independent Work: Choice, Necessity, and the Gig Economy. McKinsey Global Institute, October. http://www.mckinsey.com/global-themes/employment-and-growth/independent-work-choice-necessity-and-the-gig-economy.
68. New York Times Editorial Board (2017). The Gig Economy's False Promise, *New York Times,* 10 April.
69. Scheiber, Noam (2017). How Uber Uses Psychological Tricks to Push Its Drivers' Buttons, *New York Times,* 2 April.
70. Colvin, Geoff (2015). Humans Are Underrated, *Fortune,* 23 July. See also Colvin, Geoff (2016). *Humans Are Underrated: What High Achievers Know that Brilliant Machines Never Will,* Portfolio/Penguin.
71. Smith, Aaron (2016). Public Predictions for the Future of Workplace Automation. Pew Research Center, 10 March. http://www.pewinternet.org/2016/03/10/public-predictions-for-the-future-of-workforce-automation/.
72. Smith, Aaron and Monica Anderson (2017). Automation in Everyday Life. Pew Research Center, 4 October. http://www.pewinternet.org/2017/10/04/automation-in-everyday-life/.
73. AP-NORC (2017). Americans' Assessment of their Increasingly Automated Lives. The Associated Press – NORC Center for Public Affairs Research, 17–21 August. http://www.apnorc.org/projects/Pages/Americans-Assessments-of-Their-Increasingly-Automated-Lives.aspx.
74. Kolbert, Elizabeth (2016). Race Against the Machine, *The New Yorker,* 19 December.
75. Cohn, Viktor (1955). Robot Farm Machines Take Over Field Work, *Spokane Daily Chronicle,* 21 January. See p. 2. https://news.google.com/newspapers?id=XaQpAAAAIBAJ&sjid=nfYDAAAAIBAJ&pg=5292,5131744&dq=robot+farmer&hl=en.
76. Ford, Martin (2015). *Rise of the Robots: Technology and the Threat of a Jobless Future,* Basic Books. See p. 23
77. Belton, Padraig (2016). In the Future, Will Farming Be Fully Automated? *BBC News,* 25 November.
78. World Bank (2016). Food Security Overview. http://www.worldbank.org/en/topic/foodsecurity/overview#1.
79. Porter, Eduardo (2016). The Mirage of a Return to Manufacturing Greatness, *New York Times,* 26 April.
80. Israel High-Tech and Investment Report (2003). A Water Melon Loving Robot, Issue of September 2003. http://www.ishitech.co.il/0903ar3.htm.

81. McCurry, Justin (2016). Japanese Firm to Open World's First Robot-run Farm, *The Guardian,* 2 February.

82. Geller, Tom (2016). Farm Automation Gets Smarter, *Communications of the ACM* 59(11): 18–19.

83. Fraser, Evan and Sylvain Charlebois (2016). Automated Farming: Good News for Food Security, Bad News for Job Security? *The Guardian International Edition,* 18 February.

84. Feingold, Spencer (2017). Field of Machines: Researchers Grow Crop Using Only Automation, *CNN,* 7 October. http://www.cnn.com/2017/10/07/world/automated-farm-harvest-england/index.html.

85. Kenny, Charles (2014). Why Factory Jobs Are Shrinking Everywhere, *Bloomberg,* 28 April. https://www.bloomberg.com/news/articles/2014-04-28/why-factory-jobs-are-shrinking-everywhere.

86. Manyika, James, Jeff Sinclair, Richard Dobbs, Gernot Strube, Louis Rassey, Jan Mischke, Jaana Remes, Charles Roxburgh, Katy George, David O'Halloran, and Sreenivas Ramaswamy (2012). Manufacturing the Future: The Next Era of Global Growth and Innovation. McKinsey Global Institute, November. https://www.mckinsey.com/business-functions/operations/our-insights/the-future-of-manufacturing.

87. Collard-Wexler, Allan and Jan de Loecker (2015). Reallocation and Technology: Evidence from the US Steel Industry, *American Economic Review* 105(1): 131–171.

88. Lehmacher, Wolfgang (2016). Don't Blame China for Taking U.S. Job, *Fortune,* 8 November.

89. Bradsher, Keith (2017). A Robot Revolution, This Time in China, *New York Times,* 12 May.

90. Ross, Alec (2016). *The Industries of the Future,* Simon & Schuster. See p. 36.

91. Levinson, Marc (2017). U.S. Manufacturing in International Perspective. Congressional Research Service, 18 January. https://fas.org/sgp/crs/misc/R42135.pdf.

92. Acemoglu, Daron, David Autor, David Dorn, Gordon H. Hanson, and Brendan Price (2014). Return of the Solow Paradox? IT, Productivity, and Employment in US Manufacturing, *American Economic Review: Papers & Proceedings* 104(5): 394–399.

93. Andes, Scott and Mark Muro (2015). Don't Blame the Robots for the Lost Manufacturing Jobs. The Brookings Institution, 29 April. https://www.brookings.edu/blog/the-avenue/2015/04/29/dont-blame-the-robots-for-lost-manufacturing-jobs/. See also Graetz, Georg, and Guy Michaels (2017). Robots at Work. Unpublished paper, 11 November. http://personal.lse.ac.uk/michaels/Graetz_Michaels_Robots.pdf.

94. Petzinger, Jill (2017). Germany has Way More Industrial Robots than the US, but They Haven't Caused Job Losses, *Quartz.com,* 10 October. https://qz.com/1096642/germany-has-more-industrial-robots-than-us-impact-on-jobs-wages-inequality/.

95. Dauth, Wolfgang, Sebastian Findeisen, Jens Südekum, and Nicole Woessner (2017). The Rise of Robots in the German Labour Market. VOX: CEPR Policy Portal, 19 September. http://voxeu.org/article/rise-robots-german-labour-market.

96. Worstall, Tim (2016). The U.S. Lost 7 Million Manufacturing Jobs—And Added 33 Million Higher-Paying Service Jobs, *Forbes,* 19 October.

97. Wikipedia (2018). Toyota Production System. https://en.wikipedia.org/wiki/Toyota_Production_System.

98. Porter, Eduardo (2017). Home Health Care: Shouldn't It Be Work Worth Doing? *New York Times,* 29 August.

99. *Ibid.* See also Graham, Judith (2017). The Disabled and the Elderly Are Facing a Big Problem: Not Enough Aides, *The Washington Past,* 23 April.

100. iRobot (2018). http://www.irobot.com.

101. Newman, Jared (2018). Robots That Do Your Chores Are So Close But So Far, *Fast Company,* 29 January. See also Japan Times (2015). A Demonstration of "Laundroid," the World's First Automated Laundry-folding Robot. Video. https://www.youtube.com/watch?v=7apeh4tjsgI.

102. Cain Miller, Rebecca (2017). Amazon's Move Signals End of Line for Many Cashiers, *New York Times,* 17 June.

103. Krugman, Paul (2017). Why Don't All Jobs Matter? *New York Times,* 17 April.

104. Kessler, Sarah (2017). Wendy's Is Responding to the Rising Minimum Wage by Replacing Humans with Robots, *Quartz,* 3 March. https://qz.com/923442/wendys-is-responding-to-the-rising-minimum-wage-by-replacing-humans-with-robots/.

105. Kolhatkar, Sheelagh (2017). Welcoming Our New Robotic Overlords, *The New Yorker,* 23 October.

106. Martin, Claire (2017). A Robot Makes a Mean Caesar Salad, but Will It Cost Jobs? *New York Times,* 6 October. See also Kolodny, Lora (2017). Meet Flippy, a Burger-grilling Robot from Miso Robotics and CaliBurger, *Tech Crunch,* 7 March. https://techcrunch.com/2017/03/07/meet-flippy-a-burger-grilling-robot-from-miso-robotics-and-caliburger/. See also Peters, Adele (2018). This Crazy-looking Robot Is the Chef at a New Burger Joint, *Fast Company,* 21 June.

107. Ford, Martin (2015). *Rise of the Robots: Technology and the Threat of a Jobless Future,* Basic Books. See pp. 14–15. See also Motherboard (2015). Inside the Japanese Hotel Staffed by Robots. Video. https://www.youtube.com/watch?v=mpzIQt6l4xY.

108. Tam, Donna (2014). Meet Amazon's busiest employee —the Kiva Robot, *CNet,* 30 November. https://www.cnet.com/news/meet-amazons-busiest-employee-the-kiva-robot/.

109. Wingfield, Nick (2017). Amazon's Ambitions Unboxed: Stores for Furniture, Appliances and More, *New York Times,* 25 March.

110. Wingfield, Nick (2017). As Amazon Pushes Forward With Robots, Workers Find New Roles, *New York Times,* 10 September.

111. Schiller, Ben (2018). What Happens When An Amazon Warehouse Opens? Lower Wages, No Increase In Jobs, *Fast Company,* 2 May.

112. Collier, David A. (2018). The Service Sector Revolution: The Automation of Services, *Long Range Planning* 16(6): 10–20. See also Lohr, Steve (2018). 'The Beginning of a Wave': A.I. Tiptoes Into the Workplace, *New York Times,* 5 August.

113. Harris, Ainsley (2018). AI Could Kill 2.5 Million Financial Jobs – And Save Banks $1 Trillion, *Fast Company,* 8 May.

114. Rosenberg, Tina (2017). In Kenya, Phones Replace Bank Tellers, *New York Times,* 9 May.

115. Watson Virtual Agent Demos (2018). https://www.youtube.com/watch?v=g2f-RT0EjPg. See also https://www.youtube.com/watch?v=lwg5yAuanPg.

116. Applebaum, Benyamin and Ryan Pfluger (2017). The Jobs Americans Do, *New York Times,* 23 February.

117. Silver, Curtis (2016). Knightscope Security Robots Spotted On Uber Parking Lot and Mall Patrol, *Forbes,* 5 July. https://www.forbes.com/sites/curtissilver/2016/07/05/uber-knightscope-security-robots/#22b6f9f0d674.

118. Robinson, Melia (2017). Robots Are Being Used to Deter Homeless People from Setting Up Camp in San Francisco, *Business Insider*, 12 December. http://www.businessinsider.com/security-robots-are-monitoring-the-homeless-in-san-francisco-2017-12.
119. Bui, Quoctrung and Roger Kisby (2018). Bricklayers Think They're Safe From Robots. Decide for Yourself, *New York Times*, 6 March. See also Barron, James (2017). 21st-Century Repairman: The Robot in the Gas Main, *New York Times*, 26 December.
120. Kaplan, Jerry (2015). *Humans Need Not Apply: A Guide to Wealth & Work in the Age of Artificial Intelligence*, Yale University Press. See pp. 43–44.
121. Bureau of Labor Statistics (2016). May 2016 National Occupational Employment and Wage Estimates for the United States. https://www.bls.gov/oes/current/oes_nat.htm#53-0000.
122. Boudette, Neal E. (2017). There's a Pizza Delivery in Ford's Future, by Driverless Car, *New York Times*, 29 August.
123. Susskind, Richard and Daniel Susskind (2017). *The Future of the Professions: How Technology Will Transform the Work of Human Experts*, Oxford University Press. See especially pp. 2 and 15.
124. Kaplan, Jerry (2015). *Humans Need Not Apply: A Guide to Wealth & Work in the Age of Artificial Intelligence*, Yale University Press. See pp. 61–63.
125. Weber, Lauren and Melissa Korn (2014). Where Did All the Entry-Level Jobs Go? *The Wall Street Journal*, 5 August.
126. Lohr, Steve (2017). IBM Gives Watson a New Challenge: Your Tax Return, *New York Times*, 1 February.
127. Mancinone, Paul (2017). Mr. Watson, Don't Come In Here! *Accounting Today*, 29 March.
128. H&R Block (2018). 2017 Annual Report. http://investors.hrblock.com/static-files/954d81c4-c732-4dab-a37b-77e994c3437a. P. 1.
129. Sutton, Meg (2018). Private communication from Director, H&R Block, 1 August.
130. Lohr, Steve (2017). A.I. Is Doing Legal Work. But It Won't Replace Lawyers, Yet, *New York Times*, 19 March.
131. Blue Hill Research (2017). BENCHMARK REPORT: Ross Intelligence & Artificial Intelligence in Legal Research. *AOTMP*, 30 January. https://aotmp.com/benchmark-report-ross-intelligence-and-artificial-intelligence-in-legal-research/.
132. Le Goues, Claire, Michael Dewey-Vogt, Stephanie Forrest, and Westley Weimer (2012). A Systematic Study of Automated Program Repair: Fixing 55 out of 105 Bugs for $8 Each, *Proceedings of the 34th Annual International Conference on Software Engineering*, 3–13. See also Klieber, Will and Will Snavely (2017). Automated Code Repair in the C Programming Language, *CMU Software Engineering Institute Blog*, 16 January. https://insights.sei.cmu.edu/sei_blog/2017/01/automated-code-repair-in-the-c-programming-language.html.
133. Najar, Nida (2017). Indian Technology Workers Worry About a Job Threat: Technology, *New York Times*, 25 June.
134. Eddy, David M. (1980). Clinical Decision-Making: From Theory to Practice: The Challenge, *Journal of the American Medical Association*, 263(2): 287–290.
135. Winters, Bradford, Jason Custer, Samuel M. Galvagno Jr., Elizabeth Colantuoni, Shruti G. Kapoor, HeeWon Lee, Victoria Goode, Karen Robinson, Atul Nakhasi, Peter Pronovost, and David Newman-Toker (2012). Diagnostic Errors in the Intensive Care Unit: A Systematic Review of Autopsy Studies, *BMJ Quality & Safety* 21(11): 894–902.

136. Graber, Mark L., Nancy Franklin, and Ruthanna Gordon (2005). Diagnostic Error in Internal Medicine, *Archives of Internal Medicine*, 165: 1493–1499.

137. NationMaster (2017). Health > Physicians > Per 1,000 people: Countries Compared. http://www.nationmaster.com/country-info/stats/Health/Physicians/Per-1%2C000-people.

138. Friedman, Lauren F. (2014). IBM's Watson Supercomputer May Soon Be the Best Doctor in the World, *Business Insider*, 22 April. http://www.businessinsider.com/ibms-watson-may-soon-be-the-best-doctor-in-the-world-2014-4. See also IBM (2018). Watson for Health in Oncology home page. *https://www.ibm.com/watson/health/oncology-and-genomics/oncology.*

139. Ross, Casey and Ike Swetlitz (2017). IBM Pitched its Watson Supercomputer as a Revolution in Cancer Care: It's Nowhere Close, *STAT News*, 5 September. https://www.statnews.com/2017/09/05/watson-ibm-cancer/. See also Freedman, David H. (2017). A Reality Check for IBM's AI Ambitions, *MIT Technology Review*, 27 June.

140. Sweeney, Evan (2017). After IBM Intensely Lobbied for AI Deregulation in 21st Century Cures, the FDA Will Determine Its Fate, *Fierce Health Care*, 5 October. https://www.fiercehealthcare.com/analytics/ibm-watson-fda-21st-century-cures-artificial-intelligence-clinical-decision-support.

141. Spitzer, Julie (2018). STAT: IBM Watson Health Downsizes Its Work With Hospitals, *Becker's Health and CIO Report*, 15 June. https://www.beckershospitalreview.com/healthcare-information-technology/stat-ibm-watson-health-downsizes-its-work-with-hospitals.html.

142. Frey, Carl Benedikt and Michael A. Osborne (2013). The Future of Employment: How Susceptible are Jobs to Computerization. Oxford Martin Programme on Technology and Employment, 17 September. https://www.oxfordmartin.ox.ac.uk/downloads/academic/The_Future_of_Employment.pdf.

143. Citi GPS (2016). Technology at Work v2.0: The Future Is Not What It Used To Be. Citi GPS: Global Perspectives & Solutions, January. https://www.oxfordmartin.ox.ac.uk/downloads/reports/Citi_GPS_Technology_Work_2.pdf.

144. Global Challenge Insight Report (2016). The Future of Jobs: Employment, Skills and Workforce Strategy for the Fourth Industrial Revolution. World Economic Forum, January. http://www3.weforum.org/docs/WEF_Future_of_Jobs.pdf.

145. Manyika, James, Michael Chui, Mehdi Miremadi, Jacques Bughin, Katy George, Paul Willmott, and Martin Dewhurst (2017). Harnessing Automation for a Future that Works. McKinsey Global Institute, January. https://www.mckinsey.com/global-themes/digital-disruption/harnessing-automation-for-a-future-that-works.

146. Deveraj, Srikant, Michael J. Hicks, Emily J. Wornell, and Dagney Faulk (2017). How Vulnerable Are American Communities to Automation, Trade, & Urbanization? *Center for Business and Economic Research, Ball State University*, 19 June. https://projects.cberdata.org/123/how-vulnerable-are-american-communities-to-automation-trade-urbanization.

147. Muro, Mark, Sifan Liu, Jacob Whiton, and Siddarth Kulkarni (2017). Digitalization and the American Workforce. Brookings, November. https://www.brookings.edu/research/digitalization-and-the-american-workforce/.

148. Manyika, James, Susan Lund, Michael Chui, Jacques Bughin, Jonathan Woetzel, Parul Batra, Ryan Ko, and Saurabh Sanghvi (2017). Jobs Lost, Jobs Gained: Workforce Transitions in a Time of Automation. McKinsey Global Institute, November. https://www.mckinsey.com/global-themes/future-of-organizations-and-work/what-the-future-of-work-will-mean-for-jobs-skills-and-wages.

149. Grace, Katja, John Salvatier, Allan Dafoe, Baobao Zhang, and Owain Evans (2018). When Will AI Exceed Human Performance? Evidence from AI Experts, *Journal of Artificial Intelligence Research,* to appear. https://arxiv.org/abs/1705.08807.

150. National Academies of Science, Engineering, and Medicine (2017). *Information Technology and the U.S. Workforce: Where Are We and Where Do We Go from Here?* The National Academies Press. https://www.nap.edu/catalog/24649/information-technology-and-the-us-workforce-where-are-we-and.

151. Tingley, Kim (2017). Learning to Love our Robot Co-Workers, *New York Times,* 23 February.

152. Wakabayashi, Daisuke (2017). Meet the People Who Train the Robots (to Do Their Own Jobs), *New York Times,* 28 April.

153. Metz, Cade (2017). In the Future, Warehouse Robots Will Learn on Their Own, *New York Times,* 10 September.

154. Brynjolfsson, Erik and Andrew McAfee (2014). *The Second Machine Age: Work, Progress, and Prosperity in a Time of Brilliant Technologies,* W. W. Norton.

155. Alvaredo, Facundo, Lucas Chancel, Thomas Piketty, Emmanuel Saez, & Gabriel Zucman (2018). World Inequality Report. World Inequality Lab. https://wir2018.wid.world/.

156. Gordon, Bob (2016). Why Robots Will Not Decimate Human Jobs. LinkedIn, 19 November. https://www.linkedin.com/pulse/why-robots-decimate-human-jobs-bob-gordon/.

157. Autor, David H. (2015). Why Are There Still So Many Jobs? The History and Future of Workplace Automation, *Journal of Economic Perspectives* 29(3): 3–30.

158. The Economist (2017). The Human Cumulus: Artificial Intelligence Will Create New Kinds of Work, *The Economist,* 26 August. https://www.economist.com/news/business/21727093-humans-will-supply-digital-services-complement-ai-artificial-intelligence-will-create-new.

159. O'Reilly, Tim (2017). Using AI to Create New Jobs, *O'Reilly,* 25 May. Recorded lecture. https://www.oreilly.com/ideas/using-ai-to-create-new-jobs.

160. Friedman, Thomas L. (2017). Folks, We're Home Alone, *New York Times,* 27 September.

161. Cain Miller, Rebecca (2017). How to Prepare for an Automated Future, *New York Times,* 3 May.

162. National Academies of Sciences, Engineering, and Medicine (2017). *Building America's Skilled Technical Workforce,* The National Academies Press. https://www.nap.edu/catalog/23472/building-americas-skilled-technical-workforce.

163. Palmer, Shelly (2017). The 5 Jobs Robots Will Take Last. LinkedIn, 5 March. https://www.linkedin.com/pulse/5-jobs-robots-take-last-shelly-palmer/.

164. Baldwin, Roberto (2018). Ford Thinks Exoskeletons Are Ready for Prime Time in its Factories. Engadget, 7 August. https://www.engadget.com/2018/08/07/ford-exoskeletons-eksovest/.

165. Goodman, Peter S. and Jonathan Soble (2017). Global Economy's Stubborn Reality: Plenty of Work, Not Enough Pay, *New York Times,* 7 October.

166. Wikipedia (2017). 35-hour workweek. https://en.wikipedia.org/wiki/35-hour_workweek.

167. Peters, Adele (2018). The Four-day Work Week Is Good for Business, *Fast Company,* 20 July.

168. Darrow, Barb (2017). The Bright Side of Job-killing Automation, *Fortune,* 5 April.

169. Brown, Ellen (2017). How to Fund a Universal Basic Income Without Increasing Taxes or Inflation, *Common Dreams,* 4 October. https://www.commondreams.org/views/2017/10/04/how-fund-universal-basic-income-without-increasing-taxes-or-inflation.

170. Lowrey, Annie (2017). The Future of Not Working, *New York Times,* 23 February.
171. Pender, Kathleen (2017). Oakland Group Plans to Launch Nation's Biggest Basic Income Research Project, *San Francisco Chronicle,* 21 September. https://www.sfchronicle.com/business/networth/article/Oakland-group-plans-to-launch-nation-s-biggest-12219073.php.
172. Autor, David H. (2015). Paradox of Abundance. Appears in Subramanian Rangan (ed.) (2015). *Performance and Progress: Essays on Capitalism, Business, and Society,* Oxford Scholarship Online, September, 1-36. https://economics.mit.edu/files/11678.
173. Hyman, Louis (2018). It's Not Technology That's Disrupting Our Jobs, *New York Times,* 18 August.

Chapter 11

1. Wikipedia (2017). Robot. https://en.wikipedia.org/wiki/Robot. See also Currie, Adam (2006). The History of Robotics. *WayBack Machine Internet Archive,* 18 July. https://web.archive.org/web/20060718024255/http://www.faculty.ucr.edu/~currie/roboadam.htm. See also RobotShop Inc. (2008). History of Robotics: Timeline. http://www.robotshop.com/media/files/PDF/timeline.pdf.
2. Michaelson, Jay (2017). Golem. *My Jewish Learning.* https://www.myjewishlearning.com/article/golem/.
3. Wikipedia (2017). Frankenstein. https://en.wikipedia.org/wiki/Frankenstein. See also Shelly, Mary (1818). *Frankenstein: The Modern Prometheus,* Lackington, Hughes, Harding, Mavor & Jones.
4. Wikipedia (2017). R.U.R. https://en.wikipedia.org/wiki/R.U.R. See also https://commons.wikimedia.org/wiki/File:Capek_play.jpg.
5. Capek, Karel (1920). *R.U.R. (Rossum's Universal Robots).* (Selver, Paul and Nigel Playfair, Trans.). http://preprints.readingroo.ms/RUR/rur.pdf. See p. 28.
6. *Ibid.,* p. 52.
7. *Ibid.,* p. 63.
8. *Ibid.,* p. 72.
9. *Ibid.,* p. 88.
10. Asimov, Isaac (1950). *I, Robot,* Gnome Press. https://www.ttu.ee/public/m/mart-murdvee/Techno-Psy/Isaac_Asimov_-_I_Robot.pdf.
11. Wikipedia (2017). Three Laws of Robotics. https://en.wikipedia.org/wiki/Three_Laws_of_Robotics.
12. EPSRC (2010). Principles of Robotics. Engineering and Physical Sciences Research Council. https://www.epsrc.ac.uk/research/ourportfolio/themes/engineering/activities/principlesofrobotics/.
13. Benson, Michael (2018). What '2001' Got Right, *New York Times,* 2 April.
14. Wikipedia (2017). Blade Runner. https://en.wikipedia.org/wiki/Blade_Runner. See also Wikipedia (2018). The matrix (franchise). https://en.wikipedia.org/wiki/The_Matrix_(franchise).
15. Wikipedia (2017). Artificial intelligence in fiction. https://en.wikipedia.org/wiki/Artificial_intelligence_in_fiction.

16. Turing, Alan (1950). Computing Machinery and Intelligence, *Mind* 49: 433–460.

17. Dreyfus, Hubert L. (1965). Alchemy and Artificial Intelligence. The Rand Corporation, Report P-3244, December. http://archive.computerhistory.org/projects/chess/related_materials/text/2-4%20and%202-0.Alchemy_and_Artificial_Intelligence_1965/Rand_Corporation.Alchemy_and_Artificial_Intelligence.Dreyfus-Hubert.1965.062303008.pdf.

18. Dreyfus, Hubert L. (1972). *What Computers* Still *Can't Do*, Harper & Row. https://archive.org/stream/whatcomputerscan017504mbp/whatcomputerscan017504mbp_djvu.txt. See also Dreyfus, Hubert L. (1992). *What Computers* Still *Can't Do*, The MIT Press.

19. Papert, Seymour (1968). The Artificial Intelligence of Hubert L. Dreyfus: A Budget of Fallacies. MIT Project MAC AI Memo 154. https://dspace.mit.edu/handle/1721.1/6084.

20. Haugeland, John (1996). Body and World: A Review of What Computers Still Can't Do: A Critique of Artificial Reason (Hubert L. Dreyfus), *Artificial Intelligence* 80(1): 119–128.

21. Searle, John R. (1990). Is the Brain's Mind a Computer Program? *Scientific American* 262(1): 25–31.

22. Churchland, Paul M. and Patricia Smith Churchland (1990). Could A Machine Think? *Scientific American* 262(1): 32–39.

23. Wikipedia (2017). History of artificial intelligence. https://en.wikipedia.org/wiki/History_of_artificial_intelligence. See also Grudin, Jonathan (2009). AI and HCI: Two Fields Divided by a Common Focus. *AI Magazine*, Winter 2009, 48–57.

24. McCarthy, John, Marvin L. Minsky, Nathaniel Rochester, and Claude E. Shannon (1955). A Proposal for the Dartmouth Summer Research Project on Artificial Intelligence, *AI Magazine* 27(4): 12–14. https://www.aaai.org/ojs/index.php/aimagazine/article/view/1904/1802.

25. Wikipedia (2017). Timeline of artificial intelligence. https://en.wikipedia.org/wiki/Timeline_of_artificial_intelligence.

26. Greenemeier, Larry (2017). AI versus AI: Self-Taught AlphaGo Zero Vanquishes Its Predecessor, *Scientific American*, 18 October.

27. Kasparov, Garry (2017). *Deep Thinking: Where Machine Intelligence Ends and Human Creativity Begins*, PublicAffairs.

28. Gibney, Elizabeth (2017). How Rival Bots Battled Their Way to Poker Supremacy, *Nature* 543(7644): 160–161.

29. Weber, Bob (2017). Alberta-made Computer Wins at No-limit Texas Hold 'Em Poker, *Global News*, 2 March. https://globalnews.ca/news/3283782/alberta-made-computer-wins-at-no-limit-texas-hold-em-poker/.

30. Mozur, Paul (2017). Google's A.I. Program Rattles Chinese Go Master as It Wins Match, *New York Times*, 25 May.

31. McDermott, Drew (2015). GOFAI Considered Harmful (and Mystical). Unpublished paper, 27 June. http://www.cs.yale.edu/homes/dvm/papers/nogofai.pdf. See also Boden, Maggie (2016). On Deep Learning, Artificial Neural Networks, Artificial Life, and Good Old-Fashioned AI. *Oxford University Press Blog*, 16 June. https://blog.oup.com/2016/06/artificial-neural-networks-ai/. See also Levesque, Hector (2017). *Common Sense, the Turing Test, and the Quest for Real AI*, The MIT Press.

32. Wikipedia (2017). Expert system. https://en.wikipedia.org/wiki/Expert_system.

33. Boden, Maggie (2016). On Deep Learning, Artificial Neural Networks, Artificial Life, and Good Old-Fashioned AI, *Oxford University Press Blog*, 16 June.

34. LeCun, Yann, Yoshua Bengio, and Geoffrey Hinton (2015). Deep Learning, *Nature* 521: 436–444. This paper provides helpful pointers to important literature about deep learning.
35. Robinson, Jennifer (2016). U of T's Geoffrey Hinton: AI Will Eventually Surpass the Human Brain but Getting Jokes ... That Could Take Time, *U of T News*, 5 December. https://www.utoronto.ca/news/u-t-geoffrey-hinton-ai-will-eventually-surpass-human-brain-getting-jokes-could-take-time.
36. Lewis-Kraus, Gideon (2016). The Great A.I. Awakening, *New York Times*, 14 December.
37. Olah, Christopher (2017). Blog. http://colah.github.io/about.html.
38. Socrates (pseudonym) (2012). 17 Definitions of the Technological Singularity. *Singularity Weblog*, 18 April. https://www.singularityweblog.com/17-definitions-of-the-technological-singularity/.
39. Ulam, Stanislaw (1958). Tribute to John von Neumann, 1903–1957, *Bulletin of the American Mathematical Society* 64(3): 1–49.
40. Good, Irving John (1966). Speculations Concerning the First Ultraintelligent Machine, *Advances in Computers* 6: 31–88. https://www.sciencedirect.com/science/article/pii/S0065245808604180
41. Wikipedia (2017). Technological singularity. https://en.wikipedia.org/wiki/Technological_singularity.
42. Vinge, Vernor (1993). The Coming Technological Singularity: How to Survive in the Post-Human Era. NASA Conference Publication 10129. Paper presented at the VISION-21 Symposium sponsored by NASA Lewis Research Center and the Ohio Aerospace Institute, 30–31 March. https://ntrs.nasa.gov/archive/nasa/casi.ntrs.nasa.gov/19940022855.pdf. See pp. 1,10.
43. Kurzweil, Ray (2005). *The Singularity is Near*, Penguin Group.
44. *Ibid.*, p. 9.
45. Galeon, Dom and Christianna Reddy (2017). Kurzweil Claims That the Singularity Will Happen by 2045, *Futurism*, 5 October. https://futurism.com/kurzweil-claims-that-the-singularity-will-happen-by-2045/.
46. Bostrom, Nick (2015). *Superintelligence: Paths, Dangers, Strategies*, Oxford University Press.
47. Dowd, Maureen (2017). Elon Musk's Billion-Dollar Crusade to Stop the A.I. Apocalypse, *Vanity Fair*, 26 March.
48. Tegmark, Max (2017). *Life 3.0: Being Human in the Age of Artificial Intelligence*, Alfred A. Knopf.
49. Müller, Vincent C. and Nick Bostrom (2014). Future Progress in Artificial Intelligence: A Survey of Expert Opinion. In Müller, Vincent C. (Ed.), *Fundamental Issues of Artificial Intelligence*, Springer.
50. Mozur, Paul and John Markoff (2017). Is China Outsmarting America in A.I.? *New York Times*, 27 May. See also Metz, Cade (2018). Pentagon Wants Silicon Valley's Help on A.I., *New York Times*, 15 March.
51. See also Mozur, Paul (2017). Beijing Wants A.I. to Be Made in China by 2030, *New York Times*, 20 July. See also Manjoo, Fahrad (2017). How to Make America's Robots Great Again, *New York Times*, 25 January.
52. Mozur, Paul and Keith Bradsher (2017). China's A.I. Advances Help Its Tech Industry, and State Security, *New York Times*, 3 December.
53. McGillivray, Kate (2017). Canada Lost the Lead in Artificial Intelligence: Here's How Toronto Will Get It Back, *CBC*, 29 March. http://www.cbc.ca/news/canada/toronto/toronto-artificial-

intelligence-vector-1.4046016. See also Lohr, Steve (2017). Canada Tries to Turn Its A.I. Ideas into Dollars, *New York Times,* 9 April.

54. Metz, Cade (2017). Uber Hires an AI Superstar in the Quest to Rehab its Future, *Wired,* 8 May. https://www.wired.com/2017/05/uber-hires-ai-superstar-quest-rehab-future/.

55. Isaac, Mike and Neal E. Boudette (2017). Ford to Invest $1 Billion in Artificial Intelligence Start-Up, *New York Times,* 10 February.

56. Quora (2017). How Is Machine Learning Used in Finance? *Quora.* https://www.quora.com/How-is-machine-learning-used-in-finance. See also The Economist (2017). Unshackled Algorithms: Machine-Learning Promises to Shake Up Large Swathes of Finance, *The Economist,* 27 May.

57. Metz, Cade (2018). Facebook Adds A.I. Labs in Seattle and Pittsburgh, Pressuring Local Universities, *New York Times,* 4 May.

58. Metz, Cade (2016). Inside OpenAI, Elon Musk's Wild Plan to Set Artificial Intelligence Free, *Wired,* 27 April. https://www.wired.com/2016/04/openai-elon-musk-sam-altman-plan-to-set-artificial-intelligence-free/. See also Haikara, Nina (2017). This U of T Alum Is Leading AI Research at a Nonprofit Backed by Elon Musk, *U of T News,* 28 March. https://www.utoronto.ca/news/u-t-alum-leading-ai-research-1-billion-non-profit-backed-elon-musk.

59. Statt, Nick (2017). Elon Musk Launches Neuralink, a Venture to Merge the Human Brain with AI, *The Verge,* 27 March. https://www.theverge.com/2017/3/27/15077864/elon-musk-neuralink-brain-computer-interface-ai-cyborgs.

60. Metz, Cade (2018). A.I. Researchers Are Making More Than $1 Million, Even at a Nonprofit, *New York Times,* 19 April.

61. Lohr, Steve (2017). Intel, While Pivoting to Artificial Intelligence, Tries to Protect Lead, *New York Times,* 10 July. See also Metz, Cade (2018). Google Makes Its Special A.I. Chips Available to Others, *New York Times,* 12 February.

62. Metz, Cade (2017). Chips Off the Old Block: Computers Are Taking Design Cues from Human Brains, *New York Times,* 16 September. See also Metz, Cade (2018). Big Bets on A.I. Open a New Frontier for Chip Start-Ups, Too, *New York Times,* 14 January.

63. Frank, Aaron (2017). The Future of AI Is Neuromorphic. Meet the Scientists Building Digital 'Brains' for Your Phone, *Wired,* 6 March. http://www.wired.co.uk/article/ai-neuromorphic-chips-brains. See also Gomes, Lee (2017). The Neuromorphic Chip's Make-or-break Moment, *IEEE Spectrum,* June, 52–57.

64. Friedman, Thomas L. (2018). While You Were Sleeping, *New York Times,* 16 January. See also Wikipedia (2018). Quantum computing. https://en.wikipedia.org/wiki/Quantum_computing.

65. Vincent, James (2016). These Are Three of the Biggest Problems Facing Today's AI, *The Verge,* 10 October. https://www.theverge.com/2016/10/10/13224930/ai-deep-learning-limitations-drawbacks.

66. Metz, Cade (2017). Teaching A.I. Systems to Behave Themselves, *New York Times,* 13 August.

67. Reynolds, Matt (2017). AI Learns to Write its Own Code by Stealing from Other Programs, *New Scientist,* 22 February. https://www.newscientist.com/article/mg23331144-500-ai-learns-to-write-its-own-code-by-stealing-from-other-programs/. See also Metz, Cade (2017). Building A.I. That Can Build A.I., *New York Times,* 5 November.

68. Metz, Cade (2018). Google Sells A.I. for Building A.I. (Novices Welcome), *New York Times,* 17 January.

69. Lake, Brenden M., Ruslan Salakhutdinov, and Joshua B. Tenenbaum (2017). Human-level Concept Learning Through Probabilistic Program Induction, *Science* 350(6266): 1332–1338.
70. Lake, Brenden M., Tomer D. Ullman, Joshua B. Tenenbaum, and Samuel J. Gershman (2017). Building Machines that Learn and Think Like People, *Behavioral and Brain Sciences* 40: 1–72.
71. Yao, Mariya (2017). Understanding the Limits of Deep Learning, *Venture Beat*, 2 April. https://venturebeat.com/2017/04/02/understanding-the-limits-of-deep-learning/.
72. Marshall, Aarian (2017). After Peak Hype, Self-driving Cars Enter the Trough of Disillusionment, *Wired*, 29 December. See also Ohnsman, Alan (2018). Fatal Tesla Crash Exposes Gap in Automaker's Use of Car Data, *Forbes*, 16 April. See also Mims, Christopher (2018). In Self-Driving-Car Road Test, We Are the Guinea Pigs, *The Wall Street Journal*, 13 May. See also Hattern, Julian (2018). Tesla in Autopilot Mode Accelerated Seconds Before Crashing into Firetruck: Police, *Global News*, 25 May. See also Whiston, David (2018). U.S. Opens Probe into Fatal Tesla Crash in California as Shares Plunge, *CBC News*, 28 May.
73. Pontin, Jason (2018). Greedy, Brittle, Opaque, and Shallow: The Downsides to Deep Learning, *Wired*, 2 February. See also Marcus, Gary (2018). Deep Learning: A Critical Appraisal. Unpublished paper, 2 January. https://arxiv.org/abs/1801.00631.
74. Allen, Paul (2011). The Singularity Isn't Near, *MIT Technology Review*, 12 October. See also Kurzweil, Ray (2011). Don't Underestimate the Singularity, *MIT Technology Review*, 20 October.
75. Singularity Wikibook (2012). Collection of articles. https://archive.org/details/Singularity Wikibook/.
76. Brooks, Rodney (2017). The Seven Deadly Sins of AI Predictions, *MIT Technology Review*, 6 October.
77. Sternberg, Robert J. (1985). *Beyond IQ: A Triachic Theory of Human Intelligence*, Cambridge University Press.
78. Gardner, Howard E. (1983). *Frames of Mind: The Theory of Multiple Intelligences*, Basic Books. See also Gardner, Howard (1999). *Intelligence Reframed: Multiple Intelligences for the 21st Century*, Basic Books.
79. Wootson, Cleve R. Jr. (2017). Sophia the Robot Is Now a Citizen of Saudi Arabia, *The Washington Post*, 29 October.
80. Nass, Clifford, Jonathan Steuer, and Ellen R. Tauber (1994). Computers are Social Actors, *Proceedings of the SIGCHI Conference on Human Factors in Computing Systems*, 72–78.
81. Epley, Nicholas, Adam Waytz, and John T. Cacioppo (2007). On Seeing Human: A Three-Factor Theory of Anthropomorphism, *Psychological Review* 114(4): 864–886.
82. Donath, Judith (2017). The Robot Dog Fetches for Whom? *Medium*, 7 May. https://medium.com/berkman-klein-center/the-robot-dog-fetches-for-whom-a9c1dd0a458a.
83. Turkle, Sherry (2011). *Alone Together: Why We Expect More from Technology and Less from Each Other*, Basic Books, p. 1.
84. *Ibid.*, p. 87.
85. Newman, Judith (2014). To Siri, With Love: How One Boy With Autism Became BFF's With Apple's Siri, *New York Times*, 17 October.
86. Turkle, Sherry (2011). *Alone Together: Why We Expect More from Technology and Less from Each Other*, Basic Books, p. 105.

87. *Ibid.*, pp. 116, 125.
88. Wikipedia (2017). Uncanny valley. https://en.wikipedia.org/wiki/Uncanny_valley.
89. Tech Insider (2017). We Talked To Sophia—The AI Robot That Once Said It Would 'Destroy Humans'. 28 December. https://www.youtube.com/watch?v=78-1MlkxyqI.
90. Poniewozik, James (2017). In 'Humans,' if You Need a Marriage Counselor, See a Robot, *New York Times,* 12 February.
91. Noga, Markus, Chandran Saravana, and Stephanie Overby (2017). Empathy: The Killer App for Artificial Intelligence, *D!gitalist Magazine,* 26 January. https://news.sap.com/empathy-the-killer-app-for-artificial-intelligence/.
92. Xiao, Bo, Zac E. Imel, Panayiotis Georgiou, David C. Atkins, and Shrikanth S. Narayanan (2016). Computational Analysis and Simulation of Empathic Behaviors: A Survey of Empathy Modeling with Behavioral Signal Processing Framework, *Current Psychiatry Reports* 18(5): 49.
93. El Kaliouby, Rana (2017). We Need Computers with Empathy, *MIT Technology Review*, 20 October.
94. Schwab, Katherine (2018). AI Is Giving Brands Eerily Human Voices, *Fast Company*, 2 April. https://www.fastcodesign.com/90166206/the-future-of-branding-synthetic-voices-that-sound-100-human.
95. Metz, Cade and Keith Collins (2018). To Give A.I. the Gift of Gab, Silicon Valley Needs to Offend You, *New York Times,* 21 February.
96. Nagabhirava, Sri (2016). In Pursuit of Empathetic Machines, *Crunch Network,* 15 March. https://techcrunch.com/2016/03/15/in-pursuit-of-empathetic-machines/. See also Gershgorn, Dave (2018). Google Is Building 'Virtual Agents' to Handle Call Centers' Grunt Work, *Quartz,* 24 July. https://qz.com/1335348/google-is-building-virtual-agents-to-handle-call-centers-grunt-work/.
97. Felten, Ed (2017). What Does It Mean to Ask for an 'Explainable' Algorithm? *Freedom to Tinker,* 31 May. https://freedom-to-tinker.com/2017/05/31/what-does-it-mean-to-ask-for-an-explainable-algorithm/. See also Burrell, Jenna (2016). How the Machine 'Thinks': Understanding Opacity in Machine Learning Algorithms, *Big Data & Society,* January–June, 1–12.
98. Wikipedia (2017). CYC. https://en.wikipedia.org/wiki/Cyc.
99. Knight, Will (2016). An AI with 30 Years' Worth of Knowledge Finally Goes to Work, *MIT Technology Review*, 14 March. In 2018, Microsoft co-founder Paul Allen announced he was investing $125 million in a new project to teach machines common sense; see Metz, Cade (2018). Paul Allen Wants to Teach Machines Common Sense, *New York Times,* 28 February.
100. Swartout, W., C. Paris, and J. Moore (1991). Design for Explainable Expert Systems, *IEEE Expert* 6(3): 58–64.
101. Ananny, Mike and Kate Crawford (2016). Seeing without Knowing: Limitations of the Transparency Ideal and its Application to Algorithmic Accountability, *New Media & Society* 20(3): 973–989.
102. Crawford, Kate (2016). Can an Algorithm Be Agonistic? Scenes of Contest in Calculated Publics, *Science, Technology & Human Values* 41(1): 77–92.
103. Weinberger, David (2017). Our Machines Now Have Knowledge We'll Never Understand, *Wired,* 4 April. https://www.wired.com/story/our-machines-now-have-knowledge-well-never-understand/.

104. Knight, Will (2017). The Dark Secret at the Heart of AI, *MIT Technology Review*, 11 April.
105. Kuang, Cliff (2017). Can A.I. Be Taught to Explain Itself? *New York Times*, 21 November.
106. Gunning, David (2016). Explainable Artificial Intelligence (XAI). Program Information, Defense Advanced Research Projects Agency. https://www.darpa.mil/program/explainable-artificial-intelligence. See also Gunning, David (2016). Explainable Artificial Intelligence (XAI). Defense Advanced Research Projects Agency. Slide deck presented at Proposers Day, 11 August. https://www.cc.gatech.edu/~alanwags/DLAI2016/(Gunning)%20IJCAI-16%20DLAI%20WS.pdf.
107. Hendricks, Lisa Anne, Zeynep Akata, Marcus Rohrbach, Jeff Donahue, Bernt Schiele, Trevor Darrell. Generating Visual Explanations. *Computer Vision—ECCV 2016*, Leibe B., Matas J., Sebe N., Welling M. (Eds.). Lecture Notes in Computer Science 9908, 3–19. Springer.
108. Ribeiro, Marco Tulio, Sameer Singh, and Carlos Guestrin (2016). 'Why Should I Trust You?' Explaining the Predictions of Any Classifier, *Proceedings of the 22nd ACM International Conference on Knowledge Discovery and Data Mining*, 1135–1144.
109. Olah, Chris, Alexander Mordvintsev, and Ludwig Schubert (2017). Feature Visualization. Google Research Report, 7 November. https://distill.pub/2017/feature-visualization/.
110. IJCAI (2017). IJCAI-17 Workshop on Explainable AI (XAI) Proceedings. Meeting held on 20 August. http://home.earthlink.net/~dwaha/research/meetings/ijcai17-xai.
111. Microsoft Research (2018). Intelligible, Interpretable, and Transparent Machine Learning. https://www.microsoft.com/en-us/research/project/intelligible-interpretable-and-transparent-machine-learning/.
112. Caruana, Rich, Yin Lou, Johannes Gehrke, Paul Koch, Marc Sturm, and Noémie Elhadad (2015). Intelligible Models for HealthCare: Predicting Pneumonia Risk and Hospital 30-day Readmission, *Proceedings of the 21th ACM International Conference on Knowledge Discovery and Data Mining*, 1721–1730.
113. Banavar, Guruduth (2016). Learning to trust artificial intelligence systems: Accountability, compliance and ethics in the age of smart machines. *IBM*. IBM Position Paper. https://www.research.ibm.com/software/IBMResearch/multimedia/AIEthics_Whitepaper.pdf
114. Israelsen, Brett (2017). 'I can assure you [...] that it's going to be all right': A Definition, Case For, and Survey of Algorithmic Assurances in Human-Autonomy Trust Relationships. Unpublished paper. https://arxiv.org/pdf/1708.00495.pdf.
115. OxfordDictionaries (2018). Definition of 'responsible'. https://en.oxforddictionaries.com/definition/responsible.
116. OxfordDictionaries (2018). Definition of 'accountable'. https://en.oxforddictionaries.com/definition/accountable.
117. Crawford, Kate and Ryan Calo (2016). There Is a Blind Spot in AI Research, *Nature* 538, 20 October, 311–313.
118. Ananny, Mike (2015). Towards an Ethics of Algorithms: Convening, Observation, Probability, and Timeliness, *Science, Technology, & Human Values* 41(1): 93–117.
119. Diakopoulos, Nicholas and Sorelle Fiedler (2016). How to Hold Algorithms Accountable, *MIT Technology Review*, 17 November.
120. Danaher, John (2016). Robots, Law and the Retribution Gap, *Ethics and Information Technology* 18: 299–309.

121. OxfordDictionaries (2018). Definition of 'retribution'. https://en.oxforddictionaries.com/definition/retribution.

122. Calo, Ryan (2015). Robotics and the Lessons of Cyberlaw, *California Law Review* 103(1): 513–564.

123. O'Neil, Cathy (2016). *Weapons of Math Destruction: How Big Data Increases Inequality and Threatens Democracy*, Crown Publishers.

124. *Ibid.*, p. 143.

125. Newman, Nathan (2014). How Big Data Enables Economic Harm to Consumers, Especially to Low-Income and Other Vulnerable Sectors of the Population, *Journal of Internet Law*, December, 11–23.

126. Pasquale, Frank (2015). *The Black Box Society: The Secret Algorithms that Control Money and Information*, Harvard University Press.

127. Vincent, James (2016). Twitter Taught Microsoft's AI Chatbot to Be a Racist Asshole in Less than a Day, *The Verge*, 24 March. https://www.theverge.com/2016/3/24/11297050/tay-microsoft-chatbot-racist.

128. Caliskan, Aylin, Joanna J. Bryson, Arvind Narayanan (2017). Semantics Derived Automatically from Language Corpora Contain Human-Like Biases, *Science* 356(6334): 183–186. See also Princeton University, Engineering School. Biased bots: Human prejudices sneak into artificial intelligence systems, *ScienceDaily*, 13 April. www.sciencedaily.com/releases/2017/04/170413141055.htm.

129. Buolamwini, Joy and Timnit Gebru (2018). Gender Shades: Intersectional Accuracy Disparities in Commercial Gender Classification, *Proceedings of Machine Learning Research* 81: 1–15.

130. Barocas, Solon and Andrew D. Selbst (2016). Big Data's Disparate Impact, *California Law Review* 104(1): 671–732. See p. 677.

131. Hurley, Dan (2018). Can An Algorithm Tell When Kids Are In Danger? *New York Times*, 2 January.

132. Eubanks, Virginia (2018). *Automating Inequality: How High-Tech Tools Profile, Police, and Punish the Poor*, St Martin's Press.

133. Angwin, Julia, Jeff Larson, Surya Mattu, and Lauren Kirchner (2016). Machine Bias: There's Software Used Across the Country to Predict Future Criminals. And It's Biased Against Blacks, *ProPublica*, 23 May. https://www.propublica.org/article/machine-bias-risk-assessments-in-criminal-sentencing.

134. Angwin, Julia and Jeff Larson (2016). Bias in Criminal Risk Scores Is Mathematically Inevitable, Researchers Say, *ProPublica*, 30 December. https://www.propublica.org/article/bias-in-criminal-risk-scores-is-mathematically-inevitable-researchers-say.

135. Dressel, Julia and Hany Farid (2018). The Accuracy, Fairness, and Limits of Predicting Recidivism, *Science Advances* 4(1): eaao5580. http://advances.sciencemag.org/content/4/1/eaao5580.

136. Stanley, Jay (2017). Pitfalls of Artificial Intelligence Decisionmaking Highlighted In Idaho ACLU Case, *ACLU*, 2 June. https://www.aclu.org/blog/privacy-technology/pitfalls-artificial-intelligence-decisionmaking-highlighted-idaho-aclu-case. See also K.W. v. Armstrong (2018). *ACLU of Idaho*. https://www.acluidaho.org/en/cases/kw-v-armstrong.

137. Kehl, Danielle, Priscilla Guo, and Samuel Kessler (2017). Algorithms in the Criminal Justice System: Assessing the Use of Risk Assessments in Sentencing, *Responsive Communities Initiative*, 25 August. https://dash.harvard.edu/handle/1/33746041. See also Wikipedia (2018). Loomis v. Wisconsin. https://en.wikipedia.org/wiki/Loomis_v._Wisconsin.
138. Israni, Ellora Thadaney (2017). When an Algorithm Helps Send You to Prison, *New York Times*, 26 October.
139. Staff Report (2013). A Review of the Data Broker Industry: Collection, Use, and Sale of Consumer Data for Marketing Purposes. Committee on Commerce, Science, and Transportation, 18 December. https://www.commerce.senate.gov/public/_cache/files/0d2b3642-6221-4888-a631-08f2f255b577/AE5D72CBE7F44F5BFC846BECE22C875B.12.18.13-senate-commerce-committee-report-on-data-broker-industry.pdf.
140. Federal Trade Commission (2014). Data Brokers: A Call for Transparency and Accountability. Federal Trade Commission, May. https://www.ftc.gov/system/files/documents/reports/data-brokers-call-transparency-accountability-report-federal-trade-commission-may-2014/140527databrokerreport.pdf.
141. Etzioni, Oren (2017). How to Regulate Artificial Intelligence, *New York Times*, 1 September. See also Burt, Andrew (2018). Leave A.I. Alone, *New York Times*, 4 January.
142. Goodman, Bryce and Seth Flaxman (2016). European Union Regulations on Algorithmic Decision-making and a 'Right to Explanation'. Oxford Internet Institute, 28 June. https://arxiv.org/abs/1606.08813.
143. EU (2016). General Data Protection Legislation. Council of the European Union, 6 April. https://www.eugdpr.org.
144. *Ibid.*, p. 146–147.
145. *Ibid.*, p. 139.
146. Amodei, Dario, Chris Olah, Jacob Steinhardt, Paul Cristiano, John Schulman, and Dan *Mané* (2016). Concrete Problems in AI Safety. https://arxiv.org/abs/1606.06565.
147. Cheney, James, Stephen Chong, Nate Foster, Margo Seltzer, and Stijn Vansummeren (2009). Provenance: A Future History, *Proceedings of the International Conference on Object Oriented Programming, Systems, Languages, and Applications 2009*, 957–964.
148. Pasquier, Thomas, Matthew K. Lau, Ana Trisovic, Emery R. Boose, Ben Couturier, Mercè Crosas, Aaron M. Ellison, Valerie Gibson, Chris R. Jones, and Margo Seltzer (2017). If These Data Could Talk, *Scientific Data* 4 (5 September). https://www.nature.com/articles/sdata2017114.
149. Bass, Dina and Ellen Huet (2017). Researchers Combat Gender and Racial Bias in Artificial Intelligence, *Bloomberg*, 4 December. https://www.bloomberg.com/news/articles/2017-12-04/researchers-combat-gender-and-racial-bias-in-artificial-intelligence.
150. Bolukbasi, Tolga, Kai-Wei Chang, James Zou, Venkatesh Saligrama, and Adam Kalai (2016). Man is to Computer Programmer as Woman is to Homemaker? Debiasing Word Embeddings, *30th Conference on Neural Information Processing Systems 2016*, 1–25.
151. Dwork, Cynthia, Nicole Immorlica, Adam Tauman Kalai, and Max Leiserson (2018). Decoupled Classifiers for Fair and Efficient Machine Learning, *Proceedings of Machine Learning Research* 81(1): 1–15. http://proceedings.mlr.press/v81/dwork18a/dwork18a.pdf.
152. About OpenAI (2018). Mission statement. https://openai.com/about/#mission.

153. Chen, Sophia (2017). AI Research is in Desperate Need of an Ethical Watchdog, *Wired*, 18 September.
154. Coldewey, Devin (2017). You Should Read this Super-interesting AMA with AI Researcher Joanna Bryson, *TechCrunch*, 13 January. https://techcrunch.com/2017/01/13/you-should-read-this-super-interesting-ama-with-ai-researcher-joanna-bryson/.
155. Bryson, Joanna (2017). AI Ethics, Artificial Intelligence, Robots, and Society. http://www.cs.bath.ac.uk/~jjb/web/ai.html.
156. Schank, Roger (2018). The Fraudulent Claims Made by IBM about Watson and AI. Unpublished paper. http://www.rogerschank.com/fraudulent-claims-made-by-IBM-about-Watson-and-AI.
157. Diakopoulos, Nicholas, Sorelle Friedler, Marcelo Arenas, Solon Barocas, Michael Hay, Bill Howe, H. V. Jagadish, Kris Unsworth, Arnaud Sahuguet, Suresh Venkatasubramanian, Christo Wilson, Cong Yu, and Bendert Zevenbergen (2017). Principles for Accountable Algorithms and a Social Impact Statement for Algorithms. Fairness, Accountability, and Transparency in Machine Learning. https://www.fatml.org/resources/principles-for-accountable-algorithms.
158. ACM (2017). Statement on Algorithmic Transparency and Accountability. ACM US Public Policy Council, 12 January. https://www.acm.org/binaries/content/assets/public-policy/2017_usacm_statement_algorithms.pdf.
159. Zook, Matthew, Solon Barocas, danah boyd, Kate Crawford, Emily Keller, Seeta Peña Gangadharan, Alyssa Goodman, Rachelle Hollander, Barbara A. Koenig, Jacob Metcalf, Arvind Narayanan, Alondra Nelson, and Frank Pasquale (2017). Ten Simple Rules for Responsible Big Data Research, *PLoS Computational Biology* 13(3).
160. Compolo, Alex, Madelyn Sanfilippo, Meredith Whittaker, and Kate Crawford (2017). AI Now 2017 Report. https://ainowinstitute.org/AI_Now_2017_Report.pdf.

Chapter 12

1. Gibson, William (1982). Burning Chrome, *Omni Magazine*, July. See also Gibson, William (1984). *Neuromancer*, Penguin Group, p. 51. See also Sullivan, Mark (2009). Neuromancer Turns 25: What It Got Right, What It Got Wrong, *MacWorld.com*, 1 July. https://www.macworld.com/article/1141500/entertainment/neuromancer-25.html
2. IMDb (2017). *Her*. http://www.imdb.com/title/tt1798709/. See also the trailer, https://www.youtube.com/watch?v=WzV6mXIOVl4.
3. Wikipedia (2017). Nosedive. https://en.wikipedia.org/wiki/Nosedive.
4. Zhao, Christina (2018). 'Black Mirror' in China: 1.4 Billion Citizens to be Monitored through Social Credit System, *Newsweek.com*, 1 May. https://www.newsweek.com/china-social-credit-system-906865. See also The Late Show with Stephen Colbert (2018). Everyone In China Is Getting A 'Social Credit Score'. 8 May. https://www.youtube.com/watch?v=N4Gr-HLM7Qk.
5. Statista (2018). Most famous social network sites worldwide as of April 2018, ranked by number of active users (in millions). https://www.statista.com/statistics/272014/global-social-networks-ranked-by-number-of-users/.
6. Turkle, Sherry (1984). *The Second Self: Computers and the Human Spirit*, Simon & Schuster, p. 12.

7. Turkle, Sherry (1995). *Life on the Screen: Identity in the Age of the Internet*, Simon & Schuster, p. 26.
8. Turkle, Sherry (2011). *Alone Together: Why We Expect More from Technology and Less from Each Other*, Basic Books.
9. Turkle, Sherry (2015). *Reclaiming Conversation: The Power of Talk in a Digital Age*, Penguin Press.
10. Kraut, Robert, Michael Patterson, Vicki Lundmark, Sara Kiesler, Tridas Mukopadhyay, and William Scherlis (1998). Internet Paradox: A Social Technology that Reduces Social Involvement and Psychological Well-Being, *American Psychologist* 53(9): 117–1031.
11. Kraut, Robert, Sara Kiesler, Bouka Boneva, Jonathon Cummings, Vicki Helgeson, and Anne Crawford (2002). Internet Paradox Revisited, *Journal of Social Issues* 58(1): 49–74.
12. Hampton, Keith, Lauren F. Sessions, Eun Ja Her, and Lee Rainie (2009). Social Isolation and New Technology: How the Internet and Mobile Phones Impact Americans' Social Networks. Pew Internet & American Life Project, November. http://www.pewinternet.org/files/oldmedia//Files/Reports/2009/PIP_Tech_and_Social_Isolation.pdf.
13. Rainie, Lee and Barry Wellman (2012). *Networked: The New Social Operating System*, The MIT Press, pp. 12–13.
14. Kercher, Sophia (2017). An App for Mothers Who Missed Out on Tinder, *New York Times*, 10 May.
15. Kross, Ethan, Philippe Verduyn, Emre Demiralp, Jiyoung Park, David Seungjae Lee, Natalie Lin, Holly Shablack, John Jonides, and Oscar Ybarra (2013). Facebook Use Predicts Declines in Subjective Well-Being in Young Adults, *PLoS ONE* 8(8): e69841. See also Dotson, Taylor (2017). *Technically Together: Reconstructing Community in a Networked World*, The MIT Press, p. 2.
16. Andalibi, Nazanin, Pinar Ozturk, and Andrea Forte (2017). Sensitive Self-disclosures, Responses, and Social Support on Instagram: The Case of #Depression. *Proceedings of the 2017 ACM Conference on Computer Supported Cooperative Work and Social Computing*, 1485–1500. See also Bessière, Katherine, Sara Kiesler, Robert Kraut, and Bonka S. Boneva (2008). Effects of Internet Use and Social Resources on Changes in Depression, *Information, Communication, & Society* 11(1): 47–70. See also Bessière, Katherine, Sarah Pressman, Sara Kiesler, and Robert Kraut (2010). Effects of Internet Use on Health and Depression, *Journal of Medical Internet Research* 12(1): e6.
17. After I wrote this section, I found a 2018 book, Vaidhyanathan, Siva (2018). *Antisocial Media*, Oxford University Press. It is well described by its subtitle: How Facebook Disconnects Us and Undermines Democracy.
18. Pew Internet Research (2015). Teens, Social Media & Technology Overview 2015. http://www.pewinternet.org/2015/04/09/teens-social-media-technology-2015/.
19. Common Sense Media (2015). The Common Sense Census: Media Use by Tweens and Teens. https://www.commonsensemedia.org/research/the-common-sense-census-media-use-by-tweens-and-teens.
20. Ofcom (2015). Children and Parents: Media Use and Attitudes Report. https://www.ofcom.org.uk/__data/assets/pdf_file/0024/78513/childrens_parents_nov2015.pdf.
21. Parkes, Alison, Helen Sweeting, Daniel Wight, Marion Henderson (2013). Do Television and Electronic Games Predict Children's Psychosocial Adjustment? Longitudinal Research Using the UK Millennium Cohort Study, *Archives of Disease in Childhood* 98: 341–348.
22. Blum-Ross, Alicia and Sonia Livingstone (2016). Families and screen time: Current advice and emerging research. London School of Economics Media Policy Brief 17. http://eprints.lse.ac.uk/66927/1/Policy%20Brief%2017-%20Families%20%20Screen%20Time.pdf.

23. Gopnik, Alison (2016). Is 'Screen Time' Dangerous for Children? *The New Yorker*, 28 November.

24. Richtel, Matt (2017). Are Teenagers Replacing Drugs With Smartphones? *New York Times*, 13 March.

25. Busch, Bradley (2016). FOMO, Stress and Sleeplessness: Are Smartphones Bad for Students? *The Guardian*, 8 March.

26. Lepp, Andrew, Jacob E. Barkley, and Aryn C. Karpinski (2014). The Relationship between Cell Phone Use, Academic Performance, Anxiety, and Satisfaction with Life in College Students, *Computers in Human Behavior* 31: 343–350.

27. Homayoun, Alicia (2017). The Secret Social Media Lives of Teenagers, *New York Times*, 7 June.

28. Jolly, Jennifer (2016). In 'Screenagers,' What to Do About Too Much Screen Time, *New York Times*, 15 March. See also Screenagers (2015). https://www.screenagersmovie.com/host-a-screening/.

29. Alter, Adam (2017). *Irresistible: The Rise of Addictive Technology and the Business of Keeping Us Hooked*, Penguin Press.

30. *Ibid.*, p. 9.

31. Alter, Adam (2017). Why Our Screens Make Us Less Happy. TED2017 Talk. https://www.ted.com/talks/adam_alter_why_our_screens_make_us_less_happy#t-1360.

32. Popescu, Adam (2018). Keep Your Head Up: How Smartphone Addiction Kills Manners and Moods, *New York Times*, 25 January.

33. Harris, Tristan (2016). How Technology Hijacks People's Minds, *HuffPost*, 27 May. See also Cooper, Anderson (2017). What is 'Brain Hacking'? Tech Insiders on Why You Should Care, *CBS News*, 9 April. See also Thompson, Nicholas (2017). Our Minds Have Been Hijacked by Our Phones, Tristan Harris Wants to Rescue Them, *Wired*, 26 July.

34. Raphael, Rina (2017). Netflix CEO Reed Hastings: Sleep Is Our Competition, *Fastcompany.com*, 6 November. https://www.fastcompany.com/40491939/netflix-ceo-reed-hastings-sleep-is-our-competition.

35. Wikipedia (2017). Gamification. https://en.wikipedia.org/wiki/Gamification.

36. Bhatia, Manjeet Singh (2008). Cell Phone Dependence—A New Diagnostic Entity, *Delhi Psychiatry Journal* 11(2): 123–124.

37. Fox, Jesse and Jennifer J. Moreland (2015). The Dark Side of Social Networking Sites: An Exploration of the Relational and Psychological Stressors Associated with Facebook Use and Affordances, *Computers in Human Behavior* 45: 168–176.

38. Shakya, Holly B. and Nicholas A. Christakis (2017). Association of Facebook Use With Compromised Well-Being: A Longitudinal Study, *American Journal of Epidemiology* 185(3): 203–211.

39. Twenge, Jean M. (2017). Have Smartphones Destroyed a Generation? *TheAtlantic.com*, September. https://www.theatlantic.com/magazine/archive/2017/09/has-the-smartphone-destroyed-a-generation/534198/. See also Twenge, Jean M., Gabrielle N. Martin, and W. Keith Campbell (2018). Decreases in Psychological Well-Being Among American Adolescents After 2012 and Links to Screen Time During the Rise of Smartphone Technology. *Emotion*. Advance online publication. http://dx.doi.org/10.1037/emo0000403. See also Twenge, Jean M., Thomas E. Joiner, Megan L. Rogers, and Gabrielle N. Martin (2018). Increases in Depressive Symptoms, Suicide-Related Outcomes, and Suicide Rates Among

U.S. Adolescents After 2010 and Links to Increased New Media Screen Time, *Clinical Psychological Science* 6(1): 3–17.

40. Burke, Moira and Robert E. Kraut (2016). The Relationship Between Facebook Use and Well-Being Depends on Communication Type and Tie Strength, *Journal of Computer-Mediated Communication* 21: 265–281.
41. Clark, Melissa (2016). Workaholism: It's Not Just Long Hours on the Job, *American Psychological Association*, April. http://www.apa.org/science/about/psa/2016/04/workaholism.aspx.
42. Schreier, Jason (2017). Video Games Are Destroying the People Who Make Them, *New York Times*, 25 October.
43. ABC News (2015). Technology and 'Hard Work Pays' Attitude Drives World of Workaholics: Study, *ABC News*, 8 July. http://www.abc.net.au/news/2015-07-08/technology-breeding-a-generation-of-workaholics-study/6604548.
44. Porter, Gayle, and Nada K. Kakabadse (2006). HRM Perspectives on Addiction to Technology and Work, *Journal of Management Development* 5(6): 535–560.
45. Middleton, Catherine (2008). Do Mobile Technologies Enable Work–Life Balance? Dual Perspectives on BlackBerry Usage for Supplemental Work. In Hislop, Donald (Ed.), *Mobility and Technology in the Workplace*, Routledge.
46. Andreassen, Cecilie Schou, Mark D. Griffiths, Rajita Sinha, Jørn Hetland, amd Ståle Pallesen (2016). The Relationships between Workaholism and Symptoms of Psychiatric Disorders: A Large-Scale Cross-Sectional Study, *PLoS ONE* 11(5): e0152978.
47. The World Unplugged (2017). https://theworldunplugged.wordpress.com. See also Moeller, Susan, Elia Powers, and Jessica Roberts (2012). 'The World Unplugged' and '24 Hours without Media': Media Literacy to Develop Self-Awareness Regarding Media, *Comunicar* 20: 45–52.
48. Solon, Olivia (2018). Former Facebook and Google Workers Launch Campaign to Fight Tech Addiction, *The Guardian*, 5 February.
49. Douthat, Ross (2017). Resist the Internet, *New York Times*, 11 March.
50. Cochrane, Emily (2018). A Call to Cut Back Online Addictions. Pitted Against Just One More Click, *New York Times*, 4 February.
51. Mele, Christopher (2017). How to Log Off of Facebook Forever, With All Its Perks and Pitfalls, *New York Times*, 24 March.
52. Bowles, Nellie (2018). Is the Answer to Phone Addiction a Worse Phone? *New York Times*, 12 January.
53. Gelles, David (2018). Tech Backlash Grows as Investors Press Apple to Act on Children's Use, *New York Times*, 8 January.
54. Wilson, Mark (2018). Apple's Plan to Make Its Design Less Addictive, *Brand Knew Magazine*, 12 June. http://www.brandknewmag.com/apples-plan-to-make-its-design-less-addictive/. See also Pardes, Arielle (2018). Apple's iOS Restrictions Aren't Helping Tech Addiction, *Wired.com*, 3 June. https://www.wired.com/story/ios-restrictions-digital-wellness/.
55. Mele, Christopher (2017). Coffee Shops Skip Wi-Fi to Encourage Customers to Actually Talk, *New York Times*, 9 May. See also Stabiner, Kate (2018). What to Do When Laptops and Silence Take Over Your Cafe? *New York Times*, 13 February.
56. Morris, David Z. (2017). *Fortune*, 1 January. http://fortune.com/2017/01/01/french-right-to-disconnect-law/

57. Digital Detox® (2018). http://digitaldetox.org. Dopamine Labs (2018). https://usedopamine.com.
58. Ives, Mike (2017). Electroshock Therapy for Internet Addicts? China Vows to End It, *New York Times,* 13 January.
59. Gartner (2017). Leading the IoT: Gartner Insights into How to Lead in a Connected World. https://www.gartner.com/imagesrv/books/iot/iotEbook_digital.pdf.
60. Tibbits, Skylar (Ed.) (2017). *Active Matter,* The MIT Press.
61. Weinberger, Matt (2017). Why Amazon's Echo Is Totally Dominating—and What Google, Microsoft, and Apple Have to Do to Catch Up, *Businessinsider.com,* 14 January. http://www.businessinsider.com/amazon-echo-google-home-microsoft-cortana-apple-siri-2017-1. See also Rubin, Ben Fox (2017). Alexa, Be More Human, *CNet,* 29 August. https://www.cnet.com/html/feature/amazon-alexa-echo-inside-look/. See also Green, Penelope (2017). 'Alexa, Where Have You Been All My Life?' *New York Times,* 11 July. See also Chen, Brian X., Farhad Manjoo, and Vindu Goel (2017). HomePod Speaker and New iMacs: What We Saw at Apple's WWDC, *New York Times,* 6 June.
62. Weed, Julie (2017). Did You Pack Too Much? Your Suitcase Knows, *New York Times,* 3 July. See also Hughes, C. J. (2017). The Latest in Apartment Technology: Fridge Cams and Robotic Valets, *New York Times,* 15 December. See also Chen, Brian X. (2018). To Invade Homes, Tech Is Trying to Get in Your Kitchen, *New York Times,* 8 January.
63. Quain, John R. (2018). Alexa, What Happened to My Car? *New York Times,* 25 January.
64. Green, Penelope (2017). 'Alexa, Where Have You Been All My Life?' *New York Times,* 11 July. For a discussion of a 3-year-old girl's interaction with Alexa, and why her mom finally decided to put the device into a closet, see Botsman, Rachel (2017). Co-Parenting with Alexa, *New York Times,* 7 October.
65. Purington, Amanda, Jessie G. Taft, Shruti Sannon, Natalya N. Bazarova, and Samuel Hardman Taylor (2017). 'Alexa is my new BFF': Social Roles, User Satisfaction, and Personification of the Amazon Echo, *Proceedings of the 2017 Association for Computing Machinery.*
66. Terdiman, Daniel (2018). Here's How People Say Google Home and Alexa Impact Their Lives, *Fast Company,* 5 January.
67. Amazon (2018). Alex Lost her Voice. 2018 Super Bowl Ad. https://www.youtube.com/watch?v=J6-8DQALGt4.
68. Wakabayashi, Daisuke and Nick Wingfield (2018). Alexa, We're Still Trying to Figure Out What to Do with You, *New York Times,* 15 January. See also Rosenbloom, Stephanie (2016). Google Home Helps You Leave the House, Too, *New York Times,* 26 December.
69. Wakabayashi, Daisuke (2017). Google's New Gadgets Come with a Big Helping of A.I., *New York Times,* 4 October.
70. Maheshwari, Sapna (2018). Hey, Alexa, What Can You Hear? And What Will You Do with It? *New York Times,* 31 March. Chokshi, Niraj (2018). Is Alexa Listening? Amazon Echo Sent Out Recording of Couple's Conversation, *New York Times,* 25 May.
71. Jaquith, Todd (2017). Here's a Look at the Smart Cities of the Future, *Futurism.com,* 18 January. https://futurism.com/heres-a-look-at-the-smart-cities-of-the-future/.
72. Chen, Brian X. (2018). In an Era of 'Smart' Things, Sometimes Dumb Stuff Is Better, *New York Times,* 21 February.
73. Elgan, Mike (2018). The Case Against Teaching Kids to Be Polite to Alexa, *Fast Company,* 24 June.

74. Krueger, Myron (1983). *Artificial Reality,* Addison-Wesley.

75. AccuVein (2018). Vein illumination. https://www.accuvein.com/.

76. Wikipedia (2017). Augmented reality. https://en.wikipedia.org/wiki/Augmented_reality.

77. Isaac, Mike (2017). Mark Zuckerberg Sees Augmented Reality Ecosystem in Facebook, *New York Times,* 18 April.

78. Wikipedia (2017). Virtual reality. https://en.wikipedia.org/wiki/Virtual_reality.

79. Barnes, Brooks (2017). Virtual Reality's Potential for Magic Gets Real, *New York Times,* 19 February. See also NYTVR (2017). Discover Stories Without Limits. http://www.nytimes.com/marketing/nytvr/. See also Barnes, Brooks (2017). Virtual-Reality 'Star Wars' Attractions Coming to Disney Malls, *New York Times,* 3 August.

80. Parkin, Simon (2017). The Coming Horror of Virtual Reality, *The New Yorker,* 15 May. See also Wingfield, Nick (2017). Sticker Shock, and Maybe Nausea, Hamper Sales of Virtual Reality Gear, *New York Times,* 8 January.

81. Nwaneri, Crystal (2017). Ready Lawyer One: Legal Issues in the Innovation of Virtual Reality, *Harvard Journal of Law & Technology* 30(2): 601–627.

82. Polo, Susana (2010). The Internet Is For Infographics...About Porn, *The Mary Sue,* 6 June. https://www.themarysue.com/internet-porn-statistics/.

83. Cox, Jamieson (2015). Pornhub Is Emulating Netflix with its New Premium Streaming Service, *The Verge,* 6 August. https://www.theverge.com/2015/8/6/9108459/pornhub-premium-streaming-service-netflix-for-porn.

84. Lee. Nicole (2018). Fake Porn Is the New Fake News, and the Internet Isn't Ready: AI-generated Porn Is Just the Beginning, *Engadget,* 30 January. https://www.engadget.com/2018/01/30/fake-porn-is-the-new-fake-news-and-the-internet-isn-t-ready/.

85. Wikipedia (2018). Timeline of online dating services. https://en.wikipedia.org/wiki/Timeline_of_online_dating_services.

86. StatisticBrain (2017). Online Dating Statistics. *Statistics Brain Research Institute.* https://www.statisticbrain.com/online-dating-statistics/.

87. Rosenfeld, Michael J. and Reuben J. Thomas (2012). Searching for a Mate: The Rise of the Internet as a Social Intermediary, *American Sociological Review* 77(4): 523–547.

88. Wikipedia (2018). Online dating service. https://en.wikipedia.org/wiki/Online_dating_service.

89. Shaadi.com (2018). Meet someone for keeps. https://www.shaadi.com/.

90. Lee, Ji Hyun (2013). Hey Mom, Call Me When You Find My Wife, *New York Times,* 10 May.

91. Tugend, Alina (2016). For Online Dating Sites, a Bumpy Road to Love, *New York Times,* 24 December.

92. Gildea, Florence (2018). The End of Dating: Tinder, Porn & New Forms of Alienation. Campaign Against Sex Robots, 9 February. https://campaignagainstsexrobots.org/2018/02/09/the-end-of-dating-tinder-porn-new-forms-of-alienation-by-florence-gildea/.

93. Dimov, Daniel (2016). Pornbots—Sexual Barbies of the Future, *Infosec Institute,* 20 June. http://resources.infosecinstitute.com/pornbots-sexual-barbies-of-the-future/#gref.

94. Abyss Creations, LLC (2018). https://www.realdoll.com/.

95. Realbotix (2018). https://realbotix.com/.

96. Trout, Christopher (2017). RealDoll's First Sex Robot Took Me to the Uncanny Valley, *Engadget*, 11 April. https://www.engadget.com/2017/04/11/realdolls-first-sex-robot-took-me-to-the-uncanny-valley/.

97. Danaher, John and Neil McArthur (2017). *Robot Sex: Social and Ethical Implications*, The MIT Press.

98. McArthur, Neil (2017). The Case for Sexbots. Chapter 3 In 97. Danaher and McArthur, ibid.

99. Di Nucci, Ezio (2017). Sex Robots and the Rights of the Disabled. Chapter 5 in 97. Danaher and McArthur, ibid.

100. Danaher, John (2017). The Symbolic Consequences Argument in the Sex Robot Debate. Chapter 7 in 97. Danaher and McArthur, ibid.

101. Richardson, Suzanne (2017). What the Idea of 'Sex Robots' Tells Us About Prostitution, *Nordic Model Now!*, 10 June. https://nordicmodelnow.org/2017/06/10/what-the-idea-of-sex-robots-tells-us-about-prostitution/. See also https://campaignagainstsexrobots.org/ and https://nordicmodelnow.org/.

102. Wikipedia (2018). Bitcoin. https://en.wikipedia.org/wiki/Bitcoin.

103. Wikipedia (2018). Cryptocurrency. https://en.wikipedia.org/wiki/Cryptocurrency.

104. Popper, Nathaniel and Tiffany Hsu (2017). Bitcoin Plummets More Than 30 per cent in Less Than a Day, *New York Times*, 22 December.

105. Shiller, Robert J. (2017). What Is Bitcoin Really Worth? Don't Even Ask, *New York Times*, 15 December.

106. Average daily price of a bitcoin (2018). *99 Bitcoins*. https://99bitcoins.com/price-chart-history/?gclid=EAIaIQobChMIr7Ob-9ub2gIVyrjACh0zYgYXEAAYBCAAEgJ5FfD_BwE.

107. Popper, Nathaniel (2018). Rise of Bitcoin Competitor Ripple Creates Wealth to Rival Zuckerberg, *New York Times*, 4 January.

108. Popper, Nathaniel (2017). Bitcoin Hasn't Replaced Cash, but Investors Don't Care, *New York Times*, 6 December.

109. Popper, Nathaniel (2017). Bitcoin's Price Has Soared, but What Comes Next? *New York Times*, 8 December.

110. Currie, Antony (2017). Digital Currencies Are Growing on Faltering Foundations, *New York Times*, 29 September.

111. Popper, Nathaniel (2017). As Bitcoin Scrapes $10,000, an Investment Boom Like No Other, *New York Times*, 27 November.

112. Popper, Nathaniel (2018). As Bitcoin Bubble Loses Air, Frauds and Flaws Rise to Surface, *New York Times*, 5 February.

113. Roose, Kevin (2017). I Was Wrong About Bitcoin. Here's Why, *New York Times*, 12 December. See also Popper, Nathaniel (2018). Venture Capitalists Seek 'Safe Harbor' for Virtual Currencies, *New York Times*, 19 April.

114. Popper, Nathaniel (2017). Warning Signs About Another Giant Bitcoin Exchange, *New York Times*, 21 November.

115. Popper, Nathaniel (2015). Can Bitcoin Conquer Argentina? *New York Times*, 29 April.

116. Lee, Su-Hyun and Nathaniel Popper (2017). In South Korea, the Virtual Currency Boom Hits Home, *New York Times*, 3 December.

117. Popper, Nathaniel, Oleg Matsnev, and Ana Vanessa Herrero (2018). Russia and Venezuela's Plan to Sidestep Sanctions: Virtual Currencies, *New York Times,* 3 January.
118. Li, Cao (2017). China Bitcoin Exchange to Stop Trading Virtual Currencies Amid Crackdown, *New York Times,* 14 September.
119. Goel, Vindu and Suhasini Raj (2018). India Clings to Cash, Even as Tech Firms Push Digital Money, *New York Times,* 7 January.
120. Wikipedia (2018). Blockchain. https://en.wikipedia.org/wiki/Blockchain. For a clear explanatory video, see https://www.nytimes.com/video/business/100000005675385/baffled-by-bitcoin-heres-how-cryptocurrency-works.html?action=click>ype=vhs&version=vhs-heading&module=vhs®ion=title-area.
121. Kaushal, Mohit and Sheel Tyle (2015). The Blockchain: What It Is and Why It Matters. Brookings, 13 January. https://www.brookings.edu/blog/techtank/2015/01/13/the-blockchain-what-it-is-and-why-it-matters/.
122. Popper, Nathaniel (2018). There Is Nothing Virtual About Bitcoin's Energy Appetite, *New York Times,* 21 January.
123. Li, Cao and Giulia Marchi (2017). In China's Hinterlands, Workers Mine Bitcoin for a Digital Fortune, *New York Times,* 13 September.
124. Popper, Nathaniel (2017). Bitcoin Expansion Is Off the Table. At Least for Now, *New York Times,* 8 November.
125. Appelbaum, Binyamin (2018). Is Bitcoin a Waste of Electricity, or Something Worse? *New York Times,* 28 February.
126. Marvin, Rob (2017). Blockchain: The Invisible Technology That's Changing the World, *PCMag.com,* 29 August. https://www.pcmag.com/article/351486/blockchain-the-invisible-technology-thats-changing-the-wor. See also Tapscott, Alex and Don Tapscott (2017). How Blockchain Is Changing Finance, *Harvard Business Review,* 1 March. https://hbr.org/2017/03/how-blockchain-is-changing-finance.
127. Popper, Nathaniel and Steve Lohr (2017). Blockchain: A Better Way to Track Pork Chops, Bonds, Bad Peanut Butter? *New York Times,* 4 March. See also Orcutt, Mike (2017). Why the CDC Wants in on Blockchain, *MIT Technology Review,* 2 October. https://www.technologyreview.com/s/608959/why-the-cdc-wants-in-on-blockchain/.
128. Wikipedia (2018). Initial coin offering. https://en.wikipedia.org/wiki/Initial_coin_offering.
129. Popper, Nathaniel (2017). Initial Coin Offerings Horrify a Former S.E.C. Regulator, *New York Times,* 26 November.
130. Johnson, Steven (2018). Beyond the Bitcoin Bubble, *New York Times,* 16 January. See also Schiller, Ben (2018). Is the Blockchain's Potential for Social Impact Over-Hyped? *Fast Company,* 12 April.
131. Wikipedia (2018). List of public corporations by market capitalization. https://en.wikipedia.org/wiki/List_of_public_corporations_by_market_capitalization.
132. Mozur, Paul (2017). The World's Biggest Tech Companies Are No Longer Just American, *New York Times,* 17 August.
133. Benner, Katie (2017). Airbnb Tries to Behave More Like a Hotel, *New York Times,* 17 June.
134. Isaac, Mike (2017). Uber's C.E.O. Plays With Fire, *New York Times,* 8 September. See also Isaac, Mike and William K. Rashbaum (2017). F.B.I. Investigates Uber Software Used to

Monitor Lyft Drivers, *New York Times,* 8 September. See also Isaac, Mike (2017). Uber Engaged in 'Illegal' Spying on Rivals, Ex-Employee Says, *New York Times,* 15 December. See also Hill, Steven (2018). New Leadership Has Not Changed Uber, *New York Times,* 26 March.

135. O'Reilly, Tim (2017). Uber's Opportunity to Remake Silicon Valley—For Good, *Wired,* 29 June.

136. Hu, Winnie (2017). As Uber Woos More Drivers, Taxis Hit Back, *New York Times,* 18 March.

137. Bennhold, Katrin (2017). On London's Streets, Black Cabs and Uber Fight for a Future, *New York Times,* 4 July.

138. Fitzsimmons, Emma G. and Winnie Hu (2017). The Downside of Ride-Hailing: More New York City Gridlock, *New York Times,* 11 March.

139. *Ibid.* See also Badger, Emily (2017). Is Uber Helping or Hurting Mass Transit? *New York Times,* 16 October.

140. Manjoo, Farhad (2017). How Microsoft Has Become the Surprise Innovator in PCs, *New York Times,* 26 July.

141. Belk, Russell W. and Gülnur Tumbat (2005). The Cult of Macintosh, *Consumption, Markets and Culture* 8(3): 205–217.

142. Nicas, Jack (2018). Apple Is Worth $1,000,000,000,000. Two Decades Ago, It Was Almost Bankrupt, *New York Times,* 2 August.

143. Manjoo, Farhad (2016). Tech's 'Frightful 5' Will Dominate Digital Life for Foreseeable Future, *New York Times,* 20 January.

144. Wikipedia (2018). Facebook. https://en.wikipedia.org/wiki/Facebook.

145. Manjoo, Farhad (2017). Why Facebook Keeps Beating Every Rival: It's the Network, of Course, *New York Times,* 19 April.

146. Wakabayashi, Daisuke (2017). Why Some Online Video Stars Opt for Facebook Over YouTube, *New York Times,* 4 October. See also Wilson, Mark (2017). Facebook's Plan to Swallow the Whole Internet, *Fast Company,* 2 May. https://www.fastcodesign.com/90170454/facebooks-plan-to-swallow-the-whole-internet.

147. Dwoskin, Elizabeth and Craig Timberg (2018). How Merchants Use Facebook to Flood Amazon with Fake Reviews, *The Washington Post,* 23 April.

148. Oremus, Will (2018). Are You Really the Product? The History of a Dangerous Idea, *Slate.com,* 27 April. https://slate.com/technology/2018/04/are-you-really-facebooks-product-the-history-of-a-dangerous-idea.html.

149. Cohen, Noam (2018). Facebook Doesn't Like What It Sees When It Looks in the Mirror, *New York Times,* 16 January. See also Sorkin, Andrew Ross (2018). Failed by Facebook, We'll Return to the Scene of the Crime. We Always Do, *New York Times,* 9 April.

150. Manjoo, Farhad (2017). Why Instagram Is Becoming Facebook's Next Facebook, *New York Times,* 26 April. See also Roose, Kevin (2018). What if a Healthier Facebook Is Just... Instagram? *New York Times,* 22 January.

151. Wilson, Mark (2018). Designers Just Fixed Facebook. Your Move, Zuckerberg, *Fast Company,* 6 April. https://www.fastcodesign.com/90166785/designers-just-fixed-facebook-your-move-zuckerberg. See also Sorkin, Andrew Ross (2018). Facebook Should Consider a 'Why Me?' Button, *New York Times,* 2 April. See also Campbell-Dollaghan, Kelsey (2018). Want to Fight Back Against Facebook's Algorithm? Check Out These Tools, *Fast Company,* 21 March.

https://www.fastcodesign.com/90164935/want-to-fight-back-against-facebooks-algorithm-check-out-these-tools.

152. Phillips, Matt (2018). Facebook's Stock Plunge Shatters Faith in Tech Companies' Invincibility, *New York Times,* 26 July.

153. Rutenberg, Jim (2017). News Outlets to Seek Bargaining Rights Against Google and Facebook, *New York Times,* 9 July.

154. Wu, Tim (2018). Don't Fix Facebook. Replace It, *New York Times,* 3 April. See also Frenkel, Sheera (2018). Fact Check: What Mark Zuckerberg Said About Facebook, Privacy and Russia, *New York Times,* 11 April. See also Cohen, Noam (2018). Can Facebook Develop a Conscience? *New York Times,* 11 April. See also Porter, Eduardo (2018). Facebook Is Creepy. And Valuable, *New York Times,* 17 April. See also The Editorial Board, The New York Times (2018). Can Facebook Be Cut Down to Size? *New York Times,* 5 June.

155. Scott, Mark (2017). E.U. Fines Facebook $122 Million Over Disclosures in WhatsApp Deal, *New York Times,* 18 May.

156. Kessel, Jonah M. and Paul Mozur (2017). How Facebook Is Changing Your Internet, *New York Times* Video, 18 September. https://www.youtube.com/watch?v=cR_XVGemAnw.

157. Mozur, Paul, Mark Scott, and Mike Isaac (2017). Facebook Navigates an Internet Fractured by Governmental Controls. *New York Times,* 17 September.

158. Wikipedia (2018). Google. https://en.wikipedia.org/wiki/Google.

159. Hess, Amanda (2017). How YouTube's Shifting Algorithms Hurt Independent Media, *New York Times,* 17 April.

160. Duhigg, Charles (2018). The Case Against Google, *New York Times,* 20 February.

161. Warren, Tom (2018). Google Fined a Record $5 Billion by the EU for Android Antitrust Violations, *The Verge,* 18 July. https://www.theverge.com/2018/7/18/17580694/google-android-eu-fine-antitrust.

162. Wakabayashi, Daisuke and Michael Corkery (2017). Google and Walmart Partner with Eye on Amazon, *New York Times,* 23 August.

163. Wikipedia (2018). Alphabet Inc. https://en.wikipedia.org/wiki/Alphabet_Inc. See also Wakabayashi, Daisuke (2018). Google's Parent Company Spends Like It's Thinking of a Future Beyond Ads, *New York Times,* 23 April.

164. Wikipedia (2018). Amazon (company). https://en.wikipedia.org/wiki/Amazon_(company).

165. Streitfield, David (2017). Bookstore Chains, Long in Decline, Are Undergoing a Final Shakeout, *New York Times,* 28 December.

166. Alter, Alexandra (2017). Amazon Sets Up Shop in the Heart of the Publishing Industry, *New York Times,* 24 May.

167. Wingfield, Nick (2017). Amid Brick-and-Mortar Travails, a Tipping Point for Amazon in Apparel, *New York Times,* 30 April.

168. Corkery, Michael (2017). Scenes from Sears: 2 Locations Tell a Story of Struggle in a Tight Retail Market, *New York Times,* 24 November. See also Corkery, Michael (2018). Sears: The Original Everything Store, Files for Bankruptcy, *New York Times,* 14 October.

169. Hsu, Tiffany (2017). Retailers Experiment with a New Philosophy: Smaller Is Better. *New York Times,* 17 November.

170. Goel, Vindu (2017). Amazon, in Hunt for Lower Prices, Recruits Indian Merchants, *New York Times,* 26 November. See also Creswell, Julie (2018). Amazon, the Brand Buster, *New York Times,* 23 June.

171. Abrams, Rachel and Julie Creswell (2017). Amazon Deal for Whole Foods Starts a Supermarket War, *New York Times,* 16 June.

172. Manjoo, Farhad (2017). In Whole Foods, Bezos Gets a Sustainably Sourced Guinea Pig, *New York Times,* 17 June.

173. Wingfield, Nick and David Gelles (2017). Amazon's Whole Foods Strategy: Cheaper Kale and Avocado, *New York Times,* 24 August.

174. Wingfield, Nick (2018). Bit by Bit, Whole Foods Gets an Amazon Touch, *New York Times,* 1 March.

175. Cusumano, Michael A. (2017). Amazon and Whole Foods: Follow the Strategy (and the Money), *Communications of the ACM* 60(10): 24–26.

176. Wingfield, Nick (2018). Inside Amazon Go, a Store of the Future, *New York Times,* 21 January. See also Inside the First Amazon Go Store (2018). Video at https://www.youtube.com/watch?v=zdbumR6Bhd8.

177. Thompson, Ben (2018). Amazon Go and the Future, *Stratechery,* 23 January. https://stratechery.com/2018/amazons-go-and-the-future/.

178. Wingfield, Nick, Paul Mozur, and Michael Corkery (2018). Retailers Race Against Amazon to Automate Stores, *New York Times,* 1 April.

179. Manjoo, Farhad (2017). Amazon's Vision of Computing's Future: An Information Appliance, *New York Times,* 28 June.

180. Maheshwari, Sapna (2017). As Amazon's Influence Grows, Marketers Scramble to Tailor Strategies, *New York Times,* 31 July.

181. Wingfield, Nick (2017). Amazon's Latest Way into Your Life Is Through the Front Door, *New York Times,* 25 October.

182. Wingfield, Nick and Katie Thomas (2017). Hearing Amazon's Footsteps, the Health Care Industry Shudders, *New York Times,* 27 October. See also Ballentine, Claire and Katie Thomas (2018). Amazon to Buy Online Pharmacy PillPack, Jumping into the Drug Business, *New York Times,* 28 June.

183. Sorkin, Andrew Ross (2017). Conglomerates Didn't Die. They Look Like Amazon, *New York Times,* 19 June.

184. Kang, Cecilia (2017). Amazon Turns on the Charm Amid Criticism from Right and Left, *New York Times,* 15 October.

185. Stewart, James B. (2017). Washington Post, Breaking News, Is Also Breaking New Ground, *New York Times,* 19 May.

186. Kang, Cecilia, Nick Wingfield, and Danielle Ivory (2018). Amazon's Critics Get New Life with Trump's Attacks on the Company, *New York Times,* 22 April. See also Stewart, James B. (2018). Amazon, the Elephant in the Antitrust Room, *New York Times,* 3 May.

187. Manjoo, Farhad (2017). Tech Giants Seem Invincible. That Worries Lawmakers, *New York Times,* 4 January.

188. Manjoo, Farhad (2017). The Upside of Being Ruled by the Five Tech Giants, *New York Times,* 1 November.

189. Manjoo, Farhad (2018). Tackling the Internet's Central Villain: The Advertising Business, *New York Times,* 31 January.
190. Pangburn, D. J. (2017). How—And Why—Apple, Google, And Facebook Follow You Around in Real Life, *Fast Company*, 22 December.
191. Taplin, Jonathan (2016). Forget AT&T. The Real Monopolies Are Google and Facebook, *New York Times,* 13 December.
192. Manjoo, Farhad (2017). Tech's Frightful Five: They've Got Us, *New York Times,* 10 May. See also Kolbert, Elizabeth (2017). Who Owns the Internet? (originally published as The Content of No Content), *The New Yorker*, 28 August.
193. Casselman, Ben (2017). A Start-Up Slump Is a Drag on the Economy. Big Business May Be to Blame, *New York Times,* 20 September.
194. Roose, Kevin (2018). The Young and Brash of Tech Grow a Bit Older, and Wiser, *New York Times,* 14 March.
195. Streitfeld, David (2017). 'The Internet Is Broken': @ev Is Trying to Salvage It, *New York Times,* 20 May.
196. Herrman, John (2017). What if Platforms Like Facebook Are Too Big to Regulate? *New York Times,* 4 October.
197. Cohen, Noam (2017). Silicon Valley Is Not Your Friend, *New York Times,* 13 October.
198. Taplin, Jonathan (2017). Is It Time to Break Up Google? *New York Times,* 22 April. See also Schiller, Ben (2018). This Is How We Take Power Back from Facebook (and Every Other Monopoly), *Fast Company*, 21 March.
199. Taplin, Jonathan (2017). REVIEW—Can the Tech Giants Be Stopped?—Google, Facebook, Amazon and other tech firms are transforming the economy and labor market, with scant public debate or scrutiny; Changing course won't be easy, *The Wall Street Journal,* 15 July. For a book-length treatment, see Taplin, Jonathan (2017). *Move Fast and Break Things: How Facebook, Google and Amazon Cornered Culture and Undermined Democracy*, Little, Brown and Company.
200. Lyall, Sarah (2018). Who Strikes Fear into Silicon Valley? Margrethe Vestager, Europe's Antitrust Enforcer, *New York Times,* 5 May.
201. Kang, Cecilia and Daisuke Wakabayashi (2017). Once Cozy with Silicon Valley, Democrats Grow Wary of Tech Giants, *New York Times,* 23 January.
202. Kang, Cecilia (2017). Internet Giants Face New Political Resistance in Washington, *New York Times,* 20 September.
203. Wingfield, Nick (2018). Microsoft Tries a New Role: Moral Leader, *New York Times,* 7 May.
204. Suchman, Lucy, Lilly Irani, and Peter Asaro (2018). Google's March to the Business of War Must Be Stopped, *The Guardian*, 16 May. See also Shane, Scott, Cade Metz, and Daisuke Wakabayashi (2018). How a Pentagon Contract Became an Identity Crisis for Google, *New York Times,* 30 May. See also Wakabayashi, Daisuke and Cade Metz (2018). Google Promises Its A.I. Will Not Be Used for Weapons, *New York Times,* 7 June.
205. Feenkel, Sheera (2018). Microsoft Employees Question C.E.O. Over Company's Contract With ICE, *New York Times,* 26 July.
206. LeRoy, Greg and Maryann Feldman (2017). Cities Need to Stop Selling Out to Big Tech Companies. There's a Better Way, *The Guardian*, 3 July.

Epilogue

1. Kranzberg, Melvin (1986). Technology and History: Kranzberg's Laws, *Technology and Culture* 27(3): 544–560.
2. Markoff, John (2016). *Machines of Loving Grace: The Quest for Common Ground Between Humans and Robots*, HarperCollins.
3. O'Reilly, Tim (2017). *What's the Future and Why It's Up to Us*, Harper Business.
4. Manjoo, Fahrad (2020, expected). *Masters of Our Universe*, Simon & Schuster. For a very early preview, see Manjoo's 2012 talk, https://vimeo.com/59061411.
5. Christensen, Clayton M. (1997). *The Innovator's Dilemma: The Revolutionary Book that Will Change the Way You Do Business*, Harper Business.
6. Martínez, Antonio García (2016). *Chaos Monkeys: Obscene Fortune and Random Failure in Silicon Valley*, HarperCollins.
7. United States Securities and Exchange Commission (2012). Form S-1 Registration Statement forFacebook,Inc.,https://www.sec.gov/Archives/edgar/data/1326801/000119312512034517/d287954ds1.htm, p. 70.
8. Juma, Calestuous (2016). *Innovation and Its Enemies: Why People Resist New Technologies*, Oxford University Press.
9. Frischmann, Brett and Evan Selinger (2018). *Re-Engineering Humanity*. Cambridge University Press.

Afterword

1. Smith, Brad (2018). The rural broadband divide: An urgent national problem that we can solve. *Microsoft On the Issues*, 3 December 2018. https://blogs.microsoft.com/on-the-issues/2018/12/03/the-rural-broadband-divide-an-urgent-national-problem-that-we-can-solve/.
2. Graham-McLay, Charlotte (2018). From Encyclopedic Collector to 'Wikipedian-at-Large'. *New York Times*, 16 November 2018.
3. Kang, Cecilia (2018). California Lawmakers Pass Nation's Toughest Net Neutrality Law. *New York Times*, 31 August 2018. See also Confessore, Nicholas (2018). New York Attorney General Expands Inquiry Into Net Neutrality Comments. *New York Times*, 16 October 2018.
4. Mone, Gregory (2018). Feeling Sounds, Hearing Sights. *Communications of the ACM* 61(1), 15–17. See also Liu, Yang Liu, Noelle RB Stiles, and Markus Meister (2018). Augmented reality powers a cognitive assistant for the blind. *eLife* 7, (2018): e37841.
5. Kolhatkar, Sheelah (2017). The Disrupters. *The New Yorker*, 20 November 2017, 52-63.
6. Orlov, Laurie (2019). Real Seniors lack essential technology: who will make it happen in 2019?. Aging in Place Technology Watch, 29 December 2018. https://www.ageinplacetech.com/blog/real-seniors-lack-essential-technology-who-will-make-it-happen-2019. See also Knowles, Bran and Vicki L. Hanson (2018). The Wisdom of Older Technology (Non)Users. *Communications of the ACM* 61(3), 72–7.
7. Taplin, Jonathan (2018). *Move Fast and Break Things: How Facebook, Google, and Amazon Cornered Culture and Undermined Democracy*. Little, Brown, and Company. Data points cited appear on pp. 91, 99, 44, 80, 81, 93, 168, 164, 250. See especially Taplin's Chapter 12 where he

proposes solutions. See also Barnes, Brooks (2018). Netflix's Movie Blitz Takes Aim at Hollywood's Heart. *New York Times,* 16 December 2018.

8. Marshall, Catherine C. and Frank M. Shipman (2017). Who Owns the Social Web? *Communications of the ACM* 60(5), 52-61.
9. Rossman, Katherine (2018). PowerPoint Is the Most Efficient Way for Kids to Manage Their Parents. *New York Times,* 20 December 2018.
10. For a recent review of progress in precision medicine, see MIT Technology Review (2016). Business Report: Precision Medicine. *MIT Technology Review,* September 2016, 89-97. For a discussion of progress in and ethical dilemmas raised by genetics and AI, see Jannot, Mark (ed.) (2018). From Gene Editing to A.I.: How Will Technology Transform Humanity. *New York Times,* 18 November 2018. For a discussion of deep learning in medicine, see Hinton, Geoffrey (2018). Deep Learning—A Technology With the Potential to Transform Health Care. *JAMA*. Published online August 30, 2018. doi:10.1001/jama.2018.11100. See also Naylor, C. David (2018). On the Prospects for a (Deep) Learning Health Care System. *JAMA*. Published online 30 August 2018. doi:10.1001/jama.2018.11103.
11. Riek, Laurel (2017). Healthcare Robotics. *Communications of the ACM* 60(11), 68–78. See also Stariano, Adam, Elian Peltier, and Dmitry Kostyukov (2018). Meet Zora, the Robot Caregiver. *New York Times,* 23 November 2018.
12. Bromwich, Jonah Engel and Katie Van Syckle (2018). Tumblr Fans Abandon Ship as Tumblr Bans Porn. *New York Times,* 6 December 2018. See also Powell, Jessica (2018). The Problem With Banning Pornography on Tumblr. *New York Times,* 6 December 2018.
13. Taub, Amanda and Max Fisher (2018). Facebook Fueled Anti-Refugee Attacks in Germany, New Research Suggests. *New York Times,* 21 August 2018. See also Stevenson, Alexandra (2018). Facebook Admits It Was Used to Incite Violence in Myanmar. *New York Times,* 6 November 2018.
14. Roose, Kevin (2018). On Gab, an Extremist-Friendly Site, Pittsburgh Shooting Suspect Aired His Hatred in Full. *New York Times,* 28 October 2018. See also Frenkel, Sheera, Mike Isaac, and Kate Conger (2018). On Instagram, 11,696 Examples of How Hate Thrives on Social Media. *New York Times,* 29 October 2018.
15. Fisher, Max (2018). Inside Facebook's Secret Rulebook for Global Political Speech. *New York Times,* 27 December 2018.
16. Marantz, Andrew (2018). Antisocial Media. *The New Yorker,* 19 March 2018, 58-67. See also Lagoria-Chafkin, Christine (2018). *We are the Nerds: The Birth and Tumultuous Life of Reddit, the Internet's Culture Laboratory*. Hachette Books.
17. Fisher, Max and Katrin Bennhold (2018). As Germans Seek News, YouTube Delivers Far-Right Tirades. *New York Times,* 7 September 2018.
18. Stevenson, Alexandra (2018). Soldiers in Facebook's War on Fake News Are Feeling Overrun. *New York Times,* 9 October 2018. See also Klonick, Kate and Thomas Kadri (2018). How to Make Facebook's 'Supreme Court' Work. *New York Times,* 17 November 2018.
19. Nicas, Jack (2018). Apple News's Radical Approach: Humans Over Machines. *New York Times,* 25 October 2018.
20. Warraich, Haider (2018). Dr. Google Is a Liar. *New York Times,* 16 December 2018.
21. Peltier, Elian and Adam Satariano (2018). After Yellow Vests Come Off, Activists in France Use Facebook to Protest and Plan. *New York Times,* 14 December 2018.

22. Manjoo, Fahrad (2018). Google Tried to Change China. China May End Up Changing Google. *New York Times*, 22 August 2018. See also Swisher, Kara (2018). The Real Google Censorship Scandal. *New York Times*, 13 September 2018.
23. Heller, Nathan (2018). The Digital Republic. *The New Yorker*, 18 and 25 December 2017, 84–93.
24. Hauser, Christine (2018). Police Use Fitbit Data to Charge 90-Year-Old Man in Stepdaughter's Killing. *New York Times*, 3 October 2018.
25. Jamieson, Kathleen Hall (2018). *Cyberwar; How Russian Hackers and Trolls Helped Elect a President*. Oxford University Press. The phrase 'swung the election to Trump' appears on page 213.
26. New Knowledge (2018). The Tactics & Tropes of the Internet Research Agency. https://disinformationreport.blob.core.windows.net/disinformation-report/NewKnowledge-Disinformation-Report-Whitepaper.pdf. See also Computational Propaganda Research Project (2018). The IRA, Social Media, and Political Polarization in the United States, 2012-2018. https://comprop.oii.ox.ac.uk/wp-content/uploads/sites/93/2018/12/IRA-Report-2018.pdf. Media summaries of the findings of these reports include: Shane, Scott and Sheera Frenkel (2018). Russian 2016 Influence Operation Targeted African-Americans on Social Media. *New York Times*, 17 December 2018; Frenkel, Sheera, Daisuke Wakabayashi and Kate Conger (2018). Tech Companies Dragged Feet on Russian Interference Data, Reports Say, *New York Times*, 17 December 2018; Roose, Kevin (2018). Social Media's Forever War. *New York Times*, 17 December 2018.
27. Frenkel, Sheera and Mike Isaac (2018). Facebook 'Better Prepared' to Fight Election Interference, Mark Zuckerberg Says. *New York Times*, 13 September 2018. See also Frenkel, Sheera and Mike Isaac (2018). Inside Facebook's Election 'War Room'. *New York Times*, 19 September 2018. See also Barnes, Julian E. (2018). Russians Tried, but Were Unable to Compromise Midterm Elections, U.S. Says. *New York Times*, 21 December 2018.
28. Frenkel, Sheera and Mike Isaac (2018). Russian Trolls Were at It Again Before Midterms, Facebook Says. *New York Times*, 7 November 2018. See also Frenkel, Sheera (2018). Facebook Tackles Rising Threat: Americans Aping Russian Schemes to Deceive. *New York Times*, 11 October 2018.
29. Roose, Kevin (2018). 6 Types of Misinformation to Beware Of on Election Day. (And What to Do if You Spot Them.) *New York Times*, 5 November 2018.
30. Sanger, David E. and Sheera Frenkel (2018). New Russian Hacking Targeted Republican Groups, Microsoft Says. *New York Times*, 21 August 2018. See also Shane, Scott and Alan Blinder (2018). Secret Experiment in Alabama Senate Race Imitated Russian Tactics. *New York Times*, 19 December 2018.
31. Stamos, Alex (2018). How the U.S. Has Failed to Protect the 2018 Election — and Four Ways to Protect 2020. *New York Times*, 22 August 2018.
32. Isaac, Mike and Kevin Roose (2018). Disinformation Spreads on WhatsApp Ahead of Brazilian Election. *New York Times*, 19 October 2018.
33. Nicas, Jack (2018). Facebook Says Russian Firms 'Scraped' Data, Some for Facial Recognition. *New York Times*, 12 October 2018. See also Susskind, Jamie (2018). Chatbots are a Danger to Democracy. *New York Times*, 4 December 2018. For a recent review of social bot detection systems, designed to distinguish between messages from humans and bots, see Ferrara, Emilio, Onur Vardi, Clayton Davis, Filippo Menczer, and Alessandro Flammini (2016). The Rise of Social Bots. *Communications of the ACM* 59(7), 96–104.

34. Shimer, David (2018). With Drone Deliveries on the Horizon, Europe Moves to Set Ground Rules. *New York Times,* 31 December 2018.

35. Wallach, Wendell (2017). Toward a Ban on Lethal Autonomous Weapons: Surmounting the Obstacles. *Communications of the ACM* 60(5), 28–34. See also Evans, Hayley (2018). Lethal Autonomous Weapons Systems at the First and Second U.N. GGE Meetings. *Lawfare,* 9 April 2018. https://www.lawfareblog.com/lethal-autonomous-weapons-systems-first-and-second-un-gge-meetings. See also Chertoff, Philip (2018). Perils of Lethal Autonomous Weapons Systems Proliferation: Pre- venting Non-State Acquisition. *Centre for Security Studies, ETH Zurich,* 25 October 2018. http://www.css.ethz.ch/en/services/digital-library/articles/article.html/a4f0de69-1e0b-401e-871d-1956fa9063d3/pdf.

36. Isaac, Mike and Sheera Frenkel (2018). Facebook Security Breach Exposes Accounts of 50 Million Users. *New York Times,* 28 September 2018. See also Isaac, Mike and Kate Conger (2018). Facebook Hack Puts Thousands of Other Sites at Risk. *New York Times,* 2 October 2018. See also Perlroth, Nicole, Amie Tsang, and Adam Satariano (2018). Marriott Hacking Exposes Data of Up to 500 Million Guests. *New York Times,* 30 November 2018. See also Sanger, David E. Nicole Perlroth, Glenn Thrush and Alan Rappeport (2018). Marriott Data Breach Is Traced to Chinese Hackers as U.S. Readies Crackdown on Beijing. *New York Times,* 11 December 2018.

37. Hiltner, Stephen (2018). For Hackers, Anonymity Was Once Critical. That's Changing. *New York Times,* 22 September 2018. See also Schmidle, Nicholas (2018). Digital Vigilantes. *The New Yorker,* 7 May 2018, 30-37.

38. Sanger, David E. and William J. Broad (2018). New U.S. Weapons Systems Are a Hackers' Bonanza, Investigators Find. *New York Times,* 10 October 2018. See also Mahairas, Ari and Peter J. Beshar (2018). A Perfect Target for Cybercriminals. *New York Times,* 19 November 2018.

39. Lindquist, Ulf and Peter G. Neumann (2017). Inside Risks: The Future of the Internet of Things. *Communications of the ACM* 60(2), 26-30.

40. Zetter, Kim (2018). The Crisis of Election Security. *New York Times,* 26 September 2018. See also Electronic Frontier Foundation (2018). Election Security Remains Just as Vulnerable as in 2016. *Eff.org,* 28 September 2018.

41. Cohn, Nate and Kevin Quealy (2018). A Mysterious 'Undervote' Could End Up Settling the Florida Senate Race. *New York Times,* 9 November 2018.

42. Horton, Alex (2018). Veterans aren't getting their GI Bill payments — because VA's 50- year-old computer system broke. *The Washington Post,* 15 November 2018.

43. Conger, Kate (2018). Uber's Driverless Cars Return to the Road After Fatal Crash. *New York Times,* 20 December 2018. See also Markoff, John (2018). Urban Planning Guru Says Driverless Cars Won't Fix Congestion. *New York Times,* 27 October 2018. See also WNYC Studios (2018). Whose Streets? *On the Media,* 23 November 2018. https://www.wnycstudios.org/story/on-the-media-2018-11-23?utm_medium=email&utm_source=topic+optin&utm_campaign=awareness&utm_content=20181130+ne+nl&mkt_tok=eyJpIjoiTVRKa01XRXhNekZtT1RSayIsInQiOiJjTHBZalhEMGhlNlFXczZCUmt3RUFObVN3M1NJbkQwcXE2cXFWcVRtNjhNVGY0XC9vbUNRXC9MQXR4dlFxNUhsZ2llWmI2anlXZ0tZOUprNmZHXC8zT1BXa05DVmh6XC9GV2RuWHJDbndBbWFJbVRFc1dPdjBT-NVJGZ2Vta1dEZHRRdjcifQ%3D%3D.

44. Goel, Vindu (2018). India's Top Court Limits Sweep of Biometric ID Program. *New York Times,* 26 September 2018.

45. The Editorial Board, New York Times (2018). Did Facebook Learn Anything From the Cambridge Analytica Debacle? An even bigger data breach suggests it didn't. *New York Times,* 6 October 2018. See also Isaac, Mike and Natasha Singer (2018). Facebook Says Bug Opened Access to Private Photos. *New York Times,* 14 December 2018. See also Confessore, Nicholas, Michael LaForgia and Gabriel J.X. Dance (2018). Facebook Failed to Police How Its Partners Handled User Data. *New York Times,* 12 November 2018. See also Dance, Gabriel J.X., Michael LaForgia, and Nicholas Confessore (2018). As Facebook Raised a Privacy Wall, It Carved an Opening for Tech Giants, *New York Times,* 18 December 2018. See also Confessore, Nicholas, Michael LaForgia and Gabriel J.X. Dance (2018). Facebook's Data Sharing: 5 Takeaways From Our Investigation, *New York Times,* 18 December 2018.

46. Daisuke Wakabayashi, Daisuke (2018). Google Plus Will Be Shut Down After User Information Was Exposed. *New York Times,* 6 October 2018.

47. Valentino-DeVries, Jennifer, Natasha Singer, Michael H. Keller, and Aaron Krolick (2018). Your Apps Know Where You Were Last Night, and They're Not Keeping It Secret. *New York Times,* 10 December 2018. See also Harris, Rich, Michael H. Keller, and Jennifer Valentino-DeVries (2018). 8 Places Where Smartphones Tracked People's Movements. *New York Times,* 15 December 2018. See also Bowles, Nellie (2018). Stealing From a Cashierless Store (Without You, or the Cameras, Knowing It). *New York Times,* 13 September 2018. See also Savage, Maddy (2018). Thousands Of Swedes Are Inserting Microchips Under Their Skin. *NPR.com,* 22 October 2018.

48. Turow, Joseph, Michael Hennessy, and Nora Draper (2015). The Tradeoff Fallacy: How Marketers are Misrepresenting American Consumers and Opening Them Up to Exploitation. Unpublished paper. *Annenberg School for Communication, University of Pennsylvania.* https://repository.upenn.edu/asc_papers/521/.

49. Reuters (2018). North Korean Defectors' Personal Data Was Stolen by Hackers, South Says. *Reuters,* 28 December 2018.

50. Marr, Bernard (2018). The Amazing Ways How Unilever Uses Artificial Intelligence To Recruit & Train Thousands Of Employees. *Forbes,* 14 December 2018.

51. Gabrielle, Vincent (2018). The Dark Side of Gamifying Work. *Fast Company,* 1 November 2018. See also Rosenblat, Alex (2018). When Your Boss Is an Algorithm. *New York Times,* 12 October 2018.

52. Widdicombe, Lizzie (2018). Rate Your Boss! *The New Yorker,* 22 January 2018, 22--8.

53. Anzilotti, Eillie (2018). Inside New York City's Plan to Guarantee Lyft and Uber Drivers a Minimum Wage. *Fast Company,* 4 December 2018. See also Ghaffary, Shirin (2018). New York City has set the nation's first minimum pay rate for Uber and Lyft drivers. *Recode,* 4 December 2018. https://www.recode.net/2018/12/4/18125789/uber-lyft-drivers-wage-minimum-new-york.

54. Berg, Janine, Marianne Furrer, Ellie Harmon, Uma Rani, and M Six Silberman (2018). Digital labour platforms and the future of work: Towards decent work in the online world. *International Labour Organization,* 20 September 2018. https://www.ilo.org/wcmsp5/groups/public/---dgreports/---dcomm/---publ/documents/publication/wcms_645337.pdf.

55. Jordan, Miriam (2018). As Immigrant Farmworkers Become More Scarce, Robots Replace Humans. *New York Times,* 20 November 2018. See also Peters, Adele (2018). Inside Silicon Valley's Newest, Most Autonomous Farm Yet. *Fast Company,* 3 October 2018.

56. Deloitte Development LLC (2018). 2018 Deloitte skills gap and future of work in manufacturing study. *Deloitte Insights.* https://www2.deloitte.com/us/en/pages/manufacturing/articles/future-of-manufacturing-skills-gap-study.html.

57. Knight, Will (2016). The People's Robots. *MIT Technology Review* 119(3), 44–53.
58. Melendez, Steven (2018). Amazon and Walmart add more robots, but insist they won't terminate jobs. *Fast Company,* 15 December 2018.
59. Porter, Eduardo (2018). Hotel Workers Fret Over a New Rival: Alexa at the Front Desk. *New York Times,* 24 September 2018.
60. Son Hugh (2018). Goldman Sachs, advisor to the ultra-rich, plans to offer wealth management for the little guy. *CNBC,* 22 October 2018. https://www.cnbc.com/2018/10/22/goldman-advisor-to-the-ultra-rich-plans-wealth-management-for-all.html.
61. Subramanian, Samanth (2017). India Warily Eyes AI. *MIT Technology Review,* November/December 2017, 38–44.
62. Centre for the New Economy and Society (2018). The Future of Jobs Report 2018. *World Economic Forum.* http://www3.weforum.org/docs/WEF_Future_of_Jobs_2018.pdf.
63. Acemoglu, Daron and Pascual Restrepo (in press). Artificial Intelligence, Automation and Work. Appears in Agrawal, Ajay, Joshua Gans, and Avi Goldfarb (eds.) (2019). *The Economics of Artificial Intelligence: An Agenda.* University of Chicago Press.
64. Acemoglu, Daron and Pascual Restrepo (2018). Robots and Jobs: Evidence from US Labor Markets. Unpublished paper, 16 July 2018. https://economics.mit.edu/files/15254.
65. Heller, Nathan (2018). Take the Money and Run. *The New Yorker,* 9 and 16 July 2018, 65–9.
66. Yuan, Li (2018). How Cheap Labor Drives China's A.I. Ambitions. *New York Times,* 25 November 2018. See also Snow, Jackie (2018). The World of A.I. *New York Times,* 18 October 2018.
67. Lohr, Steve (2018). M.I.T. Plans College for Artificial Intelligence, Backed by $1 Billion. *New York Times,* 15 October 2018.
68. Fuller, Thomas and Cade Metz (2018). A.I. Is Helping Scientists Predict When and Where the Next Big Earthquake Will Be. *New York Times,* 26 October 2018. See also Kaste, Martin (2018). Facebook Increasingly Reliant on A.I. To Predict Suicide Risk. *NPR.com,* 17 November 2018. See also Singer, Natasha (2018). In Screening for Suicide Risk, Facebook Takes On Tricky Public Health Role. *New York Times,* 31 December 2018.
69. Silver, David, Thomas Hubert, Julian Schrittwieser, Ioannis Antonoglou, Matthew Lai, Arthur Guez, Marc Lanctot, Laurent Sifre, Dharshan Kumaran, Thore Graepel, Timothy Lillicrap, Karen Simonyan, and Demis Hassabis (2018). Mastering Chess and Shogi by Self-Play with a General Reinforcement Learning Algorithm. arXiv:1712.01815. See also *Schuller,* Björn W. (2018). Speech Emotion Recognition. *Communications of the ACM* 61(5), 90-99. See also Brock, Andrew, Jeff Donahue, and Karen Simonyan (2018). Large Scale GAN Training for High Fidelity Natural Image Synthesis. 28 September 2018. https://arxiv.org/abs/1809.11096. See also Schwab, Katherine (2018). A Google intern built the AI behind these shockingly good fake images. *Fast Company,* 2 October 2018.
70. Metz, Cade (2018). Finally, a Machine That Can Finish Your Sentence. *New York Times,* 18 November 2018. See also Mitchell, Melanie (2018). Artificial Intelligence Hits the Barrier of Meaning. *New York Times,* 5 November 2018.
71. Kaufman, David (2018). Watch Out Workers, Algorithms Are Coming to Replace You — Maybe. *New York Times,* 18 October 2018. See also Turkle, Sherry (2018). There Will Never Be an Age of Artificial Intimacy. *New York Times,* 11 August 2018.
72. Parnas, David Lorge (2017). The Real Risks of Artificial Intelligence. *Communications of the ACM* 60(10), 27–31. See also Kuipers, Benjamin (2018). How Can We Trust a Robot. *Communications of the ACM* 61(3), 86–95.

73. Monroe, Don (2018). AI, Explain Yourself. *Communications of the ACM* 61(11), 11–13. See also Doshi-Velez, Finale and Mason Kortz (2017). Accountability of AI Under the Law: The Role of Explanation. https://arxiv.org/abs/1711.01134.

74. Baeza-Yates, Ricardo (2018). Bias in the Web. *Communications of the ACM* 61(6), 54-61. See also Manjoo, Fahrad (2018). Here's the Conversation We Really Need to Have About Bias at Google. *New York Times*, 30 August 2018.

75. Pasquale, Frank (2018). When Machine Learning is Facially Invalid. *Communications of the ACM* 61(9), 25-27.

76. Molnar, Petra and Lex Gill (2018). Bots at the Gate: A Human Rights Analysis of Automated Decision-Making in Canada's Immigration and Refugee System. *The Citizen Lab, University of Toronto*. https://citizenlab.ca/2018/09/bots-at-the-gate-human-rights-analysis-automated-decision-making-in-canadas-immigration-refugee-system/.

77. Friend, Tad (2018). Superior Intelligence. *The New Yorker*, 14 May 2018, 44–51. See also Somers, James (2017). Is AI Riding a One-Trick Pony. *MIT Technology Review* 120(6), 29–36. See also Kumar, Ram Shankar Siva, Kendra Albert, David R. O'Brien, and Salomé Viljoen (2018). Law and Adversarial Machine Learning. Preprint. Work in progress. https://arxiv.org/abs/1810.10731.

78. Sullivan, Mark (2018). Amazon's boatload of new Echo devices move further beyond the phone. *Fast Company*, 21 September 2018. See also Newman, Jared (2018). Amazon's three-pronged plan for taking over your home. *Fast Company*, 19 December 2018. See also Manjoo, Fahrad (2018). A Future Where Everything Becomes a Computer Is as Creepy as You Feared. *New York Times*, 10 October 2018.

79. Khatoun, Rida and Sherali Zeadally (2016). Smart Cities: Concepts, Architectures, Research Opportunities. *Communications of the ACM* 59(8), 46-57. See also Kofman, Ava (2018). Google's 'Smart City of Surveillance' Faces New Resistance in Toronto. *The Intercept*, 13 November 2018. https://theintercept.com/2018/11/13/google-quayside-toronto-smart-city/.

80. Bowles, Nellie (2018). A Dark Consensus About Screens and Kids Begins to Emerge in Silicon Valley. *New York Times*, 26 October 2018.

81. Bowles, Nellie (2018). Remember Bitcoin? Some Investors Might Want to Forget. *New York Times*, 27 December 2018.

82. Manjoo, Fahrad (2018). How Apple Thrived in a Season of Tech Scandals. *New York Times*, 26 September 2018. See also Lohr, Steve (2018). Microsoft Is Worth as Much as Apple. How Did That Happen? *New York Times*, 29 November 2018.

83. Wakabayashi, Daisuke, Erin Griffith, Amie Tsang and Kate Conger (2018). Google Walkout: Employees Stage Protest Over Handling of Sexual Harassment. *New York Times*, 1 November 2018. See also Conger, Kate and Daisuke Wakabayashi (2018). Google Overhauls Sexual Misconduct Policy After Employee Walkout. *New York Times*, 8 November 2018. See also Wakabayashi, Daisuke and Cecilia Kang (2018). Google's Pichai Faces Privacy and Bias Questions in Congress, *New York Times*, 11 December 2018.

84. Confessore, Nicholas and Matthew Rosenberg (2018). Sheryl Sandberg Asked for Soros Research, Facebook Acknowledges. *New York Times*, 29 November 2018.

85. Satariano, Adam and Mike Isaac (2018). Facebook Used People's Data to Favor Certain Partners and Punish Rivals, Documents Show. *New York Times*, 5 December 2018.

86. Frenkel, Sheera, Nicholas Confessore, Cecilia Kang, Matthew Rosenberg and Jack Nicas (2018). Delay, Deny and Deflect: How Facebook's Leaders Fought Through Crisis. *New York Times*, 14 November 2018.

87. Osnos, Evan (2018). Ghost in the Machine. *The New Yorker,* 17 September 2018, 32–47.

88. Bowles, Nellie (2018). 'I Don't Really Want to Work for Facebook.' So Say Some Computer Science Students. *New York Times,* 15 November 2018.

89. Streitfeld, David (2018). Amazon Hits $1,000,000,000,000 in Value, Following Apple. *New York Times,* 4 September 2018. See also Weise, Karen (2018). Amazon Squeezes Out More Profit as Sales Growth Slows. *New York Times,* 25 October 2018.

90. Weise, Karen (2018). Last-Minute Shoppers Increasingly Trust Only Amazon to Deliver. *New York Times,* 21 December 2018.

91. Terdiman, Daniel (2018). How AI is helping Amazon become a trillion-dollar company. *Fast Company,* 5 October 2018.

92. Metz, Cade (2018). Amazon's Homegrown Chips Threaten Silicon Valley Giant Intel. *New York Times,* 10 December 2018.

93. Weise, Karen (2018). Want to See What's Up Amazon's Sleeve? Take a Tour of Seattle. *New York Times,* 23 September 2018.

94. Streitfeld, David (2018). After Protest, Booksellers Are Victorious Against Amazon Subsidiary. *New York Times,* 7 November 2018.

95. Stone, Brad (2013). *The Everything Store: Jeff Bezos and the Age of Amazon.* Little, Brown & Company.

96. Cusumano, Michael A. (2017). Amazon and Whole Foods: Follow the Strategy (and the Money). *Communications of the ACM* 60(10), 24-26.

97. Brown, H. Claire (2018). Amazon gets huge subsidies to provide good jobs— but it's a top employer of SNAP recipients in at least five states. *The New Food Economy,* 19 April 2018. https://newfoodeconomy.org/amazon-snap-employees-five-states/. See also Weise, Karen (2018). Amazon to Raise Minimum Wage to $15 for All U.S. Workers. *New York Times,* 2 October 2018.

98. Jensen, Nathan M. (2018). The Amazon HQ2 Fiasco Was No Outlier. *The Wall Street Journal,* 14 December 2018.

99. Leroy, Greg (2018). The Amazon deal is even worse than it looks and will cost NY more than it thinks. *Fast Company,* 16 November 2018. See also Garun, Natt and Shannon Liao (2018). For Queens Residents, Amazon's HQ2 Isn't Arriving Without a Fight. *The Verge,* 20 November 2018. https://www.theverge.com/2018/11/20/18093040/amazon-hq2-long-island-city-queens-resident-reactions-neighborhood-impact.

100. Conger, Kate and Cade Metz (2018). Tech Workers Now Want to Know: What Are We Building This For? *New York Times,* 7 October 2018. See also Captain, Sean (2018). How tech workers became activists, leading a resistance movement that is shaking up Silicon Valley. *Fast Company,* 15 October 2018.

101. Conger, Kate (2018). Tech Workers Got Paid in Company Stock. They Used It to Agitate for Change. *New York Times,* 16 December 2018.

102. Eggerton, John (2018). Open Markets Figures Display Google, Facebook Dominance. Broadcasting & Cable, 26 November 2018. https://www.broadcastingcable.com/news/open-markets-figures-display-google-facebook-revenue-dominance.

103. Satariano, Adam (2018). Amazon Dominates as a Merchant and Platform. Europe Sees Reason to Worry. *New York Times,* 19 September 2018.

104. Goel, Vindu (2018). India Pushes Back Against Tech 'Colonization' by Internet Giants. *New York Times,* 31 August 2018. See also Goel, Vindu (2018). India Curbs Power of Amazon and Walmart to Sell Products Online. *New York Times,* 26 December 2018.

105. Swisher, Kara (2018). Introducing the Internet Bill of Rights. *New York Times,* 4 October 2018.

106. Streitfeld, David (2018). Amazon's Antitrust Antagonist Has a Breakthrough Idea. *New York Times,* 7 September 2018. See also Khan, Lina M. (2016). Amazon's Antitrust Paradox. *126 Yale Law Journal,* 710–805. See also Wu, Tim (2018). *The Curse of Bigness: Antitrust in the New Gilded Age.* Columbia Global Reports.

Resources

Prologue

The Pew Research Center (http://www.pewresearch.org) describes itself as 'a nonpartisan fact tank that informs the public about the issues, attitudes and trends shaping America and the world. It conducts public opinion polling, demographic research, media content analysis and other empirical social science research.'

The Berkman Klein Center (https://cyber.harvard.edu) for Internet and Society at Harvard University states that its mission is 'to explore and understand cyberspace; to study its development, dynamics, norms, and standards; and to assess the need or lack thereof for laws and sanctions'.

The Citizen Lab (https://citizenlab.org), housed at the University of Toronto's Munk School of Global Affairs, does R&D at the intersection of information and communication technologies (ICT), human rights, and global security.

The Oxford Internet Institute (https://www.oii.ox.ac.uk) describes itself as 'a multidisciplinary research and teaching department of the University of Oxford, dedicated to the social science of the Internet'.

The mission of the Electronic Frontier Foundation (https://www.eff.org) is 'defending your rights in the digital world'.

The Centre for the Internet and Human Rights (CIHR) (https://networkofcenters.net/center/centre-internet-and-human-rights-cihr) states that its goal 'is to inform current public and academic debates by producing high-quality research [about technology and society] grounded in theory and empirical data'. CIHR is a collaborative network of 91 research centres located across the world, with heaviest participation from Europe and Asia.

The ACM Special Interest Group on Computers and Society (SIGCAS) (https://www.sigcas.org/) addresses 'the social and ethical consequences of widespread computer usage' with useful resources such as scholarly articles, news, and book reviews.

The Special Interest Group on Computers, Information, and Society (SIGCIS) (http://www.sigcis.org) describes itself as 'the leading international group for historians with an interest in the history of information technology and its applications'. It sponsors conferences and workshops which may be of interest to readers of this book.

The Computer Professionals for Social Responsibility (CPSR) (http://cpsr.org/) is a 'global organization promoting the responsible use of computer technology'. It was founded in 1981, and has some useful resources on its website, but has been inactive since 2008.

Chapter 1

The website of the Inclusive Design Research Centre (http://idrc.ocad.ca/) provides numerous resources relevant to understanding inclusive design and technology; see also the Special Needs Opportunity Window (SNOW), http://www.snow.idrc.ocad.ca/.

Laurie Orlov's Aging in Place Technology Trends (https://www.ageinplacetech.com) publishes 'Industry Market Trends, Research & Analysis'. She ranges broadly over technologies that do or may have application for seniors, is particularly attuned to hype, and supports her analyses with references to relevant articles.

Chapter 2

The Oxford Handbook of Internet Studies (http://www.oxfordhandbooks.com/view/10.1093/oxfordhb/9780199589074.001.0001/oxfordhb-9780199589074) describes itself as having been designed to 'bring together scholarly perspectives' on topics within the emerging field of internet studies, providing 'a synthesis and critical assessment of the research in [each] particular area'.

Common Sense Media (https://www.commonsensemedia.org/) describes itself as follows: '[We are] the leading independent non-profit organization dedicated to helping kids thrive in a world of media and technology. We empower parents, teachers, and policymakers by providing unbiased information, trusted advice, and innovative tools to help them harness the power of media and technology as a positive force in all kids' lives.'

The Takedown Project (http://takedownproject.org) is 'a collaborative effort housed at UC-Berkeley School of Law and the American Assembly to study notice and takedown procedures... [and] to understand this fundamental regulatory system for global online speech'.

Chapter 3

The American Educational Research Association (AERA) (http://www.aera.net/) describes itself as 'a national research society' that 'strives to advance knowledge about education, to encourage scholarly inquiry related to education, and to promote the use of research to improve education and serve the public good'. Its publications and conferences include quality material dealing with digital technologies in education and learning.

The Clubhouse Network (http://www.computerclubhouse.org), 'an international community of 100 Clubhouses located in 19 countries, providing youth with life-changing opportunities for over 23 years, provides a creative, safe, and free out-of-school learning environment where young people from underserved communities work with adult mentors to explore their own ideas, develop new skills, and build confidence in themselves through the use of technology'.

Chapter 4

The American Society for Artificial Internal Organs (https://asaio.com) is a forum for presenting and discussing 'the development of innovative medical device technology at the crossroads of science, engineering, and medicine'.

Norman Doidge's website (http://www.normandoidge.com) is a good starting place for learning about neuroplasticity.

SharpBrains (http://sharpbrains.com) is an independent market research firm tracking health and performance applications of brain science, with a particular focus on cognitive training exercises and games.

Chapter 5

AccessNow.org (https://www.accessnow.org) 'defends and extends the digital rights of users at risk around the world', via 'direct technical support, comprehensive policy engagement, global advocacy, grassroots grantmaking, and convenings' such as RightsCon (https://www.rightscon.org), a conference that in its seventh year brought 2,400 individuals to a meeting in Toronto, Ontario.

See additional Resources listed above in the section for the Prologue.

Chapter 6

The OpenNet Initiative (https://opennet.net) was 'a collaborative partnership of three institutions: the Citizen Lab at the Munk School of Global Affairs, University of Toronto; the Berkman Center for Internet & Society at Harvard University; and the SecDev Group in Ottawa'. Their aim was to 'identify and document internet filtering and surveillance'. Although the Initiative's ten-year research programme has drawn to a close, the website holds an entire archive of published work and data.

The Wikipedia entry on Lethal Autonomous Weapons (https://en.wikipedia.org/wiki/Lethal_autonomous_weapon) has pointers to useful resources dealing with this issue.

Chapter 7

Schneier on Security (https://www.schneier.com/) includes a blog, newsletter, book list, essays, newsreel, and list of talks, many with pointers to video recordings of them, by Bruce Schneier, one of the world's top experts on digital security.

The Caltech/MIT Voting Technology Project (http://www.votingtechnologyproject.org) 'applies social science and engineering to voting. [Their] work ranges from the functioning of voting machines to the effects of reforms on voter behavior to the assessment of voting systems.'

Chapter 8

The ACM Special Interest Group on Computers and Human Interaction (https://sigchi.org/) and the Human Factors and Ergonomics Society (https://www.hfes.org/) both deal with maximizing human control of technology and advocating for the appropriate use of technology.

The Electronics Takeback Coalition (http://www.electronicstakeback.com/) describes itself as a promotor of 'green design and responsible recycling in the electronics industry. Our goal is to protect the health and well-being of electronics users, workers, and the communities where electronics are produced and discarded by requiring consumer electronics manufacturers and brand owners to take full responsibility for the life cycle of their products.'

A good resource on the 'right to repair' movement is https://ifixit.org/right, which states: '[w]e have the right to repair everything we own. It's high time we demand the right to open, tinker with, and repair everything we own.'

Chapter 9

Since 1992, the Privacy Rights Clearinghouse (https://www.privacyrights.org/) has 'empowered individuals to protect their privacy by providing direct one-to-one assistance, creating original educational publications, and advocating for consumer-friendly policy'.

EPIC, the Electronic Privacy Information Center (https://www.epic.org), has pursued the mission of 'focus[ing] public attention on emerging privacy and civil liberties issues and... protect[ing] privacy, freedom of expression, and democratic values in the information age' since 1994.

Chapter 10

The Future of Humanity Institute (FHI) at the University of Oxford (https://www.fhi.ox.ac.uk) is a 'multidisciplinary research institute at the University of Oxford. Academics at FHI bring the tools of mathematics, philosophy and social sciences to bear on big-picture questions about humanity and its prospects.'

The Oxford Martin School Programme on Technology and Employment (https://www.oxfordmartin.ox.ac.uk/research/programmes/tech-employment) is 'investigating the implications of a rapidly changing technological landscape for economies and societies.... [to] provide an in-depth understanding of how technology is transforming the economy, to help leaders create a successful transition into new ways of working in the 21st Century'.

The O'Reilly Next:Economy Newsletter, is a weekly publication with excellent insights into the subjects covered in Chapter 10. Readers can subscribe at https://www.oreilly.com/emails/newsletters/index.html.

Chapter 11

The AINow Institute (https://ainowinstitute.org) at New York University is 'an interdisciplinary research center dedicated to understanding the social implications of artificial intelligence. [Their] work focuses on four core domains: rights & liberties, labor & automation, bias & inclusion, and safety & critical infrastructure.'

The Berkman Klein Center and the MIT Media Lab are anchor institutions of the Ethics and Governance of AI Initiative (https://aiethicsinitiative.org/), a 'a hybrid research effort and philanthropic fund that seeks to ensure that technologies of automation and machine learning are researched, developed, and deployed in a way which vindicate social values of fairness, human autonomy, and justice'.

The mission of the Future of Life Institute (https://futureoflife.org) focuses on the technology that 'is giving life the potential to flourish like never before... or to self-destruct'. Its main area of interest is AI, with the goal of keeping AI beneficial. It gives grants for research on topics such as AI safety.

The Stanford One Hundred Year Study on Artificial Intelligence (https://ai100.stanford.edu) is a project with 'leading thinkers from several institutions... [participating in]... a 100-year effort to study and anticipate how the effects of artificial intelligence will ripple through every aspect of how people work, live and play'.

Deep Mind Ethics & Society (https://deepmind.com/blog/why-we-launched-deepmind-ethics-society/), a research unit of Google's Deep Mind subsidiary, has the dual objectives of 'help[ing] technologists put ethics into practice, and help[ing] society anticipate and direct the impact of AI so that it works for the benefit of all'.

An annual conference on Fairness, Accountability, and Transparency in Machine Learning (https://www.fatml.org) brings together 'a growing community of researchers and practitioners concerned with fairness, accountability, and transparency in machine learning'.

The Council for Big Data, Ethics, and Society (https://bdes.datasociety.net/) provides 'critical social and cultural perspectives on big data initiatives', and plans to 'develop frameworks to help researchers, practitioners, and the public understand the social, ethical, legal, and policy issues that underpin the big data phenomenon'.

Chapter 12

The Center for Humane Technology (http://humanetech.com) notes that 'our society is being hijacked by technology' and states its goal as 'reversing the digital attention crisis and realigning technology with humanity's best interests'.

The Future of Computing Academy (https://acm-fca.org/about-future-of-computing-academy/) has members who 'actively engage and work on impactful projects to computing and society'.

Index